D1294156

CRIMINAL INVESTIGATION

Third Edition

Ronald F. Becker, MEd, JD
Director
Criminology and Criminal Justice Program
Chaminade University
Honolulu, Hawaii

JONES AND BARTLETT PUBLISHERS
Sudbury, Massachusetts
BOSTON   TORONTO   LONDON   SINGAPORE

World Headquarters

Jones and Bartlett Publishers
40 Tall Pine Drive
Sudbury, MA 01776
978-443-5000
info@jbpub.com
www.jbpub.com

Jones and Bartlett Publishers Canada
6339 Ormindale Way
Mississauga, Ontario L5V 1J2
Canada

Jones and Bartlett Publishers International
Barb House, Barb Mews
London W6 7PA
United Kingdom

Jones and Bartlett's books and products are available through most bookstores and online booksellers. To contact Jones and Bartlett Publishers directly, call 800-832-0034, fax 978-443-8000, or visit our website www.jbpub.com.

Substantial discounts on bulk quantities of Jones and Bartlett's publications are available to corporations, professional associations, and other qualified organizations. For details and specific discount information, contact the special sales department at Jones and Bartlett via the above contact information or send an email to specialsales@jbpub.com.

Unless otherwise indicated, photographs are under the copyright of Jones and Bartlett Publishers, courtesy of MIEMSS, or have been kindly provided by the author.

Production Credits
Acquisitions Editor: Jeremy Spiegel
Editorial Assistant: Maro Asadoorian
Production Director: Amy Rose
Senior Production Editor: Renée Sekerak
Production Assistant: Jill Morton
Associate Marketing Manager: Lisa Gordon
Manufacturing and Inventory Control Supervisor: Amy Bacus
Composition: ATLIS Graphics
Interior Design: Anne Spencer
Cover Design: Kate Ternullo
Cover Image: © Les Cunliffe/age fotostock
Chapter Opener Image: © Stephen Sweet/ShutterStock, Inc.
Associate Photo Researcher and Photographer: Christine McKeen
Text Printing and Binding: Malloy Incorporated
Cover Printing: Malloy Incorporated

Library of Congress Cataloging-in-Publication Data
Becker, Ronald F.
    Criminal investigation / by Ronald F. Becker. — 3rd ed.
        p. cm.
    Includes bibliographical references and index.
    ISBN 978-0-7637-5522-5 (hardcover)
  1. Criminal investigation.   I. Title.
    HV8073.B374 2009
    363.25—dc22
                                    2008018114
6048

Printed in the United States of America
12 11 10 09 08   10 9 8 7 6 5 4 3 2 1

Robert G. Teather
1947–2004

I would like to dedicate this book to the father of underwater investigation, Cpl. Robert G. Teather, C.V. In a time when adults have few heroes, Bob was mine. Rest in peace, Bob.

Contents

Preface

Because of popular forensic television shows, people are developing a new language called forensic-speak. Because they have seen forensic programs, people believe they understand how crime scenes are investigated and how criminals are caught. They do not. Most crimes are investigated and criminals are caught the old-fashioned way: by examining the evidence and reviewing the pathologist and autopsy reports, then canvassing neighborhoods, talking to people, interviewing witnesses, and interrogating suspects. All of this work is done by investigative personnel, not by forensic scientists or forensic technicians. The good news about all the forensic television programming is that people, including criminals, believe that if you commit a crime, forensic evidence will catch you.

The way forensic science is done on television makes it look exciting and relatively simple. Chaminade University of Honolulu offers a Bachelor of Science degree in forensic science that is certified by the Academy of Forensic Sciences. It is the most demanding science curriculum on campus. Enrollments are very high, but graduation rates are smaller. What people seem to forget is that the emphasis in the forensic sciences is on science. It is necessary to disabuse forensic science students and criminal justice students of many of the fallacies they have brought with them from watching television.

Most criminal investigation texts fail to develop the relationships among the lab, the investigation, and the courtroom. The best investigation is of little use if the evidence seized is inadmissible in the courtroom, and most laboratory results will likewise be of little use if investigators contaminate or destroy forensic evidence during the investigation. The ultimate objective of criminal investigators is to clear cases by arresting suspects, but their actions are toothless without the sanctions imposed by judges and juries. The true objective of all investigations is to present admissible evidence to a prosecutor who can then prosecute the case to the full extent of the law. In this sense, the real objective of criminal investigators is to convict criminals. The pursuit of truth and the reconstruction of crimes are admirable objectives, but they are academic exercises if the ultimate point is not to provide admissible evidence upon which convictions can be based.

A criminal investigator is just one member of a team that includes patrol officers, evidence technicians, forensic scientists, medical examiners, pathologists, and prosecutors. None of the members can function properly without the professional support of the others. Although criminal justice education is compartmentalized, there is no reason why the members of the investigative team cannot understand their interdependence and the importance of working cooperatively. This book covers the material that most criminal investigation texts do, but it highlights forensic and legal considerations that apply to specific investigative techniques. Case law is included when relevant.

The prosecutorial chain is only as strong as its weakest link. Every team member must be mindful that the defense can use the incompetence of one member of the investigative team to discredit the whole team. The admissibility of laboratory results is based on the appropriate investigation and handling of the materials provided to the lab. Positive test results are useless if investigators contaminated the samples during the course of the investigation.

Each investigation involves the gathering and packaging of evidence, whether on land, underground, or underwater. This text addresses underwater investigations in part because of the increased use of waterways and the crimes and accidents that occur on them. Dive teams around the country are learning a scientific investigative protocol for processing underwater crime scenes. All federal agencies have trained underwater investigators and are convinced that future acts of terrorism may be waterborne. The homicide investigator has overall supervisory responsibility for the recovery of underwater evidence; without some idea of how it is done, it cannot be done correctly.

The world of criminal investigation has progressed to the point that no single text can adequately prepare a competent criminal investigator for the challenges confronting investigators today. What was contained in criminal investigation texts last year may be obsolete next year, or after the next terrorist event. The best that can be done is to try and catalog investigation's best practices with an eye toward anticipating the needs of the criminal investigator in the future.

Acknowledgments

This project could not have been completed without the help of a number of people. Robert Skiff, Jim Cocke, and Tom Curtis of SIRCHIE Finger Print Laboratories, Inc., provided numerous pictures and crime scene–technician instruction that proved invaluable in the writing of this book. The students of the March 12–16, 2007 Crime Scene Technology and Evidence Collection course allowed me to attend and treated me as one of their own. Dr. William Chillcott, boat accident reconstructionist, helped me understand the lethality of recreational boating and provided some extraordinary pictures for the section on vessel accident investigation. Many of my colleagues allowed me to bounce ideas off of them in our day-to-day interaction and put up with my laboratory experiments. To these people and to all the others my failing memory has neglected to recall, thanks.

Introduction to Criminal Investigation

▶ ▶ STUDENT LEARNING OUTCOMES

Upon completion of this chapter, students will demonstrate an understanding of:

- The scientific method and how it applies to criminal investigation
- The contributions of medical science to the investigative process
- The objectives of a criminal investigation
- The members of the investigative team
- How to admit evidence during trial

■ Perspective

Many see investigation as art or magic, a matter of hunches and theories. From this perspective, arrests and convictions are fortuitous. To the contrary, investigation is largely scientific. There is room for hunch and theory, but only within the confines of a rigid methodology. An understanding of the principles of forensic science (which are the same as for science generally) is essential to successful investigations. Many investigations are resolved within hours of the commission of the crime, primarily as a result of victim and witness statements, but these statements themselves may be bolstered at the time of trial by corroborating forensic evidence (**TABLE** 1-1).

■ Fundamentals of Forensic Science

Scientists utilize a **protocol** to structure their investigations (that is, the scientific method). The terminology varies, but the steps are generally the same. The objective is to arrive at a conclusion that others can replicate by applying the same protocol. Scientists have evolved a vocabulary for discussing this protocol; many of the terms are defined in the following sections.

TABLE 1–1 **Types of Evidence**

- **Physical evidence:** Evidence that can be touched and evaluated tactually
- **Testimonial evidence:** Words communicated by testifying witnesses
- **Circumstantial evidence:** Everything that is not eyewitness testimony
- **Forensic evidence:** Physical evidence that requires scientific validation

Parsimony

According to the **principle of parsimony**, one should seek the simplest explanation for the phenomenon being examined. If an automobile refuses to start, a mechanic might list possible reasons, from the simplest to the more complex:

1. No gas
2. No spark
   a. Low water in battery
   b. Bad battery cables
   c. Bad battery connections
   d. Failed battery
   e. Failed starter

A skilled mechanic would check the battery and its connections before replacing the starter. In doing so, he or she would be applying the principle of parsimony.

Specification

In any scientific experiment, **specification** of what exactly is going to be done and how it is to be done is important. Researchers may evaluate the procedure employed to determine if anything in the setup might have affected the outcome in ways other than intended.

Scientific Method

Researchers must first decide which particular phenomenon they wish to observe. It is imperative that the working **hypothesis** formulated by the research group that is utilizing the **scientific method** include an anticipated outcome and a supposed cause (i.e., a variable being tested to see whether it is a cause of the outcome). Only one variable can be examined or changed at a time. Changing or testing more than one variable at a time would render any observed outcome useless, for it would be impossible to tell which of the variables caused the outcome.

Observation

Scientists conduct experiments under controlled conditions to determine what happens when certain variables change. In many instances, what happens cannot be observed with the naked eye. Therefore, scientists use an array of instruments to assist in the **observation** process, such as microscopes, spectrometers, chromatographs, tape recorders, and cameras, to mention just a few. Note that scientists occasionally observe with senses other than sight.

Recording

Most scientific experiments take place over time and involve complex designs. **Recording** each step of the experimental method ensures that other experimenters can replicate the results. It is replicability that moves a phenomenon from art or magic to science.

Taxonomy

After the experiment, it may be necessary to group specific characteristics of the observed phenomena in order to create a **taxonomy**. Firearms examiners use taxonomic characteristics in classifying cartridges, cases, and bullets. During examination, they focus on one characteristic at a time.

Analysis

Data can only be used if it is broken down into parts. As in the construction of a jigsaw puzzle, the placement of a piece requires a detailed examination of that piece as well as the adjoining pieces. At the crime scene, the investigator gathers information from three separate sources: people, records, and physical evidence (Osterburg and Ward, 1992). Exceptional organizational skills are required to gather information from these sources and to render that information into a useable form. The organization of the information is the first step in the analytic process. It is difficult to analyze anything when overwhelmed by incoming data. Sorting, classifying, and organizing the information allows **analysis** to begin.

Once investigators have interviewed people, reviewed records, and examined evidence, they must **synthesize** the discrete data elements into a working hypothesis. What happened? When did it happen? Where did it happen? How did it happen? Who made it happen? These are the questions investigators seek to answer. In creating a hypothesis, investigators must try to suggest answers to as many of the posed questions as possible, based not on conjecture but on an examination of the gathered data.

Hypothesis

A working hypothesis is like an incomplete jigsaw puzzle that comes together a piece at a time. To carry on the analogy, the puzzle is old and in a container other than the original; you do not know what the puzzle picture is; and you do not know if all the pieces are provided or if there are pieces that do not belong to that puzzle. A picture will nonetheless begin to form as you put pieces together. At some point, what the puzzle depicts may suddenly seem apparent, and you will be able to form a hypothesis as to the full image. If subsequent pieces show the image to be different than first guessed, the hypothesis must be revised. Any criminal investigation faces the challenges of arriving at an apparent image without sufficient puzzle pieces and of disregarding the pieces that do not fit. As the investigation progresses, new corroborating facts will be added and the interpretation of some old facts changed. This is the process whereby the hypothesis advances toward becoming a theory.

Theory

As data are added, the hypothesis begins to take on a life of its own. It becomes more solidly based and evolves into a **theory** that begins to explain and predict.

Inductive Reasoning

We all come to answers in life based on experience. A series of similar or repeated experiences allows us to generalize to conclusions. If a person has had a bad experience with drinking water in another country and then suffers a repeat episode, he or she may jump to the conclusion that water in other countries is not safe to drink. This conclusion is incorrect. It may well be that water in the particular village, city, or establishment was tainted, but generalizing to the quality of water in all other countries is an unsupported leap.

Most of life's lessons (which we might place under the rubric "common sense") are brought to us by way of **inductive reasoning**, which is also an integral part of the scientific method. When applying inductive reasoning, you must keep in mind that you are usually dealing with probabilities, not certainties.

Deductive Reasoning

Conclusions can be reached through **deductive reasoning** as well. In a valid deductive argument, if the premises are true, the conclusion must be true. Consider this argument: All other countries have poor-quality water. Canada is another country. Therefore, Canada has poor water quality. The conclusion is certain on the condition that the premises are true. Note, however, that if even one of the premises of a deductive argument is not true, the conclusion remains uncertain. As pointed out earlier, many other countries have stringent sanitation regulations, which means that the first premise of the example deductive argument, far from being known to be true, is known to be false. Therefore, the argument does not help us determine whether Canada has poor-quality water—it may, or it may not.

■ Criminal Investigation and the Scientific Method

The scientific method usually is employed only partially in a criminal investigation. Two variables dictate the determination of which parts can be used: the type of crime being investigated and the type of information available. In a homicide, investigators use a variety of skills that derive from the scientific method. The following scenario identifies the various components of the scientific method where they come into play.

It is apparent that an investigation goes through many stages in the attempt to reconstruct the past. What is not apparent is the scientific method employed in most investigations (TABLE 1-2). Investigators may lack necessary vocabulary or be ignorant of scientific method and thus attribute many conclusions reached during investigations to "street savvy," hunches, or intuition. Rather, what is really at work is the process of inductive reasoning progressing through to the use of deductive reasoning. Many of the steps may be unidentified or misidentified, but they are still there. If investigators applied the scientific method intentionally and systematically rather than unconsciously or haphazardly, they would be greatly assisted in their reconstruction of the past.

TABLE 1-2   Applying the Scientific Method

Scientific Method	Criminal Investigation
Describe the phenomenon.	Identify what crime was committed.
Build a hypothesis.	Develop a working hypothesis based on information and evidence.
Collect data.	Gather records, evidence, and corroborative or uncorroborative information.
Test the hypothesis.	Constantly review all the facts, whether consistent or inconsistent with the working hypothesis; focus the case when the facts allow; interview or interrogate the suspect.
Continue to collect data.	As the finger of suspicion begins to point, gather any and all additional corroborative data.
Arrive at a theory.	Once probable cause has been attained, arrest the suspect. Provide all evidence to the prosecution, both inculpatory and exculpatory.

Source: Osterburg and Ward (1992), 35.

CASE IN POINT

The Scientific Method at Work

A homicide investigator has been called to the scene of an apparent suicide. In the kitchen of a small rural home, a body lies next to an overturned chair and a shotgun. The right foot of the deceased is bare, and a string tied in a bow around the big toe is also tied around the trigger of the shotgun. There is a large wound in the victim's chest and considerable tissue and blood residue on the barrel of the shotgun. Behind the victim is a waist-high hole in the wall about the size of a little finger.

These facts considered in their totality give some support to the hypothesis that this was a suicide. There appears to have been no struggle, and the weapon is in close proximity to the body. The hole in the wall is a bit troubling. The investigator's experience (inductive reasoning) tells him that shot shells do not leave such a hole unless they are chambered for a rifled round (shotguns have a cartridge that contains either numerous pellets or a single projectile). He examines the shotgun (analysis) and discovers that the two chambers of the double-barreled shotgun both contain a shell. One is spent. Upon removing it, he notes that the shell contains pellets. His hypothesis that a suicide occurred does not explain the hole in the wall (synthesis). If he is wedded to his hypothesis, he may choose to ignore this anomaly. Or he may begin to ask some additional questions:

- Who was present at the time of the shooting?
- Did the hole in the wall exist prior to the shooting?
- Are there other weapons on the premises?

Pursuing answers to these questions will provide information that can be used as a basis for further reasoning.

The investigator learns that only the victim's wife was present at the time of the incident, and she does not seem to be aware of any structural flaws in the kitchen wall. She tells the investigator that there is also a 30-caliber hunting rifle in the gun cabinet in the living room. Another hypothesis begins to take shape. Could the wife have murdered her husband? There are only two possibilities if the wife is telling the truth: suicide or homicide (with the wife as the primary suspect).

The investigator notices that the victim is wearing his wristwatch on his left wrist, which suggests he was right-handed. The investigator begins to gather information that he sees as consistent with right-handedness (classification):

- The wristwatch is on the victim's left wrist.
- The victim's wallet is in his right rear pants pocket.
- The victim's right front pants pocket is worn.
- There is a pocketknife in the right front pants pocket.
- There is a ballpoint pen in the left shirt pocket.

The wife confirms that her husband was right-handed.

The investigator begins to gather information that he sees as inconsistent with right-handedness (classification):

- The right foot has been bared.
- The string is tied to the right big toe.

The investigator's assumption, based on experience and reason, is that a right-handed person would have bared his left foot and tied the string to his left big toe (induction). That the facts conflict with this assumption suggests that someone else tied the string (deduction). The investigator suspects homicide (synthesis, theory), and he has the crime scene handled in a manner appropriate for an investigation of a homicide.

(continued)

The medical examiner confirms that a hole consistent with the passage of a 30-caliber bullet through the body was made prior to the shotgun blast. The laboratory discloses that the bow tied to the victim's big toe was tied not from the victim's position but rather from a reversed position, by someone facing the sole of the foot. The prosecution's theory of the case, which it will attempt to prove by presenting forensic evidence, is that the wife shot her husband with the hunting rifle while they were both sitting at the kitchen table. She then took the shotgun and placed the barrel at her husband's chest and fired, thereby obscuring the original and fatal wound. Stripping his foot bare and tying the string to his toe was her final attempt at making the homicide look like a suicide.

■ Importance of Forensic Evidence

Forensic science in police work is becoming increasingly important, not only because of advances in science but also because of changes in the legal system. In *Miranda v. Arizona* (1966), the U.S. Supreme Court held that a suspect must be told of the Fifth Amendment protection against self-incrimination and the Sixth Amendment right to counsel during interrogations (EXHIBIT 1-1). This decision required police to rely less on confessions and more on forensic evidence in obtaining convictions.

■ Medical Contributions

As forensic science has moved into the legal forum, dentists and physicians have worked alongside scientists to bring additional tools to the investigative team. Medical examiners and forensic pathologists have been in the forefront of the medical personnel assisting in the discovery process.

Forensic Pathology

Forensic medicine has been around for years because of the close relationship between law and medicine for the better part of the 20th century onward. **Pathology** is the branch of medicine associated with the study of structural changes caused by disease or injury. The term *forensic pathology* simply adds the concept of unnatural or suspicious in front of the word denoting disease or injury.

EXHIBIT 1-1   The Fifth and Sixth Amendments to the U.S. Constitution

Fifth Amendment

No person shall be held to answer for a capital or otherwise infamous crime, unless on a presentment, or indictment of a Grand Jury, except in cases arising in the land or naval forces, or in the militia, when in actual service in time of war or public danger; nor shall any person be subject for the same offense to be twice put in jeopardy, of life or limb; nor shall be compelled in any criminal case to be a witness against himself, nor be deprived of life, liberty, or property, without due process of law; nor shall private property be taken for public use, without just compensation.

Sixth Amendment

In all criminal prosecutions, the accused shall enjoy the right to a speedy and public trial, by an impartial jury of the State and district wherein the crime shall have been committed, which district shall have been previously ascertained by law, and to be informed of the nature and cause of the accusation; to be confronted with the witnesses against him; to have compulsory process for obtaining witnesses in his favor, and to have the assistance of counsel for his defense.

There are actually two branches of pathology: anatomic, which deals with structural alterations of the human body; and clinical, which deals with laboratory examination of samples removed from the body. Most forensic pathologists are experts in both branches. Such experts are certified to perform the following functions:

- Establish cause of death
- Estimate the time of death
- Infer the type of weapon used
- Distinguish homicide from suicide
- Establish the identity of the deceased
- Determine the additive effect of trauma or preexisting conditions

The pathologist generally makes these determinations as the result of an autopsy. Injuries can cause death in a variety of ways:

- Asphyxia
    Strangulation
    Drowning
    Smothering
- Wounding or trauma
    Bullet wounds
    Stab wounds
    Blunt force
- Poison
- Burns
- Traffic accident

Autopsy

The purpose of an autopsy is to observe and make a permanent legal record of the gross and minute anatomic peculiarities of a body as soon as possible after death. Anatomic examination may be sufficient to establish cause of death if the forensic pathologist has access to other information (such as surrounding circumstances, life history, psychiatric data, and other pertinent information). Clinical, or microscopic, examination of organ parts is often necessary to further bolster the forensic pathologist's conclusions. The examination of organ parts from the body is useful in toxicology cases as well as any time alcohol or drugs are suspected. The inspection of stomach contents is part of every postmortem exam, because it may provide information as to cause as well as time of death. Clinical examination also tends to confirm hunches about age, race, sex, height, weight, and general health condition, in cases of unidentified remains.

Autopsy Interpretation

Generally, autopsy reports include a four-stage interpretive process.

1. **Contributing cause:** Usually a preexisting illness or condition. Examples are pneumonia or asthma, if the victim had either of those conditions. The preexisting illness could conceivably be the real cause of death.

2. **Mechanism:** Usually anything expressible only in medical jargon. For example, "lung sacs became obstructed and could no longer transport oxygen."

3. **Immediate cause:** This section usually gets at the cause of death. It can be expressed in medical jargon, such as "asphyxia," "contusion," and so on, or it can be expressed in layman's terms, such as "perforating gunshot wound to the head."

4. Manner of death: Whether the forensic pathologist thinks the death is a suicide, a homicide, or from accidental, natural, or unknown causes.

The general rule is that manner = mechanism + immediate cause, but there are other general rules as well. If the mechanism is undetermined, the death must be ruled as occurring in an unknown manner. This happens in some poisoning cases. If the immediate cause simply aggravated a significant preexisting condition (contributing cause), the pathologist must rule the death natural, but the law may consider the death a homicide. Most traffic fatalities are ruled accidental.

Forensic Serology

The forensic serologist determines the type and characteristics of blood, conducts blood tests, examines bloodstains, and prepares testimony or presentations at trial; he or she also analyzes semen, saliva, and other body fluids. Blood is the most common and perhaps most important evidence left at or carried away from a crime scene. Its presence can link suspect and victim to one another and to the scene of violence. Bloodstain patterns provide significant information about position and movement during the crime, who struck whom first, in what manner, and how many times. Over the years, criminals have tried many ingenious ways to hide, clean up, and remove blood evidence, but this is an area in which criminal justice technology has stayed one step ahead.

Forensic law considers blood to be class evidence (items that share certain quantifiable characteristics), but the potential exists for individualized blood typing. Today, forensic serologists can provide testimony with some degree of certainty linking a single individual, and that individual only, to a bloodstain. Consider that identical twins may have the same DNA profile but completely different antibody profiles, and you begin to see the future of forensic serology.

Forensic Toxicology

Forensic toxicology is essentially a specialty area of analytical chemistry. **Toxicology** is the science of the adverse effects of chemicals on living organisms. In general, a toxicologist detects and identifies foreign chemicals in the body, with a particular emphasis on toxic or hazardous substances. A descriptive toxicologist performs toxicity tests to evaluate the risk that exposure to a substance poses to humans. A mechanistic toxicologist attempts to determine how substances exert deleterious effects on living organisms. A regulatory toxicologist judges whether or not a substance has a low enough risk to justify making it available to the public.

A **toxin** is any material exerting a life-threatening effect upon a living organism. Poisons are a subgroup of toxins. Toxic materials exist in many forms (gaseous, liquid, solid, animal, mineral, and vegetable) and may be ingested, inhaled, or absorbed through the skin. Poisons generally either enter the body in a single dose or accumulate over time. Toxins work in minute quantities or low levels, requiring sensitive analytical instruments for detection. Some toxins have medicinal value, but many produce irreparable damage. Some toxins have antidotes; others do not. Poisons can be combated by prompt treatment, and most organ damage (except for serious central nervous system injury) may be repairable. All substances are poisons; there is none that is not a poison. Dose differentiates a poison from a remedy.

A forensic toxicologist normally is presented with preserved samples of body fluids, stomach contents, and organ parts. He or she also has access to the coroner's report, which contains information on various signs and symptoms, as well as other postmortem data.

Ordinarily, the toxicologist is not required to render an opinion regarding whether toxin levels in the body were enough to cause death. This is usually the province of the forensic pathologist. Physicians are the only ones qualified to render opinions on the physiologic effects of toxins, and forensic law allows them to provide their testimony based solely on the toxicological report (that is to say, even though they may have no personal knowledge of the case). This law can vary by jurisdiction. Toxicology responsibilities include:

- **Postmortem forensic toxicology** determines the absence or presence of drugs, chemicals, gases, metals and other volatile substances in human fluids and tissues, and evaluates their role as a determinant or contributory factor in the cause and manner of death
- **Human-performance forensic toxicology** determines the absence or presence of drugs and chemicals in breath, blood, or other fluid and their role in modifying human performance
- **Forensic urine drug testing** determines the absence or presence of drugs and their metabolites in urine to demonstrate prior use or abuse

Blood Tests for Intoxication

The best medicolegal method for determining anything close to impaired judgment is an estimate of the amount of alcohol that has flowed through the blood vessels of the brain. Theoretically, a blood sample drawn from the brain's blood vessels (or from spinal fluid) would yield the most accurate results. However, for practical purposes, blood samples to test for intoxication are usually drawn from the arm.

With blood tests, the law allows suspects to choose the laboratory that will perform the analysis. The person drawing blood therefore will take two samples at the same time (as close to the traffic stop as possible), one vial for the police and another vial for the suspect. A preservative (sodium fluoride or mercuric chloride) must be added to the vials if testing will not be accomplished within a few hours; otherwise, putrefaction begins. The vials must also not be exposed to sunlight or heat.

The most commonly used laboratory test for alcohol in a blood sample is the dichromate oxidation method (a type of chemical test). This involves using ready-made ampules (closed glass containers) containing a mix of chromium dichromate and sulfuric acid. If anything containing alcohol is introduced into this solution, oxidation will cause a residue of chromic sulfate to form. The unconsumed amount of dichromate or the chromic sulfate formed is then measured, which gives the percentage of alcohol in the sample expressed in percent weight per volume.

After a toxicologist determines when the drinking started and ended (the absorptive interval of time) and when the person last ate (one reason why police ask these questions in stops for suspected driving under the influence), he or she can then extrapolate backward in time from the blood alcohol concentration estimation to the time of driving, accounting for the full ingestion and absorption of alcohol.

Urine Tests for Intoxication

Law enforcement practice is to take two samples of urine at 30-minute intervals; preferably, the second sample should be collected after the bladder has been emptied. Again, precautions must be made to add preservative and to keep the samples from exposure to light and heat.

Urinalysis requires a bit more sophisticated laboratory equipment than blood testing. One of three laboratory methods can be used: (1) chemical tests, (2) biochemical tests, or (3) gas chromatography. Gas chromatography is the most widely used because, unlike blood tests, it can distinguish alcohol from ketones and aldehydes (a problem that exists with diabetics and people with other disorders). Although chromatography produces a printout and lends itself to quantitative analysis, it always requires the expert testimony of a scientist to be admissible in court. This is because chromatography results are subject to both quantitative and qualitative interpretation.

Forensic Odontology

Forensic odontology (dentistry) mainly involves the identification of an assailant by comparing a record of a suspect's dentition (set of teeth) with a record of a bite mark left on a victim. Other uses in law for dentists include the identification of human remains and medicolegal assessment of trauma to oral tissues.

Teeth are highly resistant to destruction and decomposition, so dental identification can be made under extreme circumstances. Forensic odontology was used to identify the bodies of Adolf Hitler and Eva Braun at the end of World War II, as well as in the investigations of the World Trade Center attacks, the Waco Branch Davidian siege, and numerous airplane crashes and natural disasters. The United States has a fairly well-developed system of dental recordation (the Universal System), so it is not surprising to find it used to identify remains. One can also approximate age solely by analysis of teeth (a bit like checking for molar eruption and wear on a horse's teeth to determine age).

At some crime scenes, criminals leave their bite impressions on food products, chewing gum, or, more commonly, on the skin of their victims, especially in cases of battery, rape, child abuse, and homicide; this permits the use of **bite mark analysis**. There are seven types of bite marks, which can be classified by four degrees of impression. Contusions are the most common type of bite mark. Incisions offer the best three-dimensional image of the teeth. When avulsions and artifacts can be combined, the result is a three-dimensional image. Bite marks on a dead body have different characteristics from those on a live body, so a forensic dentist might be able to assist with estimating time of attack or time of death. Generally, the better the bite mark, the better an expert can make a comparison with a suspect.

Forensic odontology has been used as far back as the Roman Empire to identify victims of crime. Bite mark analysis is gaining acceptance as a forensic tool. When the bite mark is not sufficiently deep to reveal the unique characteristics of each tooth, it can only be said to have "class" characteristics. However, the location, size and number of wounds can be used in establishing a profile of the offender (Douglas, 1998).

In a non-sexually-based assault, bite marks may be found on the fingers, ears, nose, chest and thorax. In cases of sexual assault where the victim is female, wounds tend to cluster around parts of the body associated with sexuality. Bite marks can be found on the neck, shoulder, arm, breast, pubic area, buttocks, and thigh. In a male victim, bite marks might be found on the arm, chest, abdomen, buttocks, penis, and scrotum.

In cases where the bite mark causes sufficient damage to the flesh, it may be possible to determine the unique characteristics of each tooth. It is then possible to match these unique characteristics to a particular individual. The size and shape of the wound will be affected by the place on the body where it occurs, because certain areas of the body bend, distorting the surface area of the skin (Saferstein, 2007). Analytical steps include:

- Is the injury in question a bite mark?
- Is the injury in question a human bite mark?

- Are there sufficient characteristics to allow the marks to be matched to a suspect?
  - Suction marks
  - Front incisor marks
  - Canines
- Marks can be swabbed for DNA from saliva.
- Photographs are taken.
- Dental casts can be made of the mark.
- Dental casts can be made of the suspect's teeth.

Forensic odontologists most often receive evidence in the form of a photograph or images stored on computer disc. The use of digital photography allows the odontologist to reduce the margin of error found with traditional analysis of photographs (Bowers, 2004).

Digital images provide accurate means of measuring bite marks. Digital images when used with software such as Photoshop allow for better control of the image visualization through the use of features such as zoom. When digital photography is used in combination with digital imaging software, transparent overlays of the victim can be made, which can be laid over a suspect's dental images. (Bowers, 2004)

Medical examiners or police investigators will call in a forensic dentist when a bite mark is discovered while conducting an autopsy or viewing a body at a crime scene. The examination of a bite mark follows predictable steps:

1. A saliva sample from the bite is obtained.
2. The forensic dentist takes photographs.
3. The forensic dentist makes multiple impressions, casts, or molds of the bite mark.

Computerized bite-analysis software exists. Once a suspect is apprehended, the forensic dentist makes one or more impressions of the suspect's teeth, compares them with the recorded bite marks, and, if called to testify, renders an opinion regarding the probability of a match. The theory underlying forensic dentistry is that no two mouths are alike (even those of identical twins are different) and that teeth, like tools, leave recognizable marks.

■ Objectives of an Investigation

It is a common misconception that every crime is solvable and that the perpetrator always leaves traces at the crime scene that inevitably lead to his or her door. What is true is that a person cannot enter a crime scene without leaving something and taking something (perhaps only something microscopic). Finding the perpetrator's traces does not guarantee a resolution to the investigation, but it is a step in that direction.

Solving a crime means different things to the public than to a criminal investigator. The public believes a crime has been solved when the perpetrator has been identified and apprehended. However, identification and apprehension are but two of the seven objectives of a police investigation:

1. Crime detection
2. Locating and identifying suspects (Before a crime scene can be processed, individual perpetrators must be removed from the premises because they pose a danger to police, investigators, and others.)

3. Locating, recording, and processing evidence while observing all constitutional considerations

4. Arresting the perpetrator(s) while observing all constitutional considerations

5. Recovering property pursuant to Fourth Amendment requirements

6. Preparing for trial, including completing accurate documentation

7. Convicting the defendant by testifying and assisting in the presentation of legally obtained evidence and statements

Presuming a crime has been committed, the search for truth and the reconstruction of the crime scene are of little value if evidence necessary to the trial of the case is lost, destroyed, or contaminated. Recognizing that the evidence recovered and the steps in its recovery are the foundations upon which the prosecution must build its case allows for a wider view of the criminal investigation process.

Finding the perpetrator is often the simplest part of the job. Obtaining evidence in support of a conviction may be more difficult. Some "successful" investigations do not result in convictions, and some "failed" investigations do result in convictions. A less-than-elegant investigation may nonetheless result in a plea bargain, whereas the best-run investigation may run out of leads.

■ Investigator's Role

The expansion of science and technology raises the question of whether the forensic scientist has replaced the criminal investigator. The answer is clearly no. On the contrary, the investigator's role has been enhanced, because the evidence collected has increased value in the hands of a forensic specialist who knows how to extract its meaning but who depends on the investigator to put its meaning into context. The investigator and the forensic scientist work cooperatively (albeit frequently physically apart). The investigator recognizes what is important physical evidence, and the scientist processes it. Because of his or her experience, the investigator knows where to look for evidence and how to weigh its significance. The scientist knows how to handle, analyze, record, and interpret forensic evidence.

Many agencies, especially those with a large volume of cases and extensive resources, place an intermediary between the criminal investigator and laboratory scientists. In these agencies, forensic technicians actually recover, tag, and bag all evidence discovered by on-scene investigators. A criminal investigator need only locate prospective evidence and then leave it to the trained technicians to process it. Note that this text will treat the criminal investigator as both the finder of evidence and the person responsible for photographing, tagging, handling, and maintaining all evidence gathered at the crime scene.

OFFICER'S NOTEBOOK

Definition of a Successful Investigation

For the purposes of this text, a successful investigation is one in which the following statements are true:

- All available physical evidence is handled competently.
- All witnesses are interviewed intelligently.
- All suspects are interrogated effectively.
- All leads are developed.
- All documentation is completed comprehensively, clearly, and accurately.

■ Selecting Investigators

A criminal investigator must possess a variety and range of skills not called for in any other profession (TABLE 1–3). In addition, the investigator must be emotionally stable, physically fit, and self-motivated. Where are such extraordinary people found?

The story of criminal investigation is the story of men and women who developed an understanding of the criminal mind and criminal motivation while on the street.

TABLE 1–3   Skills and Competencies Crucial in Criminal Investigators

- *Rational thinking (deductive and inductive reasoning).* This includes the ability to relate a large number of seemingly unrelated facts. The investigator must let facts determine a hypothesis and theory, rather than fitting facts to a preexisting theory. The hypothesis and theory must be based on scientific (objective) observation and recall.

- *Critical thinking.* The investigator must be able to "see" and not just look; to allow critical thinking to flow as facts are gathered and a hypothesis is synthesized.

- *Analytic thinking.* The investigator must recognize evidence or potential loci of trace evidence and digest information from numerous sources. He or she must have the ability to see where pieces of the puzzle may fit based on the relationship of various bits of information to other bits of information.

- *Ethics and integrity.* The investigator should possess a personal philosophy based on honor, integrity, and duty in order to avoid confusion, ambiguity, and corruption.

- *Human anatomy.* The investigator should be able to determine the nature and quality of wounds inflicted upon a victim and to separate postmortem (after death) from antemortem (before death) injuries. He or she should be able to recognize defensive wounds and possible rape.

- *Human physiology.* The investigator should know something about putrefaction (gas formation) and decomposition, as well as insect larvae cycles and marine depredation.

- *Psychology.* All human discourse is based upon concepts of worth and esteem. An ability to assess the mental state of victims, witnesses, and suspects is essential for successful interviewing and interrogation.

- *Sociology.* Effective communication depends on the ability to recognize socioeconomic factors and their effect on the language, customs, and sensitivities of victims, witnesses, and suspects.

- *Archaeology.* Like field and marine archaeologists, the criminal investigator must locate all evidence geographically (where) and temporally (when).

- *Pharmacology.* In a death or drug investigation, the investigator may need to identify controlled substances, clandestine laboratories, or death as a result of poison.

- *Firearms.* In a society that values self-defense and handguns, the investigator obviously must be able to handle, identify, and process firearms safely.

- *Language and communication.* Ninety percent of what an investigator does involves language-based communication, from interviews to court testimony.

- *Constitutional law.* Of what value is a superb investigation if, in the process, individual constitutional rights are violated, rendering evidence inadmissible?

- *Law of evidence and its admissibility.* Although it is not necessary to be a lawyer to be a competent criminal investigator, it *is* necessary to know the evidentiary predicates (formal steps required of a lawyer attempting to admit particular types of evidence) for all evidence to be admitted at the time of trial.

- *Criminalistics (forensic science).* The more an investigator knows about forensic evidence, the less likely mishandling and contamination are to occur.

Indeed, there has been a time-honored tradition of selecting prospective investigators from the ranks of patrol personnel, with little regard for education and training. It was presumed that any officer who had accrued time in the ranks possessed the basic qualifications needed by a criminal investigator, and few other departmental requirements existed. Whatever skills were required by the job could be readily picked up on the job, supplemented by a brief stint at a school for investigators.

Many agencies now have incorporated a civil service examination to standardize the requirements for criminal investigators. The future will see men and women selected as criminal investigators because of their background in science or the law. University criminal justice curricula will require more science, computer, and law courses and will favor minors in science rather than sociology or psychology. Most agencies recognize that detective candidates need:

- An active imagination
- Patience
- An ability to be a team player
- An ability to be able to communicate
- An ability to recognize his/her audience
- An understanding of search and seizure law and its application
- An understanding of *Miranda vs. Arizona* and the line of cases flowing from it
- Tenacity
- Honesty and integrity
- Good physical condition
- Excellent writing skills
- An ability to recognize discrimination and remove it from the investigative process
- An ability to testify objectively and professionally
- An ability to be a leader

■ The Legal Team

Investigators and prosecutors are the most visible members of the criminal investigation team. Mutual respect fosters communication and assists in the trial and pretrial process, but the relationship between prosecutors and police frequently is adversarial or nonexistent. Police think that prosecutors often dismiss good cases or plea-bargain cases that should be tried. In most instances, their attitude toward prosecutors is a product of a difference in the legal criteria police and prosecutors use in carrying out their duties. Whereas police need only **probable cause** to arrest a suspect, prosecutors must prove their case **beyond a reasonable doubt**—two different standards. When this fact is noted, it makes sense that conflict will sometimes arise between police, who may believe they have a good case and made a "righteous" arrest, and a prosecutor, who may not see sufficient evidence to win a conviction. Police may have done everything correctly and their case may still not satisfy the legal requirements for a conviction.

Police are bound by Fourth Amendment considerations in the delivery of their services to the community (**EXHIBIT 1-2**). Police must have probable cause to search or to seize people or property. The seizure of people is called **arrest**, and it must be predicated upon information that would convince a reasonable person that a crime has been or is about to be committed. In trying to understand the standard of probable cause, it is

EXHIBIT 1–2　The Fourth Amendment to the U.S. Constitution

The right of the people to be secure in their persons, houses, papers and effects, against unreasonable searches and seizures, shall not be violated, and no warrants shall issue, but upon probable cause, supported by oath or affirmation, and particularly describing the place to be searched, and the persons or things to be seized.

often useful to view it as requiring a 51% probability that the individual has committed or is committing a crime (i.e., it is more likely than not).

Prosecutors, on the other hand, must evaluate evidence in its entirety, including that which justifies the arrest, and must determine whether they can convict the defendant on evidence beyond a reasonable doubt. For comparison purposes, we can consider a reasonable doubt as approximately equivalent to requiring more than a 90% probability that the person has committed the crime for which he or she is charged. That 39% difference (between 51% and 90%) constitutes a considerable gap and partly explains why arrest rates are higher than conviction rates. Police and prosecutorial staff will find it easier to cultivate a good relationship if they understand and appreciate that difference.

Prosecutors prosecute those cases in which they have confidence. That confidence is based on the quantity and quality of evidence, the quality of documentation supporting an investigation, and the ability of investigative witnesses to communicate from the witness stand.

If the conditions are favorable to the prosecution, the case will be prosecuted or a severe plea bargain reached. Victories do no damage to a prosecutor's career, or to an investigator's. Victory is self-perpetuating. If an investigator's cases consistently meet the conditions described above, they will be prosecuted consistently and conviction will result frequently. If, on the other hand, a case fails to meet one of these conditions, the probability of prosecution or conviction (if the case is prosecuted) diminishes. A prosecutor who has serious misgivings about a case or about an investigator is less likely to prosecute not only the case in question but also future cases handled by that investigator.

■ Admissibility of Evidence

It is the investigator's job to collect all of the available evidence, and it is the prosecutor's and the court's job to weigh the significance of the evidence. The first threshold that evidence must pass is that of proof of admissibility in court, called the **predicate**. All investigators must have not only an understanding of the rules of evidence admissibility but also a working knowledge of the foundation upon which all types of evidence are ushered before the court. It also pays to have a working relationship with the prosecutor and an understanding of the prosecutor's style when he or she asks formal questions allowing evidence to be admitted. New prosecutors may be less familiar with required evidentiary predicates than an experienced investigator. Absent the appropriate predicate, evidence otherwise admissible will not be admitted. It is helpful if the testifying investigator can assist the prosecutor in establishing the necessary predicates and can anticipate the types of questions that will establish those predicates. For example, the predicate for admitting photographs is not complicated, but the standard could remain unmet if either the prosecutor or the testifying investigator is not familiar with the format.

All evidence has a specific predicate that must precede its submission to the court. In essence, all evidence comes to the jury through the mouth of a witness. A piece of evidence will have no bearing on the outcome of the case, despite having been appropriately handled, stored, and presented to the prosecution, if the **evidentiary foundation** (predicate) for its admissibility is lacking. Once evidence has passed the test of admissibility and is made a part of the court record, it has the potential to influence the outcome of the trial. Such evidence is said to be **probative** (more likely than not to prove a fact in issue). Evidence is not the same as a fact. Facts are derived from evidence. Evidence may tend to prove a fact, or may not, or it may be just strong enough to create a reasonable doubt.

The investigator must know what evidence is required to determine the issue of guilt; whether such evidence indicates or fails to indicate guilt; and, when guilt is apparent, whether such evidence is likely to prove guilt beyond a reasonable doubt. The success of an investigation, as already noted, depends on the evidence collected and its legal significance. It is important to remember that a verdict of acquittal does not mean the defendant is innocent, but rather that the defendant has not been proven guilty beyond a reasonable doubt. A not-guilty verdict is not always a vindication, contrary to what defendants usually claim, as evidenced by findings of negligence in a civil suit based on the same testimony and evidence.

■ Summary

In this chapter we were introduced to the world of the criminal investigator, and we discovered some of the players and some of the contributors to the methodology employed in processing a crime scene. The introduction opens the discussion of the characteristics of a criminal investigator and includes a team perspective much larger than the conventional approach. It should be pointed out at this point that the greatest investigations in the world are of little use if the evidence gathered cannot be admitted at the time of trial, and that is why the end of the introduction addresses fundamental concepts of evidence admissibility. The next chapter is a continuation of the introductory chapter and provides a brief history of criminal investigation.

■ Key Terms

analysis: Rendering information into a form that allows it to be used
arrest: To place a person in the custody of a law enforcement agency
beyond a reasonable doubt: The standard of certainty necesssary to convict someone of a crime

bite mark analysis: Comparison of bite marks on a victim to those of a known suspect

circumstantial evidence: Everything that is not eyewitness testimony

deductive reasoning: Drawing conclusions based on premises that are certain (known to be true)

evidentiary foundation: Basis for a conclusion that was determined using collected evidence; predicate

forensic evidence: Physical evidence that requires scientific validation

forensic urine drug testing: Determines the absence or presence of drugs and their metabolites in urine to demonstrate prior use or abuse

human-performance forensic toxicology: Determines the absence or presence of drugs and chemicals in blood, breath, or other fluid and their role in modifying human performance

hypothesis: Prediction of outcome made in advance of testing a particular phenomenon

inductive reasoning: Drawing conclusions based on probabilities rather than certainties

Miranda v. Arizona: Supreme Court decision that requires that a suspect be told of the Fifth Amendment protection against self-incrimination and the Sixth Amendment right to counsel during interrogations

observation: Determination of what happens in an experiment when certain variables are changed

pathology: The branch of medicine associated with the study of structural changes caused by disease or injury

physical evidence: Evidence that can be touched and tactually evaluated

postmortem forensic toxicology: Determining the absence or presence of drugs, chemicals, gases, metals and other volatile substances in human fluids and tissues

predicate: Proof of admissibility in court

principle of parsimony: Principle that one should seek the simplest explanation for the phenomenon being examined

probable cause: Information upon which a reasonable person would believe that a crime has been or is about to be committed

probative: Likely to prove a fact

protocol: Set of steps followed to arrive at a conclusion that can be replicated by others using the same set of steps

recording: Making note of each step of the experimental method employed, so that the experiment can be repeated and the results replicated

scientific method: Formulation of a hypothesis and development of a protocol to test a hypothesis, in order to identify factors causing a particular phenomenon

specification: Designation of what is going to be done and how it is to be done

synthesis: The combination of data to form a working hypothesis

taxonomy: Classification of observed phenomena into groups that share specific characteristics

testimonial evidence: Words communicated by testifying witnesses

theory: A hypothesis that is supported by data

toxicology: The science of the adverse effects of chemicals on living organisms

toxin: Any material exerting a life-threatening effect upon a living organism

■ Review Questions

1. Are all crimes solvable?
2. What are the seven objectives of a police investigation?
3. What was the significance to investigators of the U.S. Supreme Court decision in *Miranda v. Arizona*?
4. What are the steps and characteristics of a successful criminal investigation? Mention these in the course of describing such an investigation.
5. What types of skills and competencies should a criminal investigator possess?
6. What is the purpose of using the scientific method?
7. What is the principle of parsimony and how does it apply to criminal investigations?
8. What is the job of a forensic serologist?
9. How is blood alcohol concentration determined?
10. Who conducts an autopsy? Why?
11. Of what investigative value is a bite mark left on the thigh of a victim?
12. What are the analytical steps in dealing with a presumed bite mark?
13. What are the characteristics that an agency looks for in a detective candidate?
14. What is meant by "all evidence comes to the jury through the mouth of a witness"?

■ Bibliography

Bowers, M.C. (2004). *Forensic dentistry: A field investigator's handbook.* Elsevier Publishing.

Douglas, J.E., Olshaker, M. (1996). *Obsession.* New York: Scribner.

Osterburg, J.W., & Ward, R.H. (2000). *Criminal investigation: A method of reconstructing the past.* Cincinnati, OH: Anderson.

Saferstein, R. (2007). *Criminalistics.* Upper Saddle River, NJ: Prentice Hall.

■ Suggested Reading

Saferstein, R. (2007). *Criminalistics: An introduction to forensic science* (9th ed.). Upper Saddle River, NJ: Prentice Hall.

Steadman, D.W. (2003). *Hard evidence: Case studies in forensic anthropology.* Upper Saddle River, NJ: Prentice Hall.

A Brief History of Criminal Investigation

CHAPTER

2

▶ ▶ STUDENT LEARNING OUTCOMES

Upon completion of this chapter, students will demonstrate an understanding of:

- How law enforcement developed in England
- How the English system was employed in the United States
- The arrival of criminal investigation to England and the United States
- The arrival of forensic science to the United States

■ Early History

In England at the end of the 13th century, the king established a system consisting of justices of the peace and parish constables, a system that served England and the United States until 1829. This system, though inefficient, did maintain a modicum of order in the class-based agrarian societies of this era, where conflict resolution was more often the result of a tradition of deference than of law enforcement; social and geographic mobility was restricted; and transience was virtually unknown. In agrarian societies, people typically are born and die within the confines of the same community, and values important to the community are maintained through community vigilance and a series of informal sanctions, from public rebuke to ostracism. A vigilant community has little need for external sanctions. It takes a village to police its own morals and values.

In the United States and in Western Europe, the Industrial Revolution led to the urbanization of manufacturing centers. A formerly agrarian population began to evolve into a labor pool for industrial complexes. People began moving about the countryside, and community vigilance had little impact upon those who were merely passing through. The industrial centers brought strangers together in a new environment in which a sense of community was replaced by exploitation of laborers, deplorable living conditions, ghettos, and poverty. In the United States, a growing tide of European immigrants generated population pressure in northeastern and midwestern cities. The flow of immigration created cultural and religious tensions between the new arrivals and the existing inhabitants, tensions that caused resentment, segregation, and discrimination.

These evolving industrial problems were not unique to the United States. England had earlier tasted the fruit, sweet and bitter, of industrialization and discovered that the system of social sanctions, justices, and constables that had been somewhat effective in rural areas was totally inadequate to bring order to its industrial centers. In 1829, the creation of a metropolitan police department altered the London system of law enforcement.

London's police department served as a model for other British municipalities as well as for emerging American cities. The rural areas of England and the United States did not require such elaborate policing arrangements, and the simpler constabulatory system continued to served such communities and remains in place throughout much of rural America. In U.S. cities, however, population increases, high rates of immigration, and economic development made it increasingly difficult to control the violence and criminality inherent in a large urban population (Miller, 1977).

■ Law Enforcement Developments in London and New York City

London

The constabulary system was organized around a group of **constables** appointed by local justices, to whom they owed their allegiance and continued employment. The constables were responsible for patrolling their precincts and could raise an alarm should it become necessary to solicit assistance from citizens to arrest a fleeing wrongdoer. Some constables were held in low esteem, as demonstrated by the failure of the citizenry to come to their assistance and by the ridicule heaped upon them while in pursuit of criminals. (Most states still have a **hue and cry** statute in their penal codes that requires citizens to come to the aid of a police officer when requested to do so. When responding to a police officer request for assistance, a citizen is given the powers and shackled with the responsibilities of a police officer. The delegation of police powers to citizens serves as a deterrent to raising the hue and cry today.)

Thieves were the primary plague of industrial London. A burgeoning class of unemployed, displaced rural families turned to theft as a profession when they found the doors to industrial employment closed to them. Constables were ineffective in stopping the wave of crime washing over London. Merchants and others were left to their own devices in trying to protect themselves from robbery and assault. When goods were stolen, it was customary for the victim to use his or her own financial resources to hire a **thief catcher**. Many thief catchers were thieves themselves, or moonlighting constables. Although an effective method of recovering stolen goods, hiring thief catchers did nothing to deter theft and may even have encouraged it, for in many instances the thief catcher was the very person who had stolen the goods in the first place.

In 1730, Sir Thomas De Veil was appointed magistrate for the Bow Street district of London. During the 17 years he was in office, he established the most effective police operations in the London area. In 1748, Henry Fielding, best known to us as a novelist, replaced Sir Thomas and continued improving police service in the Bow Street district.

Henry and his brother John advocated a single unified police organization. They hoped to establish a systematic criminal intelligence gathering apparatus, create a coherent police administration, and develop a preventative strategy for crime management (Radzinowicz, 1986). One of Henry's plans was to promote a small force of these catchers, directing and deploying them in a coherent manner about the city of London and its suburbs. Equivalent to bounty hunters, his new monied police, the so-called Bow Street Runners, would be under a central command with appropriate administrative supervision and controls (McMullan, 1996)

Henry was also responsible for organizing the first police intelligence organization, which published its gathered criminal intelligence in the *Covent Garden Gazette*. By 1800, the Bow Street Police Office was hailed as the leading law enforcement agency in the metropolitan London area (Johnson and Wolfe, 1996).

The rising crime rate in London taxed even the Bow Street district police. It was becoming apparent that the traditional methods of law enforcement were inadequate to combat crime in London. Effective enforcement in one precinct caused criminals to move to a less-policed or less-effectively-policed district. Leaving each district to fashion its own law enforcement methodology meant that districts had no uniformity in enforcement and no common grounds for communication or for the exchange of information and policing techniques. Entire portions of London were left without any effective means of preventing or punishing crime.

The first step toward standardizing law enforcement in London came in 1785, as the result of the efforts of William Pitt the Younger, who attempted to introduce a bill establishing a police force that would have jurisdiction throughout the city. Although soundly defeated, the bill served as the blueprint for legislation passed in 1829 creating the London Metropolitan Police (Radzinowicz, 1986). The new headquarters was established at 4 Whitehall Place, and the back entrance, used by visitors, was in Scotland Yard, which led to the headquarters being called Scotland Yard.

The continued high crime rate set the stage for Sir Robert Peel, who proffered a preventive approach to law enforcement. It was the association of the Metropolitan Police with Sir Robert that gave rise to the use of **bobby** as a colloquial term for a police officer. Peel established patrol areas and patrol functions, the collection of intelligence, and the centralization of all law enforcement activities. Police officers eventually accepted the notion of uniforms, although officers originally viewed them as livery, i.e., the uniforms worn by servants. Peel's highly visible and mobile force was easily recognized, and it acted as a deterrent on metropolitan streets. The bobby came to know his beat and those who lived and worked on it. Assigning officers to areas other than those in which they lived avoided fraternization with residents. Sir Robert Peel set out the structure and the salaries of the new Metropolitan Police force:

- 8 superintendents (£200 per annum)
- 20 inspectors (£100 per annum)
- 88 sergeants (3s 6d per day)
- 895 constables (3 shillings per day) (Tobias, 1979)

The formation of an investigative branch of the Metropolitan Police was inevitable. Patrol responsibilities precluded bobbies from devoting sufficient time to the investigation of crimes whose perpetrators were not apprehended immediately. To solve this problem, carefully selected police officers took on investigative duties. These officers were chosen from the foot patrol police, giving the latter an incentive to develop

CASE IN POINT

Three men, Weskett, Bradley, and Cooper, burgled the residence of the Earl of Harrington. Fielding's network of thief takers spent two years pursuing and eventually apprehending the group. The pursuers were successful in tracing one of the stolen banknotes. They circulated information and descriptions of the thieves throughout the country, and, by following leads, they penetrated the burglar's disguises, tricks, and aliases. They fostered the betrayal of a prostitute who knew Bradley, and they apprehended Bradley shortly thereafter. Bradley testified against Cooper, who received 14 years from the King's Bench (Linebaugh, 1991).

observational skills and intelligence networks. This method of selecting investigators, along with civil service testing, is still used by most contemporary police agencies (Johnson and Wolfe, 1996).

Jack the Ripper

In the years 1888–1891 residents of London's East End regarded the name **Jack the Ripper** with terror and his name was known the world over. Jack the Ripper is the popular name given to a serial killer who killed a number of prostitutes in the East End of London in 1888. The name comes from a letter written and published at the time of the murders. The killings took place in the districts of Whitechapel, Spitalfields, Aldgate, and the City of London proper.

Suspects.   Of the many suspects bandied about at the time, only four were based on any credible evidence:

- Aaron Kosminski, a Polish Jewish resident of Whitechapel
- Montague John Druitt, a 31-year-old lawyer and schoolteacher who committed suicide in December 1888
- Michael Ostrog, a Russian-born thief
- Dr. Francis J. Tumblety, an American who was arrested in November 1888 for indecency offenses and who fled the country

Of the many murders that had occurred in 1888 that were attributed to Jack, only five are generally accepted as his work:

- Mary Ann (Polly) Nichols, murdered Friday, August 31, 1888
- Annie Chapman, murdered Saturday, September 8, 1888
- Elizabeth Stride, murdered Sunday, September 30, 1888
- Catharine Eddowes, also murdered on Sunday, September 30, 1888
- Mary Jane (Marie Jeanette) Kelly, murdered Friday, November 9, 1888

The killer cut the throats of Mary Ann Nichols, Annie Chapman, Elizabeth Stride, Catharine Eddowes, and Mary Kelly. There were abdominal mutilations in all the cases except that of Elizabeth Stride. The killer took Annie Chapman's uterus, Catharine Eddowes' uterus and left kidney, and Mary Kelly's heart.

The Letter.   Jack the Ripper's name was written at the end of a letter, dated September 25, 1888, and sent to the Central News Agency, who turned the letter over to the police.

....

Dear Boss,

I keep on hearing the police have caught me but they wont fix me just yet. I have laughed when they look so clever and talk about being on the right track. That joke about Leather Apron gave me real fits. I am down on whores and I shant quit ripping them till I do get buckled. Grand work the last job was. I gave the lady no time to squeal. How can they catch me now. I love my work and want to start again. You will soon hear of me with my funny little games. I saved some of the proper red stuff in a ginger beer bottle over the last job to write with but it went thick like glue and I cant use it. Red ink is fit enough I hope ha. ha. The next job I do I shall clip the ladys ears off and send to the police officers just for jolly wouldn't you. Keep this letter back till I do a bit more work, then give it out straight. My knife's so nice and sharp I want to get to work right away if I get a chance. Good Luck.

Yours truly
Jack the Ripper

Dont mind me giving the trade name

PS Wasnt good enough to post this before I got all the red ink off my hands curse it No luck yet. They say I'm a doctor now. ha ha. (Begg, 2001)

....

New York City

New York City had adopted a system of law enforcement similar to the one that preceded the birth of the London Metropolitan Police. New York employed a system composed of locally elected constables and justices of the peace. Just as high crime rates relegated the constabulary system to the refuse heap in London, so too in New York. The evolution of police operations in London prompted New York City to abandon the constabulary system in 1845 and institute instead a uniformed, centrally organized police force. Officers wore a badge made of copper and soon became known as **coppers** (Miller, 1977).

The constabulary system continued to work well in rural areas, where crime was deterred by community sanction and watchfulness. To this day, the only prerequisite for serving as a constable or justice of the peace is widespread recognition and public esteem.

■ The Birth of Scientific Investigation

Criminal investigation involves the application of the scientific method to the analysis of a crime scene. As forensic science evolved, so too did the need for field practitioners to understand forensic science and the information that can be obtained from evidence preserved for forensic evaluation. As early as 1248, the Chinese recognized that the body itself could contain information about the cause and method of death. A handbook entitled Hsi Yuan Lu, published in 1250, gave guidelines for the postmortem examination of bodies. It included descriptions of various wounds caused by sharp versus blunt instruments and offered advice on how to determine whether an individual found in the water had died of drowning or had been killed beforehand and whether a burned individual was dead before the onset of the fire.

Doctors and other medical practitioners who, through observation, noted certain consistencies in natural deaths and uncharacteristic aspects of violent deaths, took the first steps in the forensic journey. These practitioners were the first medical pathologists. The written records of the development of **forensic pathology** in Europe begin in 1507, when a volume known as the Bamberg Code appeared. Twenty-three years later, Emperor Charles V issued a more extensive penal code, known as the *Constitutio Criminalis Carolina,* for all the lands included in his empire. The two documents recognized the importance of medical testimony as an integral part of trials involving possible infanticide, homicide, abortion, or poisoning.

In the latter half of the 16th century, Ambrose Pare performed official medicolegal autopsies. He reported findings from the examination of the lungs of smothered children and studied the traces left by sexual assault (Thorwald, 1965). As a result of advances in knowledge about violent death, judicial authorities and the police in Europe soon began to call upon physicians to help solve fatal crimes. Most of the larger jurisdictions developed centers, commonly known as institutes of forensic medicine, where experts carried out their investigations.

■ Scientific Investigation in the United States

The historical development of scientific investigation in this country can be traced to the English coroner system. The justice courts authorized the **coroner** to attach or arrest witnesses or suspects and to appraise and safeguard any lands or goods that might later be forfeited by reason of guilt of the accused. William Blackstone wrote a succinct description of the coroner's duties at the time of King Edward I in 1272:

The office and power of a Coroner are also like those of a Sheriff, either judicial or ministerial, but principally judicial . . . And consists, first in inquiring, when a person is slain or dies suddenly, or in prison, concerning the manner of his death. And this must be upon sight of the body; for if the body be not found, the coroner cannot sit. He must also sit at the very place where death happened and the inquiry must be made by a jury of 4, 5, or 6 of the neighboring towns over which he is to preside. If any be found guilty by this inquest of murder or other homicide, the coroner is to commit them to prison for further trial and must certify the whole of his inquisition, together with the evidence thereon, to the Court of King's Bench, or the next assizes. (Latrobe, 1861, p. 6)

In 1877, the English parliament enacted a law requiring an **inquest** to be conducted whenever the coroner had reasonable cause to suspect a violent or unnatural death had occurred or when the cause of death was unknown. This had the effect of granting the coroner wide authority to investigate cases and was in sharp contrast to the practice on the European continent, where prosecutors and police began investigations. Thus, the coroner's office developed as a broad-spectrum investigative agency concerned with a large proportion of all deaths. The United States ultimately adopted an act similar to the English law. It is reflected in current statutes that empower the medical examiner's office and lay the jurisdictional foundation for the performance of a medical examination.

In 1789, a professor of physiology at the University of Edinburgh began giving lectures in legal medicine and public health. In general, professors of legal medicine, by doing research and authoring textbooks, were most responsible for establishing legal medicine and pathology as an independent scientific pursuit.

American colonists brought the coroner system from England intact. An early definition of a coroner's duties in the colonies can be found in the governor of Maryland's 1640 appointment of John Robinson to be high constable and coroner for St. Mary's County. According to the definition, the coroner, among other duties, was required "upon notice or suspicion of any person that hath or shall come to his or her death entirely within the limits of that county to warn as many inhabitants of the said county as you conveniently may to view the dead body and to charge the person with an oath truly to inquire and true verdict to grant how the person viewed came upon his or her death according to the evidence" (Browne, 1885, p. 417).

The earliest mention of a physician in connection with the duties of a coroner was in 1860 in Maryland, where the Code of Public General Laws authorized the coroner or his jury to require the attendance of a physician in cases of violent death. Eight years later, the legislature authorized the governor to appoint a physician as sole coroner of Baltimore. In Boston in 1877, the Commonwealth of Massachusetts adopted a statewide system requiring that a physician known as a **medical examiner** supplant the coroner. In 1915, New York City adopted a law eliminating the coroner's office and creating a medical examiner system, authorizing the investigation of any death resulting from criminal violence, casualty, or suicide; occurring suddenly while the person was in apparent health, was unattended by a physician, or was imprisoned; or occurring in any suspicious or unusual manner (Fisher, 1993, p. 14).

■ The Growth of Forensic Science

The latter part of the 19th century witnessed the emergence of the science of pathology as a subspecialty of medicine; at the same time, the related fields of forensic science began to develop. During this period, **Alphonse Bertillon** devised the first scientific system of identification; his anthropometric system was accepted as the most accurate method of criminal identification until the early 1900s.

Bertillon came from a family dominated by medical doctors, naturalists, and mathematicians, but his unassuming air and lack of personal grace resulted in his being assigned to an assistant clerkship in the records room of the French Surete's archives in Paris. It was his task to file identifying data on all criminals apprehended and convicted throughout France, and this tedious task was rendered additionally distasteful by his realization that virtually all of the descriptions were so vague as to be useless. In 1879, he decided, upon the basis of his observations and his knowledge of science, that no two people could have exactly the same physical characteristics. If enough measurements were taken, a high degree of individuality could be developed for each person in a police agency's files. By February 1883, his technique was shown to be successful, and it was referred to in the newspapers as *anthropometry* or *Bertillonage.* Bertillon's methods gained immediate attention. In the United States, they were widely adopted, and a central file of measurements was maintained at Sing Sing prison.

Bertillon's system was destined to be short lived, because it often provided incorrect identification. Henry Faulds, a Scottish physician working in Japan, noticed the practice of identifying pottery and sealing documents through the use of handprints and fingerprints. In 1892, Sir Francis Galton published *Finger Prints,* a book-length monograph that contained a basic system of classification (Galton, 1892). Galton's system was expanded into a practical method of categorization widely adopted throughout the world by 1903.

American fingerprinting efficiency was increased in 1924 when federal prisoner identification files maintained at the federal prison at Leavenworth were combined with the files maintained by the International Chiefs of Police at Sing Sing. The consolidated fingerprint bureau, later to be relocated to the FBI in Washington, DC, proved invaluable not only for criminal investigation but also for the identification of the victims of accidents and natural disasters (Johnson and Wolfe, 1996).

In the 1870s, a Frenchman, Albert Florence, developed a definitive chemical test for the presence of human semen, and another Frenchman, Ambroise Tardieu, discovered that dotlike blood spots under the pleura (the membrane that lines the chest and covers the lungs) were characteristic of death by rapid suffocation. In 1882, an Austrian, Eduard von Hoffmann, discovered that persons burned alive had soot in their windpipes and lungs and carbon monoxide in their blood.

A German physician, Paul Uhlenhuth, developed a test in 1901 that permitted scientists to distinguish one species of animal blood from another, while his countryman, Karl Landsteiner, discovered that human blood cells could be grouped into what came to be known as A, B, and O types. In 1915, a simple procedure for determining the blood group of a dried bloodstain was developed by Leone Lattes in Italy.

Closely related to bloodtyping is DNA matching, which now is used often in criminal investigations. Deoxyribonucleic acid (DNA) is located in all human cells, and its precise configuration is determined by heredity. DNA is the architect, foreman, and bricklayer of life. In every creature, DNA carries the coded messages of heredity and governs everything from eye color to toe length. It is present in every one of the trillions of cells in the human body. Based on the work of **Alec Jeffreys** at the University of Leicester, a method was developed to extract DNA from a specimen of blood, semen, or other tissue, slice it into fragments, and tag the fragments with a radioactive probe so that they would expose X-ray film. The resulting pattern of stripes on the film is as distinctive as a fingerprint, and Jeffreys and his colleagues named the process of isolating and reading DNA markers *DNA fingerprinting*.

In one of the first experiments conducted by Jeffreys using his new **genetic fingerprinting**, he tested a family group to see if the pattern of inheritance was as simple as he expected it to be. That experiment showed him that half of the bands and stripes were from the mother and the rest from the natural father (Beeler and Wiebe, 1988). Determining whether these characteristics held true for tissues other than blood was his next task. His team took both blood and semen and found that the genetic map was constant, regardless of the kind of cells from which the material had come. To determine test sensitivity, Jeffreys' team tested small quantities of blood and semen. A drop of blood or a tiny amount of semen was sufficient. Jeffreys clearly had developed a laboratory technique that provided seemingly irrefutable results. His concern, however, was to ensure proper identification of the forensic materials available at a crime scene. How effective would his procedure be in identifying degraded DNA? Additional testing on three-year-old blood and semen stains turned out to be equally successful.

In March 1985, Jeffreys published his first scientific report, in which he estimated that the chance of two people having the same DNA fingerprint (absent identical twins) was zero. "You would have to look for one part in a million million million million million before you would find one pair with the same genetic fingerprint and with a world population of only five billion it can be categorically said that a genetic fingerprint is individually specific and that any pattern does not belong to anyone on the face of this planet who ever has been or ever will be" (Wambaugh, 1985, p. 94).

Nevertheless, there are different methods of DNA testing. For example, in the O.J. Simpson case, the laboratory used two methods. One process, RFLP (restriction fragment length polymorphism) is more accurate but requires a large quantity of the material to be tested. The other process, PRC (polymerase chain reaction) requires only small quantities of material but may be less accurate.

■ Development of Crime Laboratories

Scientific fields such as chemistry, physics, biology, and microscopy have a long history of separate development. Although the noted German jurist Hans Gross published a textbook in 1893 detailing the application of information derived from these separate fields to criminal investigation, it was not until 1910, when Edmond Locard established the first crime laboratory in Lyon, France, that these specialties were brought together for the sole purpose of improving criminal investigation. The success of Locard's laboratory led to the formation of similar laboratories in different parts of Europe, and in 1923 the first complete crime laboratory in the United States was established in Los Angeles. In 1932, a laboratory organized within the FBI made forensic science available nationwide for the first time. This laboratory has served as the model for the formation and organization of forensic laboratories at local, state, and national levels throughout the world (Fisher, 1993).

In a modern, well-equipped forensic laboratory, experts from the fields of serology and immunology, ballistics, document analysis, fingerprinting, polygraphy, analytical chemistry, and geology work together to solve crimes and provide scientifically validated evidence. In the past decades, many of the sophisticated analytical techniques and scientific instruments developed primarily for medicine and industry have been incorporated into forensic laboratories. Technologies such as gas-liquid chromatography, infrared spectroscopy, nuclear magnetic resonance, and mass spectroscopy have found their fullest application in criminal investigation.

Although much of the testing falls to the scientists, it is the responsibility of the criminal investigator to preserve physical evidence and to exercise good judgment in determining which scientific measurements and evaluations are appropriate. The rapid expansion of scientific methods of investigation has placed special demands on the training and financial resources of police agencies. Use of sophisticated techniques requires a high level of formal education, a comprehensive knowledge of modern science, and the ability to work with highly trained professionals in anatomy, physiology, chemistry, and physics. It was under these types of pressures that the old American system of elected coroners began to give way to trained medical examiners after 1935, and the work of police detectives soon came to involve coordinating the investigations of many professional scientists and applying their discoveries to the solution of criminal cases.

The Myth of Crime Lab Invincibility

Crime lab reports seem to have an aura of invincibility about them. Maybe we believe that the reported results are based upon "science," which, in turn, can be empirically tested. Because report contents can be checked, we assume that no lab technician would falsify a report.

What happens to a piece of forensic evidence from the time of its discovery until it appears in the courtroom? First, we should realize that the discovery itself could affect the integrity of the evidence. After the evidence is discovered, it has to be collected; it is then packaged, labeled, and transported—four more chances for error. It is then stored, removed from storage, and again transported, this time to the laboratory. At the laboratory, the evidence is logged in, placed in storage, again removed from storage, kept from intermingling with other evidence, and documented properly. All of this activity occurs before any tests are performed.

Next, the evidence is taken to a clean, contamination-free work area, where it must be unpackaged properly. The item must be inspected visually and described properly in detail to document its condition before any work is performed on it. In most instances it will be photographed, weighed, and sketched. Only then will the lab technician consider beginning any laboratory work.

The technician must figure out what test or tests are appropriate, determine if sufficient amounts of the evidence exist for those tests, and then properly dissect the portion to be tested and properly prepare the testing material, all while continuing to document each step. Only then does any testing begin. Some tests might include as many as five or six separate procedures, each of which must be performed properly and documented, with the evidence afterward being repackaged, relabeled, and once again transported to storage properly. Then the technician interprets what the experiments have disclosed.

The evidence must next be removed from the lab's storage area, logged out, transported to the police evidence area, logged in, and stored properly until the prosecuting attorney decides if he or she wants more testing performed, at which point the whole process begins anew. Once tested and recorded, the evidence has to make it to the courtroom for the preliminary examination, back to storage, possibly back to the lab for more testing, back to the police, and so on.

Thus, it is clear that no other type of evidence is exposed to anywhere near as many opportunities for destruction, mishandling, contamination, or other conceivable catastrophes that can be brought on by human or natural error as forensic evidence.

■ Summary

This chapter provides a brief overview of the evolution of law enforcement in England and the United States. We also learn how the coroner's office evolved into the medical examiner's office. It must be noted that an entire academic life could be spent studying the history of criminal investigation here and in England and that the purpose of this chapter is to provide a bit of a historical perspective to our study. The ultimate objective of all the work done by criminal investigators, laboratory personnel and prosecutors is to be able to present the discovered evidence in a court of law. Recent news reports tell us of serologists and DNA technicians that have fabricated evidence in an effort to save time and effort. Even in the trial of O.J. Simpson, where the suspect was accused of multiple homicides, forensic personnel handled evidence with their bare hands and a criminal investigator lied on the witness stand. To what end is the best investigation if what we discover cannot be presented at trial?

Everything brought to the crime laboratory came from a crime scene. As such, the next chapter deals with crime scenes and the information needed to understand the nature, breadth, and scope of what is left to be processed after a crime has been committed. We usually envision crime scenes associated with single homicides. Today we must enlarge our perspective to include crime scenes as large as the Branch Davidian Compound in Waco, Texas, and the Twin Towers in Manhattan.

■ Key Terms

Alec Jeffreys: Scientist who developed the method of DNA fingerprinting

Alphonse Bertillon: Person who developed the first scientific system of identification for use in criminal investigation

bobby: Colloquial term for a police officer, which arose due to the close association of Sir Robert Peel with the Metropolitan Police Department in London

constables: Law enforcement officers in London appointed by local justices, to whom they owed their allegiance and continued employment

copper: Colloquial term for a police officer, coined because the members of the first uniformed police force in New York City wore badges made of copper

coroner: In the English coroner system, this person was authorized by the justice courts to attach or arrest witnesses or suspects and to appraise and safeguard any lands or goods that might later be forfeited by reason of guilt of the accused

forensic pathology: Area of medicine pertaining to studying the causes of human death

genetic fingerprint: The DNA fingerprint of an individual

hue and cry: Alarm sounded by constables to summon help from citizens to apprehend a criminal

inquest: A formal inquiry

Jack the Ripper: The popular name given to a serial killer who killed a number of prostitutes in the East End of London in 1888

medical examiner: A physician who works for a law enforcement agency to investigate the cause of any death that could have resulted from a crime or that occurred in a suspicious or unusual manner

thief catcher: A person hired to locate someone's stolen goods; this person was often a thief himself or a moonlighting constable

■ Review Questions

1. What type of law enforcement system was established in early colonial America? Where did it come from and what were its shortcomings?
2. What were thief catchers, and what role did they play in the evolution of law enforcement in London?
3. What was the hue and cry, and what vestiges of it remain today?
4. Who were the Bow Street Runners, and what contribution did they make to the evolution of English law enforcement?
5. How did bobbies and coppers get their names?
6. How did the office of coroner evolve, and what was its impact on the establishment of the office of medical examiner?
7. Who was Alphonse Bertillon, and what was his contribution to forensic science?
8. What is DNA?
9. What was Alec Jeffreys' contribution to the study of DNA?
10. What level of education do you think the author of the Jack the Ripper letter had?

■ Bibliography

Beeler, L., & Wiebe, W.R. (1988). DNA identification tests and the courts. *Washington Law Review* 63:903.

Begg, P. (2004). *Jack the Ripper. The facts.* London: Robson Books.

Browne, W.H. (Ed.). (1885). *Archives of Maryland.* Vol. 3. Baltimore: Maryland Historical Society.

Fisher, R.S. (1993). History of forensic pathology and related laboratory sciences. In W.U. Spitz (Ed.), *Medicolegal investigation of death* (3rd ed.). Springfield, IL: Charles C. Thomas.

Galton, F. (1892). *Finger Prints*. London: MacMillan.

Johnson, H.A., & Wolfe N.T. (1996). *History of criminal justice* (2nd ed.). Cincinnati, OH: Anderson.

Latrobe, J.G. (1861). *Justices' practice under the laws of Maryland* (6th ed.). Baltimore: Lucas.

Linebaugh, P. (1991). *The London hanged: Crime and civil society in the 18th Century*. London: Penguin.

McMullan, J. L. (1996). The new improved monied police: Reform, crime control, and the commodification of policing in London. *British Journal of Criminology* 36:85–108.

Miller, W.R. (1977). *Cops and bobbies: Police authority in New York and London, 1830-1870*. Chicago: University of Chicago Press.

Radzinowicz, L. (1986). *A history of English criminal law and its administration from 1750*. London: Stephens.

Thorwald, J. (1965). *The century of the detective*. New York: Harcourt World.

Tobias, J.J. (1979). *Crime and police in England 1700-1900*. London: St. Martin's Press.

Wambaugh, J. (1985). *The blooding*. New York: Bantam.

The Crime Scene

▶ ▶ STUDENT LEARNING OUTCOMES

Upon completion of this chapter, students will demonstrate an understanding of:

- The responsibility of all the members of the crime scene team
- How to process crime scenes big and small
- The use of templates and virtual photography in constructing crime scene sketches
- The importance of taking crime scene notes
- The importance of recording/documenting the crime scene

No matter what the crime or where the location, no two crime scenes are ever the same. Each crime scene encompasses not only the geographic area but also persons and things. Protecting the area is pointless if what is contained within it is not also protected. The entryways and exits and travel routes to and from the scene must similarly be guarded against contamination. The geographic area and the material objects within it usually can be secured easily. More difficult is preserving the people on the crime scene. Yet they must be preserved as meticulously as any other evidence.

All crime scenes contain physical evidence, that is, evidence that can be touched, seen, or otherwise perceived using the unaided senses or forensic techniques. The difficult task is to determine what is evidence and what is not. However, it is better to process too much evidence than too little. Experience will help an investigator begin to pare down what is taken from a crime scene. Each crime has its own set of evidence parameters that help in distinguishing evidence from non-evidence.

Anything taken from the crime scene should be instrumental in discovering the facts. Keep in mind that the evidence reveals the facts; when the evidence is inconsistent with a hypothesis, the hypothesis must be changed to fit the evidence—not the other way around. Numerous court cases have reduced the significance of suspects' confessions and highlighted the key role of evidentiary corroboration. The importance of crime scene processing continues to increase. Not all evidence is recognized readily as such. Often, seemingly insignificant material left at a crime scene can increase in importance as the trial approaches or during the trial. The skills of the investigator may come into play anywhere or at any time.

The crime scene includes all areas through which the participants moved while entering to commit the crime, while committing the crime, and while exiting the crime

CASE IN POINT

Searching an Outdoor Crime Scene
In a search for a semiautomatic pistol in a man-made lake in Texas, divers laid down a tarpaulin and began unloading and stacking their air tanks, search ropes, personal flotation devices, wetsuits, and other dive-related equipment. Before they found the gun, divers using underwater metal detectors discovered four live 9-mm cartridges. The cartridges were located, bagged, and tagged. By the end of the day, the handgun was discovered and appropriately processed. As the dive team members were stowing their equipment, they discovered three *more* cartridges under the tarpaulin. That team learned that areas adjacent to the crime scene may be a part of that crime scene and must be processed as such.

scene. Generally the crime scene is a single well-defined area, but it may encompass several noncontiguous areas. Because most human activity takes place in sheltered places, the majority of crimes occur inside. Buildings and vehicles are the most common crime scenes, and most crime scene processing involves these locations. However, as more and more people seek outdoor recreation, investigators will need to develop the ability to deal with outside crime scenes as well.

The outdoor crime scene and the underwater crime scene require a redefinition of what constitutes a crime scene or secondary crime scene. People must get to wherever they are going outside, and they seldom walk. The roadways they drove, the areas adjacent to a crime scene that facilitate parking, and the pathways leading to and away from an exterior or underwater crime scene may contain evidence of that passage. In underwater recovery operations, dive team members may stage their equipment and seek access to the area to be searched with little consideration that the area over which they are walking is part of a crime scene. They may begin their search activities walking around in hip-deep water, impervious to the fact that what they are walking upon may also be part of the crime scene.

Reconstructing the scene of a crime is accomplished by recording each piece of evidence in relation to permanent non-evidentiary items at the scene. The strategy is the same regardless of the location of the crime scene. Inside or outside, evidence must be recovered with some record of its relationship to the environment from which it was removed. Inability to demonstrate that relationship at the time of trial may prevent the evidence from being admitted.

■ First Response

The investigative team's most valuable investigative tool consists of the officers who arrive first on the scene. Too often these officers are excluded from the investigative "club," treated as underlings, and denied services and training that could increase the chance of investigative success. It is imperative that **first-responding officers** possess an understanding of the investigative process, including a familiarity with and an appreciation for forensic evidence and its location, processing, and handling. A telephone at a crime scene may be the most convenient phone to use, but getting to the phone and picking up the handset may destroy essential evidence. Ambling through the crime scene is preventable through education about the nature of the first-response function.

Protection of the crime scene will reduce crime scene **contamination**. All crime scenes and all evidence retrieved from a crime scene are contaminated; the goal is not to add to the contamination. Only materials handled in contamination-free laboratories can be said to be truly uncontaminated. The trick is to prevent any untoward or unnecessary contamination from occurring once the scene and its contents come into the possession of the police. Anyone entering a crime scene leaves something; anyone departing a crime scene takes something along. This kind of **transfer** is what prompts forensic scientists to search for minute materials that may have been left at the scene of the crime.

First-responding officers must protect the scene by:

- Conceptualizing the crime scene
- Establishing the boundaries of the crime scene
- Keeping unauthorized personnel and the curious out
- Detaining and separating any eyewitnesses
- Continuing security until properly relieved

While doing this, they must also obtain medical assistance for anyone at the crime scene who is injured.

The most difficult situations to deal with are those involving other agencies and media representatives. Medical examiners, emergency medical personnel, and coroners all have duties to perform. Bodies cannot be released until officials have completed their investigative analysis. Often, there will be someone making a demand for entry who may be upset by being excluded from the scene. It is vital that the police and all persons associated with a crime scene in any capacity be aware of and comply with the written policies and procedures that apply to crime scene security. Media representatives often attempt to gain access and information by invoking the First Amendment (EXHIBIT 3-1) and the people's right to know. Some police officers are only vaguely aware of the amendment and have little understanding of the cases that have established First Amendment limitations. Nowhere does the First Amendment refer to the people's right to know, nor does it refer to extraordinary rights of the press. It simply refers to the abridgment of freedom of the press. The purpose of the First Amendment is to protect the press and the public from a strong central government and the temptation it would have to censor the press. Denial of access to a crime scene does not abridge freedom of the press; journalists are free to write whatever they wish, within the confines of laws that govern the media.

In managing the press, it is important to attempt to maintain a good rapport with all representatives of the media. First responders do not have the responsibility to make any statements to the press. The public information officer should make all statements to the press, and all requests for access or statements should be referred to that officer. Media representatives have no greater right to enter a secured area than any other citizen, nor have they any greater right to information. Under no circumstances are media representatives to be allowed access to a crime scene. All information provided to the press regarding an investigation should be managed through **press pools** and public statements.

EXHIBIT 3-1   The First Amendment to the U.S. Constitution

Congress shall make no law respecting an establishment of religion, or prohibiting the free exercise thereof; or abridging the freedom of speech, or of the press; or the right of the people peaceably to assemble, and to petition the Government for a redress of grievances.

OFFICER'S NOTEBOOK

Media Checklist
- Do not contact the media unless you are trained and designated as the public information officer (PIO) or you are cleared through the PIO's office.
- Be courteous at all times. An angry press does not serve the interests of law enforcement.
- Bar all media from a crime scene and advise media representatives that an area will be set aside from which all information will be disseminated.
- "No comment" is often the standard refrain of police. It is irritating to the press and should be replaced with a more rapport-building standard, such as "The public information officer will make a statement to all press representatives as soon as the situation allows."
- Avoid all contact with the media off duty as well as on duty, unless specifically charged with that responsibility.
- Unauthorized statements quoted by the press are often claimed by the police to be misquotations or taken out of context; in reality, they are usually accurate, although uttered thoughtlessly or in haste. Think before you speak, and realize that anything you say can be recorded and broadcast.
- If you are the subject of press coverage, do not fall victim to believing the image the press is attempting to portray.

Once the boundaries of the scene have been determined and made secure, evidence must be discovered and collected and the crime reconstructed. Most evidence at a crime scene is vulnerable, and often the most effective evidence is the most easily damaged. **Trace evidence** is extremely fragile and susceptible to contamination. It is usually undetectable by the naked eye and must undergo extensive laboratory procedures before it can be preserved and used later at trial. Items of evidence such as blood, fingerprints, hairs, fibers, footwear, broken glass, paint scrapings, tread marks, footprints, and tool marks are easily destroyed, altered, or contaminated. Only people authorized by written policy to help process the crime scene should be allowed on the scene.

As important as first responders are in securing the usual crime scene, they play an even more significant role in handling witnesses and securing the area in an underwater investigation. They may have to cordon off high-use areas and contact agencies that possess authority over the waterway to reduce boat traffic and to secure the search area. Many jurisdictions treat waterways as an anomaly and believe that there is nothing to process in an underwater crime scene. This attitude sometimes has led to the inadmissibility of important evidence and the acquittal of offenders who otherwise would have been convicted. It does little good to have a properly trained dive team if the investigator in charge sees water recovery as the mere retrieval of items from beneath the water. Just as there is an appropriate protocol to be employed on dry-land investigations, so too there should be a protocol for underwater investigations.

■ Collecting, Handling, and Preserving Evidence

The objective of all criminal investigations is to win convictions, and the key to winning convictions, even when there is a confession or eyewitness testimony, is the quality of the evidence obtained at the crime scene. The evidence is of little value if it has been handled, tagged, or stored improperly. Once each item of evidence has been photographed and included in a crime scene sketch, it must be collected, preserved, transported, and stored. Improperly collected, preserved, transported, or stored evidence will be inadmissible at trial once the defense discovers any improprieties. (Issues of admissibility are dealt with in another chapter, as are chain of custody and authentication.)

The handling and packaging of evidence is a lengthy subject. Each item of evidence at the scene should be placed in an appropriate container, which should be tagged to identify it and differentiate it from all other evidence taken at the scene as well as all other evidence ever taken anywhere. Commercial evidence tags and labels are available and provide places for entering pertinent information. Once bagged and tagged, the evidence must be transported to the police evidence room. As mentioned in the chapter on chain of custody, every moment of the existence of a piece of evidence must be accounted for once that piece of evidence has been seized. Appropriate documentation will deflect any suggestion that the evidence in question has been misplaced, manipulated, or replaced. It is the evidence custodian's responsibility to ensure that any access to evidence placed in storage is legitimate and documented.

CASE IN POINT

Searching a Complex Crime Scene

On February 28, 1993, near Waco, Texas, four agents from the Treasury Department's Bureau of Alcohol, Tobacco, and Firearms (ATF) were killed and more than 20 agents were wounded when David Koresh and members of a religious cult, the Branch Davidians, ambushed a force of 76 ATF agents while they were attempting to execute a lawful search and arrest warrant. The ensuing standoff lasted 51 days, ending on April 19, 1993, when the compound erupted in flames. The fire destroyed the compound, and more than 70 residents died. The compound was situated on a 77-acre parcel of land and had multifaceted, multistoried buildings of more than 20,000 square feet (Department of the Treasury, Bureau of Alcohol, Tobacco, and Firearms, 1993).

Prior to the operation in March of 1993, the Texas Rangers were asked by the U.S. Attorney's Office to process the Davidian compound crime scene upon successful completion of the raid. The Rangers began by creating a **crime scene processing plan** that included processing the crime scene, collecting evidence, storing and maintaining evidence, and interviewing and interrogating all witnesses and suspects (Texas Department of Public Safety, 1994). This was the first time a federal agency had requested a state agency to investigate the results of federal actions.

In most investigations, the volume of evidence is not a major consideration. Evidence is documented at the crime scene using log sheets, evidence tags, and submission forms. If a crime scene produces thousands of evidentiary items, however, the process poses a greater challenge. The Waco compound produced more than 300 weapons and several hundred large items (Texas Department of Public Safety, 1994). The Rangers divided the compound into three basic search areas:

1. The main structure (building) and outbuildings
2. Aerial matters (trajectory, angles, and sources)
3. All other physical areas

The evidence was divided into three crime scene categories:

1. Arson evidence
2. Death evidence
3. All other physical evidence

(continued)

Using aerial photographs, maps, and certified engineers, the Rangers created an elaborate grid system. The vicinity around the main compound building was surveyed and sectioned using crisscross lines and stake markers. Each section was further divided into grids. Each building section perimeter followed natural foundation lineaments or existing wall planes. Each section was assigned an alphabetic designation, and each grid was assigned a numeric designation. A grid within a certain section carried the section alphabetic character as the first letter in the grid designation. For example, section A had several grids, and grid 1 of this section carried the designation A1. This method of designation enabled the investigators to identify clearly the exact location where a specific piece of evidence was found. The evidence item could be pinpointed on grid maps for courtroom purposes. The building area of the compound contained 13 sections and 53 grids. The entire compound was divided into 21 sections.

Seven search teams were created to process the crime scene. The teams consisted of the following personnel: team leader, recorder, laboratory technician, ordnance/firearms specialist, and photographer. It was the team leader's responsibility to manage the overall process and make the necessary decisions. The team leader was also the only team member to handle the evidence.

The job of the recorder was to document all pertinent information gathered by the team. The recorder completed the field note documentation when evidence was located and removed from the grid. The laboratory technician was available to handle proper packaging and identification of the recovered evidence. All technical questions were referred to the technician. The firearms and explosives expert was available to handle all weapons or ordinance discovered by the team. This team member was not actively involved in the search but served as an available resource on an as-needed basis. The photographer's responsibility was to visually document the crime scene and all evidence discovered within it. For each photo, the time, date, location, film type, camera settings, and photo sequence were listed.

One Ranger was charged with the responsibility of processing all arson evidence, and another oversaw the handling of all human remains. Whenever a member of the search group located evidence, the team leader was apprised of its discovery. The team leader examined the evidence and directed the photographer to take the necessary pictures of the item in its natural state. The item was then measured and sketched using the rectangularization method. The baseline reference points were the grid cross lines and natural wall planes. Once the proper documentation was completed, the team leader determined whether the evidence was arson material, firearms evidence, or human remains.

Once sufficient items were gathered for transportation to the evidence collection center, the team leader conveyed the evidence to an evidence custodian. The items of evidence were designated a **batch**. Each batch consisted of from 1 to 20 items, depending on their type and size. Two Rangers were assigned to be evidence custodians. The custodians maintained a large truck into which each batch of evidence was placed. The truck was used to transport the evidence to Waco, where it was stored in a specially constructed vault. The truck made the trip whenever it was full or at the end of the working day. A total of eight persons handled more than 3,000 pieces of evidence with confidence that the chain of custody could be established and communicated effectively in court (Texas Department of Public Safety, 1994).

■ Taking Notes

Note takers should record field notes while they are still under the stimuli that made something seem noteworthy, not at a later time. Field notes constitute the most readily available and reliable record of the crime scene. They do not form a logical flow of events but make up a hodgepodge of information gleaned from numerous perceptions, interviews, and measurements. In large investigations, the task of note taking sometimes seems overwhelming, but the basic principles remain the same (see Officer's Notebook).

Field notes are the building blocks the investigator uses to develop hypotheses and, later, a theory of the crime. Field notes also can stimulate the investigator's memory if and when the case goes to court. They provide the basic information for the official report,

OFFICER'S NOTEBOOK

Elements of Field Notes

The Five Ws and an H

Who
- committed the crime?
- had a motive to commit the crime?
- was the victim?
- saw what happened?
- reported the crime?
- might know something?
- were the first people on the scene?

What
- was the relationship between victim and perpetrator?
- crime was committed?
- was said and by whom?
- evidence might there be?
- evidence has been discovered?
- is missing?
- was left?
- was moved?
- was touched?

Where
- did the crime occur?
- was evidence located?
- are all the witnesses?
- were all the witnesses?
- do witnesses live?
- is the suspect?
- was entry made?
- was exit made?

When
- was the crime committed?
- was the crime reported?
- was evidence discovered?
- did the first responder arrive?
- was the scene secured?
- was the scene released?

Why
- was the crime committed?
- was the victim chosen?
- was the location chosen?
- were the criminal implements chosen?

How
- did the perpetrator gain entry?
- was the crime committed?
- did the perpetrator depart?

(continued)

Important Information
Field notes should also contain the following:
- Identification of time and date (the date and time of assignment to the case; the date and time of arrival on the scene).
- Description of the location (description of the scene upon arrival, including weather, lighting, approaches, and geographic location). Information regarding the location can be useful in establishing lines of sight and the distance of visibility.
- Description of the crime scene (broad overview that narrows to specific noticeable details, such as forced entry, disarranged furniture, bloodstains, blood spatter, and the condition of doors and windows).
- Listing of absent items. What should be at the crime scene but is missing often reveals something about the perpetrator and the nature of the crime. A serial killer might take a souvenir or **trophy** that features prominently in fantasies associated with the killings. Such a souvenir or trophy may be helpful in establishing a profile of the killer and figuring out the **killer's signature** (the pattern associated with his or her killings).
- Description of wounds on the victim. The types and locations of wounds should be recorded. If discoloration is present, its location and color should be included.
- Photograph log. The photographer should keep a separate log of photos; if the investigator takes the pictures, he or she should place an entry in the field notes for each entry. The entry should include a description of the content of the photo; the speed of the film; the shutter speed; the distance from the object photographed; the location and direction from which the photo was taken; and the date, time, and case number or name.
- Videotape log. If the investigator is taking the video, then the following information should be recorded: the type of recorder, the type of film, the type of lens or lenses, and whether artificial light was used.
- Identification of the evidence recovered and its location. All evidence must be geographically and temporally located. It is the investigator's job to record sufficient information to adequately place each piece of evidence. All measurements should be recorded, as well as the identity of the person who discovered the evidence. To identify evidence, the investigator should provide a description of the evidence and note its location, the time discovered, who discovered it, the type of container used to store it, the method of sealing the container, the markings used on tags and evidence, and where the evidence is being kept (maintenance log).

which is the foundation for trial testimony. The official report will contain numerous entries. The investigator will produce an initial report early on in the investigation; as the investigation develops and new information is discovered, the investigator will add supplemental reports to the original. The compilation of these reports, in conjunction with the field notes, allows the investigator to recollect the investigation in detail and thus form the backbone of the prosecution and the defense.

All courtroom testimony is balanced against the documentation the investigator has accumulated, including his or her field notes. At the time of trial, the investigator may use the field notes to refresh his or her memory, but doing so allows the defense an opportunity to examine the notes and conduct a cross-examination of the witness pertaining to the notes. With that risk in mind, the investigator should put nothing in the notes that he or she would not be willing to share with the defense, the judge, or the jury. An additional caveat: All notes are available to the defense upon request, and the officer testifying is not allowed to remove anything from the notebook. Each notebook

OFFICER'S NOTEBOOK

Field Notes Best Practices

- Write legibly.
- Write complete thoughts.
- Indicate date and time for all entries.
- For each case, create one set of notes in one or more notebooks.
- Share information with other investigators.
- Corroborate all information.
- Not everything is important, but err on the side of recording too much rather than too little.
- Periodically transcribe your notes in type (they make more sense, and patterns emerge more clearly).
- Organize transcriptions into categories, such as persons, places, and things; physical evidence; forensic evidence; and so on.
- Use a matrix to assist in identifying information. Variations in witness statements regarding height, weight, hair color, stature, eye color, and car color or make can be recorded in a matrix to arrive at a range for each of the identifying characteristics, to compute an average, or to discover the most common response.

should therefore contain notes about one investigation only, so that sensitive material from another investigation is not publicized inadvertently.

In some states, there is a rule of procedure that allows the defense to inquire of the witness whether there are any other writings or statements taken or made by the witness that are not included in the official report. An affirmative answer allows the defense to request a recess and an order directing the witness to obtain the documentation and return immediately with it to the courtroom. Even if the witness is not using the notes to refresh his or her memory, the defense may still obtain them if they exist.

Use of Notes

Notes are useful for the following reasons:

1. As the investigation progresses, suspects and witnesses make statements that may seem insignificant at the time but may later prove important. Field notes allow retrieval of those statements.

2. If a witness or suspect makes a statement and later adds information inconsistent with that statement, the notes will assist in impeaching the new statement and may lead to a confession.

3. It is through gathering, correlating, organizing, and comparing information that the crime scene is reconstructed and derivative evidence developed.

4. Notes are important in preparing for interviews of witnesses, interrogation of suspects, and testifying before the court.

5. Attorneys for the state and the defendant will be interested in the time, date, and manner in which evidence and information were gathered and will have a vested interest in the quality and thoroughness of all reports, notes, and entries.

Memory is always suspect and subject to extrapolation and interpolation, the grist of cross-examination. Memory corroborated by reports and notes takes on a believability not possessed by unaided memory.

■ The Walk-Through

A **walk-through** of the crime scene is conducted to develop a perspective on the nature of the crime, its commission, and the type of evidence that will be expected and searched for. The question of possible unauthorized intrusions may arise. If the scene is not consistent with the investigator's expectations, the investigator should suspect that contamination has occurred. He or she should then interview police at the scene to determine to what extent the scene has been altered by unwitting forays across the area containing the evidence.

During the walk-through, the investigator visually locates evidence or prospective sites for trace evidence. The walk-through will assist the investigator in determining the boundaries of the search, identifying focal points for the search, and discovering important evidentiary items that may need special photographic or forensic attention. Evidence that deteriorates over time or with exposure should be given processing priority. Experts may need to be invited to the scene to interpret bloodstain patterns or to process trace evidence.

The focal points of the walk-through minimally should include the following:

- The point of entry (including the method of entry)
- The point of exit
- The crime route within the premises
- Contact objects (anything touched by the perpetrator or victim)
- Waiting areas (any place the perpetrator may have waited while watching or stalking)
- Any missing objects and areas adjacent to those objects
- Any turf marking (urine or feces left as a calling card)
- Food or drink ingested or left at the scene

■ Recording the Crime Scene

The crime scene is first recorded through photography or videography or both. The video camera is a popular tool for recording crime scenes. After the walk-through and before anything is touched, examined, or moved, the scene is put on film or tape. The result is a permanent historical record of how the scene appeared at the time of the documentation. Moving anything prior to recording the crime scene is a gross mistake, for a trial court will usually exclude any photograph or videotape that does not reflect the scene as it was found.

Crime Scene Photography

Police departments across the country are coming to realize that pictures make an impression on juries—even in routine incidents. Departments are finding new ways to use photography, both as a tool for investigation and as a means to record data quickly and accurately.

Attention to a few simple rules can make pictures acceptable to most judges.

- **Do not disturb the scene.** Some courts have held that a scene is disturbed by the addition of a measuring scale and label. Leave them out of the first series of pictures. After the scene has been photographed in its original state, a second series of pictures with size references and labels can be taken.

- **Get a complete series of pictures.** It is sometimes difficult to determine what is important and what is not. Shooting the entire crime scene preserves it and allows subsequent examination for what may have been taken or added. Each important object in the scene should appear in at least three pictures: (1) an overview, (2) a mid-range shot, and (3) a close-up. The overview should cover the entire scene to bring out the relationships among the objects. The mid-range shot shows an important object and its immediate surroundings. Finally, each close-up shows detail clearly. All of these pictures are important. A close-up alone does not indicate where the object was located. An overview alone does not bring out all items sharply enough to permit a detailed examination.
- **Record all data.** A picture log will allow you to note all features that need to be considered in the pictures taken. Additionally, each log entry should include information as to camera angle and perspective. A crime scene sketch showing the location of the camera for each picture taken will be an asset when testifying.

Pictures need not be pretty or artistic to supply convincing evidence.

Photographing the Violent Crime Scene

For the purpose of criminal investigative analysis (profiling), it is important to record much more than those areas in which acts of violence took place. Photographs can be instrumental in recording the victim's lifestyle and personality, the topography and socioeconomic conditions surrounding the crime scene, and much more that is important to any investigator or analyst who is unable to visit the crime scene.

When photographing violent crime scenes, the aim should be to maximize useful information that will enable the viewer to understand where and how the crime was committed. The crime scene includes not only the immediate locality where the crime took place, but also adjacent areas where important acts occurred immediately before or after the commission of the crime. Aerial photographs are particularly important in serial rape or murder investigations, because they can geographically link crime scenes together.

Overlapping photographs should be taken of the exterior of the crime scene to show its locale in relation to the rest of the neighborhood. The photographs can be cut and pasted together to create a panoramic view of the scene. Crowds that gather at a crime scene and license plates of vehicles parked in the vicinity also must be photographed, because the killer may still be in the area observing the investigation.

Interior photographs should depict the condition of the room; articles left at the scene; and trace evidence such as cigarette butts, tool marks, and the impressions of shoe prints. In general, articles apparently in use immediately prior to the commission of the crime or that appear to have been disturbed from their customary position should be photographed.

During a rape investigation, the purpose of the photographic record is to record signs of any struggle at the scene of the attack or indications of the victim's effort to resist the attack, such as bruises, torn clothing, and so forth. Bite marks should be photographed using oblique lighting, with and without a measuring device, at the crime scene.

In a rape-homicide investigation, infrared ultraviolet photography of the body may detect latent bite marks, because hemorrhaging can occur in tissue under the skin. The location of foreign hairs and fibers, biological fluids, and stains may also be discovered and photographed.

In cases involving the sexual exploitation of children, every room in a suspect's residence should be photographed, even if no physical evidence is found during the crime scene search. Chances are the suspect has taken pictures of his exploits and concealed this material at another location. Rarely will these photographs be discarded, because they represent a trophy or remembrance of the conquest. When these photographs are recovered, they may be compared with the crime scene photos to prove they were taken in the suspect's dwelling.

In death due to asphyxia as a result of a hanging, doubt sometimes exists as to whether the occurrence is murder, suicide, or an accident. Photographing the original position of the body may help in determining the manner of death. An overview shot of the body and rope should be taken at torso and foot level. Show the height of the body above the ground; a murderer usually tries to raise the body completely, whereas the suicide victim frequently never gets his or her feet off the ground and is sometimes found in a sitting position or half-prone position. Photographs should be made that show the relative position of any object, such as a chair or stool, that appears to have been kicked from under the feet of the deceased.

If done properly, crime scene photography can greatly assist the profiler in developing a psychological and behavioral profile of the offender.

Bloodstain Photography

Videotape can be an excellent medium for documenting bloodstains at a crime scene. If a video camera is available, it is best used after the initial walk-through. This records the evidence before any major alterations have occurred at the scene. Videotape provides a perspective on the crime scene layout that cannot be perceived as easily in photographs and sketches. The value of videotaping blood evidence is that the overall relationship of various blood spatters and patterns can be demonstrated. The videotape can show the relationship of spatters to the various structures at the crime scene. In cases where the suspect may have been injured, the video camera can be used to document any blood trails that may lead away from the scene.

Whether a video camera is available or not, it is absolutely essential that still photographs are taken to document the crime scene and any associated blood evidence. Photographs can demonstrate the same type of things that the videotape does, but crime scene photographs can record close-up details, record objects at any scaled size, and record objects at actual size. These measurements and recordings are more difficult to achieve with videotape.

Infrared film can also be used for documenting bloodstains on dark surfaces. Overview, medium-range, and close-up photographs should be taken of pertinent bloodstains. Scaled photographs (photographs with a ruler next to the evidence) must also be taken of items in cases where size relevance is significant or when direct (one-to-one) comparisons will be made, such as with bloody shoeprints, fingerprints, high-velocity blood spatter patterns, and so forth. A good technique for recording a large area of blood spatter on a light-colored wall is to measure and record the heights of some of the individual blood spatters. The overall pattern on the wall, including a yardstick as a scale, is then photographed with slide film. After the slide is developed, it can be projected onto a blank wall or onto the actual wall many years after the original incident. By using a yardstick, the original blood spatters can be viewed at their actual size and placed in their original positions. Measurements and projections can then be made to determine the spatters' points of origin (Schiro, 2003).

Digital Photography

In a digital world, it is surprising that many crime scenes are still photographed with 35-mm cameras. Part of the reluctance to use digital cameras has to do with the concern that digital images are more easily altered than are images on film. In truth, if the intent is to alter an image, there is sufficient sophistication to alter the image regardless of medium. This can be countered with sworn testimony that the image has not been altered. In criminal cases, the defense may challenge the authenticity of crime scene photos at a motion to suppress or at trial, leaving the matter to the judge or the jury.

Digital images do not raise the first opportunity for the possibility of manipulation; all methods of recording images can be manipulated. If a digital photograph is altered, it can be detected by embedded information, making the possibility of successful manipulation unlikely. When working with digital images it is important to store the original image. On occasion it is necessary to use software to enhance a digital image or to use color contrast to more fully visualize the digital image. The court will resort to the original image if questions of admissibility arise.

The FBI recommends documenting any and all changes to a digital image. Some software used to manipulate digital images provides an integral recording device, documenting each alteration made with the software. These records will prove invaluable in providing enhanced images to the jury. The FBI Scientific Working Group on Imaging Technologies has addressed most of the important issues involving the use of digital photos in law enforcement. They have provided a set of guidelines that should be considered best practices by anyone considering the use of digital imagery in processing a crime scene; these guidelines are available at www.fdiai.org/images/SWGIT guidelines.pdf.

Digital Photographs in Court

All evidence admitted at the time of trial is subject to rules. Those rules may be the federal rules of evidence or state rules of evidence, or local rules promulgated by felony courts. Scientific evidence also may be subjected to a **Kelly/Fry hearing** to determine the scientific validity of the process or procedure. Rule 101 of the federal rules of evidence is most commonly employed to admit electronic recordings, computer records, computer data or scientific evidence and would also apply to the admission of digital photographs.

The use of digital imagery in courtrooms is becoming more common and acceptable. Computer-generated simulations based on accurate measurements from the crime scene have long been admissible. The same should hold true for digital photographs where testimony substantiates that the image portrays the scene as it was remembered without altheration.

Admissibility of Images

Photographs

The **predicate for admissibility** of photographs is fairly simple. The attorney wishing to enter the photographs will question the witness as follows:

....

Q: Officer, I now hand you what has been previously marked as State's Exhibit Number 1, and I ask you, do you recognize this photo?

A: Yes.

Q: What does the photo portray?

A: The scene at 47 Cypress Fairway Village on the evening in question.

Q: Is it a fair and accurate representation of the scene as you recall it? [If the witness is the photographer, the final words would be "as you photographed it?"]

A: Yes, it is.

Q: Has it been altered in any way?

A: No.

Such an exchange will lead to the admission of the photograph only if the answers indicate that the photograph accurately represents the unaltered scene.

The defense typically will cross-examine the witness vigorously in an attempt to get an admission that some item in the photo, even a small one, was moved, added, or altered in some fashion. Occasionally a small item loses its size perspective when photographed. Crime scene photographers will often add a ruler or some other device of known size with which to compare the object to establish proper size perspective. If a ruler has been added, the officer, in response to the last question of the evidentiary predicate, would answer: "A ruler has been added to demonstrate size."

All evidence should be photographed in situ before adding anything to establish size perspective. If an injured party or damaged auto has been removed from the crime scene, the officer assisting in the admission of the photo must state that the scene was altered and describe the alteration.

After presenting the predicate of admissibility, the prosecutor offers the exhibit into evidence. An offer of evidence usually begins with the prosecutor tendering the exhibit to the defense for any objections. If the defense objects (note that the likelihood of an objection increases in proportion to the importance of the exhibit to the prosecutor's case), the defense may choose to engage in a voir dire examination of the witness regarding the authenticity of the exhibit. If the judge sustains any defense objection, the prosecutor may be forced to address the objection by laying a further predicate. Having listened to the objection and the discussion pertaining to it, the testifying officer should then have a good idea of what additional predicates need be established. Once the matter of defense objections has been resolved satisfactorily, the judge will accept the exhibit as evidence. The prosecutor may now ask questions to elicit a description of the contents of the photograph and the significance of those contents.

Videotapes

Investigators rely on video recording to document crime scenes visually. The predicate for videotapes is often confused with the predicate for audiotapes. The appropriate predicate for videos combines the audiotape and still photograph predicates:

Q: Was the videotape you have described as State's Exhibit Number 3 prepared on a recording device capable of making an accurate recording?

A: Yes. [No technical data need be supplied, nor must the videographer have a technical understanding of videocassette recording to establish the predicate for admissibility. However, if the witness is a competent video technician, a brief technical description may ensue.]

Q: Who was the operator?

A: I was. [Or the witness would mention the name of the party who shot the video. It is not necessary to have actually filmed the video to be able to prove it up. All that is required is that the testifying officer has viewed the scene prior to the taping, has viewed the tape, and has determined that the film is an accurate reflection of the scene.]

Q: Have you viewed the videotape?

A: Yes.

Q: Has the videotape been altered in any way?

A: No. [Some agencies will record a voice-over account of what is on the screen to increase the viewer's understanding of the video images. If the officer testifying is not the narrator, the narration is hearsay and is probably inadmissible. If the defense objects to the voice-over, the volume can simply be turned all the way down. It may be necessary to testify that the video has been altered by the addition of a soundtrack but that the addition has not altered the video images.]

Q: When was the videotape made?

A: At 10:45 AM on May 7, 2004 [or whatever the correct time and date is].

Q: Do the pictures of the events contained in the videotape fairly and accurately reflect the scene as you recall it?

A: Yes.

Logging Photographs

Crime scene photographs should be taken in a systematic, coordinated sequence, and that sequence should be recorded by photo number and description. Panoramic and general-content shots should be taken and logged first, with more specific, detailed, and close-up shots following.

Generally, the police only get one opportunity to process a crime scene, but subsequent entries in a photo log may be predicated upon probable cause and warrant acquisition. Everything that needs to be done needs to be done correctly and completely the first time. There is no guarantee that any click of the shutter or any single roll of film will render a usable photograph. Multiple shots of all important aspects of the crime scene may save frustration and embarrassment later. Film is relatively cheap compared with a verdict of acquittal.

OFFICER'S NOTEBOOK

Elements of a Photo Log
The **photo log** should be a story that flows from the general to the specific. It should contain the following:
- Information sufficient to identify the photographer, including name, rank, badge number, and agency.
- Identifying information pertaining to all equipment and film used. The details of the equipment may vary from exterior to interior locations, as might the film speed and exposure settings. Any changes should be reflected in the photo log. Weather and ambient light conditions should be described.
- The case number (if one has been assigned) or a geographic location to which the photos can be tied. The date and time of day should also be provided.
- The chronological order in which the photos were taken.
- The disposition of the exposed film (whether the film was sent out for processing or processed in the police lab). If the photographer processed the film, development and printing information should be provided as an addendum to the photo log.

The log itself is not constructed at the crime scene. All the foregoing information will be included in the field notebook of the photographer and transferred onto a photo log sheet. Most agencies use preprinted log sheets divided into categories for ease of recording.

■ The Crime Scene Sketch

The data upon which the **crime scene sketch** is based are gathered after the scene has been completely processed and photographed but before evidentiary items have been bagged, tagged, and transported. The sketch is a measured drawing showing the location of all important items, landmarks, permanent fixtures, and physical evidence. The investigator is usually responsible for the crime scene sketch, but some agencies have drafting technicians who do the sketching. It is no surprise that a number of software programs are helpful for creating sketches, and computer-assisted drawing (CAD) is used widely as an investigative tool. There is software that can download information from surveying equipment and use it to create a visual representation based on the measurements. However, the majority of crime scene sketches are still drawn by hand and are not to scale.

Everything that is included in the sketch must be located geographically. (Measuring distance from permanent features is one method of doing this.) Eliminate all unnecessary detail from the sketch, and include only items necessary for locating evidence and establishing scene parameters.

Three basic measurement techniques are used for geographically locating evidence: rectangularization, triangulation, and baseline construction. In **rectangularization** (**Figure 3–1**), two right angles are drawn from the item being measured to the two nearest permanent objects (fixed points). The distance between the two fixed points and the same point on the evidence is measured. In **triangulation** (**Figure 3–2**), as the name suggests, three angles are measured: those of a triangle formed by the item of interest and two permanent objects (fixed points). In the **baseline** construction method (**Figure 3–3**), an arbitrary line (the baseline) of some measurable distance is drawn between two fixed points. There will be a unique line that both goes through the item of interest and intersects the baseline at a right angle; the location of the item can be determined by measuring the length of the line segment between the item and the baseline and also measuring the distance from the baseline's intersection with the line segment to one of the two fixed points.

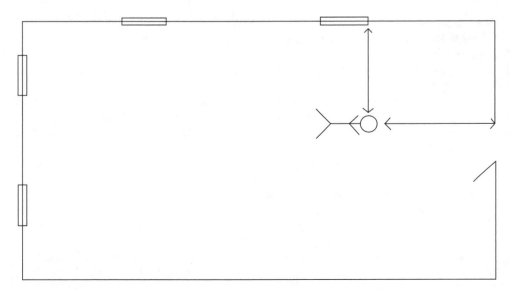

Figure 3–1 Rectangularization.

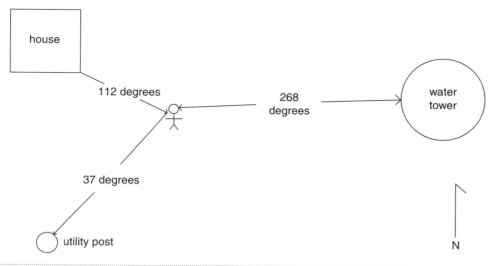

Figure 3–2 Triangulation.

Both triangulation and baseline construction work especially well outdoors, where permanent landmarks are at a distance from the item to be measured, but none of the three methods works very well when processing an underwater crime scene, where measurement of the distance between items in the water and permanent objects in the water is hampered by limited or zero visibility. A method of measurement especially designed for underwater use is discussed in the following section on underwater crime scene searches.

To be useful, a crime scene sketch must contain accurate measurements. Artistic content is not a concern. All measurements should be made from permanent objects. Indoors, walls, doorframes, window frames, and corners serve well as anchors for measurements. Outdoors, buildings, utility poles, roadways, and, less optimally, trees are generally reliable. Keep in mind that anything to which a measurement is anchored must withstand the vagaries of time. The trial may occur years after the offense. The sketch made by an investigator on the scene is not the official crime scene sketch. An initial drawing with measurements is done in pencil and later incorporated into a permanent inked or printed sketch (**Figure 3–4**).

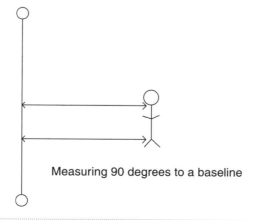

Measuring 90 degrees to a baseline

Figure 3–3 Baseline construction.

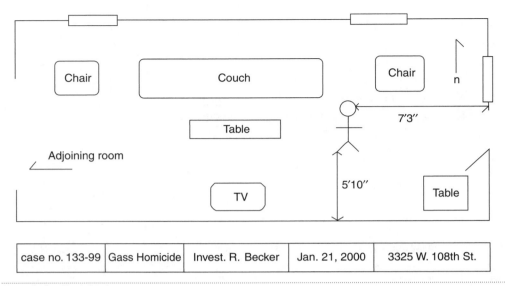

| case no. 133-99 | Gass Homicide | Invest. R. Becker | Jan. 21, 2000 | 3325 W. 108th St. |

Figure 3–4   Final sketch.

Crime scene templates are available for many different types of crime scenes. Once the crime scene has been measured and those measurements transferred to a sketch, those measurements will be used in reconstructing a more elaborate and architecturally correct diagram. Very little sophistication is required to use these templates but a very professional end product is possible (see **Figure 3–5**).

Virtual Crime Scenes

Crime Scene Virtual Tour (CSVT) provides software and instruction to police agencies to allow them to create admissible demonstrative crime scene tours (**Figure 3–6**). The software provides a distinctive virtual reality approach to crime scene investigation and reconstruction, based on 360-degree panoramic images. CSVT software integrates panoramic crime scenes images, still images, interactive maps, slideshows, texts, audios,

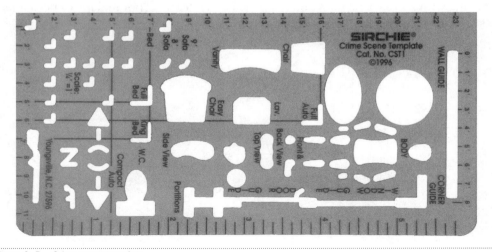

Figure 3–5   Crime scene template.

Courtesy of SIRCHIE Finger Print Laboratories, Inc.

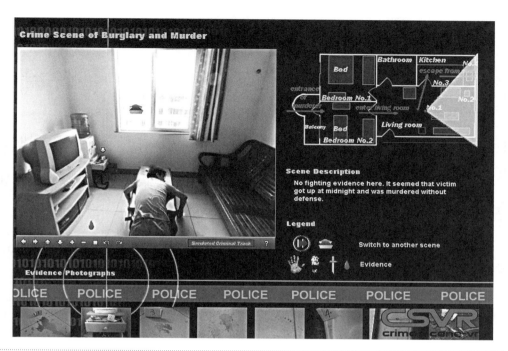

Figure 3–6   Crime scene virtual tour.

Courtesy of Crime Scene VR, www.crime-scence-vr.com

links, and thumbnails into a computer-generated searchable composite. It allows investigators to construct a three-dimensional crime scene that enables the user to wander through the scene.

With conventional photography, dozens of overlapping shots are needed to achieve a 360-degree view; with CSVT, the scene can be viewed from any room or angle, from inside or outside, without losing crime scene continuity. The program allows the user to zoom in, pan, tilt and rotate the scene, as if actually conducting a walk-through. The software allows a crime scene sketch to be added next to images, and then use the synchronized scanning function to roam the sketch while pointing out the same areas on the virtual tour, thereby orienting each piece of evidence. The program offers the opportunity to view images and relevant text at the same time, which saves the time of matching every single film photo to each piece of text. Through the links and thumbnails in crime scene virtual tour, images can be located quickly and easily rather than thumbing through a stack of documents and photos. Crime scene photos are the most common way to preserve a crime scene. Handling, displaying and storing those photos can be difficult. CSVT software provides a useful alternative to conventional crime scene displays and presentation.

A crime scene sketch is of little value if it cannot be admitted at the time of trial. As in the case of photos and tape recordings, there is a particular evidentiary foundation (predicate) that must be established in order to use sketches, maps, or diagrams:

Q: Did you participate in the preparation of the diagram that you have identified as State's Exhibit Number 2?

A: Yes.

OFFICER'S NOTEBOOK

Elements of a Crime Scene Sketch
- A scene identifier. That identifier, placed in the title box, should be either the case number or a recognizable title associated with the offense being investigated.
- Descriptive words identifying where the scene is situated.
- The date of the original sketch (rough sketch).
- The name of the investigator and the person who drew the sketch, even if they are one and the same.
- A written statement indicating the drawing's scale or noting the absence of scale.
- A directional rosette (an arrow showing which direction is north). In orienting the drawing, it is generally presumed that north is up.

Q: Are you personally familiar with the objects and locations contained in the diagram?

A: Yes.

Q: Is this a fair and accurate representation of the [search site, recovery site, location of evidence found] as you recall it?

A: Yes.

Q: Is this diagram drawn to scale?

A: No.

Generally, it is easier to testify about a diagram that is not drawn to scale. Defense lawyers may focus on minuscule measurement errors to try to undermine the credibility of the entire diagram. Reasonable approximations are much easier to defend. However, if all measurements are linked to a permanent landmark that was located on the diagram with the aid of surveying instruments, having a scale drawing may not be a problem.

■ Dry-Land Crime Scene Searches

Control and teamwork constitute the proper foundation for conducting crime scene searches. The importance of teamwork is often overlooked in the zeal of the participants to outdo each other. Each fancies himself or herself a Sherlock Holmes, and there is never a paucity of theories. The value of search teamwork becomes readily apparent when watching a dive team in operation. No one would consider traipsing about helter-skelter looking for whatever presents itself. Because of the medium in which the search is conducted, the search must be organized and methodical. In land searches, because visibility and mobility generally are not limited, organization and methodology are often sacrificed in the name of expedience.

The physical nature of a crime scene will suggest what type of search is best to employ, but the characteristics of the scene should have no effect on the quality of the search. Obviously, there will be exceptions. Large-area searches in mass-disaster investigations may have to sacrifice some quality for expedience, but in the average investigation there is no excuse for haphazard searches. Proceed slowly, for evidence not only can be contaminated by being stepped on but can be destroyed easily or overlooked entirely by the unwary. An experienced investigator will have completed the walk-through before beginning the search, and the walk-through must be conducted with trace evidence foremost in the investigator's mind.

Search Methods

The most effective search method is similar to that used by archaeologists in archaeological field digs. The area to be searched is divided into small squares (grids) approximately 1 meter by 1 meter. Each square is further divided into 4 smaller squares (each equal to one quarter of a square meter). The **grid search** begins in the northernmost of the smaller squares and progresses as one would read a book until the 1-square-meter grid has been examined completely. If trace evidence is a possibility, this is the only method that facilitates the systematic vacuuming of an indoor crime scene, with each vacuum bag representing a grid or a part of a grid (**Figures 3–7 and 3–8**). Obviously, although the grid method is thorough and comprehensive, it is very time consuming and is not appropriate for some crime scenes.

Figure 3–7   Evidence vacuum.

Courtesy of SIRCHIE Finger Print Laboratories, Inc.

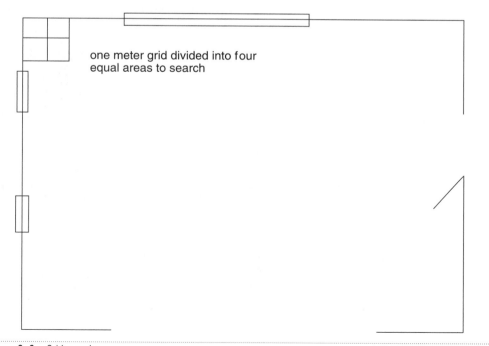

one meter grid divided into four
equal areas to search

Figure 3–8   Grid search.

One of the more common search methods employed both indoors and outdoors is the **strip search**. The search begins at one corner of a search area and continues to the opposite corner. Upon arrival at the opposite corner, the search reverses, moves 3-feet perpendicular to the line just searched and continues across to the opposite side. This pattern continues at 3-foot intervals until the entire search area has been covered. Of course, furnishings and fixtures may obstruct any search pattern. The search must continue around, over, or through whatever lies in the way.

A **spiral search** also can be used indoors or out. This involves moving in an ever-tightening or ever-expanding spiral, although starting at the outermost point and working inward is preferable. The **sector search** method is appropriate for large crime scenes. It is discussed in the Case in Point regarding the processing of complex crime scenes.

The type of crime committed, the environment in which the crime was committed, and the nature of the evidence anticipated all influence the choice of search method. In some instances, it may be necessary to conduct more than one search or to combine search methods to uncover all evidence sought. Once discovered, physical evidence usually is handled according to a predetermined protocol that includes recording field information about the evidence discovered, often through the use of field notes and evidence tags (**Figure 3–9**). That information may include, but is not limited to, the following:

- The location within the crime scene at which the evidence was obtained
- The name of the person who found the evidence

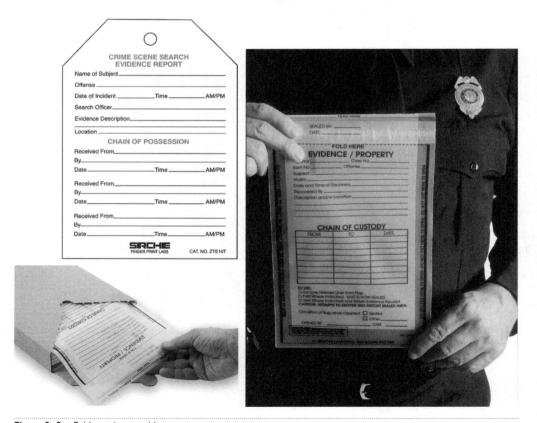

Figure 3–9 Evidence tags and bags.

Courtesy of SIRCHIE Finger Print Laboratories, Inc.

- The time and date of the finding of the evidence
- A description of any interesting characteristics unique to the piece of evidence
- The names of all participants in the search process

■ World Trade Center

The country changed on September 11, 2001. We lost our naiveté in believing we were immune to terrorist attacks from abroad and changed our focus from domestic terrorism to international terrorism. The lessons learned that day were many and crucial but perhaps most important of those lessons was that there must be a contingency plan in place for a mass terrorist event. Trying to implement one after the event is futile and frustrating.

CASE IN POINT

Large Crime Scenes

Alfred Murrah Federal Building
On April 19, 1995, at 9:03 a.m. CST, calls were received by Emergency Medical Services Authority Oklahoma City. EMS ambulances, police and firefighters had already been dispatched.

The State Emergency Operations Center was set up including personnel from military, civil defense and public safety along with the responding fire and police services. The governor called out the Oklahoma National Guard and members of the Department of Civil Emergency Management. Within the first hour, 50 people were rescued from the Murrah federal building. By the end of the day, over 180 survivors were being treated at hospitals around the city. The last survivor, a 15-year-old girl, was found under the base of the collapsed building.

Three hundred fifty tons of rubble was removed from the site each day until April 29. All of the debris was examined for body parts, explosive residue, and detonators. Canine units searched for survivors and located bodies amongst the building refuse. Rescue and recovery efforts were concluded on May 4, with the bodies of all but three victims recovered. For several days after the building's demolition, trucks hauled 800 tons of debris a day away from the site. Some of the debris was used as evidence in the trials of the conspirators.

It is important to understand that the bomb blast to the Murrah building was not devastating by itself—it just so happened that the blast was located at a critical point that undermined the whole structure of the building. Most of the damage and a vast majority of the fatalities were caused by the collapse of the building.

The FBI was on the scene immediately, because the building was under federal jurisdiction. Agents found a truck axle with a vehicle identification number (VIN). It was determined that the explosion had been contained in a 1993 Ford truck owned by Ryder Rentals of Miami, Florida. Ryder Rentals informed the FBI that the truck was assigned to a rental company known as Elliot's Body Shop in Junction City, Kansas. The FBI interviewed rental agent at Elliot's Body Shop in Junction City on April 19, 1995. The individual who signed the rental agreement provided his name, Social Security number, South Dakota driver's license, a South Dakota home address, and a destination in Omaha; the FBI's investigation determined all of the information was false.

On April 20, 1995, the rental agent was contacted again and assisted in the creation of a composite drawing. On the same day, agents interviewed three witnesses who were near the scene of the explosion prior to the detonation. The witnesses were shown a copy of the composite drawing and identified him as

(continued)

the person the witnesses had seen in front of the Murrah building. The composite drawing was shown to employees at various motels and commercial establishments in the Junction City area. Employees of the Dreamland Motel in Junction City told agents that the individual in the composite drawing had been a guest at the motel from April 14 through April 18, 1995. This individual had registered at the motel under the name of Timothy McVeigh, listed his automobile as bearing an Oklahoma license plate with an illegible plate number, and provided a home address on North Van Dyke Road in Decker, Michigan; he drove a car described as a 1970 Mercury.

A check of the Michigan Department of Motor Vehicle records showed a license in the name of Timothy J. McVeigh, date of birth April 23, 1968, with an address of 3616 North Van Dyke Road, Decker, Michigan. Further investigation showed that James Douglas Nichols and his brother Terry Lynn Nichols owned the property at that address and that the property was a working farm.

A relative of James Nichols told the FBI that Timothy McVeigh was a friend of James Nichols, who had been involved in constructing explosives and who possessed large quantities of fuel oil and fertilizer. On April 21, 1995, a former coworker of Timothy McVeigh's reported that he had seen the composite drawing on television and recognized the drawing to be Timothy McVeigh. He told the investigators that McVeigh was known to hold extreme right-wing views, was a military veteran, and was so agitated about the conduct of the federal government in Waco, Texas, in 1993, that he personally visited the site.

On April 21, 1995, investigators learned that Timothy McVeigh was arrested at 10:30 a.m. on April 19, 1995, in Perry, Oklahoma, for not having a license plate and for possession of a weapon approximately one and a half hours after the explosion at the Alfred P. Murrah Federal Building (**Figure 3–10**). McVeigh, who has been held in custody since his arrest on April 19, 1995, listed his home address as 3616 North Van Dyke Road, Decker, Michigan, listed James Nichols of Decker, as a reference, and was stopped driving a yellow 1977 Mercury Marquis.

As a result of the investigation conducted by the FBI Timothy McVeigh was indicted, tried, found guilty, sentenced to death, and executed.

FEDERAL COMPLAINT AGAINST TIMOTHY MCVEIGH

IN THE UNITED STATES DISTRICT COURT FOR THE WESTERN DISTRICT OF OKLAHOMA

UNITED STATES OF AMERICA,   No. M-95-98-H
Plaintiff   CRIMINAL COMPLAINT

v.

TIMOTHY JAMES MCVEIGH,
Defendant

I, the undersigned complainant being duly sworn state the following is true and correct to the best of my knowledge and belief. On or about April 19, 1995, in Oklahoma City, Oklahoma County, in the Western District of Oklahoma defendant(s) did, maliciously damage and destroy by means of fire or an explosive, any building, vehicle, and other personal or real property in whole or in part owned, possessed, or used by the United States, any department or agency thereof, in violation of Title 18, United States Code, Section(s) 844(f).

I further state that I am a(n) Special Agent of the Federal Bureau of Investigation and that this complaint is based on the following facts:

See attached Affidavit of Special Agent Henry C. Gibbons, Federal Bureau of Investigation, which is incorporated and made a part hereof by reference.

Figure 3–10 Alfred P. Murrah building.

Courtesy of FEMA

(continued)

/s/ Henry C. Gibbons Special Agent Federal Bureau of Investigation

Sworn to before me and subscribed in my presence, on this 21 day of April, 1995, at Oklahoma City, Oklahoma.

RONALD L. HOWLAND
UNITED STATES MAGISTRATE JUDGE

STATE OF OKLAHOMA:
COUNTY OF OKLAHOMA
AFFIDAVIT
I, HENRY C. GIBBONS, being duly sworn, do hereby state that I am an agent with the Federal Bureau of Investigation, having been so employed for 26 years and as such am vested with the authority to investigate violations of federal laws, including Title 18, United States Code, Section 844 (f).

Further, the Affiant states as follows:

1. The following information has been received by the Federal Bureau of Investigation over the period from April 19 through April 21, 1995;

2. On April 19, 1995, a massive explosion detonated outside the Alfred P. Murrah building in Oklahoma City, Oklahoma, at approximately 9:00 a.m.

3. Investigation by Federal agents at the scene of the explosion have determined that the explosive was contained in a 1993 Ford owned by Ryder Rental company.
   a. A vehicle identification number (VIN) was found at the scene of the explosion and determined to be from a part of the truck that contained the explosive.
   b. The VIN was traced to a truck owned by Ryder Rentals of Miami, Florida.
   c. Ryder Rentals informed the FBI that the truck was assigned to a rental company known as Elliot's Body Shop in Junction City, Kansas.

4. The rental agent at Elliot's Body Shop in Junction City, Kansas, was interviewed by the FBI on April 19, 1995. The individual who signed the rental agreement provided the following information:
   a. The person who signed the rental agreement identified himself as BOB KLING, SSN: 962-42-9694, South Dakota's driver's license number YF942A6, and provided a home address of 428 Malt Drive, Redfield, South Dakota. The person listed the destination as 428 Maple Drive, Omaha, Nebraska.
   b. Subsequent investigation conducted by the FBI determined all this information to be bogus.

5. On April 20, 1995, the rental agent was recontacted and assisted in the creation of composite drawings. The rental agent has told the FBI that the composite drawings are fair and accurate depictions of the individuals who rented the truck.

6. On April 20, 1995, the FBI interviewed three witnesses who were near the scene of the explosion at Alfred P. Murrah Federal Building prior to the determination of the explosives. The three witnesses were shown a copy of the composite drawing of Unsub #1 and identified him as closely resembling a person the witnesses had seen in front of the Alfred P. Murrah Building where the explosion occurred on April 19, 1995. The witnesses advised the FBI that they observed a person identified as Unsub #1 at approximately 8:40 a.m. on April 19, 1995, when they entered the building. They again observed Unsub #1 at approximately 8:55 a.m., still in front of the 5th Road entrance of the building when they departed just minutes before the explosion.

7. The Alfred P. Murrah building is used by various agencies of the United States, including Agriculture Department, Department of the Army, the Defense Department, Federal Highway Administration, General Accouinting Office, General Services Administration, Social Security Administration, Labor Department, Marine Corps, Small Business Administration, Transportation Department, United States Secret Service, Bureau of Alcohol, Tobacco and Firearms, and Veteran's Administration.

8. The composite drawings were shown to employees at various motels and commercial establishments in the Junction City, Kansas, vicinity. Employees of the Dreamland Motel in Junction City, Kansas, advised FBI agents that an individual resembling Unsub #1 depicted in the composite drawings had been a guest at the Motel from April 14 through April 18, 1995. This individual had registered at the Motel under the name of Tim McVeigh, listed his automobile as bearing an Oklahoma license plate with an illegible plate number, and provided a Michigan address, on North Van Dyke Road in Decker, Michigan. The individual was seen driving a car described as a Mercury from the 1970's.

9. A check of Michigan Department of Motor Vehicle records shows a license in the name of Timothy J. McVeigh, date of birth April 23, 1968, with an address of 3616 North Nan Dyke Road, Decker, Michigan. This Michigan license was renewed by McVeigh on April 8, 1995. McVeigh had a prior license issued in the state of Kansas on March 21, 1990, and surrendered to Michigan in November 1993, with the following address: P.O. Box 2153, Fort Riley, Kansas.

10. Further investigation shows that the property at 3616 North Van Dyke Road, Decker, Michigan, is associated with James Douglas Nichols and his brother Terry Lynn Nichols. The property is a working farm. Terry Nichols formerly resided in Marion, Kansas, which is approximately one hour from Junction City.

11. A relative of James Nichols reports to the FBI that Tim McVeigh is a friend and associate of James Nichols, who has worked and resided at the farm on North Van Dyke Road in Decker, worked and resided at the farm on North Van Dyke Road in Decker, Michigan. This relative further reports that she had heard that James Nichols had been involved in constructing bombs in approximately November 1994, and that he possessed large quantities of fuel oil and fertilizer.

12. On April 21, 1995, a former co-worker of Tim McVeigh's reported to the FBI that he had seen the composite drawing of Unsub #1 on the television and recognized the drawing to be a former co-worker, Tim McVeigh. He further advised that McVeigh was known to hold extreme rightwing views, was a military veteran, and was particularly agitated about the conduct of the federal government in Waco, Texas, in 1993. In fact, the co-worker further reports that McVeigh had been so agitated about the deaths of the Branch Dividians in Waco, Texas, on April 19, 1993, that he personally visited the site. After visiting the site, McVeigh expressed extreme anger at the federal government and advised that the Government should never had done what it did. He further advised that the last known address he had for McVeigh is 1711 Stockton Hill Road, #206, Kingman, Arizona.

13. On April 21, 1994, investigators learned that a Timothy McVeigh was arrested at 10:30 a.m. on April 19, 1995, in Perry, Oklahoma, for not having a license tag and for possession of a weapon approximately 1-1/2 hours after the detonation of the explosive device at the Alfred P. Murrah Federal Building in Oklahoma City, Oklahoma. Perry, Oklahoma, is approximately a 1-1/2 hour drive from Oklahoma City, Oklahoma. McVeigh, who has been held in custody since his arrest on April 19, 1995, listed his home address as 3616 North Van Dyke Road, Decker, Michigan. He listed James Nichols of Decker, Michigan, as a reference. McVeigh was stopped driving a yellow 1977 Mercury Marquis.

(continued)

14.   The detonation of the explosive in front of the Alfred P. Murrah Federal Building constitutes a violation of 18 U.S.C. Section 844(f), which makes it a crime to maliciously damage or destroy by means of an explosive any building or real property, in whole or in part owned, possessed or used by the United States, or any department or agency thereof.

Further, your affiant sayeth not.
/s/HENRY C. GIBBONS

Special Agent
Federal Bureau of Investigation

Suscribed and sworn to before me this 21 day of April 1995.
/s/ Ronald J. Howland
UNITED STATES MAGISTRATE JUDGE
Western District of Oklahoma

There are generally five aspects to responding to terrorism that need be considered:

- Prevention—gathering intelligence, wiretaping, surveillance
- Preparation—training, exercises, exams
- Containment—first response, hazmat, police, fire
- Investigation—federal, state, local, ICS (incident command structure)
- Rehabilitation—picking up the pieces, psychological debriefing, putting what is broke back together or back on line

The key to prevention is intelligence in all it forms:

- Human
- Signal
- Systems

The keys to preparation are training, interagency agreements, and contingency plans. The keys to containment are vulnerability analysis and first response training, equipment and commitment, and the key to investigation is recognizing that large crime scenes are most easily processed when viewed as a series of linked small crime scenes. Most of us watched as the attack on this country took place and as the buildings' infrastructures began to deteriorate (Figure 3–11). We watched as the debris was searched and bodies removed, although the investigative portion of the endeavor was not televised. Trucks crossed the Verrazano Narrows Bridge, turned off Route 440 and chugged up the incline to the Fresh Kills landfill on Staten Island, New York. Behind tight security, 800 workers from city police and fire departments; the FBI, Secret Service; Bureau of Alcohol, Tobacco and Firearms; National Guard; and outside volunteers worked 12-hour shifts. The 45,000 tons of debris yielded 256 body parts, many personal belongings, and aircraft parts.

Figure 3–11 Aerial view of the World Trade Center disaster.

Courtesy of NOAA

■ Underwater Crime Scene Searches

In February 1994, Southwest Texas State University (now Texas State University San Marcos) purchased what had been Aquarena Springs theme park. The area that had been used for an underwater theater was left intact and unused. Various faculty at the university began to consider possible uses for the park and the theater.

The criminal justice department at Southwest Texas State University entered the world of public safety diver training in July 1994, with the birth of the Underwater

Institute. The author created and was the director of the Institute. In creating a public safety diver training institute it was necessary to determine the state of public safety diving in Texas. It was noted that dive recovery operations were actually "salvage" operations conducted with little regard for an investigatory protocol or the possibility of the existence of forensic evidence. As the training curriculum and underwater research for the Underwater Institute began to take shape, it became apparent that there were some misconceptions—or myths—involved in the processing of submerged evidence. It was to these misconceptions that the Underwater Institute began to devote its attention and course instruction.

The concept of the underwater recovery of evidence as nothing more than a salvage operation represented a major myth that continued to surround the police underwater recovery operation. Agencies also cling to other myths, or misconceptions, about the underwater recovery of evidence. These include the ultimate objective and composition of the dive recovery team, the forensic value of submerged evidence, the assumptions concerning accidents, and the ability to locate submerged items geographically

Myth 1: The dive recovery team's ultimate objective is to recover a submerged item. If agencies continue to view this process as a salvage operation, then they will conclude that the ultimate objective of dive teams is to find and recover the item sought and return it safely. Both represent admirable objectives but remain shortsighted and a product of traditional law enforcement policy, practice, and perspective. However, convicting criminals of the unlawful acts they commit (simplistic but fundamental to scientific processing of an underwater crime scene) represents the true objective of a dive recovery team.

Myth 2: The dive team is made up of a primary diver, safety diver, line tender, on-scene commander, and others involved solely in the recovery process. Embracing the former myth gives rise to this one. However, when agencies recognize that winning convictions constitutes the primary objective of dive recovery teams, they realize that first responders, investigators, crime laboratory personnel, and prosecutors are dive recovery team players as well. First-responding officers set the tenor of underwater investigations, just as they do in land-based operations. These officers have the responsibility of ensuring crime scene integrity and witness identification, segregation, and initial interviews; barring access by all unauthorized personnel, including the media, medical personnel, and curious bystanders; and recognizing the potential location of all forensic evidence, including routes of entry and exit, and protecting these sites. Because these officers play a pivotal role in underwater investigations, agencies should train them in the fundamentals of processing an underwater crime scene, including exactly what they must protect, and provide them with descriptions of other team members' roles. Often, investigators, crime laboratory personnel, and prosecutors also lack an understanding of the scientific approach to processing an underwater crime scene. For example, if only divers realize that submerged evidence has as much forensic value as evidence found on land, then investigators may fail to understand the crucial steps that divers must take to preserve not only the items recovered but the need to collect water and samples of the bottom and surrounding areas as a control for laboratory analysis. Applying the concept of background contamination to underwater evidence collection demonstrates how bottom samples can allow laboratory personnel to exclude the background as the source from which any trace evidence might have originated.

Myth 3: All submerged evidence is bereft of forensic value. Often, water serves as a preservative for forensic evidence that becomes lost only as a result of the recovery method employed, that is, salvaging. For example, in the true account of a modern murder mystery, a serologist determined that a blood specimen that was submerged for three years in salt water was human blood (Bugliosi, 1992). Also, investigators found fiber evidence on the body of a murder victim even though the perpetrator had disposed of the body in a river (Deadman, 1984). Therefore, while most submerged evidence possesses potential forensic value, all too often, investigators unknowingly overlook, contaminate, or destroy this evidence during the recovery process.

Myth 4: All submerged firearms are bereft of forensic value. Firearms constitute the most neglected evidentiary item recovered from water. A variety of places exist on a firearm that may retain forensic material. For example, fingerprints often remain on protected surfaces, especially on lubricated areas, such as the magazine of a semiautomatic pistol or the shell casing of the rounds in the magazine from the individual's thumb that pushed it into the magazine. Using small-particle reagent, it is possible to recover wet fingerprints without the necessity of air drying first. Also, if the perpetrator carried the weapon in a pocket, under an automobile seat, or in a glove compartment, the firearm could retain a variety of fibers on its sharp edges, especially on sights and magazine levers. Finally, weapons used in contact wounds may have "barrel blowback" (e.g., blood, tissue, bone, hair, or fabric) stored in the barrel of the firearm (Spitz, 1993). When deposited in water, a weapon primarily fills through the barrel. The water serves as a block for any material deposited inside the barrel. The material resides there until a pressure differential (i.e., raising it to the surface) releases the water in the barrel. Unfortunately, such critical evidence frequently is lost due to traditional recovery methods, expedience, and ignorance. If divers hold recovered firearms by the barrel and raise them over their heads as they surface, they drain the contents of the weapons and lose potentially crucial evidence. To avoid this, divers should package weapons in water, while in the water, and obtain a bottom sample to ensure that any fibers or other material found on the weapons are not the product of immersion.

Myth 5: Submerged vehicles are simply stolen. To resolve this myth, investigators should consider two questions. Are all stolen vehicles immediately reported as stolen?

Are all stolen vehicles immediately reported as having been used in a crime? Most investigators realize that they should consider all stolen submerged vehicles as crime vehicles (i.e., stolen for use in the commission of another crime) until proven otherwise. In doing so, they can understand that the conventional recovery method (towing by the axle) seriously alters, contaminates, or destroys any evidence. What should they do instead?

Before instituting the recovery of a submerged vehicle, investigators should catalog any information that may become important later but that the recovery method may alter or destroy. Divers can conduct this cataloging process by compiling a *swim-around checklist*. Divers can complete this checklist even in the worst water conditions through touch alone or other means, such as recording the VIN and license number by using a water bath. By pressing a clear plastic bag filled with water against the license plate and their masks to the other side, divers get a clear medium through which they can see the information; a camera can take a picture using the same process. The swim-around checklist allows divers to record the location of any occupants of the vehicle; the condition of the windshield, windows, headlights, and taillights; and the contents of the glove compartment. It also helps divers determine if the keys were in the ignition and if the accelerator was blocked. This information can prove essential during the subsequent investigation of the incident. Lifting should be done using air bags as opposed to tow trucks, thereby preserving the internal integrity of the vehicle.

Myth 6: All drownings are accidents. Experienced homicide investigators generally presume that all unattended deaths are murders until proven otherwise, except when they occur in the water. Many investigators have participated in the recovery of a presumed accidental drowning victim only to have some serious subsequent misgivings as to the mechanism of death. Therefore, investigators should employ the same investigatory protocol afforded deaths on land to deaths on or in the water. By processing the bodies of drowning victims correctly, investigators can obtain a variety of forensic evidence. For example, divers should place bodies in body bags to avoid losing transient evidence, such as hair or fibers, and to ensure that any injuries that occur during the recovery process are not mistaken for wounds inflicted before death. Bagging bodies in the water reveals damage to the body bags that corresponds to injuries to the bodies that may occur during the recovery process. Bagging bodies in the water also keeps the clothing intact. For example, shoes can contain dirt, blood, glass, gravel, or other debris from a prior crime scene, which may prove valuable to investigators and laboratory personnel. Because shoes become lost easily, divers should bag feet, with the shoes intact, to prevent loss and possible contamination during the recovery operation or subsequent transportation of the body to the medical examiner's office.

Myth 7: All air disasters are accidents. This myth coexists with another one: Air crash disasters happen somewhere else. Since September 11, 2001, this particular myth takes on poignancy heretofore absent in America's collective unconscious. Aircraft crashes can and do occur in every part of the world. Moreover, because most of the world is covered in water, many aircraft crashes occur in the water. For every large commercial airliner that crashes into water (or on land), several hundred airplanes with a seating capacity of less than 10 crash into oceans, lakes, and rivers (Teather, 1994). With this in mind, jurisdictions with any type of body of water within its boundaries can recognize that they may have to conduct an underwater recovery of an aircraft. If they assume that such incidents always are accidents, they may overlook, contaminate, or destroy critical evidence that may indicate that the crash resulted from criminal intervention. Investigators also must understand the purpose of the recovery operation in aircraft crashes. To identify passengers and to determine what caused the crash constitute the two primary purposes. However, investigators must remember that when an aircraft crashes, even in water, it generally becomes a mass of twisted, convoluted, and shredded metal, and the occupants usually have sustained massive, often disfiguring, fatal injuries (Teather, 1994). Conducting underwater recoveries of such incidents requires the establishment of contingency plans before an aircraft disaster occurs. In addition, divers involved in the underwater recovery of aircraft and the victims involved in such disasters must have the necessary training and equipment to carry out the operation effectively.

Myth 8: It is not necessary or possible to locate submerged items geographically. This myth has evolved because most underwater recovery operations occur in conditions of limited visibility. However, divers can find a 2000-year-old submerged vessel; sketch the area where they found it; recover, label, and measure all of the pieces in relation to each other; reconstruct the vessel on land; and tell by the placement of the cargo in the hold what ports the vessel visited and in what order it visited them (Becker, 2000). The techniques exist if the need does. Situations where dive recovery teams need to employ such techniques could include an accident reconstruction where one vehicle came to rest in the water. The position of the vehicle would reveal the direction of travel as well as the approximate speed on impact. In a weapon recovery, the position of the weapon in the water may determine its relevance. If divers discover a weapon 500 yards from where a witness places the individual disposing of the weapon, some serious questions could arise about the case. Investigators must understand the importance of properly marking and recording the location of the recovery site. Failure to do so may result in the loss of the site, in the event that more than one dive is necessary, and considerable expense in time and effort in relocating the site and the evidence at the site; inability to orient parts of a dismantled motor vehicle, vessel, or airplane, or dismembered body; or evidence subsequently being rendered inadmissible at the time of trial (Becker, 1995).

Myth 9: The only successful recovery operation is one that discovers the evidentiary item sought. This is a relatively recent myth added as the result of the author's experience in serving as a consultant for the Honolulu Police Department during a recovery operation for a pipe that had been used in a homicide. The possibility of trace evidence remaining on the pipe was slim but possible (especially on ragged or threaded ends). The media were present in force, because the number of homicides in Hawaii is small and a search underwater for a murder weapon a major media event. Based on the information provided by the suspect, a search area was selected and a search pattern employed and executed. The pipe was not found. Everyone left disappointed. That disappointment led to the inclusion of this myth. In reality a successful underwater search occurs in one of two ways: (1) the item sought is found, or (2) There is sufficient confidence in the team, their equipment, and search integrity that it can be stated unequivocally that the item sought is not there. The second point allows the focus of the search to shift confidently to a new location.

Myth 10: All underwater operations begin at the water's edge. In considering how crime scenes generally are treated, it should be apparent that whatever is in the water did not materialize there. It had to get there in some fashion. Just as in any dry-land investigation, there are points of access, exit, and staging that must be considered as part of the crime scene. Whoever put the item in the water got there somehow. That somehow is part of the crime scene. This became most apparent in a recovery operation for a firearm: The dive team brought a tarp, laid it on the ground and staged their dive equipment upon it. After the discovery of the pistol, the team packed the dive gear, removed the tarp, and found five expended shell casings underneath. Although it was apparent that they were from the recovered pistol, they had been trod upon to the point that their forensic usefulness was compromised.

A major focus in land investigations is on witnesses. Witnesses are as important to the underwater recovery team as they are to any investigative effort. When dealing with drownings or abandoned evidence where witnesses are available, the dive team should not rely on investigators to gather information pertaining to the **last seen point (LSP)**. The dive team has the responsibility of independently establishing the last seen point. A thorough examination of possible witnesses by a member of the dive team may provide data overlooked or misinterpreted by the investigating officers. That information may reduce the time and effort expended in the search of the applicable areas.

In lake drownings, the victim often is found on the bottom within a radius from the last point seen equal to the depth of the water. For example, if the victim drowned in 30 feet of water, the body will likely be found on the bottom within a 30-foot radius from

---

CASE IN POINT

Establishing a Last Seen Point

The effectiveness of developing a last point seen and the futility of not using one was demonstrated when a boat sank in a lake surrounded by a residential community. The first divers on the scene inquired of individuals in the general area in which the boat sank, then cleared the area of all civilians. They searched for five days without success. A second team was later dispatched and began canvassing the houses overlooking the area in question. Using a boat placed on the lake as a reference point, various witnesses placed the point at some distance from that first determined to be the last seen point. The sunken boat was discovered shortly after the new search began. The first divers relied on conjecture fueled by haste instead of using a search strategy that began with interviews based on a floating reference point. Although the second team spent a day seeking and interviewing witnesses, their total time on-site was only two days, and their efforts culminated in success.

---

the point on the bottom directly below the last point seen topside. In establishing the last point seen, it is often helpful to place a diver or a boat in the water and allow the witness to direct the diver to that point. Each interview should be conducted at approximately the location of the eyewitness at the time of the last sighting.

In moving water, a last seen point becomes the demarcation point for determining body drift. A body sinks at the average of 2 feet per second in moving water. To determine the speed of the current it would be necessary to drop something floatable in the water, follow its unobstructed flow for one minute, then measure the distance. That would give us the number of feet the current is moving in one minute. (For feet per second, divide the feet per minute rate by sixty seconds.) It is necessary to convert the current from minutes to seconds because the sink rate figure is measured in seconds. To be able to use the sink rate and the current speed together, these figures must be of the same unit, that is, seconds.

Once we have calculated the current speed in feet per second, using a sink rate of 2 feet per second we are now ready to calculate how far down stream the body may have moved.

$$\frac{\text{Current (ft/min)}}{60} = \text{current speed in ft/sec}$$

$$\text{seconds to sink to bottom} \times \text{current speed} = \text{distance traveled}$$

Thus, if the current is traveling at 180 ft/min and the depth is 20 feet:

$$\text{current speed: } \frac{180}{60} = 3 \text{ ft/sec}$$

$$\text{sink rate: 2 ft/sec, i.e., 10 seconds to sink to bottom}$$
$$\text{distance traveled: 10 sec} \times 3 \text{ ft/sec} = 30 \text{ ft}$$

All information gathered from witnesses or other investigators is geared to assist in the recovery of physical evidence. Witnesses possess different perspectives, and each witness's perspective may color the information given. Any information provided by investigators pertaining to the search area should be corroborated if possible.

Although the recovery of drowning victims gets the most media exposure, underwater recovery teams spend much of their time in the water seeking evidence, usually in the form of a weapon, stolen property, or abandoned drugs. As waterway recreation and transportation expand, so will crimes committed on the waterways. Underwater investigators work on a broad range of crimes and crises, including but not limited to boat arson, suicides, homicides, drownings, abandoned contraband, abandoned weapons, abandoned vehicles, vehicle entombment, vessel and aircraft crashes, and attachment of contraband to keels.

The first step in any underwater investigation is to locate the underwater crime scene. It is helpful to think of the recovery of underwater evidence as an extension of the overall investigation.Underwater investigation should be conducted just as meticulously as investigations on land.

As in any investigation, a search cannot begin until a reasonable search area has been delineated and all information that might reduce the size of the search area has been gathered and considered. Much frustration and wasted underwater searching can be avoided by not entering the water too soon. In most cases requiring police divers, the life of the victim is not in question. Bad weather and surface conditions should be considered before anyone is ordered into the water. Barring a hurricane, bottom conditions on one day will be virtually the same the next day. Postponing the dive until better diving conditions are available should always be kept as an option by the team leader. No evidence is so important that it warrants risking the life of a diver.

Divers are often asked to recover an item of evidence that is partially visible or has already been located. When the resting place of the item can be ascertained from the surface, it is not necessary to initiate search procedures. When the recovery team must conduct a search, the following general procedures should be used.

Search Briefing

Once the area of the search has been described, the team leader should conduct a **search briefing**. The briefing should cover the methods to be employed and the role of each participant. The dive team will probably be eager to get into the water, but a lack of planning will likely result in a fruitless initial search, leading to wasted time and a duplication of effort. An integral part of the briefing is documenting the dive (see the Officer's Notebook).

OFFICER'S NOTEBOOK

Elements of the Dive Report
The following information should be obtained and documented for inclusion in the **dive report:**
- Witnesses interviewed (names, addresses, and telephone numbers)
- Dive team members
- Time, date, and location of search
- Persons present
- Purpose of search
- Time divers arrived
- Time search began
- Method of search
- Weather conditions
- Water conditions (temperature, depth, tide, and current)
- Bottom conditions
- Equipment availability (vessels, tow trucks, and barges)
- Time and date of and reason for search termination

Currents

Currents are important for two reasons. First, the diver may need mechanical assistance to maintain a position. Second, police not familiar with underwater operations may exaggerate the effect of the currents when locating the search area. In river searches in which fast currents are evident, it may be necessary to affix a line across the river and anchor it securely on both sides. Once that line is anchored, another line can be tied to it perpendicularly to deploy a rubber raft. Divers can be tended from the raft, and safety divers can be stationed in the raft to facilitate ease of access.

Surf, Waves, and Tide

Turbulent surface activity in shallow water may affect items lying on the bottom. Again, the effect of surf and waves may not be as great as expected, and search operations should begin at the point of entry. Obviously, tides and crashing surf may move material shoreward or out to sea, but assumptions made as to the degree of movement may be erroneous. The tide characteristics of a potential dive site can affect the search in a number of ways. When investigators interview witnesses about the last point seen, they must take the tide into consideration, because it can influence the witnesses' distance perception. If possible, witnesses should be interviewed at the scene at approximately the same tidal flow as occurred during the incident in question. In areas of significant tidal flux, low tide allows investigators to search the area without needing to enter the water.

Marking the Perimeter

The preliminary briefing should be followed by dispatching divers to mark the perimeter of the area to be searched with buoys and, if necessary, to place a dive flag visible to any vessels that may be using the area. Generally a rectangle is used to describe the perimeter, with each corner marked with buoys that are visible not only to team participants but also to the crews of nearby vessels. These buoys should be large enough not to be ignored.

Once the divers have marked the perimeter, they should locate it geographically (by transit, compass, tape measure, or range finder) and sketch or plot it on a site map. If a site map is drawn or available, plastic overlays can be used to plot the search area on the overlay without permanently marking the map itself. If the search area must be expanded, the overlay can be replaced. Investigators should keep each overlay as a permanent part of the dive record so that testimony regarding the search can be supported by the plastic overlays. Once the search area has been marked, the recovery process can begin.

The Underwater Search

It is not always necessary to launch a search using large numbers of divers and expensive equipment. In water of high visibility, for centuries fishermen have used a simple device—a glass-bottom bucket—to locate underwater schools of fish. This same device should be part of every recovery team's equipment. For example, Edmund Scientific of New Jersey makes an inflatable cone with a glass bottom and a viewfinder top designed specifically for clear-water use. Putting police personnel in the water is not always the most effective use of their time.

Search Patterns and Methods

In water of limited visibility or having an irregular bottom structure, divers may search using a search pattern. In **blackwater diving**, lines must be sunk to which divers can be tethered while conducting a search by feel, handheld sonar, or metal detector. Handheld sonar can be used in conjunction with any of the search patterns described in this section. A sonar unit emits a beep when it senses an item protruding from the bottom. As the diver descends, the beep becomes louder. Once the diver senses an item, he or she should mark its location with a buoy before the search is interrupted. If the item sensed is not the object sought, the search can be taken up again at the point the item was first sensed. The same approach should be used when the diver is operating a handheld metal detector. Most detectors use dials and audible signals to assist in locating metal. (It would be helpful if sonar and metal-detecting devices also produced a vibration that increases in intensity as the object being sensed draws closer.)

Often, divers conduct low-visibility and no-visibility searches without the assistance of electronic devices. Engaging in a hand search is like crawling through visually impenetrable mud wearing gloves, attempting to identify by touch the things the hand grasps or touches. All the senses focus on the hand and fingers, and the sense of touch heightens to the point that a diver wearing gloves is able to touch a pull tab from a soft drink can and identify it without picking it up. A hand search must be undertaken with diligence and perseverance. A systematic search method will prevent duplication of efforts and will facilitate documentation and in-court testimony.

The offense being investigated will affect the nature and scope of the search, as will existing currents, tidal conditions, water depth, visibility, wind direction, and known bottom structure. It is the recovery team leader's responsibility to determine, based on the relevant variables, which search pattern to employ. Search patterns have different attributes and are able to meet different search requirements, but every search should have certain basic attributes:

- The search should begin at a predetermined point, have predetermined midpoints and changes of direction, and end at a predetermined location or upon discovery of the item sought.
- Surface personnel and searchers should communicate through line signals or be in voice contact.
- The searchers should deploy buoys to mark points of interest or items of evidence.
- The search pattern should be simple.
- The search should use divers and resources effectively.
- The search should allow a large safety margin and provide adequate support for the divers.

Most searches involve a **line tender** (a surface component) and a diver or divers. All divers should be competent in line tending. Working as a team, the diver provides the labor, and the tender provides the direction and support. The tender is the diver's lifeline and is responsible for keeping notes regarding the diver's location, direction, duration, and depth. In cases where a diver is unable to determine air consumption and depth, it will fall to the tender to provide that information. Each tender will need a compass, timepiece, flotation device, and notepad. The compass is for recording search direction and termination points, and the watch is for estimating air consumption and time at depth. A basic rule of thumb based on fatigue and ability to focus suggests that divers should be limited to 20-minute searches. When the call out provides sufficient divers, extended time should be unnecessary. After 20 minutes, air consumption becomes a concern, as do focus and fatigue. The more divers means less air time per diver.

Although a **random search** is no pattern at all, inserting a number of divers at a search site and having them cast about may prove successful if the area is small and visibility is good. In clear water with a bottom layered with sediment, it is important for the divers not to go too deep and agitate the sediment, prohibiting a subsequent patterned search if the random search is unsuccessful.

Sweep searching is the most commonly employed method for searches conducted contiguous to an accessible shoreline, bridge, dock, pier, or in a river whose current requires that a line be stretched across the river. The diver is tethered to the tender by a quarter-inch polypropylene line and swims (crawls) in ever-broadening arcs. The tender line remains taut, and the tender and diver remain in continuous communication through line signals. The farthest reaches of the arcs should be determined by the tender, using landmarks, placed buoys, or compass bearings. The tender should record the terminus of the arcs in his or her notebook and include a sketch of the search site and search pattern.

When the bottom drops quickly, it may be best to employ a parallel pattern to avoid running the diver into the shore and to reduce the number of times the diver's ear must equalize pressure because of a change in depth. Underwater obstacles can be addressed in one of three fashions: by raising the tender line, by conducting the search up to the obstacle and beginning again on the other side of the obstacle, or by placing a flotation device in the middle of the tender line, thereby raising the line off the bottom.

If the area to be searched is relatively free of obstructions and close to the shoreline, a **parallel search** pattern allows lengthy passes along the shoreline, extending outward (**Figure 3–12**). Markers should be placed on the shore at the farthest reaches of the pattern. The tender moves back and forth between these two markers, paralleling the diver. At the furthest reaches of the pattern, two tugs on the tender line communicate to the diver that it is time to turn around and go back the other way, but at a slightly greater distance from the shoreline. The amount of line fed to the diver at each direction change is determined based on visibility. For hand searches, it should be an arm's length.

Circular searches are generally boat-based. They are useful for searching areas in which the line tender is not able to work from shore. In shallow water, the line tender is at the center of the circle in a boat, feeding line to the divers, who swim 360 degrees, then stop and change direction (**Figure 3–13**). At the point where the diver changes direction, the tender feeds additional line. The line tender directs the search using a landmark, an anchored buoy, or a compass bearing to determine when the change of direction should occur. Changing direction is less disorienting than swimming in concentric circles and does not require the tender to continue turning in circles.

In a circular search, the tender can feed the line to the diver using an anchored swivel, or the line can be self-fed. A diver can conduct a circular search without a boat or circle board. A submerged diver, acting as the tender and the center of the search pattern, uses compass bearings or an orientation line to determine the needed directional changes and direct the search.

Snag searching (**Figure 3–14**) can utilize an arc pattern, a parallel pattern, or a circular pattern. The size of the item sought and the number of submerged obstructions determine the applicability of this technique. Its value is that it allows large areas to be searched in a short period of time. The tender allows more line to the diver than would be used in a hand or visual search.

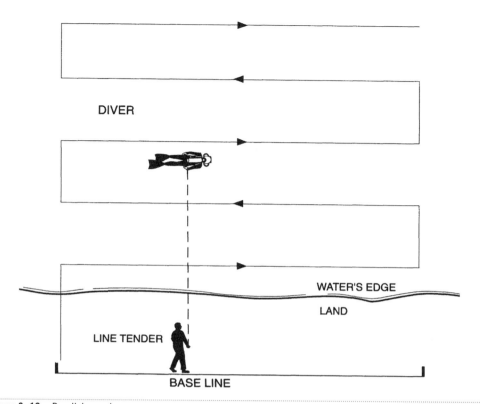

DIVER

WATER'S EDGE

LAND

LINE TENDER

BASE LINE

Figure 3–12 Parallel search.

Reprinted with permission from R. Becker, *Processing the Underwater Crime Scene: Underwater Investigative Techniques*, ©1995, Charles Thomas Publishing Company

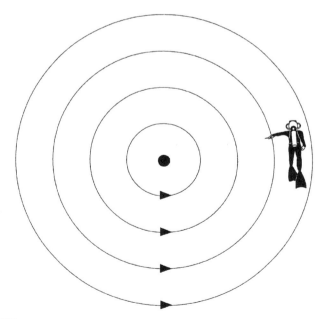

Figure 3–13 Circular search.

Reprinted with permission from R. Becker, *Processing the Underwater Crime Scene: Underwater Investigative Techniques*, ©1995, Charles Thomas Publishing Company

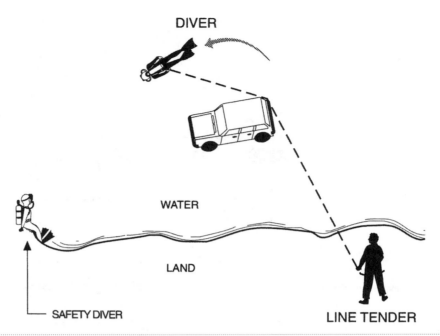

Figure 3–14   Snag search.

Reprinted with permission from R. Becker, *Processing the Underwater Crime Scene: Underwater Investigative Techniques,* ©1995, Charles Thomas Publishing Company

In clear water, a **compass search** can be conducted without a tender. Using compass bearings, divers submerged in the water can direct the course of the search. A compass search works best when there are two divers, one maintaining the compass heading and the other conducting a visible investigation of the bottom. Mark the furthest reaches of the search with a buoy so that the next pass is at a consistent distance from the last pass.

Relocating the Search Site

It may be necessary to continue searching a site beyond the first day. In such cases, the accurate plotting of each day's search pattern will prevent duplication of effort or the need to guess where previous searches left off. Once evidence has been found, it may take days to process and recover the evidence completely. Returning to the precise location is essential, but floating buoys left unattended may disappear, so the location should be marked permanently.

If the search party includes a transit operator, the location can be preserved by triangulation. Often divers will attempt to use compass bearings to triangulate their position. Although subject to significant margins of error (depending on the distance of the objects used for triangulation), in many instances compass bearings are all that are available. When a compass is used to locate a site, the objects from which bearings are taken should be greater than 30 degrees apart. When plotted on a map, these bearings should be sufficient to direct the team to the general location. In addition to the compass triangulation, a buoy should be sunk 4 or 5 feet below the surface at the exact spot to facilitate rapid detection of the search site or the evidence being recovered.

An agency with extensive resources might consider acquiring submersible transponders that emit a signal that can be picked up on handheld sonar. Obviously, such a transponder makes relocating a search site simple. Anyone competent in navigation skills should have no trouble in plotting the location of the search site using typical navigational instruments and shoreside landmarks. Numerous commercial **global positioning systems (GPSs)** are available. Although these devices are not as accurate as an instrument stabilized on a tripod and calibrated for accuracy, they are a reasonable addition to the equipment inventory.

Searches conducted out of the sight of land pose an additional problem. Typical navigational techniques, including sextant-based techniques, can only approximate the position of a vessel at sea. Radio beacons affixed to various well-known permanent landmarks allow vessels at sea with radio direction finders (RDFs) to triangulate their positions with a modicum of certainty. Someone with a GPS device can use satellites to compute his or her position to a heretofore unattainable degree of accuracy. Such a device can be used on land or at sea, as long as it is able to receive signals from one of the satellites to which it is calibrated.

The Temporal and Geographic Location of Evidence

After the team has located evidence, the usual next step is to retrieve it. Remember, the officer recovering the evidence will be responsible for testifying as to the method used in locating, marking, sketching, measuring, photographing, bagging, and tagging the evidence and maintaining the chain of custody. A team member must record all details pertaining to the dive site prior to the recovery of any evidence. The boundaries of the recovery site should be marked with buoys and the entire area plotted on a site chart. This chart must be large enough to contain measurement information about each piece of evidence to be recovered. The methods used to record available information will vary depending on the size of the recovery area, nature of the items to be recovered, available time, weather conditions, water conditions, visibility, bottom conditions, seriousness of the offense, and personnel demands.

Failure to mark and record the location of the recovery site properly may result in losing the site (an important setback if more than one dive is necessary), may cause considerable expenditure of time and effort in rediscovering the location, may render the evidence inadmissible at the time of trial, or may make it impossible to orient the parts of a dismembered or dismantled auto, vessel, airplane, or body.

In airplane crashes, body parts—arms, hands, legs, and feet—may be strewn over the site (Wagner and Froede, 1993). Reconstruction of the bodies may require anthropological assistance. Often the fastest way to associate severed limbs with a torso is by recording the location of the body parts relative to the seat or seats to which the parts were closest. By referring to the seating chart, body parts can be associated readily with the passenger who had been occupying the seat nearest to where the body parts were found.

Photography is the most effective method of recording. Where visibility allows, the camera should be the first piece of equipment on the site. The team should photograph all evidence where it is found. After it is measured, sketched, and tagged, the photographer should photograph the evidence again and then bag it.

Measuring Evidence

Trilateration is a method of measurement in which the diver need not rely on sight for accuracy (**Figure 3–15**). Objects in the water are measured from two known locations

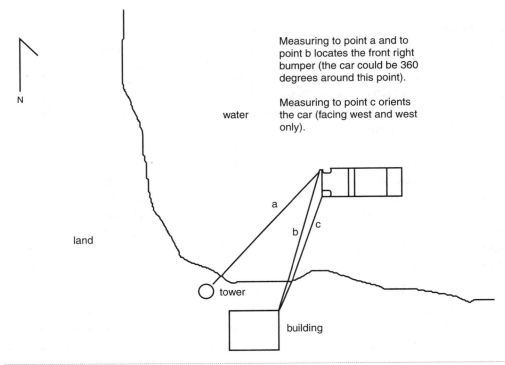

Measuring to point a and to point b locates the front right bumper (the car could be 360 degrees around this point).

Measuring to point c orients the car (facing west and west only).

N

water

land

tower

building

a

b

c

Figure 3–15   Trilateration.

on the shore. The end of the tape to be read is on shore at the prelocated position, and the diver moves the tape to a point on the object being measured. The shore-based end of the tape is then moved from one known position to the other. It is important to note that this measurement will only give you the location of the object being measured, not its orientation. To orient the object, two more measurements must be taken from a different point on the submerged item.

■ Mass Disasters

Human-made mass disasters are disasters in which human factors are involved. The most common human-made mass disasters are aircraft crashes. Aircraft crashes are especially visible because of the attention accorded them by the media, the great number of airports, the great number of aircraft, and the potential for large numbers of injured and dead. There are an estimated 2000 aviation fatalities nationally each year.

In every aircraft crash, local authorities will be first on the scene. Their conduct will often determine the success or failure of the accident investigation and will play an important role in the successful identification of the dead. The primary objectives are to recover bodies, identify the bodies, and reconstruct the events leading to the crash. The objective of the first-responding team is to secure the scene from any and all trespass. With any exterior crime scene—and air crashes in water are no exception—it is helpful to establish three separate zones of security emanating from the scene center. The zone immediately surrounding the center should not be penetrated by anyone other than forensic specialists with specific authorization, and a ledger should be kept that lists who enters, the time of entry, the time of departure, and what was removed. The second zone should be accessible by only those actively involved in the investigation. The third zone should function as a perimeter from which all traffic approaching the crime scene from any direction can be monitored. The opportunity for looting can be great in a mass disaster.

A mass disaster plan should be developed for each community and each department, including, if necessary, procedures for underwater recovery operations. All unauthorized people, including unauthorized police personnel, should be kept away from the crash site. The presumption in an airline crash should be that the incident was caused by criminal acts until proven otherwise, and the entire scene should be treated and processed as a crime scene.

On June 24, 1975, Eastern Airlines Flight 66 crashed in New York. Police on the scene gave each body a consecutive number, removed all valuables from the bodies, and put all recovered jewelry and wallets into manila envelopes. The envelopes were then sent to the property room, with the intention being to prevent theft. The bodies were lined up on the tarmac and covered with sheets. All this was done before any efforts were made to use wallet contents, jewelry, or body position to identify the victims. Later, when the personal

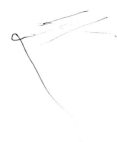

OFFICER'S NOTEBOOK

Aircraft Crash Protocol

In Texas, the Southwest Texas State University Underwater Institute gathered statewide information to provide all jurisdictions with a list of resources in the event of an aircraft crash. The following list is indicative of the type of information necessary to form a contingency plan.

1. Your name and agency affiliation
2. Salvage vessel (describe its size and capacity)
3. Salvage equipment (describe equipment and location)
4. Warehouse (for airplane parts and passenger luggage; describe size, furnishings, and equipment)
5. Refrigerated storage (for bodies and body parts; describe size, furnishings, and equipment)
6. Forensic pathologist (to assist in determining cause of death; provide name and location)
7. Forensic anthropologist (to assist in reassembling body parts; provide name and location)
8. Funeral director (to assist in forwarding or preparing bodies; describe equipment, name, and location)
9. Forensic odontologist (to assist in dental identification; provide name and location)
10. Ambulance service (to transport the injured or body parts)
11. Hospital (to receive the injured and to provide medical and dental records for the deceased)
12. Divers (equipped with gear and training for contaminated and hazardous materials; describe gear and training and provide names of divers)
13. Communication equipment (describe type and number)
14. Mobile housing (to accommodate manpower needs)
15. Psychologist (to provide debriefing for participants)
16. Food service (to feed participants)
17. Sanitation facilities (to meet participants' needs)
18. Shuttle craft (to transport divers and searchers; describe size, power, and capacity)
19. Any other equipment or services that might assist in the response to an in-water air crash

property envelopes that supposedly contained the personal effects of the passengers were examined, officials found that all valuables had been removed or lost in handling.

Although gathering and inventorying personal effects is important, it is more important not to remove any of these materials until the entire wreck site has been searched and photographed and all remains have been photographed in relation to debris and personal effects. Most underwater investigators use 35-mm cameras and color film. Video footage often reveals a perspective that may be lost in still photography. The entire underwater site should be shot in overlaying strips, the video footage should be overdubbed with narrative, and finally the site should be documented using conventional 35-mm still shots.

The recovery and identification of passengers is generally the most time-consuming part of an air crash investigation, especially if that investigation is taking place underwater. Identification can be positive or presumptive. A **positive identification** is identification beyond reasonable doubt. Positive identification is based on pre- and postmortem comparisons of dental records, fingerprints, palm prints, and footprints or on DNA profiling. A **presumptive identification** is an identification that is less than certain. A presumptive identification requires several points of inconclusive comparison that cumulatively establish the legal identity of the body.

The easiest way to begin an underwater air crash investigation is to obtain a passenger list and seating assignment. The investigation is likely to be hampered by the fact that many of the bodies will have been torn asunder, disfigured, or mutilated as a result of impact or deceleration. A group of body parts and personal possessions may be near an assigned seat, giving some clue as to their identity. It may take time to obtain the information necessary to begin identification, such as the flight manifest, the seating assignment, medical and dental records, and information provided by family members and employers. In most cases, positive identifications are made on the basis of comparison of teeth and dental records. Few people today have not had dental work done on their teeth. That dental work is as individual as fingerprints.

Fingerprint comparison is the next most common method of identification. It has been estimated that only 25% of the American population have fingerprints on file. Only a single fingerprint is necessary to confirm identification.

If body fragmentation is extensive, identification becomes more difficult. For presumptive purposes, a single finger, foot, part of a dental prosthesis, or jaw can identify a passenger as having died in the crash. There are 206 bones in the body, and any one of

OFFICER'S NOTEBOOK

On-Scene Conduct
- Keep the search scene secure and organized, and anticipate attempts at covert photography.
- All briefings and debriefings of dive team members should be done in private.
- Recovery team members should arrive at the site together rather than straggle in individually.
- Conduct and conversation should reflect the gravity of the situation at all times.
- The release of information pertaining to victims should be done by authorized personnel only.
- All statements to the media should be prepared statements and should be read to media representatives (copies of such statements should be kept as part of the file).

them may have specific characteristics that will allow identification when compared with antemortem X-rays. Such identification will allow a death certificate to be issued. An unidentified individual hampers the investigation and places the burden of an unsettled estate upon the next of kin.

In all crashes, the specter of a human-caused explosion hovers. All clothing, personal effects, and body parts should be handled in the same fashion as for a known bombing. Any investigation should search for detonator components. Aircraft parts should be recovered and documented like any other evidence. Even in the case of a crash where there is confirmation of accidental causes, those causes will be best discovered and corroborated by treating the recovery operation as a criminal investigation.

Investigators of an air crash are subject to pressures to move quickly to determine the cause and forestall the clamor of relatives trying to determine if their loved ones were passengers. Those pressures should not affect the quality of the investigation. An underwater recovery is an especially time-consuming operation, and the public, media, and federal agencies must learn to accept that. It is akin to an underwater archaeological excavation and brings into play the full range of underwater skills used in recovering, measuring, and processing evidence. Further, time, diligence, and patience—the main requisites of an underwater excavation—are anathema to the public and the media. Fortunately, once the human remains have been recovered, there is little reason to hurry the investigation of an air crash. (See EXHIBIT 3-2 for guidelines for dealing with the media.)

Salvage techniques occasionally have been used for the rapid recovery of underwater evidence. The public now expects these techniques to be employed in any underwater investigation of an air disaster. It is necessary to help the public understand that a full and complete archaeological recovery operation has important benefits that are worth the extra time needed. Public relations in this type of situation require a masterful touch, but the investigation should involve a complete archaeological examination and excavation of the scene to ensure that no evidence of identification and causation (criminal endeavor) is overlooked. Although a good working relationship with the press is desirable, it is best for recovery team members to leave the establishment of such a relationship to the persons assigned to that task.

EXHIBIT 3-2   Do's and Don'ts for Dealing with the Media

Do	*Don't*
Be firm	Be unnecessarily gruff
Be specific	Be pedantic
Be courteous	Make any on-record statements
Designate press pool area	Apologize or make exceptions
Escort media representatives from the crime scene	Enjoy it
Advise media representatives of press releases	Make press releases
Encourage coverage	Assist in coverage
Recognize First Amendment rights	Allow photos to be taken
Encourage investigative reporting	Allow access to witnesses
Keep lines of movement open	Take no for an answer
Keep lines of communication open	Allow media to be obstructive

CASE IN POINT

September 11, 2001

The enormity of the World Trade Center crime scene (approximately 16 acres), coupled with the sheer mass of 140 million tons of debris, made the job of recording evidence unearthed during the recovery and clean-up effort extremely difficult (**Figure 3–16**). From the outset, investigators required careful documentation of each piece of evidence as it was uncovered by firefighters and other recovery crew members. The precise location of evidence—which ranged from human remains and building debris to scraps of airliner metal—aided in the reconstruction of the event.

Early on, the process of (1) identifying each piece of evidence and (2) recording its location within the mountain of snarled metal and concrete was conducted manually. Handwritten notes describing each item, coupled with rough measurements or estimates of its location, were made by those clearing and processing the crime scene, along with notes on the date and time of discovery. A tracking number was assigned to each item. Later, these notes were entered into a database. The process was slow and difficult. Mismatched numbers and inaccurate estimates of location inevitably arose under the difficult conditions. Moving around on the debris field seeking points of reference for handheld measurement created the potential for serious on-site accidents among the ruins.

Recognizing the problems, New York Fire Department officials enlisted the help of Links Point (Norwalk, CT), a firm specializing in wireless data-transmission systems that incorporate GPS technology for a range of tracking applications. Links Point's solution included the use of handheld terminals manufactured by Symbol Technologies, Inc. (Holtsville, NY), which contained integrated barcode scanners and customized software from Links Point. The handheld terminals also had built-in radio transceivers for sending information to host computers.

Equipped with this state-of-the-art equipment, the task of recording data immediately became safer and faster, and much more accurate. Using a handheld terminal, a firefighter, when finding evidence,

Figure 3–16   World Trade Center.

Courtesy of Andrea Booher/FEMA Photo News

was able to key in a brief description of the object. A barcode was attached to the object, serving as a unique "serial number," which was later rescanned to retrieve information from a database. Onsite, the firefighters scanned the item's barcode. Simultaneously, its location was recorded by a GPS link, which is accurate to within three feet. Additionally, the application software electronically time-stamped the data transaction with the date and hour of the recording.

All this information was instantly uploaded into one of a number of laptops set up as host computers for the evidence-recovery effort. In this way, an accurate database of all items was created, assigning specific locations for each within a large gridwork covering the recovery site.

On the night of September 12, 2001, the Fresh Kills Landfill on Staten Island was designated a secondary crime scene, and trucks began arriving from Ground Zero with steel and crushed debris that was once the World Trade Center. Over the next 10 months, an operation to recover human remains, personal effects, and the objects of everyday life from tons of material was undertaken by the New York Police Department, an FBI evidence recovery team, 25 state and federal agencies, and 14 private contractors. Thousands of detectives, agents, and forensic evidence specialists worked around the clock to recover remnants of the lives lost at the World Trade Center. Over 1.7 million hours were spent working at the landfill. Those 1.7 million hours revealed

- 4,257 human remains, which resulted in the identification of over 300 individuals to date
- Approximately 4,000 personal photographs
- $78,318.47 in domestic and foreign currency
- 54,000 personal items, such as identification cards and driver's licenses
- 1,358 vehicles, including 102 fire apparatus and 61 Police Department vehicles

■ Summary

If an investigator can process a homicide, then in all likelihood that same investigator can employ techniques borrowed from a homicide crime scene investigation in processing any other type of crime scene. It is for that reason that homicides were the grist for discussing crime scene processing in this chapter. Much of what we see in the movies deals with the pursuit and apprehension of criminals, not with the day-to-day tedium associated with interviewing witnesses, canvassing neighborhoods, and digesting information gleaned from the crime scene. Much of the work of the criminal investigator is dictated by what is left at the crime scene. How the investigator processes that crime scene and handles the evidence found there determines to a large degree the ultimate success of the investigation.

The next chapter deals with legal issues associated with criminal investigations. It is impossible to conduct a competent investigation without having a fundamental understanding of the law that applies. In the main, what investigators need to know is contained in the Fourth, Fifth, and Sixth Amendments and the U.S. Supreme Court cases interpreting those amendments. The following chapter provides that information.

■ Key Terms

baseline: Arbitrary line of some measurable distance drawn between two fixed points; also, a construction method used to geographically locate evidence

batch: Group of a defined number of pieces of evidence, used to track and store those items for later use

blackwater diving: Diving done to collect evidence in water of limited visibility. In this type of diving, investigators must sink lines to which divers can hold while conducting a search by feel, handheld sonar, or metal detector

bottom structure: The composition of the floor of an area where divers will search for evidence. Knowing this helps decide what equipment will be needed for the dive

circular search: Boat-based searches that are useful for searching areas in which the line tender is not able to work from shore. In shallow water, the line tender is at the center of the circle in a boat, feeding line to the divers, who swim 360 degrees, then stop and change direction. At the point where the direction is changed, the tender feeds additional line to the divers

compass search: Search done in clear water, in which divers submerged in the water direct the course of the search using compass bearings

contamination: Materials and other factors added to crime scenes that were not there at the time of the crime and can affect the proper collection and interpretation of evidence negatively

crime scene processing plan: Plan created to carry out a systematic investigation of a crime scene

crime scene sketch: A measured drawing showing the location of all important items, landmarks, permanent fixtures, and physical evidence at a crime scene

dive report: Report documenting the details of the dive, including the people involved, the reason for the dive, and the conditions during the dive

first-responding officers: First officers to arrive at the crime scene. They are responsible for protecting the crime scene from any avoidable contamination in order to preserve it for investigation purposes

five Ws and an H: Who, what, where, when, why, and how

global positioning system (GPS): A device that uses satellites to compute position

grid search: Search method in which an area to be searched is divided into small squares approximately 1 meter by 1 meter, each of which is further subdivided into 4 smaller squares. The search begins in the northernmost of the smaller squares and progresses as one would read a book until the 1-square-meter grid has been examined completely

Kelly/Fry hearing: Hearings to determine the scientific acceptability of the testimony to be offered

killer's signature: The pattern associated with a person's killings

last seen point: Last location where a drowning victim was on top of the water; used to locate that person under the water

line tender: The surface component of an underwater search

parallel search: Search pattern done in areas relatively free of obstructions and close to the shoreline; it allows lengthy passes along the shoreline, extending outward

photo log: Recording of the people involved, equipment used, and conditions under which crime scene photographs were taken

positive identification: An identification beyond reasonable doubt

predicate for admissibility: The requirements that need to be met in order to use an item as evidence in a trial

press pool: A group of journalists authorized to cover an event

presumptive identification: An identification that is less than certain and requires several points of inconclusive comparison that cumulatively establish the legal identity of the body

random search: Method used by divers for searching that has no pattern, but which can be useful when a number of divers are placed in a small area with good visibility

rectangularization: Basic measurement technique used for geographically locating evidence, in which two right angles are drawn from the item being measured to the two nearest permanent objects (fixed points), and then the distance between the two fixed points and the same point on the evidence is measured

search briefing: A meeting that takes place once the search area has been described to cover the methods to be employed and the role of each participant in the search

sector search: A search method that is appropriate for large crime scenes

snag search: Search method that can be used with an arc pattern, a parallel pattern, or a circular pattern; it allows large areas to be searched in a short period of time

spiral search: A search method that involves moving in an ever-tightening or ever-expanding spiral; it can be used indoors or out

strip search: Search method that begins at one corner of a search area and continues to the opposite corner. Upon arrival at the opposite corner, the search reverses, moves 3 feet perpendicular to the line just searched, and continues across to the opposite side. This pattern continues until the search is complete

sweep search: The most commonly employed method for underwater searches conducted contiguous to an accessible shoreline, bridge, dock, pier, or in a river whose current requires that a line be stretched across the river. The diver is tethered to the tender by a quarter-inch polypropylene line and swims in ever-broadening arcs

trace evidence: Evidence left at the scene of a crime that usually cannot be seen with the naked eye and that requires the assistance of lights or reagents to visualize

transfer: The process whereby a person entering and exiting a crime scene leaves something and takes something

triangulation: Basic measurement technique used for geographically locating evidence; in this technique, three angles are measured, those of a triangle formed by the item of interest and two permanent objects (fixed points)

trilateration: A method of measurement that does not rely on a diver's sight for accuracy. Objects in the water are measured from two known locations on the shore

trophy: Remembrance or souvenir of a conquest; a body part

walk-through: Passing through a crime scene to survey the scene and determine what type of search method should be employed

■ Review Questions

1. Why is it important to secure the crime scene?
2. What part of the crime scene is the most difficult to preserve?
3. What is physical evidence?
4. What is meant geographically by the term *crime scene?*
5. What is the importance of the first-responding officer to the investigative team?
6. What is crime scene contamination, and what role does it play in the processing of a crime scene?
7. What is transfer, and what is its significance to a crime scene?
8. What are the eight elements of an appropriately protected crime scene?
9. What rights do the press have to view a crime scene?

10. What is trace evidence, and what precautions must be provided to ensure that such evidence is not destroyed?

11. What are field notes, and what role do they play in the criminal investigation?

12. What are the five Ws and the H of crime scene investigation?

13. What kind of information should be recorded pertaining to recovered evidence?

14. What is a walk-through and what purpose does it serve?

15. Where does photography come into play in processing the crime scene? What is photographed and when is it photographed?

16. What is the appropriate predicate for the admissibility of crime scene photographs?

17. What information is included in a crime scene photo log?

18. What are triangulation, rectangularization, and trilateration?

19. What information should be included on a crime scene sketch?

20. What is the appropriate predicate for the admissibility of a crime scene sketch?

21. Describe three dry-land and three underwater search techniques.

22. How does processing a complex crime scene differ from processing a less complex crime scene?

23. Describe the search plan employed by the Texas Rangers at the Branch Davidian compound near Waco, Texas.

24. In underwater searches for drowned victims, what is the last point seen, what is its significance, and how is it determined?

25. What should the presumption be in a mass disaster?

26. List three rules of crime scene photography.

27. Discuss the type of photographs that should be taken at a crime scene.

28. Why photograph blood stains?

29. How should a violent crime scene be photographed?

30. When should a crime scene be photographed?

31. What problems might arise in using a digital camera to record a crime scene?

32. Of what value are virtual crime scenes to the investigation of a crime?

33. Of what use are templates in creating a crime scene sketch?

34. What was the major factor in the capture of Timothy McVeigh?

35. How far downstream might an adult body travel if the water is travelling 180 ft. per minute with a depth of 20 feet?

36. What is a successful underwater recovery operation?

■ Bibliography

Becker, R.F. (1995). *The underwater crime scene.* Springfield, IL: Charles Thomas.

Becker, R.F. (2000). *Criminal investigations.* Gaithersburg, MD: Aspen.

Bugliosi, V. (1992). *And the sea will tell.* New York: Ivy.

Deadman, H.A. (1984). *Fiber evidence and the Wayne Williams trial. FBI Law Enforcement Bulletin* 53(5) 10–19.

Department of the Treasury, Bureau of Alcohol, Tobacco, and Firearms (1993). *Investigation of Vernon Wayne Howell a.k.a. David Koresh.* Washington, DC: Government Printing Office.

Schiro, G. (2003). Louisiana State Police Crime Laboratory. http://www.crime-scene-investigator.net.

Spitz, W.V. (1993). *Drowning in medicolegal investigation of death* (3rd ed.). Springfield, IL: Charles Thomas.

Teather, R.G. (1994). *Encyclopedia of underwater investigations.* Flagstaff, AZ: Best.

Texas Department of Public Safety (1994). *Criminal investigative report, David Koresh.* Austin: Texas Department of Public Safety.

Wagner, G.L., & Froede, R.C. (1993). Mass disasters. In W.U. Spitz (Ed.), *Medicolegal investigation of death* (3rd ed.). Springfield, IL: Charles C. Thomas.

■ Suggested Reading

Bass, G.B. (1968). *Archaeology under water.* New York: Frederick A. Praeger.

Blackman, D.J. (1973). *Marine archaeology.* London: Martin Robertson.

Brylske, A. (1984). *PADI rescue diver manual.* Santa Ana, CA: PADI.

Cleator, P.E. (1973). *Underwater archaeology.* New York: Holt, Rinehart and Winston.

Falcon-Barker, T. (1964). *Roman galley beneath the sea.* New York: McGraw-Hill.

Linton, J.S. (1986). *The dive rescue specialist training manual.* Fort Collins, CO: Concept Systems.

Lonsdale, M.V. (1989). *SRT diver.* Los Angeles: Lonsdale.

Marx, R.F. (1990). *The underwater dig.* Houston, TX: Pisces Books.

Teather, R.G. (1983). *The underwater investigator.* Fort Collins, CO: Concept Systems.

Williams, J.C.C. (1972). *Underwater surveying by simple graphic photogrammetry with obliques. Underwater archaeology: A nascent discipline.* Paris: Unesco.

Wood, M. (1985). *Dive control specialist handbook.* Fort Collins, CO: Concept Systems.

The Law of Search and Seizure

CHAPTER
4

▶ ▶ STUDENT LEARNING OUTCOMES

Upon completion of this chapter, students will demonstrate an understating of:

- Due process of law
- Warrantless searches and seizures pursuant to the Fourth Amendment
- The guarantee against self-incrimination as contained in the Fifth Amendment
- The implication of *Miranda v. Arizona* for criminal investigations

■ The U.S. Constitution and Due Process

The U.S. Constitution is a blueprint for the building of a democratic government. It outlines the structure of our government and the powers granted to the three branches. The authors of the Constitution realized that they had not included guarantees of individual freedom, despite the fact that violations of the colonists' individual rights laid the foundation for the American Revolution. The Founders amended the Constitution to include guarantees that addressed the original grievances against the English crown. The first 10 amendments of the U.S. Constitution, known as the Bill of Rights, form the groundwork of **due process**. As a student of criminal justice, you will study parts of the Bill of Rights—specifically, those rights considered to be criminal procedural rights, which are contained in the Fourth, Fifth, and Sixth Amendments to the U.S. Constitution. These three amendments and their case law interpretations have established the fundamentals of due process.

The Bill of Rights was not intended to apply to the states. It was the object of the drafters of the Constitution to protect the citizens of the colonies from an oppressive central government, a government insensitive to the rights of its citizens, a government that levied abuses upon its citizenry—in short, a government like that of England. After passage of the Fourteenth Amendment (**EXHIBIT 4-1**), the U.S. Supreme Court began

EXHIBIT 4–1   The Fourteenth Amendment to the U.S. Constitution

Section 1. All persons born or naturalized in the United States, and subject to the jurisdiction thereof, are citizens of the United States and of the State wherein they reside. No State shall make or enforce any law which shall abridge the privileges or immunities of citizens of the United States; nor shall any State deprive any person of life, liberty, or property, without due process of law; nor deny to any person within its jurisdiction the equal protection of the law.

to interpret the due process guaranteed in this amendment as the same due process guaranteed in the Bill of Rights. Bit by bit the Bill of Rights was incorporated into the Fourteenth Amendment until virtually all of it had been made part of this amendment's due process clause.

The Fourteenth Amendment contains three separate but equally important clauses:

1. The privileges and immunities clause
2. The due process clause
3. The equal protection clause

We will be most concerned with the **due process clause** as we study searches and seizures. The Supreme Court has embraced the Fourth, Fifth, and Sixth Amendments as the touchstones that limit the discretion available to police in conducting searches of people and places and in seizing people and things.

The Fourth Amendment

The Fourth Amendment provides two guarantees that assure citizens due process when confronted by police seeking to conduct a search or to seize a person or thing. First, it proclaims that "the right of the people to be secure in their persons, houses, papers, and effects, against unreasonable searches and seizures, shall not be violated." The most important part of this procedural safeguard is that all searches and seizures must be reasonable. The Supreme Court has gone to significant lengths to define what kind of searches and seizures are reasonable. An understanding of **reasonableness** as promulgated by the Court can only be achieved by examining some of the salient cases that provide the definition of reasonableness.

Second, the amendment proclaims that "no warrants shall issue, but upon probable cause, supported by oath or affirmation, and particularly describing the place to be searched, and the persons or things to be seized." When we think of seizures, we generally think of things other than persons, but the Fourth Amendment provides for the restrictions on police conduct in effecting an arrest. Disputes pertaining to this clause generally arise in regard to the **probable cause** requirement for a warrant to search or arrest. Probable cause to arrest is information upon which a reasonable person would believe that a crime has been committed or is about to be committed. Probable cause to search is the minimum information a reasonable person would need to have to believe that an item is where it is purported to be. Not only must police have reasonable information that the item in question is contraband, the fruit of a crime, or otherwise illegal to possess, but they must also have reasonable information as to the location of the item.

Expectation of Privacy

As citizens we believe we have a right of privacy that is enforceable through the Fourth Amendment. An examination of the Fourth Amendment carries no mention of privacy; in fact an examination of the Bill of Rights carries no mention of privacy. How is it we have come to recognize a right of privacy, a right protected under the U.S. Constitution? The U.S. Supreme Court in *Griswold v. Connecticut* (1965) found a right of privacy in the Bill of Rights and lodged firmly in the Fourth Amendment. Griswold was the Executive Director of the Planned Parenthood League and Dr. Buxton a licensed physician who served as Medical Director of the League. The League provided information, instruction, and medical advice on how to prevent conception to a married couple. Provision of such information was a violation of Connecticut statute. Griswold and Dr. Buxton were found guilty of having violated state statute and were fined $100. Their appeals were of no avail until they reached the U.S. Supreme Court. Justice Douglas, writing for a majority, found that information of the type provided in this case was a matter of personal privacy. Although the word "privacy" was found nowhere in the Constitution, Justice Douglas described the right of privacy as a penumbral right, emanating from within the Third, Fourth, Fifth, and Eighth Amendments to the Constitution and enforceable through the Fourteenth Amendment's due process clause. In time, the right of privacy came to be lodged and subsumed within the Fourth Amendment.

The question left unanswered by *Griswold* was what types of privacy were protected. The Court left the concept wide latitude for interpretation. In *California v. Greenwood* (1988) the Court had to deal with an unusual set of circumstances. The Greenwoods were using and selling drugs. Complaints by neighbors about the noise and traffic at the Greenwood residence put police on notice. Seeking probable cause for a warrant, the police placed the Greenwood residence under surveillance. They confirmed the noise and traffic, but also noticed the Greenwoods placed their garbage on the curb for pickup. The police contacted the garbage collectors and asked them to pick up the Greenwood's garbage, keep it separate, and give it to them. Upon examination of the contents of the garbage, police discovered evidence of narcotics use. A warrant was issued, a search conducted, and narcotics were found. The Greenwoods claimed that they had an "expectation of privacy" in their garbage, which was manifest in the fact the garbage bag was opaque, closed, and under the control of the Greenwoods. The Court held that the Greenwoods may have had an expectation of privacy in their garbage, but not all expectations of privacy were protected under the Fourth Amendment. Only those expectations that society accepts as reasonable are protected. Because garbage outside the **curtilage** of the home is available to marauding pests, children, and adults, it is also available to the police. Garbage placed in the public domain outside the curtilage of the home does not have an expectation of privacy recognized by the Court.

Since September 11, 2001, new legislation has been passed providing what is seen as extraordinary power to federal law enforcement agencies. The PATRIOT Act is often cited as the death of the Fourth Amendment. It should be noted that many of the things addressed by the Act as violative of the Fourth Amendment in fact are not. The Fourth Amendment protects the right of the people to be secure in their persons, houses, papers, and effects. The primary abuse that this amendment addressed was the colonial practice of law enforcement and military personnel entering into a residence to seize a person or thing. The primary protection is to homes, people, and things associated directly with people and their homes. The right does not protect against:

- Books checked out at the library
- Videos checked out at video stores
- Hospital records
- Photographs taken in public
- Videos taken in public

It has become popular to complain about these things and invoke illusory rights within the Fourth Amendment as having been violated. There are state tort laws that protect privacy and property rights that have nothing to do with the Fourth Amendment.

The Fifth Amendment

Because of the colonists' experience at the hands of a government that denied them the right to remain silent and allowed coerced confessions to be used against them in colonial courts presided over by British jurists, the drafters of the Bill of Rights included a provision that specifically forbade the government from requiring that a person incriminate himself or herself. Through later Supreme Court decisions, the self-incrimination clause of the Fifth Amendment took on unprecedented significance in American jurisprudence.

The clause provides testimonial protection, with its focus being the spoken word (and in some instances, the written word). It is important to understand the testimonial nature of the protection offered by the amendment when considering police conduct. A videotape of a person performing badly during a field sobriety test is as incriminating as an admission that he or she is in fact intoxicated. Yet, the videotape is admissible at the time of trial, whereas the confession is not, at least absent certain judicially required warnings explaining the right to remain silent. At first glance, there seems to be little difference in the potential effects upon the jury of the videotape and a confession. It is not the impact that is the determining difference, but the nature of the self-incriminating evidence. One is an instance of verbal self-incrimination prohibited by the Fifth Amendment; the other is not.

The Supreme Court has laid down a further condition for the applicability of the Fifth Amendment: The admission or verbal statement must have resulted from an attempt on the part of the police to solicit such a statement or must have occurred during the gathering of criminal evidence.

The Sixth Amendment

The Sixth Amendment requires that a person caught up in the criminal justice system be provided legal representation. When dealing with the police, at what point is a citizen entitled to the assistance of counsel? The answer is: at the point where he or she asks for such assistance. The Supreme Court, however, has determined that this fundamental right may not be known, may be forgotten, or may be unevoked because of intimidation or fear. In a far-reaching decision in *Miranda v. Arizona* (1966), the Court required that a

---

CASE IN POINT

Pennsylvania v. Muniz, 1990

In the case *Pennsylvania v. Muniz* (1990), an officer stopped Muniz's vehicle and directed him to undergo standard sobriety field tests, which unbeknownst to him were videotaped. He performed poorly and was taken into custody. At the station, he was booked, and as part of the booking process he was asked for seven standard pieces of information, including his name, address, height, weight, eye color, date of birth, and age. He was also asked to give the year in which his sixth birthday occurred. The videotape and the answer to the question about his sixth birthday were admitted at the time of trial over the objection of the defendant's lawyer. Muniz was convicted of driving under the influence.

The Supreme Court held that police may ask routine questions of a person suspected of driving while under the influence and may videotape their responses without violating the defendant's Fifth Amendment right prohibiting self-incrimination. The routine questions and the videotape do not elicit testimonial responses that are protected by the Fifth Amendment. The question about Muniz's sixth birthday, however, was not a routine question. It was designed to elicit an incriminating response during a criminal investigation (a response that was testimonial in nature) and was therefore in violation of the Fifth Amendment.

series of warnings be provided whenever a citizen is subjected to an interrogation while in the custody of the police. These warnings, in recognition of the landmark nature of the case, are commonly known as **Miranda warnings**.

The Sixth Amendment contributed to the content of those warnings: "In all criminal prosecutions, the accused shall enjoy the right . . . to have the assistance of counsel for his defense." Although the amendment speaks specifically of "criminal prosecutions," the Court has presumed that the investigation of a criminal offense begins the prosecutorial process and thus brings into play the right to the assistance of counsel.

■ The Exclusionary Rule

History

In *Weeks v. United States* (1914), the Supreme Court decided that evidence obtained (seized) as a result of an illegal search, arrest, or interrogation would not be admissible at the time of trial (excluded). This case applied only to the federal government and its law enforcement agencies. Not until 1961 did the states feel the brunt of the holding in the Weeks case.

In addition to imposing federal constitutional standards on police within the states, the Court, in *Mapp v. Ohio* (1961), indicated that both the Fourth and Fifth Amendments were the genesis of the **exclusionary rule**, which meant that the exclusionary rule would govern illegal searches and seizures and also that illegally obtained confessions would be excluded at the time of trial.

CASE IN POINT

Mapp v. Ohio, 1961

In 1961, three Cleveland police officers went to the residence of Dolree Mapp looking for a person who was wanted for a recent bombing. The officers demanded entrance but were refused. After the arrival of other officers, the police broke down the door. Mapp demanded that she be shown the search warrant authorizing the intrusion into and the search of her home. When a paper was held up by one of the officers, Mapp grabbed the paper and placed it in the bodice of her blouse. The police forcibly removed the paper and handcuffed Mapp. A search of the house produced no bomber but did produce some drawings and books that the police believed to be obscene. The materials were admitted into evidence during trial over Mapp's objection. Dolree Mapp was convicted of possession of obscene materials.

The Supreme Court held that the exclusionary rule promulgated in *Weeks* and applicable in federal cases was also applicable in state criminal proceedings. There were three questions that the Court had to address in the *Mapp v. Ohio* (1961) case:

1. Was there a warrant?
2. If not, was there an exception to the warrant requirement?
3. If the search was in fact illegal, what remedy should be applied?

There was no warrant produced at the time of trial, although the probable cause the police had could have been best used to obtain a warrant. There are few exceptions to the warrant requirement that override the privacy inherent in a person's home. A prior panel of Supreme Court justices, in *Wolf v. Colorado* (1949), had determined that the exclusionary rule born in *Weeks* did not apply to the states. That Court believed that there were sufficient state remedies available to a person who had been illegally arrested or searched and that it was unnecessary to extend federal protection against such police conduct. Yet in this case, *Wolf v. Colorado* (1949) was overturned and the exclusionary rule was extended to the states.

The logical extension of the exclusionary rule as a deterrent to police misconduct in conducting searches, seizures, or interrogations is to exclude any evidence discovered as a result of an illegally conducted search, seizure, or interrogation. An illegally obtained confession is excluded, and any evidence discovered as the result of the confession is likewise excluded. Such evidence is referred to as **derivative evidence** and is subject to the exclusionary rule. The idea that evidence can be derivatively tainted is commonly called the **fruit-of-the-poisonous-tree doctrine**.

Exceptions

The easiest way to avoid the impact of the exclusionary rule is to obtain a search warrant and execute that warrant legally—that is, in a manner consistent with the authorization contained within the warrant. Remember that the presumption regarding searches and seizures is that, absent a warrant, all searches and seizures of persons and things are presumed unconstitutional. However, Supreme Court justices are not able to foresee all situations, and most rules have exceptions. The Court has defined the exclusionary rule further to assist police in determining what conduct is acceptable in conducting searches and seizures. The object of the exclusionary rule is to deter police misconduct. If important evidence is excluded, it may be impossible to obtain a conviction based on the remaining evidence.

The Inevitable Discovery Exception

In an effort to ameliorate the impact of the exclusionary rule, the Court proffered the **inevitable discovery doctrine** in the 1984 case *Nix v. Williams* (see Case in Point). Simply stated, the doctrine allows derivative evidence that would generally be rendered inadmissible by the fruit-of-the-poisonous-tree doctrine to be admitted if the evidence would have been discovered anyway, without the assistance of the illegally seized evidence.

CASE IN POINT

Nix v. Williams, 1984

On December 24, 1984, a 10-year-old girl was kidnapped from a YMCA in Des Moines, Iowa. A man later determined to be Williams was seen carrying a large bundle wrapped in a blanket with two skinny white legs protruding. Williams's car was later found 160 miles east of Des Moines. Articles of clothing belonging to the missing child and a blanket were found at a rest stop between the YMCA in Des Moines and where the car was found. The car and the YMCA became the east and west boundaries for a massive search. Williams was arrested in Davenport, close to where the car had been found, and arraigned. The attorney for the defendant was told that Williams was to be returned to Des Moines. The attorney told the transporting police that they were not to interrogate his client. During the return trip, one of the officers engaged Williams in conversation. Knowing him to be a lay preacher, the officer began what became known as the "Christian burial speech," in which he told Williams that the girl should be given a Christian burial before a snowstorm prevented the body from being found. Williams agreed to take the officers to the child's body. The body was found about two miles from where the search party was searching.

At the trial, a motion to suppress was denied, and Williams was convicted of first-degree murder. On appeal, it was determined that the evidence was wrongfully admitted as a product of an illegal interrogation (interrogation in the absence of the suspect's lawyer). At the second trial, the prosecutor did not offer Williams's statement into evidence and did not seek to show that Williams had led the police to the body, but rather that the body would have been discovered had the search continued. Williams was convicted of murder.

The Court decided that, although fruit-of-the-poisonous-tree evidence is usually inadmissible, it may be admissible if the state can prove that the evidence would have been discovered anyway by legal means. The state must prove through police testimony the inevitability of the discovery; simply saying it would have been inevitable is not sufficient.

The Good Faith Exception

The most significant exception to the exclusionary rule, the **good faith exception**, results from the Supreme Court's decision in *United States v. Leon* (1984). Acting on information provided by an informant, police began a drug investigation. Three deputy district attorneys prepared and reviewed an affidavit for a search warrant and, in response to the affidavit, a state court judge issued the requested warrant. A search of the premises disclosed large quantities of drugs. The defendant was indicted, but his motion to suppress evidence was granted based on the fact that the affidavit and warrant contained insufficient probable cause. The court dismissed the case against the defendant.

The Fourth Amendment allows the use of evidence obtained by officers acting in reasonable reliance on a search warrant issued by a neutral and detached magistrate, even if the warrant is ultimately found to be invalid. Once the officer has complied with the prerequisites for obtaining a warrant, there is little more that the officer can do to comply with the law. Further, there is little deterrent value in penalizing the officer for the magistrate's error. Any evidence seized in a search conducted pursuant to a warrant that was issued by a neutral and impartial magistrate, appearing valid on its face, and procured without fraud on the part of the police is immune to exclusion. It goes without saying that the prudent officer will obtain a search warrant whenever possible. The value of the warrant is not only that it ensures that probable cause in fact exists, but also that it avoids lengthy pretrial suppression motions because it affords immunity to police pursuant to the "good faith" holding of *United States v. Leon* (1984).

■ Search Warrants

The basic presumption inherent in the Fourth Amendment is that warrantless searches of and arrests in someone's home are illegal. Absent **exigent circumstances**, police may not enter a private home to make a routine, warrantless arrest (*Payton v. New York,* 1980). Exigent circumstances occur when the suspect may destroy or secrete evidence or abscond. They never justify the warrantless entry of a residence for the purposes of effecting a search or an arrest for an offense other than a felony. The warrant is not only a law enforcement tool, but also an absolute necessity when dealing with a person and his or her residence.

A warrant represents the authority of the state mediated by an impartial magistrate. It may be easy to find a law-and-order judge who will give the police anything they want. But remember, if the warrant is patently lacking in probable cause, the officer may still be held civilly liable for false arrest or criminal trespass; the judge has absolute immunity from suit for any action arising from his or her judicial duties. It is far better to find a judge who will require the officer to get the necessary probable cause. This type of judge is an asset and will assist in providing competent assessments of probable cause for good searches and arrests.

A good search also benefits the prosecutor, who now can demand that the defendant demonstrate a failure of probable cause before having to prove otherwise. The amount of time and effort required to defend probable cause pursuant to a warrant is less than

OFFICER'S NOTEBOOK

Warrant Procedures

The **warrant procedure** comprises three individual actions on the part of the police:

1. Drafting an affidavit that on its face establishes, to the satisfaction of a neutral and detached magistrate, sufficient probable cause
2. Serving the warrant
3. Preparing and rendering the search warrant return

Experience and preparation are the keys to preparing an adequate search **warrant affidavit**. It is better to provide too much information than not enough. A competent magistrate will not ask any questions pertaining to probable cause and the information contained in the affidavit. The language used should be free of jargon and abbreviations because defense counsel will scrutinize it should the matter progress to trial or to a suppression motion. Real skill is required to be able to draft readable, legally sufficient search warrant affidavits.

It goes without saying that everything contained in an affidavit should be true or corroborated. Known falsities abrogate the "good faith" defense against defective warrants. The affidavit is a legal road map that tells the magistrate what has been done in obtaining probable cause and what is going to be done with it. Each legally sufficient affidavit includes the following:

- A statement outlining the facts the officer believes constitute probable cause
- A description of what the probable cause allows to be sought
- Identification of the places the probable cause allows to be searched

Keep in mind that the search is not over until the things sought have been found or the possibilities for searching have been exhausted. When filling out the affidavit, the officer should include the smallest item sought supported by the probable cause. A warrant for a rifle allows only those places that can house a rifle to be searched legitimately. A warrant for a rifle and ammunition increases the scope of the search and allows a search of those places that could house a rifle or rifle ammunition. Exceptions to the warrant requirement are discussed later in the chapter, but during a search, anything found that is illegal to possess, even if it was not included in the warrant, is seizable if the place where it is discovered is a possible location for the items being sought.

Every search warrant (**EXHIBIT 4–2**) must contain certain essentials to meet constitutional and legal muster. All warrants contain the following:

1. Authorization by a magistrate in the name of and by the authority of the state
2. Authorization to seize specifically described items
3. Issuance based on probable cause
4. A specific location (to be confused with no other)
5. Authorization granted to a specifically named officer
6. A return that includes the following:
   a. Date of the search
   b. Items seized
   c. Name of the serving officer
   d. Signature of the serving officer
   e. Signature of the issuing magistrate

The **return** is an itemized inventory of all the property seized by the executing officers. It is prepared in duplicate, and a copy is left with the defendant or, in his or her absence, at the residence. The original is returned to the issuing magistrate no later than 24 hours after service of the warrant.

EXHIBIT 4–2 **Search Warrant**

STATE OF TEXAS
SEARCH WARRANT

THE STATE OF TEXAS
To the Sheriff or any Peace Officer of _____ County, Texas or any Peace Officer of the State of Texas

Greetings:
Proof by affidavit being made this day, before me, by _____ (name of officer) a Peace Officer under the laws of Texas, that there is probable cause to believe that in the herein described (building, premises, or vehicle) is located the following property, possession of which is a violation of the laws of Texas or constitutes evidence of a violation of the laws of Texas, and is particularly described as follows:

controlled substances to include:
marijuana and associated paraphernalia
cocaine and associated paraphernalia
crack cocaine and associated paraphernalia

The described (building, premises, or vehicle) should be searched by reason of the following grounds:
Possession of the above described controlled substances is evidence of violation of the Texas Health and Safety Code.

You are therefore commanded at any time day or night to make an immediate search of the residence at *337 Sisterdale Road, Sisterdale, Texas* more specifically described as:

A single family dwelling located on the property of Filmore Duckworth and wife Dusty, attached outbuildings including a farm shop, barn, and garage.

Herein fail not, but have you then and there this Warrant within three days, exclusive of the day of its issuance and exclusive of the day of its execution, with your return thereon, showing you how you have executed the same, files in this court.

Issued this the _____ day of _____ 2004, at _____ o'clock am/pm

_____
Judge

without a warrant, and evidence obtained pursuant to a warrant is more readily accepted by the court than evidence obtained without the benefit of a warrant.

■ Warrantless Searches Based on Probable Cause

The Fourth Amendment protects persons and their houses, papers, and effects against unreasonable searches and seizures. There is only one method whereby that protection may be waived—the obtainment of a warrant based on probable cause. A careful examination of the Fourth Amendment will disclose no mention of any exceptions to the warrant requirement. The most important word in the evaluation of the Fourth Amendment is the word *warrant;* in context, its significance is paramount and should not be mitigated by any interpretation that suggests that exceptions to the warrant requirement are the norm. They are not. We concentrate on the exceptions because it is to these that police must often resort as a result of exigencies, not to avoid basic Fourth Amendment requirements, but to respond to rates of crime that did not exist at the time the amendment was drafted, when the low levels of mobility and transience and a sense of community often served to suppress misconduct.

The history of exceptions to the Fourth Amendment can be divided into two periods. In the first, probable cause provided the basis for most exceptions, thereby making probable cause the most important part of the Fourth Amendment. In the second, the issue of reasonableness came to play a more important role. Clearly, the focal point of the amendment has changed, depending upon its application.

Search Incident to Arrest

The law of arrest, although governed by the Fourth Amendment, has long recognized probable cause as an exception to the warrant requirement outside the home. One of the first issues that arose as a result of allowing arrests based on probable cause was the latitude granted to the police to search the arrestee. There is a definite safety concern in waiting to search a person until a warrant can be obtained. Police would be at substantial risk in placing suspects in their vehicles without first searching them, and the back seats of police cars would become repositories for undiscovered contraband and evidence. Once the suspect had been taken to the jail for booking, the danger would continue to increase if a warrant was not awaiting the suspect's arrival. The suspect might be placed in and among a jail population while in possession of a weapon or drugs. The Supreme Court addressed this potentially volatile situation in *Chimel v. California* (1967).

The purpose of such a search is to protect the police and the public and to prevent the destruction of evidence. The Court was of the opinion in *Chimel v. California* (1967) that the probable cause of the arrest gave the probable cause to search required by the Fourth Amendment.

Chimel establishes the scope of a **search incident to an arrest** in an individual's home. The Court went on to say that the area under an arrestee's immediate control is that area into which he might reach (an arm's span). The Court presumed that the suspect was going to be removed immediately from the premises. In those instances where it is necessary to move the defendant about the premises, another arm's-span search might be authorized (e.g., if a semiclad suspect requests to clothe himself, the officers could subject the area where he intends to seek clothing to another search incident to arrest). In fact, if the suspect is transferred to another officer, that officer may perform another search of the suspect's person before placing him or her in the officer's vehicle, even though the suspect was previously searched by an officer at another location. It is a good rule of thumb, however, not to use the movement of the suspect about the

---

CASE IN POINT

Chimel v. California, 1967

Chimel was suspected of having robbed a coin shop. The police, who had an arrest warrant but no search warrant, went to the suspect's home. Chimel was not there, but his wife admitted the police. Upon Chimel's arrival at his home, the police took him into custody. The police asked for consent to search the premises. Consent was denied, but the police conducted a search nonetheless. A search of the entire house disclosed coins that had been stolen from the coin shop. The coins were introduced at trial over the defendant's objection. Chimel was convicted of robbery. The Court decided that, after making a legal arrest, the police may search the area within the suspect's immediate control to ensure that the suspect does not have access to a weapon or evidentiary items.

> ### CASE IN POINT
>
> **United States v. Ross, 1982**
> Police stopped Ross based on a reliable informant's tip that Ross was dealing drugs out of the trunk of his car. After the stop and arrest, the police searched the interior of the vehicle and found a bullet. That bullet provided probable cause to believe that the vehicle could have contained a gun. The trunk was opened, and a paper bag containing heroin was searched. A later search of the trunk at the station disclosed a bank bag of money. The Court held that the arrest of Ross was based on probable cause provided by an informant and that the search of the interior of the vehicle was justified incident to the arrest of Ross. The search of the trunk was justified upon the finding of the bullet; that provided probable cause to believe that the vehicle contained a firearm. The search of the containers in the trunk was "reasonable" in that they could have contained the weapon that was being sought.

house to justify further searches; for safety's sake, the suspect should be removed from the premises as soon as possible.

The **arm's-reach concept** promulgated in *Chimel* was elaborated upon in dealing with the high mobility and compactness of an automobile. The most straightforward way of applying *Chimel* to automobile searches is to recognize that everywhere within an automobile is within an arm's reach (except the trunk). The Supreme Court has determined that when a suspect is arrested in a vehicle, the immediate area is defined as the entire passenger compartment of the vehicle, including closed but not locked containers (*New York v. Belton,* 1981).

In 1982, the Court addressed the propriety of the police searching the trunk of a car whose driver had been lawfully arrested. The Court held that probable cause to stop and search a vehicle justifies the search of every part of the vehicle and its contents, including any containers in which the contraband sought might be secreted. In many instances, the search of the vehicle, as of the person, is focused not on any particular evidence, but rather on any evidence that might be uncovered. When searches are performed on packages or luggage in the trunk, individual probable cause must be satisfied. That is, the police must be looking for something in particular when searching the trunk, and the thing they seek must be based on probable cause, although a warrant or exigent circumstances are not required.

This exception to the warrant requirement of the Fourth Amendment is based on the amendment's probable cause clause and reasonableness requirement. The probable cause for the arrest establishes the requisite probable cause for the search. A search incident to arrest can never be legal if the arrest giving rise to the search is not legal.

■ Warrantless Searches Based on Reasonableness

Consent Searches

The most important tool in a police officer's arsenal against crime is the **consent search**. A consent search need not be supported by any quantity of cause or any individual suspicion. The notion of police requesting permission to search is at odds with the self-concept of many officers, according to which they demand, they do not ask. Getting police out of cars and onto the streets ameliorates this difficulty. An officer needs no probable cause to engage a citizen in a conversation, nor to request permission to search a citizen's person, auto, or effects, as long as the officer remembers that the citizen is free to decline to give consent. A citizen's declination should not result in retaliation or threat. Consent must be voluntary—that is, free from psychological or physical coercion.

In *Bumper v. North Carolina* (1968), the U.S. Supreme Court determined that consent given based on the false assertion of the police that they were in possession of a valid search warrant was coerced. The term *consent search* itself is virtually an oxymoron, in that, because permission was given, the Fourth Amendment does not apply (as long as consent was voluntary, was given by a person legally able to give consent, and the scope of the search was within the given or inferred consent). A proper consent search for Fourth Amendment purposes is a search in which the Fourth Amendment plays no direct role. In a sense, a properly conducted consent search is not really a search. However, a consent given by a person illegally in custody is not really a consent, and anything seized (derivative evidence) as a result of that consent would be excluded (*Florida v. Royer,* 1983).

Most departments provide consent forms for officers, realizing that written consent is more effective than oral consent at the time of a suppression motion. The question that invariably arises with respect to a consent to search is whether the consent was given voluntarily and knowingly. The requirement for voluntariness is self-explanatory and predicated upon a coercion-free consent. A written consent goes a long way toward proving voluntariness if it also contains an admonition to the citizen that consent must be freely given and not as the product of coercion. The requirement for knowing is not self-evident; it too is more easily proven if a written consent form provides an additional caveat indicating that consent may be withheld, suspended, withdrawn, or limited in scope or duration (*Florida v. Enio Jimeno,* 1991).

In *Schneckloth v. Bustamonte* (1973), the U.S. Supreme Court clearly relieved the police of the responsibility of having to provide consent warnings comparable to those required in the *Miranda* decision. At the same time, however, it indicated that the burden would be on the police and the state to prove that the consent was given knowingly. The Court went on to say that the touchstone of knowing consent was sufficient. In other

CASE IN POINT

Florida v. Enio Jimeno, 1991

Enio Jimeno was overheard discussing the pick up of drugs by Dade County police. Police officers followed Jimeno, and, when he failed to stop at a stop sign, pulled him over. The officer told Jimeno that he believed Jimeno was involved in a drug transaction and that he would like permission to search the vehicle. Jimeno gave consent, and officers found a bag of cocaine on the passenger-side floor of the automobile. Jimeno was arrested and charged, but the Florida courts granted a motion to suppress, which claimed the consent to search the vehicle was not consent to search individual containers found within the vehicle.

The U.S. Supreme Court held that the scope of a search is defined by the object being sought. Jimeno had been told by the officer that he believed Jimeno had been involved in a drug transaction and that the officer was looking for drugs. The Court was of the opinion that it was reasonable for the police to interpret the consent given to include consent to search containers within the vehicle that might bear drugs.

The Court went on to say that containers that could be opened easily, and had no additional indices of an expectation of privacy could be opened, but that locked containers would need specific consent or a warrant. The Court was very specific about the right of a citizen to limit the scope of the search to which he or she gave consent, but it held that if consent is given to search for a particular thing, the search may include unlocked containers that may contain the thing sought without requiring further or more explicit consent.

words, to give consent, a citizen has to be of an age and possess the education, intelligence, cultural familiarity, and language skills to understand that he or she is free to withhold, withdraw, or limit consent without fear of recrimination. The officer obtaining consent therefore has the responsibility of providing testimony that the consent giver had the sophistication necessary to presume that he or she had the right to withhold, withdraw, or limit consent, a heavy burden in light of the situations in which consent is generally sought. The prudent officer will use a consent form with warnings about coercion and the citizen's rights (EXHIBIT 4-3). Absent a consent form, the next best approach is to utter an oral warning outlining the citizen's rights (which must be given in the same fashion in court as on the street).

Memory is not a reliable source for ensuring that a citizen's rights have not been violated, nor his or her will overborne. Departments should provide consent warning cards for officers similar to those provided for Miranda situations. Although approved by the Court, the worst-case scenario for the officer is to obtain consent without providing some kind of warning. The end result will be that the officer will be confronted on the witness stand with the task of explaining the considerations employed in determining the age, intelligence, education, cultural familiarity, and language skills of the person from whom the consent was obtained.

The courts have long abhorred general searches (what one might call fishing expeditions). Remember, the Fourth Amendment requires that the particular thing sought and the place in which it is believed to be must be cited in a warrant. The scope of a valid consent search was addressed by the Supreme Court in *Florida v. Enio Jimeno* (1991), which established the basis for determining how far a search based on consent could go and what the responsibility of the officer was in requesting consent to search.

Emergency Searches

Police or firefighters may find themselves on premises to provide a service other than to arrest, interrogate, interview, or search. If police are brought to the premises to deal with an emergency, any evidence discovered in the course of handling the emergency is admissible despite the fact the police had no probable cause or warrant to enter the premises. The entry would be reasonable under the Fourth Amendment and exempt from any warrant or probable cause requirement (*Mincey v. Arizona*, 1978). The discovery would fall within the plain-view doctrine (discussed in a following section), abrogating the need for particularized suspicion, probable cause, or a warrant. The item discovered would have to meet the requirements set forth later in the chapter.

The **emergency exception** to the warrant requirement only justifies entry to the premises without probable cause or a warrant. Another exception to the warrant requirement would be necessary to justify the inadvertent discovery of contraband or evidence.

Exigent Circumstances Exception

Similar to the emergency exception, and sometimes considered as part of that exception, is the exception for situations in which the police are concerned that a criminal may destroy evidence or abscond from the scene. If the police have probable cause to believe that a felony has been committed and that the evidence may be destroyed in the time that it takes to procure a warrant, a warrantless entry may be made. A search of the premises based on the probable cause justifying the entry is permissible. Any entry based on exigent circumstances will be the subject of vigorous examination at the suppression

EXHIBIT 4–3   Consent Search Forms, in English and Spanish

CONSENT TO SEARCH

I _____ , having been informed of my constitutional right not to have a search made of the building, premises, and/or vehicle consent to such search, and hereby authorize Officer _____ , a police officer of the City of _____ , _____ County, Texas to conduct a search of the building, premises and/or vehicle. This consent is given with full knowledge of my right to refuse to grant consent, withdraw consent, or to limit consent in scope or duration. This authorization is given to allow the search of the building, premises, and/or interior of my vehicle, containers, locked or unlocked, the glove compartment, and the trunk of the automobile for anything that is illegal to possess. Upon discovery of contraband or evidence I also consent to the seizure of those items by the searching officers. This consent has been granted voluntarily and without threats or promises of any kind. Signed this _____ day of _____ 2008.

Signature of person granting consent _____

Signature of officer(s) requesting consent _____

Police Department

_____ County, Texas

CONSENTIMIENTO DE REGISTRO

Yo, _____ habiendo sido informado de mis derechos constitucionales de no permitir el registro de mi edificio, premisas, y/o automovil (es) consiento al mencionado registro, por medio de la presente, dandole la autoridad al _____ .

Y _____ , quienes son oficiales de policia de la ciudad de _____ , del Condado de _____ , Texas, y otros oficiales policias que pudieran asistir en el registro, para conducir unregistro completo de los siguientes edificios, premisas y/o automovil (es) descritos:

Lugar: _____ , Condado de _____ , Texas.

Descripcion: _____

_____

Estos oficiales estan autorizados por mi, para llevarse papeles, materiales o cualquier otra propiedad que deseen, dandome un recibo. Este permiso escrito es dado por mi, a los oficiales mencionados anteriormente voluntariamente y sin ninguna amenaza o promesa de nungun tipo.

Fecha: _____ , _____ .   Hora: _____ m.

Firma: _____

Testigos: _____ _____

Informacion de lo ejecutado

Este consentimiento de registro fue dado el dia _____ del _____ , _____ , y fue ejecutado el dia _____ del _____ , a las _____ .

La propiedad descrita abajo fue confiscada por los signientes oficiales de policia mencionados en el consentimiento de registro:

_____

_____

_____

La mencionada propiedad fue encortada en el lugar designado y descrito en el consentimiento de registro.

_____

_____

Oficiales Ejecutando El Registro

> ## OFFICER'S NOTEBOOK
>
> ### Requirements for Plain-View Searches
>
> The Supreme Court has laid out the following specific requirements for the admissibility of evidence discovered in "plain view":
>
> - The officer must be on the premises legitimately.
> - The item viewed must have been found through **inadvertent discovery** (access was not gained through subterfuge for the purpose of examining the premises).
> - It is immediately apparent that the item is evidence, contraband, or otherwise illegal to possess.

hearing. Police will be required to prove the probable cause as well as the exigency that justified entry without a warrant.

Plain-View Searches

Often evidence will come to the attention of an officer who is on a citizen's premises for a reason other than a search, an arrest, or exigent circumstances. The courts have unanimously recognized that when police are **legitimately on the premises** and recognize contraband or evidence in plain view, it is unreasonable to think that the same contraband or evidence will be there at the time the police return with a warrant.

The court does not treat a plain-view discovery as a search. Because a search was not anticipated and access to the premises was not gained for the purposes of conducting a search, the Fourth Amendment does not apply. If the item to be seized is immediately recognizable as illegal to possess, then no search was necessary to reveal that to the police; thus, once again, the Fourth Amendment does not apply. If any manipulation of the item in question occurs, however, a search in fact has occurred and must be justified pursuant to the Fourth Amendment or one of its exceptions. The **immediately apparent** requirement establishes that no search was necessary to discover the items or to identify them as illegal to possess (*Coolidge v. New Hampshire,* 1971).

Open-Field Exception

The open-field exception is often confused with the plain-view exception, but when they are examined in light of the Fourth Amendment, it becomes easy to distinguish between the two. The Supreme Court has held that open fields are not protected by the Fourth Amendment. The only concern the Court has is in defining an **open field**. The Fourth Amendment protects a citizen's home and by extension the area around the home that is used in the course of daily living, known as its curtilage. Any area outside the curtilage of the home is an open field and is unprotected by the Fourth Amendment. Therefore, any examinations of such areas are, with regard to the Fourth Amendment, not searches.

The police need no excuse for treading upon an open field. They need no justification for looking for whatever they choose once in that field. Their conduct is not subject to constitutional scrutiny if it has been determined that the area in question is not a house or its curtilage but rather an open field. There is no legally-on-the-premises requirement because there are no premises.

If the area of interest to the police is an open field that is fenced and posted to prohibit trespassing, they can enter without further justification. They may have committed

CASE IN POINT

Oliver v. United States, 1984

Police received a tip that Oliver was growing marijuana on a noncontiguous plot of land near his house. Police located the area in question, determined it was not contiguous to Oliver's home or farm, and, although it was fenced and posted, found a path leading through a locked gate to a field of marijuana surrounded by trees that kept the field from the public view. Oliver was arrested and convicted of manufacturing a controlled substance. The question raised was whether the field searched was protected by the Fourth Amendment. Oliver's position was that the field was not within public view, in fact demonstrated an expectation of privacy by the signs, fencing, and locked entrance, and therefore was not an "open field." The Supreme Court determined that since this land was not involved in the activities of daily living, it was not curtilage and therefore not protected under the Fourth Amendment. The fact that Oliver had demonstrated an expectation of privacy in the field and that it was not subject to cursory public view was not persuasive to the Court. The justices said that although the police officers' conduct may have been subject to criminal or civil sanction for trespass, it did not violate the Fourth Amendment, since the area was an open field.

  The Court's interpretation of the open-field doctrine suggests that the area in question need not be a field, nor need it be open, to fall within the exception. Fenced yards have been considered open fields when viewed by the police from the air. Because the same view is available to any member of the public, it is also available to the police.

a criminal trespass, but they have not rendered their conduct subject to the exclusionary provisions of the Fourth Amendment. Unlike in the case of the plain-view exception, there is no "legitimately on the premises" requirement, nor any "inadvertent discovery" requirement. Once the trespass has been completed, the police may search wherever and for whatever they choose without fear of having their evidence suppressed. Once an item is found, it may be handled and examined to determine if it is in fact evidence or contraband without rendering it inadmissible.

Vehicle Inventories

From the outset, it is important to recognize that an inventory is not a search. An **inventory** is an administrative procedure that is governed by the Fourth Amendment as it applies to administrative procedures. Because it is not an effort to obtain evidence and is civil rather than criminal in nature, Fourth Amendment requirements are relaxed. The purpose of a **vehicle inventory** is to:

- Ensure that a citizen's property is accounted for properly
- Protect the police from spurious claims of theft
- Protect the public and the police from the possibility of explosive devices secreted in the vehicle

  The inventory may be conducted at the scene or after a vehicle has been impounded. If an inventory is used as a method for conducting an otherwise illegal search, the inventory procedure has been violated and the evidence is suppressible. The attack on a vehicle inventory can be based on either of two claims: (1) no procedure for taking a vehicle inventory has been standardized in written form in a policy and procedures manual, or (2) the guidelines for an existing procedure were not followed correctly. Proof of either will establish that a search has been conducted and that an attempt has been made to describe it as an inventory. Many texts refer to an inventory procedure as an inventory search, but it cannot be both an inventory and a search. It is a bad habit to refer to the procedure as an inventory search, for it lays the semantic foundation for impeachment of the officer's credibility.

Stop and Frisk

Police encounter citizens in a variety of suspicious circumstances that do not give rise to probable cause. Society expects police officers to act on their suspicions in their efforts to "protect and serve." However, citizens are free from unnecessary restraint in our society, and the Fourth Amendment thus requires probable cause (TABLE 4-1). The U.S. Supreme Court has provided law enforcement the necessary tools to act on reasonable suspicion. A police officer may detain a citizen if the officer has reasonable suspicion that the citizen has committed or is about to commit a crime. The officer's suspicion must be based on articulable facts rather than mere speculation. The facts may be a product of an officer's training, education, and experience. Such a **stop** is not a seizure as provided for in the Fourth Amendment, but rather is a temporary detention similar to a traffic stop, where the motorist knows that, after a brief interruption, he or she will be allowed to continue driving (absent certain infractions).

If, during the course of a temporary detention, a police officer becomes fearful that the person detained may possess a weapon, the officer may conduct a pat-down **frisk** of the outer clothing to ensure that the subject is not armed. This frisk is not a search, but is a reasonable intrusion upon a person's expectation of privacy based again on articulable facts that give rise to a fear or concern that the subject is armed (*Terry v. Ohio*, 1968).

Police Roadblocks

It might appear that police stopping motorists for the purpose of determining their sobriety would be a serious intrusion upon a citizen's freedom to come and go and would therefore constitute an unconstitutional seizure. The answer to that proposition depends on whether the detention was for the purpose of assessing sobriety or for some other law enforcement purpose.

Sobriety Checkpoints

The Michigan Department of State Police had been using sobriety checkpoints since 1986. State police stopped all vehicles passing through the checkpoint and briefly examined their drivers for signs of intoxication. Should the field tests and the officer's observations suggest the driver was intoxicated, the driver was arrested. A citizen group of motorists

TABLE 4-1   Standards of Proof

Standard	Explanation
Criminal Law	
Beyond a reasonable doubt	Trial sufficiency of evidence (99%)
Clear and convincing	Some sanity determination
Probable cause	Legal sufficiency of evidence (more likely than not; 51%)
Reasonable suspicion	Foundation of investigatory detentions (less than 51%)
Significant government interest	No particularized suspicion
Civil Law	
Preponderance of the evidence	Comparable to probable cause

> **OFFICER'S NOTEBOOK**
>
> **Frisk Criteria**
> Two separate thresholds of causation must be crossed before an officer is entitled to stop and frisk a suspect. The two quanta of cause must be satisfied independently of one another.
> 1. The officer must have a reasonable suspicion that the suspect has committed or is about to commit a crime (this is the quantity of cause necessary for detaining the suspect).
> 2. The officer must also have a reasonable suspicion that the individual is carrying a weapon and poses a threat to the officer or others (this is the quantity of cause necessary for frisking the suspect).

filed a request for an injunction and a declaratory judgment with the Michigan courts. The state courts ruled that the checkpoints were a violation of the Fourth Amendment requirement for probable cause, or at least reasonable suspicion. The Michigan Court of Appeals affirmed the holding of the trial court, saying that sobriety checkpoints do not deter drunk driving.

The United States Supreme Court (*Michigan Department of State Police v. Sitz,* 1990) held that the roadblocks were a seizure under the Fourth Amendment. The Court went on to say, however, that the seizures were a limited intrusion on motorists and therefore reasonable in light of the significant government interest in reducing highway deaths, injuries, and property damage caused by intoxicated drivers.

Drug Interdiction Checkpoints

The city of Indianapolis operated vehicle checkpoints on its roads in an effort to interdict unlawful drugs. Motorists who were stopped at such a checkpoint filed suit, claiming that the roadblocks violated the Fourth Amendment. The District Court denied their request for a preliminary injunction, but the Seventh Circuit reversed, holding that the checkpoints contravened the Fourth Amendment.

The Supreme Court in its opinion briefly addressed the exceptions to the Fourth Amendment requirement of individualized suspicion. The Court's position is that a search or seizure is unreasonable under the Fourth Amendment absent individualized suspicion of wrongdoing, for which there are limited exceptions. For example, the Court has upheld brief, suspicionless seizures at a fixed checkpoint designed to intercept illegal aliens (*United States v. Martinez-Fuerte,* 1976) and at a sobriety checkpoint aimed

> **CASE IN POINT**
>
> ***Minnesota v. Dickerson,* 1993**
> Police suspected Dickerson of possessing crack cocaine after having watched him enter and depart a known crack house. Dickerson was detained and subjected to a pat-down search (frisk) for weapons. The officer conducting the frisk detected something in Dickerson's jacket pocket. By manipulating the pocket's contents between his fingers, the officer recognized what he believed to be crack cocaine. Obviously, the pat down for weapons does not include the right to seek other evidence or contraband, but the court in this case postulated that a "plain feel" exception might exist if the officer was able to determine during the frisk that something he touched on the person of the suspect was identifiable solely by touch and was illegal to possess. In the end, though, the Court in the *Dickerson* case held that the manipulation of the item in Dickerson's pocket exceeded a frisk and constituted a separate and independent search not founded on probable cause; thus, anything discovered as a process of that search was not admissible because it was illegally seized.

at removing drunk drivers from the road (*Michigan Department of State Police v. Sitz,* 1990). The Court has also suggested that a similar roadblock to verify drivers' licenses and registrations would be permissible to serve a highway safety interest (*Delaware v. Prouse,* 1979). However, the Court has never approved a checkpoint program whose primary purpose was to detect evidence of ordinary criminal wrongdoing.

The detection of ordinary criminal wrongdoing is what principally distinguishes drug interdiction checkpoints from those the Court has previously approved, which were designed to serve purposes closely related to the problems of policing the border or the necessity of ensuring roadway safety. Attorneys for Indianapolis said that the Sitz and Martinez-Fuerte checkpoints had the same ultimate purpose of arresting those suspected of committing crimes. Securing the border and apprehending drunken drivers are law enforcement activities, and authorities employ arrests and criminal prosecutions to pursue these goals. The Court was not persuaded and expressed a concern that if this case were to be granted the same latitude as border searches, driver's license checks, and sobriety checkpoints, then there would be little check on the authorities' ability to construct roadblocks for almost any conceivable law enforcement purpose. The Court went on to say that the checkpoint program is also not justified by the severe and intractable nature of the drug problem. The gravity of the drug threat alone cannot be the deciding factor in questions concerning what means law enforcement may employ to pursue a given purpose.

The Court was not swayed by the argument that sobriety checkpoints, driver's license checkpoints, and drug interdiction checkpoints could all be conducted simultaneously. They held that if drug interdiction checkpoints could be justified by their lawful secondary purposes of keeping impaired motorists off the road and verifying licenses and registrations, then authorities would be able to establish checkpoints for virtually any purpose so long as they also included a license or sobriety check. The Court therefore left it to local tribunals to determine the primary purpose of the checkpoint program (*City of Indianapolis v. Edmond,* 2000).

■ Summary

Much of what police do must be considered within the context of the rights that each citizen among us enjoys. Police often see the U.S. Constitution as an impediment to law enforcement and criminal investigation. A broader understanding of the U.S. Supreme Court cases regarding the Fourth and Fifth Amendments serve as tools that can be added to a toolbox used to assure that all searches and seizures of persons and things are done constitutionally. It is this perspective that we must consider when recognizing that we only get one chance to process a crime scene.

One of the most challenging forms of evidence awaiting the homicide investigator is blood evidence. It is the most common evidence found at a homicide crime scene and requires special attention to detail, handling, and packaging. The next chapter introduces us to blood evidence and the evidentiary considerations appertaining thereto.

■ Key Terms

arm's-reach concept: Concept established in *Chimel v. California* (1967), in which it was ruled that a house search may be conducted in the area under the arrestee's immediate control, that is, the area into which he or she might reach; when applied to automobiles, the entire passenger compartment of the vehicle, including closed but not locked containers, can be searched

consent search: A warrantless search that is voluntarily permitted by a person who is legally able to give consent; the scope of the search must be within the given or inferred consent

curtilage: The area surrounding a home that is used in the course of daily living

derivative evidence: Evidence found as the result of a confession or the seizure of other evidence; usually used to denote evidence that is tainted by being acquired as a result of illegally obtained original evidence

due process: The conduct of legal proceedings according to established rules and principles

due process clause: A constitutional provision that prohibits the government from unfairly or arbitrarily depriving a person of life, liberty, or property

emergency exception: Exception to the warrant requirement; it states that if police are brought to the premises to deal with an emergency, then any evidence discovered in the course of handling that emergency is admissible despite the fact the police had no probable cause or warrant to enter the premises

exclusionary rule: Rule resulting from *Weeks v. United States* (1914) that excludes evidence at the time of trial that was obtained (seized) as a result of an illegal search, arrest, or interrogation

exigent circumstances: Circumstances that occur when the suspect may destroy or secrete evidence or abscond

frisk: A pat-down search of the outer clothing of a person to ensure that the subject is not armed, conducted when the officer has a reasonable suspicion, based on articulable facts, that the subject is armed

fruit-of-the-poisonous-tree doctrine: Common name for the idea that evidence can be tainted derivatively

good faith exception: Exception to the exclusionary rule that allows evidence obtained illegally to be used in trial when the officers obtaining the evidence had reason to believe that they were operating under a warrant that was issued properly

immediately apparent: Immediately recognizable as illegal to possess, with no search having been necessary to reveal that to the police

inadvertent discovery: One of the original elements of a plain-view discovery of evidence; meant to convey the accidental discovery of an item that is illegal to possess. It is no longer an element of the plain-view exception, based on *Arizona v. Hicks* (1987)

inevitable discovery doctrine: Doctrine that allows derivative evidence that would generally be rendered inadmissible by the fruit-of-the-poisonous-tree doctrine to be admitted if the evidence would have been discovered anyway, without the assistance of the illegally seized evidence

inventory: An administrative procedure that accounts for a citizen's property

legitimately on the premises: Legally allowed to be in a location despite not having a warrant; in such cases, officers are allowed to collect evidence that is in plain view and likely will not still be there when the officers return with a warrant

Miranda warnings: Warnings read to a suspect in police custody that inform the suspect of his or her constitutional rights

open field: Any area outside the curtilage of the home; an open field is unprotected by the Fourth Amendment

probable cause: A reasonable ground to suspect that a person has committed or is committing a crime or that a place contains specific items connected with a crime

reasonableness: The quality of being fair, proper, or moderate under the given circumstances

return: An itemized inventory of all the property seized by the officers executing a warrant

search incident to an arrest: Search that is allowed when an officer is carrying out an arrest authorized by an arrest warrant

stop: Detaining a citizen, which is allowed when an officer has reasonable suspicion, based on articulable facts rather than mere speculation, that the citizen has committed or is about to commit a crime

vehicle inventory: Accounting for the items contained within a vehicle

warrant affidavit: Document that establishes, to the satisfaction of a neutral and detached magistrate, sufficient probable cause

warrant procedure: Three individual actions on the part of the police, that is, (1) drafting an affidavit that on its face establishes, to the satisfaction of a neutral and detached magistrate, sufficient probable cause; (2) serving the warrant; and (3) preparing and rendering the search warrant return

■ Review Questions

1. What portion of the Fourth Amendment pertains to arrests?
2. What portion of the Fourth Amendment pertains to searches?
3. What are exigent circumstances, and how do they affect the warrant requirement of the Fourth Amendment?
4. In what amendment or amendments do we find the equal protection, privileges and immunities, and due process clauses? Of what importance is the due process clause to the rights of citizens of various states?
5. What area may police search when arresting a felon in his or her home pursuant to a lawful warrant? What case supports this type of search?
6. What is the fruit-of-the-poisonous-tree doctrine?
7. What is the exclusionary rule, and how did it come to be applied to the states?
8. What are the elements of a plain-view exception to the warrant requirement?
9. What exception to the exclusionary rule did *United States v. Leon* (1984) establish? How does this exception assist police in avoiding civil liability?
10. What is derivative evidence, and what effect does the exclusionary rule have on it?
11. What is contained in a legally sufficient search warrant affidavit?
12. What is the role of voluntariness in obtaining consent to search?
13. What is the open-field exception to the warrant requirement, and what role does curtilage play in applying the exception?
14. How would a defense attorney try to attack the validity of a vehicle inventory?
15. What are the two quanta of cause that must be satisfied before an officer can engage in a legal stop and frisk?
16. What does the PATRIOT Act allow law enforcement to do that they could not do before?

■ Key Legal Cases

Arizona v. Hicks, 480 U.S. 321 (1987).
Bumper v. North Carolina, 391 U.S. 543 (1968).
Chimel v. California, 395 U.S. 294 (1967).
California v. Greenwood, 486 U.S. 35 (1988).
City of Indianapolis v. Edmond, 000 U.S. 99-1030 (2000).
Coolidge v. New Hampshire, 403 U.S. 443 (1971).
Delaware v. Prouse, 440 U.S. 648 (1979).
Florida v. Enio Jimeno, 499 U.S. 934 (1991).
Florida v. Royer, 460 U.S. 491 (1983).
Griswold v. Connecticut, 381 U.S. 479 (1965).
Mapp v. Ohio, 367 U.S. 643 (1961).
Michigan Department of State Police v. Sitz, 496 U.S. 444 (1990).
Mincey v. Arizona, 437 U.S. 385 (1978).
Minnesota v. Dickerson, 508 U.S. 366 (1993).
Miranda v. Arizona, 384 U.S. 436 (1966).
New York v. Belton, 453 U.S. 454 (1981).
Nix v. Williams, 467 U.S. 431 (1984).
Oliver v. United States, 466 U.S. 170 (1984).
Payton v. New York, 455 U.S. 573 (1980).
Pennsylvania v. Muniz, 496 U.S. 582 (1990).
Schneckloth v. Bustamonte, 412 U.S. 218 (1973).
Terry v. Ohio, 392 U.S. 1 (1968).
United States v. Leon, 468 U.S. 897 (1984).
United States v. Martinez-Fuerte, 428 U.S. 543 (1976).
United States v. Ross, 456 U.S. 798 (1982).
Weeks v. United States, 232 U.S. 383 (1914).
Wolf v. Colorado, 338 U.S. 25 (1949).

Blood Evidence

▶ ▶ STUDENT LEARNING OUTCOMES

Upon completion of this chapter students will demonstrate an understanding of:

- Bloodstain pattern analysis
- Bloodstain mechanics
- How to field test for blood
- How to package and handle blood evidence

Because blood is a very common source of evidence at a crime scene, it must be handled as physical evidence to be tagged and bagged; in addition, everyone entering the scene must take care not to disturb the patterns of blood, which can reveal as much to the trained eye as the results of the laboratory testing of the blood itself. The interpretation of bloodstain patterns requires careful planned experiments utilizing surface materials comparable to those found at the crime scene. Whoever is assigned the responsibility of interpreting these stains must be given first access to the crime scene so that the blood patterns may be photographed before other crime scene processing activities obscure them (**Figure 5–1**).

Herbert L. MacDonell (1971) has made an in-depth study of bloodstain patterns. The following are a few sample findings:

- **Surface texture** provides the foundation for blood pattern interpretation. The harder and less porous a surface, the more contained the pattern.
- When a drop of blood hits a hard, smooth surface, it breaks up, splashing smaller droplets about it. These smaller droplets travel in the same direction as the original drop, leaving a pattern that is teardrop shaped, with the pointed end directed toward the place of origin.
- The **circular distortion** of a stain on a flat surface will allow determination of the angle of impact. The more nearly perpendicular the angle of impact, the more circular the blood drop stain. As the angle increases, the stain becomes more elongated. The elongation allows a trigonometric determination of the point of origin (MacDonell, 1993).

There is a computer program that greatly simplifies the data handling and computations necessary to apply the formulas devised by MacDonell and others. This program

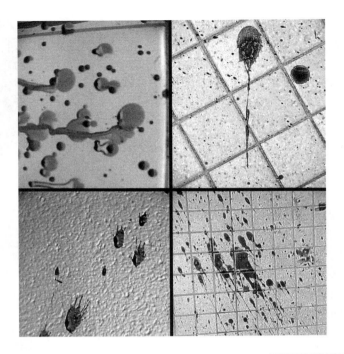

Figure 5–1   Blood stain pictures.

Courtesy of Dr. Steve Gilbert

can graphically represent the position of the victim at the instant blood was shed, making manual reconstruction of the point of origin unnecessary. The program can analyze blood spatter on floors and walls; it cannot reconstruct a three-dimensional point of origin from patterns on surfaces of oblique orientation (Eckert and James, 1993).

■ Bloodstain Interpretation

The examination and interpretation of bloodstains cannot occur at a scene that has not been preserved or through which the first-responding police officers have trod unnecessarily. Bloodstain interpretation may be accomplished by direct examination of the crime scene or by careful examination of color crime scene photographs. Investigators who examine photographs must also examine clothing and weapons along with any other physical evidence. Autopsy reports can also be helpful. However, interpretation should leave hospital records, postmortem examinations, autopsy reports, and autopsy photographs for last. Often these reports contain conjectural statements that may affect the interpretation. Once the investigators begin interpretation, they should rely on these secondary resources for corroboration rather than formulation.

Bloodstain interpretation can provide myriad pieces of information:

- The origin of the blood drops
- The distance from origin to impact
- The direction of the impact
- The type of impact
- The number of blows, stabs, or shots

- The position of the victim and the assailant at the time of the bloodshed
- The movement of the victim and the assailant during the bloodshed
- The movement of the victim and the assailant after the bloodshed

The study of fluids in motion forms the basis for hypotheses regarding the location, shape, size, and **directionality** of bloodstains relative to the forces that produced them.

■ Bloodstain Mechanics

Free-Falling Blood

As a drop of blood falls, the surface tension of the drop minimizes surface area, causing the drop to acquire a spherical shape. A spherical drop will not break up until acted upon by a force other than gravity. When a drop of **free-falling blood** strikes a nonporous, smooth horizontal surface, the result is a circular bloodstain. A rough-textured surface will cause the surface tension to rupture and create a stain with **spines**. The degree of distortion of the stain is a product of the texture of the impact surface, not the distance fallen (Laber, 1985). The diameter of the stain is a product of the volume of the drop, the distance fallen, and the texture of the impact surface.

Maximum diameters are achieved when the height of the blood source allows the blood drop to reach its **terminal velocity**. MacDonell (1971) has established that for a 0.05-ml drop of free-falling blood, the terminal velocity is 25 feet per second, which is achieved after the blood falls a distance of about 20 feet. Drops of smaller volume have smaller terminal velocities, and drops of larger volume have higher velocities. Blood drops in excess of 0.05 ml will produce bloodstains with a greater diameter at a shorter falling distance. Investigators should derive conservative estimates as a result of experimentation that uses comparable surface textures and angles of impact. Investigators are able to recognize the types of bloodstains resulting from free-falling blood drops based upon their size, shape, and distribution at a crime scene. The interpretation process can incorporate information about velocity, possible source, and movement.

Impact Angles

Free-falling blood dropping vertically and striking a horizontal surface at 90 degrees will produce circular bloodstains. Blood dropping on a nonhorizontal surface produces elongated, oval-shaped stains—the greater the angle, the greater the elongation. The narrowest end of the stain will point in the direction of travel and away from the point of origin. This angle can be calculated by measuring the width and length of the bloodstain. **Angle of impact** calculations are now usually done with the help of computer software.

Point of Convergence

When a body is subjected to force sufficient to cause bleeding, the blood released will strike various surfaces at a variety of angles. A **point of convergence** is a common point to which individual bloodstains can be traced (**Figure 5–2**). Stains on a surface, when traced through their long axis, will come together at a point on that surface, showing the direction from which they came and their direction of travel. For example, bloodstains on a floor will lead back along the floor to a common point—the point at which lines drawn through the long axes of the stains would intersect.

Point of Origin

The point of convergence, which is a point on the plane of the surface on which the blood drops fell, assists in determining where the blood came from—the **point of origin**,

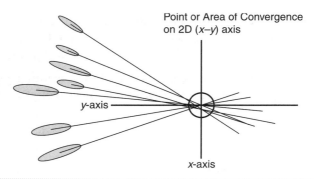

Figure 5–2   Point of Convergence photo.

in other words. This latter is the point (or set of points) in three-dimensional space at which the body was located at the time it was struck and began to throw off drops of blood. The point of origin is determined by projecting angles of impact of well-defined bloodstains back to an axis constructed through the established point of convergence. In other words, the point of convergence shows the general direction the blood traveled. By examining the bloodstains, one can see a distortion in the shape of the drop due not to the surface texture but to the angle at which the blood drop hit the surface. This distortion reveals the impact angle of the blood. Strings can be projected from each measured bloodstain at its angle of impact back to an axis perpendicular to the plane on which the bloodstains are located and passing through their point of convergence. The place where these strings come together is the point or the set of points in space from which the bloodstains are likely to have originated.

Low-Velocity-Impact Bloodstains

Secondary blood splashing (**ricochet**) may occur as a result of the deflection of large volumes of blood after impact on a **target surface**. **Splashed** bloodstain patterns usually have a large central area and peripheral spattering, with the spatter appearing as elongated, oval-shaped spots. These patterns are often produced when pools of blood are disturbed by objects such as shod feet, or when large volumes of blood fall from a source such as a victim's wound. The larger the quantity of splashed blood, the greater the spatter.

Medium-Velocity-Impact Bloodstains

When a strong force strikes an exposed source of blood, the blood is broken up into many small droplets. When these droplets strike a target surface, they produce bloodstain patterns that are readily distinguishable from patterns produced by **dripped** blood, which is associated with low-velocity force or impact (Eckert and James, 1993).

Projected Blood

When large quantities of blood undergo medium- or high-velocity impact, the blood is forcibly **projected** upon a target surface or surfaces and creates distinctive patterns. When blood is directed horizontally or vertically downward with more force than gravity alone would exert, the resulting pattern has a periphery of spinelike extensions and a streaking secondary spatter. Blood released under arterial pressure forms this type of pattern, and the process of release is referred to as **arterial gushing** or **spurting**. The resulting stains are characteristic and readily identified by appearance and shape. Arterial gushing is common at crime scenes where a shooting or stabbing has occurred.

Cast-off Blood

In blunt trauma cases, often the assailant swings the weapon repeatedly at the victim. These repeated blows may create a pattern as blood is flung from the weapon on each successive blow. If a weapon has produced blood, it will often adhere to that weapon. During the backswing away from the victim, the blood on the weapon will be thrown off and travel tangentially to the arc of the swing, striking nearby surfaces such as walls, ceilings, floors, and other objects in its path. The initial blood that is cast from a weapon during the backswing may strike a target surface and produce circular stains at 90 degrees. These stains often appear on walls or ceilings. As the backswing continues past its apex, the remaining blood is cast off a greater distance at a greater angle and will produce oval-shaped stains. Determination of the angle of impact and the convergence of these cast-off bloodstains allows a reconstruction of the position of the victim and assailant.

Numerous **cast-off patterns** will allow a reconstruction of the movements of the victim and assailant as well as their relative positions at the time the cast-off patterns were produced. They also allow an estimation of the minimum number of blows struck. The number of distinct patterns or trails of cast-off stains equals the minimum number of blows struck plus one, because the first blow does not produce a cast-off pattern. If more than one blow was struck on the same plane, the cast-off patterns may overlap, which is the reason only the minimum number of blows struck may be estimated (MacDonell, 1971).

Flow Patterns

Flow patterns indicate the direction of travel of flowing blood. Pooled blood behaves like pooled water. The direction of travel of either is dependent upon gravity. Flow patterns may be seen on the body of the victim as well as on the surface upon which the victim is lying. Flow patterns and blood pooling may reveal movement of a victim during or after bloodshed or alteration of the crime scene. Blood flow patterns on the victim should be consistent with the victim's injuries and subsequent pooling. Any inconsistencies suggest that the injuries were not sustained at the crime scene and that the victim was transported there after injury or death.

A blood source that collides with an object moving at a speed between 5 and 25 feet per second will produce **medium-velocity blood spatter**. In order to create a medium-velocity blood pattern, the blood source must be exposed prior to impact. Medium-velocity bloodstains range from 1 mm to 4 mm in diameter and are often characterized by a pattern in which streaks radiate away from the area of impact. Interrupted radial patterns suggest that the assailant's body and clothing may have intercepted part of the splashing blood.

High-Velocity-Impact Bloodstains

A collision between a blood source and an object moving in excess of 100 feet per second will create a **high-velocity-impact pattern**. The high-velocity impact creates a mist of showering blood that, because of its low density, does not travel far. High-velocity-impact bloodstains are generally associated with gunshot injuries. Spatter from a gunshot is multidirectional. **Backspatter** may occur if the assailant and weapon are proximate to the victim upon impact. The assailant and the weapon may bear evidence of blood spatter. The amount of backspatter is affected by the type of weapon and ammunition, the muzzle-to-target distance, the position of the victim at the time of impact, and the physiological characteristics of the struck area (Stephens and Allen, 1983). In the case of contact wounds, the barrel of the weapon may contain flesh, bone, and blood residue from **barrel blowback** (or **drawback**). Barrel blowback also may cause backspatter on hands and clothing. High-velocity **forward spatter** is generally a product of a gunshot exit wound. This type of spatter can assist in determining the location of the victim at the time of the wounding.

■ Testing Blood Evidence

Because of the violent nature of criminal homicide, blood is commonly found at the crime scene. The investigator may encounter blood evidence in one or more of four general areas:

1. On the victim
2. At the crime scene
3. On a weapon
4. On the assailant

Police, prosecutors, and experts all want to know the answer to three things when confronted with dried blood found at a crime scene:

1. Is it blood?
2. Is it human blood?
3. How closely related is it to the blood of known or discovered suspects?

In answering the first question, forensic scientists can use a variety of chemical tests known as **presumptive determinants** (presumptive because some substances other than blood test positive as well). The blood tests fall into two categories: **catalytic** and crystal. The crystal tests are considered to be confirmatory and are much more sensitive than the catalytic tests.

Catalytic Tests

The most commonly used reagents for presumptive blood tests are o-toluidine, phenol-phthalein, luminol, and leucomalachite green. A positive result serves as a preliminary step in determining the origin of the stain.

Phenolphthalein Test

Formerly, the most common test used in determining whether a stain was blood was the benzidine color test. Because of the carcinogenic nature of benzidine, that test has been replaced with the **phenolphthalein test** (Higaki and Philip, 1976). When a blood specimen is mixed with phenolphthalein and hydrogen peroxide, the hemoglobin in the blood will cause a deep pink color to form. This test is not conclusive, because some other substances will cause the same reaction, but the result is strongly suggestive. Phenolphtalein is considered one of the most reliable of the crime scene blood tests. When applied to an unknown stain, if blood, it will produce a pink reaction. The reagent may be used from a bottle (which introduces shelf time into the equation) or ampoules (which are more expensive but have indefinite shelf lives). Reagent ampoules are contained inside a plastic applicator (**Figure 5–3**). To be used, the reagent ampoules must be crushed and then the plastic applicator shaken for 30 seconds. A piece of moistened contact paper is rubbed over the stain (a cotton swab can be used) and the phenolphthalein applicator rubbed lightly across the dampened transfer stain. A pink reaction indicates the stain is blood.

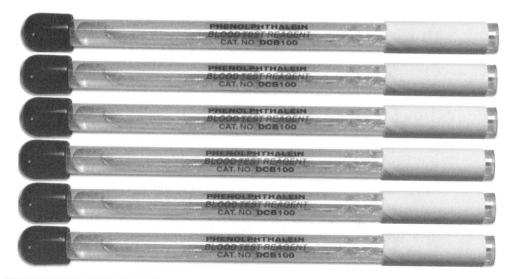

Figure 5–3   Phenolphthalein dischaps (disposable chemical applicators) reagent.

Courtesy of SIRCHIE Finger Print Laboratories, Inc.

Luminol Test

As the name suggests, the reaction of luminol with blood causes luminescence—a light change, not a color change. Luminol is dispensed as a spray upon the surface to be examined. The sprayed object or area must be viewed in the dark—the darker the surroundings, the greater the luminescence. The **luminol test** is very sensitive and allows application to large areas or to areas that may appear to be blood free but might still carry a residue of blood after a hasty cleaning. Luminol can be applied specifically to a small area using an ampoule applicator or to large areas by spraying (**Figure 5–4**). Luminol does not interfere with DNA testing, making it an appropriate choice for many investigators. The luminescence caused by luminol when contacting blood can only be viewed in the dark, making application difficult at best. Using a red light allows the eyes to adjust to the darkness and provides enough light to work by. When luminescence occurs, the eyes have adjusted to the dark, making even dim stains highly visible. Luminol may provide a reaction even after the scene has been cleaned.

O-Toluidine Test

The **o-toluidine test** uses a reagent that is a mixture of o-toluidine base and ethanol. O-toluidine droplets, followed by 3% hydrogen peroxide droplets, are applied to a suspect specimen. If a rapidly developing blue color appears, the strong suspicion is that the specimen is blood.

Leucomalachite Green Test

The **leucomalachite green test** uses a low-sensitivity reagent consisting of 1 g of leucomalachite green powder, 100 ml of glacial acetic acid, and 150 ml of distilled water, with the entire mixture diluted with hydrogen peroxide. The application of this reagent produces a characteristic green color in the presence of blood. Many investigators consider this the most sensitive of the reagents. A positive reaction produces a purple response.

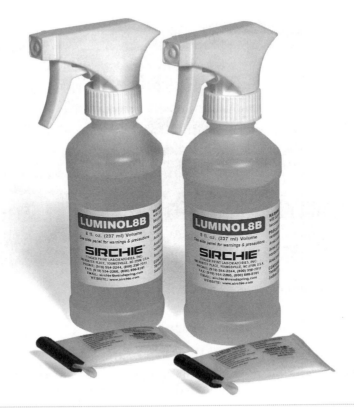

Figure 5–4 Luminol8 (spray bottle).

Courtesy of SIRCHIE Finger Print Laboratories, Inc.

Crystal Tests

Once it has been satisfactorily determined that a specimen is in fact blood, the next step is to establish the species of origin. The **precipitin test** is based on the fact that when animals are injected with human blood, antibodies are formed that react with the invading human blood in an effort to neutralize the presence of the human blood. The antibodies can be recovered by bleeding the animal that was injected and isolating the blood serum. (Blood clots when fibrin in the animal's blood traps the red blood cells from the human blood; if the clotted material is removed, a pale yellow liquid known as blood **serum** is left.) This serum, known as human blood antiserum, contains antibodies that will react with human antigens (Saferstein, 1990).

The test can be conducted in a capillary tube. The bloodstain is placed on top of the human antiserum. If the blood is human, it will react with antibodies in the antiserum and form a cloudy ring where the blood and the human antiserum meet in the capillary tube. The reaction will occur with bloodstains as old as 15 years. In one criminal trial, a precipitin test produced a positive result from bloodstains on a piece of cloth that had been immersed in salt water for more than 3 years (Bugliosi, 1992).

Blood Typing

Antigens are chemical structures residing on the surface of each red blood cell. **Blood types** are determined by the kind of antigen on the surface of these cells. Although numerous antigens exist on the surface of each red blood cell, the ones used for typing are the A, B, O, and Rh antigens.

Characteristics of Blood Types

Blood types are distinguished by the following antigens:

- Type A blood has A antigens on its surface.
- Type B blood has B antigens on its surface.
- Type AB blood has both A and B antigens on its surface.
- Type O blood does not have either A or B antigens on its surface.
- Rh-positive blood has D antigens on its surface.
- Rh-negative blood does not have D antigens on its surface.

For every antigen, there is an **antibody**. Each antibody name has the prefix anti- followed by the name of the corresponding antigen. An antibody will react with its specific antigen. If serum containing anti-B is added to red blood cells carrying the antigen B, the antibodies will attach themselves to the cells, creating a network of linked cells through a process called **agglutination**.

- Type A blood has A antigens and anti-B antibodies.
- Type B blood has B antigens and anti-A antibodies.
- Type AB blood has AB antigens and neither anti-A nor anti-B antibodies.
- Type O blood has neither A nor B antigens and both anti-A and anti-B antibodies.

The process of cell linking allows blood to be typed. In typing blood, only anti-A and anti-B serum are required. Blood of type A will be agglutinated by anti-A serum, blood of type B will be agglutinated by anti-B serum, AB blood will be agglutinated by both anti-A and anti-B serum, and blood of type O will not be agglutinated by either anti-A or anti-B serum. Both anti-A serum and anti-B serum are available commercially.

OFFICER'S NOTEBOOK

Absorption-Elution Technique for Typing Dried Bloodstains

The absorption-elution technique involves four distinct steps:

1. Antiserum is placed on the stained material.
2. The antiserum is removed by washing the bloodstained material.
3. The stained material is heated at 56°C, thereby breaking the antibody–antigen bond (elution).
4. Either A cells or B cells are then combined with the eluted antibodies, and the presence or absence of agglutination is observed.

This test requires that anti-A serum, anti-B serum, and anti-H serum be added to separate stain samples. The samples are incubated overnight at 4°C to allow the antibodies in the antiserum to combine with their specific antigens. The stain samples are then washed in a cold saline solution. To separate the antigens from the antibodies, a small amount of saline solution must be added to each sample. The samples are again incubated for 20 minutes at 56°C. The heat separates the antibodies from the antigens in the sample and produces an antiserum specific to the blood type of the stain. Known A, B, and O cells are added, and the absence or presence of agglutination is observed. If A cells are agglutinated, the stain was type A. If both A and B cells are agglutinated, the stain was type AB. If only O cells are agglutinated, the stain was type O. If only type B cells are agglutinated, the stain was type B (Miller and Brown, 1990).

Typing Dried Blood

Red blood cells rupture upon drying, leaving nothing to agglutinate. Although agglutination can no longer be used to type the dried stain, the antigens that were present on the wet stain are still present in the dried stain and can be identified by indirect means. The current method of typing dried bloodstains is the absorption-elution technique (see Officer's Notebook).

■ Handling Blood Evidence

In crime scenes at which a violent crime occurred, often blood is transferred from the victim to the assailant. It is the probability of this type of transfer that makes homicide investigators pay special attention to blood and bloodstained clothing. In an effort to preserve what may become important evidence, investigators collect all the clothing from the victim as well as samples of the underlying strata upon which the body rested. Even what appear to be unstained portions of clothing may be gathered. In many cases, blood may not be visible but may still respond to appropriate laboratory testing. All bloodstains should be measured and photographed prior to handling.

Packaging of bloodstained clothing is critical. Heat and moisture can reduce the viability of antigens. Time is of the essence. Bloodstains should be submitted for laboratory testing immediately. Not only does the passage of time corrupt bloodstains, but it also raises serious questions about efficiency and the chain of custody. Airtight containers may cause condensation of moisture within the container and result in the growth of bacteria that can destroy blood.

In many investigations, the determination that a stain is human blood may be sufficient. In other investigations, blood type may assist in identifying human blood on an assailant's clothing. However, it takes DNA characterization of blood to link a bloodstain to a particular individual. Any information as to the relative positions of the victim and the assailant during the attack can only be accomplished through blood pattern analysis.

Collecting Blood

Blood is usually recovered as fresh blood, clotted blood, spatters, smears, or flakes. Wet blood on clothing can be siphoned off with a sterile eyedropper and placed in a clean vial (marked with date, time, etc.). The remainder of the garment can be allowed to air dry, then rolled in paper to prevent rubbing and placed in a paper bag. Plastic bags may allow moisture to condense onto the interior surface of the plastic, contaminating the bloodstain. If several garments are involved, each should be placed in a separate bag. The tagged bags and tagged vials should be submitted as soon as possible to the laboratory (the time of submission should be noted in the investigator's report or the evidence log).

OFFICER'S NOTEBOOK

Collecting Bloodstained Samples

All bloodstained clothing should be packaged separately in paper bags. If stains are wet, they should be air dried prior to packaging. Blood deposited on surfaces that do not lend themselves to packaging should be allowed to dry and then scraped onto a clean piece of paper. A control sample must also be submitted, to prove that the positive results of any testing were from the sample submitted and not something previously deposited on the surface and lying under the sample.

CASE IN POINT

A Telling Drop

In one case involving an open-field death, the female victim was found face down with knife wounds to the front of her body. A cursory examination of the body revealed a single circular dried blood droplet on her buttocks. Investigators discussed various ways of retrieving the blood after having photographed it. Determining that the blood would probably not survive handling and moving of the body, they decided to remove it prior to movement of the body. The circumference of the blood drop indicated that it fell perpendicular to the victim's reclining body, probably as a result of a wound to the assailant. Mutilating the body was thought to be the only option until an evidence technician suggested lifting the droplet like a fingerprint. The efforts to lift it were successful, and analysis of the droplet played a prominent role in the identification and subsequent conviction of the murderer.

Dried bloodstains can be recovered by using a cotton swab dampened with distilled water. The swab is rotated upon the dried stain until the cotton turns rust colored. The swab should then be placed in a sealed vial and tagged.

Dried flakes can be scraped onto a piece of filter paper or lifted from the surface using a fingerprint lifter (or transparent tape). The flakes and paper should be placed in a clean pillbox, then sealed and tagged. Each flake of dried blood should be boxed separately, and its location should be identified on the crime scene sketch.

Handling Guidelines

Unnecessary exposure of blood to heat, moisture, and bacterial contamination will shorten the survival time of its antigens. It is important that all bloodstained material be submitted for testing without delay. Each moment the material is not delivered to the laboratory must be accounted for and explained. Because of the importance of blood evidence, the investigators should devise a delivery protocol to get bloodstained material from the crime scene to the laboratory as quickly as possible. Such a protocol will prevent embarrassing questions on cross-examination and reduce the risk of a challenge to evidence based on deterioration of the specimen.

All containers in which blood is placed should be saved and available at the time of trial in case of questions pertaining to the collection and handling of the evidence. It is important that as much of the blood as possible be preserved at the scene and at the laboratory. The defense may request court permission to conduct independent tests, especially if DNA testing has been performed.

■ Summary

What was once called blood spatter analysis is now referred to by the Federal Bureau of Investigation as **bloodstain pattern analysis**. Bloodstain analysis is one of the staples of crime scene investigation that requires specific expertise in interpretation and collection. The role of the investigator is to recognize it and bring to bear the appropriate expertise to identify, interpret, and preserve blood stain evidence. The amount of information that can be had from a bloodstain analyst is amazing, but only if the stains have been preserved in the condition in which they were deposited. In the beginning of this chapter it was noted that blood at homicide crime scenes is very common. Just as common is the destruction of those stains. The primary responsibility of all parties to a crime wherein blood stain evidence is present is to preserve it and to record it.

Blood stains on clothing can be a way to identify a suspect; the next chapter discusses other ways of identifying a suspect including fingerprints, composite drawings, lineups, and DNA evidence.

■ Key Terms

agglutination: The process by which blood cells link together to form clumps

angle of impact: Angle at which a blood drop hits a surface, relative to the horizontal plane of that surface; the angle can be calculated by measuring the width and length of the bloodstain

antibody: Substance that will react with its specific antigen

antigens: Chemical structures residing on the surface of each red blood cell

arterial gushing (spurting): Blood exiting under pressure from a breached artery

backspatter: Blood that is directed toward the energy source causing the spatter

barrel blowback (drawback): The blood residue found in a gun barrel as a result of a large-caliber contact wound; it is backspatter contained in the gun barrel

blood stain pattern analysis: The FBI nomenclature for analyzing blood stains left at a crime scene

blood type: The type of antigens found on red blood cells

cast-off pattern: The pattern produced by a bloody object in motion (such as a weapon) resulting in blood projected (thrown) onto a surface other than the impact site

catalytic test: A presumptive blood test

circular distortion: The stain that results from blood striking a flat surface at an angle; the more nearly perpendicular the angle of impact, the more circular the blood drop stain

directionality: The direction of a drop of blood from point of origin to point of impact

drip pattern: The pattern created by blood dripping into blood; in this pattern, round blood spatters occur at the periphery of the central bloodstain

flow pattern: Pattern that indicates the direction of travel of flowing blood

forward spatter: Blood that travels in the same direction as the force causing the spatter; forward spatter is often associated with gunshot exit wounds

free-falling blood: Blood that has not been acted on by a force other than gravity; when a drop of free-falling blood strikes a nonporous, smooth, horizontal surface, the result is a circular bloodstain

high-velocity impact pattern: Pattern caused by the collision of a blood source with an object moving in excess of 100 feet per second, resulting in a mistlike dispersion that travels only a short distance

leucomalachite green test: Test used to determine if a specimen is blood. When a reagent (consisting of 1 g of leucomalachite green powder, 100 ml of glacial acetic acid, and 150 ml of distilled water, with the entire mixture diluted with hydrogen peroxide) is applied to blood, it turns a characteristic green color

luminol test: Very sensitive test used to determine if a specimen is blood; if an object or area that has been sprayed with luminol emits light (as viewed in the dark), it was likely covered by blood

medium-velocity blood spatter: Spatter caused by a blood source colliding with an object moving at a speed between 5 and 25 feet per second

o-toluidine test: Test used to determine if a specimen is blood. If a blue color rapidly appears after an application of o-toluidine droplets followed by an application of 3% hydrogen droplets, the specimen is likely blood

phenolphthalein test: Test used to determine if a specimen is blood; the hemoglobin in a blood specimen mixed with phenolphthalein and hydrogen peroxide will cause a deep pink color to form

point of convergence: A common point to which individual bloodstains can be traced

point of origin: Point from which the blood drop began moving toward the surface on which it left a stain; this location can be determined by projecting the angles of impact of the bloodstains back to an axis constructed through the point of convergence

projected: Directed forcefully onto a surface

ricochet: Secondary blood splashing that may occur as a result of the deflection of large volumes of blood after impact with a primary target surface to a secondary target surface

serum: The portion of blood fluid that remains after coagulation; it contains antibodies

spine: The pointed-edge pattern that radiates away from a drop of blood that has struck a target surface

splash: A (projected) pattern created by a low-velocity impact upon the surface of a pool of blood with a volume 0.10 ml or greater

surface texture: Composition of materials in a given surface that provides the foundation for blood pattern interpretation

target surface: Surface onto which blood is deposited

terminal velocity: The maximum speed to which a free-falling drop of blood can accelerate in air; this velocity is approximately 25.1 feet per second

■ Review Questions

1. What role does surface texture play in a blood pattern deposit?
2. If a blood drop stain is perfectly round, what can be said about the direction from which it fell?
3. What shape does free-falling blood take?
4. What is the bloodstain impact angle and what does it say about the crime?
5. How does point of convergence differ from point of origin?
6. Is it necessary to know the point of convergence to determine the point of origin? Why?
7. What is ricochet blood?
8. What are the differences among high-, medium-, and low-velocity bloodstains?
9. Why do cast-off bloodstain patterns only suggest the minimum number of blows delivered to the victim?
10. What are the various tests for determining whether a blood sample is in fact blood and, if so, whether it is human blood?
11. How is blood typed?
12. Can dried blood be typed, and, if so, how?
13. How is phenolphthalein used to test for blood?
14. How is luminol used to test for blood?

■ Bibliography

Bugliosi, V. (1992). *And the sea will tell.* New York: Ivy Books.

Eckert, W.G., & James S.H. (1993). *Interpretation of bloodstain evidence at crime scenes.* Boca Raton, FL: CRC Press.

Higaki, R.S., & Philip M.S. (1976). A study of the sensitivity, stability and specificity of phenolphthalein as an indicator test for blood. *Canadian Society of Forensic Science Journal* 9, 97–99.

Laber, T.L. (1985). Diameter of a bloodstain as a function of origin, distance fallen and volume of drop. *International Association of Blood Pattern Analysts News* 2(1), 12–16.

MacDonell, H.L. (1971). Interpretation of bloodstains: Physical considerations. In C. Wecht (Ed.), *Legal medicine annual.* New York: Appleton-Century-Crofts.

MacDonell, H.L. (1993). *Bloodstain patterns.* Corning, NY: Laboratory of Forensic Science.

Miller, L.S., & A.M. Brown (1990). *Criminal evidence laboratory manual* (3rd ed.). Cincinnati, OH: Anderson.

Saferstein, R. (1990). *Criminalistics: An introduction to forensic science.* Englewood Cliffs, NJ: Prentice Hall.

Stephens, B.G., & Allen T.B. (1983). Backspatter of blood from gunshot wounds: Observations and experimental simulation. *Journal of Forensic Sciences* 23, 437–439.

Suspect Identification

CHAPTER
6

Upon completion of this chapter students will demonstrate an understanding of:

- A basic history of the evolution of fingerprinting
- The various methods of developing fingerprints
- The importance of photographing fingerprints
- Lifting fingerprints
- A basic introduction to DNA typing

Often an investigator is confronted with a plethora of physical evidence but no suspect to whom the evidence relates. Technicians and laboratory equipment form the front lines of the battle in the investigation in these cases. Three identification methods require the services of a forensic or investigative specialist: fingerprint comparison, DNA comparison, and composite drawing. A more common identification method, the police lineup, involves investigators, witnesses or victims, and a known suspect. This chapter discusses the investigative, scientific, and legal aspects of these four identification methods.

■ Biometric Identification

The government has long attempted to identify people by biological characteristics, from bumps on a person's head to the ridges on his or her fingers. New trends in identification involve the use of iris patterns and voice recognition systems. Banking and government agencies are the primary users of **biometric identification** systems, and biometrics has become a growth industry. The state of Connecticut began to use fingerprint scanning in 1996 as a way to deter welfare fraud, and both the Department of Defense and the Department of Veterans Affairs are considering using digitized fingerprinting systems to identify employees.

All biometric systems require similar equipment, including a high-resolution scanning device to digitize an image of some part of the human body and a computer to run the pattern-recognition and sorting software for the specific type of identification in use. Various biometric systems scan human body parts, including fingerprints, irises and retinas, faces, and hands, and software and scanning devices are also being developed to identify signatures and voices.

Iris Scanning

Iris scanning has generated much interest in biometric measurement. The iris has several advantages as an identifying body part: It is an integral part of the body and is not easily modified. Unlike fingerprints, the iris can be imaged from a distance. Iris patterns are unique. No two persons have the same iris pattern; in fact, no two eyes have the same iris pattern. The patterns are stable throughout life and only change in a highly predictable manner as the pupil opens and closes (Lerner, 2000).

Sensar Incorporated has developed camera technology that identifies a person's head and then locates the eyes and the irises. The IriScanAA algorithm locates the outer and inner borders of the iris and detects and excludes the eyelids if they get in the way. The system uses a mathematical technique called wavelet analysis to translate the image of the iris into a digitized pattern. Wavelet analysis breaks down the image into a set of spatially limited waves called an **iris code**. This code is defined in a coordinate system (grid). Once an iris code is prepared, the computer compares a specific individual code against a group of codes (iris patterns) previously stored in the computer. The computer calculates the number of agreements and disagreements between two iris codes. Because the iris code is so short, it can be compared quickly with large databases at a rate of 100,000 codes per second (Lerner, 2000).

Digital Fingerprints

Fingerprinting is the most widespread biometric technology and the one favored by most government agencies. In **digital fingerprinting**, an individual places a finger on an optical scanner, which creates and saves a digitized image of the person's fingerprint. Software then searches the fingerprint image for the location of **minutiae**, points where a finger friction ridge ends or splits in two. Minutiae are highly individualized and can be used to recognize an employee or can be compared to a database of stored fingerprints of criminals in search of a match. Portable digital scanners are being developed that will allow the investigator to scan crime scene fingerprints directly into a computer and communicate them to a national database for comparison and storage.

Other biometric techniques are under development, but all of them have a higher error rate than either iris scanning or digital fingerprint imaging. Hand dimensions remain relatively stable but are not sufficiently unique to distinguish people in a large population. There has been considerable research on facial recognition, but faces vary depending on expression and are easy to disguise or alter. Voice identification is desirable for remote access applications; however, a person's voice varies with emotion, age, and health, so this approach has not reached the application stage.

■ Fingerprints

Fingerprint identification began over 4000 years ago when King Hammurabi used fingerprint seals on contracts. Nearly 600 years before Marco Polo visited China, the law book of Yung-Hwui required that a husband in a divorce decree had to seal the document with a fingerprint. In 1823 a graduate student named Johannes Purkinje described fingerprint types in his doctoral thesis and classified them into nine major groups.

In general, however, until the late 19th century there was no unified system of physical identification beyond a general description of age, weight, marks, and scars. With Alphonse Bertillion's new measurement system, people were looking at ways to catalog suspects. In 1888, Sir Francis Galton met with Sir William Herschal. Out of that meeting arose a classification system based on various points of identification in a fingerprint, known as *Galton details.* In the 1890s, Sir Edward Richard Henry, Inspector General of Police in Bengal, India, experimented with Sir William Herschal's system of using Indian natives' palm prints on contracts. Henry eventually joined the Metropolitan Police of London and initiated his fingerprint identification system, which is the basis for the modern American fingerprint system.

Friction skin is made up of ridges running parallel to one another and is found on the soles of the feet and the palms of the hands. These **friction ridges** run in parallel rows that form patterns. The individual ridges form various shapes or characteristics that do not appear in the same place or sequence from one finger to another.

A close examination of the friction ridges reveals that all along their length the surface is broken in an irregular fashion by sweat pores. The pores are openings for the ducts leading from the sweat glands found in the subcutaneous tissue. The human body has three kinds of sweat glands:

- Eccrine glands are found on all parts of the body and are the only sweat gland found on the palms of the hands and the soles of the feet.
- Apocrine glands are located in the pubic, mammary, and anal areas.
- Sebaceous glands are located on the forehead, chest, back, and abdomen and produce an oily secretion, sebum.

All three kinds of glands secrete water as well as many different organic and inorganic substances. Water is secreted to help control body temperature. As the water moves to the surface it evaporates and picks up waste products from other parts of the body. Only the sebaceous glands secrete oily substances; fingers touching those areas are likely to pick up oily residues and transfer them upon contact, leaving fingerprints.

Television, books, and movies often emphasize the value of fingerprints in solving serious crimes. Until the advent of computer technology, however, that value was mostly mythical. Fingerprints were used to inculpate or exculpate based on a suspect group. A search of fingerprint files for the match to a fingerprint found at the scene of a crime occurred only in fiction. The classification system used in categorizing stored fingerprints and the large number of fingerprints stored made it impossible to check through a fingerprint collection manually looking for a match. Computers have turned art into reality. Automated fingerprint identification systems now allow police to do what screenwriters and movie directors have long pretended they could.

The possibilities offered by this technology can only be appreciated when we consider the size of the fingerprint database the federal government has collected. The FBI has been receiving copies of fingerprint cards from all state and federal agencies that require employees to be fingerprinted. They have copies of all the prints of persons who served in wars from Korea to Iraq. Additionally, they have copies of all persons arrested and booked, as a juvenile or an adult, for a misdemeanor or a felony.

Fingerprint Individuality

No two fingers have yet been found that have identical characteristics. **Fingerprint individuality** is not dependent on age, size, gender, or race. The identifiable aspects of a fingerprint are called minutiae (ridge characteristics). The shape, location, and number of minutiae individualize a fingerprint.

There is no agreement as to how many ridge characteristics must be shared by a discovered print and the fingerprint of a suspect before they can be said to be a match.

After a three-year study, the International Association for Identification determined that "no valid basis exists for requiring a predetermined minimum number of friction ridge characters which must be present in two impressions in order to establish positive identification" (Saferstein, 2007, p. 435). In each and every instance when identification is made between two impressions, that identification is the product of a comparison done by an expert. The value of the expert opinion is based upon the following criteria:

- The number of comparable ridge characteristics
- The knowledge of the expert
- The experience of the expert
- The ability of the expert to explain how the comparison was done
- The quality of the testimony of the adverse expert

Fingerprint Immutability

From birth to death, a person's fingerprints retain their classifiable characteristics. The hands and fingers will grow and the print will enlarge with that growth, but the ridge characteristics remain **immutable**. Efforts to eradicate prints are futile, and the scar tissue that results from attempts to do so is as individual as the small number of ridge characteristics that may have been destroyed.

Fingerprints are a mirror image of the friction ridge skin of the palm, fingers, and thumb. It is the friction ridges that are reproduced by the black lines of an inked fingerprint impression. When examined under a microscope, the friction ridges of the fingers reveal a single row of pores that are ducts through which sweat is deposited. That sweat, along with body oils that have been picked up when the fingers touch other parts of the body, may be deposited upon a touched surface. The touching may result in a transfer of sweat and oils in the shape of finger friction ridges (a fingerprint) onto the surface touched.

Prints deposited onto a surface but invisible to the naked eye are known as **latent prints**. Technically, only prints that cannot be readily seen with the unassisted eye are latent prints, yet police frequently use the term latent to refer to any fingerprint left at a crime scene, whether visible or not. Fingerprint characteristics must be gleaned by computer or by an individual examination of the pattern (**Figure 6–1**). A magnified examination of the pattern will reveal the individual characteristics that make up the pattern (**Figure 6–2**). When done by hand, the work of determining fingerprint characteristics is tedious and painstaking.

Classifying Prints

Fingerprints fall into three classes based on general patterns. The most common class is the loop; about 65% of the population has loop patterns on at least one finger. Approximately 35% of the population has a whorl pattern on a finger or thumb, and only about 5% of the population has arches.

Loop Patterns

Loops must have one or more ridges that enter from one side of the print, recurve, and exit from the same side. Loops are divided into two groups: ulnar loops, which open toward the little finger, and radial loops, which open toward the thumb (**Figure 6–3**).

Additionally, a loop pattern must have a core and a delta. The **core** is the centermost point of the loop at the apex of the innermost ridge of the loop. The **delta** is a two-sided

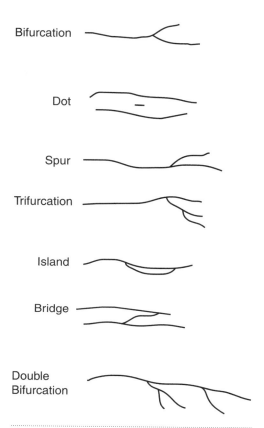

Bifurcation

Dot

Spur

Trifurcation

Island

Bridge

Double
Bifurcation

Figure 6–1 Fingerprint characteristics.

Figure 6–2 Fingerprint enlarger.

Courtesy of SIRCHIE Finger Print Laboratories, Inc.

triangular shape to one side of the loop that resembles a river delta (loop prints have only one delta per print). These two points are necessary for classifying a print based on the number of friction ridges between the delta and the core of the loop.

Whorl Patterns

As is often the case in things technical, the classification of **whorls** is needlessly confusing. The confusion arises as a result of the four groupings into which a whorl pattern may fall: (1) plain whorl, (2) central pocket loop whorl, (3) double loop whorl, and (4) accidental whorl (**Figure 6–4**). The problem, for those unaccustomed to fingerprint classification, is that the word *loop* is used in distinguishing among whorl patterns but is also used as the name of a nonwhorl pattern. It helps to keep in mind that the names of the two loop patterns, radial and ulnar, are related to the radial and ulnar bones in the arm. The terms *central pocket loop* and *double loop* refer to loops occurring inside whorls—central pocket loop whorls and double loop whorls. Remember that a radial and an ulnar loop each have only one delta, and that any whorl pattern has a minimum of two deltas. What appears to be a loop having two deltas is a double loop whorl or a central pocket loop whorl. Any pattern that is not covered by one of the categories or is a combination of two patterns is called an **accidental**.

Figure 6–3 Loop pattern.
Courtesy of the Federal Bureau of Investigation

Figure 6–4 Whorl pattern.
Courtesy of the Federal Bureau of Investigation

Arch Patterns

The least common pattern is also the simplest to classify. **Arches** are either plain or tented (**Figure 6–5**). A plain arch is formed by friction ridges entering from one side of the print and exiting on the opposite side, rising to a peak in the center of the ridge to form a hill-like pattern. A tented arch, instead of rising gently to the center and sloping easily away, thrusts up in the center and falls quickly away.

Understanding fingerprint patterns is essential for doing fingerprint comparisons. Once two prints are seen to have the same pattern, they can be examined further for similarities in ridge numbers and configuration.

Detecting Prints

Although police often use the term *latent print* to describe all fingerprints found at a crime scene, many of the prints discovered are visible and should not be called latent. Any investigator, lawyer, or expert who unartfully uses "latent" to describe a visible print can expect to be challenged on competent cross-examination. Such a simple point is

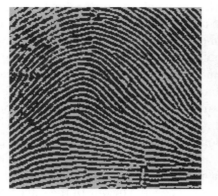
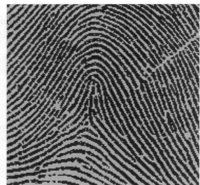

Figure 6–5 Plain arch and tented arch.
Courtesy of the Federal Bureau of Investigation

not lost on jurors, who generally are swayed by simple reasons to find one witness more believable than another.

There are three distinct types of prints found at a crime scene and a fourth type used by police: (1) visible prints, (2) plastic prints, (3) latent prints, and (4) inked impressions. Just as a photographic print is a representation of, but not identical to, the original scene, a fingerprint is a representation of, but not identical to, the actual finger skin friction ridges.

Visible Prints

Visible prints are readily identifiable as fingerprints with the unassisted eye. Fingers that have been in contact with a colored material such as toner, ink, blood, paint, oil, or chocolate leave visible prints. Once the material has soiled the fingers, the material may be transferred to a surface with which the ridges come into contact.

Plastic Prints

If fingers come into contact with a soft material such as soap, wet putty, wet cement, wet plaster, or dust, a ridge impression may be left sufficient for performing comparisons. As children, most of us have placed hand, foot, or finger impressions in wet cement. In Hollywood, a cultural artifact has been built around celebrities embedding their hands and feet in a wet cement pavement, leaving hand- and footprints. These are **plastic impressions**, and they can be used for fingerprint comparisons. If a movie star were a suspect in a crime and refused to allow inked impressions to be taken by the police, the star's concrete hand impression could probably be compared with a print at the scene of the crime to help determine the star's guilt or innocence.

Latent Prints

Body perspiration and oils may conspire to leave invisible residues on surfaces that if **visualized** (made visible) would constitute a usable impression of the finger skin friction ridges. Visualizing latent prints requires the use of techniques, chemicals, and powders appropriate for the type of surface upon which the prints repose. **Developing prints** on a nonabsorbent surface requires a different approach than developing prints on a softer, more absorbent surface (**Figure 6–6**). The following section provides details.

Developing Prints

Fingerprints discovered on absorbent surfaces can be made visible through the application of powder. The type of powder to use depends on a number of variables.

Powders

Latent prints may be developed (visualized) by applying one of a variety of **fingerprint powders** available from distributors of fingerprinting equipment. These powders differ in

---

OFFICER'S NOTEBOOK

Handling Visible Prints

It is important that visible prints be photographed immediately (**Figure 6–6**). They can often be preserved by bagging the object upon which they were found, by rendering the surface upon which they were found small enough to be bagged, or by being lifted (see the description of the lifting of latent prints later in this chapter). A dry bloody fingerprint on the body of a victim can be lifted using lift tape, avoiding mutilation of the body in an attempt to preserve the print. Any efforts to lift prints should be preceded by taking a set of photographs in case the lifting procedure is not successful.

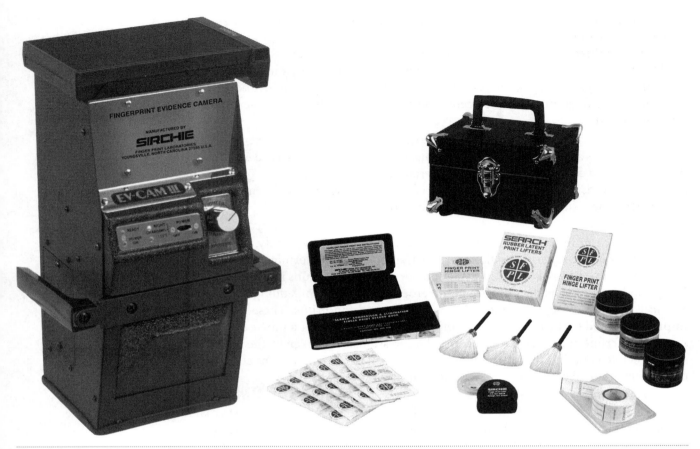

Figure 6–6   Fingerprint camera and fingerprint kit.

Courtesy of SIRCHIE Finger Print Laboratories, Inc.

color, consistency, density, and polarity. Whatever powder is selected may be applied by brush or by magnetic wand or blown onto the latent print. The powder will cling to the fluids that created the fingerprint. Excess powder can be removed by whirling a feather brush above the print (**Figure 6–7**). On backgrounds that are complicated or distracting, fluorescent powders offer advantages over convetional powders. They are applied in the same fashion but ultraviolet light is necessary to view them. Using ultraviolet light requires an orange filter to see the fluorescent prints. The print can be lifted as any other powdered print but must use a specialized camera and lights to be photographed (see **Figures 6–8 through 6–10**).

Chemical Development

The most common chemical used for developing latent prints on porous surfaces such as paper and cloth is **ninhydrin**. Ninhydrin chemically reacts with the amino acids in sweat and renders a purple-blue print. (The color is similar to that of old-fashioned mimeographed handouts.) Ninhydrin (triketohydrindene hydrate) is sprayed on the surface that is being checked for prints. The chemical is commercially available in fuming spray cans and wet wipes for ease of application. The development time, which ranges between 1 and 24 hours, can be hastened by heating the specimen to 100°C. Diaza-fluoren one (DFO) can produce a similar result and is more reliable. It is a fluorescing ninhydrin

Figure 6–7   Fingerprint brush and use of brush to develop the print and remove excess fingerprint powder.

Courtesy of SIRCHIE Finger Print Laboratories, Inc.

analog and is useful on porous surfaces, including paper. DFO is also used to develop weak blood stains but requires ultraviolet light for fluorescing.

Superglue fuming is gaining acceptance in technical circles for the development of fingerprints on nonporous surfaces, such as Formica, metal, or plastic bags. Superglue is cyanoacrylate ester, which is the chemical that develops the print. Cyanoacrylate fumes

---

OFFICER'S NOTEBOOK

Capturing Prints with Powders

Technical expertise is needed for the selection of the appropriate powder for the print, surface composition, and surface color. Light powders are best for dark surfaces, and dark powders are best for light surfaces. The method whereby the print is visualized is referred to as the *development* of the print (heavy hands do not an investigator make). On horizontal surfaces, once the print is developed, the technician can write in the excess powder around the impression his or her name, the date, the crime scene location, and the case number. The information written in the excess powder can be lifted at the same time as the impression, thereby creating a record that is part of the impression. If the surface is horizontal, a *tag board* (a white piece of rigid cardboard) can be propped up against the vertical surface or taped next to it; the same information is recorded upon this board.

Once developed and tagged, the print should be photographed. What may seem like an obsession with photography will make sense to anyone who has lost a print during the lift process or misplaced a print once lifted. Also, photographs of prints found at the crime scene and taken from the suspect can be enlarged and presented to the jury during expert testimony to assist the jury in understanding why the defendant and only the defendant could have left the print.

Figure 6–8 Feather duster.

Courtesy of SIRCHIE Finger Print Laboratories, Inc.

Figure 6–9 Flourescent powder.

Courtesy of SIRCHIE Finger Print Laboratories, Inc.

are created when superglue is heated or placed on a piece of cotton with sodium hydroxide. The item upon which the latent print is impressed must be placed, along with the superglue, in an airtight container and allowed to work (**Figure 6–11**). After five hours, the fumes will begin to adhere to the latent print and produce a hard whitish deposit in the form of the deposited print. A handheld cyanoacrylate wand can be used at the crime scene to develop latent prints in lieu of powder. Superglue is useful on non-porous surfaces and works well on Styrofoam and plastic bags. The developed prints can be dusted with powders and photographed in place.

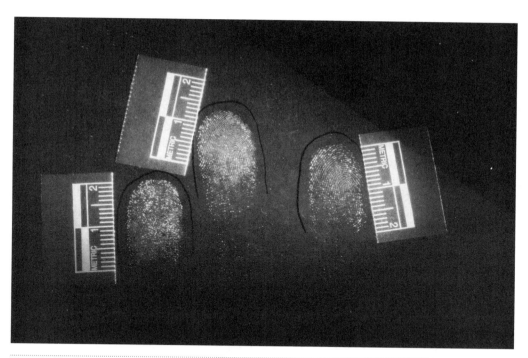

Figure 6–10 Flourescent print.

Courtesy of Maine State Police Crime Laboratory

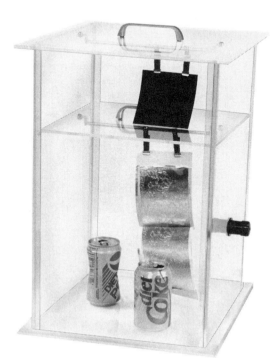

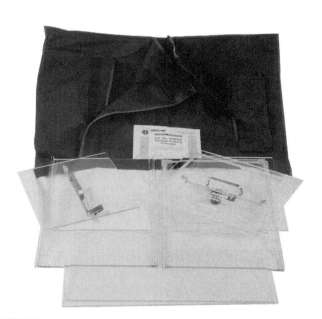

Figure 6–11 Superglue fuming in airtight box (also shown disassembled).

Courtesy of SIRCHIE Finger Print Laboratories, Inc.

Prints on paper can best be developed by exposing the surface to iodine fumes or crystals. A variety of commercial products provide iodine in a form appropriate for fuming, such as in ampoules that are dispensed using a breath-activated fuming gun or, for larger surfaces, an electronically fired fuming gun (**Figure 6–12**). Single sheets of paper can be developed for fingerprints by using dry iodine crystals. By placing the sheet of paper in a plastic bag, then breaking the ampoule that holds the iodine crystals, a series of wave-like motions can run the crystals across the surface of the paper. As the crystals cross the paper, they adhere to the oils and fatty deposits (**Figure 6–13**). Developed prints must be fixed or photographed immediately, because the reaction is temporary and will fade; commercial fixing agents are available. If the investigator is going to employ a series of methods to develop prints, he or she should use iodine crystals before ninhydrin and silver nitrate development.

Silver nitrate can be used to develop prints on paper; it reacts with the chlorides in skin secretions to form silver chloride, which turns gray when exposed to light. These developed prints are very fragile and will turn as black as the background in very short order. Photographs must be taken as soon as the prints are developed. Silver nitrate can be used on paper, cardboard, plastics and unvarnished, light-colored woods. When considering using a series of developers, silver nitrate (**Figures 6–14 and 6–15**) should be used after ninhydrin and iodine.

In processing the underwater crime scene, a process that can be used on wet metal and glass surfaces would be an advantage. One such process is the application of small particle reagent (SPR). SPR is a suspension of fine molybdenum disulfide particles that adhere to the fatty components of skin secretions, forming a gray deposit. The reagent is spayed on the suspect surface, given a few seconds to develop, then gently washed away. Wherever a print resides, it can be developed further by additional applications of SPR

Figure 6–12   Iodine fuming guns and use of breath-activated gun to develop fingerprints.

Courtesy of SIRCHIE Finger Print Laboratories, Inc.

Figure 6–13 Iodine ampoule photo.

Courtesy of SIRCHIE Finger Print Laboratories, Inc.

Figure 6–14 Silver nitrate spray.

Courtesy of SIRCHIE Finger Print Laboratories, Inc.

Figure 6–15 Silver nitrate developed print.

© Mikael Karlsson/Alamy Images

until the print is of photographic quality. Conventional lifting methods can be used to lift and preserve the developed prints.

Another process useful to the underwater investigator is the use of adhesive-side powders to develop fingerprints from the adhesive side of tapes. In homicide crime scenes, duct tape is a one common type of evidence; often, the perpetrator leaves prints on overlapping tape on a victim or balled up discarded tape. During an underwater investigation workshop taught at Chaminade University, the author submerged balled up and folded pieces of duct tape in water for 24 hours. The tape was removed from the fresh water and allowed to dry. Once dry, the tape was untangled and unfolded using an adhesive remover (such as Undo). The tape was left to dry and weighted on the ends to prevent it from curling as it dried. Once dried, an adhesive side powder was mixed with a film developer from Kodak called Photo-Flo, and applied to the adhesive side of the tape. The mixture was applied with a camel hair brush and allowed to sit for about 10 seconds, after which the mixture was washed from the tape with a slow steady stream of water. It was possible to recover fingerprints placed on the tape. It is not necessary to lift the prints when they have been developed; they can be preserved by placing lift tape over the developed prints on the adhesive side of the duct tape (see **Figure 6–16**). TABLE 6–1 provides information about the development methods that are appropriate for surfaces with different characteristics.

Fluorescence and Alternate Light Sources

The earliest use of fluorescence to visualize fingerprints occurred when it was discovered that the blue-green light of the argon-ion laser made sweat fluoresce (like the black-light posters of the 1960s). It was later discovered that the treatment of fingerprints with ninhydrin and then zinc chloride or with the dye rhodamine 6G after superglue fuming caused fluorescence and sensitivity to laser light. Further experimentation focused on the use of alternate light sources as a method of visualizing fingerprints (Saferstein,

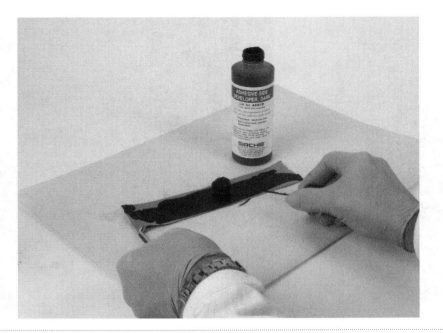

Figure 6–16 Duct tape developed prints.

Courtesy of SIRCHIE Finger Print Laboratories, Inc.

TABLE 6-1   Guide to Surfaces and Development Methods

Surface Characteristics	Development Methods
smooth, non-porous	powders, iodine, SPR, superglue
rough, non-porous	SPR, superglue
paper, cardboard	iodine, ninhydrin, DFO, silver nitrate, powders
vinyl, rubber, leather	iodine, SPR, superglue, powders
unfinished wood	ninhydrin, powders, silver nitrate
wax and waxed surfaces	powder, superglue
adhesive surfaces	adhesive-side powders

Courtesy of SIRCHIE Finger Print Laboratories, Inc.

1995). Today, there are numerous products that use light to visualize fingerprints, and they have decreased the time and effort necessary to find and develop fingerprints.

One word of caution: The use of various powders and chemicals to develop fingerprints can interfere with the gathering of blood-related evidence. All common fingerprint developers affect the tests used to classify bloodstains.

Handling and Preserving Prints

As with plastic and visible prints, once an investigator has developed a latent print, he or she must prepare and preserve it for possible use in the laboratory and courtroom. First, it must be photographed. Next, the investigator should attempt to remove the print from the crime scene, either by preserving the item upon which the print lies or by **lifting** the print. Numerous manufacturers provide specialized adhesive lifters (**Figure 6-17**).

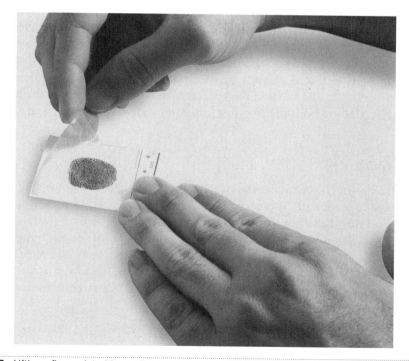

Figure 6-17 Lifting a fingerprint with an adhesive lifter.

Courtesy of SIRCHIE Finger Print Laboratories, Inc.

Figure 6–18 Fingerprint comparator.

Courtesy of SIRCHIE Finger Print Laboratories, Inc.

A lifter is a transparent tape that is placed on the powdered print with the adhesive side down. When the tape is removed, the fingerprint powder is removed with it. The lifter is provided with a black or white card upon which the transparent tape and powdered print can then be placed, adhesive side down. The colored card provides contrast to the colored powder used, helping to visualize the print. Lift tape comes in a variety of sizes and configurations so that the right type can be chosen for the size, number, and location of the prints to be lifted. Lifted fingerprints can be checked against the fingerprints of a suspect by sending both to the crime laboratory for classification and comparison (**Figure 6–18**).

■ DNA Typing

In every creature, DNA carries the coded messages of heredity, governing everything from eye color to toe length. It is present in every one of the trillions of nucleated cells in the human body. Based on the work of Alec Jeffreys at the University of Leicester, a method was developed to extract DNA from a specimen of blood, semen, or other tissue; slice it into fragments; and tag the fragments with a radioactive probe so that they expose X-ray film. The resulting pattern of stripes on the film is a so-called DNA fingerprint, and the process for isolating and reading DNA markers is known as DNA fingerprinting (see Chapter 2).

Restriction Fragment Length Polymorphism Analysis

As researchers uncovered new variations and applications of the original technique, the term *DNA typing* came to be applied to the forensic use of DNA comparisons. The method

CASE IN POINT

DNA Solves an Early Case

Based on his groundbreaking research and his publications, Alec Jeffreys at the University of Leicester was called upon to resolve an immigration case involving a boy who was living in Africa with his father but who had been born in Britain of Ghanaian parents. The boy wanted to return to Britain and live with a woman he claimed was his mother, but the immigration service believed the woman to be his aunt and had denied him British residency.

Jeffreys had to somehow match the genetic fingerprint of the child with that of a father who was not present to supply a DNA sample. The genetic fingerprints of the undisputed children of the woman in question were taken. The intent was to match those fingerprints with those of the mother, thereby establishing the fingerprint of the absent father. When Jeffreys compared the pattern of the boy with those of his ostensible brothers and sisters, the reasonable conclusion was that the man had fathered all of the children (Wambaugh, 1985).

devised by Jeffreys is called **restriction fragment length polymorphism (RFLP) analysis**. The initial research in DNA focused on inherited diseases. Today, forensic research has developed a significant body of literature for use in criminal investigations. Growing out of paternity contests and immigration cases, DNA typing has quickly become the forensic tool of the century.

Inside each of 60 trillion cells in the human body are strands of genetic material called chromosomes. Arranged along the chromosomes, like beads on a thread, are nearly 100,000 genes (the fundamental units of heredity). The genes instruct the body cells to make proteins, which determine everything from hair color to a person's susceptibility to diseases. In the nucleus of all human cells is a ribbon of deoxyribonucleic acid (DNA). The ribbon is a twisted double strand, referred to as a double helix. It is 2 microns wide, but, if uncoiled, it stretches to 6 feet in length. DNA is a **polymer**, that is, a very large molecule made by linking together a series of repeating units. In DNA, the repeating units are nucleotides. A **nucleotide** is composed of a sugar molecule, a phosphorus-containing group, and a nitrogen-containing molecule called a base. There are only four types of bases associated with DNA: adenine (A), thymine (T), guanine (G), and cytosine (C).

The twin strands of the double-helix configuration are connected, like the rungs of a ladder, by pairs of bases, in a process called base pairing. The average human chromosome has DNA containing 100 million **base pairs**. All the human chromosomes taken together contain about 3 billion base pairs. DNA is like a book of instructions. The alphabet used to create the book is simple: A, T, G, and C (i.e., adenine, thymine, guanine, and cytosine). Because of the shapes of the structures involved, a G can link only to a C, and an A can link only to a T; the DNA of the strands is complementary. The order in which these chemicals are arranged defines the role and function of a DNA molecule (Saferstein, 1995). Portions of the DNA molecule contain sequences of A, G, C, and T bases that randomly repeat themselves (tandem repeats). As with any genetic trait, these repeating sequences are inherited from the parents.

The key to understanding DNA typing lies in understanding that among the world's population there are numerous possibilities for the number of times a particular sequence of base letters is repeated on a DNA strand. The possibilities increase with the number of chromosomes, because each chromosome contains different lengths of repeating sequences. In RFLP DNA typing, **restriction enzymes** are used to cut up chromosomes into hundreds of fragments, some containing repeating sequences from the DNA molecule. These fragments (restriction fragment length polymorphisms) will be cut into different lengths, depending on the length of the repeating sequences.

Once the DNA molecules have been cut up by the restriction enzyme, the resulting fragments must be sorted out, which is accomplished through electrophoresis. Electrophoresis separates materials according to their migration rates across a starch or agar gel. When the gel is electrically charged, substances that possess an electrical charge, such as DNA, will migrate across the gel. The longer the DNA fragment, the greater the resistance to the migration. The shorter fragments move farther and faster across the gel. The movement of the various-sized fragments sorts them by length.

When the electrophoresis process is completed, the double-stranded fragments of DNA are chemically treated so that the strands separate from each other. The fragments are then transferred to a nylon membrane much the way lipstick is blotted from the lips. This transfer process is called Southern blotting, named after Edward Southern, its originator (Saferstein, 2007).

At this juncture, the DNA fragments, although transferred to the nylon membrane, cannot be seen. In order to visualize them, the nylon membrane is treated with radioactively treated fragments containing a base sequence complementary to the cut, migrated fragments. Such complementary base sequences are called *probes,* and the process of attaching the probes to the fragments to be identified is called *hybridization.* If one were attempting to identify RFLPs composed of repeats of the sequence TAG, for example, one would use a probe consisting of the complementary sequence ATC. Note that once the double strand has been separated, the single remaining strand can be hybridized.

The next step is to place the nylon sheet against X-ray film and expose it for several days. As the radioactivity of the probes decays, it strikes the unexposed film. When the film is processed, bands appear where the radioactive probes stuck to the fragments on the nylon sheet (**Figure 6–19**). The length of each fragment is determined by running

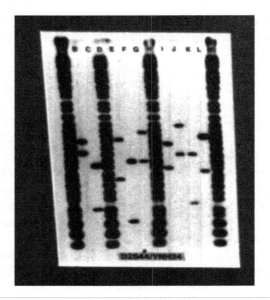

Figure 6–19 DNA radiogram.

known DNA fragment lengths alongside the test specimens and comparing the distances they migrated across the gel plate (Waye and Fourney, 1993). A typical DNA fragment pattern will show two bands (one RFLP from each chromosome). When comparing the DNA fragment patterns of two or more specimens, one looks for a match between the band sets. Individualization cannot be accomplished with a single probe; however, by using additional DNA probes, each of which recognizes different repeating DNA segments, a high degree of discrimination or near individualization can be achieved (Saferstein, 1995).

Polymerase Chain Reaction Analysis

Many forensic specimens contain only limited amounts of DNA, making them unsuitable for RFLP analysis. **Polymerase chain reaction (PCR)** procedures replicate limited quantities of DNA and generate reliable copies of what was previously subanalytic or degraded DNA. Each cycle can double the quantity of DNA (Fierro, 1993). PCR has enabled laboratories to develop DNA profiles from extremely small samples of biological evidence. The PCR technique replicates exact copies of DNA contained in a biological evidence sample without affecting the original, much like a copy machine. RFLP analysis requires a biological sample about the size of a quarter, but PCR can be used to reproduce millions of copies of the DNA contained in a few skin cells.

Because PCR analysis requires only a minute quantity of DNA, it can enable a laboratory to analyze highly degraded evidence for DNA. On the other hand, because the sensitive PCR technique replicates any and all of the DNA contained in an evidence sample, greater attention to contamination issues is necessary when identifying, collecting, and preserving DNA evidence. These factors may be particularly important in the evaluation of unsolved cases in which evidence might have been improperly collected or stored.

Advances in DNA Analysis

When properly documented, collected, and stored, biological evidence can be analyzed to produce a reliable DNA profile years, even decades, after it is collected. Just as evidence collected from a crime that occurred yesterday can be analyzed for DNA, so too evidence from an old rape kit, bloody shirt, or stained bedclothes may contain a valuable DNA profile. Newer DNA analysis techniques enable laboratories to develop profiles from biological evidence invisible to the naked eye, such as skin cells left on ligatures or weapons. These new analysis techniques, in combination with an evolving database system known as the **Combined DNA Index System (CODIS)**, make a powerful argument for reevaluating unsolved crimes to look for potential DNA evidence.

Unsolved cases should be evaluated by investigating both traditional and nontraditional sources of DNA. Valuable DNA evidence might be available that previously went undetected in the original investigation. If biological evidence is available for testing or retesting in unsolved case investigations, it is important that law enforcement and the crime laboratory work together to review evidence. Logistical issues regarding access to and the cost of DNA analysis will be a factor, as well as issues related to the discriminating power of each technology and how it might affect the outcome of the results. Laboratory personnel can provide a valuable perspective on which evidence might yield valuable and probative DNA results. Finally, if previously tested biological evidence produced a DNA profile but excluded the original suspect, revisiting those exclusion cases for the purpose of comparing them with DNA databases might prove to be very valuable to solving old cases.

Short Tandem Repeat Analysis

Short tandem repeat (STR) analysis evaluates specific regions (loci) that are found on nuclear DNA. The variable (polymorphic) nature of the STR regions that are analyzed for forensic testing intensifies the discrimination between one DNA profile and another, such that the likelihood that any two individuals (except identical twins) will have the same 13-loci DNA profile can be as high as 1 in 1 billion or greater. The FBI has chosen 13 specific STR loci to serve as the standard for CODIS. The purpose of establishing a core set of STR loci is to ensure that all forensic laboratories can establish uniform DNA databases and, more important, share valuable forensic information.

Mitochondrial DNA Analysis

Mitochondrial DNA (mtDNA) analysis allows forensic laboratories to develop DNA profiles from evidence that may not be suitable for RFLP or STR analysis. Whereas RFLP and PCR techniques analyze DNA extracted from the nucleus of a cell, mtDNA technology analyzes DNA found in the mitochondrion. Old remains and evidence lacking nucleated cells—such as hair shafts, bones, and teeth—that are not amenable to STR and RFLP testing may yield results if mtDNA analysis is performed.

Y-Chromosome Analysis

Several genetic markers that have been identified on the Y chromosome can be used in forensic applications. Y-chromosome markers target only the male fraction of a biological sample. Therefore, this technique can be very valuable if the laboratory detects complex mixtures (multiple male contributors) within a biological evidence sample. Because the Y chromosome is transmitted directly from a father to all of his sons, it can also be used to trace family relationships among males. Advancements in Y-chromosome testing may eventually eliminate the need for laboratories to extract and separate semen and vaginal cells (e.g., from a vaginal swab of a rape kit) prior to analysis.

Combined DNA Index System

The Combined DNA Index System (CODIS) is a computer network that connects forensic DNA laboratories at the local, state, and national levels. Every state in the nation has a statutory provision for the establishment of a DNA database that allows for the collection of DNA profiles from offenders convicted of particular crimes. CODIS software enables state, local, and national law enforcement crime laboratories to compare DNA profiles electronically, thereby linking serial crimes and identifying suspects by matching DNA profiles from crime scenes with profiles from convicted offenders.

DNA database systems that use CODIS contain two main criminal indices (the convicted-offender index and the forensic index) and a missing-persons index. The convicted-offender index contains DNA profiles of individuals convicted of specific crimes, ranging from certain misdemeanors to sexual assault and murder. Each state has different qualifying offenses for which persons convicted of the offense must submit a biological sample for inclusion in the DNA database. The forensic index contains DNA profiles obtained from crime scene evidence, such as semen, saliva, or blood.

When a DNA profile is developed from crime scene evidence and entered into the forensic (crime scene) index of CODIS, the database software searches thousands of DNA profiles of individuals convicted of offenses such as rape and murder. Similar to the Automated Fingerprint Identification System (AFIS), CODIS can aid investigations by efficiently comparing a DNA profile generated from biological evidence left at a crime scene against convicted offender DNA profiles and forensic evidence from other cases contained in CODIS.

CODIS can also aid investigations by searching the missing persons index, which consists of the unidentified-persons index and the reference index. The unidentified-persons index contains DNA profiles from recovered remains, such as bone, teeth, or hair. The reference index contains DNA profiles from related individuals of missing persons so that they can be periodically compared to the unidentified-persons index.

A match made between profiles in the forensic index can link crime scenes to each other, possibly identifying serial offenders. Based on these forensic matches, police in multiple jurisdictions or states can coordinate their respective investigations and share their leads. Matches made between the forensic and convicted-offender indices can provide investigators with the identity of a suspect or suspects. It is important to note an offender hit typically is used as probable cause to obtain a new DNA sample from that suspect so the match can be confirmed by the crime laboratory before an arrest is made.

Design of CODIS.   CODIS is implemented as a distributed database with three hierarchical levels (or tiers): local, state, and national. All three levels contain forensic and convicted-offender indices and a population file (used to generate statistics). The hierarchical design provides state and local laboratories with the flexibility to configure CODIS to meet their specific legislative and technical needs.

- **Local DNA Index System (LDIS):** Typically, the LDIS installed at crime laboratories is operated by police departments or sheriffs' offices. DNA profiles originated at the local level can be transmitted to the state and national levels.
- **State DNA Index System (SDIS):** Each state has a designated laboratory that operates the SDIS, which allows local laboratories within that state to compare DNA profiles. SDIS also is the communication path between the local and national tiers.
- **National DNA Index System (NDIS):** The NDIS is the highest level of the CODIS hierarchy and enables qualified state laboratories that are actively participating in CODIS to compare DNA profiles. NDIS is maintained by the FBI under the authority of the DNA Identification Act of 1994.

Limitations of Using CODIS.   The more data contained in the forensic and offender indices of CODIS, the more powerful a tool it becomes for law enforcement, especially in its application to unsolved case investigation. However, because many jurisdictions are in the process of developing and populating their DNA databases, there are convicted-offender and forensic casework backlogs that continue to grow. As states recognize the crime-solving potential of DNA databases, they continue to expand the scope of their convicted-offender legislation, which increases the number of samples to be collected and analyzed by the DNA laboratory. As a result, more than 1 million uncollected convicted-offender DNA profiles are "owed" to the system.

Handling DNA Evidence

Because of the O.J. Simpson trial, the country discovered the effects of mishandling blood evidence. We watched on national television as a forensic technician, trained and experienced in handling blood evidence, in fact handled and packaged prospective DNA evidence with his bare hands. The defense was quick to raise issues of contamination and violation of a scientific protocol. The cumulative impact of questionable investigative conduct loomed over the jury during its deliberations. The guidelines in the Officer's Notebook are provided to avoid mishandling DNA-bearing evidence.

> **OFFICER'S NOTEBOOK**
>
> **Guidelines for Handling DNA-Bearing Evidence**
> - Wear gloves. Change them between handling each item of evidence.
> - Use disposable instruments or clean the instruments thoroughly before and after handling each evidence sample.
> - Avoid touching the area where you believe DNA may exist.
> - Avoid touching your face, nose, and mouth when examining and packaging evidence.
> - Put dry evidence into new paper bags or envelopes; do not use plastic bags.
> - Do not use staples.
> - Handle all evidence as though a jury were watching.
> - Photograph or videograph the handling and packaging process.

Sample Contamination

Any crime scene is unlikely to meet the hygienic standards characteristic of research and medical laboratories. Defendants tend to believe that anything less than absolute purity in body samples raises questions as to the reliability of the DNA typing process (**TABLE 6–2**). The word *contamination* raises the specter of something unnatural or careless happening to the samples before they reach the laboratory. It is imperative for an expert in DNA analysis who is called as a witness to address the nature of the environment in which DNA samples were deposited and to explain that contamination and age are an integral part of the nonsterile real world. Possible questions include the following:

- The question is not one of contamination but rather of how much contamination, is it not?
- Can the contaminants be removed from the sample without altering the sample?
- Were the contaminants removed before the typing protocol began?
- Could you describe the nature of the contaminants present and the method of removal?
- How was the sample contaminated?

TABLE 6–2   DNA Defenses and Responsible Parties

Defense	Responsible Party
Contaminated crime scene	The nature of the crime
Improper labeling	Investigator (technician)
Improper handling	Investigator (technician)
Improper packaging	Investigator (technician)
Broken chain of custody	Investigator (technician, laboratory)
Contaminated lab sample	Laboratory
Improper lab protocol	Laboratory
Acceptabillity of protocol	Laboratory witness
Acceptabillity of expert	Laboratory witness

CASE IN POINT

The Innocence Project

The Innocence Project at the Benjamin N. Cardozo School of Law, created by Barry C. Scheck and Peter J. Neufeld in 1992, is a nonprofit legal clinic. The Project only handles cases in which postconviction DNA testing of evidence can yield conclusive proof of innocence. Because it is a clinic, students handle the casework while being supervised by a team of attorneys and clinic staff.

Most of the clients are poor, forgotten, and have used up all of their legal avenues for relief. The hope they all have is that biological evidence from their cases still exists and can be subjected to DNA testing. All Innocence Project clients go through an extensive screening process to determine whether DNA testing of evidence could prove their claims of innocence. Thousands currently await evaluation of their cases.

As a forerunner in the field of wrongful convictions, the Innocence Project has grown to become much more than the court of last resort for inmates who have exhausted their appeals and their means. The Project is helping to organize the Innocence Network, a group of law schools, journalism schools, and public defender offices across the country that assists inmates trying to prove their innocence whether or not the cases involve biological evidence that can be subjected to DNA testing. Project managers consult with legislators and law enforcement officials on the state, local, and federal level, conduct research and training, produce scholarship, and propose a wide range of remedies to prevent wrongful convictions while continuing work to free innocent inmates through the use of postconviction DNA testing (Innocence Project, 2003).

- Where did the contamination occur?
- Was the contamination a result of laboratory handling?
- Was the contamination a result of police handling?
- Was there enough of the sample to run more than one test?
- Were additional tests run?
- Were the results the same?
- Were known samples that were contaminated with similar contaminants cleaned and typed?
- Were the results consistent with the results for uncontaminated samples?

Contamination is only a problem if left to the defendant to use as an issue with which to obfuscate or confuse. The jury should be comfortable with the idea that all forensic DNA samples are contaminated and that nothing unique or unusual happened to the samples in question.

■ Composite Identifications

Often the only way to identify a suspect is to translate a verbal description into something police and the media can use easily (**Figure 6–20**). Although all-points bulletins historically have provided a verbal description of the suspect sought, a more elaborate method of identification is available through the services of artists, computers, and kits with interchangeable facial features.

A **sketch artist**, given a description, can create a picture that, through continual refinement based on witness input, begins to bear a strong resemblance to the suspect. Most agencies do not have the financial resources to employ a person with the artistic skills necessary to provide an artist's rendition, and so a number of manufacturers have

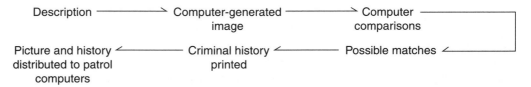

Figure 6–20 Flowchart showing the process of generating a suspect's composite picture and criminal history for use by patrol officers.

produced kits that offer predrawn facial features from which to choose. By selecting the one feature that best meets the witness's verbal description, a nonartist can begin to construct a **composite picture**.

Not surprisingly, there are software programs that render composite drawings by means of mouse commands and pull-down menus. These programs pose queries to which the witness provides a response. Because the questions are not suggestive of an answer, the final product tends to be more objective than an artist's sketch. A computer program such as Compusketch provides more than 100,000 selections from which the witness can choose, and the choices can be superimposed to the satisfaction of the witness. The final product is a laser-printed computer rendition of the facial features of the suspect ready to be distributed. Often such images are photo quality.

There are obvious advantages to distributing sketches rather than verbal descriptions to a patrol force. Most agencies require that a photograph and the fingerprints of every arrested adult suspect be taken and stored. The mug shots make up an agency's **rogues' gallery**, a ready supply of photographs for witnesses to leaf through in the attempt to

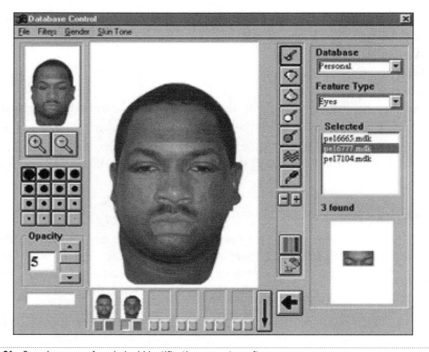

Figure 6–21 Sample screen of a criminal identification computer software program.

Courtesy of SIRCHIE Finger Print Laboratories, Inc.

identify a perpetrator. The gallery is generally divided into either offense categories or categories based on modus operandi (the method employed by the perpetrator). The gallery may be further divided into patrol areas, precincts, or neighborhoods. In addition to a photo, identification information is also recorded, such as scars, hair color, height, weight, tattoos, and age. Computer programs can retrieve photos that meet a set of typewritten descriptors or are similar to a composite drawing (**Figure 6–21**). When a typewritten description or a composite drawing is entered into the computer, a search is made of the computer's database, and mug shot matches are identified. One of the problems associated with looking at mug shots is the viewer burnout that is bound to occur. Restricting the number of mug shots a witness has to peruse avoids or at least postpones viewer overload.

■ Lineups

In virtually every criminal trial, there must be an identification of the suspect. The prosecution has a responsibility to identify the defendant as the person who perpetrated the offense or was arrested for the offense charged. Often, a prior identification has taken place at the hands of a witness or victim. That pretrial identification generally occurs in one of two ways: a review of the rogues' gallery or a viewing of a police lineup. The controlling case pertaining to police pretrial lineups is *United States v. Wade* (1967). It should be noted that the requirement from *Wade* that counsel be present applies to **postindictment lineups,** not to preindictment lineups (lineups conducted before an indictment is handed down).

Lineups traditionally have been used by police to identify suspects. Their format is generally the same, although the number of participants varies (the range is from 4 to 10). The participants are selected on the basis of their similarity to the suspect in gender, age, race, build, coloring, and so on. The participants are allowed to select the position in which they stand. Each position is designated by a number, and the background is calibrated to allow witnesses to better assess height and weight. The idea behind requiring legal representation at lineups is that the presence of counsel averts prejudice in the selection and display of the participants.

CASE IN POINT

United States v. Wade, 1967
Officials were conducting an investigation of the robbery of a federally insured bank in which two men with pieces of tape affixed to their faces stuffed the bank's money into a pillowcase and fled. A federal indictment was returned prior to the arrest of Wade. Fifteen days later, without notice to his counsel, Wade was placed in a lineup to be viewed by bank personnel. Wade was identified as the robber. At trial, witnesses who had made the lineup identification testified that they had seen Wade earlier in the custody of officials. At trial, the witnesses identified Wade and reconfirmed their lineup identification. Wade was convicted of robbery.

The U.S. Supreme Court concluded that there was grave potential for prejudice, intentional or not, in the pretrial lineup. The Court stated that counsel itself can often avert prejudice and ensure a meaningful confrontation at trial. For Wade, the postindictment lineup was a critical stage of the prosecution and therefore one at which he was entitled to counsel. The Court said that both Wade and his counsel should have been notified of the impending lineup, and counsel's presence should have been a prerequisite for conducting a lineup, absent an intelligent waiver.

OFFICER'S NOTEBOOK

Crucial Factors in Lineup Identification

The following questions are relevant to both preindictment and postindictment lineups.

- Did the witness have the opportunity to get a good look at the suspect at the time of the offense? Various ingredients come together to make an adequate opportunity: time viewed, weather conditions, visibility, lighting, and the visual acumen of the viewer.
- How much attention was the witness paying to what was happening and to what he or she was seeing at the time of the offense?
- How certain is the witness that the suspect is the same person perceived at the crime scene?
- How much time has passed from the commission of the crime to the identification?
- How consistent is the identification with the original report provided to the police?
- Was there anything about the lineup that pointed to the suspect as the person to choose?

The last issue is the one of most concern to the courts. If there was something that suggested one participant over another—position, clothing, or whatever—any further inquiry into the quality of the lineup would be preempted, because suggestibility is fatal to a lineup whenever it may occur.

Some investigators believe that the presence of legal counsel at postindictment lineups serves as an obstacle to the successful completion of the investigation. The prudent investigator will welcome the input of defense counsel and recognize that such input will assist in conducting a constitutionally permissible lineup. It is better to find out during the lineup what objections, if any, the defendant's lawyer might raise than to wait until trial and discover that an impermissible lineup was conducted.

■ Summary

In every instance in which fingerprints are left at a crime scene, it becomes a game of hide and seek to ferret out where they may have been left. Because most fingerprints are invisible, it becomes important to preserve the entire scene for those with the expertise in locating, developing, photographing, and lifting such prints. It is important to remember that no matter how expert the processing, fingerprints will be destroyed during development and lifting; that is why photographing fingerprints is part of the protocol. Additionally, photographs can be enlarged for trial exhibits. At the time of trial it is helpful for the jury to see the development and lifting process. One of the best courtroom demonstration aids for fingerprinting is the overhead projector. A fingerprint can be left on the glass of the projector, and when the projector is turned on, the jury can watch the development and lifting process, enlarged, on screen, and with a live narrative.

One of the skills every investigator must have is the ability to manage people at a crime scene. It might be said that a crime scene is processed only as well as the investigator in charge can manage people. The next chapter introduces us to the concept of crime scene management and the ways in which those management skills might be employed.

■ Key Terms

accidental: Any fingerprint pattern that is not covered by one of the categories or is a combination of two patterns

arches: The least common fingerprint patterns; they are either plain or tented

base pair: Pair of two of the four types of bases (A, T, G, and C) in DNA; pairing of bases helps form the double-helix configuration of DNA

biometric identification: Identifying people by biological characteristics

Combined DNA Index System (CODIS): Database system that can aid investigations by efficiently comparing a DNA profile generated from biological evidence left at a crime scene against convicted offender DNA profiles and forensic evidence from other cases contained in the database

composite picture: Picture drawn of a suspect by selecting the one feature that best meets the witness's verbal description and continuing refinement based on witness input

core: In fingerprints, the centermost point of the loop at the apex of the innermost ridge of the loop; this shape is always found in a loop pattern

delta: A two-sided triangular shape found to one side of a loop that resembles a river delta; this shape is always found in a loop pattern

developing prints: Making fingerprints visible by applying a powder or chemical

digital fingerprinting: Digital recording of a fingerprint made by having an individual place a finger on an optical scanner, which creates a digitized image of the person's fingerprint

fingerprint individuality: The shape, location, and number of minutiae that individualize a fingerprint

fingerprint powders: Powders used to develop fingerprints by clinging to the fluids that created the fingerprints

fingerprints: Mirror images of the friction ridge skin of the palm, fingers, and thumb

friction ridges: Ridges on fingers that are the identifiable characteristics of fingerprints

immutable: Unchangeable; refers to the retention of fingerprint characteristics throughout a person's life

iris code: Set of spatially limited waves that is produced by wavelet analysis of the iris

latent prints: Prints deposited onto a surface that are invisible to the naked eye

lifting: Removing a fingerprint from a crime scene by sticking a print developed with powder to transparent tape and then placing the tape (adhesive side down) on a black or white card

loops: Fingerprint pattern that has one or more ridges that enter from one side of the print, recurve, and exit from the same side, as well as a core and a delta

minutiae: Points where a finger friction ridge ends or splits in two; these are highly individualized

mitochondrial DNA (mtDNA) analysis: Analysis of DNA found in the mitochondrion, used to develop DNA profiles from evidence that may not be suitable for RFLP or STR analysis, such as hair, bones, and teeth

ninhydrin: The most common chemical used for developing latent prints on porous surfaces; it reacts chemically with the amino acids in sweat and renders a purple-blue print

nucleotide: The repeating unit of DNA

plastic impression: Fingerprints left on soft materials such as soap, wet cement, or dust that can be used for fingerprint comparisons

polymer: A very large molecule made by linking together a series of repeating units

polymerase chain reaction (PCR): Technique used to replicate exact copies of DNA contained in a biological evidence sample without affecting the original material

postindictment lineup: Lineup conducted after an indictment is handed down, during which counsel must be present

restriction enzymes: Substances used to cut up chromosomes into hundreds of fragments

restriction fragment length polymorphism (RFLP) analysis: Analysis of the banding pattern formed by cutting DNA with restriction enzymes, separating the fragments, exposing the fragments to DNA probes, and looking at the pattern of radioactive bands that results from the radioactive probe binding to the DNA fragments; several probes are used to create a profile for an individual

rogues' gallery: A ready supply of photographs for witnesses to leaf through in the attempt to identify a perpetrator

short tandem repeat (STR) analysis: A forensic analysis that evaluates specific regions (loci) that are found on nuclear DNA

sketch artist: Person who can create a picture that, through continual refinement based on witness input, begins to bear a strong resemblance to a suspect

superglue fuming: Technique used for the development of fingerprints on nonporous surfaces

visualize: To make visible

whorl: Fingerprint pattern having a minimum of two deltas; this pattern is classified into four groupings: (1) plain whorl, (2) central pocket loop whorl, (3) double loop whorl, and (4) accidental whorl

■ Review Questions

1. What is it about fingerprints that suggests individuality?
2. Why is it incorrect to refer to visible fingerprints at a crime scene as latent prints?
3. What is it that leaves fingerprints?
4. What are fingerprint patterns, and of what value are they to the criminal investigator?
5. How is a latent print visualized, developed, and lifted?
6. Why is it important to photograph a fingerprint that the investigator plans to lift anyway?
7. What is superglue fuming?
8. For what is ninhydrin spray used?
9. How would you develop fingerprints on the sticky side of duct tape?
10. What is small particle reagent used for?
11. What are iodine crystals used for?
12. What chemical is used to test for blood that luminesces under ultraviolet light?
13. What is a composite picture, and in what ways might an investigator obtain one?
14. What is a suggestive lineup?
15. What is the main legal difference between a preindictment and a postindictment lineup?
16. What is a rogues' gallery, what is in it, and how is it created?
17. Describe different ways of analyzing DNA evidence.
18. What is CODIS? Describe the three-tiered identification system.

19. Discuss crime scene DNA contamination.

20. What is STR?

21. How does mitochondrial DNA differ from nuclear DNA?

22. List the considerations in the handling and packaging of items that may bear DNA evidence.

23. Describe the Innocence Project. What is its objective?

■ Bibliography

Fierro, M.L. (1993). Identification of human remains. In W.U. Spitz (Ed.), *Medicolegal investigation of death.* Springfield, IL: Charles C Thomas.

Innocence Project (2003). http://www.innocenceproject.org.

Lerner, E. (2000). Biometric identification. *Industrial Physicist* 6(1), 18–21.

Saferstein, R. (2007). *Criminalistics: An introduction to forensic science* (9th ed.). Englewood Cliffs, NJ: Prentice Hall.

Wambaugh, J. (1985). *The blooding.* New York: Bantam.

Waye, J., & Fourney M. (1993). Forensic DNA typing of highly polymorphic VNTR loci. In R. Saferstein (Ed.), *Forensic science handbook* (Vol. 3, pp. 298–327). Englewood Cliffs, NJ: Prentice Hall.

■ Key Legal Case

United States v. Wade, 388 U.S. 218 (1967).

Managing Criminal Investigations and Cultivating Sources of Information

CHAPTER

7

▶ ▶ STUDENT LEARNING OUTCOMES

Upon completion of this chapter students will develop an understanding of:

- How crime scenes can be managed
- An incident command system
- A national incident management system
- How surveillance is conducted
- How serial homicides can be profiled
- The role of informants in the investigative process

■ Managing the Criminal Investigation

Traditionally, the detective who was on duty and took the call for investigative assistance conducted the investigation. Whoever was present became the owner of the new case. In departments where specialists investigated crimes, each detective would be in the rotation and responsible chronologically for the next case. For example, all burglary detectives would remain in the rotation, adding new cases as they were received. Each detective's caseload continued to increase and was lightened only when the detective cleared a case or determined the case could not be solved with the available evidence and information.

The major source of motivation for investigating cases in this system was the probability of clearing the case quickly and thus remove it from one's caseload. Administrators evaluated the success of various investigators by the rate at which they cleared cases. It should not be surprising that those cases with the greatest potential for arrest were the ones upon which investigators focused their time and energy. A new concept in criminal investigation accomplishes the same thing. **Managing criminal investigations** (MCI) is designed to determine which crimes are most solvable and to use limited investigative resources to solve them. It does not rely upon traditional notions of ease of solvability as the primary indicators, however.

All successful investigations can be evaluated based on one of five possible outcomes:

1. Arrest
2. Cleared offense

3. Accepted for prosecution

4. Plea-bargained

5. Conviction

All of these outcomes further depend on the management of the investigation and the allocation of available resources.

MCI begins with recognizing that the way detectives—and patrol officers—are utilized at crime scenes is a waste of resources and manpower. Much of what is done during a preliminary investigation lays the foundation for a successful investigation. However, much of what needs to be done initially at a crime scene does not require the attention of a detective and could easily be accomplished by the first-responding patrol officer or officers.

Preliminary Investigation

In managing crime scenes, the **preliminary investigation** is the most important aspect of any investigation. The preliminary investigation is the police agency's first response to a report that a crime has been committed. As in every investigation, the primary objectives include the following:

- Determine who committed the crime, while making sure not to contaminate, lose, or destroy evidence.
- Ensure that all evidence discovered is handled so as to foster admissibility at the time of trial.
- Apprehend the perpetrator(s).
- Obtain a conviction.

In MCI, the first-responding officer collects evidence that will help identify the individual responsible for the crime and that will lead to the subsequent arrest and conviction of that person, thus relieving the investigative team of the responsibility of gathering relevant crime scene evidence.

Generally, first-responding officers render assistance to victims, take names, secure the crime scene, and restrain witnesses and suspects. First-responding officers record their perceptions and conduct interviews, which can be vital to the success of the investigation. Investigators then arrive on the scene, debrief the first-responding personnel, and release

---

OFFICER'S NOTEBOOK

Crucial Elements of the Preliminary Investigation

The framework of the preliminary investigation is based on several major areas that the first-responding officer must address. The officer must:

- Decide if an offense has actually occurred and, if so, which offense.
- Determine if the lapse of time between the crime's occurrence and the notification of police was normal.
- Note any discrepancies in witness or victim statements.
- Determine if the facts provided by the victim and witnesses are supported by the physical facts.
- Identify the victim and the time and place the crime took place.
- Identify any solvability factors that could lead to the successful conclusion of the investigation.

them to return to their duties. Investigators launch a very structured examination of the premises and either supervise the recovery and processing of evidence or recover and process it themselves. They determine the nature of the crime, attempt to identify the victim, and make an informal assessment of the factors that will be helpful in solving the crime. Detectives devote substantial time and effort to processing the crime scene time that could be better used in pursuing the investigatory steps that might lead to clearing the crime. Thus, MCI is designed to address these initial activities. Patrol personnel could conduct this preliminary investigation as readily as investigators. Giving the patrol officers responsibility for the preliminary investigation frees investigators to investigate. Subsumed within this proposition is the idea that patrol personnel receive proper training in the recognition, discovery, recovery, and preservation of all evidence that may be obtained at a crime scene.

Solvability Factors

As stated in earlier chapters, not all crimes can be solved. The sheer number of crimes is such that most metropolitan police agencies cannot field sufficient personnel to conduct the necessary investigations. In allocating investigatory personnel, more can be accomplished with less if patrol staff do preliminary investigations and gather input regarding solvability. Solvability input is used to determine where to best employ investigators and investigative resources.

The Rochester, New York, Police Department has identified 12 **solvability factors:**

1. Were there any eyewitnesses to the crime?
2. Has the suspect been identified by name?
3. Has the location of the suspect been determined?
4. Has a description of the suspect been obtained?
5. Has the suspect been identified?
6. Did the property taken have recognizable marks, numbers, or identifiable characteristics?
7. Has a modus operandi (MO) been discovered and identified?
8. Is there significant physical evidence left at the crime scene?
   a. Blood
   b. Body fluids
9. Was a vehicle involved?
   a. Was a description obtained?
   b. Was a license number obtained?
10. Did the search of the crime scene disclose anything that could be connected to an identifiable suspect?
11. Will additional investigation or media assistance increase the probability of solving the crime?
12. Is it possible that someone other than the suspect committed the crime?

During the preliminary investigation, the officer responsible processes the crime scene while keeping in mind these 12 solvability factors; crimes are seldom solved unless one or more of these factors exists. Their existence is of little consequence, however, if the preliminary investigator is not prepared to discover them.

The discovery of solvability factors determines whether or not a **follow-up investigation** is conducted and what direction that follow-up investigation will take. The absence of solvability factors at the time of the preliminary investigation may be overcome at a later date with the acquisition of information that was not available or not discovered at the time of the preliminary investigation. In other words, a closed case can be reopened.

The key to success in a preliminary investigation is the same as in any investigation: documentation. The decision to halt or continue the investigation is based on the documentation provided by the preliminary investigator. An incomplete preliminary is of no value to the managers of the investigation in determining what resources to deploy. It is imperative that preliminary investigators have not only the necessary investigative skills to ferret out solvability factors but also the discipline to document their findings correctly. It is often easier to find personnel who can identify the findings of an investigation than it is to find personnel who can identify and document investigative findings. It deserves repeating that in the world of criminal trials, if it is not documented, it does not exist. If evidence is not documented, it cannot be included in unchallenged courtroom testimony; thus, it makes little sense to conduct an investigation whose outcome will not be admissible at the time of trial.

Upon completion of the preliminary investigation, the case is submitted along with a recommendation for either further action or that no further action be taken. The recommendation has value if the following are met:

- All potential witnesses have been interviewed or accounted for.
- A thorough crime scene search has been conducted.
- All solvability factors present have been identified.
- Every reasonable investigative effort has been made.
- Documentation reflects the investigative effort and the basis for the discovered solvability factors.

Crime-Scene Processing During the Preliminary Investigation

Students often ask how much evidence should be collected at a crime scene. The usual response is to err on the part of collecting too much as opposed to too little, but not all investigations warrant a full crime-scene processing. Violent crimes should and will receive more attention than nonviolent crimes solely because of limited manpower and resources. What follows is a set of guidelines for managers of criminal investigations to use in determining how much evidence to collect at a given crime scene and how much effort should be applied in collecting that evidence.

- If a suspect is arrested at or near the scene, any physical evidence from the crime scene will be useful in the prosecution.
- If a suspect has been identified but not arrested, any physical evidence can be used to corroborate the identification.
- If there are sufficient leads to make it possible that the suspect will be identified, any physical evidence should be collected to corroborate any future identification.
- If there are peculiar circumstances to the crime, it may indicate a pattern. Physical evidence may be useful in corroborating the identification of a suspect traced through investigation of other crimes in the series.

Conviction Is the Objective

As mentioned in earlier chapters, the relationship between police and prosecutors is not always cordial. It is of little value to place blame for this historic development other than to recognize that it exists and must be overcome for investigations to have meaning. MCI requires investigating patrol officers to communicate with criminal investigators, who communicate with their supervisors, who manage investigations, who in turn communicate with the prosecutor's office. If MCI is to prove effective, there must be a change in investigatory procedure as described, but there also must be a change in how cases are prepared for trial. Prosecutors must be involved in those cases that have sufficient solvability factors to warrant additional investigation. That prosecutorial input can direct and assess the handling of the investigation, witnesses, and evidence. With early intervention by the prosecutor's office, there should be no surprises in initiating criminal proceedings, preparing the case for trial, or negotiating a plea agreement. In Costa Rica, prosecutors attend any felony crime scene as it is being processed. Costa Rican prosecutors are more intimately involved in their cases than their counterparts in the United States. Having a prosecutor present as a legal resource helps prevent constitutional violations that may jeopardize the introduction of evidence or statements. Additionally, prosecutors have a working relationship with criminal investigators as well as a first-person understanding of the crime, the crime scene, the evidence, and the people involved. Prosecutors may also provide legal counsel that reduces the incidence of errors that jeopardize the case.

With oversight from and communication with the prosecutor's office, it should be routine to evaluate the case periodically to assess progress toward obtaining evidence, witness statements, suspect identification, and, ultimately, conviction.

Managing Criminal Investigations

There are a number of potential benefits associated with MCI:

1. *An increase in arrests and in case clearance.* With investigators focusing their attention on follow-up investigations of cases with sufficient information to support a successful outcome and not wasting time on unsolvable cases, both arrests and clearances should increase.

2. *A readily available cohort from which to draw future detectives.* Preliminary investigators will have demonstrated the temperament, patience, and discipline required of criminal investigators and will have served in a proving ground for promotion into those positions.

3. *Reallocation of personnel and resources.* Investigators will be able to focus on solvable cases.

Incident Command System

The **incident command system (ICS)** is a management tool designed to enable effective domestic incident management by integrating a combination of facilities, equipment, personnel, procedures, and communications within a common organizational structure. An incident command system is used to organize both near-term and long-term field-level operations for a broad spectrum of emergencies, from small to complex incidents. It is normally structured to facilitate activities in five major functional areas:

- Command
- Operations

- Planning
- Logistics
- Finance
- Administration (Department of Homeland Security, 2004)

Acts of biological, chemical, radiological, and nuclear terrorism represent particular challenges for the traditional ICS structure. Events that are geographically dispersed will require extraordinary coordination among federal, state, local, and nongovernmental organizations. The initial response to most domestic incidents is typically handled by local 911 dispatch centers and emergency responders within a single jurisdiction. In other instances, incidents that begin with a single response within a single jurisdiction may expand rapidly to multidiscipline, multijurisdictional incidents requiring significant additional resources and operational support. In such cases, the ICS provides a flexible core mechanism for coordinated and collaborative incident management. When a single incident covers a large geographical area, multiple local ICS organizations may be required. Effective cross-jurisdictional coordination is vital.

National Incident Management System

On February 28, 2003, President Bush issued Homeland Security Presidential Directive (HSPD)-5, which directed the Secretary of Homeland Security to develop and administer a **National Incident Management System (NIMS)**. According to HSPD-5, this system would provide a consistent nationwide approach for federal, state, and local governments to work effectively and efficiently together to prepare for, respond to, and recover from domestic incidents, regardless of cause, size, or complexity. To provide for interoperability and compatibility among federal, state, and local capabilities, the NIMS would include a core set of concepts, principles, terminology, and technologies covering the incident command system; multiagency coordination systems; unified command; training; identification and management of resources (including systems for classifying types of resources); qualifications and certification; and the collection, tracking, and reporting of incident information and incident resources (Department of Homeland Security, 2004).

The NIMS uses a systems approach to integrate the best of existing processes and methods into a unified national framework for incident management. This framework forms the basis for interoperability and compatibility that will, in turn, enable a diverse set of public and private organizations to conduct well-integrated and effective incident management operations. The core set of concepts and principles includes:

- Utilizing an incident command system for command and management
- Preparedness, including cross-agency training and agreements
- Resource management, which involves vulnerability studies and resource inventories
- Communications and information management, including using open lines and computers dedicated to the response to an incident
- Supporting technologies, including voice and data communication systems, information management systems, and data display systems (Department of Homeland Security, 2004)

Both ICS and NIMS are the future in managing crime scenes that require a multijurisdictional response. All state public safety agencies will become conversant in the language of NIMS and ICS, because all future grants will be predicated on the premise that the agency submitting the proposal is NIMS, ICS qualified. Training in NIMS can be had through public safety agencies or online through a variety of Web sites including an independent study at Department of Homeland Security, Federal Emergency Management Agency, Emergency Management Institute.

■ Sources of Information

One of the most important tasks performed by police investigators is to gather **intelligence** (information). Although gathering intelligence has traditionally been viewed as a military function, police investigators understand the need to discover and cultivate sources of information for cases under investigation as well as crimes yet to be committed. Many agencies have an intelligence organization or department whose sole responsibility is to gather information. Most police investigators gather information on a much less formal basis. It is the less formal process that is discussed in this chapter.

Every crime has an abundance of information that can be gathered, from forensic evidence to witness, victim, and suspect input. The investigator's job is to recognize the prospective sources of information. If an investigation runs into an information dead end, the reason may be that the investigator has overlooked a source of information or has not recognized the importance of information already gathered.

Community Policing and Criminal Investigation

When we think of community policing we often think of police on foot walking beats. In truth, community policing is as diverse as communities. In any community, law enforcement personnel can assist in maintaining safety. One of the creative uses of community policing involves using community police teams to address all the needs of a given community: traffic enforcement, emergency response, first response, and investigation of all crimes (as opposed to utilizing various felony departments within an agency). The team is managed from within rather than by an external hierarchical structure, which enables immediate decision making and direct accountability. People within a given community get to know the community team that provides services for them. In fact, the team becomes part of the community's resources, problem solvers, and leaders. Responses to problems are almost immediate, and responding team members have a pretty good idea what to expect at any given location, because they most probably have been there before. This approach to community policing streamlines police services, including crime scene investigation.

Eyewitnesses and Victims

The most common sources of information are witnesses and victims. What someone sees, hears, smells, or touches carries great weight in the courtroom. Defense lawyers challenge all circumstantial evidence as unreliable. **Circumstantial evidence** is all evidence other than eyewitness testimony. The reality is that eyewitness testimony is the least reliable evidence available to the investigator and prosecutor. The inconsistencies in eyewitness testimony are the materials from which defense lawyers build cross-examinations. An investigator should begin to worry when eyewitness information does not bear any inconsistencies. No two people experience an event using the same senses. No two perspectives are ever the same. Gross descriptions should be very similar in content, but the fine details will vary from witness to witness.

An investigator turns first to witnesses and victims as sources of information when beginning to attempt to answer the who, what, when, where, and sometimes why and how of a crime. Witnesses and victims provide the first **leads** of the investigation—the descriptions of persons, places, events, and things. As hard as witnesses and victims may try to provide the information that the investigator seeks, they are not trained observers, and their recall may be sporadic and general rather than concise and specific. Of course, recollection is often a product of the inquiry that gives rise to it (see Officer's Notebook).

Informants

The word *informant* has taken on negative connotations, although any citizen providing information to police, including witnesses and victims, is an informant. Although an informant is simply one who provides information, the use of informants can get legally complex when the motivation for providing information to the police is added to the mix. Most citizens will provide information readily and voluntarily. The problem is that the average citizen does not have the ties to the criminal community that would garner inside information about past and future crimes. Doctors, bakers, and candlestick makers generally do not travel in the same circles as criminals and their associates. The question, therefore, is how investigators can get a criminal or a criminal's affiliate to provide the investigators with information. There are two ways in which such information and people come to the assistance of the police: if the informants have a separate agenda to further, or if they are products of cultivation.

Informants with an Agenda

An informant may be motivated by a personal agenda that will be somehow furthered if the police act on the information provided. That agenda may include vengeance for past grievances (real or imagined) suffered by the informant and his or her crew or operation. Although information gained through this motive may be highly suspect, it nonetheless deserves a response. Information of serious criminal wrongdoing coming into the hands of the police should not be ignored, regardless of the source. Informants

OFFICER'S NOTEBOOK

Working with Witnesses and Victims

The skills of a successful intelligence gatherer are a lifetime in the making. In gleaning information from citizens, it is best to use language that is familiar to those being interviewed and that is free of jargon. Kilometers and meters (or yards and feet) may be foreign terminology to a witness, for example. Using measurement terms familiar to the witness will result in more accurate results. When asking questions about a vehicle, the investigator may only be able to discover the color and vehicle type. Requesting the witness to compare the vehicle in question with vehicles currently in the vicinity can be more helpful than asking if the vehicle was a compact, subcompact, mid-sized car, sedan, and so on. Likewise, when asking questions about a suspect's body type, the investigator should consider having the witness compare it with the body types of those present. The resulting information is likely to be more accurate than if the witness is required to guess the suspect's weight and height and express them in pounds and in feet and inches. The most efficient way of getting a good physical description is to construct a composite drawing. Most people are more comfortable thinking graphically instead of linearly or physiologically.

As for weapons, the unsophisticated witness may be able to distinguish between a pistol (semiautomatic) and a revolver but may be unable to provide much else in the way of information. With prompting and with visual guidance, the witness may be able to guess the barrel length as well as the caliber (a finger-sized hole as opposed to a pencil-sized hole) and possibly the color. It should be kept in mind that the witness's attention was on the gaping hole in the barrel, perhaps to the exclusion of everything else.

acting out of vengeance usually require anonymity, and it becomes the responsibility of the investigator to corroborate the information provided, if possible.

Sometimes an informant provides information about a competitor as a way of weakening or dispensing with the competitor. Although the police may be reluctant to help one criminal against another, the information is often about a crime of such seriousness that a response is required. It would be a mistake to presume that the informant with an agenda has been cultivated. The informant is using the police and is not inclined to provide information that does not result in some personal advantage.

Cultivating Informants

There are many terms used to refer to informants: confidential informant (CI); person providing information (PPI); cooperating person, party, or individual; or just informant. As noted, the most valuable informants are criminals and their associates—valuable in terms of the volume of information provided to the police. These informants often place themselves in situations that compromise their ability to keep secrets. When arrested, often the only thing a criminal has to trade is information about acquaintances involved in or planning criminal activities.

Every experienced investigator has **snitches** on the street for whom he or she is willing to go a long way to protect their identity and longevity. These street sources provide the bulk of information to police. How does someone become a snitch? Many snitches travel the edges of criminality without actually committing a crime, but by rubbing shoulders with those who do. These same individuals also may fantasize about being a police officer or assisting the police and may voluntarily assist an investigator once approached and identified as a nonplayer. The problem with informants of this type is that they are easily influenced and may turn over on the investigator as easily as they did on the criminal. Reliability is a perennial problem with informants.

The more common reason for someone to begin acting as a snitch is survival. Contrary to popular belief, the police do not arrest every criminal for every crime committed in their presence. Some criminals are informally worked by an investigator or an officer. Patrol officers often provide investigators with leads or information about past or pending crimes. Occasionally a suspect will be taken into custody for a relatively minor offense. Drug users in particular suffer greatly during periods of incarceration, because of the pain of withdrawing from the substance to which they are addicted. An occupational hazard of addiction is the possibility of having to provide police with information or face a weekend in jail. In lieu of processing the offense for which a suspect has been arrested, the investigator will offer a deal to the suspect: As long as the suspect provides an ongoing flow of information to the investigator, the investigator will continue to hold the charges in abeyance. Most misdemeanors have a statute of limitations of two years and allow leverage to be applied during that period. Obviously, informants of this type are highly unreliable and can disappear or align themselves with a criminal element that can provide a modicum of protection or pose a greater threat than the offense being used as leverage.

The most useful information is an offer during ongoing investigations in which serious charges can be brought. Federal grand juries often conduct investigations over long periods of time, especially investigations that involve drug traffickers or organized crime. Persons caught up in the international narcotics trade or in the web of crime family homicides may be given the opportunity to accept immunity for the information they can provide. Investigations on the state level often result in plea bargaining or in getting an informant to introduce an undercover agent to criminals at a certain rung in the criminal ladder. There is great danger inherent in these operations, in that the informant may choose to compromise the information provided or the officer given the introduction. Yet informants, for all their inherent problems, are an indispensable element in the war on crime, especially the war on drugs.

Informant Reliability

If information provided by an informant is to be used to establish probable cause, it must first meet certain legal requirements. The history of **hearsay** in providing probable cause is illustrative of the courts' distrust of hearsay and informants. To understand the courts' lack of appreciation for informants and hearsay, it is necessary to consider three cases dealing with these issues: *Draper v. United States* (1959), *Spinelli v. United States* (1969), and *Illinois v. Gates* (1983).

As a result of *Spinelli v. United States,* hearsay upon which police could rely in establishing probable cause must have continued to meet the test set forth in *Aguilar v. Texas* (1964), now commonly known as the two-pronged test. Both prongs had to be satisfied before informant information could be used to establish probable cause—that is, the informant must be reliable and the information must be reliable as well. It would appear the Court believed that any citizen providing information to the police must have done so on a prior occasion, and independent corroboration of the information by the police was to be expected. A failure of either prong of the two-prong test rendered the information legally unusable.

The Court did not leave us with the *Spinelli* standard. Although the test is still a good place to start in determining informant reliability, the Court set it aside in the case of *Illinois v. Gates* (1983). The Court had to come to grips with the reality of a drug war that was neither being won nor waged effectively. Law enforcement was provided more latitude in its battle against drugs, and the Court provided one more weapon by abrogating the *Spinelli* standard.

CASE IN POINT

Draper v. United States, 1959

A Denver narcotics agent had received word from an informant that Draper was going to Chicago to bring back heroin. He was to travel by train the morning of September 8th or 9th. The informant, who had previously provided reliable information, gave a detailed description of Draper, including the clothes he would be wearing, and said that he would be walking fast. Denver police set up surveillance of all trains arriving on the two mornings in question. On the second day, police observed a person matching the description of Draper. He exited the train and walked fast. He was arrested. Heroin and a syringe were seized in a search pursuant to the arrest. Draper was convicted of transporting heroin.

The question of first impression to the Court was, can information that would not be admissible at the time of trial because it was hearsay be used to establish probable cause to effect an arrest? There was no doubt that the information provided by the informant was hearsay. Hearsay evidence is any out-of-court statement made by someone other than the person testifying. The officer cannot testify at trial to what he has been told without violating the hearsay rule. The Court in *Draper* said that the corroboration of the information by the police and the fact that the informant had proven reliable in the past allowed the information to be used in forming probable cause for the purposes of a search. The Court said that there was probable cause in this case because the informant had been employed specifically for that purpose and had provided reliable information in the past. The Court thus felt it would have been dereliction of duty to have ignored the information.

> ## CASE IN POINT
>
> ### Spinelli v. United States, 1969
>
> Spinelli came to the attention of the FBI, who placed him under surveillance. He was watched entering an apartment building. A check of the phone records at the apartment confirmed what an informant had said about phone numbers being used by Spinelli in a bookmaking operation. A search warrant affidavit was written as a result of the informant's bookmaking tip and the investigators' corroboration of that tip. A warrant was issued based on the affidavit, and evidence of Spinelli's racketeering was discovered that laid the foundation for his conviction for interstate travel in aid of racketeering.
>
> It was this case that the U.S. Supreme Court used to promulgate its two-pronged test for informant reliability. Keeping in mind the misgivings the courts had of this type of hearsay information, it is not surprising that the Supreme Court was concerned with the credibility not only of the informant but also of the information provided. It held that the evidence gathered from the surveillance was insufficient to establish probable cause and that the information provided by the informant lacked indices of reliability.

Surveillance

Watching people, places, and things may not be exciting, but it is a necessary component of many criminal investigations. Perhaps the most tedious of all investigative tasks, surveillance is nonetheless an important source of information and can also corroborate information that would otherwise be useless for establishing probable cause and confirming suspicions. Surveillance may be part of an ongoing investigation or an operation to prevent a crime from occurring. The most common reason for placing a person, a place, or a thing under surveillance is to locate a suspect. Surveillance may be continuous or periodic, intense or casual. The type of surveillance best chosen is determined by the seriousness of the situation (offense), the availability of personnel, and the sophistication of the suspect.

The key to successful surveillance is planning. The Navy SEALS refer to the seven Ps: Prior proper planning prevents piss-poor performance. Although indecorous, it does bring home the importance of planning in any team operation. Experience is needed to

> ## CASE IN POINT
>
> ### Illinois v. Gates, 1983
>
> The Bloomingdale, Illinois, police department received an anonymous letter dated May 3, 1978, containing information that Gates was planning to fly to Florida and his wife was planning to drive her car to Florida on May 3rd so that she and Gates could drive back to Bloomingdale with large quantities of drugs. The letter also indicated that Gates and his wife had more than $100,000 worth of drugs in their home. Acting on this tip from an anonymous and never-before-used informant, the police discovered that Gates had made reservations for a May 5th flight to Florida. The DEA placed Gates and his wife under surveillance and discovered that he had taken the May 5th flight and had stayed in a hotel room registered to his wife. The couple left the following morning, and a search warrant for Gates' home and car was issued based on the informant's tip and the corroboration of the officers.
>
> Upon arriving home, Gates found the police waiting. A search of the house and car disclosed marijuana and other illegal items. Gates was convicted of violating state drug laws. The Court abandoned the two-pronged test of Spinelli and replaced it with a more flexible ***totality of the circumstances*** test. The Court ruled that the task of the police in drafting an affidavit for a search warrant and of a magistrate in issuing that warrant is to determine whether, given all the circumstances, "there is a fair probability that the evidence sought will be found in a particular place."

conduct proper surveillance. Being able to react spontaneously to an unforeseen development requires imagination, stamina, and courage.

The most common type of surveillance involves a suspect on the move, either on foot, in a car, or in the air. Usually police use an auto in conducting surveillance. A lack of personnel and resources means that only one auto might be available. Unfortunately, it is fairly easy to detect a single surveillance auto, because it must stay behind the subject and within view. Career criminals check periodically for **tails** and are often successful in eluding (shaking) a tail. Important cases justify using multiple autos for surveillance and expending the required resources.

Following someone on foot is a tricky business. The unaware or unsophisticated suspect is easy to follow if the surveillance is from afar and the tail understands the basic rules of foot surveillance. The suspect may enter a building or a vehicle to test for a tail. In one-car or one-person surveillance, when the suspect enters a building, it is best not to follow the suspect into the edifice but rather await his or her exit. Should there be more than one entrance, the officer should watch the entrance that the suspect used. Generally people will exit through the same portal they entered—unless suspicious of a tail, in which case the entry into the building may have been for the sole purpose of shaking the tail.

A **stakeout** is a type of surveillance that requires great patience and many departmental resources. Places and things are generally the focus of a stationary surveillance. Houses, autos, or hidden contraband may draw the attention of investigators.

Deciding the vantage point for fixed surveillance requires imagination and an appreciation of the characteristics of the setting and the people who live and work in the area. Police observers must be unobtrusive and draw no attention to themselves or their position. Fixed surveillance is generally conducted for the following reasons (Gilbert, 1998):

- To gather evidence pertaining to a place, persons, or activities
- To establish probable cause for a search or arrest warrant
- To apprehend suspects
- To corroborate information provided by an informant
- To assess access routes for a tactical response
- To protect undercover operatives

OFFICER'S NOTEBOOK

Multivehicle Surveillance

In planning multivehicle surveillance, all participants must be aware of the various techniques employed by suspects to detect a tail and the methods of foiling such efforts. Changes of directions by the suspect to run a "square" in order to watch following vehicles can be dealt with by maintaining autos on parallel routes. When the vehicle turns, a radio message conveys to operatives that a parallel vehicle should take up the surveillance. Entry into a parking lot or garage requires a vehicle to watch the entrance and/or exit while the tailing vehicle either drives by the parked suspect or parks with the suspect vehicle in view. The surveillance should then be continued by a trailing vehicle at the entrance or exit.

The suspect may ignore traffic control devices or double back along his or her route of travel. Both tactics are generally unsuccessful in multivehicle surveillance if the officers involved have planned for their possibility. Obviously, in multivehicle and multiofficer surveillance, radio communications become an important element of the operation. More and more citizens have police scanners and monitor radio traffic. A secure channel should be maintained or cell phones should be used for communication.

OFFICER'S NOTEBOOK

Essential Considerations When Planning Surveillance

1. Who will watch?
2. When will watching take place?
3. What will be watched?
4. How long will the person, place, or thing be watched?
5. Will surveillance be sporadic or continuous?
6. Who will pay for the watching?
7. When will the watching cease?
8. Under what circumstances should watching be forsaken?
9. From where will watching take place?
10. What information is to be recorded?
    a. Documentary
    b. Audio
    c. Video (photographic)
11. What are the team members' roles?
    a. Watchers
    b. Gofers (errand runners)
        i. Food and drink
        ii. Equipment
    c. Problem solvers
    d. Recorders
        i. Notes
        ii. Photos
        iii. Videotapes
        iv. Tape recordings

Often police will conduct a fixed surveillance and make audio recordings through the use of wiretaps or bugs. Whichever device is used, a warrant for the use of the device may be necessary. The two cases that provide the answers to questions involving intrusions into someone's spoken word are *Katz v. United States* (1967) and *On Lee v. United States* (1952).

The *Katz* decision overruled a prior decision in *Olmstead v. United States* (1928), which held that wiretapping did not violate the Fourth Amendment unless there was some trespass into a "constitutionally protected area." According to the Katz test, a search has been conducted whenever there is a reasonable expectation of privacy and that expectation has been breached. The Constitution protects people rather than places, and the Fourth Amendment is portable.

The *Katz* case established the basis for all wiretaps. All states have specific procedural statutes governing the issuance of wiretap orders, as does the federal government. There is a widely recognized exception to the *Katz* standard, however—an exception that has also been codified in most states. This issue is seen in the case *On Lee v. United States* (see Cases in Point).

Legal Trends in Surveillance

As a result of innovations in electronic technology, there is virtually nothing today's police officers cannot hear, see, or follow. Parabolic microphones, sonic wave detectors, digital audio bugs, and "bionic ears" allow officers to listen to conversations just about

CASE IN POINT

Katz v. United States, 1967

Defendant Katz was a bookmaker running a "wire" operation. He used a public telephone booth to call in street wagers to a site nearby that had a phone bank for accepting illegal wagers. The FBI suspected Katz of bookmaking and had him under surveillance. His routine use of the public telephone gave rise to additional suspicion, although short of probable cause. The FBI determined that because the telephone booth was visible to the public, there was no Fourth Amendment protection for those using the telephone inside. They placed a listening device on the outside of the booth without physically trespassing into the booth and recorded the defendant's conversations. Katz was convicted of transmitting wagering information across state lines.

The U.S. Supreme Court determined that any type of wiretapping that violated a person's reasonable expectation of privacy was a search under the Fourth Amendment and must be accompanied by a warrant or an exception to the warrant requirement. The Court held that Katz did not shed his right to Fourth Amendment protection because he made his call from a public place. One who uses a public telephone and shuts the door has demonstrated an expectation that conversations taking place therein are to be kept private. Considering the circumstances of this case, the Court felt that Katz should have been able to presume that the words he uttered into the mouthpiece were not to be broadcast to the world.

anywhere. Even wiretaps have become much more sophisticated: They can now intercept conversations occurring over cell phones, satellite phones, and between computers. Officers can also utilize night vision technology, thermal infrared imaging, helicopter surveillance with forward-looking infrared (FLIR) devices, and tiny video cameras that can be hidden in such things as eyeglasses and smoke detectors.

As a general rule, court authorization is not required to use **enhancement technology** to obtain better picture or sound quality provided that police are legitimately situated when the interception is made. As the U.S. Supreme Court observed, there is nothing in the Fourth Amendment that prohibits police from augmenting the sensory faculties bestowed upon them at birth with such enhancement as science and technology affords them (*People v. Arno*, 1979).

Acquisition technology surveillance devices do not merely enhance sights or sounds; they actually permit officers to acquire sights and sounds that they would not otherwise have been able to perceive from a legitimate vantage point. Examples include hidden

CASE IN POINT

On Lee v. United States, 1952

On Lee was suspected of selling opium. A federal undercover agent and former acquaintance of On Lee entered On Lee's laundry wearing a radio transmitter while engaging him in conversation, all of which was being monitored by offsite federal agents. The conversations played a significant role at trial in winning a conviction of On Lee for selling opium. The Court held that there was no trespass onto On Lee's premises, in that it was open to the public and entry was invited. No trespass occurred, but was there a breach of On Lee's reasonable expectation of privacy? The Court felt that as long as the police have the permission of one of the parties to the conversation, eavesdropping on or recording the conversation is not a Fourth Amendment issue. Because a person assumes the risk that whatever is said to another person may be reported to the police, it follows that if the police are invited to share in that conversation, there is no violation of the suspect's constitutional rights.

listening devices and wiretaps. As a general rule, a warrant or other court order is required to use acquisition technology (*Katz v. United States,* 1967).

Some devices coming onto the market are so technologically sophisticated that a reasonable person could not envision that they would be able to enhance or acquire that which was intercepted. Defendants may argue that a warrant is required whenever officers want to utilize surveillance equipment that is highly sophisticated, regardless of whether it is also highly intrusive. At present the courts have rejected the argument that a warrant is required to utilize a surveillance device merely because it is "sophisticated" or technologically complex (*United States v. Knotts,* 1983). In dealing with new technology, it would be wise to remember that the more sophisticated a form of technology, the greater the likelihood that warrantless use will constitute an unreasonable intrusion. What is considered sophisticated today, however, will be on the journey to obsolescence tomorrow.

Police also rely on vehicle tracking devices to follow a car as it is driven on public streets. These devices can be attached secretly to the suspect's vehicle or personal property. A warrant is not required to attach a tracking device to a car if the car is parked in a public place. A warrant is not required to follow a tracking device placed on a vehicle so long as the vehicle remains on public streets or in public places. In *United States v. Knotts* (1983), the Supreme Court held that "a person traveling in an automobile on public thoroughfares has no reasonable expectation of privacy in his movements from one place to another."

If a tracking device has been hidden inside a movable item, a warrant is not required to track it as it is carried to the home. Once the item is carried into the residence, however, a warrant is required to continue tracking its movements because the tracking device is transmitting information "that could not have been obtained through visual surveillance" (*United States v. Knotts,* 1983).

One of the most effective methods of conducting surveillance is to do so from an airplane or helicopter. A warrant is not required to conduct aerial surveillance over public or private property, because air traffic is such a common part of our daily lives that people cannot reasonably expect privacy from the air unless the flight is being conducted in an unusually intrusive manner (*Florida v. Riley,* 1989). Surveillance from aircraft or helicopters may be conducted without a warrant as long as the following are true:

1. The aircraft has a legal right to be at the altitude permitted by FAA regulations.
2. The flight is conducted in a "physically nonintrusive manner."
3. If a helicopter is used, it is not flown at unusually low altitudes, absent exigent circumstances.

Officers who are conducting aerial surveillance are free to use binoculars, camera equipment, or other surveillance technology to enhance that which is visible from the air.

Thermal imaging forward-looking infrared devices, commonly known as FLIRs, are mounted under aircraft in gimbaled housings and are used to detect heat sources. The most common use is in nighttime high-speed pursuits. Thermal imaging devices have also been used in cases where the police have reason to believe that marijuana is being grown inside a home, business, or other structure. The U.S. Supreme Court has held that the government may not use a device that is not in general public use to explore details of a private home that would previously have been unknowable without physical intrusion, ruling that such surveillance would be a Fourth Amendment search and therefore presumptively unreasonable without a warrant (*Kyllo v. United States,* 2001). It would appear that the use of FLIRs for identifying marijuana in open fields and unenclosed areas of curtilage would be constitutionally acceptable.

Binoculars and telescopes can function as either enhancement or acquisition devices, depending on their proximity to the target. If they are used merely to enlarge or clarify something visible to the naked eye, they are enhancement devices that require no legal authorization. On the other hand, a warrant may be required to utilize devices that acquire images that could not be seen from a suitable vantage point. Regarding night-vision binoculars, the courts have agreed that the use of artificial means to illuminate a darkened area does not constitute a search (*Oregon v. Wacker*, 1993).

Thanks to modern technology, officers can overhear people talking just about anywhere; however, an intercept order is required if the parties to the conversation reasonably expect privacy. Like wiretaps, listening devices are acquisition technology; thus, a court order or the consent of a party to the conversation is required if the device has been hidden inside the suspect's home, private office, or any other place in which a reasonable expectation of privacy exists (*United States v. McIntyre*, 1978).

In this vein, although the courts have not yet decided, it would appear that the use of parabolic microphones would be constitutionally permissible if the conversations that were being listened to or recorded were taking place in public subject to being overheard by the casual listener. Similarly, under federal law, the term **electronic communication** means in-transit electronic impulses, sounds, and other signals transmitted over wire, radio, or microwave. Absent issues of national security or investigation of organized crime, a federal court order or consent is necessary to intercept electronic communications if the transmission is not "readily accessible to the general public."

Police may videotape anything that occurs in a public place, open fields, or any place not subject to a recognized expectation of privacy (*Lopez v. United States*, 1963). Similarly, although looking through windows may not be nice, it is lawful under certain circumstances:

1. The window was uncovered or only partially covered.
2. The police were in a place they had a legal right to be or were invited to be.
3. The officers' observations were made with the naked eye or enhanced by binoculars (*People v. Camacho*, 2000).

The use of dogs to detect drugs, explosives, or other contraband does not constitute a search as long as the activity takes place in a public forum. In addition, the warrant-less inspection of garbage left for pickup in a public place does not constitute a search. Once the garbage is placed outside of the curtilage of the home, it no longer enjoys the protection of the Fourth Amendment (*California v. Greenwood*, 1988).

Useful information is available from the phone company, namely, information dealing with incoming calls, outgoing calls, addresses, payment histories, and residential histories. There is no recognized expectation of privacy in these records in that the phone company and not the suspect keeps them (*Smith v. Maryland*, 1979).

Interviewing

An investigation always involves interviewing and sometimes, with luck, interrogation. Investigators **interview** witnesses or persons with information; after a suspect is in custody, the investigator moves from interviewing to **interrogation**. Whereas the goal of interviewing is to gather information, the goal of interrogation is to establish the truth.

Because interrogation is such a crucial part of an investigation, this topic is addressed in its own chapter (Chapter 8).

Victim Interviews

In preparing for a victim interview, the investigator must factor into the equation the emotional state of the victim. The preparation should include any and all information gathered by the officers who were first on the scene. Their written reports may give some insight as to the nature of the crime, the background of the crime, and the emotional condition of the victim. It would be a mistake to rely solely on the written information. A person-to-person conversation with the responding officers could prove useful. It is a wise investigator who checks the criminal history of victims and all other sources of information to assess the credibility of the information about to be received.

The first meeting with the witness can be fruitful or disastrous, depending on the effort the investigator has put into preparing for the interview. The nature of the offense can tell much about the likely mental state of the victim. When dealing with property crimes, an investigator can generally expect to find a very angry victim. The frustration the victim has experienced in attempting to protect his or her property and in attempting to understand how this could have happened to him or her often manifests as anger. The perpetrator is unavailable as a subject on which to vent hostility, so it often falls to the investigator to field the victim's anger. This is not an easy thing to do, but a sympathetic, patient, and nonaccusatory demeanor can go a long way toward defusing the anger and establishing rapport.

It is impossible to be irrational and rational simultaneously. An effective approach in dealing with emotionally distraught people is to ask questions that require a processing of information rather than a simple automatic response. Focusing these questions away from the victim and the offense will require the victim to focus on providing factual information. The first question or questions may be ignored, but continued efforts to elicit factual information likely will be successful.

Crimes against the person usually result in a broader range of emotions, some of which may be hard to defuse. Rape victims, assault victims, and relatives of homicide victims have an array of responses that may require professional help to sort out. Some-

OFFICER'S NOTEBOOK

Examples of Data-Processing Questions

The following are typical data-processing questions:

- Do you live here alone? What is your home phone number? What is your work number? Who else lives with you? How long have you lived here? Where did you live prior to this location? Who are the members of your family? What are their names?
- Are you employed? Who is your employer? How long have you worked there? What do you do there? Is any special training required to do your job?
- Do you know your neighbors? Are they home? Do you know their names and telephone numbers?

It is difficult to answer such questions appropriately (i.e., by providing the right kind of information) and to be hysterical simultaneously. Perseverance may be necessary for many victims, but once the bridge has been crossed, the anger level should be reduced to levels that will allow offense-specific questions to be asked.

times only time can begin to heal the emotional wounds suffered by the victim. It takes an experienced investigator to know when to push and when to allow time to do its healing. If the victim needs professional help, the investigator may be most successful in gathering information by recognizing this fact and by giving the victim the names of resources that can provide that help.

Interviewing Reluctant Witnesses

People are reluctant to talk to the police for a variety of reasons: prior experience with the police, culturally influenced views regarding the police and cooperation with the police, fear of the police or of those who may be pursued by the police, language barriers, or alignment with the criminal element within the community. When encountering a reluctant witness, the investigator must attempt to discover the basis for the reluctance and determine what approach, if any, might mitigate the underlying reasons for the lack of cooperation.

Most commonly, people simply prefer not to get involved. Giving information to the police, although only minimally disruptive to their routines, may eventually result in injury to them or to family members. Pleas for help that focus on the civic responsibility of citizens may be useful. An explanation of the importance of cooperating may ring true. One might suggest that if the witness were the victim, he or she would want others to assist in the apprehension of the offender. It is generally a bad ploy to try to intimidate a person into cooperation. This tactic usually will result in more antagonism and perhaps escalate into an unnecessary confrontation.

The victim of certain types of crimes may be reluctant to cooperate with the police. The elderly who do not wish to appear senile or naive may disguise their concerns with ambivalence or lack of cooperation. Assurance that the type of victimization to which they fell prey is not at all unusual or a reflection upon them or their age may open closed doors. A female rape victim may harbor resentment toward men generally as a result of her experience and may flatly refuse to talk to male police and investigators. A male officer may arrange for the assistance of a female officer and thus provide the victim with a listener with whom she is comfortable. Before presuming that a female rape victim is uncooperative, a male investigator might ask if she would prefer to talk to a woman officer or a doctor. Should she request a physician, the male investigator should spend some time with the interviewer beforehand discussing the types of information that the investigator would like to obtain. If she requests a female officer, the male officer should inform the interviewer about the crime. When dealing with any witness who is highly emotional, the investigator should gather the information carefully and with sensitivity and treat it skeptically. All information should be documented and corroborated later through a follow-up interview.

Interviewing Children

Children are notorious for telling investigators more than they want to know. No matter what age a child witness is, the investigator must be an active listener—not someone who is merely asking specific questions and wants only specific answers, but someone who is genuinely interested in the child and what the child has to say. In addition, the interview should be conducted in a place that provides the child with a sense of comfort, familiarity, and security. It is best to have a parent in attendance during the interview, and many states have statutes that require a parent to be in attendance throughout the interview. Preschool children have difficulty thinking in measured units, be they units of time, weight, or distance. They often talk with a free flow of consciousness and touch on material that ranges far and wide from the matter under investigation. An investigator needs to exhibit great patience and care in managing the course of the interview. Patience and an appreciation of children are the basic prerequisites for interviewing children; the rest can be learned.

Children process information differently than do adults. They think in concrete rather than abstract terms, they do not organize their thoughts, and their narratives wander. Also, they may not understand why lying is bad, nor why the truth is important. A child's world revolves around himself or herself; thus, the more the questions pertain to the child, the more information will be provided. Keep in mind also that children have a limited attention span (it lengthens with age). Questions should be kept short and the questioning period brief. If necessary, conduct the interview in sessions. Finally, children know when interviewers like them and are comfortable with them. If an interviewer is not comfortable, the child will not be comfortable.

Investigators who conduct interviews with children should understand the basics of how a child's memory works, which is different from that of adults. Memory-associated development occurs over time and includes attention, language, conversational tracking, scripting, and source monitoring (Poole and Lamb, 1998).

Each of these is covered in the following sections.

OFFICER'S NOTEBOOK

Tips for Interviewing Children

It is important that a child be given an explanation for the interview as well as certain ground rules. A child witness should be told the following:

- Who is going to conduct the interview
- What is going to be sought
- Why it is being sought
- Why it may be necessary to tell the story more than once (to police, psychologists, social workers, investigators, and so on)
- What happens with the information gathered
- What more may be expected of the child
- That police, investigators, prosecutors, and judges are there to protect the child

The interviewer should select his or her words carefully, with an emphasis on clarity and understandability. The interview should begin with questions the child can answer easily and successfully and progress to the more nebulous queries only after the child has been put at his or her ease.

- Conduct the interview in an environment that is comfortable for the person being interviewed.
- Establish rapport. Allow a brief period of introduction.
- Pay attention—both to what is being said and what isn't.
- Listen actively.
- Do not interrupt.
- Allow a free flow of information even if the information is irrelevant.
- Encourage narrative responses.
- Ask open-ended questions.
- Give the impression that time is not of the essence.
- Be patient.
- Be courteous.
- Be professional.

Because perception relies on attention, attention plays a large part in governing what aspects of an event a child will remember, what parts of an interview he or she will understand, and to which questions a child will respond (Reisberg, 2001). Attention is affected not only by brain development but also by a child's interest in and familiarity with a task, which affect the amount and duration of attention they give to it (Anderson et al., 1986). Interviewers should not only seek to eliminate distractions (such as toys and clutter) when talking to children, but should also make sure that the child is familiar with and understands the purpose and form of the interview.

A child's verbal repertoire has a huge impact on conversational ability. The more words a child knows, the more options the interviewer has in forming questions and the more options the child has in crafting responses. Crafting questions in language that a child of a particular age and developmental stage can comprehend is a skill unto itself. The ability to remember and report is linked to the ability to speak. The younger the child, the more limited the vocabulary, which results in very limited communication and very limited response and imagery (Greenhoot et al., 1999).

Many researchers who have studied children's autobiographical accounts comment on how difficult it can be to get children to talk about the desired subject in response to open-ended questions. Although it is recognized that open-ended questions are a more reliable interviewing technique that provides less suggestibility for generating a particular answer, it may be an exercise in futility in getting a child to respond to such questions and, if responding, to respond to the specific topic of interest to the interviewer. Children may need a prompt to initiate focus on the subject. The question "What happened today?" may not precipitate a response or may precipitate a response irrelevant to the subject of interest. Achieving relevance may require mild prompting such as "What happened at school during spelling today?" Such prompting questions should only be used to begin the conversation; open-ended questions are the method of choice once the child begins to respond (Steward and Steward, 1996, as cited in Poole and Lamb, 1998). A child may not be able to maintain focus on the subject of the inquiry and may drift to other, more interesting topics. If the interviewer does not recognize topic drift when it happens, there is a great opportunity for misunderstanding or misinterpretation of a child's responses (Poole and Lamb, 1998).

A script is an understanding of what is supposed to happen based on what has happened in the past. It provides some security, in that for much of what we encounter on a daily basis, we either have encountered it before or have encountered something similar enough to allow us to fashion a generalized workable response. Scripts reduce the effort needed to get through routine events. Schemata can produce automatic expectations of what will happen in a familiar context; therefore, when actual events contradict expectations, scripts can also cause inaccurate reconstructive recollection of events (Ceci and Bruck, 1995).

Children who are interviewed multiple times may develop scripts about the subject matter of the interviews even if they had no actual experience with the event in question (Ceci and Bruck, 1995). If children are exposed repeatedly to suggestive information about the investigation during interviews or conversations with family or others, their developing scripts may cause them to give progressively more complete and believable testimony about an event they may not have experienced (Ceci and Bruck, 1995). The effects of scripting make it crucial that interviewers resist conducting suggestive and repetitive interviews and learn to gather the information they need in as few interviews with as few questions and prompts as possible.

The boundaries between a child's concept of reality and fantasy are not rigidly defined. For instance, children may believe that something pretend can become real, so it is difficult for them to decide with certainty whether an event was real or imagined (Ceci and Bruck, 1995). Identifying the source of memories for real events is challenging, but is a necessary component of nonsuggestive interviewing (Poole and Lamb, 1998).

One source-monitoring task that is particularly difficult for children is discriminating between information they received through their own experience and that received through other sources (Poole and Lamb, 1998). Source-monitoring skills have major implications for interviewing children. To give accurate testimony, children need to be able to distinguish whether they or someone else really did something or just pretended and whether their information about it comes from their experience or from a conversation or other source. Interviewers need to keep their questions grounded in reality and to question sources of information whenever possible. The first step in source monitoring is to interview those who have interacted with the child prior to and in anticipation of the interview. From medical personnel to teachers and parents, it is important to learn what such sources know and what and how it was related to the child (Poole and Lindsay, 2001).

No two child witnesses will respond the same way to interviewers or interview techniques. Police interviewers must appreciate the typical developmental cognitive skills of each child witness to better determine how to interview a particular child. Along with that information, they should develop an instinct for the potential hazards that can befall the unsuspecting interviewer.

There are many ways in which interviewing procedures can be suggestive. Through word choice, praise and punishment, and disproportionately attending to some information, interviewers can have a significant effect on the responses they get from children they interview (Ceci and Bruck, 1995). Interviewers' choices of words can reveal important information and assumptions even in questions that sound ordinary. Poole and Lindsay (2001) recommend that interviewers use neutral language and avoid words such as abuse, bad, and hurt when investigating allegations of abuse.

Another common form of suggestion or leading in interviews comes from the attention that interviewers pay to or withdraw from certain topics. When children say something inconsistent with the interviewer's hypothesis or bias, it frequently gets ignored (Ceci and Bruck, 1995). The method of attending, ignoring, rewarding, and punishing can heavily sway children's testimony (Ceci and Bruck, 1995). Interviewers should practice reinforcing children for any information they give, including saying "I don't know" (Poole and Lamb, 1998). Also, interviewers should think through their assumptions about a case and challenge them so that they will be more likely to entertain multiple hypotheses and conduct nonleading interviews (Ceci and Bruck, 1995).

Time considerations are also a potential hazard. The longer a child has to wait between witnessing an event and being interviewed about it, the less complete and accurate his or her report will be (Poole and Lamb, 1998).

Although children may need direct prompts to begin speaking about an event, it is best to use open-ended lines of questioning whenever possible. Interviewers often have suspicions about the event they are asking a child about and intentionally or unintentionally ask close-ended questions that guide the child to confirm their suspicions (Ceci and Bruck, 1995). Interviewers should orient children to the topic of the interview, using specific prompts if they need to (Steward and Steward, 1996, as cited in Poole and Lamb,

1998). They should also check periodically to confirm that the child is still on topic and that his or her responses pertain to the event in question (Poole and Lamb, 1998). Beyond any directive questions or prompts needed to orient children to the topic at hand, interviewers should rely on open-ended questions (Ceci and Bruck, 1995).

Avoid repeated questions and interviews. Children involved in investigative interviews often undergo 6 to 12 or more official interviews during the course of an investigation (Ceci and Bruck, 1995). Children can develop a script for an event they may not have experienced just by undergoing a series of interviews about it (Ceci and Bruck, 1995). Furthermore, repeated closed and specific questions often lead children to change their answers (Poole and Lamb, 1998). Social rules about conversation dictate that when someone asks you a question a second time it is generally because you failed to answer it satisfactorily the first time. Children may not understand that in some contexts a question is repeated to generate more information, not to encourage recantation of the original answer (Poole and Lamb, 1998).

It is not hard to imagine that after multiple interviews, children's testimony could be contaminated easily, even though it may not be possible to gather all the information available in only one interview. If numerous interviews are necessary, it is critical that interviewers use nonleading and open-ended questions and limit the number of interviews as much as possible (Poole and Lamb, 1998).

In addition to the interviews to which children may be subjected, they may also talk with their parents, friends, and teachers about the event or the interview. Suggestion, leading questions, and misinformation can come from sources other than the investigator's interview (Ceci and Bruck, 1995). It is important for the interviewer to return to the source of the answers being offered by the child. It might prove useful to begin with questioning the child about what he or she has been told about the event in discussions with parents, friends, teachers, and so forth. Once it has been determined that other sources may have shaped the child's perspective, it helps to query the child often as to the source of the information; for example, "Is that what your mom told you?"

Criminal Profiling

When investigators speak of **profiling**, they may be referring to the profiling of a drug courier, rapist, violent offender, or serial killer. This section focuses on the FBI Investigative Support Unit, which deals with serial homicides. The word *profiling* has fallen on bad times of late, used to describe the behavior of police who single out people of color. The word has been used legitimately long before the practice of police profiling. Investigators have profiled serial offenders, serial rapists and serial killers before the word became associated with a highly suspect activity. Although race is part of a serial profile, in that we know most serial killers are white and serial killers kill intraracially, police conduct should never be based on a single attribute. As a general rule of thumb, the use of race in contemporary law enforcement is constitutionally suspect.

Investigating killings that appear to bear no relationship to the world of the deceased has long been a challenge for homicide investigators. If a homicide investigation does not identify a suspect within 24 hours of the homicide, the probability of clearing the homicide decreases over time. Since 1978, the FBI has provided local and state law enforcement agencies a psychological resource and database to assist in investigations of homicides that meet certain criteria. Included are homicides that are serial in nature, random, without motive, or sexually oriented; homicides in which the victims are unidentified; and cases in which missing persons may be homicidal victims.

The **Violent Criminal Apprehension Program (VICAP)** collects, sorts, analyzes, and categorizes data on serial homicides in an effort to uncover hidden relationships among homicides, victims, and modi operandi. If one crime or disappearance has characteristics similar to those of others, links can be made that may assist in the apprehension of a perpetrator who otherwise would remain free. Because many small and rural agencies are unaware of what is happening outside their jurisdictions, VICAP provides assistance in identifying serial killers, their victims, and their crimes.

A major source of research and development on criminal profiling today is the Investigative Support Unit, which was started as the Behavioral Science Unit in the late 1950s by two FBI employees. Now a part of the National Center for the Analysis of Violent Crime (NVC), which is one of the major components of the Critical Incident Response Group (CIRG), it consists of agents and professionals with training in behavioral or forensic science as well as consultants from the mental health professions. This unit has amassed large amounts of data on the backgrounds, family characteristics, current behaviors, and psychological traits of various types of criminal offenders, partly obtained from interviews with dozens of convicted criminals such as serial murderers.

Criminal profiling is used mostly by behavioral scientists and the police to narrow down an investigation to those suspects who possess certain behavioral and personality features that are revealed by the way a crime was committed; the idea is that behavior reflects personality (Douglas and Olshaker, 1996). The primary goal is to aid local police in limiting and refining their suspect list so they can direct their resources where they might do the most good. Profiling in itself, however, does not identify a specific suspect. Instead, profilers sketch a general biographical description of the most likely type of unknown suspect.

Profiling Multiple Murderers

Multiple murderers are usually divided into three basic categories: serial, mass, and spree killers. The **serial killer** is someone who has murdered on at least three occasions, with emotional cooling-off periods between each incident, whereas a **mass murderer** kills four or more victims in one location in one incident, with the killings all part of the same emotional experience. Finally, a **spree killer** is defined as someone who murders at two or more locations, with no emotional cooling-off period between the homicides (Douglas and Olshaker, 1999). The emphasis here is on serial killers.

Along with manipulation, domination, and control, a significant motivation for many serial killers is sexual. The offender is also likely to mentally relive his killings, often with the help of souvenirs or trophies, such as a bracelet or a body part taken from the victim. Most continue to kill until they are stopped.

Much of what we know about serial-offender profiling is a product of the many interviews FBI behaviorists have conducted with captured serial killers. Those interviews revealed that many serial killers had three characteristics in common. These characteristics have come to be known as the serial killer's trilogy and suggest an underlying frustration with lack of control (Douglas and Olshaker, 1999):

1. Enuresis (bed-wetting)
2. Cruelty to small children and/or animals
3. Starting fires

In most cases, the offender establishes a comfort zone, that is, an area close to where he lives or works, where he feels emotionally and physically comfortable. As confidence and experience grows, so does the area of activity.

In multiple homicides, the killer is usually of the same race as the victim. This characteristic of the serial killer led profilers astray in the Washington Beltway sniper case, in which snipers John Lee Malvo and John Allen Muhammad engaged in random shootings of victims who were primarily white. The victim selection of these two snipers led law enforcement personnel to presume that the killers were white. The modus operandi suggested that more than one killer was involved.

To be able to assess the behavior of any unknown suspect, it is vital to separate the suspect's modus operandi from his or her signature. The **modus operandi (MO)** is what an offender has to do to commit the offense. The **signature** is what makes the crime atypical and distinguishable from other crimes and other criminals.

Serial killers can be characterized into one of two categories: *organized killers* plan their crimes, display control at the scenes of crime, leave few or no clues, and target strangers, while *disorganized killers* do not plan their crimes, and their crime scenes reflect it. The scene will show evidence of haphazard behavior and unnecessary and undirected violence, leaving a disheveled crime scene that may retain clues (see TABLE 7-1).

Disorganized crime scenes may be a product of ever-escalating fantasy-driven scenarios in the killer's head that do not compare to the reality of the homicides. The thrill or satisfaction encountered in the first killings begins to dissipate or the satisfaction expected was not

TABLE 7-1   Profiling Serial Killers

Organized	Disorganized
• Intelligent	• Average to below average intelligence
May have higher education	• Socially inept
Above average intelligence (though not the mythical geniuses of literature)	• Local
• Socially competent	Opportunistic target selection
Uses guile and charm to capture his victim	Kills and manipulates the body at the scene
• Manipulative	Leaves the body at the scene
• Sexually competent	• Sexually incompetent
• Geographically mobile	• Manual laborer
• Occupationally mobile	May be unemployed
• Masculine	Uses tools at hand to effect his fantasy
• Lives with a partner	• May revisit the site
Has a history of being a domestic abuser	Masturbatory fantasies
• Selects targets carefully	• Will take souvenirs
Has a "play room"	
Has a dump site	
May pose the body	
Has a comfort zone	
• Will take trophies	
• May take souvenirs	
May give them as gifts	
• Looks like us	

realized. Although sex plays a prominent role in serial homicides, the primary motivation is a quest for control and power. As violence at the scene escalates, the amount of evidence left increases and detection and apprehension become more likely.

Profiling Stages

The FBI has established five behavioral stages in profiling and a sixth apprehension stage; the author has included a seventh conviction stage (TABLE 7-2).

The first stage involves collecting all information available about the crime, including physical evidence, photographs of the crime scene, autopsy reports and pictures, witness testimony, extensive background information on the victim, and police reports. The validity of a psychological profile depends on the quality of the information provided by the investigating agency, which in turn depends on the quality of the crime scene processing. Murders that are motiveless, are sexually oriented, and that demonstrate the presence of psychopathology lend themselves best to profiling. Essential documents and information include the following:

1. Crime scene photos, measurements, lab results, and itemized lists of evidence recovered. The photos should reflect any staging (posing of the victim), signature evidence (trophies, souvenirs, or torture marks), and tools of torture. The test information might include the results from blood analysis, DNA fingerprinting, fingerprint development, blood-spatter analysis, toxicology tests, and the autopsy. Copies of the death certificate and the medical examiner's or pathologist's report should also be part of the package.
2. All offense, investigation, and supplemental reports, including witness statements.
3. Information on the victim's background:
   - Criminal history
   - Family history
   - Marital history
   - Employment history
   - Educational background
   - Physical condition
   - Attire at time of death
   - Residence address
   - Work address
   - Race, religion, ethnicity, and gender

TABLE 7-2 Profiling Stages

Stage 1	Collecting evidence and information
Stage 2	Using this information to fashion questions and patterns regarding the crime and criminal
Stage 3	Reconstructing the behavior of the offender and the victim
Stage 4	Constructing a tentative description of the most likely suspect or suspects
Stage 5	Concentrating on suspects that match the profile
Stage 6	Apprehending the suspect
Stage 7	Obtaining the conviction of the defendant based on the evidence found in the case

The amount of information left at the crime scene and the quality of its processing determine the level of detail and quality of the profile. As serial killers continue in their killing, they learn. Their learning curve is reflected in how the crime scenes are left.

In the second stage, the profiler uses the information gathered to fashion questions and patterns regarding the criminal and the crime. At this stage, the investigator can ask:

- What type of homicide has been committed—mass murder, spree killing, or serial murder?
- What is the primary motive for the crime—sexual, financial, personal, or emotional disturbance?
- What level of risk did the victim experience?
- What level of risk did the murderer take in killing the victim?
- What was the sequence of acts before and after the killing?
- How long did these acts take to commit?
- Where was the crime committed?
- Was the body moved?
- Was the body found where the murder had taken place?

In stage three the profiler attempts to reconstruct the behavior of the offender and the victim. Again, this reconstruction is a process of asking the right questions:

- Was the murder organized (suggesting a killer who selects victims carefully)?
- Was the murder disorganized (indicating an impulsive killer)?
- Was the crime staged to mislead the police?
- What motivations were revealed by such details as the cause of death, location of wounds, and the position of the body?

Some general profiling rules include the following:

- Brutal facial injuries point to killers who know their victims.
- Murders committed with whatever weapon happens to be available reflect greater impulsivity than murders committed with a gun and may reveal a killer who lives fairly near the victim.
- Murders committed early in the morning seldom involve alcohol or drugs.

At stage four, profilers construct a tentative description of the most likely suspects. That description may include information regarding the suspect's:

- Race
- Sex
- Age (emotional age may not be consistent with chronological years)
- Marital status
- Living arrangements
- Employment history
- Psychological characteristics
- Probable reactions to the police
- Past criminal record
- Geographic comfort zone (Plotting the locations of the homicides or the recovery of victims may reveal a geographic area in which the killer feels most comfortable

obtaining victims, killing victims, or disposing of their bodies; discovery of such an area indicates that the killer has a permanent residence nearby and is not a traveling murderer.)

- Occupation (Tools used and the marks left on the body of victims, referred to as a signature, may be associated with the killer's occupation. If the bodies are tool pinched, are bruised, have ligature marks, or are restrained by wire twisted together but no tools were left at the crime scenes, the tools probably are valuable to the killer and may have uses other than torture.)
- Type of fantasy or psychopathy (for example, the taking of souvenirs or trophies may offer psychologists insight into the mental disorder at work)
- History of violence, probability of future slayings, and the kind of evidence likely to occur at future crime scenes

In stage five, investigators concentrate on suspects matching the profile. The intent is that the application of the prior five stages will result in stage six, the apprehension stage. As in all criminal investigations, the ultimate objective is to win a conviction of the defendant based on the evidence obtained in the case. Thus, a seventh stage should be added to the prior six, in which emphasis is placed on the importance of handling and packaging evidence correctly and respecting the constitutional rights of all suspects. It does little good to have created a profile that results in the apprehension of the suspect if in the interim evidence is contaminated, lost, or destroyed or a suspect is provided a constitutional appellate issue.

In gathering information from a crime scene, investigators need to remember that what is absent sometimes is as important as what has been left. A thorough investigation should thus include a canvass of the premises with a knowledgeable friend or relative of the victim to determine what, if anything, is missing.

Profiling, though in its infancy, is moving closer to becoming a science all the time. The profiler of today is part sage, part cop, and part psychologist and depends on experience and a large smattering of luck. The FBI has taken its profiling show on the road, providing training and certification to police interested in learning the art of profiling. A national and international association is being formed to provide participants from all over the world a place to come in order to learn about profiling and share their experiences.

Modus Operandi

The identification of a suspect may be the product of how the crime was committed. The methods employed by the perpetrator to commit the crime may be so unusual as to bear noting. It is these methods, or MOs, that may be an unintended clue to the offender's identity. Most crimes are so typical in terms of motive or methods as to be indistinguishable from one another. (In such cases, only evidence particular to the suspect, victim, or their relationship is likely to be useful). Determining the MO in these types of cases will provide little information apart from generalizations that will not lead to a suspect or his or her identity. It is the uniqueness of a crime that qualifies an MO as workable.

Experienced investigators have encountered criminals whose MOs are so identifiable as to serve as a signature for the offender. The FBI developed the Violent Criminal Apprehension Program (VICAP) in an effort to collect into databases crime scene information unique enough to be identifiably the work of particular offenders. Although the database contains information that surpasses that contained in an offender's MO,

OFFICER'S NOTEBOOK

Roof Top Slaying

Francine Elveson was a 26-year-old teacher of handicapped children at a local day care center. Weighing 90 pounds and standing less that 5 foot tall, she brought a rare empathy and sensitivity to her students, being mildly handicapped herself with kyphoscoliosis, or curvature of the spine. Shy and not very socially oriented, she lived with her parent in the Pelham Parkway House apartments.

She had left for work as usual at 6:30 in the morning. About 8:20, a 12-year-old boy who also lived in the building found her wallet in the stairwell between the third and fourth floors. He had no time to do anything with it and still be on time for school, so he kept it until he came home for lunch, and then gave it to his father. The father went to the Elveson apartment a little before 3:00 that afternoon and gave the wallet to Francine's mother, who then called the day-care to let Francine know her wallet had been found. Mrs. Elveson was told her daughter had not shown up for work that day. Instantly alarmed, she and her other daughter and a neighbor began a search of the building.

On the roof landing at the top of the stairwell, they came upon Francine's nude body, beaten by blunt-force trauma so severely that the medial examiner later found that her jaw, nose, and cheeks had been fractured and her teeth loosened. She had been spread-eagled and tied with her own belt and nylon stockings around her wrists and ankles, though the medical examiner determined she was already dead when this was done. Her nipples had been cut off after death and placed on her chest. Her underpants had been pulled over her head to cover her face, and bite marks were on her thighs and knees. The several lacerations on the body, all of them shallow, suggested a small pocketknife. Her umbrella and pen had been forced into her vagina and her comb was placed in her pubic hair. Her earrings had been placed on the ground symmetrically on either side of her head. The cause of death was determined to be ligature strangulation with the strap of the victim's own pocketbook. On her thigh the killer had scrawled, "You can't stop me," and on her stomach he had written, "Fuck you," both with the pen that had been inserted into her vagina. The other significant feature of the scene was that the killer had defecated near the body and covered the excrement with some of Francine's clothing.

Traces of semen were found on her body. There were no defense wounds on the hands or blood traces or skin fragments under fingernails. The only tangible piece of forensic evidence was a single negroid hair found on the body during the autopsy.

The initial attack occurred when Francine walked down the stairs. After she was battered unconscious she was carried up to the roof landing. The autopsy indicated that she had not been raped.

Francine's parents said she sometimes took the elevator, sometimes the stairs, with no particular regularity. The occupants of the dwelling were about 50% African American, 40% white, and 20% Hispanic.

Based on the information provided in this chapter: Was this an organized or disorganized crime scene? Why? Who would you want to talk to? Why?

there is little question that MO is included and was probably the starting point for the collection of the data.

Most agencies have a rogues' gallery of photographs of past offenders. In the old days, these photographs were placed in books, and victims were asked to examine mug shots of prior offenders in the hopes of identifying the perpetrator. Today it should be no surprise that many agencies have their rogues' gallery digitally entered into a computer system that includes information about a particular criminal's MO. The gallery can be searched by criteria such as gender, race, age, name, height, weight, hair color, visible markings, eye color, or modus operandi.

Modus operandi is further subdivided into the following elements:

- Time of day
- Location

- Property at issue
- Indoor vs. outdoor
- Types of buildings involved (commercial or residential)
- Signatures
- Particular entry methodology or words
- Particular exit methodology or words
- Clothing
- Weapon
- Soiled scene
- Disguise
- Con (pretending to be on the premises legitimately relative to a particular job or status)
- Victim targeting
- Branding (whatever is left or taken unrelated to the commission of the crime)

Coupling faces with MOs allows the database to serve a dual purpose as a compilation of mug shots and as a database of MOs and their association with particular individuals, particular behaviors, and particular places with a criminal history.

Crime Mapping

Crimes are not geographically random. For a moment in time, crimes, victims, and offenders all exist at the same place at the same time. The lure of targets and their geographic availability determine where people decide to commit crimes. Mapping crimes provides insight into the where and, derivatively, perhaps the why of crimes. Mapping can help law enforcement identify the areas in which citizens need protection. The simplest of maps can be used to direct patrols to where concentrations of crimes suggest the most help is needed. Police administrators use maps to record criminal trends and to assist in the allocation of staff and resources. Criminal investigators use maps to help develop profiles of serial offenders and to geographically isolate a serial offender's comfort zone.

Crime mapping in its essence is not new; police have long used pushpins in maps to isolate areas of criminal activity and to delineate the working area for particular offenders. Today, however, geographic information system (GIS) software allows police to produce digital maps. The same GIS software used to map crime locations can be used to calculate crime density (number of crimes per square mile). These density values can be used to create a map that uses color to represent different values among land units within the study area.

Data from sources other than law enforcement can be used in crime mapping and analysis. Census data can be used to examine a particular crime and the locations at which it is occurring with respect to demographic factors. A large cluster of homicides in high-population areas allows a correlation to be drawn between homicides and population density. Data pertaining to vacant housing units may represent a concentration of certain drug, violent, or property crimes. Police departments use computer-mapped crime locations to pinpoint hot spots, that is, areas with high concentrations of crime. Hot-spot analysis can be conducted using spatial and temporal analysis of crime (STAC) software. The Illinois Criminal Justice Information Authority developed this software, which draws ellipses based on the densest concentrations of mapped incidents.

As with all computer-generated data, the end result is only as good as the information going in: garbage in, garbage out. Databases are tools that assist law enforcement in the management of information. No matter how sophisticated the instrument used to manage, organize, or manipulate information, the usefulness of the analysis is directly proportionate to the time, care, quantity, and reliability of the data upon which the analysis is based.

■ Summary

When we watch investigations on television, everyone appears to know what their responsibilities are and addresses them. There seems to be no clear-cut management or leadership. Contrary to what is portrayed in the movies, each crime scene is the responsibility of the investigator assigned the case. That assignment includes within it the understanding that the investigator in charge knows how to manage the people who will be assisting in the processing of the crime scene, from first responding officer to forensic personnel working at his/her direction. The assignment also assumes the investigator knows how to apply the appropriate protocol for the type of crime being investigated. In the old days that skill came from on-the-job training; today, crime scene management is taught to all investigators as police recruits and during investigator's school. There is nothing natural about managing people or a location; it is a learned process. This chapter discussed various management methods but more importantly draws attention to the fact that those working on a crime scene do not manage themselves, nor does the location manage itself.

This chapter briefly touched on interrogation. The next chapter discusses the subject in depth. Today people believe that most crimes are cleared through the use of forensic evidence. That is probably not a bad belief, it is just not the truth. Most serious crimes are cleared by skillful interrogations, and the key to a skillful interrogation involves preparation. The next chapter will reveal the secrets to a successful interrogation.

■ Key Terms

acquisition technology: Technical devices that permit officers to acquire sights and sounds that they would not otherwise have been able to perceive from a legal vantage point; such technology requires a warrant or other court order

circumstantial evidence: All evidence other than eyewitness testimony

electronic communication: In-transit electronic impulses, sounds, and other signals transmitted over wire, radio, or microwave

enhancement technology: Technical devices that allow augmentation of sound or picture quality; such technology does not require a warrant or other court authorization

follow-up investigation: Investigation of a crime that is conducted if solvability factors are found during the preliminary investigation

hearsay: Any out-of-court statement made by someone other than the person testifying

informant: One who provides information

incident command system (ICS): A management tool that integrates multiple resources

intelligence: Information

interrogation: The formal questioning of a suspect conducted in a controlled environment and performed in an accusatory manner in order to learn the truth

interview: A conversation with witnesses or victims in order to elicit information

leads: The initial descriptions of persons, places, events, and things related to an investigation

managing criminal investigations (MCI): Concept designed to determine which crimes are most solvable and to use limited investigative resources to solve them

mass murderer: Someone who kills four or more victims in one location in one incident; the killings are all part of the same emotional experience

modus operandi (MO): What an offender has to do to commit the offense in question; literally, a *manner of operating*

National Incident Management System (NIMS): A method of coordinating the supervision of multiple agencies working together

preliminary investigation: The police agency's first response to a report that a crime has been committed

profiling: Technique used mostly by behavioral scientists and the police to narrow down an investigation to those suspects who possess certain behavioral and personality features that are revealed by the way a crime was committed

serial killer: Someone who has murdered on at least three occasions, with emotional cooling-off periods between each incident

signature: A factor or factors that make the crime atypical and distinguishable from other crimes and other criminals

snitch: Criminal or person who associates with criminals who gives information to police about acquaintances involved in or planning criminal activities

solvability factors: Information about a crime that can provide the basis for determining who committed the crime

spree killer: Someone who murders at two or more locations, with no emotional cooling-off period between the homicides

stakeout: A type of stationary surveillance that generally focuses on places and things and requires great patience and many departmental resources

tail: Automobile surveillance of a suspect

totality of the circumstances: Test used to determine if information supplied by an informant is legally usable; it states that such information is legal if, given all the circumstances, there is a fair probability that the evidence sought will be found in a particular place

Violent Criminal Apprehension Program (VICAP): Program that collects, sorts, analyzes, and categorizes data on serial homicides in an effort to uncover hidden relationships among homicides, victims, and modi operandi

■ Review Questions

1. In MCI, who conducts the preliminary investigation?
2. In MCI, how is it determined if a follow-up investigation is to be conducted?
3. In MCI, who conducts the follow-up investigation?
4. What are solvability factors?
5. What are the 12 solvability factors identified by the Rochester Police Department?
6. Who are informants, and what service do they provide to law enforcement?

7. What risks or limitations are inherent in dealing with informants?

8. What is hearsay evidence, and how does the exclusion of hearsay evidence apply to information provided by informants?

9. What cases have played a role in determining whether information from informants can be used to establish probable cause? Discuss the importance of each case.

10. What is a stakeout and when is it used?

11. What is the Violent Criminal Apprehension Program (VICAP), and what service does it provide to the law enforcement community?

12. Discuss the first six FBI profile stages.

13. What is the seventh stage that might be added to the FBI profile stages?

14. What kind of questions might be posed after viewing crime scene photos, reports, and statements?

15. What is the difference between an organized and a disorganized crime scene? What does it tell you about the offender?

16. What is the difference between a mass murder and a serial homicide?

17. What is the difference between a serial murder and a spree killing?

18. What is GIS, and how is law enforcement using it?

19. When interviewing children, what effect do leading questions have on the credibility of the interview?

20. What effect does a child's linguistic ability have on the quality of an interview?

21. List four ways that suggestibility may influence the results of an interview with a child.

22. Explain how someone else might influence a child's testimony during an interview.

23. Discuss ways to avoid the hazards associated with child interviews.

24. What would be the advantage, if any, of having a prosecutor at the crime scene during processing?

25. In large crime scenes such as the attack on the World Trade Center in New York on September 11, 2001, who was in charge of processing the crime scene?

26. List the core principles of NIMS.

■ Bibliography

Anderson, D.R., Lorch, E.P., Field, D.E., Collins, P.A., & Nathan, J.G. (1986). Television viewing at home: Age trends in visual attention and time with TV. *Child Development* 57, 1024–1033.

Ceci, S.J., & Bruck, M. (1995). *Jeopardy in the courtroom: A scientific analysis of children's testimony.* Washington, DC: American Psychological Association Press.

Department of Homeland Security. (2004). *National Incident Management System,* www.dhs.gov

Douglas, J. E., & Olshaker, M. (1996). *Mind hunter.* New York: Pocket Books.

Douglas, J. E., & Olshaker, M. (1999). *The anatomy of motive.* New York: Scribner.

Gilbert, J.N. (1998). *Criminal investigation* (4th ed.). Englewood Cliffs, NJ: Prentice Hall.

Greenhoot, A.F., Ornstein, P.A., Gordon, B.N., & Baker-Ward, L. (1999). Acting out the details of a pediatric check-up: The impact of interview condition and behavioral style on children's memory reports. *Child Development* 70, 363–380.

Poole, D.A., & Lamb, M.E. (1998). *Investigative interviews of children: A guide for helping professionals.* Washington, DC: American Psychological Association Press.

Poole, D.A., & Lindsay, D.S. (2001). Children's eyewitness reports after exposure to misinformation from parents. *Journal of Experimental Psychology: Applied* 7, 27–50.

Reisberg, D. (2001). *Cognition* (2nd ed.). New York: W.W. Norton & Company.

■ Key Legal Cases

Aguilar v. Texas, 378 U.S. 108 (1964).
California v. Greenwood, 486 U.S. 35 (1988).
Draper v. United States, 358 U.S. 307 (1959).
Florida v. Riley, 488 U.S. 445 (1989).
Illinois v. Gates, 462 U.S. 213 (1983).
Katz v. United States, 389 U.S. 347 (1967).
Kyllo v. United States, 533 U.S. 27 (2001).
Lopez v. United States, 373 U.S. 427 (1963).
Olmstead v. United States, 277 U.S. 438 (1928).
On Lee v. United States, 343 U.S. 747 (1952).
Oregon v. Wacker, 317 Or. 419 (1993).
People v. Arno, 90 Cal. App. 3d 505 (1979).
People v. Camacho, 23 Cal. App. 4th 824 (2000).
Smith v. Maryland, 442 U.S. 735 (1979).
Spinelli v. United States, 393 U.S. 410 (1969).
United States v. Knotts, 460 U.S. 276 (1983).
United States v. McIntyre, 582 F.2d 1221 (9th Cir. 1978).

Interrogation

▶ ▶ STUDENT LEARNING OUTCOMES

Upon completion of this chapter students will demonstrate an understanding of:

- The Supreme Court's holding in *Miranda v. Arizona*
- The circumstances that give rise to Miranda warnings
- How to conduct a successful interrogation
- How to record the confession

One of the most effective trial exhibits that the prosecution can present to a jury is a confession. The impact of this type of evidence is one of the reasons that the U.S. Supreme Court promulgated guidelines for law enforcement agents eliciting confessions. Confessions are obtained through **interrogations**, the most daunting type of interview that an investigator can conduct. An interrogation is comparable to a chess match, in which a number of standard moves may be used to initiate contact. But at some point during every interrogation, standard moves cease to be available and spontaneity must take over. This is when a criminal investigator demonstrates his or her real skill as an interrogator. The best-planned interrogations, like the best-planned trials, often go awry. It is when an interrogation does go awry that a novice interrogator will undergo baptism by fire and be reborn, it is hoped, as a better practitioner of the art of interrogating offenders.

Preplanned opening moves may serve well with new offenders or in establishing rapport with career criminals, but the preparation for the interrogation is what carries an investigator beyond the opening game. An investigator's familiarity with the crime, the modus operandi of the crime, the suspect, the evidence to date, and the crime scene determines whether he or she can make it to the end game when playing against a seasoned, hostile, or psychopathic offender. Seasoned offenders and psychopaths often enjoy doing battle with police, whom they believe to be intellectually inferior. Too often, the interrogator's lack of preparation proves them correct (Gilbert, 1998).

Interrogations usually take place at the police station, in a sparsely furnished room with no windows or distractions. This spartan environment is designed to disarm the suspect and place him or her at a disadvantage. Separation from the things he or she is familiar with can be traumatic for the uninitiated. For the experienced offender, it is just one more in a long series of places he or she would rather not be.

Interrogative technique is unique to the interrogator. Successful interrogators, however, tend to:

- Show respect for the suspect's constitutional rights
- Show respect for the dignity of the worst among us
- Possess an understanding of human and conversational dynamics
- Maintain control over passions and prejudice
- Exhibit confidence and professionalism
- Exhibit self-respect as well as respect for the law and the criminal justice system

The interrogation environment created by police is inherently intimidating. The Supreme Court has been concerned with the intimidating aspects of interrogation in determining whether confessions obtained by investigators are voluntary. Two cases demonstrate the Court's concern and establish guidelines for ensuring that statements obtained from suspects are voluntary and not a product of coercion, whether explicit or implicit: *Escobedo v. Illinois* (1964) and *Miranda v. Arizona* (1966).

The *Escobedo* case raised two questions that the Court ultimately would address in its *Miranda* decision:

1. Do the rights recognized by the Court apply only to serious offenses for which the suspect is in custody and requests the services of an attorney?
2. At what point does an investigation begin to focus on one person?

The two elements giving rise to the need for *Miranda* warnings are *custody* and *interrogation*. The absence of either removes the need to provide such warnings. There are a number of cases of which every investigator should be aware. These cases, briefly described here, define the boundaries of interrogation and the types of situations in which *Miranda* warnings are not required.

- *New York v. Quarles*, 467 U.S. 649 (1987). Public safety concerns exempt police from having to provide *Miranda* warnings. A response to an inquiry about the location of an abandoned weapon may be incriminatory, but it also serves the

CASE IN POINT

Escobedo v. Illinois, 1964

Escobedo v. Illinois centered on the following question: When does an interview become an interrogation? Escobedo was wanted for murder and was arrested and interrogated. After his arrest, police told him that someone had witnessed the murder and had identified him as the perpetrator. Escobedo refused to admit the offense and instead stated that he wished to speak with his lawyer. Escobedo's lawyer arrived at the police station and requested an opportunity to speak with his client. He was not allowed access to his client. During the course of various station-house interrogations, Escobedo repeatedly requested to speak with his lawyer and finally admitted to some of the facts of the murder and incriminated himself. He was charged with and convicted of murder.

The Supreme Court held that when an interview is no longer one of general inquiry about a crime but begins to focus on one person who has been taken into police custody, that interview has become an interrogation, and the Sixth Amendment right to counsel is in effect. A failure to warn the suspect at this stage of the criminal justice process that he or she has the right to remain silent and the right to the services of an attorney is constitutionally impermissible, and any information obtained may not be used against the suspect in a court of law.

CASE IN POINT

Miranda v. Arizona, 1966

Miranda v. Arizona centered on the following question: What must police tell a person they intend to interrogate? Charged with rape and kidnapping, Miranda was arrested, taken to the police station, and questioned. The interrogation extended over a two-hour period, at the end of which Miranda signed a written confession. He was convicted of rape and kidnapping. The Supreme Court concluded that, whoever the suspect and whatever that suspect's sophistication, it is necessary to provide the suspect a warning as a counterweight to the intimidating characteristics of a hostile environment. The warning must be sufficient to ensure that any statements provided by the suspect are voluntary and not the product of an overborne will.

The custodial interrogation of a suspect has inherent intimidating characteristics that only a constitutional warning can obviate. Any warning promulgated by the police must minimally apprise the suspect that:

- He or she has the right to remain silent.
- Any and all statements made by the suspect can and will be used against him or her in a court of law.
- He or she has the right to the services of an attorney during questioning.
- He or she has the right to an appointed counsel if unable to afford counsel.

The Court went on to define what it meant by "custodial interrogation," which applies to those situations in which a suspect is entitled to *Miranda* warnings: "We mean questioning initiated by law enforcement officers after a person has been taken into custody or otherwise deprived of his freedom of action in any significant way."

public interest because it pertains to safety; therefore, it does not raise the need for *Miranda* warnings.

- *McNeil v. Wisconsin,* 501 U.S. 171 (1990). A suspect's invocation of the Fifth Amendment right to remain silent with regard to a particular offense does not constitute an invocation for other offenses for which the suspect has not yet been charged. The invocation of the Fifth Amendment right to remain silent prohibits police from inquiring into any aspects of the offense in question, but they may initiate further interrogation about unrelated offenses until the right to remain silent is again invoked. The invocation of the Fifth Amendment right against self-incrimination is specific to an offense.
- *Texas v. Cobb,* 532 U.S. 162 (2001). A suspect's invocation of the Sixth Amendment right to counsel with regard to a particular offense does not constitute an invocation for other offenses for which the suspect has not yet been charged. The invocation of the Sixth Amendment right to counsel prohibits police from inquiring into any aspects of the offense in question, but they may initiate further interrogation about unrelated offenses until the right to counsel is again invoked. The invocation applies to the offense in question and any factually related offenses.
- *Oregon v. Elstad,* 470 U.S. 298 (1985). *Miranda* warnings may "cure" a previously voluntarily provided unwarned confession if the warnings are provided prior to the elicitation of a subsequent statement.
- *Connecticut v. Barrett,* 479 U.S. 523 (1987). A suspect who has refused to give a written confession may still be urged to provide an oral confession as long as he or she has not invoked the right to remain silent.

- *Duckworth v. Eagan,* 492 U.S. 195 (1989). The *Miranda* warnings need not be given exactly as suggested by the Supreme Court or as written in police procedural manuals as long as they convey to the suspect his or her Fifth and Sixth Amendment rights.
- *Pennsylvania v. Muniz,* 496 U.S. 582 (1990). Because the Fifth Amendment provides *testimonial* protection—that is, protections regarding a person's testimony—behavior and communications designed to gather nonevidentiary information are not covered. DWI roadblocks typically involve routine questioning of a stopped motorist. The questions may elicit responses that eventually prove incriminating, but they were designed to gather routine information. Answering such questions is not considered to be self-incriminatory and therefore is not protected by the Constitution. Should videotape recordings of responses to these routine questions be made, they too are constitutionally permissible.
- *Davis v. United States,* 114 S.Ct. 2350 (1994). After a suspect voluntarily waives his or her rights as described in *Miranda,* investigators may continue the interrogation until the accused affirmatively asserts his or her rights.
- *Brewer v. Williams,* 430 U.S. 387 (1977). Interrogations may be direct or indirect, explicit or implicit. An investigator cannot attempt to accomplish indirectly what he or she cannot accomplish directly. In *Brewer,* a conversation between officers in a police vehicle was intended to and did elicit an incriminating statement from the suspect in the back seat. The Court held that the statement was the functional equivalent of a confession because of the officers' knowledge of the suspect's sensitivity toward religious issues; therefore the subject's statement was inadmissible.
- *Arizona v. Mauro,* 481 U.S. (1987). Recorded self-incriminatory conversations between two persons, one of whom gives consent for the recording, do not rise to the level of an interrogation and do not require *Miranda* warnings.

It is not unusual for the defense attorney, during trial, to request the testifying officer to recite the *Miranda* warnings to the jury just as they were provided to the defendant. The best practice is to read the warnings from a card. The defense attorney may ask whether the reason it is necessary to read them is because of the officer's inability to recall them, or the attorney may request to see the card (which he or she is entitled to do) and then ask the witness to recite the warnings. The reason for reading the warnings is simply to ensure that no misunderstanding occurs as the result of a possible misstatement of the warnings. In response to the request to recite the warnings without benefit of the card, the witness should state that it would be unprofessional, in that a recitation from memory may result in a misstatement of the warnings.

To see the problem, consider the following version of the warnings:

You have the right to remain silent. Anything you say may be held against you in a court of law. You have the right to the services of an attorney. If you cannot afford one, one will be provided for you. Do you understand these warnings as I have explained them to you?

If you recognized that the *may* in the second sentence could be problematic, you have a lawyer's penchant for verbal exactitude. The word *may* suggests an alternative and constitutes a hint of impermissible coercion through unauthorized bargaining. The

OFFICER'S NOTEBOOK

Interrogation Tips

- Pick the time—to suit the investigator.
- Pick the place—to isolate the person being interrogated.
- Provide *Miranda* warnings, even if they have been provided in the past.
- Maintain eye contact. The eyes are the windows to the soul, and penetrating eye contact is disconcerting to the guilty.
- Record the interrogation, including the *Miranda* warnings.
- Transcribe the interrogation and have the person interrogated sign the transcription, making any corrections he or she feels necessary.
- Treat the person being interrogated with respect and dignity.
- Be patient.
- Be professional.
- Be honest.
- Do not play games.
- Do not deprive the person being interrogated of sleep, food, cigarettes, or use of toilet facilities.
- Do not say or do anything you would not want a jury to hear.

defense would make the most of it by intimating that if this error were made, many other serious errors might have been made as well. It is prudent to read *Miranda* warnings both on the street and in the courtroom. Those who do read the warnings will not risk falling victim to a skillful cross-examiner.

■ Successful Interrogations

A **successful interrogation** results in a guilty criminal suspect's making a confession or admitting participation in an illegal activity. Often, guilty suspects leave the interrogation room without making an admission. Interrogations can fail for many reasons. Some are foreseeable. Once investigators have identified these factors, they can consider and act upon them to increase the probability of successful interrogations. Certain components are crucial to every successful interrogation. These major components are:

- Preparing for the interrogation
- Distinguishing between interrogations and interviews
- Developing persuasive themes and arguments
- Establishing a set plan
- Building a good relationship with the interrogation subject
- Allowing enough time for the interrogation

Preparing for the Interrogation

Preparation is the most important factor in conducting a successful interrogation. Factors to consider when preparing interrogations include:

- The setting and environmental considerations
- Knowledge of case facts
- Familiarity with the subject's background
- The method used to document the confession

Setting and Environmental Factors

Successful interrogations require that interrogators, not subjects, control not only the topics of discussion but also the physical environment. Officers should conduct interrogations only when they can ensure privacy and control of the environment. A good setting is a small, controlled, sound-insulated room void of distractions. A setting free from diversions forces the subject to respond only to the interrogator's inquiries. It also gives investigators a much better opportunity to observe the subject's verbal and nonverbal responses to the questions. The further the situation gets from a controlled setting, the higher the chance that the interrogation will fail. Often, only one good interrogation opportunity exists. Risking that opportunity in an unacceptable environment may be a poor investigative decision (Aubrey and Caputo, 1986).

Knowledge of Case Facts

Understanding case facts remains critical to any interrogation, but some facts may prove more important than others. Knowing how a crime occurred can be an effective tool of persuasion. If investigators can tell a suspect how a crime was committed, the suspect may give the reasons for his or her involvement in the incident.

Familiarity with the Subject's Background

Acquiring adequate background information about a suspect is another critical factor in achieving a successful outcome. A subject's feelings, attitudes, and personal values directly affect the nature and outcome of an interrogation. Individuals often make the choice to confess based on their emotions, and then defend their positions or choices with logic. When interrogators understand a suspect's goals, needs, and conflicts, they can use this information to persuade a suspect that confessing the truth is in the suspect's best interest (Decker and Denney, 1992).

Documenting Confessions

Investigators should plan the details of **documenting the confession** before beginning the interrogation. Best practices for interrogation is for all interactions with a suspect to be videotaped with a sound recording. Any allegations of coercion or overreacting can best be rebutted by providing a complete videorecording of what transpired before, during, and after a suspect makes an incriminating statement. Additionally, a verbatim transcript of the entire interrogation should be made. Not a transcript of only the incriminating statement but of every word that transpired between interrogators and the suspect.

OFFICER'S NOTEBOOK

Elements of a Plan for Documenting a Confession
- Who will obtain the waiver of rights?
- Will the statement be a stenographic recording?
- Will the suspect write out the statement?
- Will the statement be recorded orally?
- Who will witness the statement?
- Will the statement be a narrative or in question-and-answer format?

Once the entire process has been recorded and transcribed, the portion containing the incriminating statement can be cut from the transcript. All this is necessary in the event that the confessing suspect recants the confessions and alleges coercion.

Distinguishing Between Interrogations and Interviews

Investigators must understand the distinction between interviewing and interrogating suspects. Interviews are the pathways to interrogations: an interview should precede every interrogation. Through the interview, investigators learn about the suspect and his or her needs and fears. The information gathered during the interview will be used to fashion the arguments and themes used throughout the interrogation.

In interrogations, investigators lead, and subjects follow. Investigators do not seek information. They do not take notes. They only want to obtain truthful admissions or confessions. Continuing to obtain erroneous or fabricated facts while trying to secure truthful admissions causes investigators to lose the advantage in the interrogation process. Once investigators determine that interrogation is warranted, obtaining the truth from the subject becomes their only goal (Aubrey and Caputo, 1986).

Developing Persuasive Themes and Arguments

Lack of arguments and themes to persuade subjects to tell the truth stands as a major cause of interrogation failure. Experience provides investigators with an ever-increasing supply of arguments. Conducting more interrogations gives investigators additional ideas and a wider variety of themes to pursue.

Preparation allows investigators to plan their themes and arguments before interrogating subjects. Certain themes and arguments remain universally available, including the following:

- Minimizing the crime
- Blaming the victim
- Decreasing the shamefulness of the act
- Increasing guilt feelings
- Appealing to the subject's hope for a better outcome

Knowing what is important to a suspect gives interrogators plenty of topics and helps them avoid running out of subjects.

Building a Good Relationship

Suspects may confess for no other reason than their respect for and trust in their interrogators. Investigators must build a good **relationship** with suspects. Anything that appears more important than the suspect or the relationship may prove detrimental to the interrogation process.

The perspectives, values, and goals of suspects and investigators diverge dramatically. It is necessary for an investigator to view an interrogation, a crime, and life experiences from the suspect's point of view. As investigators realize and understand these differences, interrogations become more personal and more effective.

Allowing Enough Time

Successful interrogations require a certain amount of time to complete. That time is unique to each investigation and to each suspect. Suspects make critical life decisions based on their personal needs and wants and their perceived ideas about their situations balanced against the themes, arguments, and facts presented by interrogators. Such a complicated process requires ample time to conclude successfully.

■ The Reid Technique

John E. Reid, who established a private polygraph firm in 1947 in Chicago, developed the **Reid technique**. The technique represents the cumulative experiences of dozens of associates who used the technique successfully to solve thousands of crimes since 1997. The training was first made available to the public in 1974, and more than 200,000 investigators have been trained in these techniques.

The Reid technique describes a three-part process for conducting a successful interrogation:

1. Factual analysis: This stage represents the collection and analysis of information relative to a crime scene, the victim, and possible suspects. Factual analysis helps determine the direction an investigation should take and offers insight regarding the possible offender.

2. Interview of possible suspects: This highly structured interview, referred to as a behavior analysis interview, is a nonaccusatory question-and-answer session intended to elicit information from the subject in a controlled environment. The clinical nature of the interview, including the asking of specific behavior- provoking questions, is designed to provide the investigator with verbal and nonverbal behavior symptoms that either support probable truthfulness or deception.

3. Accusatory interrogation: If the investigator believes that the subject has not told the truth during the nonaccusatory interview, the third part of the technique is employed, which is the accusatory interrogation.

The purpose of an interrogation is to elicit the truth. The persuasive efforts used during an interrogation must be balanced against the possibility that the suspect is innocent of the offense. The techniques must be effective enough to persuade a guilty suspect to tell the truth, but not so powerful as to cause an innocent person to confess.

All deception is motivated by the desire to avoid the consequences of telling the truth. These consequences may be social (going to prison, losing a job, paying a fine) or personal (feelings of embarrassment, shame, or humiliation). The investigator who tells a suspect, "You're in a lot of trouble and face the rest of your life behind bars," has made it psychologically very difficult for the suspect to tell the truth. The common technique, used by interrogators nationwide, of informing the suspect about the possible sentence facing him or her if convicted should be avoided.

The interrogator should also refrain from using hard **descriptives** such as *murder, rape,* and *theft* in favor of the less harsh concepts of *taking a human life, nonconsensual sex,* and *taking,* respectively. It is psychologically much easier to admit *causing a person's death* than it is to admit to *murdering* that person. In addition, the investigator should portray an understanding and compassionate demeanor toward the suspect that allows the suspect to feel better about himself and less guilty about the crime he has committed. Another technique to reduce the perceived consequences of a crime involves more active persuasion. In this instance, the suspect is told that his or her crime could have been much worse and that it is fortunate that the suspect did not engage in the more serious activity.

Every person who has committed a crime will have justified that crime in some way. A crime against a person is often justified by blaming the victim. Crimes against property may be justified in a variety of ways. The employee who steals may justify the theft because she is underpaid and overworked; the auto thief blames society for not providing him a sufficient standard of living. Over time, criminals develop a victim's mentality. Criminals convince themselves and each other that they are the casualties of an unjust and unfair criminal justice system. Although the criminal may accept that what he did was wrong, the criminal believes he deserves special consideration because of his unique situation. An important part of the victim mentality is the urge to protect this victim image, to the extent of making a self-serving yet incriminating statement. The procedures employed in the Reid technique reinforce the guilty suspect's own justification for the crime and culminate by taking advantage of the suspect's victim mentality.

Steps of the Reid Technique

John Reid divided interrogation into different steps because he observed that suspects often go through identifiable stages during a successful interrogation (for complete coverage of this method, see Inbau, Reid et al., 2004). Suspects often begin by denying involvement in the offense. The guilty suspect eventually becomes quiet and withdrawn. At some point the guilty suspect starts to mentally debate whether or not to confess. It is at this stage that the investigator seeks the first admission of guilt. Once this admission is offered, the suspect is generally willing to disclose the details of his or her crime through standard questioning procedures.

Step 1: Positive Confrontation

In the first step, the investigator advises the suspect that the investigation clearly indicates that he or she is responsible for the commission of a crime. This, of course, may not be a true statement. However, to persuade a guilty suspect to tell the truth, the investigator must often exaggerate his or her confidence in the suspect's guilt and the evidence and information in the possession of the police.

Following this direct positive confrontation, the investigator makes a transition statement. An example of a transition statement is, "We have everything we need to tie you to this crime; now's the chance to tell your side of the story." The transition statement is psychologically important in that it offers a pretense for the interrogation other than to elicit a confession. The concept of understanding why the crime was committed is attractive to the guilty suspect, who believes outside circumstances were responsible for his committing the crime. Finally, the transition statement allows the investigator to become more understanding and compassionate, encouraging the suspect to respond.

Step 2: Theme Development

A **theme** is a monologue in which the investigator offers moral or psychological excuses for the suspect's criminal behavior. The theme is not designed to plant new ideas in the suspect's mind but merely to reinforce the justifications that already exist in the guilty suspect's mind.

Criminals mentally distort the motives and circumstances surrounding their crime. They do not accept the true reasons behind their behavior. They have found some justification that, in their mind, either excuses or excepts their behavior, often with a victim-mentality embellishment. It is the investigator's job to determine what this fallacious

OFFICER'S NOTEBOOK

The Reid Technique
- Step 1: *Positive confrontation.* The investigator advises the suspect that the investigation clearly indicates that he or she is responsible.
- Step 2: *Theme development.* The investigator offers moral or psychological excuses for the suspect's criminal behavior.
- Steps 3 and 4: *Talking through denial.* If a suspect is permitted to voice too many denials, he becomes committed to that position and no amount of persuasion will allow him to save enough face while telling the truth.
- Step 5: *Focusing attention.* Behavioral signs include dropped barriers (uncrossing arms or legs), a less tense posture, and inability to maintain eye contact.
- Step 6: *Responding to passivity of the interrogation.* The interrogator condenses theme concepts to one or two central elements.
- Step 7: *Alternative questioning.* The question posed is one that presents two choices to the suspect regarding the crime he or she has committed. The choices generally contrast a positive and a negative choice.

justification might be and turn it into a theme that will allow the suspect to buy in, reducing in his or her mind the criminal consequences of his or her behavior.

Steps 3 and 4: Talking Through Denials

Most guilty suspects will offer denials during theme development. An important principle with respect to denials is that the more often a suspect denies involvement in an offense, the more difficult it is for that person to tell the truth. If a suspect is permitted to voice too many denials, he becomes committed to that position and no amount of persuasion will allow him or her to save enough face while telling the truth. For this reason, the investigator will discourage the suspect from offering weak denials by simply maintaining a flow of words.

It is important to recognize that the interrogator does not prevent a suspect from offering a denial—he or she simply makes the suspect socially uncomfortable when denials are made. A guilty suspect's denials become weaker and less persistent as the investigator continues on with his or her theme. Once the suspect recognizes that his denials are not dissuading the investigator's confidence in his guilt, he often psychologically withdraws. His mind is focused on the consequences of his crime and he is content to allow the investigator to continue to talk and simply tunes him or her out.

Step 5: Focusing Attention

Once the suspect begins to withdraw, it is important for the interrogator to redefine the suspect's focus. That focal change should be directed toward the interrogator. The change in focus should be gradual, not abrupt. For the first time during the interrogation, the suspect may begin to think about telling the truth. The behavioral signs at this stage of an interrogation include dropped barriers (uncrossing arms or legs), a less tense posture, and an inability to maintain eye contact.

Step 6: Responding to Passivity of the Interrogation

The tempo of the interrogation slows. The investigator condenses theme concepts to one or two central elements, and moves into the next step of the process, which is designed to elicit the initial admission of guilt.

Step 7: Alternative Questioning

This step is the point to which the interrogator has been heading since the beginning. There is but one time during the course of an interrogation where an **alternative question** will elicit a truthful response. It is the skillful investigator who recognizes that point in time. The question presents two choices to the suspect regarding the crime he or she has committed. The choices generally contrast a positive and a negative choice. Accepting either choice, of course, results in an admission of guilt. The psychology of the alternative question relies on the guilty suspect's victim mentality. An example of an alternative question in a homicide case might be, "Did you plan on doing this since the day you got married, or did it pretty much happen on the spur of the moment because of the fight you had?" or, "Did you pull the trigger or did your partner?"

In those instances in which a suspect accepts the positive side of the alternative question, the suspect's agreement with the investigator's question is an admission of guilt that must be preserved. The admission should lead to an oral confession, which in turn should result in a recorded or written confession. A **confession** is a statement acknowledging personal responsibility for a crime, including details only the guilty person would know.

■ Written Statements and Confessions

Written statements are permanent records of the pretrial testimony of accused persons. They may be used in court as evidence attesting to what was told to investigators; to refresh the memory of the people who made the statements; and to refresh the memory of investigators.

Miranda warnings and the signing of a **waiver** form stating that the suspect understands his or her rights pursuant to *Miranda v. Arizona* and voluntarily waives those rights in making any written statements must precede all written confessions. The confession is generally recorded using one of three accepted methods: narrative, question-and-answer, or a combination of narrative and question-and-answer.

The narrative method allows the interviewee or person executing the statement to record the information in his or her own words as desired. That is ideal if the person is articulate and does not compile a mass of irrelevant information. The narrative is used more often with a complainant or witness than with a victim or suspect.

In the question-and-answer method, the investigator can limit the information presented to that which is pertinent. Two disadvantages of using this method are: (1) it is time-consuming for the investigator and (2) it may suppress some valuable information that might have been volunteered had the narrative method been used.

A combination of the preceding two methods normally produces the best results. The person being questioned is first allowed to tell his or her story, and then the investigator elicits specific information previously omitted. This method or the question-and-answer method is most often used when taking a statement from an accused suspect.

Confession Law

Confession law is the area of law dealing with the proper technique for legally obtaining a confession, and the rights guaranteed a suspect when he or she is deciding whether to give a confession. Key developments in this area are summarized in TABLE 8-1.

TABLE 8–1   Key Developments in Confession Law

Case	Ruling
Brown v. Mississippi (1936)	Physical coercion violates the Fourth Amendment.
Chambers v. Florida (1940)	Psychological coercion violates the Fourth Amendment.
Ashcraft v. Tennessee (1944)	Psychological coercion is not admissible.
Haley v. Ohio (1948)	Relay teams of interrogators are inherently coercive.
Payne v. Arkansas (1958)	Holding a suspect incommunicado is coercive.
Miranda v. Arizona (1966)	Suspects must be read their rights before questioning.
United States v. Ferrara (1967)	Promises of light bail may be permissable.
Frazier v. Cupp (1969)	Police can say that an accomplice is cooperating.
Harris v. New York (1971)	Confession can be used in court to impeach testimony.
United States v. Arcediano (1974)	Promises of federal instead of state prison are approved.
Beckwith v. United States (1976)	Custody, not focus of suspicion, triggers *Miranda*.
Brewer v. Williams (1977)	Established functional equivalence test for custody.
United States v. Fike (1977)	No need to re-*Mirandize* a suspect unless day(s) have passed.
North Carolina v. Butler (1979)	Waiver of *Miranda* does not have to be written.
California v. Braeske (1980)	Requests to speak off the record must be honored.
Rhode Island v. Innes (1980)	No functional equivalent if police talk to each other.
Edwards v. Arizona (1981)	*Miranda* is waived if suspect initiates conversation.
California v. Prysock (1981)	*Miranda* warnings do not have to be read ritually.
New York v. Quarles (1987)	Established public safety exception.
Duckworth v. Eagan (1989)	*Miranda* warnings do not have to be read precisely.
Illinois v. Perkins (1990)	Police can pose as inmates to extract confessions.
Minnick v. Mississippi (1990)	Interrogation stops when the suspect requests an attorney.
Pennsylvania v. Muniz (1990)	*Miranda* warnings do not apply to drunk drivers.
Arizona v. Fulminate (1991)	Technically deficient confessions do not overturn convictions.
Davis v. United States (1994)	Suspect must make an unambiguous request for an attorney.

■ Summary

Interrogations have always been a concern to the American people. Our collective historical experience with England during the colonial period as reflected in the Declaration of Independence and later in the Bill of Rights highlights the major grievances that the American colonists had with the English government. Prominently situated in the Fifth Amendment is the prohibition against self-incrimination. Although national emphasis has changed law enforcement focus to forensic evidence, the confession that is a product of understanding constitutional constraints is still the grist that makes the law enforcement mill turn.

In the next chapter we discuss firearm and cartridge class characteristics and the methods used by firearms examiners to identify and compare firearms, cartridges, cartridge cases and projectiles. The United States has an infatuation with the handgun and it is employed commonly in armed robberies, aggravated assaults and homicides. Handling firearm evidence requires an appreciation for what forensic personnel are looking for and making sure that the handling and packaging assists in the preservation of any trace evidence.

■ Key Terms

alternative question: A two-pronged question that presents two choices (generally a positive and a negative choice) to the suspect regarding the crime he or she has committed; accepting either choice results in an admission of guilt

confession: A statement acknowledging personal responsibility for a crime, including details only the guilty person would know

confession law: Area of law dealing with the proper technique for legally obtaining a confession, and the rights guaranteed a suspect when he or she is deciding whether to give a confession

descriptives: Words that yield vivid mental images

documenting the confession: Recording a suspect's confession; the method used to do this should be planned

interrogation: The formal questioning of a suspect, conducted in a controlled environment and performed in an accusatory manner in order to learn the truth

preparation: The most important factor in conducting a successful interrogation; it involves considering the setting and environment, knowing the case facts, being familiar with the subject's background, and determining the method used to document the confession

Reid technique: Technique for conducting a successful interrogation that describes a three-part process to be used during the interrogation

relationship: Connection between the suspect and the interrogator during an interrogation; a good relationship must be built in an attempt to get a confession from a suspect

successful interrogation: Interrogation that results in a criminal suspect's making a confession or admitting participation in an illegal activity

theme: Monologue in which the investigator offers moral or psychological excuses for the suspect's criminal behavior

waiver: Conscious act of giving up rights or privileges

■ Review Questions

1. What role did the case of *Escobedo v. Illinois* play in the evolution of confession law?
2. When does an interview become an interrogation?
3. What role did *Miranda v. Arizona* play in the evolution of confession law?
4. Under what circumstances must a person be given the warnings pursuant to *Miranda v. Arizona*?
5. List the cases that contributed to the evolution of confession law. What was their contribution?
6. What is the three-part process used in the Reid technique?
7. List four themes that an interrogator may incorporate into an interrogation.

8. Describe (in detail) each of the seven steps in the Reid technique.

9. Discuss the method of documenting a confession.

10. What is a waiver, and how is one obtained?

■ Bibliography

Aubrey, A.S., & Caputo, R.R. (1986). *Criminal interrogation* (3rd ed.). Springfield, IL: Charles C. Thomas.

Decker, D., & Denney, J. (1992). *You've got to be believed to be heard.* New York: St. Martin's Press.

Gilbert, J.N. (1998). *Criminal investigation* (4th ed.). Englewood Cliffs, NJ: Prentice Hall.

Inbau, F.E., Reid, J.E., et al. (2004). *Criminal interrogation and confessions* (4th ed.). Sudbury, MA: Jones and Bartlett.

■ Key Legal Cases

Arizona v. Mauro, 481 U.S. (1987).

Brewer v. Williams, 430 U.S. 387 (1977).

Connecticut v. Barrett, 479 U.S. 523 (1987).

Davis v. United States, 114 S.Ct. 2350 (1994).

Duckworth v. Eagan, 492 U.S. 195 (1989).

Escobedo v. Illinois, 378 U.S. 478 (1964).

McNeil v. Wisconsin, 501 U.S. 171 (1990).

Miranda v. Arizona, 384 U.S. 436 (1966).

New York v. Quarles, 467 U.S. 649 (1987).

Oregon v. Elstad, 470 U.S. 298 (1985).

Pennsylvania v. Muniz, 496 U.S. 582 (1990).

Texas v. Cobb, 532 U.S. 162 (2001).

Firearms Investigation

CHAPTER
9

▶ ▶ STUDENT LEARNING OUTCOMES

Upon completion of this chapter students will demonstrate an understanding of:

- The difference between ballistics and firearms examinations
- The types of firearms used by offenders
- Class characteristics of firearms
- Class characteristics of cartridges, cartridge cases, and projectiles
- Issues associated with the introduction of firearms evidence at the time of trial

■ Physical Evidence

For the purposes of our discussion in this chapter, we can break evidence down into two broad categories: physical evidence and testimonial evidence. **Physical evidence** is evidence that can be handled, examined, tested, seen, felt, or tasted. It can be as small as a gene or as large as an automobile. **Testimonial evidence** encompasses the testimony of witnesses and of defendants. All physical evidence is **circumstantial evidence** and is only partial proof of a crime. Indeed, all evidence is circumstantial except eyewitness identification or a confession by the defendant. The closer to certainty evidence brings us, the more it loses its circumstantial nature.

From an investigative viewpoint, the most important aspect of physical evidence is its transferability. **Transfer** of evidence provides the basis for much of what forensic technicians and forensic laboratories do. Whenever two objects meet, some evidence of the meeting remains to establish that in fact a meeting did occur. In particular, whenever a person comes in contact with a crime scene, something is left and something is taken away. Often what is left or taken is microscopic (trace evidence) and requires forensic skills to discover, handle, and evaluate.

All investigators cannot be forensic scientists, but all investigators must appreciate the potential loci of forensic evidence. These loci depend on the nature of the crime and the evidence left at the scene of the crime. Lack of an understanding of the potential loci of evidence at a crime scene can result in contamination or destruction of the trace evidence. Types of evidence that may transfer include the following:

- A vehicular collision may leave visible paint on the fender of each vehicle. Even if the paint is visible to the naked eye, forensic analysis will be needed to verify that the residues discovered are of the same paint. The color alone is not sufficient.

- In a kidnapping case, fibers from the interior of a suspect's automobile may match those taken from the clothing of the abductee. Again, color comparison is only the beginning; fiber analysis must be used to establish that the fibers came from the same source.
- Burglary tools, like other tools, leave distinctive marks on surfaces when applied with force. Microscopic examination of surface marks and of the face of a suspected tool may convince a jury that the tool was the one used in breaking into the burglarized premises.

Investigators have the responsibility to determine what crime was committed, the avenues of egress and exit used by the criminal, and the possible location of forensic evidence. It is the forensic evidence left behind that will allow the investigators to place both the suspect and the victim at the scene of the crime and to reconstruct the events that led up to and occurred during and after the offense. Thus, every investigator needs to appreciate what forensic technicians and laboratory scientists do, how they do it, and where they do it, for they are an important part of the investigative team and may make the difference between a successful and failed investigation as well as a successful and failed prosecution.

The physical evidence found at a crime scene often includes a **firearm** or firearm components. It is imperative that the investigator understand what type of forensic evidence is available to the firearms examiner.

■ Ballistics and Firearms Identification

The identification of firearms is often incorrectly referred to as ballistics. **Ballistics** is actually the study of projectiles in motion. Ballistic studies involve four discrete areas:

- Interior ballistics is the study of the motion of projectiles in the gun barrel and the conversion of the chemical energy of the cartridge propellant into the kinetic energy of the projectile.
- Transitional ballistics deals with the transition from the projectile's passage through the gun barrel to the projectile's flight through the air.
- Exterior ballistics deals with projectile flight from the muzzle end to the target (taking into account air resistance, gravity, wind, and elevation).
- Terminal ballistics is the study of the interaction of the projectile with the target.

Firearms identification, on the other hand, is concerned primarily with the identification of firearms by the examination of their fired bullets and cartridges; it is only tangentially related to ballistics.

National Integrated Ballistics Information Network

The National Integrated Ballistics Information Network (NIBIN) is a nationally interconnected, computer-assisted ballistics imaging system used by firearms examiners to obtain computerized images of bullets and **cartridge cases**. These images can be compared with images already entered into the system. The system is made up of federal, state, and local law enforcement crime laboratories. The Bureau of Alcohol, Tobacco, Firearms and Explosives (ATF) is responsible for the development and deployment of the system nationally.

Prior to the creation of NIBIN, the FBI and ATF established their own computerized ballistics imaging systems. NIBIN was established to incorporate the FBI's Drugfire system and the ATF's Ceasefire system. The system uses the ATF's imaging system and the secure, high-speed telecommunications network of the FBI.

Recent bills introduced in Congress would require all manufacturers to supply a spent cartridge and bullet for inclusion in the system before being allowed to sell or import the firearm. This would increase significantly the ability to trace firearms used in crimes. Presently, the participation of federal, state, and local law enforcement agencies in NIBIN is restricted by law to the ballistics imaging of data associated with only those guns used in crimes.

Comparisons of bullet and cartridge case marks historically were accomplished by firearms examiners using comparison microscopes. This process was accurate but slow and labor intensive. In the early 1990s, the ballistics imaging and matching process was computerized. Digital cameras were used to photograph bullets and cartridge cases and scan them into a computer. These images were then analyzed by a software program and stored in a database, making ballistics matching faster. When the computerized system was connected across numerous law enforcement agencies through a telecommunications system, it allowed the rapid comparison of bullets and cartridge cases used in crimes from different jurisdictions. The use of computerized images of bullets and cartridge cases streamlines chains of custody for those bullets and cartridge cases that are to be used in court.

NIBIN is composed of several computer-connected networks. The goal is for NIBIN data to be shared nationally. The ATF has more than 80 offices around the country that serve as repositories for the deposit and retrieval of ballistic images. Four different types of integrated ballistics identification systems (IBIS) make up the NIBIN network:

- **Regional server:** The central data repository for the region, in which all images are stored and bullet/cartridge casing correlation requests are executed
- **Digital acquisition system (DAS) remotes:** An IBIS system composed of a microscope and a computer unit that allows image acquisition or evaluation. These systems are linked to a regional server, where the images are stored and bullet/cartridge casing comparison or correlation requests are sent
- **Rapid brass identification (RBI):** A portable cartridge casing system that allows on-site digital capture of fired cartridge casings for transmission to a central IBIS for processing, comparison, and storage
- **Matchpoint:** A desktop computer connected to a DAS remote by LAN (local area network), allowing bullet/cartridge analysis

IBIS technology is designed to be used without extensive computer training or sophistication. Once entered, a sample that results in a hit (a possible match with a database record) provides demographic information about the crime; images of the correlated bullet casing, which includes the breech face, firing pin, and ejector marks; and images of the correlated bullet, including lands and accidentals.

If the image is captured at a DAS remote, the data is sent to the regional server for comparison. A hit results in the correlation data being returned to the DAS remote. Images captured by a RBI system are sent by telephone to the cooperating DAS remote. The images are transmitted to the regional sever for comparison in the region's database. Again, a hit results in the correlation data being returned to the cooperating DAS, and the RBI user is notified by telephone. Ejected cartridge casings found at a crime scene can be digitized right at the scene. The information can be transmitted to a laboratory, where a technician can use the system to conduct a search. If a hit is found, results can be returned to the personnel at the scene while the investigation is still in progress.

The IBIS analysis system does not provide matches—it provides correlations, a short list of possible matches. The final analysis for a match is conducted by a firearms examiner through a comparison microscopic.

■ Types of Firearms

Firearms examiners generally come into contact with five types of firearms: pistols, rifles, assault rifles, machine guns, and shotguns.

Pistols

Pistols are handheld firearms designed to be fired with one hand. Pistols are either single-shot, single-action revolvers; double-action revolvers; or self-loading pistols (commonly referred to as "automatic" pistols) and fully automatic handheld pistols. If a pistol is fully **automatic**, it continues to fire as long as the trigger is depressed and ammunition is available. The pistols called automatics are incorrectly identified and should be referred to as **semiautomatic** or self-loading (**Figure 9–1**). Some self-loading or semiautomatic pistols store the recoil energy of the barrel in coiled springs, and then use this energy to extract the expended cartridge casing from the firing chamber, eject it from the weapon, cock the firing mechanism preparatory to firing the next round, and load a live round into the firing chamber. Self-loading pistols may also work on a blowback principle. In

Figure 9–1   Revolver (top) and semiautomatic pistol (bottom).

Courtesy of Austin Police Department, Austin, Texas

blowback-operated pistols, the bolt and barrel are held together only by the inertia of the bolt and the pressure of the recoil spring. The recoil of the cartridge provides the energy for extraction, ejection, cocking, and loading (Wilbur, 1977). Glock has manufactured a fully automatic handgun that looks like the semi-automatic firearms it manufactures. The primary difference is in the barrel of the fully automatic Glock 18C, which has two parallel compensator ports about a half-inch long on the top front and two ports on the side of the barrel that reduce recoil. The weapon comes with a standard clip and a 30-round clip.

Revolvers may have either a single or double action. Single-action revolvers must be cocked manually before each firing. Double-action revolvers are cocked by the pull of the trigger. There is a high-powered hunting pistol that fires a single high-velocity rifle cartridge. This weapon combines the power of a rifle with the portability of a handgun. It is breech loaded with a single cartridge and must be broken open to eject each round and load a new round.

Rifles

Rifles are weapons designed to be used with two hands and fired from the shoulder position. There are single-shot rifles, lever-action rifles (fed by magazine), bolt-operated rifles (fed by clip or magazine), semiautomatic rifles (fed by clip or magazine), and automatic rifles (fed by clip or belt). Lever-action and bolt-action rifles use the manual manipulation of a lever or turnbolt to extract and eject each expended cartridge, cock the firing mechanism, and load a live round into the firing chamber. Semiautomatic and automatic rifles are blowback, recoil, or gas operated. Gas-operated rifles use a portion of the hot propellant gases trapped from the barrel by a gas piston to extract, cock, and load. Automatic rifles use limited-capacity magazines, whereas light machine guns generally fire belted ammunition.

Assault Rifles

During the two decades following World War II, the world's armies replaced their bolt-action and semiautomatic rifles with assault rifles (**Figure 9–2**). An **assault rifle** is a hand-carried, shoulder-fired semiautomatic or automatic weapon in a rifle caliber. One of the problems with wartime use of assault rifles is the hard use to which they are put. Often field use is much different than the circumstances under which the rifle was tested while being developed. The M16, a Vietnam-era standard-issue assault rifle, was notorious for building up carbon from expended rounds and then locking the bolt in the open position. Metal Storm, a contractor to the U.S. government, is field testing an electronically fired assault weapon. The only moving parts are the projectiles themselves. Early testing allows rounds to be fired so quickly that three rounds hit the target in the same hole before the firearm recoils. The electronic weapon can be manufactured in any configuration from pistol to howitzer, and the effects are impressive. Technology never sleeps; what we see as cutting-edge technology today is obsolete tomorrow.

Machine Guns

Submachine guns and **machine guns** are fully automatic weapons (**Figure 9–3**). Machine guns load their ammunition from magazines or from belts. Because of the recoil, machine guns are fired from a tripod or bipod (unless you are John Wayne or Rambo). Submachine guns, which are automatic weapons designed to be fired while being held in the hands, fire pistol cartridges (Hogg, 1977).

Figure 9–2   AR15 assault rifle (top) and .223-caliber AR15 Bushmaster (bottom).

Courtesy of Austin Police Department, Austin, Texas

Figure 9–3   Uzi (top left), Tech 9 (top right), and Mac 10 (bottom).

Courtesy of Austin Police Department, Austin, Texas

All the types of weapons discussed to this point are **rifled firearms**. Their barrels (**Figure 9–4**) have a set of spiraling lands and grooves within them. The **lands** of the rifling are the raised ridges that bite into the surface of the bullet and give it a rotational motion as it moves down the barrel; the **grooves** of the rifling are the recessed areas between the lands. The rifling grips the fired bullet and engraves its surface with land and groove impressions. The microscopic imperfections of the rifling produce patterns of parallel scratches called striations (or striae). Rifled firearms may be characterized by their **caliber**, or bore diameter. The bore diameter of a rifled barrel is the diameter measured from the

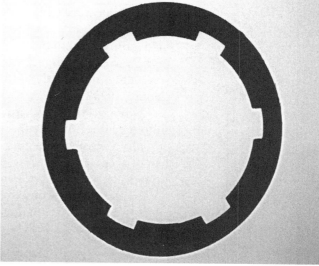

Figure 9–4 Barrel rifling.

Courtesy of Austin Police Department, Austin, Texas

tops of opposing lands. The caliber and bore diameters of American weapons normally are given in inches, whereas those of other weapons are given in millimeters. Many manufacturers and users express caliber in both inches and millimeters.

Shotguns

Shotguns, like rifles, are designed to be fired from the shoulder, but they are smooth-bore weapons, having no lands or grooves in the barrel (**Figure 9–5**). Unless firing a slug round, shotguns fire multiple projectiles, called pellets. Shotguns may have single or double barrels. Single-barrel shotguns may be single-shot weapons or repeaters. Repeating shotguns have magazines from which rounds are loaded into the weapon, either manually with a pump action or semiautomatically (Hatcher et al., 1977).

Shotguns are referred to by their bore diameters. These diameters are expressed in **gauge** measurements (**Figure 9–6**). When all firearms fired spherical lead balls, their bore diameters or gauges were expressed as the number of such lead balls that could be made from 1 pound of lead (e.g., 10 lead balls having the same diameter as the interior of the barrel of a 10-gauge shotgun should weigh 1 pound). The exception to this measurement scheme is the .410-gauge shotgun, which has a bore diameter of .410 inches (Nonte, 1973).

Military Police System, Tennessee, has developed a 12-gauge shotgun called the Auto Assault 12 Automatic Shotgun, which fires at a relatively slow rate of 300 rpm and employs a recoil dampening mechanism that allows it to be fired automatically without loss of accuracy. This weapon is manufactured from corrosion-resistant, high-impact, heat-treated stainless steels and high-impact plastics and requires no lubrication. Rounds are fed from an 8-round magazine, or a 20- or 32-round drum. The Auto Assault 12 (AA12) Automatic Shotgun also features a quick-change barrel system. Barrel lengths range from 13 to 18 inches.

Figure 9–5   Shotguns (top to bottom): semiautomatic, double barrel (over and under), double barrel (side by side), and pump action.

Courtesy of Austin Police Department, Austin, Texas

Figure 9–6   Shotgun shells (left to right): .410 gauge, 28 gauge, 20 gauge, 16 gauge, and 12 gauge.

Courtesy of Austin Police Department, Austin, Texas

■ The Firing Mechanism

The firearms examiner needs to know how certain components of a firearm's firing mechanism perform. The **breechblock** is the part of a firearm's action that supports the base of the cartridge in the chamber when it is fired. The **firing pin** is the part of the firearm's action that strikes the cartridge primer in order to fire it. Breechblocks may be finished with an end mill, by turning on a lathe, or by hand filing. The breechblocks of semiautomatic pistols are usually finished by filing vertically down through the ejector slot in the slide. This gives a characteristic direction to the striations imparted to the soft metal of the primer caps of fired cartridges. Firing pins are turned on lathes or filed flat by hand (Hatcher et al., 1977).

■ Ammunition

Types of Bullets

The three most commonly used bullets (**Figure 9–7**) in rifled firearms are lead-alloy bullets, semi-jacketed bullets, and fully jacketed bullets. Lead-alloy bullets are harder than pure lead bullets and less likely to produce lead fouling of the rifling. Pure lead .22-caliber bullets may be coated with a very thin film of copper. This film has a tendency to flake off the surface of the bullet, removing the striations produced by the rifling (Mathews, 1962).

Jacketed bullets consist of a lead core surrounded by a jacket of harder material. Jackets are commonly made of a copper-nickel alloy or mild steel. Semiautomatic pistols use fully jacketed bullets because the noses of the bullets must slide up a ramp as rounds are chambered (Nonte, 1973).

A semi-jacketed bullet has a copper-alloy or aluminum jacket that covers only the side of the bullet, leaving the nose exposed. This type of bullet is designed to mushroom on impact so that most of its kinetic energy is expended in the target. A hollow-point bullet has a hollow in the exposed lead core at the nose of the bullet. A soft-point bullet

(A)

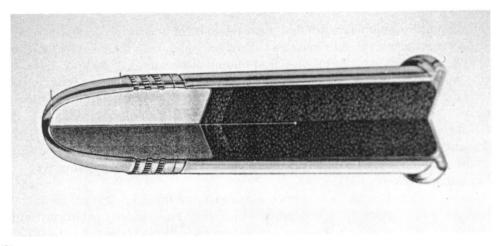

(B)

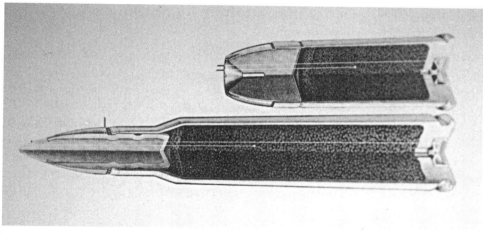

(C)

Figure 9–7 (A) Pistol bullets: lead (top row), copper jacketed (middle row), and body armor piercing and Teflon-coated armor piercing (bottom row). (B) Illustration of a .22 caliber rimfire cartridge. (C) Cutaway views of piston centerfire cartridge (bottom) and rifle centerfire cartridge (top).

Courtesy of Austin Police Department, Austin, Texas

is a semi-jacketed bullet with a soft metal plug inserted in its nose. Both the soft metal insert and the thinner jacket facilitate bullet expansion.

Another approach to obtaining proper expansion of a semi-jacketed bullet is to place a hard metal insert in the nose of the bullet. Bronze-point bullets are special bullets intended for hunting. Upon impact, the bronze point is forced back into the bullet's core, causing it to mushroom.

Frangible bullets are composed of powdered iron or powdered iron with an organic binder. These bullets are used in shooting galleries and in urban law enforcement because they disintegrate on impact without the danger of a ricochet or penetration through thin walls.

Steel-jacketed armor-piercing bullets have an extremely hard steel jacket surrounding a tungsten carbide core. The hardness of the jacket generally prevents the rifling of the weapon from marking the projectile.

A special-purpose bullet has been developed by Remington called an accelerator cartridge. The projectile is a normal .223-caliber soft-point bullet pressed into a .30-caliber plastic grommet (sabot). Upon firing, the bullet and the sabot exit the barrel, and at some distance from the muzzle the bullet separates from the sabot and continues along its trajectory as the sabot falls away. There are no identifiable rifling marks on such a bullet.

Bullets may have round noses, pointed noses, or flat noses. Their bases may be flat or boat-tailed. The shape of a bullet is dictated by a number of considerations, including aerodynamics. Boat-tailed bullets are designed to reduce turbulence in the wake of the bullet, thereby reducing bullet drag.

The media has given much coverage to a Teflon-coated bullet that is reputed to be a cop killer. It is a green projectile, supposedly covered with a Teflon substance that will allow penetration of police body armor. In truth, the cartridge is an armor-piercing round, and the Teflon coats the projectile to protect the hard metal of the projectile from damaging the lands and grooves in the barrel. The Teflon has nothing to do with the penetrating characteristics of the projectile.

Propellants

Smokeless powders are classified as degressive burning, neutral burning, or progressive burning. Degressive-burning powder grains burn from the outside in; the surface area consequently decreases, as does the burning rate of the grain. Solid, uncoated powder grains burn in a degressive manner. Neutral-burning powders have perforations so that the burning of the outside of the grains is balanced by the burning on the interiors of the perforations; the net effect is that the surface area remains relatively constant, as does the burning rate. Progressive-burning powders are coated with a deterrent material that slows down the initial burning of the powder grains; once the deterrent coating is burned off, the burning rate goes up (O'Connor, 1965).

The manipulation of powder burning rates through variations in grain size, shape, and coating is necessary because of the variations in caliber, barrel length, and chamber size among firearms. When a weapon is fired, the **propellant** begins to burn, generating hot gases. These gases expand, forcing the bullet from the cartridge casing into the barrel. Once the bullet begins to move, the volume available to the gases generated by the burning propellant increases. If the production of gases stopped immediately after the unseating of the bullet into the barrel, further travel of the bullet down the barrel would cause the pressure behind it to fall. At the point where the pressure exerted on the bullet was balanced by the frictional force acting between the bullet and the barrel, the bullet would come to a stop. To prevent this, the powder must continue to burn as the bullet proceeds down the barrel. Burning of powder after the bullet exits the barrel wastes energy because none of the energy released after the bullet exits the barrel can be converted into kinetic energy. The weight (amount), grain size, and burning rate of a cartridge's propellant must be adapted to the type of firearm intended to fire it.

Primers

The centerfire cartridge is a 19th-century invention. Eventually, it supplanted the rimfire cartridge in all but the smallest calibers. Centerfire ammunition manufactured in the United States uses the Boxer primer (named for its inventor, E.M. Boxer, a colonel in the British army). This **primer** consists of a metal cup containing a small amount of primer material placed between the cup and a small metal anvil. When the weapon is fired, its firing pin crushes the primer material between the cup and anvil; the flame from the primer's explosion reaches the propellant through a large flash hole in the base of the cartridge. Centerfire cartridges manufactured outside the United States use the Berdan primer (named after its inventor, Hiram Berdan, a colonel in the Union army during the American Civil War). Cartridge cases that accept the Berdan primer have a conical anvil as an integral part of their bases. The primer cap is simply a small metal cup containing a pellet of primer compound. Two or three small holes spaced evenly around the anvil communicate the flash of the primer through the base of the casing to the propellant (Tarassuk and Blair, 1979).

Beginning in 1900, primers based on potassium chlorate began to appear as replacements for mercury fulminate primers, but their residue proved as corrosive as the residue of the latter. Modern primers are exclusively nonmercurial and noncorrosive. A typical centerfire primer produced today will contain lead styphnate, antimony sulfide, barium nitrate, and tetracene (O'Connor, 1965).

Cartridge Cases

Cartridge cases are available in a wide variety of shapes and sizes (**Figure 9–8**). Differently shaped cases are intended for use in different types of firearms. Revolvers fire straight-rimmed cartridges; the rims prevent the cartridges from falling through the revolver's cylinder. Self-loading pistols fire straight rimless cartridges; because they are clip fed, there is no need for a rim. Cartridge cases may have cannelures rolled into them near their mouths; these cannelures prevent the bullets from inadvertently being pushed back into the cases. A bullet may also be held in place by crimping the mouth of the cartridge onto the surface of the bullet.

The heads of cartridges frequently bear stampings that provide information about the maker of the cartridges. For instance, the letters R-P on the head of a cartridge case indicate that Remington-Peters made it. A cartridge also may carry markings identifying the nominal caliber of its bullet.

Shot Shells

Most shotgun ammunition contains pellets, although some commercially available shot shells have either a single-round ball or a rifled slug. Shotgun pellets come in a variety of sizes, from 000 buckshot (0.36 inch in diameter) down to Number 12 birdshot (0.05 inch in diameter). The larger the shot number, the smaller the shot. The number of pellets of each size making up the load of a shot shell depends on its gauge. For example, 12-gauge Number 1 buckshot cartridges generally contain 16 pellets, whereas a 16-gauge Number 1 buckshot cartridge generally contains 12 pellets. Shotgun pellets may be lead, lead alloy, or soft steel. Concern that waterfowl might eat toxic lead pellets has generated a movement to replace all lead-based shot with the more environmentally sound nontoxic soft steel shot. At one time, shot shells were made completely of brass. These brass shells have disappeared and have been replaced by shells with brass bases and paper or plastic sides.

The pellets in the shot shell are separated from the propellant by one or more over-powder wads (**Figure 9–9**). These wads are used to separate the propellant gases from the shot and to cushion the pellets during their acceleration up the barrel. Wadding is made of cardboard, felt, or plastic. In modern shot shells, the pellets are held in a plastic cup

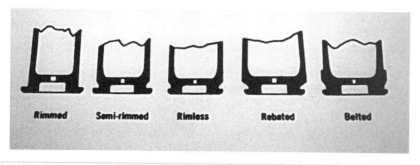

Figure 9–8 Types of cartridge rims.

Courtesy of Austin Police Department, Austin, Texas

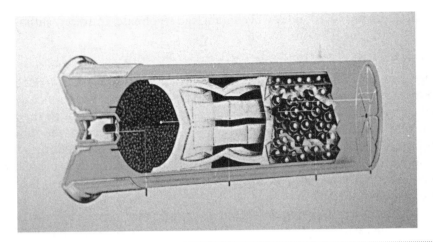

Figure 9–9 Shot shell components: primer, powder, wadding, and shot.
Courtesy of Austin Police Department, Austin, Texas

that prevents their deformation through contact with the interior of the shotgun barrel. The plastic cup in some applications also serves as a wad.

■ Firearms and Forensics

The Early History of the Examination of Firearms

The history of contemporary **firearms examination** may have begun with the work of Dr. Albert Llewellyn Hall, a practicing physician in Buffalo, NY. In 1931, Hall published an article in the *American Journal of Police Science* titled "The Missile and the Weapon" (Hall, 1931). This article concerned the possibility of matching fired bullets to the weapon that fired them based on microscopic examination of the striations on the bullets.

The first firearms case in the United States should have established the precedent for the admissibility of firearm comparison testimony. In *Commonwealth v. Best* (1902), the Supreme Judicial Court of the Commonwealth of Massachusetts permitted the introduction of the results of comparative examinations of markings on bullets. The case was ignored until the 1930s. The widespread acceptance of comparisons of bullet markings took nearly a quarter of a century. Courts seemed willing to allow the introduction of cartridge case comparisons but were extremely reluctant to allow the admission of tes-

CASE IN POINT

The Brownsville Shooting
On the night of August 13, 1906, unknown persons shot up downtown Brownsville, TX, killing a local barkeeper. Local civilian witnesses claimed that black soldiers carried out the shooting. During the ensuing Senate investigation, an Army officer and a civilian technician from the U.S. arsenal at Springfield, MA, examined the firing impressions and extractor marks on cartridges found in the streets of Brownsville the day after. These examiners found that most of the cartridges had been fired from rifles of B Company, 25th Infantry. Being unable to fix blame on a specific soldier and believing that a conspiracy of silence existed among the personnel of the 25th Infantry, the War Department dishonorably discharged all 167 enlisted men in the battalion (Lane, 1971).

timony pertaining to comparison of bullets, firing-pin impressions, or extractor marks. The readiness of courts to accept comparisons of marks on cartridges but not rifling marks on bullets may have been due to the greater visibility of the marks on cartridges and to the absence of a comparison microscope. The first use of firing pin impressions and extractor marks as evidence occurred during the investigation of the Brownsville massacre (see Case in Point).

Examination of Weapons

As an examination protocol, test-firing is not necessarily the first step. There is a possibility that the weapon was last used in a homicide involving a contact wound. If the barrel was in contact with the body upon firing, there may be blood and tissue in the barrel as a result of barrel blowback. The weapon's bore also may have fibers from its owner's pockets. There is also a possibility that the weapon, its components, and its ammunition may retain fingerprints.

Once the firearm has been processed for fingerprints and trace evidence, a complete identification of the weapon should be made. The identification should include the following class characteristics:

- Make or manufacturer
- Type (revolver, pistol, etc.)
- Caliber
- Serial number
- Model
- Number of shots
- Barrel length

The make, manufacturer, and model are determined from names, trademarks, and proof marks placed on various components of the weapon. The caliber of the weapon may be indicated by the name or by trademark information. A weapon may be modified by fitting a different-caliber barrel to the weapon's frame.

The **National Firearms Act of 1968** requires retailers to record the serial number of a weapon and the name of its purchaser. Because of the importance of the serial number for tracing a firearm's owner, a criminal may remove the stamped serial number by grinding. If the grinding does not go deep enough into the metal, a stamped serial number may still be recovered by chemical etching, electrochemical etching, or ultrasonic cavitation. Many firearms have parts of the serial number stamped into internal components. Handguns often have the serial number stamped at different locations on the frame.

CASE IN POINT

St. Valentine's Day Massacre

In 1929, Calvin Goddard was called to Chicago to examine the fired bullets and cartridges in the St. Valentine's Day massacre. He was able to determine that the victims of the gangland execution had been killed with two different Thompson submachine guns, one with a 20-round magazine and the other with a 50-round drum magazine (Goddard, 1930). Goddard's impressive performance led to the establishment of a private forensic laboratory in Chicago under Goddard's direction. This laboratory later became the Chicago Police Department Crime Laboratory. Also in 1929, Goddard testified in *Evans v. Commonwealth* (1929), which became the precedent-setting case for the admissibility of comparisons of rifling marks.

In a case involving an accidental firing or a firing that occurred during a fight or struggle, the amount of force required to pull the trigger may be important. The trigger pull may be measured by gradually increasing the amount of weight hanging from the weapon's trigger while the weapon is held vertically with the mechanism cocked. The measurement should be made with the actuating force applied to the trigger at the same spot that the finger of a person firing the weapon would be placed.

In Costa Rica all firearms must be registered immediately after purchase with the Organismo Investigacion Judicial (federal police). Part of the registration process includes a test firing of the firearm and a retrieval of the projectile, which is placed in federal files as a control sample to which any unknowns can be compared. In the United States, manufacturers are providing an expended cartridge case and projectile to the Bureau of Alcohol, Tobacco, Firearms and Explosives for each of the firearms they manufacture for the same reason.

Examination of Bullets

In the absence of a suspect weapon, a firearms examination is confined to the determination of **class characteristics** of the bullets, such as caliber, direction of twist of the rifling, **degree of twist**, number of lands and grooves, and width of the lands and grooves (**Figure 9–10**). With these data, the firearms examiner may be able to determine the make and model of the firearm that fired the bullets. If there are two or more fired bullets that exhibit the same class characteristics, they are then examined under a **comparison microscope** to determine if the bullets were fired by the same weapon.

Before class characteristics of bullets are determined, the bullets should be examined for the presence of **trace evidence** such as blood, hairs, fibers, wood splinters, glass particles, paint, concrete, or soil particles. A bullet may pick up blood, hairs, and fibers as it passes through a shooting victim. Trace evidence such as wood splinters or glass particles embedded in a bullet indicate that the bullet may have passed through an intermediate object such as a door, wall, or window. Paint, concrete, or soil particles may be found if a bullet ricochets off a hard surface.

Caliber

The caliber of an undeformed fired bullet may be measured with a micrometer. The diameter of interest is the diameter across the land impressions (which, on the expended bullet, will be indentations made by the barrel lands). Allowance must be made for the

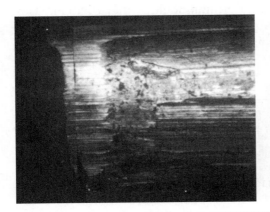

Figure 9–10 Bullet comparisons.

Courtesy of Austin Police Department, Austin, Texas

fact that firearm calibers are merely nominal indications of the true bore diameters. A group of Colt pistols, all nominally .38-caliber weapons, were found to have bore diameters ranging from 0.348 to 0.395 inch.

The caliber of an intact but badly deformed bullet may be estimated from its weight. The determination of caliber by weight will rarely allow the examiner to specify a particular caliber for the bullet, but certain calibers may be eliminated as possibilities. When the bullet is fragmented, an accurate weight can no longer be obtained. In such a case, the caliber of the bullet may be estimated by measuring the widths of a land impression and an adjacent groove impression (Mathews, 1962).

Number of Lands and Grooves

In bullets recovered intact, the number of lands and grooves can be determined by counting them. In cases where bullets are badly deformed, measurement of the width of the land and groove impressions may be combined with knowledge of the caliber of the bullet to calculate the number of lands and grooves. Because manufacturers use a specific number of grooves in their firearms and this number is generally constant for a given make and model, the number of lands and grooves is an important class characteristic (Mathews, 1962).

Rifling Twists

The direction of twist of the rifling may be determined by inspection of the fired bullet if it is not badly deformed. The rifling may spiral either to the left or to the right. Left-hand twist rifling is often referred to as Colt-type rifling, and right-hand twist rifling is often referred to as Smith-and-Wesson-type rifling.

Land and Groove Width

The width of the land and groove impressions may be measured using a filar micrometer, traveling microscope, or toolmaker's microscope. Measurements are made perpendicular to the axis of the bullet. Observing that the land impressions on a bullet are wider than the groove impressions allows the firearms examiner to eliminate certain makes and models of firearms. Land and groove impressions that are of a markedly different width than the other impressions on the bullet may reflect a defect in manufacture that is extremely rare (Mathews, 1962).

Bullet Comparisons

Bullet comparisons are made using a comparison microscope. A comparison microscope consists of two compound microscopes, each with its own objectives, stage, and focusing adjustments. The microscopes are joined by a comparison bridge, a system of prism mirrors that brings the images of the two microscopes together so that they may be compared side by side through a single ocular. The images of the two microscopes may be superimposed or they may be viewed side by side, with the field of view divided equally between the two microscopes. The bullets to be compared are attached to short cylindrical bullet holders. The bullet holders slip onto the shafts of the bullet-manipulating mechanisms, which in turn are attached to the microscope stages. The bullet-manipulating mechanisms are provided with universal joints so that the bullets may be oriented at any angle.

Once the bullets are mounted, the examiner begins the search for matching patterns of striations. The limited expansion of jacketed bullets leads to only occasional contact with the bottoms of the grooves, and only the base may be upset sufficiently to seat well in the barrel's rifling. Therefore, the initial examination is most likely to discover a pattern of striations near the base of the bullet. A land impression on a test-fired bullet is compared successively to each land impression on the suspect bullet until a match is obtained or it is determined that no match is possible. Once a match has been made with a pair of land impressions, the bullets are rotated synchronously to see if other matching striation patterns may be observed. If both bullets were fired from the same barrel, numerous matching patterns will be evident. Marks other than land and groove striations may be observed.

Skid marks are caused by the bullet sliding over the beginnings of the lands at the breech end of the barrel. Shaving marks occur when a revolver bullet in the cylinder is not lined up perfectly with the barrel. The bullet will strike the edge of the forcing cone (the flared opening in the revolver's frame in front of the cylinder where the fired bullet enters the barrel), and a portion of the bullet will be shaved off on the side striking the forcing cone. Comparing shaved spots on a bullet may be difficult. Test firing may not always result in a similar shaving, and many shots may have to be fired before a similarly shaved bullet can be obtained.

In an effort to avoid detection, criminals may flatten, bend, or shorten the barrel of a firearm. Flattened barrels may be restored to round, bent barrels may be straightened, or bullets may be forced through the barrels. The marks on bullets fired through the barrel at its original length may not match the marks on bullets fired through a shortened barrel.

The examination of fired bullets may lead to any one of three conclusions:

1. The questioned bullet was fired from the suspect weapon.

2. The questioned bullet was not fired from the suspect weapon.

3. The results of the examinations are insufficient to reach a final determination.

Examination of Cartridges

In examining a fired cartridge case, the examiner using a low-power microscope will note the following:

- Size
- Shape
- Type (rimmed, semirimmed, rimless, belted, rimfire, centerfire)
- Size of firing pin impression
- Position of firing pin impression
- Location of extractor marks
- Location of ejector marks
- Any other accidental marks (any mark other than those caused in the manufacturing process)

The shape and location of the firing pin impression on the cartridges of bullets shot from a .22-caliber, single-shot, breech-loading rifle can serve to identify the make and model of the rifle. The relative positions of the extractor and ejector marks on cartridges from self-loading pistols allow the same determination (Mathews, 1962). If a suspect firearm is available and if the class characteristics of cartridges from that weapon match those of the questioned cartridge, the examiner fires test shots with the suspect weapon in order to obtain fired cartridges for comparison purposes. The cartridges then are placed inside an iris diaphragm that attaches to the bullet-mounting devices in the comparison microscope. Comparison of the various marks on the fired cartridges begins with the firing pin impressions, firing pin drag marks, and breechblock marks. A match of these marks would show that the same weapon fired both cartridges.

After the examiner evaluates these marks, he or she compares the extractor marks, ejector marks, chambering marks, and magazine (clip) marks. A match of any of these types of marks indicates that the two cartridges have been run through the action of the same weapon but does not establish that they ever passed through the barrel. Cartridge case class characteristics include:

- Caliber (headstamped)
- Manufacturer (headstamped)
- Composition (copper, cupronickel)
- Rim type (rim less, rimmed, semi-rimmed, belted)
- Primer (center fire, rim fire)

Examination Objectives

Whenever a firearm is discharged in the commission of a crime, physical evidence is likely to be available. Such evidence in the hands of a competent firearms examiner may prove valuable in answering a number of questions. Residue from firing a firearm will remain on surfaces until removed. Barrel blowback will deposit unignited powder, which is expended as a black cloud, on the firearm and the hand and forearm of the individual firing it. Gunshot residue tests can be conducted to determine if residue is present on an assailant's or victim's hand. Although the FBI no longer tests for gunshot residue because of lack of demand and expense, gunshot-residue testing in the field is still an important investigative tool.

Generally speaking the objective of firearms examination includes:

- Matching/identifying projectiles
- Matching/identifying cartridge cases
- Matching/identifying cartridges
- Matching/identifying extractor marks
- Matching/identifying ejector marks
- Match/identifying lands and grooves
- Matching/identifying firearms
- Matching firing pin impressions
- Matching machine marks on cartridge case heads
- Matching striations on projectiles
- Assessing trigger pull
- Examining powder residue

OFFICER'S NOTEBOOK

Questions a Firearms Examiner Aims to Answer
- Can the crime scene bullet or cartridge casing be linked to a suspected weapon?
- Is the recovered weapon capable of being fired?
- Can the weapon be accidentally fired?
- What is the trigger pull?
- Can the serial number be restored?
- Can the type of gun be determined from an examination of the class characteristics of a bullet or cartridge case recovered at the crime scene?

■ Legal Aspects

A Virginia case decided in 1897, *Dean v. Commonwealth*, was the first in which an appellate court approved of testimony regarding the similarity between fatal and test bullets (weight was the compared variable). Beginning with *Jack v. Commonwealth*, a Kentucky case decided in 1928, expert testimony concerning firearms identification began to receive objective appellate appraisal. A year later, this same court, in *Evans v. Commonwealth* (1929), rendered the first exhaustive opinion treating firearms identification as a science and sanctioning its use for the purpose of establishing the guilt of the accused. Today, the accuracy of firearms identification is common knowledge, and ample case law upholds the admissibility of firearms evidence when presented by a qualified expert.

As with other expert testimony, the witness is permitted to testify that in his or her opinion a particular bullet was fired from a certain weapon. The expert's testimony is confined to his or her areas of special knowledge. For example, a witness whose expertise concerns only the identification of bullets by means of their microscopic markings would not be permitted to testify on the issue of whether a certain wound was caused by a particular weapon or whether the bullet traveled a particular trajectory prior to striking the victim. In situations in which bullets are mutilated beyond identification or the suspect weapon cannot be fired, an expert still may be permitted to testify regarding other relevant matters. Even though the condition of fatal bullets may preclude an identification of the evidence weapon, an identification is permissible on the basis of cartridge case breech face imprints, firing pin impressions, or ejector and extractor marks (*Williams v. State*, 1960).

Class Characteristics

A firearms expert may be able to identify only the class characteristics of a badly deformed bullet. That expert may still testify to the fact that the fatal bullets were fired from a gun having characteristics similar to those of the gun obtained from the accused and had physical characteristics like those of the bullets in the accused's gun (*State v. Bayless*, 1976).

Cartridge Evidence

Identification based upon a comparison of breech face imprints, firing pin impressions, and extractor and ejector marks was recognized by the courts in *State v. Clark* (1921). This Oregon case allowed the expert to testify that "a peculiar mark on the brass part of the primer" matched that found on a cartridge fired from the suspect weapon.

In Montana, another case was decided based upon comparative evidence (*State v. Vuckovich*, 1921). The expert in this case testified that a peculiar crimp on an empty shell found at the scene of the murder was similar to a mark on shells fired from the defendant's pistol. Evidence was introduced to show that the "firing marks made by the lands and grooves of the barrel of the pistol were the same" on both the test and the fatal bullets. This decision confirmed the acceptability of using shells and bullets as comparative evidence.

Chain of Custody

As with all evidence, the chain of custody of weapons, shells, and bullets must be unbroken and documented. If it is necessary for more than one examiner to handle the evidence, that should be recorded and the documentation should be available to the defendant upon request. Every moment of the existence of the evidence from the time it entered into the possession of the state (through the hands of law enforcement personnel) to its introduction at the time of trial must be accounted for and supported by the appropriate chain-of-custody documentation.

Long periods of time may elapse between the time shots are fired and the time the bullets or shells are collected. In *State v. Boccadoro* (1929), a bullet fired into the ground a year or two prior to the commission of the murder under investigation was recovered and identified as having been fired by the murder weapon. In *State v. Lane* (1951), shells dropped into a river during target practice months before their recovery were admitted. The time the shells spent underwater was to be considered when assigning weight to the evidence, but it was not detrimental to admissibility. In *Commonwealth v. Ellis* (1977), bullets that had been fired into an oak tree four months prior to the homicide were recovered and matched to the bullets found at the scene of the crime.

The destruction of ballistics evidence before the defendant has had an opportunity to conduct his or her own tests may be a violation of a defendant's constitutional rights to due process and of the confrontation assurances of the Sixth Amendment. Where the destruction is inadvertent, the courts have been unsympathetic to such claims. The state inadvertently destroyed the alleged murder weapon and bullets in the case of *People v. Triplett* (1965), and the defendant contended that this destruction denied him his right to confront the state's firearms expert with his own expert's analysis of the physical evidence. The court rejected this assertion, refusing to take an absolutist view of the confrontation clause.

Expert Testimony

The testimony of the expert does not require a concomitant introduction of the test bullets themselves. In fact, little is to be gained by entering the bullets as evidence. The expert will take photographs of the comparison microscope views and have them enlarged for courtroom use. The greater the number of comparisons of striations on bullets or casing markings on shells, the easier it will be to convince the jury that the bullets were fired from the same firearm. Photographs of the matching bullets and shells are not required; the oral testimony of the expert is considered to be sufficient to get the matter before the jury (*Commonwealth v. Ellis,* 1977). However, it bolsters the expert's testimony for the jury to receive a detailed explanation of the comparisons upon which the expert has based his or her opinion. Additionally, photo enlargements go a long way in defusing the defendant's allegations that not enough points of comparisons were ascertainable to support a positive identification.

Tests performed by firearms examiners need not be conducted in the presence of the accused (*State v. Aiken,* 1967). It was held to be an error in *Johnson v. State* (1971) to admit prosecution evidence in a case where the fatal bullet was not made available for an examination by the defense. But when the bullet, shell, or weapon is made available for an examination by a defense expert, it is reasonable to condition the test upon the presence of a state expert. The court in *State v. Nutley* (1964) held that because firearms identification is a relatively exact science with a common methodology, no prejudice to the defense is incurred by prosecution representation.

Defense Questions

In each case involving firearms identification, a litany of defense questions present themselves. Many of the questions raised by the defendant should have been raised by the

---

OFFICER'S NOTEBOOK

Pretrial Questions That Must Be Answered

Although not exhaustive, the following list contains questions that could prove embarrassing if not addressed prior to trial.

- Did the bullet recovery technique used in the test firing record and preserve the total capability of the firearm to produce microscopic striation marks? It is possible that the medium into which the bullet was fired could impart striations independent of those caused by the weapon fired. It is also possible that the medium into which the bullet was fired could cleanse some of the markings that would have occurred if the bullet had been fired into a less resistant medium (water, ballistic gel, etc.).

- Did two successively fired test bullets and/or casings contain the same microscopic striation marks necessary for specific identification? The more rounds that must be fired to achieve a similar result, the more suspect becomes the reliability of the comparison. The obvious question (especially in those cases involving a few points of comparison) is, "How many rounds would you have fired in order to obtain a match?"

- Did the bullet and/or casing marking details change with subsequent firings? If so, then all markings on all casings may be suspect. It is important that the examiner keep records of the order of the firing of the bullets to avoid any suggestion that the weapon randomly imparts bullet striations and case markings.

- Was the bore of the weapon changed in any way since the time of the firing of the questioned bullet? If so, the expert must be prepared to explain and demonstrate the effect, if any, of the changes on the riflings or markings on the bullets and cases tested.

- Were the bullets, cases, and primers used in the laboratory tests of the same composition as those in question? Any differences in composition of the tested materials will be focused upon by the defense at the time of trial. The testifying expert must be ready to challenge any assertions that the testing materials affected the markings produced by the suspect weapon.

---

examiner or by the attorney expecting to call the firearms examiner as a witness. The primary challenge to firearms evidence is:

- Chain of custody
- Authentication (that the evidence in question is the same as taken from the crime scene)
- Evidence handling
- Age of examining equipment
- Calibration of examining equipment
- Examiner's expertise
- Number of the evidentiary samples in the population
- Number of the evidentiary firearms in the population
- Likelihood that an exact duplicate is possible

■ Submerged Firearms

The recovery of a firearm from under water is a straightforward proposition. No expensive lift equipment is necessary, and the time involved in the recovery is minimal once the firearm has been located. The location and mapping of a firearm should be handled in the same fashion as for any other important submerged evidence. The recovery method usually employed is simply to hand the weapon to someone on shore or in a boat. Weapons are handled in such a cavalier fashion because of a lack of appreciation of the effect of water on ferrous metals and of the possibility that transient evidence could remain on the firearm.

Recovery Purposes

The recovery and preservation of firearms serves four purposes:

1. Medicolegal examination
2. Ballistic comparisons
3. Weapon identification
4. Fingerprint examination

The likelihood of discovering fingerprints on a weapon that has been submerged even for a short period of time is remote. However, there are parts of the firearm that may still render a classifiable latent print. Any ammunition in the weapon may retain fingerprint impressions. The ammunition in these weapons should be considered live and the weapon loaded until rendered otherwise. A firearm retrieved from salt water after lengthy submersion may appear relatively unaffected.

When a firearm is retrieved and maintained properly, preservation techniques may allow ballistics tests to be conducted on the weapon and its ammunition. All firearms need to be preserved for testing, and preservation begins when the divers who recovered the weapon immediately immerse it in water.

Serial Numbers

Every firearm is stamped with a variety of numbers. The serial number is useful in determining the original ownership of the weapon (**Figure 9–11**). The serial number may be more readily apparent upon discovery by the dive team than later, after mishandling and oxidation have occurred. One of the initial acts of the underwater investigator should be to record and photograph the serial number in the water if visibility allows. Once rusting begins—and it happens very quickly—retrieval of the serial number may be difficult or impossible.

Serial numbers are usually stamped with hard metal dies. These dies strike the metal surface with a force that allows each digit to sink into the metal to a prescribed depth. Restoration of serial numbers can be accomplished because the metal crystals in the stamped zone are placed under a permanent strain that extends a short distance beneath the original numbers. When an **etching agent** is applied, the strained area will dissolve at a slower rate than the surrounding corroded metal, permitting the underlying number pattern to appear. The ability to recover serial numbers using etching acids is determined by the extent of the corrosion of the firearm. Obviously, it is essential to retard the corrosion by not exposing the firearm to oxidizing agents.

OFFICER'S NOTEBOOK

Submerged Weapon Handling Tip

Once a weapon is retrieved and subjected to the air, oxidation will begin immediately, and thorough rusting may occur in less than an hour, rendering ballistic examination impossible. It is therefore crucial to keep the weapon immersed in water until the preservation procedure can be started.

Figure 9–11   Revolver serial number.

Courtesy of Austin Police Department, Austin, Texas

Other Trace Evidence

If a handgun was placed in a pocket or under a car seat prior to submergence, fabric from the pocket or debris and fiber from the auto floor may still adhere to protruding portions of the weapon (sights, safeties, clip releases, hammers).

Barrel Blowback

In addition to fingerprint and ballistic evidence, a firearm, especially a handgun, may contain hair, tissue, blood, and fibers. The muzzle blast of a gun fired in contact with a body and the negative pressure in the barrel following discharge may cause blood, hair, tissue fragments, and fabric to be found several inches back inside the barrel (Spitz, 1993). Retrieving a weapon by inserting something into the barrel will only serve to dislodge and destroy any trace evidence. It is best to hold the weapon by the trigger guard or the checkered portion of the grip or stock.

The notion that a submerged firearm is bereft of any relevant forensic information is erroneous. The notion that human tissue, hair, and blood will be displaced from the barrel of a firearm as a result of submersion is also erroneous. Vincent Bugliosi (1992) described the testimony of an FBI serologist who testified during the trial of Buck Walker for the grisly deaths of Mac and Muff Graham. The serologist testified that after three years' submersion in the Pacific Ocean, a metal container in which it was believed that Muff Graham had been dismembered, burnt, and submerged tested positive on a phenolphthalein screening test. The phenolphthalein screen is sensitive to a drop of blood in ten thousand parts of water. However, this screen only determines if the sample in question is blood, not whether the blood is human. The serologist went on to describe a second test that he performed, called a ouchterlony screen, that does determine if a blood specimen is human. After three years of submersion and sand, water, and marine intrusion, the serologist was still able to determine that the cloth sample removed from the submerged case was stained with human blood.

■ Physical Evidence Predicates

Every investigation involves physical evidence, and every investigation should antici-pate the need to authenticate each item discovered. Authentication of physical evidence is fairly standard and should pose no admissibility problems for the testifying officer. Occasionally defense lawyers will stipulate to the authenticity of large quantities of evi-dence when they are convinced that the testifying witness is competent in establishing the appropriate predicate. The stipulation avoids the dramatic effect of the prosecution focusing on each piece of evidence.

Often it will take more than one witness to lay the complete predicate for a piece of evidence. For example, a recovery team diver recovers a handgun and, after proper measuring and handling, gives it to an evidence technician to check for latent prints on the ammunition contained in the magazine. The evidence technician discovers latent prints and manages to lift one successfully. A suspect has inked fingerprint impressions taken. The latent print and the inked impression are forwarded to the crime laboratory for comparison. It will take the testimony of four witnesses before the laboratory analysis can be admitted as evidence:

1. The diver who discovered the handgun will identify the weapon and attest to the fact that it is the one found, describe the method employed in discovery, and testify that the weapon has not been altered.

2. The technician who lifted the latent print will extend the custody chain, identify the weapon, identify the latent print, describe the method whereby a latent print was lifted, and attest that the print has not been altered.

3. The officer who took the inked impression of the suspect will identify the inked impression, identify the defendant from whom the impression was taken, and attest that the impression has not been altered.

OFFICER'S NOTEBOOK

Proper Technique for In-Court Authentication of Physical Evidence

Q: You have in your hand a _____ [handgun, knife, bat, hatchet, shirt, gasoline can, etc.] that you have identified as State's Exhibit 4. When and where did you first see it?

A: [Officer gives time, date, and location.]

Q: How do you know that this is the same _____ that you recovered?

A: [Officer describes identifying characteristics. If there are no specific identifying characteristics that distinguish this item from all others, then it should be marked and that mark described.]

Q: Is the _____ in the same or substantially the same condition as when you found it?

A: [Officer describes any alterations.]

4. The laboratory technician will extend the custody chain for both the inked and latent prints, identify both, and express an opinion regarding the laboratory comparison that was made.

For a sample courtroom examination of a fingerprint expert, see Appendix A.

As each witness testifies, the prosecutor will request that provisional admissibility be allowed the exhibit, pending the anticipated cumulative testimony of all four witnesses. After all four witnesses have testified, the prosecutor should have overcome any objections as to the authenticity of the exhibit offered, and the court should allow the exhibit into evidence.

■ Summary

Firearms are the most common weapon used in homicides in the United States. The historical relationship with firearms and violent confrontation of our Western past is alive and well in the American proclivity to use firearms to commit crimes and resolve conflict. The good new is that firearm evidence at crime scenes is readily found and recovered and easily identifiable. National ballistics databases make the identification of firearms evidence quicker and more accessible.

Hawaii has the most restrictive handgun ownership procedure in the country. Before a person can buy a handgun, he or she must first complete an NRA firearms safety training course, demonstrate firearm competency, and complete a written final examination. Upon completion of the examination, the instructor provides a certification of completion that will allow a person to take that certificate to a gun store and purchase the firearm of his/her choice. The buyer receives a document describing the firearm, including serial number, that must be taken to the Honolulu Police Department for registration. Upon completion of the registration process, the registrant receives a permit to own the handgun described. The registration is returned to the gun store and the buyer can now take possession of his /her handgun. The training and registration process may in part account for the relatively low homicide rate in Hawaii. The Hawaiian process may be a reasonable compromise between gun control and gun owner advocates.

Confrontation to resolve a dispute may result in death. The next chapter introduces us to the specific nature of death investigations in all its manifestations from manslaughter to capital murder.

■ Key Terms

assault rifle: A hand-carried, shoulder-fired semiautomatic or automatic weapon in a rifle caliber

automatic: Firearm that continues to fire as long as the trigger is depressed and ammunition is available

ballistics: The study of projectiles in motion

breechblock: The part of a firearm's action that supports the base of the cartridge in the chamber when it is fired

caliber: The diameter of the bore of a gun

cartridge case: That part of a cartridge that contains the powder and primer; it is the part of the cartridge that accommodates the projectile (bullet)

circumstantial evidence: All evidence other than eyewitness testimony

class characteristics: Characteristics used to identify a firearm, including caliber, direction of twist of the rifling, degree of twist, number of lands and grooves, and width of the lands and grooves

comparison microscope: Microscope that can be used to examine two or more fired bullets that exhibit the same class characteristics and determine whether the bullets were fired by the same weapon

degree of twist: The grooves inside the barrel of a gun spiral at a particular angle, with some steeper (greater) than others; degree of twist is an identifying characteristic of the firearm that includes the number of twists, the angle of the twist, and whether or not the twist is to the left or the right

etching agent: Agent used to visualize serial numbers on a firearm that is corroded

firearms: Weapons from which a shot is discharged; firearms examiners generally come into contact with five types of firearms: pistols, rifles, assault rifles, machine guns, and shotguns

firearms examination: Examination of the fired bullets and cartridges of a firearm to determine the weapon that fired them

firing pin: The part of the firearm's action that strikes the cartridge primer in order to fire it

gauge: Measurement used to refer to bore diameters; when all firearms fired spherical lead balls, their bore diameters or gauges were expressed as the number of such lead balls that could be made from 1 pound of lead (e.g., 10 lead balls having the same diameter as the interior of the barrel of a 10-gauge shotgun should weigh 1 pound)

grooves: The recessed areas between the lands of the rifling

jacketed bullet: Bullet that consists of a lead core surrounded by a jacket of harder material, commonly a copper-nickel alloy or mild steel

lands: The raised ridges of the rifling that bite into the surface of the bullet and give it a rotational motion as it moves down the barrel

machine gun: Fully automatic weapon that is fired from a tripod or bipod because of the recoil; machine guns fire ammunition from magazines or from belts

National Firearms Act of 1968: Act that requires retailers to record the serial number of a weapon and the name of its purchaser

physical evidence: Evidence that can be handled, examined, tested, seen, felt, or tasted

pistol: Handheld firearm designed to be fired with one hand; pistols are single-shot, single-action revolvers; double-action revolvers; or self-loading (semiautomatic)

primer: A metal cup containing a small amount of primer material placed between the cup and a small metal anvil

propellant: Powder that begins to burn when a firearm is fired; the pressure increase caused by the burning powder propels the bullet from the firearm

revolver: Type of pistol that can be single-action or double-action

rifle: Weapon designed to be used with two hands and fired from the shoulder position

rifled firearm: Type of firearm whose barrel has a set of spiraling lands and grooves

semiautomatic: Self-loading weapon

shotgun: Firearm that is designed to be fired from the shoulder; unlike a rifle, it is a smooth-bore weapon, having no lands or grooves in the barrel

submachine gun: Fully automatic weapon that is designed to be fired while being held in the hands; submachine guns fire pistol cartridges

testimonial evidence: Evidence that encompasses the testimony of witnesses and of defendants

trace evidence: Evidence such as blood, hairs, fibers, wood splinters, glass particles, paint, concrete, or soil particles that can be picked up by a bullet after it is shot and can indicate the materials through which it traveled

transfer: The process whereby two objects that meet leave evidence of their meeting; in particular, refers to the fact that a person entering and leaving a crime scene leaves something and takes something

■ Review Questions

1. What are the differences among physical evidence, testimonial evidence, and circumstantial evidence?

2. Transferability is an important forensic concept for investigators to understand. Why?

3. What is the difference between firearms examination and ballistics?

4. Why is a pistol that fires each time the trigger is pulled misnamed if referred to as an "automatic"?

5. What role do lands and grooves play in a bullet's flight and in the examination of a suspect bullet?

6. What is the measure for expressing the size of a shotgun or a shotgun shell? How is it determined?

7. Who was Calvin Goddard, and what did he contribute to the field of firearms examination?

8. Is there a truly fully automatic pistol?

9. Is there a fully automatic shotgun?

10. What are the primary ways that a firearm is challenged when efforts are made to admit it into evidence?

■ Bibliography

Bugliosi, V. (1992). *And the sea will tell.* New York: Ivy Books.

Goddard, C.H. (1930). St. Valentine's Day massacre: A study in ammunition tracing. *American Journal of Police Science* 1, 60–78.

Hall, A.L. (1931). The missile and the weapon. *American Journal of Police Science* 2, 311–321.

Hatcher, J.S., Jury, F.J., & Weller, J. (1977). *Firearms: Investigation, identification and evidence.* Harrisburg, PA: Stackpole.

Hogg, I.A. (1977). *The encyclopedia of infantry weapons of World War II.* New York: Thomas Y. Crowell.

Lane, A.J. (1971). *The Brownsville affair: National crisis and black reaction.* Port Washington, NY: Kennikat.

Mathews, J.H. (1962). *Firearms identification, Vol. 1.* Springfield, IL: Charles C. Thomas.

Nonte, G.C. (1973). *Firearms encyclopedia.* New York: Harper & Row.

O'Connor, J. (1965). *Complete book of rifles and shotguns.* New York: Harper & Row.

Spitz, W.U. (1993). Injury by gunfire. In W. U. Spitz et al. (Ed.), *Medicolegal investigation of death* (3rd ed.), Springfield, IL: Charles C. Thomas.

Tarassuk, L., & Blair, C. (1979). *The complete encyclopedia of arms and weapons.* New York: Simon & Schuster.

Wilbur, C.G. (1977). *Ballistic science for the police officer.* Springfield, IL: Charles C. Thomas.

■ Key Legal Cases

Commonwealth v. Best, 62 N.E. 748 (1902).

Commonwealth v. Ellis, 364 N.E.2d 808 (1977).

Dean v. Commonwealth, 32 Gratt (V.) 912 (1897).

Evans v. Commonwealth, 19 S.W.2d 1091 (1929).

Jack v. Commonwealth, 222 Ky. 546, 1 S.W.2d 961 (1928).

Johnson v. State, 249 So.2d 470 (Fla. App. 1971).

People v. Triplett, 243 N.W.2d 665 (1965).

State v. Aiken, 434 P.2d 10 (1967).

State v. Bayless, 357 N.E.2d 1035 (1976).

State v. Boccadoro, 144 A. 612 (1929).

State v. Clark, 196 P. 360 (1921).

State v. Lane, 223 P.2d 437 (1951).

State v. Nutley, 129 N.W.2d 155 (1964).

State v. Vuckovich, 203 P. 491 (1921).

Williams v. State, 333 S.W.2d 846 (1960).

Death Investigation

▶ ▶ STUDENT LEARNING OUTCOMES

Upon completion of this chapter students will demonstrate an understanding of:

- The different types of homicides
- A homicide investigative protocol
- The types of wounds made by firearms
- Postmortem changes in the decedent

Murder is the least common of all crimes, the crime cleared most often, and the offense that receives the greatest attention from law enforcement and the media. As in all investigations, the crime scene is often the greatest source of information about the offense and the offender, especially in the case of stranger murders and serial murders.

Not all homicides require the attention of the police. A **homicide** is the taking of a human life by another human. The circumstances of the homicide determine if it was justifiable or was **murder**, the killing of another with malice aforethought. Criminal homicide is defined by state statute and may be further subdivided into categories such as capital murder (murders for which, due to the circumstances of the murder, capital punishment may be imposed), murder (homicide with malice aforethought), and manslaughter (homicide with the absence of malice aforethought). Many states still use degrees to distinguish one type of homicide from another, with first-degree murder being murder with malice aforethought.

Every murder has specific elements that must be proven at the time of trial, referred to as the **corpus delicti** of the offense. The use of this term, which in Latin means *body of the crime,* often misleads the public and the media into thinking that the state must produce a corpse in order to convict someone for murder. In fact, the term is used in law to refer to the material evidence in a criminal homicide case that shows that a crime has been committed (evidence that may include the victim's corpse, of course). All criminal homicides require the state to prove the following:

- There has been a death of a human being (which may be difficult to prove absent a body, this fact in turn explaining the tendency of perpetrators of premeditated murders to try to dispose of the body).
- The death was caused by another person's illegal act or failure to act.

The legal questions that often plague a homicide investigation usually revolve around **proximate cause** and **causation**. The question of proximate cause concerns the conduct of the agent and the consequences of that conduct. The illegal act must be close in time and space to the death of the deceased. There is no problem in determining that a person who shot a gun was responsible for the consequences when the projectile struck the person at whom the gun was aimed. Proximate cause may become an issue, however, in more convoluted scenarios. Firing a shot into a construction site for the purpose of shooting a personal enemy but instead causing a person on the construction site to jump instinctively and drop a concrete block so that it strikes and kills another person two stories below may be tragic, but the person firing the shot has not murdered the person upon whom the block has fallen. The chain of cause and effect is too tenuous to establish the causal element of the corpus delicti of murder.

The question of causation most often arises in situations in which an individual is seriously injured by another but does not die immediately or shortly after the assault. The greater the time from the illegally caused injury until death, the more attenuated becomes the relationship between the injuring act and the death. Most states address the causation question by statute, requiring that the death occur within a particular time frame after the illegal act causing the injury.

Most police agencies do not have homicide investigators and evidence technicians, although most metropolitan agencies do. It therefore is necessary in many small or rural agencies for all patrol officers to process their own crime scenes. Assignment is on a first-come, first-serve basis, and the responding officer is also the officer responsible for the investigation and preparation of the case for trial.

■ Who Kills?

Americans report over 16,000 murders each year, most of which occur in large cities. Most murder victims are white; however, in proportion to the population, blacks are more often both victims and offenders. Criminal homicide is the leading cause of death among black males 25 to 34 years of age. Most murders are committed using a firearm and are perpetrated by the young, those 20 to 24 years old. Men are more likely to be killed in the kitchen, whereas women are more likely to be killed in the bedroom. Criminal homicide is predominantly the domain of men; women commit only 10% of criminal homicides. To the advantage of the police, only 20% of homicides are stranger murders; the rest are homicides in which a casual or close personal relationship exists between victim and offender. The number of stranger murders is growing, presumably as a result of additional gang- and drug-related violence (*Uniform Crime Reports*, 1975–2005).

■ Homicide Investigations

Any death that is considered to be suspicious or is unattended by medical personnel should be treated as a murder until proven otherwise. As noted in the section in Chapter 3 on underwater investigations, the presumption in the case of drownings has been exactly the opposite.

Often a cursory examination of the homicide crime scene will indicate that the death in question was natural or accidental. Once it has been determined that the victim is dead and medical assistance is of no use, the investigation can begin. Investigators need to be aware that a person drowned in cold water may not be dead but, rather, in a state in which the mammalian skin reflex has shut down all physiological signs. Cardiopulmonary resuscitation of the victim of such a drowning should continue until terminated by qualified medical personnel.

Numerous persons will be in a hurry to move the deceased, but any movement of the deceased should be done by the investigators or by medical personnel under the direction of the investigators. Once the coroner or medical examiner arrives, the medical personnel will likely ask to remove the body—for their own convenience. They have better things to do than hang around a crime scene. The body should not be removed until the investigator has gathered whatever information he or she is seeking, regardless of how long that may take. In some crime scenes, the body is positioned and staged. Body parts may be arranged in a particular fashion. Once the scene has been cleared of unnecessary personnel (there should have been none to start with), the investigator can begin a closer examination of the body and the crime scene and may thereby uncover relationships between the staging of the body and other aspects of the crime scene.

The Investigative Protocol

Until it has been conclusively determined that the death in question was accidental or a product of natural causes, the investigator should follow the protocol outlined in the Officer's Notebook. In jurisdictions that have homicide investigators and departments, it may prove helpful to remember who is on the investigative team.

OFFICER'S NOTEBOOK

Protocol at the Scene of a Death
1. Preserve the crime scene.
2. Retain and segregate witnesses.
3. Conduct a walk-through of the crime scene.
   a. Mentally locate evidence.
   b. Mentally locate access and exit points and look for evidence of forced entry.
   c. Navigate the crime scene without damaging or contaminating trace or blood evidence. (If this is not possible, then ensure that trace and blood evidence are photographed and tagged and bagged, or arrange for blood specialists to evaluate blood pattern evidence.)
   d. Determine what is to be photographed.
   e. Determine from what vantage point the best photos can be obtained.
   f. Determine what, if anything, appears to be missing.
   g. Attempt to construct a scenario based on your observations.
4. Search the premises for evidence.
   a. Navigate the crime scene without damaging or contaminating trace or blood evidence.
   b. Locate all evidence (mark the location of evidence with distinctive markers in order to relocate the evidence and to prevent its destruction or contamination during further searching).
5. Record the crime scene.
   a. Take field notes that reflect your first impressions and construct an overall description of the crime scene and the evidence.
   b. Photograph the scene based on impressions gathered during the walk-through.

(continued)

6. Locate all evidence geographically and temporally. The measurements should be taken without disturbing the evidence. If this is not possible, then they should be taken after collection of the evidence, using evidence markers placed in the same positions as the evidence collected.
7. Collect and preserve all evidence.
   a. Maintain an evidence log.
   b. Bag and tag all evidence.
   c. Where necessary, place an identifying mark on the evidence itself.
8. Identify the victim.
   a. Search for identifying documentation on the victim's body and confirm identification by talking with friends and relatives.
   b. If the victim is not readily identifiable, seek secondary evidence of identification and appropriate tools, such as
      i. Medical records
      ii. Dental records
      iii. Radiographs
      iv. Composite drawings
      v. Assistance from a forensic anthropologist
      vi. Fingerprints
      vii. Jewelry
9. Ascertain cause and mechanism of death, utilizing documents such as the following:
   a. Autopsy report
   b. Medical examiner's report
   c. Pathologist's report
   d. Toxicological report
10. Gather information.
    a. Conduct interviews with the following:
       i. Relatives
       ii. Neighbors
       iii. Employers
       iv. Coworkers
    b. Run a criminal history.
    c. Check business records.
    d. Compare the modus operandi to that of other crimes and criminals.
    e. Collect samples of writing, voice, hair, blood, and so on from the pool of suspects.
11. Interrogate suspects.
    a. Corroborate all statements using existing information.
    b. Allow a free flow of information.
    c. Do not express or imply any intimidation.
    d. Provide Miranda warnings.

The Investigative Team

The first responder maintains crime scene integrity, retains and segregates witnesses, and arrests suspects. It is important to remember that the first responder is a team member and to acknowledge the contribution he or she makes toward attaining the objective of all criminal investigations, which is winning a conviction.

The medical examiner pronounces the deceased dead, determines the cause and mechanism of death, and provides medicolegal information pertaining to death (the events that occured prior to, during, and after death). A show of appreciation for the work done by the medical examiner may go a long way toward creating a good working relationship. The first place and time that the investigator and medical examiner talk about the case should not be at the courthouse just prior to trial.

Forensic scientists provide technical information about evidence obtained at the crime scene and may collect evidence at the crime scene. Knowing what forensic scientists do and how they do it will assist the investigator in searching, processing, and interpreting crime scenes.

Investigators analyze, process, and synthesize information for the purpose of providing legally sufficient evidence at the time of trial.

Prosecutors utilize the work product of the rest of the team to convict the guilty party. Too often, other team members view prosecutors as adversaries or as people who will derail an investigation because of legal niceties or technicalities. The duty of all team members is to work together to obtain the conviction of criminals. Without the other members, the efforts of the investigator would be rendered useless. Each member of the team will make a contribution that will ultimately allow the investigator and trier of fact to determine the cause of death, the nature of the death (homicide, either justifiable or mitigated; natural causes; accident; or self-inflicted injury), and who caused the death.

■ The Staged Crime Scene

As investigators evaluate a crime scene, a picture should begin to develop regarding the human dynamics involved in the crime being investigated. This picture may be elusive in a homicide investigation. Any facts that appear inconsistent with the developing picture of how the crime was committed should place investigators on notice. These details may contain peculiarities that serve no apparent purpose in the commission of and motive for the crime. This confusion may be the result of a crime scene that has been **staged** prior to the arrival of the police.

Staging may occur for two reasons:

1. To direct the investigation away from the most logical suspect. In this case, it is the offender who attempts to redirect the investigation. He or she may be an overly cooperative witness providing misinformation.
2. To protect the victim or victim's family. This occurs for the most part in rape-murder crimes or autoerotic fatalities. The family member or person who finds the body performs this type of staging in an attempt to restore some dignity to the victim. These people are trying to prevent the shock that may be brought about by the position, dress, or condition of the victim. They may stage an autoerotic fatality to look like a suicide, perhaps even writing a suicide note. They may even go so far as to make the death appear to be a homicide.

For both rape-murders and autoerotic fatalities, investigators need to obtain an accurate description of the body's condition when found and to determine exactly what the person who found the body did to alter the crime scene. Scrutiny of forensic findings, crime scene dynamics, and victimology will probably reveal the true circumstances surrounding the death (Douglas and Munn, 1992).

Forensic Inconsistencies

Offenders who stage crime scenes usually make mistakes because they arrange the scene to resemble how they believe it should look. In so doing, offenders experience a great deal of stress and do not have the time to fit all the pieces together logically. As a result, inconsistencies in forensic findings and in the overall big picture of the crime scene will begin to appear. Forensic inconsistencies might include the following:

- Forensic results that do not fit the crime
- Discrepancies between witness/survivor accounts and forensic results
- Inconsistencies between autopsy reports and witness statements
- Unexplained toxicological findings
- Manipulation of a friend or relative to discover the body
- Items that were removed
- Items that were left
- Items that were repositioned

It is the responsibility of the crime scene investigator to question anything that appears not to fit a particular crime scene. In arriving at a working theory of the case, it may be easiest to address all those pieces that fit, but it is often the pieces that do not fit readily that tell the full story. It may take additional time and effort to pursue those nagging little pieces, but they may be the clues to the ultimate and correct resolution of the investigation. In many instances it is what does not fit that is most important—but only if you recognize it.

Autoerotic Asphyxiation

There is a segment of the population that finds **autoerotic asphyxiation** sexually gratifying. The physical pleasure from autoerotic asphyxia comes with the reduction of oxygen to the brain, or hypoxia. Reduced oxygen to the brain creates a semihallucinogenic, semilucid state. Proponents claim it is pleasurable in its own right without the necessity of bondage or genital manipulation. Autoerotic behavior is not criminal however it is a dangerous form of masturbation. Every autoerotic death has its own personal script; masturbation is a deeply personal, sexual act. "For certain individuals, the preferred or exclusive mode of producing sexual excitement is to be mechanically or chemically asphyxiated to or beyond the point at which consciousness or perception is altered by cerebral hypoxia (diminished availability of oxygen to the brain)" (Dietz, 1989).

The pleasure is best understood as residing in a fantasy. The fantasy may be fueled by bondage and masochistic behavior. Bondage and masochism are widely practiced without the element of hypoxia. Some involved in what is known by practitioners as *edge play* or *breath play* involve asphyxia in their activities. These activities may be practiced with a partner or partners or solo. Autoerotic asphyxiation is solo breath play.

What is unique to the autoerotic asphyxiation incident is the fantasy object associated with the masturbatory activity. Every fantasy requires an object to fulfill it. It may be complex ligatures, pornographic paraphernalia, women's undergarments, or perhaps some masochistic element. All of these objects assist the fantasy and accelerate sexual arousal. Once the investigator identifies the fantasy object or objects, the autoerotic behavior will begin to explain itself. Many individuals who engage in autoerotic asphyxia may do so in concert with genital masturbation and insertion of objects into bodily orifices for further sexual stimulation.

Parents or loved ones may alter the scene of autoerotic asphyxia victims out of shame and embarrassment; they wish to hide the truth from the police and the public. Part of that shame is based on ignorance. The conduct in question is masturbation; it may have taken a complex arrangement to facilitate masturbation, but what has taken place is not a crime and is shameful only because others have defined it as such.

Arising from the fear, ignorance, and shame associated with this activity are a variety of myths that have caught the national imagination.

- **Myth: Decedents tend to be young boys.** Data suggest that an age range of 14 to 30 is a more accurate reflection of the ages of people participating in autoerotic asphyxiation.
- **Myth: Autoerotic fatalities occur only in men.** Women masturbate, and women who engage in dangerous forms of autoerotic behavior can die from it. Asphyxia and trauma are not gender-specific activities. Although female occurrences are not as frequent as male occurrences, they do exist.
- **Myth: Nudity, or partial nudity, is always a feature in autoerotic death scenes.** Although nudity can be a feature of an autoerotic fatality, it is not a necessary feature.
- **Myth: Most autoerotic deaths are characterized by transvestitism.** Transvestitism is recurrent and persistent cross-dressing by a heterosexual male for which there is no explanation other than sexual excitement. There are widespread anecdotal reports of male decedents being discovered wearing female undergarments or clothing; however, the data do not support the claim that most autoerotic deaths are characterized by transvestitism. In fact, transvestitism occurs in only a small portion of autoerotic death cases (Turvey, 1995).

In order to identify cases of autoerotic asphyxiation, it is necessary to cast off societal labels and evaluate the scene objectively without the interference of social prejudices and with an understanding of the lengths to which friends and relatives will go to keep the underlying behavior a secret. The Officer's Notebook provides criteria for this objective evaluation.

OFFICER'S NOTEBOOK

Objective Criteria to Be Used in Determining Autoerotic Death
- Evidence of a physiological mechanism for obtaining or enhancing sexual arousal that provides a self-rescue mechanism or allows the victim to voluntarily discontinue its effect
- A reasonable and demonstrable expectation of privacy
- Evidence of solo sexual activity
- The presence of sexual fantasy objects
- Evidence of prior dangerous autoerotic practice. A complex arrangement of ligatures and bondage devices will often use walls, doors, ceilings, and so forth. An examination of the bondage arrangement may reveal prior similar use
- No apparent suicidal intent
  - There have been no prior attempts at suicide
  - Depression has not been reported
  - No divesting of important personal possessions has occurred
  - No morbid conversations regarding self-destruction have occurred

■ Recovering Human Remains*

Looking for buried human remains requires the recognition of **burial indicators**. Time since burial, ground moisture, and terrain will affect these indicators. In any search for buried remains, it may well be that the body was dismembered and that more than one burial site is involved. The search must consider large as well as multiple small burial sites.

Burial site indicators include the following:

- **Disturbed vegetation:** Whenever a hole is dug in the ground, the vegetation in and around the hole is disturbed. Adjacent areas that were disturbed during digging will also show signs of vegetation disturbance.
- **Soil compaction:** The natural decomposition of buried remains leaves a void in the soil. Time and rain cause the soil above the remains to sink to fill the void, forming a depression in the surface above the body. This depression is sometimes called a compaction site. A secondary depression may also be noted inside the primary depression. This is caused by the deterioration of the corpse's abdominal cavity.
- **New vegetation:** The new growth will not be as mature as growth in the surrounding area.
- **Soil disturbance:** When a grave is dug, the layers of the soil are disturbed. The soil under the ground is layered. Some areas have very shallow layers or multiple layers within a very few inches from the surface, whereas others have layers several feet thick. At different depths, the soil varies in color. These different colors represent the different layers of soil. Once the layers are disturbed, no amount of effort and precision can replace them exactly. Digging not only disturbs the soil layers in the grave, but also disturbs the surface soil around the grave. There will always be some residue left after refilling a hole. The residue will be a different color than the surrounding surface soil.

Multiple indicators may be present at any site.

Not all terrain lends itself to the discovery of visual burial indicators. In some instances it may be necessary to utilize tools in the search.

- **Infrared photography:** Uses the difference in temperature between the buried body and the temperature of the soil around or on top of it. Infrared photography may also indicate the difference in temperature of disturbed and undisturbed soil.
- **Methane detector:** As organic objects decompose, they produce methane gases. The longer the body has been buried, the less likely it is that methane gas can be detected.
- **Aerial photography:** A comparison of aerial photographs of the suspected area taken over a period of years might disclose a possible burial site. Aerial photos could show a vegetation disturbance occurring where a body is buried.
- **Probe:** A four-foot metal rod approximately three-eighths of an inch in diameter with a wooden T-shaped handle is poked into the ground. When pushing the probe into the ground, the investigator can feel a difference in the pressure needed to push the probe into undisturbed and disturbed soil.

---

*The material in this section was adapted from a series of lectures by Dr. M. L. Goff at his 2003 "Handling Human Remains Workshop," held each summer at Chaminade University of Honolulu.

OFFICER'S NOTEBOOK

Processing the Burial Site

After the site is photographed and sketched and vegetation is cleared away, photos should be taken of the new "clean" site. Using rope or string, set up a grid for the purpose of locating the items by measurements and for ease in placing the items on a sketch. Take close-up photographs of all items prior to their removal. Package the remains of the deceased, and, if the body has skeletonized and been disarticulated, bag body parts separately. If the body is intact, lace it on a backboard that is covered with a white sheet and then place in a *new* body bag.

Surface Recovery

Once the search is completed and the body located, the recovery site must be defined. Extreme scattering of the bones, body parts, or physical evidence by animals frequently occurs. Therefore, the area encompassing the scattered remains may be a few feet or several yards. This area must be processed (see Officer's Notebook).

Once the surface of the site has been cleared of all remains and evidence, the next step is to examine and excavate the top 6 inches of soil for any further evidence or bones. In some instances the remains have gone through a self-burial. Objects placed on the surface of the ground may work their way into the ground. The extent to which this occurs will depend on the object's weight, the density of the ground, the terrain of the area, the time elapsed, and the weather conditions.

For example, the author investigated a homicide in Montana in which the victim was lured to the side of a mountain, ostensibly to participate in a party and to partake of drugs (LSD). He was struck from behind on a game trail some distance from the mountain road and repeatedly hit with large rocks until dead. His body was then rolled off the trail and left. The murder went undiscovered for over a year. The victim was an Alaska native who had been passing through the area. Because he was not a local resident, no one reported him missing. As criminals are likely to do, the perpetrators talked to friends during parties and even acted out the murder. But no one reported the story to the police until a hunter discovered a human skull in a draw at the bottom of the same mountain where the deceased was dispatched. Investigators immediately cordoned off the area and planned and initiated a search. Various bones were strewn across the mountain, and human hair of the same color as the decedent's was found entangled in the brush. It was possible to trace the movement of the body down the hill by the hair and bones that were strewn from the trail to the bottom. Many of the bones had been gnawed and some cracked. Only about 30% of the body was actually recovered over a large area. The two young men who had committed the murder confessed when confronted with the evidence.

Excavation Techniques

Once the investigator has located and defined the burial site, he or she can choose the method of excavation. Three methods of excavating the ground around the body, and, ultimately, the body itself, are recommended:

1. **Hole:** As the name indicates, a hole is dug, uncovering the remains as the soil is removed from over and around the body.

2. **Trench:** A trench is dug next to the remains to a depth of 2 feet below the upper body level. The trench must be at least the length of the body and approximately 2 feet

wide. This trench will provide sufficient room to work and collect evidence and the remains. Using this method, three of the four walls of the grave can be defined.

3. Table: A table is dug by trenching all around the body, usually leaving a table approximately 4 feet wide by 7 feet long and extending 2 feet beyond the depth of the body. This method will leave all four walls of the grave intact plus provide sufficient room to work around the body.

Regardless of which method the investigator uses, he or she must estimate the position of the body under the ground prior to excavation. With a generous estimate, excavating a hole, trench, or table can be done without fear of disturbing the remains.

With any of these methods, investigators should remove soil in strips approximately 12 inches wide and 6 inches in depth and should hand-check and sift the soil as the different layers are removed. Anything that is not soil could be evidence or bones!

Anthropological Considerations

Because the remains in question are usually badly decomposed or skeletonized to some degree and little soft tissue may remain, a forensic anthropologist is an essential member of any recovery team. Forensic anthropologists can assist investigators by answering several important questions:

1. Are the remains in question human?
2. Is there evidence of a homicide?
3. What are the ascertainable victim characteristics (e.g., age, gender, ethnic origin, stature)?
4. Do the remains exhibit any indications of premortem and/or postmortem trauma that may assist the medical examiner or coroner in determining the cause and/or manner of death?
5. Is there anything associated with the body that will assist in identifying it?

The ability of the forensic anthropologist to answer these questions is dependent upon the amount of the skeleton recovered and the amount of damage done during the recovery.

The skull is typically the first part of the skeleton to decompose. As a result, the skull often can be found great distances from the main concentration of the remains. Gravity (if the body is on a sloping hill or any incline) and the activity of scavenging animals (such as rodents, bears, coyotes, wolves, or canines) can result in the skull being displaced after it has decomposed enough to be separated easily from the rest of the body.

Damage to important skeletal elements can occur if recovery personnel do not handle the remains appropriately. The skull and mandible are important in determining gender, laying the foundation for facial reconstruction, and determining ethnic origin. Inadvertent damage can occur to the bones during transportation. To avoid such damage, package all bones in separate bags.

■ The Autopsy

The government can order an **autopsy** in every state when there is suspicion of foul play. In addition, in most states, an autopsy may be ordered if someone dies unattended by a physician or if the attending physician is uncomfortable signing the death certificate. Many autopsy services have a sign that reads, "This is the place where death rejoices to teach those who live." Usually it is written in Latin: "Hic locus est ubi mors gaudet succurrere vitae."

In performing an autopsy, a pathologist first examines the outside of the body (**Figure 10–1**). The pathologist opens the body with a Y-shaped incision from shoulders to midchest and down to the pubic region. These incisions cut deeply, down to the rib cage and breastbone. If the head is to be opened, the pathologist makes a second incision across the head; joining the bony prominences just below and behind the ears, this cut is deep enough to expose the skull. The scalp and the soft tissues in front of the chest then are retracted back. To enter the chest cavity, he or she must cut the cartilages that join the ribs to the breastbone. The pathologist removes and examines the breastbone and attached rib cartilages. The skull vault is opened using two saw cuts, one in front and one in back. The top of the skull is removed, and the brain is very carefully cut free of its attachments from inside the skull.

The pathologist inspects chest organs, including the heart and lungs, and takes blood from the heart to check for bacteria in the blood. He or she may send blood, urine, bile, or the fluid of the eye for chemical study and to look for medicine, street drugs, alcohols, and/or poisons. The pathologist examines the heart; generally, the first step following its removal is sectioning the coronary arteries that supply the heart with blood.

The first dissection in the abdomen is usually done to free the large intestine. Using the **Virchow method**, the pathologist will begin removing organs individually. The pathologist removes the intestines and opens them using special scissors. The pathologist saves a section of any removed organ in preservative solution. He or she weighs the major solid organs (heart, lung, brain, kidney, liver, spleen, and sometimes others) on a grocer's scale. The smaller organs (thyroid, adrenals) get weighed on a chemist's triple-beam balance.

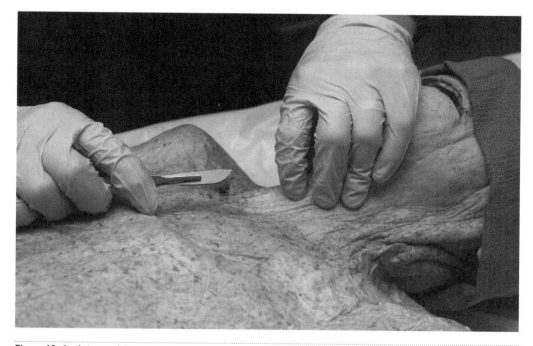

Figure 10–1 Autopsy picture.

The lungs are almost never normal at autopsy. The pathologist weighs both lungs together, then each one separately. Dissecting the lungs can be done in any of several ways. All methods reveal the surfaces of the large airways and the great arteries of the lungs. The air spaces of the lungs are evaluated based on their texture and appearance.

In order to examine the inner structure of the liver, the pathologist removes and weighs it, and then cuts it into 1-cm slices. The kidneys are weighed and dissected. The urinary system may be removed as one piece, and the digestive system down to the small intestine (the esophagus, stomach, pancreas, duodenum, and spleen) as another single piece. Once these organs are opened, a portion of the gastric contents is saved to check for poison.

Before the autopsy is over, the brain is usually suspended in fixative for a week so that the later dissection will be clean, neat, and accurate. When the internal organs have been examined, the pathologist may return all but the portions that have been saved to the body cavity. The pathologist usually replaces the breastbone and ribs in the body, sews the skull and trunk incisions shut, and then washes the body and forwards it to the funeral director.

The pathologist submits the saved tissue to the histology lab to be made into microscopic slides. When these are ready, the pathologist examines the slide sections, looks at the results of any lab work, and reports his or her final conclusions. For a complete autopsy report, see Appendix C. The University of Leicester has a Web site that allows interactive autopsy education at www.le.ac.uk/pathology/teach/va/titlpag1.html.

■ Identifying the Deceased

Most criminal homicide investigations involve readily identifiable victims. Sometimes, however, a body is not readily identifiable because it has been disfigured or dismembered or has deteriorated over time due to putrefaction. A disfigured, dismembered, or decaying body may be identified through scientific assessment of the body parts. A victim's height, age, sex, and race may be determined by a forensic anthropologist if enough of the right bones have been uncovered. Sex can be assessed from the overall size of the bones or the skeleton. The width and structure of the pubic bone provide added evidence regarding the victim's sex. Race can best be assessed by examining the skull, for skull conformation varies with race. (If the victim was of racially mixed parentage, the constellation of physical characteristics of the skull may be of little help in determining race.) The long bones of the leg may also assist in racial classification, because the femur bones of African Americans tend to be relatively straight whereas the femur bones of whites are somewhat arched. Age can be determined by dental development of the skull, skeletal size, and whether the epiphysis of the long bones in the legs is fused.

Dental work is distinctive and useful in identifying bodies that are otherwise unidentifiable. Dental identifications can be accomplished if a tentative identification of the body has been made and dental records are available to confirm that identification. Missing-person reports often give the initial impetus for a dental or medical comparison.

Physicians and hospitals can provide medical records once a tentative identification of the body has been made. Even skeletal remains can disclose identity if bone fractures are observed. Radiographs (X-rays) may assist in identifying the deceased if corresponding medical records are available. The body is much like a history book, cataloging life's physical traumas. Many people, in the course of life, have had bone fractures, surgery, or herniated discs for which they have sought medical treatment. Many have received dental treatment regularly. Medical and dental records constitute a repository of identifying information waiting to be discovered.

Other physical features may assist in identifying the deceased, such as tattoos, birthmarks, scars, physical deformities, or handicaps. Many citizens have been fingerprinted sometime during their lives. The number includes all those who have served in the military, been arrested, or worked for a government agency. The investigator should obtain a legible and classifiable full set of fingerprints and palm prints to be forwarded to the FBI's identification division. Not all fingerprint searches will be successful; although a sizable portion of Americans have been fingerprinted, the majority have not. For obvious reasons, women are poorly represented in the fingerprint records maintained by the FBI (fewer women than men have been arrested, served in the military, or been in government service).

■ Window-of-Death Determinations

Most criminal homicide investigations try to establish a time of death in order to:

- Establish the victim's movements prior to death
- Establish the victim's activities prior to death
- Establish a suspect and witness pool
- Corroborate suspects' alibis
- Establish some parameters for the investigation
- Clarify anomalies at the crime scene

The only time of which an investigator can be sure at the outset of a criminal homicide investigation is the time the body was discovered. There is no method that can establish precisely the moment of death. Investigators begin by determining a window of time in which the death must have occurred and then reduce the time frame whenever and however they can—often by discovering people whom the victim encountered before death. Discovering these people means tracing the movements of the victim between the time the victim was last seen and the time the body was found. In addition to the information gathered by investigators, valuable insight can be gained from the following:

- The medical examiner
- The pathologist
- A forensic entomologist
- The autopsy report
- A toxicology report

At its first stage, the **window of death** spans the period between the last time a witness interviewed by the police saw or heard the victim and the time the body was found. Additional input from the crime scene and the body of the deceased can help reduce the window, as can medical data and information gathered from newly discovered witnesses whom the victim encountered prior to being slain.

The medical examiner determines the cause of death (accident, suicide, or criminal homicide), and he or she or a forensic pathologist may determine the mechanism and manner of death (brain damage resulting from blunt trauma, loss of blood from a gunshot wound, etc.). The medical examiner and the forensic pathologist also can employ methods to narrow the window of death, all of which involve treating sequential changes in the deceased as a postmortem clock. The physicochemical characteristics and changes evaluated may include the following:

- Postmortem cooling (algor mortis)
- Ocular changes
- Postmortem lividity (livor mortis)
- Postmortem rigidity (rigor mortis)
- Cadaveric spasm
- Stomach contents
- Putrefaction

Algor Mortis

Postmortem body temperature declines progressively until it reaches the surrounding temperature, a process known as **algor mortis**. Under normal conditions, the body cools at a rate of 2°F per hour during the first hours and at a slower rate thereafter (the average rate of loss is 1.5°F per hour during the first 12 hours and 1°F per hour for the next 18 hours). The skin of the human body cools first and rapidly; therefore, skin temperature is not helpful in determining temperature decline. The temperature changes in the inner core of the body carry the greatest weight, because these are slower and more regular. Most forensic pathologists assess core temperature hourly by measuring rectal temperature. Although the postmortem cooling of a body may be used in approximating the time interval since death, the level of accuracy remains low. This does not mean that postmortem temperature measurements are of no use in determining the postmortem interval, only that any body-cooling data need to be viewed cautiously (Knight, 1988).

A number of variables affect postmortem cooling:

- Increased body fat and clothing may each decrease the cooling rate.
- Wind and moving air may accelerate body cooling.
- Immersion in cold water accelerates body cooling.
- Ambient temperatures affect the cooling rate as follows: The cooler the air around the body, the more rapid the postmortem cooling. Conversely, the warmer the air around the body, the slower the cooling. Indeed, if the temperature around the body is greater than the body temperature, the body temperature will increase rather than decrease.

Ocular Changes

The eyes often exhibit the first signs of postmortem change. When the eyes remain open, a thin film can be seen on the corneal surface within minutes after death. This film will escalate into **corneal clouding** within 2 to 3 hours of death. If the eyes are closed, the filming and clouding may be delayed by 24 hours or longer (Bray, 1985).

Postmortem Lividity

In deaths occurring other than as a result of drowning, a purplish-blue discoloration will occur because of the settling of blood by gravity. This gravitational movement of blood to the lowest point is referred to as **livor mortis** (Figure 10–2). In addition to the discoloration resulting from gravity pulling capillary blood to the bottommost point, there may be pale areas where the skin was pressed against a hard surface or object, preventing sedimentation. The blood pulled to the bottommost point of the body, if left undisturbed, begins to coagulate after approximately 2 hours and becomes immune

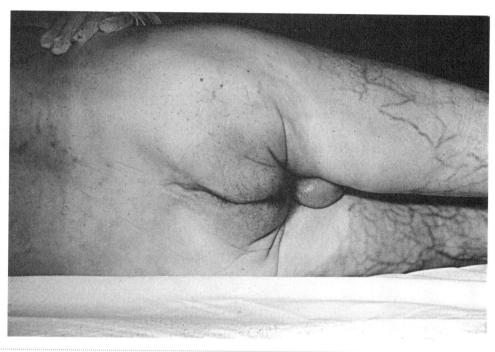

Figure 10–2 Postmortem lividity.

Photo courtesy of Steven Hanson, former Chief Investigator Bexar County MEO

to the effects of gravity. If a person died on a hard floor face upward, areas on the back and legs not in contact with the floor would turn purple-blue. The buttocks, shoulders, and heels would be pale white because of the intrusion of the hard surface on the sedimentation process.

The development of **lividity** is a gradual and progressive process that may begin as early as 20 minutes after death. Lividity in areas inconsistent with the pull of gravity strongly suggests that the body was moved after death and after the onset of lividity (Coe and Curran, 1980).

Postmortem Rigidity

Following death, the muscles of the body first become flaccid and then become increasingly stiff. The stiffness of the muscles, which eventually freezes the joints, is known as **rigor mortis**. This stiffening develops and disappears at a similar rate in all muscle groups but is first evident in the smaller muscles, which led early investigators to believe that rigor began at the head and progressed downward. The only reason rigor is evident in the head first is because of the comparatively small mass of the muscles throughout the head.

In average circumstances, rigor becomes apparent within 30 minutes of death and increases progressively to a maximum within 12 hours. It remains for about 12 hours and then progressively disappears within the following 12 hours. The progression of rigor may be modified by a variety of factors. Rigor is accelerated by hot environmental conditions, death by electrocution, and premortem vigorous exercise. Conversely, cold slows chemical decomposition and the onset of rigor. Another variable that may affect the onset of rigor is muscle mass, which is absent in children, the elderly, and the chronically underweight. The appearance of rigid limbs in positions inconsistent with gravity should raise a strong suspicion that the body was moved after the onset of rigor (Simson, 1976).

Cadaveric Spasm

Cadaveric spasm is a phenomenon more common among drownings than dry-land deaths. However, there have been instances of dry-land cadaveric spasm. In deaths accompanied by great excitement or tension, a forceful contraction or seizure is converted almost immediately into rigor, dispensing with the stage of muscle flaccidity. This rigor is not a product of chemical decomposition but rather a response during life to impending death and the accompanying anxiety or excitement. Bodies are found with eyeglasses or other possessions clutched firmly in hand, and on occasion pistols must be removed forcibly from the hand.

Stomach Contents

Often the presence of food in the stomach and its appearance may be helpful in determining an approximate time of death. The type of food itself may be instrumental in determining the activities of the deceased just prior to death. Time calculations are based on the fact that the stomach empties at a rate that can be estimated. The reason the rate can only be estimated is that it is determined by the amount and type of food, drug, or alcohol ingested as well as the physical and emotional condition of the deceased.

The stomach does not empty immediately. Only small amounts of food are emptied per minute and only after the food has been reduced to small particles. Therefore, food will be retained longer in the stomach of an individual who does not chew his or her food completely. Drugs and alcohol also affect the rate at which food is emptied from the stomach. The ingestion of alcoholic beverages with a meal delays stomach emptying, as does the ingestion of narcotics. Emotional stress also may delay stomach emptying for many hours. Those suffering emotional or physical shock associated with the ingestion of food will suffer a delay in stomach emptying. Finally, extremely cold or extremely hot weather may also affect the rate at which the stomach empties (Perper, 1993). Cold retards stomach emptying; heat accelerates stomach emptying.

Putrefaction

The rate that the body decomposes as the result of bacterial and microorganismal action depends primarily on environmental temperatures and the prior physical state of the decedent. It is generally accepted that **putrefaction** in air is more rapid than putrefaction in water, which in turn is more rapid than putrefaction in soil. One week in air equals two weeks in water and eight weeks in soil.

Exposure to cold also delays decomposition. It therefore is necessary to determine the ambient temperatures to which the body has been exposed when assessing rate of decomposition. A body lying outdoors in cold weather will decompose much slower

---

CASE IN POINT

New York Medical Examiner Dr. Michael Baden was able to determine the contents of a dead woman's last meal. Investigators were able to associate those contents with the menu of a restaurant at which the women had been seen. Interviewing employees revealed the name of a man with whom the decedent departed the restaurant. The stomach contents led ultimately to the arrest and conviction of her slayer.

Figure 10–3 Gloving.

Reproduced from Teather, Robert. *Encyclopedia of Underwater Investigation.* Best Publishing Company, 1994

than a body resting indoors in a heated environment or outdoors during the summer. The fact of warm days and cold nights must also be taken into consideration in the case of outdoor deaths. In general, decomposition begins within 24 to 30 hours of death, and its start can be seen in the greenish discoloration of the right lower abdominal area. The discoloration is followed by gaseous bloating and a greenish discoloration of the face, along with fluids being purged from the mouth. As decomposition continues, the tongue swells and protrudes from the mouth, and the eyes bulge. The discoloration of the face begins to spread to the chest and arms within about 48 hours. Discoloration of the skin may be so pronounced that the racial classification of the body may be mistaken.

As decomposition progresses, the skin begins to slip, and after three days the body becomes bloated. The shedding of the skin of the hands, including the fingernails, is called **gloving;** the shedding of the skin around the feet and legs is called **stocking.** The gloves, once shed, can render fingerprints, but the skin may be inside out, rendering a reverse print. Taking prints from gloves (**Figure 10–3**) should be done by persons trained in the proper process (Perper, 1993).

All of the seven methods used by medical personnel to arrive at a time of death are fraught with variables that affect the accuracy and reliability of any time frame proffered. All data must be viewed as approximations and be used accordingly. Although trying to determine the time of death may seem like an exercise in futility, a good estimate of the window of death will help the investigator focus his or her activities where they need to be focused—on the period surrounding the commission of the homicide.

■ Forensic Entomology

Insects process dead animal remains. Many use decomposing tissue as a source of food and as a place to raise their young. Insects have a highly developed sense of smell, which helps them locate decomposing animal tissue. Flies are attracted by the odor of the decomposition gases, blood, and purged body fluids. Insects are responsible for the consumption of all parts of the animal carcass except the skeleton. A decomposing body can be viewed as a succession of environments for different groups of specialized insects. The basic pattern of succession of insects is constant around the world (Smith, 1986).

In essence, a decomposing body provides a buffet for insects, but the line is only open to certain insects at certain times.

Insect Colonization of a Corpse

Insects process human bodies the same way they process any other animal. **Forensic entomology** is based on the analysis of insects and other invertebrates that sequentially colonize a decomposing body and the rates at which various stages of their offspring develop. Entomological information can be extremely useful in determining the manner of death, whether the cadaver has been moved from one site to another, and the length of the postmortem interval.

Flies, whose larvae are capable of living in a semiliquid environment, are the first insects to homestead decomposing remains. Maggots, which are fly larvae, are responsible for the consumption of the cadaver's organs and tissues. Only much later, when the corpse has dried out to a large extent, do the species of other insect groups, notably beetles, move in and continue the process (Hall, 1948).

Frequently, blowflies arrive minutes after death. Blowflies begin to lay eggs immediately or first feed on the purged fluids. On bodies that have not suffered trauma, flies initially feed and lay eggs in the natural body openings, specifically, the ears, nose, mouth, anus, and genitalia. Open wounds are attractive to colonizing flies. Blowfly eggs measure 2 to 3 mm and are elongated, white to yellow, and readily visible to the naked eye, having the appearance of grated cheese. During colder months, the quantity of blowfly eggs on a corpse may be reduced substantially, and the eggs may be difficult to locate, having been laid in areas that provide protection from the elements (under eyelids, in ear canals, or within the nostrils). The laid eggs generally hatch within one to three days. When hatched, the wormlike creatures produced are called larvae or maggots. The larvae grow rapidly, passing through three distinct physiological changes (instars). Large numbers of larvae hatch together and move around in the corpse in a mass (see **Figures 10–4 and 10–5**).

Blowfly larvae become fully grown within several days to several weeks, depending upon the species, the environmental conditions, and the number of larvae present. After reaching the third instar, larvae undergo a dramatic change: They crawl away from the corpse, burrow down into the soil, and secrete a hardened outer skin or casing around their body, a process referred to as pupation. Within the pupal case, a larva undergoes a complete physical reorganization and eventually emerges bearing all of the characteristics of the adult fly. Blowfly pupae are resilient and may remain buried in the soil beneath the corpse for hundreds of years. Blowfly pupae can supply valuable information long after the body has decomposed.

Following invasion of the corpse by blowflies, a wide variety of other types of insects colonize the remains. The successive nature of the colonization process enables forensic entomologists, when supplied with a representative sample of the insects present, to provide forensically meaningful information concerning the circumstances of the death.

Insect larvae not only can reveal information that aids in the estimation of the time of death but also can be used in the identification of poisons or drugs ingested by the deceased prior to death. Larvae can be pureed in a blender and subject to an examination that will reveal toxic substances present in the corpse at the time of death. It should be obvious that this type of testing requires a substantial number of larvae (Beyer, Enos, and Strajie, 1980).

Figure 10–4 Maggot picture.

Figure 10–5 Pupal case.

Entomological Evidence

In a criminal investigation, there may be an interest in finding out *when* a victim died, as well as an interest in finding out *how* the victim died. Entomological evidence may assist in both these determinations.

Cause of Death

Poison can be traced in blood, urine, stomach contents, hair, and nails. On a body, maggots may be a source of information about how the victim died. Over time it will be impossible to sample stomach contents, urine, and blood from the corpse because of advanced decomposition, but it may still be possible to sample maggots or empty pupal cases on or around the remains. What would have been found in the blood, urine, or stomach contents might be reflected in the composition of the bodies of the maggots.

Some chemicals may influence the life cycle of the maggot. Knowledge of drug use in the victim is important not only in finding the cause of death, but also in estimating the time of death. High dosages of cocaine accelerate the development of some sarcophagids. Malathion, an insecticide, is taken orally when used in a suicide. The presence of malathion in the mouth may lead to a delay in the colonization of the mouth.

The sites of blowfly infestation on the corpse may be important in determining the cause of death, or at least in reconstructing the events leading to death. If a body has been subjected to perimortem trauma or mutilation, a heavy infestation of the injured locations may be evident. Blowflies may oviposit (lay eggs) in wound sites

---

CASE IN POINT

Insects Can Tell a Story

Sixty specimens of insects were found in two separate seizures of cannabis (marijuana) in New Zealand. Only one species was known to occur in New Zealand. Eight other species were native only to Asia:

Coleoptera

- *Bruchidius mendosus* (Bruchidae): Distributed throughout Southeast Asia, but not known in Indonesia or the southern tip of the Malayan Peninsula.
- *Tachys* species (Carabidae): An abundant tropical genus normally found along the banks of streams or lakes.
- *Stenus basicornis* (Staphylinidae): Distributed throughout Southeast Asia; usually found on the banks of streams or lakes.
- *Azarelius sculpticollis* (Tenebrionidae): A rare species known only in Sumatra and Borneo. It lives as a "guest" in the nests of termites.
- *Gonocnemis minutus* (Tenebrionidae): Found in Thailand; lives as a "guest" in the nests of termites.

Hymenoptera

- *Parapristina verticellata:* A pollinator of the fig (*Ficus microcarpa*), which is distributed throughout the Indo-Australian region, from India and South China to New Caledonia.
- *Tropimeris monodon* (Chalcididae): Known from northwest India to Sumbawa in Indonesia.
- *Pheidologeton diversus* (Formicidae): Restricted in distribution to Southeast Asia from India to Indochina, including Singapore and West Indonesia. It is most common in the Indo-Malaysian region, including Thailand.

By plotting the distribution of these species and studying the degree of overlap, it was possible to suggest that the cannabis originated in the Tenasserim region between the Andaman Sea to the west and Thailand in the east. From the known habits of the insects, it was surmised that the cannabis was harvested near a stream or lake with fig trees and termite nests nearby.

instead of the more common natural body openings. Blowflies will oviposit in the facial region, followed by the genital and anal regions. If there is a sexual assault prior to death, leading to bleeding in the genital or anal region, blowflies will be more likely to oviposit there.

Moving the Body After Death

After death, a succession of fungi, bacteria, and animals will colonize the dead body. The substrate on which the body is lying also will change over time. Leakage of fluids from the dead body will lead to the disappearance of certain insects, and other insects will increase over time. An entomologist may be able to determine the postmortem interval by the insects on or under the body. If an analysis of the insects in the soil suggests a short postmortem interval, and the analysis of the insects on and in the body suggests a longer postmortem interval, the difference may be a product of the body having been moved from the site of death.

Insects and Drugs

Many arthropods are found together with stored products, which may include drugs. Because illegal drugs often are grown or manufactured in one country and sold in others, it may be possible to determine the source of growth or manufacture. If insects are discovered with the drugs, it may be possible to determine their point of origin. An appreciation of the biology of the insect species found with the drugs may say something about the surroundings where the drugs were produced or packed.

For example, in a homicide committed on Oahu in Hawaii, Dr. Lee Goff was asked to examine the body and consult with the police. In particular the police were concerned

OFFICER'S NOTEBOOK

Handling Insect Evidence

Representative samples of all adult and immature insects should be collected from the corpse as well as from inside and beneath the body. Once collected, adult flying insects can be placed immediately in 70% ethanol or isopropyl alcohol diluted with water to a ratio of 1:1. Crawling insects from the surface and within the body should be collected using forceps or fingers. Insects on the ground beneath the corpse can be collected most easily by scooping up the top few centimeters of soil and placing it in a plastic bag. The plastic bag containing the soil should be chilled to prevent further growth of the insects before they are extracted and preserved. A careful examination of the soil beneath the corpse is important, particularly in cases of advanced decay. When skeletal remains are encountered in a field, examination of the bones and surrounding soil must be made prior to skeletal removal. Close examination of bone cavities should produce insect remains, and examination of the cranial vault should prove fruitful.

Representative samples of the fly larvae, including the largest individuals present, should be collected and immediately divided into two subsamples. One subsample can be preserved immediately in ethanol; the other should be saved alive for raising to the adult stage. Sufficient numbers of individuals should be collected to ensure that a representative sample of the insect population is present. Specimens for rearing should be placed alive in small cups filled with vermiculite or a similar inert substance. Living specimens to be reared should not be placed in sealed plastic bags or sealed vials for longer than 12 hours.

Containers holding the preserved and living specimens should be labeled with the appropriate data, such as date and time collected; location of the remains; area of the body from which removed; and the name, agency, and telephone number of the collector. Because climatic conditions have a profound effect on the development of immature insects, acquiring the most accurate available weather data describing conditions at the location where the corpse was found is critical. Whenever possible, maximum and minimum temperatures at the scene should be recorded (Lord and Burger, 1983).

with the small red marks on the woman's legs. Dr. Goff informed the police that the marks were made by chiggers and that there was only one place on the island these insects were found. That place coincided with the recovery location of the body. Police inquired of the deceased woman's boyfriend if he had ever been to that location. His denial precipitated an examination of his legs, where chigger bites were noted.

Collection and Preservation of Insects

Accurate forensic determinations depend on the proper collection, preservation, and husbanding of entomological specimens. Investigators must be able to recognize adult and immature stages of insects that colonize tissue and be familiar with the proper techniques for their collection and preservation.

■ Gunshot Wounds

Firearms are involved in over two thirds of all criminal homicides in the United States. Handguns are used most commonly. When a firearm is discharged, smoke containing abundant soot and gunpowder is ejected from the muzzle in addition to the bullet. Deposits of these substances around a bullet hole are called smudging, tattooing, or powder stippling. By examining the pattern of these deposits, it is possible to estimate the distance from which the bullet was fired. The terminology most often used by medical examiners and forensic pathologists to describe the range at which a bullet was fired is as follows:

- **Contact wound:** Results when the firearm is discharged with the muzzle in contact with the body.
- **Close-range wound:** A wound made by a firearm discharged with the muzzle close enough to deposit gun smoke on the body or clothing.
- **Distant wound:** A wound made by a firearm discharged with the muzzle far enough away that gun smoke is not deposited on the body or clothing.

Contact Wounds

When a firearm is fired with the muzzle against a clothed part of the body, the bullet hole in the fabric touching the muzzle sometimes is surrounded by a flat ring caused by the heated barrel. The loose fringes of fabric in the center of the bullet hole usually are turned outward, away from the body, as a result of the expanding gases escaping back through the wound. Soot in varying amounts also is deposited behind the clothing on the body. Not only will the outer surface of the garment show gun smoke deposits, but the inner surface of the garment may also, even if there are no apparent gun smoke deposits on the outside surface. The deposits on the inner surface of clothing result from the muzzle blast spreading smoke between the skin and the clothing; deposits are most likely to occur if the shot passes through several layers of fabric or if the shot was fired through a pocket. Each layer is blackened individually on both sides of the fabric, whereas the skin and wound may have no gunpowder or soot. The bright yellow flame extending from the muzzle at the time of discharge scorches clothing and adjacent skin and singes hair up to a distance of 3 inches. Soot, but little gunpowder, will be deposited (Spitz, 1993).

If clothing does not intervene between the firearm's muzzle and the skin, all the gun smoke will enter the wound—unless the firearm is a revolver whose cylinder fits loosely against the barrel, in which case gun smoke may spew from the cylinder as well as the muzzle. Additionally, if the cylinder does not fit correctly against the barrel and the alignment is not correct, particles of bullet shavings may be found on or may have penetrated the skin, even in the case of a contact wound. Small bullet fragments around a wound are referred to as **fouling**.

In contact wounds to the head, the wound may be star shaped because of tears radiating from the sides of the wound (**Figure 10–6**). These tears are the result of the sudden release of firearm gases into a confined space. When a high-powered rifle is fired when in contact with the head, the gas generated is so great as to cause massive cranial destruction. It may be impossible to identify the deceased through facial recognition. A high-powered discharge under the chin or in the mouth will cause an overexpansion or bloating of the head and face. Damage to the head is so severe that finding the entrance wound may be impossible (Spitz, 1993). The muzzle blast of a firearm discharged in contact with a body creates a negative pressure at the barrel following discharge, which may cause blood, hair, tissue, and fabric to be forced back up into the barrel.

Close-Range Wounds

Wounds caused by shots fired from a gun close enough to leave gunpowder residue around the wound are classified as close-range wounds. The diameter and density of

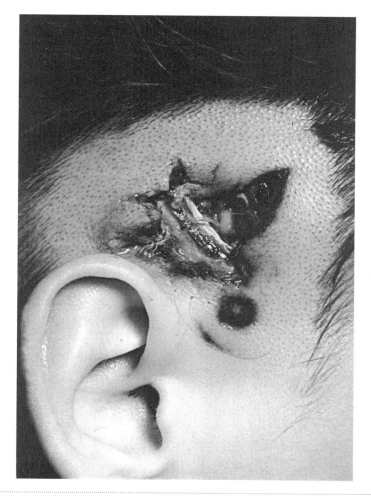

Figure 10–6 Contact wound to the head.

Photo courtesy of Steven Hanson, former Chief Investigator Bexar County MEO

the pattern of particles on the body assist in estimating the distance from which the shot was fired. These patterns differ with different guns and different ammunition. Residues from the firing of a handgun can occur when the gun is as far away as 18 inches; a rifle shot will leave residues when the rifle is as far away as 3 feet. At greater distances, the debris emitted from the barrel lacks the power to reach the body.

Determining the muzzle-to-target distance in close-range wounding requires testing the weapon originally used with the same type of ammunition originally used. Different ammunition will produce different results fired from the same weapon. Gunpowder residue can be visible when the shot fired was twice the distance from the body as the length of the barrel of the weapon. Generally, as the distance between the muzzle and the body increases, the pattern of residue on the body increases in size and the particle density decreases. In the firing of a handgun, little gunpowder and soot are deposited on the body when the distance exceeds 7 inches. Gunpowder residue is distributed circumferentially around a wound. When more residue is discovered on one side than the other, it is possible that the shot was fired at an angle (**Figure 10–7**). Powder residue will be more densely deposited on the side from which the shot was fired (Federal Bureau of Investigation Laboratory, 1970).

Distant Wounds

A wound caused by a shot fired at a distance that leaves no gun smoke residue is called a distant wound. The appearance of a wound caused by a shot fired at 10 feet is no different from that of a wound caused by a shot fired at 100 feet. Most handguns will leave no gunpowder residue at distances in excess of 2 feet. High-powered rifle wounds differ little in external appearance from those of any other projectile fired at a distance. The exit wound, however, may be large and ragged, much different from entrance and exit wounds made by a bullet fired from a handgun. The extent of external damage may justifiably lead investigators to conclude that the firearm in question was a high-powered rifle (shotguns wounds are discussed next).

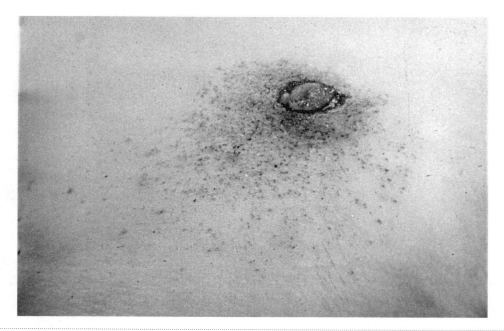

Figure 10–7 Angled powder residue.

Photo courtesy of Steven Hanson, former Chief Investigator Bexar County MEO

Direction of Fire

In determining the **direction of fire**, it is essential to properly identify the **entry wound** and the **exit wound**. The relationship between the entrance and exit wounds may reveal the direction from which the projectile was fired. Entrance wounds reveal a missing sphere of flesh carried into the wound by the projectile (**Figure 10–8**). Exit wounds have no missing flesh; if the skin around the wound were replaced, including all the jagged edges, there would be a complete covering of the exit hole. An entrance wound is often smaller than the caliber of the bullet that created the wound, whereas the exit wound is substantially larger. The skin at the point of entry is stretched by the penetrating bullet and returns to its original size after penetration. Any guess as to the caliber of a bullet based on the entrance wound diameter would be approximate and unreliable.

An entrance wound will have an **abrasion ring**, a circular or oval bruising of the tissue immediately around the bullet hole that results from the bullet scraping the skin as it penetrates (**Figure 10–9**). The abrasion will be circular and of uniform width if the bullet strikes the body perpendicularly, scraping all sides of the wound equally. If the bullet strikes the body at an angle, the hole itself will be round but the abrasions surrounding the wound will be oval because the length of the bullet has scraped along the skin as the tip of the bullet penetrates. The length of the abrasion depends on the angle at which the projectile struck the body.

Medical examiners and pathologists often are asked to position the assailant and the victim relative to the bullet pathway (or pathways). It is at this point that the information provided by the investigator becomes important to the medical examiner. Notes, measurements, and sketches are crucial in determining the resting place of the deceased. A horizontal bullet track through the chest of the victim may have been inflicted while the parties were standing, with the assailant pointing the gun directly at the victim's

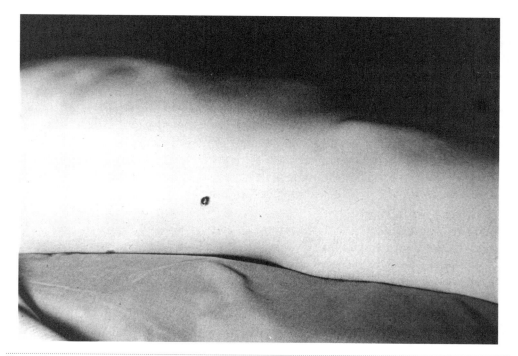

Figure 10–8 Entry wound.

Photo courtesy of Steven Hanson, former Chief Investigator Bexar County MEO

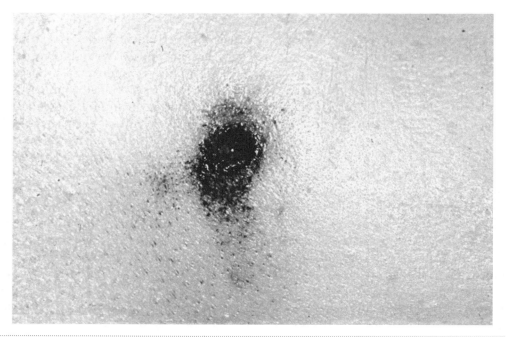

Figure 10–9 Marginal abrasions.

Photo courtesy of Steven Hanson, former Chief Investigator Bexar County MEO

chest parallel to the ground, or while the victim was lying face up on the ground, with the assailant pointing the weapon down at the victim's chest (Spitz, 1993).

Shotgun Wounds

Shotguns are used often in criminal homicides. Reconstruction of the distance of shotgun fire is similar to the process used for other firearms, although the diversity of shotgun ammunition and the use of pellets make the determination of firing distance more complex. The number of pellets in a shot shell depends on pellet size. The largest pellets are 00 Number 12 buckshot, and the smallest pellets are 270 Number 9 birdshot. The gauge of a shotgun equals the inside bore measurement. The smallest shotgun is a .410, and the largest is a 12-gauge. The bore of a shotgun is smooth but may taper at the end or have affixed to the barrel end a cylinder smaller than the bore diameter. This small cylinder is called a choke and is designed to keep the pellets from spreading too quickly. In conducting tests for determining firing distance, it is imperative that the same type and number of shot be used as was used in the criminal homicide.

Shotgun Contact Wounds

Most wounds inflicted with a shotgun in contact with the body will result in a wound diameter approximately the same as the diameter of the shotgun's bore. Because the pellets have no time to spread and thus remain in a mass, they enter the body as a single projectile, creating marginal abrasion around the perimeter of the wound, as in the case of other contact firearm wounds. Contact wounds to the head cause remarkable damage, and skull fragmentation and tissue reorganization typically render the face unrecognizable. Head, brain, and bone tissue may be spread over a wide area. It is necessary for all dispersed bone and tissue to be recovered, for it will be used in the facial reconstruction and will allow a more precise determination of the pellets' entryway. If the contact wound is to somewhere other than the head, the muzzle flame may be large enough and intense enough to ignite clothing that is not fire retardant.

Close-Range Shotgun Wounds

A shotgun discharged at a distance of less than 5 feet will allow the pellets to remain in a single mass until they reach the body. As in contact wounds, the entry hole will be approximately the same size as the bore diameter. The margins of the wound will evince abrasions, but the pattern will be less concentric and more scalloped in appearance as a result of the pellets' tendency to separate. Because of the scalloping, the pattern is called a cookie-cutter pattern. At a firing distance beyond 6 feet, the diameter of the wound increases, because the pellets continue to spread out. At a firing distance of less than 6 feet, most shotguns will deposit powder and soot on the clothing or skin.

Distant Shotgun Wounds

The wound pattern that occurs when a shotgun is fired at distances greater than 6 feet depends on the length of the barrel, size of shot, powder load, gauge of the shotgun, and choke characteristics. With small shot, pellets entering the skin produce round wounds. With large shot, such as 00 buckshot or Number 4, the wounds cannot be distinguished by the naked eye from bullet wounds. Along with the small penetrating holes caused by the pellets, there may be a larger, nonpenetrating abrasion caused by the shotgun wad. This wad is a component of all shotgun shells containing pellets and is often found in the wound or elsewhere at the scene. Investigators can derive a significant amount of information from the wadding. The diameter of the wad corresponds to the gauge of the shotgun and will often disclose manufacturing characteristics that help identify the manufacturer of the shot shell (see **Figure 10–10**).

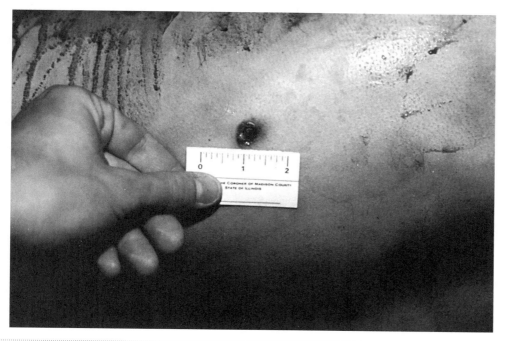

Figure 10–10 Shotgun wound pictures.

© Charles Stewart & Associates

■ Sharp-Force Deaths

Homicides

Homicides from stabbings are second in number only to firearm deaths. In dealing with sharp-force homicides, investigators must distinguish between two types of wounds:

- Cuts occur when a sharp-edged object is drawn over the skin with sufficient pressure to separate it; cut wounds are longer than they are deep.
- Stabs, on the other hand, are deeper than they are long, for they involve the penetration of a pointed instrument into the depth of the body.

Sharp-force homicides generally do not produce bruising in the vicinity of the stab wound. If there is bruising present, it is most probably the product of the fist holding the weapon coming into contact with the body (**Figure 10–11**). Bruising of the edges of a stab wound suggests that the entire blade penetrated the body. If a suspect's knife is recovered, the pathologist may match the abrasion around the stab wound with the handle of the suspect weapon.

In most homicidal throat slashings, the assailant is behind the victim. With the assailant in this position, a slash of the neck runs from left to right if the assailant was right-handed and in the opposite direction if he or she was left-handed. Homicidal cuts of the throat are often single and deep (**Figure 10–12**).

The depth of a stab wound does not depend on the length of the blade alone (**Figure 10–13**). Actually, the depth of a knife wound frequently exceeds the length of the blade that caused it. The body surface dents as the result of the thrust of the fist holding the knife. The amount of pressure needed to inflict a stab wound is minimal; less than 2 pounds of pressure is required to penetrate the skin. Once the tip of the blade has pen-

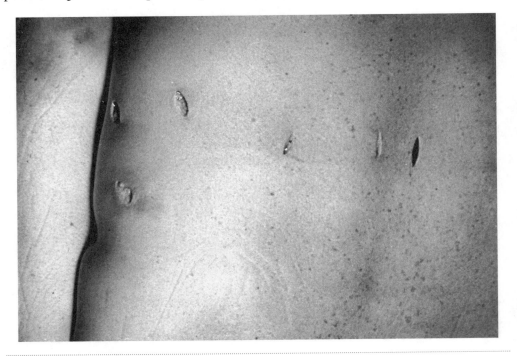

Figure 10–11 Bruising around a stab wound.

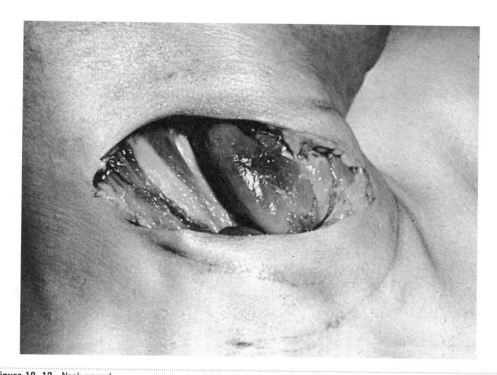

Figure 10–12 Neck wound.

Photo courtesy of Steven Hanson, former Chief Investigator Bexar County MEO

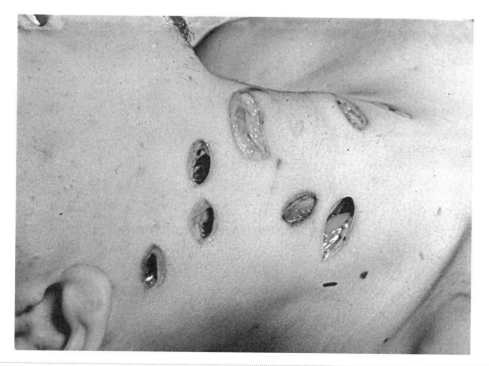

Figure 10–13 Stab wounds to the neck.

Photo courtesy of Steven Hanson, former Chief Investigator Bexar County MEO

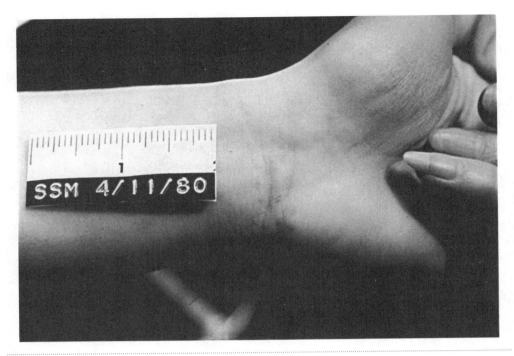

Figure 10–14   Hesitation marks.

Photo courtesy of Steven Hanson, former Chief Investigator Bexar County MEO

etrated the skin, the amount of force needed to penetrate inner organs is minimal. The same or a similar force is required to make a shallow wound as to make a deep wound (Spitz, 1993).

Self-Inflicted Stab Wounds

Suicidal stabbings are often accompanied by cuts in other areas, most often the wrist. Suicidal cuts will be parallel and of variable depth, with sharp-angle edges indicative of sawing. Frequently, numerous superficial, parallel cuts resembling scratches are noted, indicating repeated trials before the buildup of sufficient courage for the final deep gash that severs major blood vessels. Such superficial cuts and evidence of sawing are referred to as **hesitation wounds** or **hesitation marks** (**Figure 10–14**). Hesitation cuts on the wrists are usually horizontal, with right-handed persons cutting the left wrist and left-handed persons cutting the right wrist (Spitz, 1993).

■ Summary

In our society we see the taking of a human life as the most grievous of offenses. We spend more human resources and money on death investigations than on any other, and it is the easiest of crime scenes to contaminate. Everything we know about processing a crime scene and forensic protocols comes into play in the death investigation. It would be presumed that it is these investigations in which we would apply our best efforts. It may seem highly unlikely that well-trained investigators and forensic staff would not bring their best game, but habits have a way of catching up with us. We hear of forensic technicians handling evidence without wearing gloves. We hear of serologists fabricating reports. As in all human endeavors we will become the victims of our habits. If we treat all homicide investigations as the crime of the century, when the crime of the century does come along, our habits will not betray us.

In investigating assaults, it is best to view them as a homicide that went bad. The next chapter will introduce us to the many different types of assault that can occur, including sexual assault. As you will discover in the next chapter the most important evidence in an assault is the victim.

■ Key Terms

abrasion ring: A circular or oval bruising of the tissue immediately around the bullet hole that results from the bullet scraping the skin as it penetrates

algor mortis: Postmortem drop in body temperature

autoerotic asphyxiation: Type of masturbation during which sexual excitement is produced by being mechanically or chemically asphyxiated to or beyond the point at which consciousness or perception is altered by cerebral hypoxia (lack of oxygen)

autopsy: Examination of a deceased body that can be ordered when there is suspicion of foul play

burial indicators: Indications of the presence of buried remains; these include disturbed vegetation, soil compaction, new vegetation, and soil disturbance

cadaveric spasms: A forceful contraction or seizure that is converted almost immediately into rigor, dispensing with the stage of muscle flaccidity; occurs in deaths accompanied by great excitement or tension

causation: The production of an effect

corneal clouding: A thickening of the thin film seen on the corneal surface within minutes after death; clouding occurs 2 to 3 hours after death

corpus delicti: The material evidence in a criminal homicide case that shows that a crime has been committed; in Latin it means "body of the crime"

direction of fire: Direction from which the projectile was fired; the relationship between the entrance and exit wounds may reveal this information

entry wound: The wound that results when a projectile enters a body; such wounds reveal a missing sphere of flesh carried into the wound by the projectile

exit wound: The wound that results from a projectile exiting a body; such wounds have no missing flesh, and if the skin around the wound were replaced, including all the jagged edges, there would be a complete covering of the exit hole

forensic entomology: The analysis of insects and other invertebrates that sequentially colonize a decomposing body and of the rates at which various stages of their offspring develop

fouling: Small bullet fragments around a gunshot wound

gloving: The shedding of the skin of the hands, including the fingernails

hesitation wounds (hesitation marks): Superficial, parallel cuts from repeated trials made before the final deep gash that causes death

homicide: The taking of a human life by another human

lividity: A purplish-blue discoloration on the lowest points of a body that are not in contact with a hard surface

livor mortis: The gravitational movement of blood to the lowest point after deaths occurring other than as a result of drowning

murder: Homicide with malice aforethought

proximate cause: A cause that directly produces an event and without which the event would not have occurred; a cause that is legally sufficient to result in liability

putrefaction: The decomposition of the body

rigor mortis: Stiffness of the muscles after death, which eventually freezes the joints

staged: Crime scene in which the body or items were moved from the way they were when the crime occurred

stocking: The shedding of the skin around the feet and legs

Virchow method: Rudolf Virchow developed an autopsy method that included the removal and examination of each organ.

window of death: A window of time in which the death must have occurred, initially spanning the period between the last time a witness interviewed by the police saw or heard the victim and the time the body was found; investigators then reduce the time frame whenever and however possible

■ Review Questions

1. What, if anything, is the difference between homicide and murder?
2. What is the corpus delicti of criminal homicide?
3. How do proximate cause and causation come into play in criminal homicide investigations?
4. List two reasons for staging a crime scene.
5. What kind of forensic inconsistencies would suggest that a crime scene has been staged?
6. What is the presumed attraction of autoerotic hypoxia?
7. List the myths associated with autoerotic asphyxiation.
8. List four burial indicators.
9. Of what assistance is a forensic anthropologist in the recovery of human remains?
10. What effect do scavengers have on human remains?
11. When is an autopsy performed?
12. What does "Hic locus est ubi mors gaudet succurrere vitae" mean?
13. What might an anthropologist deduce from a human skull?
14. How can time of death be ascertained, and what is a window of death?
15. What type of physicochemical changes does a body undergo after death? What are livor mortis, rigor mortis, and algor mortis?
16. Explain how gloving results from putrefaction.
17. What service might a forensic entomologist provide to a criminal investigator?
18. What is insect pupation, and what role can it play in criminal homicide investigations?
19. What are the differences between contact wounds, close-range wounds, and distant wounds?
20. What is firearm smudging, tattooing, or stippling?
21. What are the characteristics of an entry wound, and how do they differ from the characteristics of an exit wound?

22. What is an abrasion ring?

23. How might stomach contents of the deceased be of use to the investigator?

24. What was Dr. Lee Goff's specialty and how did it assist the Honolulu Police Department?

■ Bibliography

Beyer, M., Enos, W., & Strajie, M. (1980). Drug identification through analysis of maggots. *Journal of Forensic Science* 25, 411–412.

Bray, M. (1985). The eye as a chemical indicator of environmental temperature at the time of death. *Journal of Forensic Science* 29, 389–395.

Coe, J., & Curran, J. (1980). Definition and time of death. In W.J. Curran, A.L. McGarry, & C.S. Petty (Eds.), *Modern legal medicine, psychiatry, and forensic science.* Philadelphia: F.A. Davis.

Dietz, P.E. (1989). Televised-inspired autoerotic asphyxiation. *Journal of Forensic Science* 34(3), 58.

Douglas, J., & Munn, C. (1992, February). *Violent crime scene analysis: Modus operandi and staging. FBI Law Enforcement Bulletin.*

Federal Bureau of Investigation Laboratory (1970, September). *Gunpowder and shot pattern tests. FBI Law Enforcement Bulletin.*

Goff, M.L. (2003). "Handling Human Remains Workshop." Chaminade University of Honolulu.

Hall, D. (1948). *The blowflies of North America.* Baltimore: Monumental Printing.

Knight, B. (1988). The evolution of methods for estimating the time of death from body temperature. *Forensic Science International* 36, 47–53.

Lord, W., & Burger, J. (1983). Collection and preservation of forensically important entomological materials. *Journal of Forensic Science* 28, 936–941.

Perper, J. (1993). Time of death and changes after death: Anatomical considerations. In W.U. Spitz et al. (Ed.), *Medicolegal investigation of death* (3rd ed.). Springfield, IL: Charles C. Thomas.

Simson, L. (1976). Thyrotoxicosis: Postmortem diagnosis in an unexpected death. *Journal of Forensic Science* 21, 831–832.

Smith, K. (1986). *A manual of forensic entomology.* London: British Museum.

Spitz, W.U. (1993). Drowning. In W.U. Spitz et al. (Ed.), *Medicolegal investigation of death* (3rd ed.). Springfield, IL: Charles C. Thomas.

Turvey, B.E. (1995). *An objective overview of autoerotic fatalities.* Available from Knowledge Solutions, 1271 Washington Avenue, #274, San Leandro, CA 94577-3646 or at http://www.corpus-delicti.com/auto.html.

Uniform Crime Reports. 1975–2005. Washington, DC: Federal Bureau of Investigation.

CHAPTER
11

Assault

▸ ▸ STUDENT LEARNING OUTCOMES

Upon completion of this chapter students will demonstrate an understanding of:

- What constitutes an assault
- The assault investigative protocol
- Police responses to domestic violence
- Police responses to child abuse
- Investigating domestic violence and child abuse
- The legal justifications for the use of force

The crime scene processing and the criminal investigation of an assault are very similar to those for a homicide. The major difference is that assaults do not result in death, even though that may have been the intent of the assailant. There are over a million reported assaults committed each year (Crime in the United States, 1990, 1991). Over 50% of reported aggravated assaults result in arrests. National victim surveys indicate that the actual number of assaults committed annually far exceeds the number reported to the police. As a practical matter, investigating assaults as an attempted murder is an excellent strategy.

There are, however, some differences in the way jurisdictions define assault. First, there is general agreement as to what constitutes an **aggravated assault**. All jurisdictions treat a physical attack that results in serious bodily injury and that is perpetrated in the course of another felony or involves the use of a deadly weapon as an aggravated assault. The difficulty arises in defining a **simple assault**. Historically, attacks on another have been called **battery**, and the threat to commit an attack upon another was called an assault. News commentators often report that the assailant committed **assault and battery**. Many jurisdictions have dropped the term battery from their penal codes and have replaced it with simple assault. Those jurisdictions define a simple assault as a threat to cause bodily injury, an offensive contact or touch, or an attack that does not cause serious bodily injury.

Assault arrests are generally made by patrol officers. These officers happen upon assaults in progress or respond to dispatches for assaults in progress. Their arrival and the circumstances often result in an arrest and extemporaneous investigation based on their observation of the assailant and victim, with little need for a subsequent investigation.

TABLE 11-1   Wife Battering Profile

Male	Female
Battering role model	Dysfunctional family
Insecure	Lacks self-esteem
Possessive	Confuses possessiveness with love
Impulse control problem	Sees anger as an admirable male characteristic (machismo)
Hits out of frustration and feelings of inadequacy	Believes behavior prompted correction
Apologizes	Wants to believe apology
Hitting escalates	Believes she can prevent hitting
Apologizes	Frightened not to accept apology

Most agencies do not expend tremendous time or resources on simple assaults unless they are a product of domestic violence (**TABLE** 11-1). In the vast majority of cases, victims of assault know their assailant and often refuse to file a complaint against the attacker.

One of the most frustrating aspects of law enforcement is the reluctance of an assaulted spouse to file a formal complaint against his or her assailant. The call to police is made out of fear and panic. The service requested is protection and removal of the offending spouse. These **domestic assaults** often occur on weekends in the early hours of the morning. Once the offender has been removed from the home, the remaining spouse (usually the wife) has time to reflect on the consequences of formal prosecution. Recognizing that her husband may lose his job if he does not report for work on Monday or if the employer discovers that he has been charged with a criminal offense, the assaulted woman, who may have only limited financial resources, forgoes signing the necessary complaint. State legislatures have addressed this anomaly by not requiring spousal complaints in domestic violence situations and requiring that an arrest be made if there is any evidence of violence. The bulk of reported assaults are domestic in nature and do not require the services of an investigator or require much in the way of an investigation (also see Domestic Violence section on page 265).

■ Aggravated Assault

The investigator in aggravated assault cases may confront a traditional crime that is accompanied by an assault (**TABLE** 11-2). Rapes, drug deals gone awry, extortion, robbery, and burglary frequently include an assault.

TABLE 11-2   Assaultive Crime Typology (From Least to Most Assaultive)

- *Terroristic threat:* Threat of violence with ability to carry out the threat
- *Reckless endangerment*: Recklessly engaging in conduct that poses imminent danger of serious bodily injury
- *Assault:* Offensive contact or threat
- *Aggravated assault:* Contact and serious bodily injury or use of a deadly weapon
- *Homicide:* Intentionally, knowingly, or recklessly causing the death of another

OFFICER'S NOTEBOOK

Handling Aggravated Assault

In any investigation in which an aggravated assault is involved, the following steps should be taken in the indicated order.

1. **Triage** of the victim
2. Render first aid and summon medical assistance
3. Preserve the crime scene
4. Question the victim and witnesses
5. Process the crime scene

Triage of the Victim

Injuries are often deceptive. Although there may be no external evidence of bleeding, blunt weapon attacks may cause internal damage. It is not the role of the investigator to make a medical determination, but he or she should inquire into the type of injuries received and the method by which they were received. If blunt trauma has occurred, especially to the head, medical services should be sought. Keep in mind that an aggravated assault may easily be the product of a friendly dispute that escalated, especially if the dispute was accompanied by alcohol or drug use. The victim may not have the mental alacrity to assess the severity of the injuries suffered and may therefore refuse medical help.

Rendering First Aid and Summoning Medical Assistance

The first obstacle may be to convince the victim that medical assistance is necessary. Hollywood portrayals to the contrary, the first responsibility of every officer arriving at a scene where injury has occurred is to provide first aid, even if the perpetrator is within arm's reach. This responsibility extends not only to victims injured at the hands of assailants but also to suspects and offenders injured by police. It may seem surprising, but a police officer who has just shot an assailant attempting to take the life of another police officer has an immediate responsibility, after disarming the assailant, to provide assistance for the injuries just inflicted (see the Case in Point).

Preserving the Crime Scene

All too often, by the time an investigator arrives at the scene of an aggravated assault it has been rearranged and trampled upon by a variety of people. One major obstacle to this type of investigation is the difficulty of assessing what damage was caused during the assault by the parties and what damage was caused by friends, police, and medical personnel. It is the first responders' responsibility to ensure that this type of damage is kept to a minimum and to record any changes to the scene occuring prior to and during their tenure at the scene. The way to preserve this type of scene is to keep all admitted and possible witnesses available and sequestered.

Questioning the Victim and Witnesses

Assaults occurring in taverns and clubs are notorious for going unseen. The major evidence in this type of investigation generally will come from the victim and the witnesses. It is important to determine if the victim was actually a victim of an assault or a perpetrator who did not fare well in his or her assaultive attempt. In virtually every assault

CASE IN POINT

Medical Assistance Imperative

In 1996 the author provided expert testimony in a federal civil rights suit filed against a local Texas police officer and agency. A Texas Department of Public Safety officer was involved in an altercation with a man who was intoxicated and much bigger and stronger than the officer. The suspect attempted to subdue the officer with blows from a flashlight to his head. During the struggle, the suspect attempted to withdraw the officer's weapon. Repeated blows to the officer's head did not succeed in dislodging his grip. Wresting the weapon from the suspect, the officer fired. His call for assistance at the onset of the scuffle was answered, and local officers arrived on the scene.

The Texas Department of Public Safety officer was in shock and suffering from head injuries and was unable to render assistance to the offender. The local officers who arrived on the scene assessed the condition of the offender and decided to await the arrival of the emergency medical staff without offering any assistance to the offender, who bled to death before he was treated. Medical testimony established that basic first aid would have kept the offender alive until the emergency medical service arrived. The family of the deceased filed a federal civil rights suit against the local officers and their agency for failure to provide medical assistance to the deceased. The case is instructive, for not only is there a moral imperative to provide medical assistance to all who are injured, but there also may be legal repercussions for failing to do so.

that is not a domestic violence offense, the offender will raise the idea of self-defense at trial or during pretrial motions. The investigator should keep in mind that one object of the investigation is to anticipate this defense and defuse it by obtaining sufficient information and evidence to establish unequivocally who was the assaulter and who was the victim.

The victim's rendition of facts will be different from the suspect's and should be recorded if possible. Information about what preceded the assault must be gathered. This kind of information will help uncover the motive for the assault and also establish that an assault in fact occurred. Simply because two people were fighting and one was injured does not mean that an assault occurred. Some states allow a **mutual combat** defense. If two parties agreed to step into the parking lot for the purpose of involving themselves in an altercation, there may or may not have been an assault. In states with mutual combat statutes, an assault may have occurred if the following criteria were met:

- The terms of the agreement were exceeded (e.g., rather than engaging in an agreed fistfight, one of the parties hits the other over the head with a beer bottle).
- One party attempted to withdraw from the combat and the other did not allow withdrawal (the shield of self-defense could be raised by the party who attempted to withdraw).
- One party attempted to terminate the combat and the other did not allow termination.

By interviewing the witnesses and gathering information about what preceded the assault, the investigator will flesh out his or her understanding of what took place and perhaps why it took place. Interviewing witnesses will assist in corroborating what the investigator has learned from the victim, the offender, or the crime scene. In those instances where the victim is unable to be interviewed, the only reliable information will be what the crime scene reveals and what the witnesses provide. If the investigator is lucky, the witnesses will help ascertain motive and assist in defusing any self-defense shield thrown up at a later date. The witnesses may also help make sense of a trampled crime scene and describe any weapons used.

Processing the Crime Scene

The scene itself should be handled as if it were the scene of a homicide—which it may end up being if the injuries are so severe as to cause death. The investigator should conduct a search focused on weapons, blood evidence, fingerprints, and trace evidence, and he or she should evaluate the scene based on the information received from the witnesses, victim, and offender.

If possible, after processing the scene, the investigator should do a walk-through with the victim and the suspect, who can each provide a narrative of the events prior to, during, and after the assault from his or her unique perspective. It is important to remember that the victim's injuries and the clothing are evidence, and the investigator has the responsibility to obtain and process the clothing for forensic examination and to record all injuries photographically.

If the assault is committed with a firearm, the defendant will probably allege that the weapon fired accidentally or during a struggle. Powder stippling, gun smoke residue, and barrel blowback will all assist in corroborating or negating the defendant's accidental firing claim. Additionally, the angle of entry may help in establishing the relative positions of the participants at the time of the shooting. Consequently, the **medical examination** must contain a forensic component out of the ordinary for the emergency room. The investigator may have to accompany the unconscious shooting victim to the hospital to retrieve clothing and to ensure that a forensic examination is made of the victim and the victim's injuries.

Photographs of the victim's injuries should be taken as soon as possible after their infliction. Injuries will heal, and the hospital may not make a **photographic record** of the injuries. A verbal description of injuries contained in the medical records is not as effective with a jury as are photographs (preferably color photographs). The best advice that an investigator can receive about investigating aggravated assaults is to view an aggravated assault as a murder that failed.

Elements of Proof

In prosecuting an aggravated assault, the state must prove that (1) the defendant was the aggressor, (2) the victim was seriously injured and/or (3) a deadly weapon was used, and (4) no justifications exist excusing the assault.

■ Domestic Violence

Officers responding to domestic abuse calls need to have a full understanding of the complex social, economic, and psychological issues that surround acts of domestic violence. That understanding can only be obtained as the result of specific training pertaining to such issues as the following:

- The cycle of domestic violence
- Investigating domestic violence
- Providing resources for the domestically abused

Types of Abuse

Domestic violence is a pattern of coercive control founded on and supported by violence or the threat of violence. The abuse may take the form of physical violence, sexual violence, emotional abuse, psychological abuse, or some combination of these elements.

Emotional abuse takes the form of a systematic degrading of the victim's self-worth. This may be accomplished by calling the victim names, making derogatory or demeaning comments, forcing the victim to perform degrading or humiliating acts, threatening to kill the victim or the victim's family, controlling access to money, and acting in other ways that imply that the victim is crazy. Psychological battering involves all of the features of emotional abuse, but also consists of at least one violent episode or attack on the victim to maintain the impending threat of additional assaults. Destruction of property is violence directed at the victim even though no physical contact is made between the batterer and the victim. This includes destroying personal belongings, family heirlooms, or even the family pet.

The Cycle of Violence

Police generally become involved in a domestic abuse situation once it has reached a flash point. However, in most domestic abuse cases, physical abuse occurs during one of the three phases that make up the cycle of violence (Walker, 1979):

1. Tension building
2. Battering
3. Honeymoon

By becoming familiar with the features of each phase in this cycle, responding officers can help victims understand that the cycle of abuse is likely to continue if nothing is done to address the underlying causes.

Stage 1: Tension Building

During the first—and usually the longest—stage, tension escalates between the couple. Excessive drinking, illness, jealousy, and other factors may lead to name calling, hostility, and friction. Unless some type of professional intervention occurs at this point, the second phase of the cycle becomes virtually inevitable.

Many women recognize these signs of impending violence and become more nurturing or compliant or just stay out of the way. Some women will accept their partner's building anger as legitimately directed at them. Such a woman may come to believe that if she does her job well, he will remain calm. If she fails, the resulting violence is her fault.

Stage 2: Battering

Many batterers do not want to hurt their partners, only to control them. However, this is the stage where the victim, the batterer, or responding officers may be assaulted or killed. Unless the battering is interrupted, the violence during this phase will escalate beyond the level of violence used in prior abusive situations. The batterer intends to emphasize control through violence: If that control was not sufficiently created during the last battering session, then in the mind of the batterer it was because not enough violence was used. Serious injury or death may occur because batterers may reach the point in their evolution at which they cannot or will not stop. After a battering episode, many victims consider themselves lucky that the abuse was not worse, no matter how severe their injuries. They often deny the seriousness of their injuries and refuse to seek medical attention.

Law enforcement officers who respond immediately after a violent episode may find an abusive perpetrator who appears extremely calm and rational. His calm demeanor is deceptive; he has just released his anger and vented his tensions at his victim. The batterer may point to the victim, who may be highly agitated or hysterical because of the abuse, and attempt to blame her for the violence. The victim may, in fact, respond aggressively against officers who attempt to intervene. Officers should be aware that this reaction might be due to the victim's fear that more severe retaliation awaits her if officers arrest the batterer. The victim also may feel desperate about the impending loss of financial support or even emotional support she receives from the abuser. Although officers should not make any false promises, they should reassure the victim that the mechanisms are in place for the criminal justice system to help. Officers have a responsibility to provide a complete, professional investigation so that the system will work. A haphazard investigation or a lack of concern by responding officers could result in a violent abuser's being released from jail to retaliate against a vulnerable victim.

Stage 3: Honeymoon

The last stage of the cycle is a period of calm, loving, contrite behavior on the part of the batterer. The victim wants to believe that her partner really can change. She feels responsible, at least in part, for causing the incident, and she feels responsible for her partner's well-being. It is at this stage that many victims request that complaints against batterers be dropped.

Handling the Cycle of Violence

The cyclic nature of domestic violence has prompted most states to pass laws requiring the following:

- In cases of obvious physical violence, police must affect an arrest.
- An inquiry must be made as to the availability of firearms on the premises.
- If firearms are on the premises, they must be taken into police custody.
- The victim must be provided written materials describing available support services.
- The victim must be told that he or she can be removed to a safe house.
- A complete investigation of the abusive circumstances must be made.
- A records check of the assailant must be performed; outstanding warrants must be executed.
- Interviews of neighbors, friends, coworkers, and relatives must be conducted.
- A signed medical records release and an examination of medical records to document prior incidents of suspected abuse are required.

It is the intent of legislatures and police agencies that the victim be protected and that the suspect be prosecuted. If that means the case must go forward with a reluctant victim, it is to the investigation and documentation that the prosecution must turn for a conviction. The goal of officers responding to domestic violence should be to develop a case that can be prosecuted even if the victim becomes resistant to testify.

Although most domestic relationships involving violence include some type of cycle, not all violent relationships go through each phase as described previously. However, most domestic abuse cases follow a pattern corresponding, in some way or another, to the cycle of violence.

OFFICER'S NOTEBOOK

Tips for Interviewing Victims of Domestic Violence

- The introduction should be brief, making it clear who you are and why you are investigating.
- Once consent to the interview has been granted, spend some time being human and getting to know the victim.
- Once the victim is at ease, lay out clearly the parameters of the interview. It will help the victim focus his or her thoughts, and serve as a tool for keeping the victim on track.
- Ask permission to take notes or record the interview. There are pluses and minuses to each method, but one way or another the information received must be documented.
- Try to focus the questioning in an organized fashion. Start with the first time the victim knew there were problems in the relationship and move forward from there. Get as much detailed information as possible. When this incident happened, was there anyone else present? Did he or she call the police?
- Tie down the date of prior incidents whenever possible. No one will remember exact dates, but ask what time of year it was. Was it winter or summer? Was it before the Christmas incident she mentioned, or after? Approximate dates can be critically important in locating documents and corroborating information with other witnesses.
- Always ask for the names and contact information for other people who may have information— friends of the victim, roommates, coworkers, social service agencies he or she dealt with, where he or she went to school. Each interview will likely yield four or five other potential witnesses, each of whom has a piece of the picture.
- Ask for permission to recontact the victim if questions come up later, and ask him or her to contact investigators if anything else comes to mind. Often the process of remembering will cause the victim to recall other details or incidents.

Source: Adapted from Tanya Brannan, Purple Berets, "Violence Against Women," http://www.purpleberets.org/violence_investigatingdv.html.

■ Investigating Child Abuse

Investigation of potential incidents of child abuse is a critical and sensitive matter. Protection of children and fairness to parents are complementary, not mutually exclusive, ends. Balancing these interests is a very difficult and challenging law enforcement responsibility. Physical and sexual abuse of children may be camouflaged as accidental injuries. Investigators frequently must determine whether a child's accident or illness was caused by a parent or caretaker. However, it is often difficult even for medical personnel to discriminate between injuries and illnesses that are accidental and those that are intentional. The information in this part of the chapter can help law enforcement personnel to determine if it is likely that abuse has occurred.

Identifying Child Abuse

Investigators must determine whether the explanation for an injury is believable. Police should begin their investigation by asking the caretaker for an explanation of the child's bruises or injuries. This is best done by asking the question, "How did the accident happen?"

All bruises must be investigated. If bruises are found on two or more planes of a child's body, investigators should be even more suspicious (e.g., a child has bruises on his buttocks and stomach). The caretaker's explanation is that the child fell backward in the living room of the family home. This might explain the bruises on the buttocks, but not the stomach bruises. If a discrepancy exists between the reported cause of an injury and the injuries seen, law enforcement personnel should investigate further.

Investigators should also keep in mind the following points:

1. All other children in the home should be examined for possible signs of child abuse.

2. Victims of physical abuse often have been intimidated and will usually support the abuser's version of how their injuries occurred to avoid further injury. They also feel that the abuse was just punishment because they were bad.

3. A physical examination of the child in suspected cases of maltreatment must be done and the data recorded precisely.

4. Laboratory data should be obtained to support or refute the evidence of abuse.

5. If the reported history of an injury or injuries changes during the course of an investigation, or if there is conflict between two adult caretakers as to the cause of injury, the likelihood of child maltreatment increases.

6. The demeanor of the child's parents or caretakers is sometimes revealing. For example, the mother's assessment of her pregnancy, labor, and delivery will often provide insight into her attitude about her child as well as give an indication of whether there is something about the child that is influencing her behavior.

7. Investigators should ask questions in an unobtrusive manner; for example:
   - Was this a planned pregnancy?
   - Did you want the baby?
   - Do you like the baby?
   - How did the accident happen?
   - What were you doing just before the accident?
   - Who was at home at the time of the accident?
   - What do you feed the baby? How often? Who feeds the baby?

8. Information about a child's birth and his or her neonatal and medical history are critical elements in investigations. Hospital records can confirm or eliminate the existence of birth injuries.

9. Any child may be abused, and child abuse occurs in all levels of society. However, there are some factors that increase a child's risk of abuse. These include the following:
   - Premature birth or low birth weight
   - Being identified as "unusual" or perceived as "different" in terms of physical appearance or temperament
   - Having a variety of diseases or congenital abnormalities
   - Being physically, emotionally, or developmentally disabled (e.g., mentally retarded or learning disabled)
   - Having a high level of motor activity, being fussy or irritable, or exhibiting behavior that is different from the parents' expectations
   - Living in poverty or with families who are unemployed
   - Living in environments with substance abuse, high crime, and familial or community violence

A careful examination of the circumstances and types of injuries and an assessment of the child and family should be carried out.

Types of Injuries

Bruises

Bruises are due to the leakage of blood into skin tissue and are produced by tissue damage from a direct blow or a crushing injury. Bruising is the earliest and most visible sign of child abuse. Early identification of bruises resulting from child abuse can allow for intervention and prevent further abuse.

Bruises seen in infants, especially on the face and buttocks, are suspicious and should be considered nonaccidental until proven otherwise. Injuries to children's upper arms (caused by efforts to defend themselves), the trunk, the front of their thighs, the sides of their faces, their ears and neck, genitalia, stomach, and buttocks are also more likely to be associated with nonaccidental injuries. Injuries to their shins, hips, lower arms, forehead, hands, or the bony prominences (the spine, knees, nose, chin, or elbows) are more likely to signify accidental injury.

It is important to determine the ages of bruises to see if their ages are consistent with the caretaker's explanation of the times of injury. Age dating of bruises can often be determined by looking at the color of the bruise.

Bruises will sometimes have a specific configuration. This may enable law enforcement officers to determine whether bruises are accidental or nonaccidental. One of the easiest ways to identify the weapon used to inflict bruises is to ask the caretaker, "How were you punished as a child?"

The pattern of a skin lesion may suggest the type of instrument used. Bruise or wound configurations from objects can be divided into two main categories: those from fixed objects, which can only strike one of the body's planes at a time, and those from wraparound objects, which follow the contours of the body and strike more than one of the body's planes. Hands can make either kind of bruise, depending on the size of the offender's hands and the size of the child. Examples of fixed and wraparound objects include the following:

- Fixed objects: Coat hangers, handles, and paddles
- Wraparound objects: Belts, closed-end (looped) cords, open-end cords (closed-end cords leave a bruise in parallel lines; open-end cords leave a bruise in a single line)

Injuries inflicted by human hands, feet, or teeth or those inflicted by belts, ropes, electrical cords, knives, switches, gags, or other objects will often leave telltale marks (e.g., gags may leave down-turned lesions at the corners of the mouth). These marks may also help in the investigative process. For example, the size of bite marks may help to determine the biter's approximate age; their shape may help identify whose teeth made the marks.

In some cases, however, bruises are acquired innocently, through play and accidental falls, or when a child has a defect in his or her clotting mechanism. The medical diagnosis of clotting disorders requires blood tests and interpretation of those tests by qualified physicians. Investigators must never jump to conclusions and must make a complete investigation of all aspects of suspected child abuse. However, their first duty is to secure the safety of the child quickly.

Eye Injuries

External eye injuries are so common in children that they are seldom clear-cut evidence of abuse. Some types of eye injuries, however, may raise a red flag for the knowledgeable investigator.

- Two black eyes seldom occur together accidentally.
- The "raccoon eyes" associated with accidental and nonaccidental fractures at the base of the skull may look similar to each other, but raccoon eyes from nonaccidental trauma usually are associated with more swelling and skin injury. The history helps distinguish between them.
- Hyphema, the traumatic entry of blood into the front chamber of the eye, may be the result of a nonaccidental injury caused by striking the eye with a hard object, such as a belt buckle. The child will complain of pain in the eye and have visual problems.
- Retinal hemorrhages are the hallmark of shaken baby syndrome and are only rarely associated with some other mechanism of injury.
- Nonaccidental trauma must always be considered in a child under 3 years of age who has retinal hemorrhages or any traumatic disruption of the structures of the globe of the eye (e.g., the lens or retina) or the skin around the eye.

■ Summary

Investigating allegations of child abuse is a challenge, both in recognizing the abusive characteristics of the injuries children receive and in recognizing that kids are active, prone to accidents, and injure easily. Equally as challenging is the provincial notion that only poor people abuse their children. Child abuse is pervasive and knows no racial, gender, or socioeconomic boundaries.

Child abuse is difficult to investigate because children are reluctant to communicate the abuse to anyone. Though they are being abused by a parent, that does not mean that they do not love that parent. Sadly, abusive parents may also love the child they abuse but not be able to manage their anger and violent response to the often loud and disconcerting behavior of children. Whatever happens from an investigative point of view, it must be remembered that psychological intervention is necessary for the child and perhaps the parent. The first responsibility is to remove children from abusive environments, followed as closely as possible by providing services that will reduce the impact of the child's abusive history.

■ Legal Justifications for the Use of Force

It should not be surprising that assault is one of the most common offenses committed. The adventure movies popular today typically have an antihero rather than a hero—a character with attitude.

One can purchase a beer with attitude, a car with attitude, or clothes with attitude; date a man or woman with attitude; or be a spectator at a sporting event whose participants exhibit attitude. **Attitude** may best be defined as an aspect of an individual's personality that immediately puts all others on notice that this individual "takes nothing from nobody at no time." Attitude has become so prevalent in our society that a woman without it is perceived as unliberated and a man without it is viewed as less than masculine. If two motorists with attitude arrive at an uncontrolled intersection, what must be the outcome? If two persons with attitude enter a dispute, what must be the outcome? It is no accident that the streets of our cities seem to be under siege, given the prevalence of street attitude (never relinquish the right of way), road rage (attitude with a car and gun), and leisure-time assaults (attitude hierarchies). Attitude has replaced courtesy, compassion, and consideration. It is a fuel that, lit with a spark, can flare up into an assault.

Because of the common notion that the United States is crime-ridden, legislators in some states have enacted **concealed handgun laws** and have broadened the circumstances in which a person may use force, including **deadly force**, in defense of self and property. Concealed handgun laws and expanded rights to use force add an element to homicide and aggravated assault investigations that investigators must be aware of.

An example of such legislation is found in Chapter 9 of the Texas Penal Code, entitled "Justification Excluding Criminal Responsibility." In the section dealing with the use of force to protect persons, the code allows citizens to use reasonable and necessary force in self-defense to the degree that they reasonably believe the force is immediately necessary to protect themselves against others' use or attempted use of unlawful force (Vernon's Annotated Penal Code, Section 9.31(a)). Of course, the statute goes on to list the many situations in which such force cannot be used, including the following:

- In response to verbal provocation alone (in Texas, **fighting words** do not justify the use of force)
- Resisting an arrest or search, whether it is legal or illegal (unless unnecessary force is being used by the police)
- The actor consented to the exact force used by the other

Additionally, a person may use deadly force to protect his or her person if:

1. A reasonable person in the actor's position would not have retreated
2. It is reasonably believed that deadly force is necessary either
   - to protect against another's unlawful use of deadly force, or
   - to prevent the imminent commission of aggravated kidnapping, murder, sexual assault, aggravated sexual assault, robbery, or aggravated robbery

The Texas legislature also has provided for persons to use force to protect their property from trespass (for real property) or to retrieve stolen property if recovery of the property is possible. Unique to Texas is the provision that use of deadly force is justified to protect property in cases where the citizen is attempting to prevent arson, burglary, robbery, aggravated robbery, theft at night, or criminal mischief during the nighttime or the flight of an individual who has committed burglary, robbery, aggravated robbery, or theft during the nighttime and is escaping with property.

An investigator must know not only the elements that make up assault and aggravated assault but also have an understanding of the legal justifications for the use of force. The existence of a seriously injured victim does not always establish that an assault occurred. Furthermore, a breach of the statutes justifying the use of force could constitute an assault. Knowing what is and what is not an assault is not as easy as it once was nor as it might appear to be.

■ Summary

As long as people marry, or have children, or drink alcoholic beverages, or use drugs, there will be assaults. It was once thought that domestic violence only occurred in the lower socioeconomic world. We now know it happens at all levels of our society. In the real world of policing it seems that assault calls occur at the same places, and that ultimately the call involves injury or death. That perspective is consistent with our understanding of the battering cycle for abused women and children. Today's disturbance is tomorrow's assault.

Recognizing that assaults leave as much evidence on the person assaulted as on the surrounding area is the first step in determining what to process at an assault crime scene. The first priority in any assault is to provide medical assistance where necessary. Pursuing the assailant is not part of the investigation. Protecting the victim as a person and as a crime scene is the most important part of the investigation.

The next chapter discusses the various forms of robbery current in our society today. Street muggings and robberies at gunpoint are the tried and true robbery methods. Burglaries and robberies are hard to clear, there is seldom a relationship between the robber and the robbed, and the police have little evidence with which to conduct an investigation.

■ Key Terms

aggravated assault: A physical attack that results in serious bodily injury and that is perpetrated in the course of another felony or involves the use of a deadly weapon

assault and battery: The threat to commit an attack upon another, and then the attack

attitude: An aspect of an individual's personality that immediately puts all others on notice that this individual "takes nothing from nobody at no time"

battery: An attack on another

concealed handgun laws: Laws that allow the use of force, including deadly force, in defense of self and property

deadly force: Force that results in death

domestic assault: Assault that occurs in the home, usually committed by a person's spouse

fighting words: Verbal provocation

medical examination: Examination of the effects of an assault on the victim's body, in order to help determine the circumstances of the assault

mutual combat: Defense to a charge of assault, contending that the two parties agreed to involve themselves in an altercation

photographic record: Photographs (preferably color photographs) taken of an assault victim's injuries

simple assault: A threat to cause bodily injury, an offensive contact or touch, or an attack that does not cause serious bodily injury; the term is used in jurisdictions that have dropped the term *battery* from their penal codes

triage: Determination of the severity of a person's wounds in order to decide if medical treatment is necessary

■ Review Questions

1. What is the difference between an assault and a battery?
2. What is simple assault?
3. What is aggravated assault?
4. What is the most common type of assault, and what investigative needs arise?
5. What is triage? Why is it an important component of an assault investigation?
6. How does self-defense come into play in assault charges?
7. What can an investigator do to defuse the self-defense shield raised by the defense in assault cases?
8. What is mutual combat, and what role does it play in determining whether an assault occurred?
9. Why is a medical examination important in an assault investigation?
10. Why is a photographic record of a victim's injuries important in an assault investigation?
11. What elements must the state prove in establishing that an aggravated assault took place?
12. What is attitude, where does it come from, and how does it contribute to the notion that our society is under siege by criminals?
13. What are fighting words, and do they legally justify a violent response?
14. What legal justifications are there for using force? Give examples of each.
15. What are the provisions of the Texas statute granting homeowners an expanded right to use force to defend themselves and their property?

■ Bibliography

FBI, Crime in the United States. (1990, 1991). *Uniform Crime Reports.* Washington, DC: U.S. Government Printing Office.

Vernon's Annotated Penal Code. (1997). Chapter 9, Section 9.31(a), Justification excluding criminal responsibility.

Walker, L.E. (1979). *The battered woman.* New York: Harper and Row.

Robbery

12

▶ ▶ STUDENT LEARNING OUTCOMES

Upon completion of this chapter students will demonstrate an understanding of:

- The different types of robberies
- The methods of investigation for various types of robberies
- The identification of robbery modus operandi
- The difference between modus operandi and signature
- A robbery checklist
- The value of a prosecutorial summary

The crime that visits urban streets and places the populace in fear for their safety consists primarily of robberies, not the gangland slayings and drive-by shootings that fill the evening news. Those most likely to be afraid of robbery are women and the elderly. Those most commonly robbed on the street are men and juveniles. Robbery, although defined differently in different jurisdictions, has common elements. It involves the taking of the property of a person by another with the intentional, knowing, or reckless causing of bodily injury or the intentional or knowing threatening of imminent bodily injury or death (**TABLE 12-1**).

Robberies can be simple or aggravated. Jurisdictions may categorize robberies based on weapon use or injuries caused. Typically, a person is held to have committed **aggravated robbery** if he or she (1) commits robbery and (2) causes serious bodily injury to another or (3) uses or exhibits a deadly weapon or (4) causes bodily injury to another person or threatens or places another person in fear of imminent bodily injury or death if the person is 65 years or older or is disabled.

Robberies fall into two broad categories depending upon the use or threat of the use of force:

- Strong-arm robbery, often referred to as common-law robbery, involves the use of physical force or the threat of the use of physical force absent a weapon.
- Armed robbery involves the use of a deadly weapon. The weapon does not have to be a firearm—any weapon that in its use or intended use may cause serious bodily injury qualifies.

Robbery in some jurisdictions is considered to be a crime of property, because the basic objective is theft. The FBI, for purposes of gathering data for its *Uniform Crime*

TABLE 12-1   The Probability of Violence in Various Types of Robbery

Type	Probability of Violence
Vehicle robbery	Low to moderate
Bump-and-grab	Low to moderate
ATM robbery	Low to moderate
Residential robbery	Low to moderate
Commercial robbery	Moderate to high
Carjacking	High
Street robbery	High

Reports, regards it as a crime against the person, for the theft is from a person and the threat or use of violence is against the person, not the thing taken. No matter the category, robbery is a felony in all jurisdictions—and a higher-degree felony if it is aggravated. It is interesting to note that the definition of aggravated robbery given earlier, taken from the Texas Penal Code, treats a robbery as aggravated if it is perpetrated upon the elderly or the disabled: the two kinds of victims least likely to be robbed but most in fear of being robbed because of media sensationalism.

Although there are over half a million reported robberies a year, many more go unreported. National surveys suggest the actual number is more than a million. Most are committed with a weapon, and the weapon of choice is the handgun. Only 25% of all robberies reported are cleared by arrest (Crime in the United States, 1989, 1990). Many crimes are reported to the police as robbery. Anyone who has had something stolen is likely to refer to the crime as a "robbery" when in legal fact it may be a theft or burglary (see Chapter 14). What people call the offense is irrelevant as long as police appropriately identify the offense and charge the offender.

■ Robbers

Although robbers come from all walks of life and, like people generally, have a range of motivations, they fall into several broad categories. The most tiresome and easily caught is the **career robber**, who has chosen robbery as his or her life's work. Career robbers are responsible for the majority of robberies committed. The tiresome aspect arises from the fact that these individuals are released again and again to reoffend. The capture of these robbers has been facilitated by the creation of police programs that keep track of reoffenders and their **modi operandi (MO)**.

Opportunistic robbers are not necessarily lifetime offenders. They are amateurs who prey upon others as the opportunity presents itself. Victims are randomly and hastily selected more because of the favorable circumstances than the loot they may relinquish. Amateur robbers are often violent and reckless, attacking without warning, preparation, or consideration of profit potential. They focus on individuals who are in the wrong place at the wrong time and who are least likely to offer resistance. Women and the elderly would be the preference, but they tend to stay away from the isolated areas favored by opportunistic robbers. Most robberies occur in the early hours of the morning before daylight in dark, unprotected areas of the city.

Substance-habituated robbers commit robbery to support a habit. These robbers have graduated to robbery from other less lucrative criminal activities. They seek immediate cash rather than stolen goods that must be fenced. Occasionally, they rob drugstores or dealers to obtain drugs directly, but most often they commit robberies as their need for a drug increases and their ability to purchase the drug decreases. The frequency of these robberies and the amount taken often are clues to the drug dependence that fires these robbers. They will not rob until their drug needs go unaddressed and will attempt to steal enough to purchase the drug quantity necessary to sustain them. Drug users are generally not under the influence of drugs when they rob, for it is the absence of drugs that motivates the robberies. Alcohol abusers, on the contrary, are generally under the influence of alcohol when they rob (Zawitz, 1988).

■ Robberies

Street Robberies

Most robberies occur on the streets of our cities (see Table 12–1 for a list of types of robberies and the attendant risk of violence). A typical attack involves a young robber and a vulnerable victim. Muggings and purse snatchings occur on the street. If a mugging or purse snatching includes violence or the threat of violence, it is a robbery. **Street robberies** often involve more than one offender. The mere presence of a number of menacing youths demanding money and jewelry is sufficient for the victim to produce all valuables. If a request for spare change is made from such a menacing group but with no threats accompanying the request, the victim may believe that violence is implied and volunteer all his or her valuables; without a threat or **show of force**, however, the encounter does not rise to the level of a robbery or theft. The objective of a street robbery is to acquire the victim's money, wallet, credit cards, identification, or jewelry. A street robbery can occur so quickly that the victim, celebrating his or her escape without injury, may not be able to provide much, if any, information to police.

Automatic teller machines (ATMs) are a fertile hunting ground for robbers, and ATM robbers have designed special methods to employ during **ATM robberies**. They may lie in wait for the victims to make a withdrawal and rob them upon completion of the transaction or abduct the victims and transport them to various locations to be able to maximize the amount of money stolen, because many machines restrict the amount that can be withdrawn and the number of withdrawals in a 24-hour period. Fortunately, many banks provide security guards and video cameras at their ATM locations. These video cameras have assisted investigators in identifying and apprehending a variety of street thugs who, unbeknownst to themselves, were filmed in passing by or across the street from an ATM. In investigating any kind of street crime, investigators should examine the environment for the presence of ATMs and their accompanying video cameras.

Residential Robberies

Often a burglary that goes wrong becomes a residential robbery, assault, or rape. Most burglars are content stealing from homes in which the occupants are absent. Occasionally, occupants return or the burglar was mistaken about the absence of the occupants. In such cases, what was intended to be a burglary now becomes a **residential robbery**—if force is used in dealing with the occupants and possessions are removed from the person of the occupants.

As the prevalence of ATM robbery demonstrates, crime adapts to changes in society. More and more people travel and take their valuables with them, and thus criminals have developed a repertoire of techniques to take full advantage of people's mobility. For example, hotels and motels are common sites for robbery. Further, the criminals committing these crimes enter when the travelers are in residence for the purpose of relieving them of their possessions, rather than burglarizing the rooms, because they have discovered that travelers generally carry their valuables on their forays.

As a variation on this theme, some robbers gain entrance to people's houses by misrepresenting themselves as repair persons, city inspectors, or police officers. The victims are selected based on the location and value of their homes. The occupants may be robbed, raped, assaulted, or killed. Some of these residential robberies may be drug-related, and in such robberies, drugs or large quantities of cash typically are targeted. The victim of a robbery in which drugs or a large stash of money was taken will be reluctant to admit the exact nature of the crime, but the criminal history of the victim may be helpful in determining motive.

Commercial Robberies

Most **commercial robbery** sites are small businesses such as liquor stores and convenience stores. By far the favorite sites are convenience stores, because they are operated by one or two persons, their high visibility allows ease of **casing**, public access makes entry simple and unremarkable, and their location on interstates and major thoroughfares makes escape easy (in some parts of the country they are called "stop and robs"). By casing the premises, robbers can determine peak business periods in an effort to avoid witnesses and logistical difficulties.

Experienced robbers eventually begin to weigh the risks against the benefits of small robberies and start to aim at higher targets. Robbers may progress from convenience stores to businesses that specialize in a product or service. The robbery of a jewelry store or a savings institution requires planning and associates if it is to be done effectively. Occasionally a lone offender will rob a bank—usually a branch office that has one employee. Generally banks and jewelry stores require more manpower and planning. The planning makes the investigation more difficult, but the increase in the number of felons increases the probability that someone will make a mistake or speak about one of the robberies. The perpetrators of a **specialty robbery** may have received inside information from an accomplice or may have had firsthand employment experience in the particular business robbed or in the same industry.

Vehicle Robberies

Commercial vehicles are often robbery targets, especially taxicabs and delivery trucks. Taxicabs are most vulnerable, because they have cash readily available and the drivers may be lulled into taking a passenger to an isolated location where the offense can be committed. Taxicab robbers tend to be violent, and the drivers are often assaulted or murdered. Possibly because a robber has engaged in conversation and has been under visual scrutiny for a lengthy time, he or she might be concerned about identification by the driver and perceive murder as a prevention against prosecution (dead men cannot testify). A **delivery van robbery** is typically a crime of opportunity perpetrated by a group of young men who have observed the van making a delivery and deduced that cash must have been received for products delivered. The group will often aggressively and violently attack the driver and remove valuables from the victim after seriously injuring him or her.

Truck hijacking is a specialty crime committed by well-armed and experienced offenders. In a truck hijacking, an entire transport vehicle and its cargo are taken. The vehicle is selected because of its cargo, and knowing what the cargo is generally requires inside information. The robbers park another truck at an isolated location and offload the stolen cargo into this truck. The driver is usually released unharmed and may have been the source of the inside information. Traditionally, liquor, cigarettes, and high-tech consumer goods are stolen.

Another specialty crime is the robbery of passengers in a vehicle. Two methods have developed. In the **bump-and-grab** method, robbers in a vehicle select a vehicle they think contains occupants with valuables. The victims' vehicle is selected based on its monetary value or the fact that it is a rental in a tourist area. The robbers bump the rear of the target vehicle and stop to examine the damage. When the occupants of the bumped vehicle exit, the robbery takes place. The prevalence of this practice in some tourist centers has prompted legislation prohibiting rental agencies from displaying anything on their vehicles that indicates they are rented. Young robbers without a vehicle may pick a strategic location at a traffic intersection and await a potential target. Looking for an auto with a purse, briefcase, or laptop computer on the seat, the **smash-and-grab** thief uses a pipe or other device hidden in his or her clothing to break the passenger-side window and grab the valuable spotted.

An especially frightening type of vehicle robbery is **carjacking**. Instead of smashing windows of vehicles stopped at intersections, robbers commandeer cars that have stopped and steal the vehicle and the possessions of the occupant(s). In some cases the occupants are kidnapped, taken to an isolated location, and assaulted, raped, or murdered. Because of the fear of carjackings, the United States Congress has made carjacking a federal crime punishable by up to 15 years in prison, or life imprisonment if death is the result of the carjacking (Rand, 1994).

■ Modus Operandi

Because of the confusion and psychological trauma associated with robberies, victims' perceptions are questionable and often not very helpful. The major tool of the investigator in identifying a robber is the method employed in the robbery, along with personal characteristics of the robber cited by witnesses (**TABLE 12–2**). Robbers tend to specialize and to develop a repertoire of behaviors that have proven successful in the past and that they believe will continue to be successful. It is their belief in methods of proven efficacy that is an investigator's greatest ally. The traits and techniques developed early in a career of robbery remain with the robber in later stages. These include the following:

- Target selection procedure
- Robber's attire or disguise
- Method of entry (if not a street robbery)
- Words or notes employed
- Weapons chosen and used
- Type of force or intimidation used
- Manner of the loot grab
- Departure signatures (if any)
- Method of departure

TABLE 12–2   Personal Traits and Methods of Operation of Robbers

Age

Gender

Socioeconomic class

Literacy

Geographical domain

Target specialty

Predilection for violence

Words used

Weapon of choice

Method of entry

Clothing

Power needs: The power needs of a robber are reflected in how he or she treats victims. Robbery is a predator crime, and often the power and control exercised over the victim are as much incentives to commit robbery as are the valuables that can be obtained, especially in the case of the young amateur robber.

Target Selection

In street robberies, targets are usually determined by opportunity, but there may be some selection process (e.g., women, the elderly, and the disabled may be the victims of choice). Robberies other than the street variety require some type of **target selection**. That selection may have taken minutes or months, depending on the sophistication and experience of the robber and the nature of the target selected. Hitting a convenience store does not require a lot of preparation, but a bank or jewelry store robbery or a truck hijacking does.

The selection criteria employed by the robber give the investigator a place to start. The answers to two questions—why and how was this target selected?—are the first insights into the robber's modus operandi. If the target could not have been selected without some prerobbery scrutiny, then the investigator must inquire throughout the community whether any strange persons or automobiles have been noticed.

Attire or Disguise

Robbers tend to select clothing and disguises that have proved functional and successful. Most robbers do not engage in extensive planning and restrict themselves to casing the places and persons to be robbed. Robbers have limited wardrobes and better things to do with their money than to buy an array of masks or disguises. Robbers are likely to select, consciously or unconsciously, clothing that hides a weapon, is comfortable, and allows a free range of motion. Just as we all have favorite clothing and just as professionals have preferred attire for specific tasks, so do robbers. A description of clothing is important when **tracing** the identity of offenders. The investigator depends on witnesses when gathering this information and should allow the witnesses to describe attire in their own way and in their own time. Such information may be helpful in uncovering patterns and connecting robberies.

Method of Entry

Entry access is significant in robberies, as it is in homicides and burglaries. Additionally, the behavior of the offender prior to and during entry may be unique. Entry behavior includes all conduct prior to entry up to the demand for valuables or a show of force. Habit creeps into all of our behaviors, and robbers are no exception. In convenience store robberies, the offender often will enter the store posing as a customer and may handle merchandise, engage in conversation with the clerk and witnesses, or use the restroom. Anything handled by the suspect should be processed for fingerprints. Convenience store video footage not only is useful in making a visual identification of the offender but also may assist the investigator in retracing the intruder's steps and reveal possible locations of fingerprints or footprints.

Words and Notes Employed

If a financial institution is the target of a robbery, the request for money must be conveyed in some fashion. The words used are important in figuring out the modus operandi of the robber. The words may be written or spoken and may reveal more about the offender than he or she recognized. The type of paper used is informative. Was the note prewritten, typed, or handwritten, or was it a pasted collage? What type of paper was used? What does the note show about the robber's command of grammar and syntax? Did the robber use paper available at the crime scene? What words were chosen to convey the robber's demand, whether written or spoken?

Although not case determinative, answering these questions adds information that will assist the investigator in fashioning an MO for the robber. An MO is often as revelatory as a criminal profile and may be thought of as information upon which a profile can be partly based. In essence, compiling information about a robber's MO allows the investigator to get into the mind of the robber and determine with some certainty whether the offender will rob again, the type of target that will be selected, the chance of violence during future robberies, and the geographical area within which the robber is comfortable operating. The information gathered by the investigator not only helps in tracing the identity of the offender but also helps sometimes in connecting the robber with prior robberies and allows limited predictions about his or her future conduct.

Weapons Chosen and Used

Robbers have a large range of weapons from which to choose. The choice of weapon may reflect amateur versus experienced status and planned versus opportunistic target selection. A knife is an amateur's weapon of choice, and its use suggests that the robber selects targets opportunistically and has limited resources and experience. If a firearm is used, the choice of weapon may reflect the sophistication and power needs of the robber. Sawed-off shotguns are very intimidating, limited in firepower, and often selected out of a need to feel powerful and hence to carry a weapon capable of causing devastating tissue damage, despite the fact that a shotgun is difficult to secrete upon one's person, difficult to transport, and less likely than a handgun to be disposed of upon completion of the robbery. Handguns are the weapon of preference for most robberies, with semiautomatic firearms providing additional firepower and range. A revolver may be selected in the early stages of a robber's career because of its cost and simplicity. Amateurs will use the same weapons over and over, whereas a more professional robber will select weapons commonly owned by ordinary citizens (thereby reducing their identifiability) and will dispose of each weapon used immediately upon completion of the robbery.

Hollywood movies portray modern professional robbers as equipped with fully automatic submachine guns and **sound suppressors** (the correct name for a silencer).

It should be noted that unless a handgun or submachine gun is equipped with an integral sound suppressor, dissipating the gases that cause the sound means dissipating the gases that operate the bolt, so only one shot can be fired before manually recocking the weapon. Also, sound suppressors are only effective when used with weapons that fire bullets at speeds less than the speed of sound. There are two sounds that occur as the result of a firearm discharge. In weapons that fire a round at speeds in excess of the speed of sound, one crack occurs at the barrel and the other where the bullet breaks the sound barrier. This second sound is impossible to suppress. Submachine guns are less available and less likely to be disposed of than more common weapons. If a submachine gun is used in the commission of a robbery, it is likely to be used again.

Type of Force or Intimidation Used

The offender brings force to bear in some fashion during the course of a robbery. That show of force may also become part of the robber's **habit pattern**. We all relegate to habit those things we do so often that thinking about them becomes unnecessary and a waste of time: which shoe we put on first, which arm we wash first in the shower, how we insert the key into the ignition of our auto, where we carry our car keys, which buttons we button first on our shirts. Many of our habits can tell an observant person something about who and what we are. So too do robbers fall victim to habit patterns that are specific to the offenses they commit. We call such habits a robber's MO, but they may be indicative of habits that transcend the crime and reflect who and what the offender is, independent of the offense being investigated.

The language used by a robber is such a habit pattern. The words selected for the purpose of committing the offense indicate the type of language with which the offender is most comfortable. The choice of words is not accidental; the robber has picked them and rehearsed them. The words said may be what the victim best remembers about the offender or they may be the only thing upon which multiple victims can agree. It is a safe assumption that the words selected have been used in the past and will be used again in the future.

Conversations between offenders in multiple-person robberies can also reveal something about the offenders and their relationships. Professional robbers will keep conversation to a minimum and may restrict communication to nods and gestures. Their original demand may be a collage constructed on nondescript paper. Yet most robberies are charged with excitement and require spontaneous decisions to address the ever-changing circumstances, eliciting verbal responses from the offenders. These responses may add to the profile that is developing of the offenders and their relationships with each other. Spontaneous comments may provide names and demonstrate that the robbers know the layout, the geographical area, the security system, or police procedures. It is important to glean every word uttered and every gesture made by the robbers. The investigator will want to ask each victim when that victim first realized that a robbery was in progress and what the robbers said or did to convey that message.

Manner of the Loot Grab

The loot taken was obtained in a particular fashion—by request, demand, gesture, or self-help. It is important to determine exactly how the robber grabbed the loot. In the robbery of a bank, if the robber directed the teller not to include **bait money** (bills that have had their serial numbers recorded and have been set aside specifically to be given to robbers so they can be traced), several questions are raised:

- Has the robber worked in a financial institution?
- Has the robber learned about bait money through experience (suggesting the possibility of a criminal record)?
- Has the robber been provided with inside information?

Departure Signature

Every robbery comes to an end. Of potential significance is the manner in which the robber exits the premises and the robber's actions toward witnesses and victims—what he or she does to them or has them do. If they have been bound, trace evidence will be present. If they were directed to lie face down on the floor, a **departure signature** may be in the making. Any last comments or behaviors unnecessary to the completion of the robbery may become the robber's trademark or signature, as though he or she were signing a just finished letter or work of art. A signature is a part of the robber's MO and sometimes is the most obvious connection between the robbery being investigated and others committed previously. A signature can occur at any time during the course of the robbery, depending on the imagination and psychological need for recognition of the offender. A kiss to women victims, a slap, or a beverage taken in celebration are examples of signatures left by robbers.

Method of Departure

One of the most valuable variables of the modus operandi is how the robber escapes the scene—on foot, in a car, or on a motorcycle or bicycle. The most easily traceable element of the offense may be the method of escape. Victims may be able to provide the make, model, and color of the vehicle. They may even recognize the vehicle as one they have seen before in the neighborhood. This is the type of information that may be gathered from a canvass of the neighborhood. Some people are reluctant to approach the police with information, even if they know that information to be relevant. It is more difficult for a person to shirk his or her civic responsibility when looking into the eyes of a hardworking, courteous investigator who is trying to protect the neighborhood and its citizens. It should not be assumed that all witnesses have been rounded up by the first-responding officers, nor that all witnesses have come forth voluntarily.

OFFICER'S NOTEBOOK

Goals of Gathering Information

By gathering all the information possible at a robbery crime scene, the investigator is working toward three separate but interdependent goals:

1. Reconstruction of the robbery
2. Identification of the robbers
3. Construction of the MO and comparison of it with those of other robberies

A complete MO is never forthcoming. The objective of the investigator is to gather as much information as possible in the hopes of being able to construct a working hypothesis as to the offender's MO. By comparing the MO in one case with those of similar robberies, the names of prior offenders may arise as possible suspects.

■ Processing the Robbery Crime Scene

The crime scene in a robbery includes the robbers' modes of arrival and departure. It may extend to the area from which a vehicle used in a robbery was stolen and to the location of the vehicle after it has been abandoned. It may include a motel room where the robbers planned the crime and to which they returned to divide the spoils. It is necessary to see a robbery as a dynamic entity, with a beginning and end apart from the person robbed or from the place where the coerced transfer of money or goods occurred. Much of the investigative effort will be focused on determining the beginning point and end point of the robbery. Although not immediately forthcoming, they become evident during the course of the investigation,

The robbery scene itself may be of evidentiary value, based on what the offender or offenders did while at the scene. The possibility of finding fingerprints, footprints, trace evidence, or tire tracks depends on what the robbers did and whether the investigator discovers what they did. If the investigation revealed that a vehicle had been parked at a particular location for an extended period of time while robbers cased the site, there may be evidence of that wait. Tire tracks, litter, or footprints in adjacent soil may be the product of a lengthy surveillance, and the knowledgeable investigator may be able to discover such evidence and use it to good effect. The doorway through which entry was made may reveal fingerprints. The cash register or display cases handled by the robbers may render fingerprints, as may any merchandise handled by an offender while posing as a customer. It is the investigator's job to determine which, if any, of these potential repositories of evidence may exist.

Vehicles recovered after a robbery may contain a wealth of forensic evidence. It is impossible to operate a motor vehicle without leaving some type of trace evidence (see Officer's Notebook). In one robbery homicide, for example, a black plastic bag was tied with a cord around the victim's head. Upon arrest of the suspect, a box of plastic garbage bags and a spool of cord were found in the trunk of his car. An examination of the striations imparted to the bags during the manufacturing process identified the bag in the homicide as having come from the box of unseparated bags. Also, the end of the

---

OFFICER'S NOTEBOOK

Examples of Trace Evidence to Look for in Vehicles

- Fibers (on seat backs, roof liner, and door frames)
- Soil
- Broken glass, asphalt, gravel (carried in the soles of the shoes)
- Hair on headrests and roof liner
- Fingerprints (on all glass surfaces, door handles, dashboard, and radio controls)
- Cigarettes and litter (in ashtray; on floor; in glove compartment; behind sun visors; on, under, and behind seats)
- Tire treads (impressions and residue, which may be identifiable in dirt or gravel)
- Saliva (left on cigarettes, cups, or discarded bandanas or other items used as a mask)
- Trace materials (fiber, blood, dirt, glass, any of which may be on both robber and victim if physical contact between them occurred)
- Tool marks (identifiable characteristic marks left by knives, pry bars, and other instruments used at the crime scene)
- Rope and tape

rope at the crime scene had been cut, and when that rope and the rope on the spool in the suspect's trunk were viewed under a comparison microscope, there was little doubt that the former had been cut from the spool.

The discharge of firearms at a robbery opens up another realm of forensic evidence. The most common evidence will be shell casings and spent bullets. Both casings and bullets have substantial evidentiary value. Firearms identification, discussed in Chapter 9, is applicable in any investigation in which a firearm is used or suspected.

■ Robbery Checklist

Every crime is unique and requires an investigation tailored to the crime, the victim, and the situation. Yet enough commonalities exist among investigations to allow the creation of a checklist for the purpose of ensuring that all investigative issues have been addressed. The checklist in the Officer's Notebook is illustrative only, and the steps need not follow each other in the order given. The list is best used to determine if an investigation has addressed all the potential sources of information that may be available.

■ Prosecutorial Summary

Every case must become transmittable and understandable. The coming together of all aspects of the investigation in a concise, objective, and usable format constitutes the culmination of the investigation. The summary should be contained in a notebook that is divided into identifiable sections and should include an index or a table of contents (see Officer's Notebook).

OFFICER'S NOTEBOOK

Checklist for Processing the Scene of a Robbery
1. Triage the injured.
2. Provide first aid.
3. Contact emergency medical assistance.
4. Identify any victims.
   a. Ascertain that a robbery has occurred.
   b. Interview victims (sooner rather than later).
5. Separate witnesses.
   a. Identify witnesses.
   b. Interview witnesses.
   c. Canvass the community.
6. Provide a broadcast dispatch.
   a. Describe the suspect or suspects.
      i. Gender
      ii. Race
      iii. Clothing
      iv. Physical characteristics (height, weight, hair color)
      v. Identifiable characteristics (scars, tattoos)
      vi. Weapons

(continued)

    b. Describe the vehicle.
       i.   Direction of travel
       ii. Time of departure
       iii. Number of occupants
       iv. Make, model, year, and color
       v. License number
       vi. Stolen status

7. Search the surrounding area (if applicable). Contact hostage negotiators if hostages were taken or the situation becomes barricaded.

8. Process the crime scene.
    a. Locate the scene (which may include a wide geographic area).
    b. Protect the scene (including people, places, and things).
       i. Log all traffic in and out.
       ii. Handle and package evidence.

9. Identify a modus operandi.

10. Utilize street sources of information.

11. Prepare the case for trial (a case summary or prosecutorial summary is a good tool [see the following section]).

Producing a **case summary** (also known as a prosecutorial summary) helps to organize information, refresh memory, and make the results of the investigation understandable and usable. If an investigation culminates in an arrest, the investigator not only must understand the results of the investigation but also must communicate those results to the team member who will try the case. A thoroughly prepared prosecutor will have a much better chance of winning a conviction or achieving a reasonable plea bargain than one who is ill-informed about the investigation.

OFFICER'S NOTEBOOK

Elements of a Case Summary

1. Copies of all documents gathered (witness statements, offense statements, supplemental statements, and a narrative report of the investigation)

2. A list of all relevant parties
— Defendant(s)
— Witnesses
— Victim
— Officers
— Investigators
— Laboratory personnel

3. A list of all relevant evidence
— What it is
— Where it is
— Who obtained it
— When it was obtained
— What its relevance is
— How it was discovered

4. Copies of the results of all lab tests

5. Copies of all photos or fingerprints taken to be used

■ Summary

   In this chapter we looked at common robbery and specialized robbery. In most street robberies the victim is traumatized to the extent that little useful information is generally available. Most victims of robbery are so pleased to be released unhurt that other considerations pale. In robberies, as in most other "stranger" crimes, the probability of apprehending the offender is remote, and as time passes that probability lessens. We do know that robbers have turf and that in most cases they will rob again. Absent genuine efforts to catch robbers through stings and surveillance, patrol response is likely to be of little help.

   Because robberies occur predominately on the street there is little useful evidence available to responding officers. The area surrounding the robbery should be canvassed for individuals who saw something or who recognized the offenders. In truth most robbers are caught either in the act or in the act of selling or pawning items taken from their victims.

   Robbery victims report a sense of violation that is often associated with rape victims. Their worlds have come to a crashing halt and they are confronted with the possibility of personal injury or death. The intrusion into the pockets and personal effects violates one of the areas we hold as most private and inviolable. In the next chapter we will discuss sexual assault, its history and investigatory protocols.

■ Key Terms

aggravated robbery: Robbery in which the person (1) commits robbery and (2) causes serious bodily injury to another or (3) uses or exhibits a deadly weapon or (4) causes bodily injury to another person or threatens or places another person in fear of imminent bodily injury or death if the person is 65 years of age or older or is disabled

ATM robbery: Robbery that occurs at an automatic teller machine; the robbers may wait for the victims to make a withdrawal and rob them upon completion of the transaction or abduct the victims and transport them to various locations to be able to maximize the amount of money stolen

bait money: Bills that have had their serial numbers recorded and have been set aside specifically to be given to robbers so they can be traced

bump-and-grab: Method used to rob people in vehicles, in which robbers bump the rear of the target vehicle and stop to examine the damage; when the occupants of the bumped vehicle exit, the robbery takes place

career robber: Criminal who has chosen robbery as his or her life's work; career robbers are responsible for the majority of robberies committed

carjacking: Robbery in which robbers commandeer cars that have stopped and steal the vehicle and possessions of the occupant(s)

case summary: Compilation of all aspects of the investigation in a concise, objective, usable format that constitutes the culmination of the investigation; also known as a prosecutorial summary

casing: Evaluating a chosen robbery site in order to determine peak business periods in an effort to avoid witnesses and logistical difficulties

commercial robbery: Robbery at a place of business, typically, convenience stores

delivery van robbery: Typically a crime of opportunity perpetrated by a group of young men who have observed a van making a delivery and deduced that cash must have been received for products delivered; the group often will attack the driver aggressively and violently and remove valuables from the victim after seriously injuring him or her

departure signature: Any last comments or behaviors unnecessary to the completion of the robbery that become the robber's trademark or signature, as though he or she were signing a just finished letter or work of art

entry access: The entry point chosen by a robber to gain access to the site of the robbery

habit patterns: Things done so often that thinking about them becomes unnecessary and a waste of time; when these habit patterns are a consistent part of a person's robberies, they are called the robber's modus operandi

modus operandi (MO); plural modi operandi: Method of operation; robbers often repeat their MO, which can be useful in figuring out who committed a particular crime

opportunistic robbers: Amateurs who prey upon others as the opportunity presents itself; these robbers focus on individuals who are in the wrong place at the wrong time and who are least likely to offer resistance

residential robbery: Robbery in a residence, which is usually the result of burglaries gone wrong because the occupants return or the burglar was mistaken about the absence of the occupants; for an incident to be a residential robbery, force must be used in dealing with the occupants, and possessions must be removed from the person of the occupants

show of force: Use of violence or the threat of violence

smash-and-grab: Method used to rob people in vehicles, in which the thief uses a pipe or other device hidden in his or her clothing to break the passenger-side window and grab valuables

sound suppressor: The correct name for a silencer; it is only effective when used with weapons that fire bullets at speeds less than the speed of sound

specialty robbery: Robbery in which the robber(s) may have received inside information from an accomplice or may have had firsthand employment experience in the particular business robbed or in the same industry

street robbery: A theft that occurs in the streets; it includes violence or the threat of force and often involves more than one offender

substance-habituated robber: A person who commits robbery to support a drug habit

target selection: Selection of a person or location for committing a robbery.

tracing: Using evidence to identify and locate a criminal

truck hijacking: A specialty crime committed by well-armed and experienced offenders, in which an entire transport vehicle and its cargo are taken

■ Review Questions

1. What is the difference between a simple robbery and an aggravated robbery?
2. What is an opportunistic robber, and how does an opportunistic robber differ from a career robber?
3. What is a street robbery?
4. How might one defend against a street robbery?
5. What social and technological changes have led to the creation of new types of robbery?
6. What are specialty robbers, and what do they specialize in?

7. What is the difference between a bump-and-grab robbery and a smash-and-grab robbery?

8. How is a carjacking conducted?

9. What does it mean to say that a robber has a modus operandi?

10. What is a case summary, and what value does it have?

11. What should be contained in a case summary?

12. What would you include in a robbery checklist? Why?

■ Bibliography

FBI, Crime in the United States. (1989, 1990). *Uniform Crime Reports*. Washington, DC: Bureau of Justice Statistics.

Rand, M.R. (1994). Carjacking. *Crime Data Brief*. Washington, DC: Bureau of Justice Statistics.

Zawitz, M.W. (1988). *Report to the nation on crime and justice*. Washington, DC: Bureau of Justice Statistics.

Sexual Assault

CHAPTER 13

Upon completion of this chapter students will demonstrate an understanding of:

- The elements of sexual assault
- Gathering evidence in the sexual assault investigation
- Interviewing the sexual assault victim
- Profiling the serial sexual offender
- Pornography and criminality

Human sexual conduct has historically been one of the dark corridors of human behavior. As human sexuality has become more open, it has received a certain amount of social and academic acceptance and become the focus of intelligent discussion. It is no surprise that sexual repression and the absence of sexual candor have redounded to the disadvantage of women. Repressed sexuality has as its adjuncts ignorance and discrimination. Much of the sexually disordered thinking prevalent in our society is the result of hundreds of years of repressed human sexuality. Some of that repression continues to taint the way sexual assault is treated by society and by law enforcement.

The only thing more dangerous than our history of sexual repression is the imagined segregation of men and women into two separate camps: potential rapists and potential victims. The data on rape that are bandied about and that form the foundation of political positions can be biased and misleading. Contributing to the bias is the difficulty of defining rape and the intentional skewing of the definition. In many surveys, women acknowledge they have been victims of rape in amazingly large numbers. As serious as the problem is, it can be exaggerated by defining rape so as to advance a political agenda. Some unwanted, nonconsensual contact is not rape. Some unforced sexual intercourse is not consensual. Because of the reluctance in the past to honestly discuss sexual aberrations and illegal sexual conduct, we can easily be saddled with working definitions of rape that are not legally relevant.

Traditionally, sexual assault has required corroboration beyond the testimony of the victim. In common law, rape was defined as forced sexual penetration by a person other than a spouse. It was a male-specific crime and could not be committed by a husband upon his wife. Additionally, for the force element to apply, there had to be evidence of resistance. Two **standards of resistance** evolved: maximum and reasonable resistance.

TABLE 13-1   Potential Charges Arising from Sexual Assault

- *Assault:* Offensive contact or threat
- *Aggravated assault:* Contact causing serious bodily injury or use of a deadly weapon
- *Sexual assault:* Rape without serious injury
- *Aggravated sexual assault:* Rape with serious injury or use of a deadly weapon
- *Kidnapping:* Abduction
- *Aggravated kidnapping:* Kidnapping for ransom, for purposes of taking a hostage, or with a deadly weapon
- *False imprisonment:* Restraint of another

Predominantly male investigators, judges, and juries saw death as preferable to succumbing to rape. A woman who survived rape was often shunned (socially ostracized) by her community and her family. It was forgivable for a husband to abandon a wife who had been raped and for a man to abrogate the marriage contract if his fiance was raped.

As severe as these responses seem in retrospect, basic attitudes toward rape have carried over into contemporary society. Why is it necessary to protect the identity of a rape victim? What is it we are protecting him or her from? Why is there still some unclean taint affixed to someone who has been raped that restrains disclosure of his or her identity? If we had really come of age in our understanding of rape and empathy for those who are raped, no one would be reluctant to come forth and report rape, and the entire community would coalesce behind the victim in support. We would not hide the victim's identity; we would loudly disavow the deed and rally to his or her cause. The idea that there is something about being raped that requires a victim's identity to be kept secret is a vestige of our past ways of dealing with sexuality and rape.

■ Elements of Sexual Assault

Sexual assault generally involves penetration or contact without consent (or, in the case of a minor, with or without consent). See TABLE 13-1 for a list of charges that can arise from sexual assault.

Legislatures have removed the **gender-specific** aspects of prior legislation, recognizing that women can sexually assault men, women can sexually assault women, and men can sexually assault men. Most penal codes contain language that prohibits the following:

- Penetration of the anus or female organ of another person by any means without the person's consent
- Penetration of the mouth of another person by the sexual organ of the actor without the person's consent

When children are at issue, the statutes prohibit the following:

- Contact or penetration of the sexual organ of a child with the mouth, anus, or sexual organ of another person
- Contact or penetration of the mouth, anus, or sexual organ of a child with the anus or sexual organ of another person

The question of consent, when children are at issue, is not material. Adult consent (or lack thereof) is usually defined in detail by statute. Adult consent is generally held to be lacking in the presence of the following:

- Use of physical force or violence
- The threat of physical force or violence with the ability to carry out the threat
- Unconsciousness or inability to resist
- Mental disease or defect that affects the ability to give consent
- Alteration of a person's ability to resist through the covert introduction of drugs

The elements of sexual assault are multitudinous and complex. A proper investigation begins with understanding what the elements of a sexual assault are and assessing the evidence that may be available to support those elements. Sexual assault cases are difficult to prove, and many rapists have gone free because of lazy or half-hearted investigations that failed to substantiate the necessary elements of rape through corroborative evidence. The good news is that three of the most unacceptable common-law provisions regarding rape have been abolished: spousal immunity, the relevance of the victim's sexual history, and resistance requirements.

Spousal Immunity

Spousal immunity has died and been buried. Spousal abuse statutes now include provisions prohibiting nonconsensual sex between marriage partners. Some states include the prohibition in their rape or sexual assault statutes. There is little probability that the spousal relationship will provide a defense against a charge of nonconsensual intercourse. The notion that sex was a husband's right and a wife's duty has lingered long enough; no one will mourn its passing.

Past Sexual Conduct

Additionally, most jurisdictions prohibit fishing exhibitions into the sexual past of the victim. It was not uncommon for the defense to argue that the survivor was "promiscuous," or wore provocative clothing, or used suggestive language. Under contemporary legal standards, it does not matter what the victim has done. As a practical matter, the conduct of the victim at or near the time of the assault will be paraded before the jury, as will the victim's behavior, language, and clothing. Some change in social standards has accompanied legal changes, and juries are less likely to find suggestive behavior, clothing, or language a substitute for consent.

Resistance

The resistance requirement has been dropped from the statutes of most jurisdictions. Nonetheless, the absence of injury or the absence of an application of force will be used to bolster the defendant's position that intercourse was consensual. The average juror still expects an unwilling participant to resist and further expects there to be evidence of that resistance. In aquaintance-rape cases, the absence of injury, torn clothing, or other evidence of rape is often seen as evidence of consent. In these cases, the evidence is generally the victim's word against the accused's word, and juries generally will not convict without corroborative evidence. Perhaps it is possible for a couple to date, have sex, and, the next morning, have differing opinions as to whether the sex was consensual. Given

CASE IN POINT

Florida v. William Kennedy Smith
The William Kennedy Smith case is an example of a sexual assault case that proper investigation could have prevented. There was no corroboration of the alleged offense, the victim's clothing was intact, and there was no physical evidence that resistance took place. The victim voluntarily placed herself in a risky position, in the company of a man whom she had just met, and went with him to an isolated area of a beach in the wee hours of the morning. It was a classic example of "he said, she said," complicated by the ingestion of alcohol. Had this case not involved a high-profile defendant, the likelihood is that an objective assessment would have taken place and a decision made that there was not enough evidence to prosecute.

CASE IN POINT

People v. Orenthal James Simpson
A perfect example of the **fallacy of innocence** is the O.J. Simpson case. The criminal jury found him to be not guilty, but a civil jury based on the same evidence and testimony found him civilly responsible for the deaths of Nicole Simpson and Ronald Goldman. The difference can be found in the quantity of proof necessary to find culpability. In a criminal case, jurors have to convict based on evidence beyond a reasonable doubt (equivalent to a probability of more than 90%). In a civil case, a jury is instructed to render a verdict based on the preponderance of the evidence (more likely than not, or a probability equivalent to 51%). The criminal jury may not have thought Simpson was innocent, but only that the state had not provided sufficient evidence to find him guilty beyond a reasonable doubt.

that many of these liaisons involve the ingestion of alcohol or drugs, good judgment is often missing and an accurate reconstruction of what happened by either party may be impossible. Juries are not immune to being influenced by the realities of today's dating protocol, and, absent some suggestion of coercion, they will likely acquit the suspect accused of date rape. Bear in mind that a verdict of not guilty is not a finding that the defendant is innocent, only that there was insufficient evidence to convict.

Aggravated Sexual Assault

Sexual assault, in most jurisdictions, is raised to the level of **aggravated sexual assault** if serious bodily injury results, a deadly weapon was used, or the victim was kidnapped. In some jurisdictions, the step up to aggravated sexual assault occurs if the assault was committed:

- By a public servant acting under color of law
- In retaliation against a public servant
- In retaliation against a witness, informant, or person reporting a crime

■ The Forced Sexual Assault Investigation

Once the police have been notified of a sexual assault, they should follow a protocol that does not vary in its essential elements from investigation to investigation (see Officer's Notebook). The victim, although a person, should be treated as part of the crime scene and thus processed for forensic and trace evidence. Failure to recognize the

> **OFFICER'S NOTEBOOK**
>
> **Basic Elements of a Sexual Assault Investigation**
>   1. Provide medical assistance to the victim.
>   2. Protect the crime scene.
>   3. Establish an evidentiary link between the assailant and victim.

possibility of evidence on the victim's person may result in the destruction of valuable forensic evidence.

It is incumbent upon the police agency to ensure that all parties responding to a sexual assault dispatch be trained in applying the protocol. The absence of specialized training for officers responding to sexual assault cases is partly responsible for the historical reluctance victims have exhibited to report sexual assaults. Police have not always been sensitive to the physical, psychological, and emotional needs of sexual assault victims and have inadvertently contributed to their victimization. Their insensitivity, coupled with the defense strategy of placing blame on the victim, explains why sexual assaults have so often gone unreported. Assault victims have been unwilling to be victimized by the police and the courts after having been victimized by their assailants.

In the past, sexual assault and child abuse cases were assigned to women officers or the newest person on the force. Men were not comfortable handling these types of cases and avoided assignment to them. It was thought that female officers, solely because of their gender, brought a level of sensitivity to sexual assault investigations that male officers could not. The truth is that there are women who are emotionally insensitive and poorly prepared to investigate sexual assaults, just as there are men who have the necessary skills. The abilities required to be a successful **sex crimes investigator** are not gender specific and can and must be learned.

Modern agencies have addressed past indiscretions and have trained their personnel to handle sexual assault victims. Many agencies have specially trained teams whose only responsibility is to respond to sexual assault cases. They, along with specially designated attorneys who have also undergone inservice training on how to prepare and prosecute sexual assault cases, understand what is required for the successful investigation of sexual assaults and the successful prosecution of the assailants.

Medical Attention and Examination of the Victim

As in all situations in which a victim has undergone a physical attack, the primary responsibility of the officer first responding to the scene is to triage the victim. That responsibility is greater in sexual assaults. The victim, fearing the perceived shame associated with being raped, may decline medical treatment. It is at this early juncture that the skill of the specially trained sex crimes investigator must come into play.

The medical attention sought is not solely for the purpose of providing treatment but also for the purpose of providing forensic evidence. To prove that sexual assault of an adult occurred, it must be shown that penetration took place. Showing this can only be accomplished through a medical examination and the collection of physical evidence from the person of the victim. Use of force may be proven by the presence of injuries to the body or ligature marks on the body. All injuries must be noted by the examining physician and photographed. It should not be presumed by the investigator that the physician will take photographs of the injuries. A request should be made directly to the physician, and, if necessary, a police photographer of the same sex as the victim should be provided to photographically record all relevant body markings under the supervision of the medical personnel.

Many people who are raped delay reporting the incident. Any delay can hinder the investigation, because the victim may have showered or destroyed soiled clothing and bed linen. Not only do such actions remove corroborating evidence from the reach of the investigator, but the defense may question why the victim did not call police immediately. In an effort to defuse this tactic, the investigator should record the mental and emotional condition of the victim, following evaluation by the examining doctor.

Today, all hospitals and emergency rooms are aware of the procedure to be employed in examining a sexual assault victim. **Sex crimes kits** have been available for a long time and should be standard equipment in all doctor's offices (**Figure 13–1**). However, it would be prudent for investigators to carry rape kits in their cars so that they can provide them to examining physicians, along with appropriate instructions on how to use them to collect evidence.

The medical examination of a sexual assault victim should include **hair brushings** and samples. During the assault, the head of the victim may have come into contact with the body or head of the assailant. The purpose of gathering hair samples is twofold: to obtain any foreign blood, tissue, fibers, or hair that may have come from the assailant, the assailant's vehicle or clothing, or the assault location; and to obtain control samples of the victim's hair so that when a suspect has been identified, it may be determined whether hair on the suspect's person or clothing came from the victim.

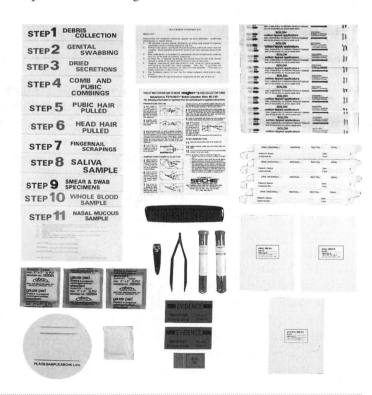

Figure 13–1 Sex crimes kit.

Courtesy of SIRCHIE Finger Print Laboratories, Inc.

Evidence hair must be kept separate from control hair, and the separation is accomplished by using an uncontaminated hairbrush for evidence brushing. Once all evidence has been removed and the brush used has been packaged along with the attached hair and evidence, a sampling of control hair is obtained by pulling hairs from the victim's head. The sample of control hairs is then packaged separately.

Investigators should also collect pubic hair brushings and samples from the victim. Pubic hair evidence must be obtained for the same reasons and in the same way as head hair evidence. It cannot be emphasized too strongly that all brushings and **pluckings** must be packaged separately, along with the brush or comb used. Each package must be marked and identified properly. It may be a good idea to have a member of the sexual assault team who is of the same sex as the victim attend the examination and retrieve each piece of evidence and control sample.

Proof of penetration is required to establish sexual assault. It will be necessary to obtain **swabbings** of the mouth, anus, and vaginal cavity in an effort to corroborate the victim's statement that penetration occurred. The victim is likely to recall what part of the body was penetrated, and the physician can focus the examination on that area. Occasionally a victim is so badly injured that he or she either does not recall the entirety of the assault or is unconscious. In this case, all three areas need to be swabbed. The swabbing is done to detect the presence of seminal fluid or spermatozoa. For each swabbing taken, a separate package must be used. Along with the swab and any attached evidence, there must be a separately packaged unused swab as a laboratory control to defuse any suggestion that the swab used was contaminated. It is part of the medical protocol to prepare slide smears for microscopic examination from swabbings. These slides must also be packaged and appropriately marked. The physician may also obtain an oral and vaginal rinse. Each rinse should be placed in an evidence vial and appropriately labeled. Again, as with all forensic examinations, there should be a control sample of the rinsing material packaged separately.

Fingernail and toenail **scrapings** may be obtained in an effort to detect hair, fibers, blood, or tissue from the assailant. Toenail scrapings may reveal dirt or fibers from a vehicle floor or assault location. Each hand and foot should be processed separately and the scrapings placed in separate bags. The instrument used to obtain the scrapings should be provided as a control and packaged separately.

All clothing not washed or destroyed by the victim should be obtained. Each item should be packaged separately. Plastic bags should not be used. Paper bags will not affect the clothing or any evidence on the clothing. If the victim is conscious and wearing the clothing he or she wore at the time of the rape, a "catch paper" should be used to capture any evidence that may be dislodged during disrobing. If the victim is unconscious, the catch paper should be placed beneath the body to accomplish the same objective. The catch paper should be folded, edges inward, to avoid loss of evidence and then separately packaged.

Interviewing the Victim

Initial Interview
The initial interview must address the who, what, and where of the assault. A description of the assailant will be valuable in communicating a description to patrol officers. What was done during the assault will provide a perspective to the investigator for the examination that is to be conducted by medical staff and the accompanying gathering

of physical evidence from the body of the victim. Where the assault occurred will lend further structure to the investigation and the possible locations of forensic evidence left at the scene of the assault.

Interviewing sexual assault victims is a very delicate process and requires special training for the interviewer or interviewing team. In most instances a woman who has been sexually assaulted harbors residual fear that may generalize to all adult males. Many agencies with crisis intervention teams have men and women on the team with the necessary training and empathy required to conduct the first interview. It is this interview that is the most difficult and the most important. It will be the inclination of all concerned to forestall the interview, thereby reducing any additional emotional trauma to the victim. That is a luxury that is not available to the sexual assault investigator or team. Much of the evidence sought is fragile. It will dissipate, be destroyed, or be contaminated if not attended to immediately. Victim comfort is always a consideration, but it must be recognized that the investigation cannot go forward without some discomfort to the victim. The sooner and more professionally that discomfort is dealt with, the better. There are those victims who are so traumatized that an immediate initial interview is impossible. It must be remembered that the initial interview is the first step in the investigation. The investigation cannot begin without it. Time is the friend of the assailant.

In most instances the interview should be conducted in private with a health care worker present. Family and friends should be excluded unless the interview cannot be

OFFICER'S NOTEBOOK

Elements Sought in the Interview of a Sexual Assault Victim
The initial interview should attempt to gather the following information:
1. A narrative of the assault
2. A description of the assailant
3. Any outstanding characteristics of the assailant that will assist in constructing an MO
   a. Assault method
   b. Words spoken or threats made
   c. Weapons used
   d. Salutatory comments or gestures
4. What the victim was doing prior to the assault
5. What the victim was doing during the assault
6. What the victim did after the assault
7. What the assailant was doing during the assault
8. What the assailant did after the assault
9. Whether a vehicle was used
   a. Make
   b. Model
   c. License number
10. Where the assault took place (perform a walk-through addressing each point of contact during the assault)
11. The names of any persons who may have witnessed the entry or the exit of the assailant
12. The names of any persons who may have witnessed the assault
13. Any necessary medical information
    a. Points of penetration
    b. Injuries
14. Points of body-to-body physical contact

conducted without the presence of the third party (child victims are handled differently). Soliciting a narrative from the victim is the best approach but may be difficult in light of the trauma suffered. If questions are needed to prompt responses, those questions need to be considered very carefully to ensure there are no suggestions of challenge to the victim's circumstances. Any inconsistencies in the victim's rendition should be attributed to the emotional state of the victim and not to conscious deception.

From the initial interview the investigator will be able to suggest to medical personnel the scope and breadth of the physical examination that the victim must undergo. It is also from this interview that the parameters of the search will be constructed of the victim's person as well as the physical surroundings in which the assault occurred.

Follow-up Interview

The initial interview will give police, investigators, and medical personnel a starting place. Once the investigation has been launched, numerous questions will arise that will require revisiting the victim and his or her story. Time will have allowed the victim to regain composure and dignity. The second interview should be more detailed, focusing on the specific words spoken and the specific acts in question. Questions of resistance can be addressed. Issues of reputation will have to be pursued in an effort to defuse defense efforts at discrediting the victim based on prior relationships and reputation. Further descriptions of the events of the assault and of the assailant can be developed. Even the most thorough investigators will find themselves returning to the victim for any additional information that will help clear the case. Interviews should be kept to a minimum and should be based on new perspectives rather than something that was overlooked in the initial or follow-up interview.

Gathering Evidence

Chapters 5 and 6 addressed DNA printing and blood typing. These laboratory procedures are most productive in assault cases in which blood, semen, or saliva have been detected. Of course, DNA typing is of value only when a suspect or suspects are at hand. It is in anticipation of locating a suspect that DNA testing is performed.

Semen is the reproductive fluid that normally contains **spermatozoa**, the male reproductive germ cells. The presence and appearance of spermatozoa are highly important to the value of semen as tracing evidence. Following their discharge from the male, spermatozoa may remain in an active state for up to 15 hours. **Seminal stains** not deposited within the body of the victim may remain intact for lengthy periods of time. Not all seminal samples contain spermatozoa. Some men have a condition called **aspermia** that prevents spermatozoa from appearing in their seminal fluids. If a seminal sample is to be tested for DNA, the evidence must first be tested to determine if it contains sperm. It is the sperm cell that contains the DNA.

Seminal stains may be found in three localities: on the victim, at the crime scene, and on the suspect. Semen located on the victim may be discovered on any exterior surface of the body or within any of the body orifices. An examination of the crime scene with ultraviolet light may reveal traces of semen, especially in areas and on things related to the assault, such as beds, towels, washcloths, paper towels, toilet paper, and carpeting. Most humans secrete blood into their other bodily fluids. Chemical analysis of a secretor's semen, saliva, or gastric juices may reveal blood type. Additionally, the enzyme **diaphorase** is present in sperm only in humans. It exists in three distinctive forms: The most common form appears in 50% of the male population, the second most common appears in 40%, and the least common is present in only 10%. The discovery of the enzyme is useful in eliminating innocent subjects and can be useful in tracing the assailant (Gilbert, 1998).

Hair and fibers are commonly found at the sexual assault crime scene or on the person of the sexual assault victim. Proper processing and handling may provide corroborative evidence that will assist in the prosecution. Seldom will fiber or hair evidence alone result in a conviction. Hair and fiber evidence are suggestive rather than determinative trace evidence. Fingerprints and DNA identifications are determinative, for only one person can have a particular fingerprint or DNA print. Hair and fiber, however, cannot be so specifically identified.

Hair

It is presently impossible to identify a human hair as coming from any single head or body, although hair can provide support in placing a suspect at a crime scene. Hair grows out of the skin from a hair follicle. It extends from the root in the follicle into a shaft culminating at a tip. The shaft is composed of a cuticle, a cortex, and a medulla (**Figure 13–2**).

The **cuticle** is made of overlapping cells that have keratinized (hardened) and flattened to form scales. Human cuticle scales are alike, but they differ from the cuticle scales of other species. Thus, the cuticle, although incapable of picking out an individual, is useful for determining if the hair in question is human.

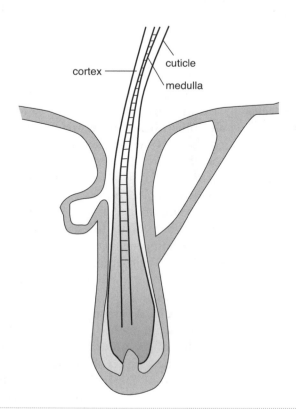

Figure 13–2 Structure of hair.

The **cortex** of the hair is made up of cells that are aligned parallel to the length of the hair. The cortex is impregnated with the pigment granules that give hair color. The shape, distribution, and color of these granules allow forensic scientists to ascertain individual points of comparison when looking at hair gathered at the scene of a crime and hair from a suspect.

The **medulla** of the hair appears to form a central canal running through the center of the hair. The medullary index, which is expressed as a fraction, denotes the diameter of the medulla relative to the diameter of the hair shaft. The index for humans is generally less than one third; for other animals, it is greater than one half. Not all hairs have medullae, and when they do exist, they may be classified as continuous, fragmented, or interrupted. Human hair, except for the hair of native Mongolians, has either no medulla or a fragmented medulla. Mongoloid hair usually has continuous medullation (Saferstein, 1995).

Hair examination determines if the hair retrieved at the scene of a crime is human and, if so, whether it is similar to hair from a suspect. Note that the morphology of hair may differ not only from one individual to another but also within a single individual. The determination that a sample hair probably comes from a particular suspect will depend on the ability of the forensic scientist to establish a match with regard to color, length, and diameter; the character of the medulla; and the shape, color intensity, and distribution of the pigment granules in the cortex. It should be remembered that hair is class evidence and that it is not possible to determine with certainty that the sample came from one individual and no other.

It is generally readily apparent to the educated eye from which part of the body hairs come. Scalp hairs show little diameter variation and have uniform distribution of pigment color. Pubic hairs are short, wiry, and curly, with a wide variation in shaft diameter. Beard hairs are coarse, normally triangular in cross section, and have blunt tips from repeated cutting. Often race can be determined, especially if the sample consists of Caucasian or Negroid head hair. Negroid hairs are normally kinky and contain dense, evenly distributed pigments. Caucasian hairs are usually straight or wavy, with very fine to coarse pigments that are even more evenly distributed than pigments in Negroid hair. However, racial intermarriage has become so common that these characteristics may not be determinative.

As stated earlier, hair is presumptive class evidence, but a new DNA procedure that allows for the replication of small quantities of DNA has proven very successful. Polymerase chain reaction DNA typing may allow an amplification of the small amounts of DNA found in the human hair root or follicle. Although current DNA typing cannot yet individualize hair, there is a reasonable expectation that future research will improve the technology to the point that DNA will reveal enough information to provide for the near complete individualization of a single hair (Saferstein, 1995). Currently, mitochondrial DNA may allow a sequencing to establish a match between a questioned and known hair. This process is used for the exclusion or association of two hairs, as opposed to a true DNA printing.

Fibers

In every situation in which two persons come into contact, transference of various materials occurs. In any offense in which there is contact, transferred hairs and fibers may serve to identify the offender. The value of fiber evidence lies in the ability of the forensic scientist to narrow the number of possible sources of origin. The mass production of garments reduces the effectiveness of fiber identification, but demonstrating that the suspect possesses a garment of the type from which the fiber in question may have come can have a substantial impact on the jury. It will fall to the defense to establish that many garments are made of the same fabric and thus discredit the validity of the match. In many investigations, there is a transfer of more than one type of fiber. A case study of the use of fiber evidence is given in the Case in Point.

CASE IN POINT

Fiber Evidence in the Atlanta Child Murders

In February of 1982 in Fulton County, Georgia, a jury returned a guilty verdict on two counts of criminal homicide against Wayne Bertram Williams. During the course of the trial, evidence was admitted linking Williams to the murder of Nathaniel Cater and Jimmy Payne in April and May of 1981 as well as to the murder of 10 other young men. The telling evidence in the case was the association of fibrous debris removed from the bodies of 12 murder victims with objects from Williams' environment. Fiber evidence can corroborate other evidence in a case; it is used to support other testimony and validate other evidence presented at a trial. This was not the situation in the Williams trial. Other evidence and other aspects of the trial were important, but were used to support and complement the fiber evidence, not the other way around. The hair and fiber matches between Williams' environment and 11 of 12 murder victims discussed at the trial were so significant that these victims were positively linked to both the residence and automobiles that were a part of the world of Wayne Williams.

Before Williams became a suspect in the Nathaniel Cater murder case, the Georgia State Crime Laboratory located a number of yellowish green nylon fibers and some violet acetate fibers on the bodies and clothing of the murder victims whose bodies had been recovered during the period of July 1979 and May 1981. The yellowish green nylon fibers were generally similar to each other in appearance and properties and were considered to have originated from a single source. This was also true of the violet acetate fibers.

Initially, the major concern with these yellowish green nylon fibers was determining what type of object could have been their source. The fibers were very coarse and had an oval cross-sectional appearance, tending to indicate that they originated from a carpet or a rug. The oval cross-sectional shape of these fibers, however, was unique, and initially the manufacturer of these fibers could not be determined. A number of different chemists agreed that the yellowish green nylon fiber was very unusual in cross-sectional shape and was consistent with being a carpet fiber.

In February 1981, an Atlanta newspaper article publicized that several different fiber types had been found on two murder victims. Following the publication of this article, bodies recovered from rivers in the Atlanta metropolitan area were either nude or clothed only in undershorts. It appeared the article had forewarned the murderer, and victims were now being disposed of in rivers in this undressed state to prevent fibers from being found on their bodies. On May 22, 1981, a four-man surveillance team of personnel from the Atlanta Police Department and the Atlanta office of the FBI were situated under and at both ends of the James Jackson Bridge over the Chattahoochee River in northwest Atlanta. Around 2:00 AM a loud splash alerted the surveillance team to the presence of an automobile being driven slowly off the bridge. The driver was stopped and identified as Wayne Bertram Williams.

Two days after Williams' presence on the bridge, the nude body of Nathaniel Cater was pulled from the Chattahoochee River, approximately one mile downstream from the James Jackson Parkway Bridge. A yellowish green nylon carpet-type fiber, similar to the nylon fibers discussed above, was recovered from the head hair of Nathaniel Cater. Search warrants for Williams' home and automobile were issued and executed. An initial association of fibers from Cater and other murder victims was made with a green carpet in the home of Williams. Associations with a bedspread from Williams' bed and with the Williams family dog were also made at that time. An apparent source of the yellowish green nylon fibers had been found.

Because of the unusual cross-sectional appearance of the nylon fiber and the difficulty in determining the manufacturer, it was believed that this was a relatively rare type and therefore would not be present in large amounts (or in a large number of carpets).

It was determined that the yellowish green nylon fiber was manufactured by Wellman Corporation and no others. It was also determined that fibers having this cross-sectional shape were manufactured and sold during the years 1967 through 1974.

Through numerous contacts with yarn spinners and carpet manufacturers, it was determined that the West Point Pepperell Corporation of Dalton, Georgia, had manufactured a line of carpet called "Luxaire," which was constructed in the same manner as the Williams carpet. One of the colors offered in the Luxaire line was called "English Olive," and this color was the same as that of the Williams carpet (both visually and by the use of discriminating chemical and instrumental tests).

It was learned that the West Point Pepperell Corporation had manufactured the Luxaire line for a five-year period from December 1970 through 1975; however, it had only purchased Wellman 181B fiber for this line during 1970 and 1971. In December 1971, the West Point Pepperell Corporation changed the fiber composition of the Luxaire line to a different nylon fiber, one that was dissimilar to the Wellman 181B fiber in appearance. Accordingly, Luxaire carpet like the Williams carpet was only manufactured for a one-year period. This change of carpet fiber after only one year in production was yet another factor that made the Williams carpet unusual.

To any experienced forensic fiber examiner, the fiber evidence linking Williams to the murder victims was overwhelming. But regardless of the apparent validity of the fiber findings, it was during the trial that its true weight would be determined. Unless it could be conveyed meaningfully to a jury, its effect would be lost. Juries are not usually composed of individuals with a scientific background, and therefore it was necessary to educate the jury in what procedures were followed and the significance of the fiber results. In the Williams case, more than 40 charts with over 350 photographs were prepared to illustrate exactly what the crime laboratory examiners had observed.

During the course of the trial the fiber matches made between fibers in Williams' environment and fibers from victims Payne and Cater were discussed. In discussing the significance or strength of an association based on textile fibers, it was emphasized that the more uncommon the fibers, the stronger the association. None of the fiber types from the items in Williams' environment by definition were common fiber types:

1. Station wagons
2. Throw rug
3. Blue rayon fibers
4. Bedroom bedspread
5. Bedroom carpet
6. Williams family dog
7. Backroom carpet square (yellowish green synthetic fibers)

One of the fibers linking the body of Jimmy Ray Payne to the carpet in the 1970 station wagon driven by Williams was a small rayon fiber fragment recovered from Payne's shorts. Data were obtained from the station wagon's manufacturer concerning which automobile models produced prior to 1973 contained carpet made of this fiber type. These data were coupled with additional information from Georgia concerning the number of these models registered in the Atlanta metropolitan area during 1981. This allowed a calculation to be made relating to the probability of randomly selecting an automobile having carpet like that in the 1970 Chevrolet station wagon from the 2,373,512 cars registered in the Atlanta metropolitan area. This probability was 1 chance in 3,828, a very low probability representing a significant association.

Another factor to consider when assessing the significance of fiber evidence is the increased strength of the association when multiple fiber matches become the basis of the association. As the number of different objects increases, the strength of an association increases dramatically.

(continued)

Studies have been conducted in England that show that transferred fibers are usually lost rapidly as people go about their daily routine (Pounds and Smalldon, 1975). Therefore, the foreign fibers present on a person are most often from recent surroundings. The fibrous debris found on a murder victim reflects the body's more recent surroundings, especially important if the body was moved after the killing. Accordingly, the victims' bodies in this particular case were not only associated with Williams but were apparently associated with Williams shortly before or after their deaths.

Although from these findings it would appear that the victims were in the residence of Williams, there was one other location that contained many of the same fibers as those in the composition of various objects in his residence: Williams' station wagon. The environment of a family automobile might be expected to reflect, to some extent, fibers from objects located within the residence. This was true of the 1970 station wagon. The automobile would be the most logical source of the foreign fibers found on both Payne and Cater if they were associated with Williams shortly before or after their deaths. It should also be pointed out that two objects, the bedspread and the blanket, were portable and could have at one time been present inside the station wagon. Both Payne and Cater were recovered from the Chattahoochee River. Their bodies had been in the water for several days. Some of the fibers found on these victims were like fibers in the compositions of the bedroom carpet and bedspread except for color intensity. They appeared to have been bleached. By subjecting various known fibers to small amounts of Chattahoochee River water for different periods of time, it was found that bleaching did occur.

Two crime laboratory examiners testified during the trial and concluded that it was highly unlikely that any environment other than that present in Wayne Williams' house and car could have resulted in the combination of fibers and hairs found on the victims and that it would be virtually impossible to have matched so many fibers found on Cater and Payne to items in Williams' house and car unless the victims were in contact with or in some way associated with the environment of Wayne Williams. Of the nine victims who were killed during the time period when Williams had access to the 1970 station wagon, fibers consistent with having originated from both the station wagon carpet and the bedroom carpet were recovered from six of these victims. The finding of many of the same fiber types on the remaining victims, who were recovered from many different locations, refutes the possibility that Payne's and Cater's bodies picked up foreign fibers from the river. The fact that many of the victims were involved with so many of the same fiber types, all of which linked the victims to Williams' environment, is the basis for arguing conclusively against these fibers originating from a source other than Williams' environment.

Source: This account of the use of fiber evidence in the Wayne Williams trial, by Harold A. Deadman, Special Agent, Microscopic Analysis Unit, Laboratory Division, Federal Bureau of Investigation, Washington, DC, is reprinted in part from the *FBI Law Enforcement Bulletin,* March and May 1984.

Types of Fibers

For forensic purposes, fibers may be classified into two categories: natural and manufactured. **Natural fibers** come from animals or plants. Common animal fibers include wool, mohair, cashmere, and furs. The most common plant fiber is cotton. The widespread use of white cotton in clothing has made its value in fiber comparison negligible, although the presence of dyed cotton in a combination of colors may serve to enhance its probative value. **Manufactured fibers** have all but replaced natural fibers in the garment and fabric industry. The first machine-made fibers were manufactured from raw materials derived from cotton or wood pulp. These materials were processed and the cellulose extracted. The cellulose was chemically treated and dissolved in a solvent before being forced through the holes of a spinning jet to produce **regenerated fibers**. Most of the commonly manufactured fibers are produced from chemicals. These synthetic fibers include trade name fibers such as Orlon.

Fiber Analysis

The forensic value of fibers depends on the scientist's ability to trace their origin and compare known fiber samples with unknown fibers from a crime scene, victim, or offender. The first step in the tracing process is to examine the fibers microscopically to determine fiber color, diameter, shape, lengthwise striations, and the pitting of fiber surfaces with delustering particles added by the manufacturer to reduce shine (Saferstein, 1995).

Two fibers that appear to be of the same color will show, if viewed under a microscope, numerous differences in the dyes used. Most fibers are impregnated with a mixture of dyes to obtain a particular color or shade. It is a stroke of luck for an investigation when the forensic examiner can show that the suspect fiber and the control fiber have the same **dye composition**. Fiber color can be determined more precisely through a chromatographic separation of the materials that compose the dyes (see the sections on chromatography in Chapter 15). The dye from each fiber to be chromatographed must be extracted using a suitable solvent, and then drops of the solution placed onto a thin-layer chromatographic plate. The dye components of the suspect fiber will separate on the thin-layer plate and can be compared with the dye components of control fibers (Laing, 1990).

A demonstration that two fibers have the same dye composition does not prove sameness of origin. Both must be shown to have the same chemical composition before it can be concluded that the samples probably come from the same source. Only a single fiber from the crime scene may be available for analysis, so it is important to apply nondestructive methods for chemical comparisons.

Synthetic fibers are manufactured by melting a polymeric substance or dissolving it in a solvent and then forcing it through the very fine holes of a spinneret. The polymer emerges as a very fine filament, with its molecules aligned parallel to the length of the filament. Just as the regular arrangement of atoms produces a crystal, so the arrangement of the fiber's polymers will cause crystallinity in the finished fiber. Light passing through a synthetic fiber emerges polarized, perpendicular, and parallel to the length of the fiber. Depending on the class of fiber, each material will have a characteristic index of refraction. Chemists are able to determine what index of refraction a particular synthetic fiber possesses. The polymers that make up a manufactured fiber, like any organic substance, will selectively absorb infrared light in a characteristic pattern. Infrared spectrometry provides a rapid and reliable method for identifying the fiber class to which a sample fiber belongs. The infrared microspectrophotometer combines a microscope with an infrared spectrophotometer, allowing for an infrared analysis of a single strand of a fiber.

Chemical substances are composed from basic structural units called molecules. The molecules of most materials comprise just a few atoms. For example, a water molecule is made up of two atoms of hydrogen and one atom of oxygen. **Polymers** are formed by linking together a large number of molecules, as many as several thousand. A polymer can be pictured as a long repeating chain, with each link representing the basic structure of the polymer. The repeating molecular units in the polymer are joined together end to end. By simply varying the chemical structure of the basic molecules and weaving them together, chemists have been able to synthesize glues, plastics, paints, and fibers (Saferstein, 1995).

Gathering Fiber Evidence
Fiber evidence can be found at any crime scene. It is generally overlooked, dislodged, destroyed, or contaminated. The task of the investigator interested in detecting and preserving fiber evidence (or any other trace evidence, for that matter) is to identify and preserve potential **trace evidence carriers**.

OFFICER'S NOTEBOOK

Collecting Fiber Evidence

Articles of clothing that the investigator suspects carry fiber evidence should be packaged in a paper bag. Each article should be packaged in a separate bag to avoid **cross-contamination.** Care must be taken to avoid contact with other areas of the crime scene and other objects at the crime scene, as well as with the investigators themselves. Any item suspected of containing trace evidence should not be moved from its discovered location until it is folded and placed in a paper bag, which should be done immediately. Moving an item to another location to fold or bag it may result in lifting fibrous or other trace materials from that location.

Car seats should be covered with polyethylene sheets to protect fiber evidence. Knife blades should be covered and bagged to protect any possible adhering fibers, tissue, blood, or hair. If a body is believed to have been wrapped in or laid upon a blanket or carpet, adhesive tape can be used to pick up fibers from the exposed areas upon which the body may have rested. Vacuuming is the least desirable method of recovering trace evidence but may be necessary in some situations. A different vacuum bag should be used for each item vacuumed, and each vacuum bag should be placed in a separate paper bag. It may be necessary for an investigator to remove a fiber from an object, which should be done using clean forceps. The fiber is then placed on a clean piece of white paper, which is folded with a pharmacist's fold and put inside another container (Saferstein, 1995).

As in the Wayne Williams case, bodies are often disposed of in a watery repository. It is wrong to assume that because a body has been submerged, it contains no evidence of forensic value. The underwater investigator's responsibility is not to retrieve fiber evidence but to prevent loss, destruction, or contamination of any evidence that lingers on the body. This objective can only be accomplished by appropriate bagging of the body before retrieval. The Williams case shows the need for bottom samples to demonstrate that the watercourse in which the body was deposited was not the source of the fibers found on the body.

There is no analytical technique that will allow a fiber strand to be associated conclusively with any single garment. The value of fiber evidence is enhanced if other types of physical evidence linking a person or an object to a crime or victim accompany it.

■ Sexual Assailant Profiling

Dr. A. Nicholas Groth (1977) has developed a rapist typology comprising two major classifications, each with two subclassifications:

1. Power rapist
    a. Power-reassurance rapist
    b. Power-assertive rapist
2. Anger rapist
    a. Anger-retaliatory rapist
    b. Anger-excitation rapist

Power-Reassurance Rapist

The goal of the **power-reassurance rapist** is to assert power over the victim. He is obsessed with proving his manhood (reassurance), selects his victim through prior observation, and uses weapons of opportunity and verbal attacks. The following are characteristics of a power-reassurance rapist.

- Rapes between midnight and 5 AM every 7 to 20 days
- Selects victims by watching
- Seeks victims roughly his own age
- Seeks victims who live alone
- Generally attacks victims in their home
- Uses weapons of opportunity
- Attempts to hide his identity
- Asks victims to remove clothing rather than forcibly removing it
- Engages in vaginal sex
- May ejaculate prematurely
- May be impotent
- Seeks validation from victims
- Feels socially inadequate
- Has no intimate female relationships
- Is employed in menial jobs
- May have prior arrests for peeping or burglary
- Does not use a vehicle (first rapes are within walking distance from his home)
- May apologize for his conduct
- May take a souvenir (Groth, 1977)

Power-Assertive Rapist

The **power-assertive rapist** seldom plans his attack or stalks his victim. His victims are typically of the same race and age group as his. His tools are charm and a facile tongue. Because his rapes are generally a product of opportunity, it is difficult to predict his behavior. The power-assertive rapist

- Rapes between 7 PM and 1 AM (often selecting victims from bars and lounges)
- Selects victims based on opportunity
- Uses charm or a con to establish contact with victims
- Physically dominates victims
- Has a weapon of choice (often a knife)
- Instructs victims not to look at his face
- Is body-conscious
- Frequents singles bars
- Enjoys physical labor
- Is married or divorced
- Has a prior record for domestic violence
- Drives a flashy vehicle (Groth, 1977)

Anger-Retaliatory Rapist

The **anger-retaliatory rapist** vents his anger upon and attempts to punish the opposite sex. His method of humiliation and punishment is sexual assault. The stimulation that precipitates his anger involves a stressor that typically relates to women, often a product of his work or family relationships. He assaults spontaneously, quickly, and violently. Any resistance on the part of the victim fuels his anger. The anger-retaliatory rapist

- Rapes at any hour
- Selects victims based on opportunity

- Selects victims within his zone of comfort (the area with which he is familiar, usually near work or home)
- Selects victims roughly his own age
- Overcomes victims rapidly and violently
- Uses weapons of opportunity, including hands, feet, and teeth
- Beats victims before, after, and during rape
- Uses degrading language
- Has a prior history of domestic violence and fighting
- Has an explosive temper
- Drinks, often to excess
- May work in construction
- Is married and is abusive to wife and children (Groth, 1977)

Anger-Excitation Rapist

The **anger-excitation rapist** is the most dangerous of the four. He may be sadistic and inclined to cause serious injury or death. He enjoys the victim's response to pain and is sexually excited by it. He plans his rapes in detail to foster his dark and sadistic fantasies. His motivation is the physical and psychological domination and the terrorizing of his victims. His attacks become more ritualized and brutal as he gains experience and discovers that the prior level of violence did not provide the satisfaction he sought. He often will abduct his victims in order to take them somewhere he can brutalize them without interruption. The anger-excitation rapist

- Plans his assaults carefully
- Incorporates his fantasies into the assault plan
- Attempts to hide his identity
- Wears gloves initially
- Becomes more violent in the face of resistance
- Rapes at any time
- Selects victims from anywhere
- Uses brutality to subdue his victims
- Remains calm during assault
- Removes victims' clothing by cutting it off
- May make video recordings of his assaults
- Feels no remorse (Groth, 1977)

Of particular importance is the length of time the assailant remains at the scene of the crime. The longer he is there, the higher the probability of his having left trace evidence. Because the offender is likely to have committed other sexual assaults, it is possible to recognize patterns that may assist in predicting future conduct. The mobility of American society makes it possible for an offender to commit crimes in many different jurisdictions. It is imperative that sex crime information be compiled into computer databases and that jurisdictions share their information.

■ Nuisance Sex Crimes

There are over 60,000 sex offenders incarcerated in the United States today, the majority for sexual assault and other violent sex crimes. Recent research has suggested that many of these violent sexual offenders have histories of sexual behaviors that are considered nuisance behavior. Nuisance sexual behaviors are sex acts that cause no obvious physical harm to the practitioners or their victims. The importance of recognizing nuisance sexual behaviors is that some practitioners move into more serious sexual offenses.

Most of us have heard of the word "fetish," and Internet searches will disclose a large number of Web sites specializing in fetishistic behavior. A **paraphilia** is a condition in which a person becomes obsessively responsive to and dependent upon an unusual stimulus or fantasy (the **fetish**) necessary to maintain sexual arousal or achieve orgasm. Paraphilia (also known as fetishism) is seldom a single deviant behavior but rather a laundry list of activities with sexual connotations. Not all paraphiliacs graduate into violent sexual offenders, but some do. It is for this reason that a passing familiarity need be developed with the more common paraphilias, including the following:

- **Scoptophilia (voyeurism):** Sexual arousal by watching the private, intimate behaviors of others. Many burglaries are perpetrated for the theft of intimate apparel rather than valuables. Voyeurism seems to have been a common pastime of many sex-related murderers.
- **Exhibitionism:** The deliberate, inappropriate exposure of one's (usually a male) genitalia.
- **Bestiality:** Sex with animals. It is known that serial killers often experience a constellation of characteristics known as the serial killer trilogy: enuresis, pyromania, and animal torture. Animal torture is a form of bestiality called zoosadism (Holmes and Holmes, 2002).
- **Gerontophilia:** The use of an elderly person for sexual purposes. Some serial offenders concentrate on elderly women. Those who sexually assault the elderly are involved in sadistic gerontosexuality. Although elderly women are not often the targets of sexual assaults, when they are, they are more likely to be injured or killed.

Pornography and Criminality

There have been lengthy and heated debates on the role that pornography plays in violent criminal behavior. For each study that concludes there is a relationship between pornography and sex crimes, another disputes that finding. What we do know is that pornography has become more available today through the Internet. We know that pornography is no longer solely the purview of men, and we know that child pornography is illegal. Forty-eight states have passed laws concerning child pornography, and the federal government is still wrestling with the United States Supreme Court to find a federal statute that stands constitutional scrutiny.

Although most people have no interest in child pornography and find it offensive, pedophiles comprise the largest group of individuals who view, exchange, and sell child pornography. The Internet has brought these people together to facilitate the viewing of child pornography and is also the vehicle through which pedophiles originate contact with children. By cruising children's chat rooms, pedophiles can locate and seduce children into meetings that lead to abuse or abduction. The Internet allows pedophiles to discuss "hunting grounds" and tactics. They may also trade in abducted children.

It is unrealistic to believe that law enforcement will eradicate child pornography from the Internet, considering the global resources that are not susceptible to United States regulation. The approach of law enforcement has been proactive. Many federal and state agencies use the tools of the pedophile to monitor pedophilic behavior. An astute understanding of the predatory nature of the pedophile and the computer tactics used to find children and child pornography has allowed law enforcement to increase the risk to pedophiles of hunting for children in public forums.

The efforts of law enforcement have driven pedophiles further underground and fostered affinity groups. Seeking to legitimize their position in a permissive social atmosphere, many pedophiles have "come out" and joined Internet groups that have stated philosophies pertaining to the "health benefits" of "loving children." Numerous Web sites of such groups exist, who as a result of police pressure have organized and seek the protection of the First Amendment in putting forth a position that attempts to justify their deviance. Pedophile chat rooms, bulletin boards, and photo exchanges are available on the Internet in numbers that make restriction impossible. It is only through parental and community vigilance that children can be protected.

Historically, a paraphiliac was an island unto himself or herself. Informal means of identification were developed and groups formed. Most practitioners were discreet, if not invisible within mainstream society. The sexual revolution of the 1960s brought many of these individuals forward, and society as a whole became more tolerant of "deviant" sexual behavior. The media have brought what heretofore has been branded deviant into our living rooms on cable and into movie theaters. The Internet has demonstrated that no matter how unusual the behavior, there is an interest group for it out there somewhere.

■ Summary

In this chapter we traced the history of sexual assault and the early impediments to successful sexual assault investigation and prosecutions. The key to sexual assault investigations, as in all other investigations, is training. For the investigation of sexual assaults, those agencies that have specialized sexual assault investigation teams seem to fare better in the investigation and in gaining the trust and cooperation of the victim to assure a knowledgeable, believable, and successful trial witness. It might be worth pointing out at this point: no matter the quality of investigation, without a confident, competent witness the trial outcome will not be satisfying to the state, the victim nor the investigator.

The most important part of this chapter deals with interviewing the victim and collecting evidence from the victim. It is imperative that both are done with sensitivity while understanding the long-range goals of the investigation. Explaining to the victim what is going to happen and why goes a long way in procuring the victim's cooperation and trust. It would seem that one of the unspoken objectives of sexual investigations is to convince the victim that she was not at fault and that what happened to her in no way diminishes her as a woman or as citizen.

Sexual assault can be the afterthought or a primary motivation in burglaries. Home burglaries that are interrupted by a women living alone may result in rape. It then becomes necessary to process the crime scene for both rape and burglary. The next chapter discusses the nature of the burglary investigation.

■ Key Terms

aggravated sexual assault: Sexual assault in which serious bodily injury results, a deadly weapon was used, or the victim was kidnapped

anger-excitation rapist: Type of rapist who plans his rapes in detail and may be sadistic and inclined to cause serious injury or death; his motivation is the physical and psychological domination and the terrorizing of his victims

anger-retaliatory rapist: Type of rapist who vents his anger upon and attempts to punish the opposite sex with sexual assault

aspermia: A condition that prevents spermatozoa from appearing in a male's seminal fluids

cortex: Portion of the hair shaft that is made up of cells that are aligned parallel to the length of the hair; useful for determining hair color and ascertaining individual points of comparison

cross-contamination: The spreading of trace evidence from one item to another item that did not contain that trace evidence when the crime occurred

cuticle: Portion of the hair shaft that is made of overlapping cells that have keratinized (hardened) and flattened to form scales; useful for determining if the hair in question is human

diaphorase: Enzyme that exists in three distinctive forms and is present in sperm only in humans; the discovery of the enzyme is useful in eliminating innocent subjects and can be useful in tracing the assailant

dye composition: The mixture of dyes used to obtain a particular color or shade

fallacy of innocence: The false belief that a person who is found not guilty in a trial is innocent

fetish: An object or body part whose real or fantasied presence is psychologically necessary for sexual gratification and is an object of obsession

gender-specific: Limited to one gender

hair brushings: Head hair and pubic hair samples gathered to obtain any foreign blood, tissue, fibers, or hair that may have come from the assailant, the assailant's vehicle or clothing, or the assault location, and to obtain control samples of the victim's hair so that when a suspect has been identified, it may be determined whether hair on the suspect's person or clothing came from the victim

manufactured fibers: Machine-made fibers

medulla: Portion of the hair shaft that appears to form a central canal running through the center of the hair

natural fibers: Fibers that come from animals or plants

paraphilia: A condition in which a person becomes obsessively responsive to and dependent upon an unusual stimulus or fantasy necessary to maintain sexual arousal or achieve orgasm; also known as fetishism

pluckings: Samples of control hair that are obtained by pulling hairs from the victim

polymer: A very large molecule made by linking together a series of repeating units

power-assertive rapist: Type of power rapist who seldom plans his attack or stalks his victim and whose rapes are generally a product of opportunity

power-reassurance rapist: Type of power rapist whose goal is to assert power over the victim and prove his own manhood

regenerated fibers: Manufactured fibers made of processed raw materials that are chemically treated

scrapings: Particles under the fingernails and toenails that may be obtained in an effort to detect hair, fibers, blood, or tissue from the assailant

seminal stains: Traces of semen that may be found in three localities: on the victim, at the crime scene, and on the suspect; use of an ultraviolet light is helpful for locating seminal stains

sex crimes investigator: Investigator who has been taught to be sensitive to the physical, psychological, and emotional needs of sexual assault victims, and has been trained in what is required for the successful investigation of sexual assaults

sex crimes kit: Assortment of equipment that is useful for collecting evidence of a sex crime from a victim

spermatozoa: The male reproductive germ cells

spousal immunity: The notion that sex was a husband's right and a wife's duty, and therefore that sexual assault by a person against his spouse was not a crime

standards of resistance: Two standards, maximum and reasonable resistance, that evolved for the force element to apply in the common-law definition of rape

swabbings: Specimens taken with a swab from the mouth, anus, and vaginal cavity to detect the presence of seminal fluid or spermatozoa

synthetic fibers: Fibers that are produced from chemicals

trace evidence carriers: Items on which trace evidence is likely to be found

■ Review Questions

1. What role has victim resistance historically played in the prosecution of rapists?
2. What is a gender-specific crime, and how does the concept apply to sexual assaults?
3. What is spousal immunity?
4. What makes a sexual assault into a case of aggravated sexual assault?
5. Why is it incorrect to view a jury's verdict of acquittal as establishing the defendant's innocence?
6. What type of training should a sex crimes investigator receive?
7. What is typically included in a rape kit?
8. Why are hair pluckings (as opposed to hair brushings) needed in rape investigations?
9. What is aspermia and what importance might it have in a sexual assault investigation?
10. What is the significance of the enzyme diaphorase?
11. What three components make up a human hair?
12. What is the significance of continuous medullation in human hair?
13. What is a regenerated fiber?
14. What is a polymer?
15. Who is Wayne Bertram Williams?
16. Who is Dr. A. Nicholas Groth, and what did he contribute to the study of sexual assailants?
17. What are trace evidence carriers?
18. What are the characteristics of a power-reassurance rapist?
19. What are the characteristics of an anger-excitation rapist?
20. Why have women historically been reluctant to report rapes?
21. What is a paraphilia?
22. Why should nuisance sexual behaviors be of interest to the police?
23. List three paraphilias that may escalate into more serious behavior.

24. What role has the Internet played in fetishistic behavior?

25. What role does the Internet play in child pornography?

■ **Bibliography** ▬▬▬▬▬▬▬▬▬▬▬▬▬▬▬

Gilbert, J.N. (1998). *Criminal investigation.* Upper Saddle River, NJ: Prentice Hall.

Groth, A.N. (1977). Rape: Power, anger and sexuality. *American Journal of Psychiatry* 134, 11–17.

Holmes, S.T., & Holmes, R.M. (2002). *Sex crimes.* Thousand Oaks, CA: Sage Publications.

Laing, D.K. (1990). The standardization of thin-layer chromatographic systems for comparisons of fiber dyes. *Journal of Forensic Science Society* 30, 299–304.

Pounds, C.A., & Smalldon, K.W. (1975). The transfer of fibers between clothing materials during simulated contacts and their persistence during wear. *Journal of Forensic Science Society* 15, 29–37.

Saferstein, R. (1995). *Criminalistics: An introduction to forensic science.* Englewood Cliffs, NJ: Prentice Hall.

Theft and Burglary

Upon completion of this chapter students will demonstrate an understanding of:

- The different types of burglary
- Entry techniques used to facilitate a burglary
- Tool marks and other impressions left at burglary crime scenes
- The different types of motor vehicle theft

In common law, taking the property of another for the purpose of depriving that person of ownership was called **larceny**. It required three basic elements:

1. A taking
2. **Asportation** (movement of the items taken)
3. An intent to deprive the owner

All three elements are problematic in our contemporary understanding of theft. In many instances, a person may be convinced to voluntarily part with his or her property, which is obviously counter to the common-law notion of "taking." Some things are so large as to prohibit movement, such as a house, land, and trees, yet today, through fraud, a person may have his or her house, land, or trees stolen. Clearly, for larceny to make sense today, there must have been an evolution of the elements. Taking may now be real or constructive, and asportation may also be real or constructive.

In common law and presently in some jurisdictions, there are numerous types of theft, with different names and definitions, in which one of the traditional elements of theft is lacking. Theft by false pretext, for example, occurs when a person voluntarily relinquishes property under some pretext that allows the thief to deprive the owner of the property. Theft by embezzlement occurs when a person entrusted with property uses the property to his or her own advantage (**conversion**) and with the intent to deprive the owner of possession.

Over time, legislatures and the judiciary have recognized many related offenses that differ in some degree from basic theft, and the result has been an ever-expanding and confusing network of theft-related statutes. Many jurisdictions, aware of the imaginativeness of thieves, decided to consolidate the theft offenses into one statute, forsaking the categories of theft by false pretext, conversion by a bailee, shoplifting, theft from a person, acquisition of property by threat, swindling, swindling by worthless check, embezzlement, extortion, receiving or concealing embezzled property, receiving or concealing stolen property, credit card theft, theft of trade secrets, forgery, and fraud. These special types of theft indicate how earnestly criminals work to separate people from their property.

Theft has come to be defined as an unlawful intentional appropriation of property. Intent to deprive ownership is questionable as an element in only one type of theft: joyriding. Many jurisdictions have added a new section to their penal codes. In addition to statutes prohibiting theft of a motor vehicle, which involves intent to permanently deprive ownership, there are now statutes dealing with **unauthorized use of a motor vehicle**. The lesser deprivation reduces the seriousness of the offense in those jurisdictions that recognize joyriding as differing from outright theft.

Once theft offenses were consolidated, the magnitude of a theft offense became based on how much was taken. Excepted from this consolidation were the offenses of burglary and robbery. The elements of burglary differ in significant degree from those of theft, and burglary is still treated as a separate and more serious offense than theft. Because of the personal confrontation and threat of personal violence involved in robbery, it too is treated as a separate and more serious offense (see Chapter 12 for a discussion of robbery).

■ Burglary

Types of Burglary

Most burglaries are products of opportunity perpetrated by noncareer burglars. Open doors and windows are an opportunist's invitation. Uncollected mail and newspapers are also an invitation. Originally, burglary was referred to as **breaking and entering** and may still be called that by investigators. Burglaries in common law required a *breaking* (forced entry) component and a physical entry into the premises. Today, neither element is required but both generally are present. The breaking component is lacking when someone originally invited onto the premises extends the visit and secrets himself or herself upon the premises to await an opportunity to commit theft. It is also lacking when entry is made through openings inviting access. Finally, there are those cases in which the burglar does not physically intrude onto the premises at all but, for example, pokes a stick through an open window to withdraw a purse on a nearby table.

Most officers understand the statutory elements of a burglary. In most jurisdictions, a **burglary** involves (1) a person who (2) enters or remains on the premises (3) of another (4) without effective consent of the owner (5) for the purpose of committing a felony or theft. Keep in mind that misdemeanor theft rises to a felony when coupled with an unlawful entry of a dwelling. Often burglaries are further subdivided into burglaries of:

- Dwellings
- Dwellings with residents present
- Commercial establishments
- Other structures
- Vehicles

When charging a suspect, confusion may arise because of unspoken aspects of the burglary elements. If a person, while supposedly on a business trip, enters his or her own home after the family is asleep and steals numerous valuable items so that an insurance claim can be made, has a burglary been committed? Which element is missing?

A person cannot burglarize his or her own home: It must be the premises of another. Where would you find the answer to that question? The statute only implies the answer. Try this one: A person trains a monkey to gather bright, shiny objects and throws the monkey through an open window. The animal returns with a cache of jewelry. Has a burglary been committed? Strictly speaking, entry by a person is required. A monkey is not a person. Has a burglary been committed? Where would you go to find the answer? The point is that statutory language and elements may not be sufficient to determine what crime has in fact been committed. It is necessary to be aware of various state court decisions that have interpreted the statute.

Penal codes come in two versions: annotated and unannotated. Annotations are short summaries of court decisions that have helped to interpret vague or ambiguous portions of a statute. Every investigator should have an annotated copy of the appropriate penal code and be familiar with the code elements as well as the court interpretations. How else would it be possible to figure out the crimes involved in a situation like the following? A man follows his wife to the home of a friend and sees her in an amorous tryst with the man of the house. The irate husband backs his pickup into the living room, hoping to crush the occupants. What crimes have been committed? Traffic violations, trespass, criminal mischief, disorderly conduct, reckless conduct, assault, aggravated assault, attempted murder? Probably the most serious offense will determine the charge ultimately brought. The most likely offense for the prosecution to prove would be aggravated assault. However, the behavior in question also constitutes a burglary. Did you get that? If not, go back to the elements of burglary and examine each with respect to the irate husband scenario.

Most burglaries occur at night, usually between 10:00 PM and 2:00 AM. It is during this time that a burglar has the best chance of entering a dwelling without being identified. The career burglar will have ascertained that the dwelling is vacant and may look for clues that the occupants are not at home. Burglaries of residences are riskier than burglaries of commercial sites, because they may be interrupted by the arrival of the residents and they generally carry a higher statutory penalty than commercial burglaries. Less risk is associated with commercial burglaries, except for the security measures taken by the owners to prohibit unlawful entry. Commercial burglaries also require greater planning and may require specific expertise, such as knowledge of computer and security systems, lock picking, safe cracking, and the value of items to be stolen.

Residential burglars focus on homes, condominiums, and apartments in the affluent sections of a community. Most home security measures, short of electronic surveillance, can be overcome easily. The professional burglar generally will seek valuables that can be transported easily, preferring money, negotiable securities, jewelry, and small art objects of value. Some professionals may specialize in art or jewelry and use a network established to provide ready disposal of the stolen items. Drug addicts compose a significant portion of household burglars and steal to support their habits. (A habit is often referred with a dollar amount, as in "I got a $250-a-day Jones [habit].") They will steal items for which a professional would not put himself or herself at risk. Amateur burglars do not specialize, nor do drug addicts. They steal whatever may be turned for a profit.

As much as the public deplores burglars and thieves, it supports their efforts, in a sense. Burglars would have no market if nonburglars refused to buy stolen merchandise. The **fence** (seller) is the middleman necessary to let the majority of us who purchase stolen property pretend we have not been involved. As in most con games, it is our desire to get something for nothing that allows us to be conned and to blindly (or not so blindly) support the theft industry. If a deal looks too good to be true, then it probably is too good to be true and involves either a con or stolen property. A too-good-to-be-believed deal should put the citizen on notice that this is something better passed by.

Juveniles form a subclass of amateur burglars. Amateurs are often armed and pose a serious threat of violence to unsuspecting returning residents. Juveniles characteristically resort to unnecessary destruction and bravado during the commission of their burglaries. Because the burglaries are usually committed by several juveniles working together, bravura is expected and displayed. They may eat the residents' food, drink their beverages, wear their clothes, use the phone, leave disparaging notes on mirrors or walls, and soil the house with feces or urine. Although the results of the juvenile burglars' gross behavior can be unpleasant, the tremendous amount of trace evidence left at the scene makes positive identification of suspects easy.

The professional burglar plans his or her crime, its execution, the departure from the site, and the disposal of stolen goods. The nature and quality of the burglary will determine the level of detail required in the planning as well as the number of people needed to pull off the burglary. The most successful professional burglars work alone and hit big, infrequently, and discreetly.

Entry Techniques

Burglers use various tools in gaining entry to the premises or to locked containers. Some of the more common techniques to gain entry include the following (Osterberg and Ward, 1992):

- Doors and window faces can be pried using a **jimmy**, and locks can be picked using burglar picks or commercially designed pick systems that have a pistol-grip handle and interchangeable picks.
- The lock cylinder can be knocked out of a lock by using a slap hammer.
- Windows can be broken and doors kicked down.
- By smashing a store window, a burglar can grab the displayed items.
- By cutting out a glass pane with a glass cutter, a burglar can reach through, unlock, and open the window or door.
- Credit cards or other thin, flexible devices can be slipped between the lock and the doorjamb to force the lock back.
- Hinge pins on a door may be removed, allowing the whole door to be removed.
- Adjacent walls may be removed or penetrated to facilitate entry.
- Explosives and heavy tools may be used to open safes.
- Bump keys can be used to jar loose the lock pins.

Tool marks and entry evidence are important for identifying the modus operandi and the individual burglar.

Tool Marks and Other Impressions

A **tool mark** is any impression, cut, gouge, or abrasion caused by a tool coming into contact with another object (Saferstein, 1995). Impressions can be found at burglary crime scenes on door and window frames through which entry was made. These impressions are made with screwdrivers, crowbars, or other devices used to pry doors and windows open. An impression itself usually renders only class characteristics indicating the type of tool, although it can have unique characteristics that allow it to be matched to a single tool. A tool retains machined marks from its manufacture, just as do firearms. These marks and striations are changed as the result of nicks and breaks in the tool's working surface that occur as the tool is used and misused. The pattern and shape of these modifications are altered by continued use, further individualizing the imperfections. It is unlikely that any two tools will have manufacturing striations, wear markings, and breaks that are exactly the same. It is these small imperfections that allow the crime laboratory to determine that the impressions at the crime scene were left by a suspect tool.

If a tool edge is scraped against a surface that is softer than the metal of the tool, it will leave a series of markings that reflect the pattern of the tool edge. These markings and the imperfections on a suspect tool can be compared in the laboratory through the use of the comparison microscope. The comparison may show an association between the marks and the tool. The more individualized the tool edge pattern, the more definitive the comparison.

In handling tool mark impressions it is important to relegate the mark to a photographic record, first from an intermediate distance and then a close up. Once the impression has been photographed it is ready to be worked. A molded impression of the marks should be taken. If the portion of the entry way bearing a tool mark can be removed and transported to the laboratory, a molded impression may not be necessary. Do not examine the marking with the aid of a ballpoint or metal probe. Any marks made to the impression that were not a product of the original tool may render the impression inadmissible at the time of trial.

Forced entry usually is accomplished with the aid of tools, the indentations left can be lifted and preserved with a casting compound similar to Durocast that Sirchie Laboratories makes (**Figure 14–1**). The putty-like material enables castings to be made on

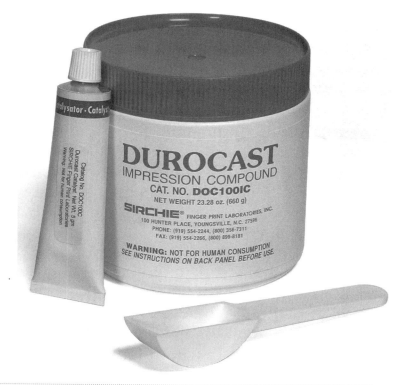

Figure 14–1 Durocast pictures-bottle.

Courtesy of SIRCHIE Finger Print Laboratories, Inc.

horizontal or vertical surfaces. The casting material can be molded into a piece long and wide enough to cover the tool mark. Once pressed gently into the tool mark and allowed to dry, the casting material can be removed and a reverse impression of the tool mark has now been transferred to the casting material, which should then be bagged and tagged as would any other evidence (**Figure 14–2a through 14–2d**).

There may be impressions other than tool marks left at a burglary crime scene, such as shoe or **tire impressions**. The major task of the investigator is to preserve a reproductive cast of any such impression until it can be transported to and examined by the crime laboratory. The first step in processing any impression, whether of a tool, shoe, or tire, is to preserve it through photography, bringing out as much detail from as many different

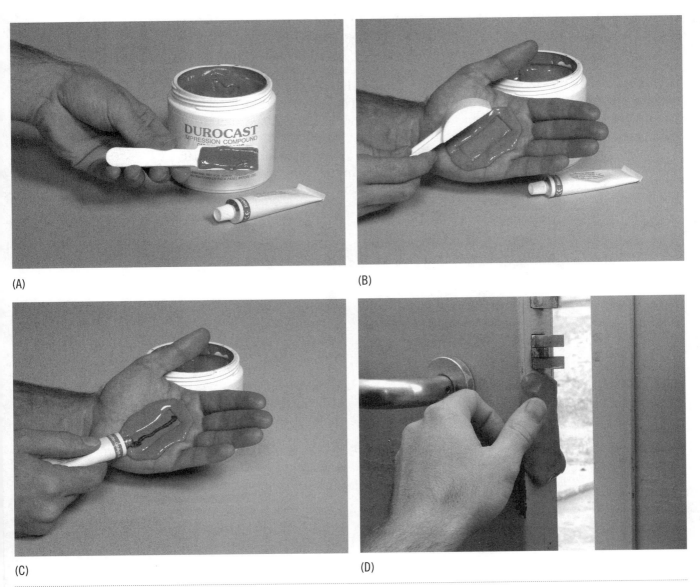

(A)

(B)

(C)

(D)

Figure 14–2 Durocast pictures-application.

angles and heights as possible. Photographs are not the preferred laboratory specimens but can supplement and support reproductive casts should the casts for lab comparisons be lost, damaged, or destroyed. Tire impressions can be duplicated by inking the suspect tread with fingerprint impression ink and running the inked tire over paper (**Figure 14–3**). The best impression involves the entire circumference of the tire, not just the suspect location. A new device is available from evidence equipment manufacturers that involves a print-out system. Some defects will not be visible unless the tire is under load. The new system uses two sheets of paper affixed back to back. One sheet facing the other is treated with carbon (much like old typewriter carbon paper). Once the tire is run over the two sheets, the carbon-sided page leaves an impression of the tire tread on the clean piece of paper opposite it (**Figure 14–4a and 14–4b**). The carbon-treated side is then removed and the side with the transferred impression is treated as any other evidence (**Figure 14–5**).

Shoe impressions may be taken at a crime scene or from a suspect. Crime scene shoe impressions require that the investigator record the footprints photographically and then make a casting of the impression. Something needs to be placed around the footprint to serve as a dam. Anything that is immersed in the tread impression should not be removed, any loose debris may be removed, but the margins of the shoe impression are very fragile and must be avoided. The impression should be prepared by spraying a commercial hardener onto the surface. After a few minutes to allow the hardener to dry, a light coating of release agent can be applied. This will allow removal of the cast without bringing attached soil. In the old days, plaster of Paris was used to cast footprint impressions; it worked well, but shrunk in the drying process by about 10%. New casting materials dry without shrinking. Many of these new casting solutions come premixed with a hardener embedded into the package (**Figue 14–6**). Shelf life is indefinite as long as

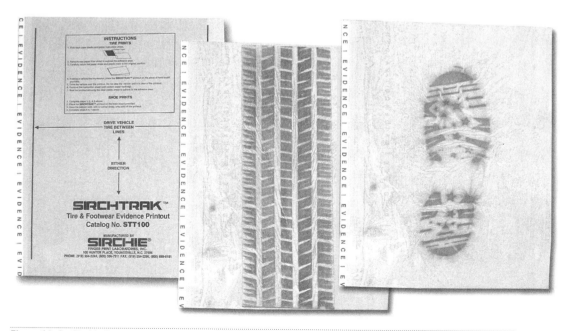

Figure 14–3 Sirchtrak.

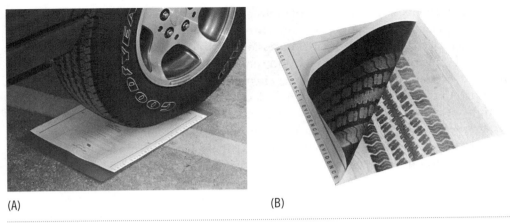

(A)   (B)

Figure 14–4   Tire impressions.

Courtesy of SIRCHIE Finger Print Laboratories, Inc.

Figure 14–5   Tire track.

Courtesy of SIRCHIE Finger Print Laboratories, Inc.

Figure 14–6   Shake and cast.

Courtesy of SIRCHIE Finger Print Laboratories, Inc.

the hardener ampoule is not broken and mixed with the casting material. Breaking the hardener ampoule and mixing it makes the material time dependent.

It is important not to pour the mixture directly onto the impression; it can destroy ridge character. Pouring the mixture onto a spoon held close to the surface of the impression will prevent damage to the impression. Once the contents of the package have been poured over the impression to a depth of no more than half of an inch (12.7 mm) and into the dam, all that is left to do is to wait for the casting material to dry. Once dry, the impression can be removed from the frame and tagged and bagged. Nothing should be removed from the bottom of the casting to avoid damage to the impression. The lab can remove it without causing damage.

Impressions in snow pose a real challenge to the investigator. Snow is highly fragile and subject to changes in the weather. Because most gypsum-based casting materials generate heat during the curing process, it is necessary to provide something to insulate the shoeprint from the casting material. Impression wax is sold in an aerosol applicator that can be sprayed over the print; once the impression is protected, the casting material can be poured (**Figures 14–7 through 14–9**).

Making an impression of a suspect's shoe used to be done by inking the bottom of the shoe and pressing it onto paper; today new methods are available. Once again, it is best to take an impression under load. Footwear impression lifts use a Styrofoam-type substance in a long box; the suspect steps into the box and onto the foam. The suspect's weight should be controlled so that the suspect does not step all the way through the

Figure 14–7   Placement of the dam.
© By Ian Miles-Flashpoint Pictures/Alamy Images

Figure 14–8   After pouring.
© Pablo Paul/Alamy Images

Figure 14–9 Cast footprint (mud and sand).

© 67 photo/Alamy Images

foam to be bottom of the box, thereby losing the impression. Once the impression has been laid, the same procedure for casting a footprint is used (**Figure 14–10**). In this case, once the casting material has dried and hardened, the foam can be torn away from the cast. The remaining cast is then tagged and bagged.

Commercial electrostatic dust lifters consist of a high voltage power supply, a nickel-plated steel ground plate, and a metallized lifting mat. In the old days it required two

Figure 14–10 Bio-foam box.

Courtesy of SIRCHIE Finger Print Laboratories, Inc.

lifting mats, a positively charged mat and a negatively charged mat; today only one sheet is used along with a metal ground plate. The mat is gently floated onto the dust print to be lifted. Once the mat is in place, a fingerprint ink roller can be used to smooth the surface of the mat. As high voltage is applied to the lifting mat, it takes on a negative charge and the ground plate becomes positive (**Figure 14–11**). Any dust present under the mat will take on a positive charge and will then be attracted to the negatively charged collection mat. A dust print that is transferred to the lifting mat will appear as a precise mirror image of the original print (**Figure 14–12**).

The value of a footprint is determined by the number of class characteristics that match the class characteristics of a suspect item. Agreement in size, shape, or design can only prove that the item in question may have made the impression; a definitive identification cannot be made on the basis of class characteristics alone. It is the presence

Figure 14–11 Electrostatic dust print lifter.

Courtesy of SIRCHIE Finger Print Laboratories, Inc.

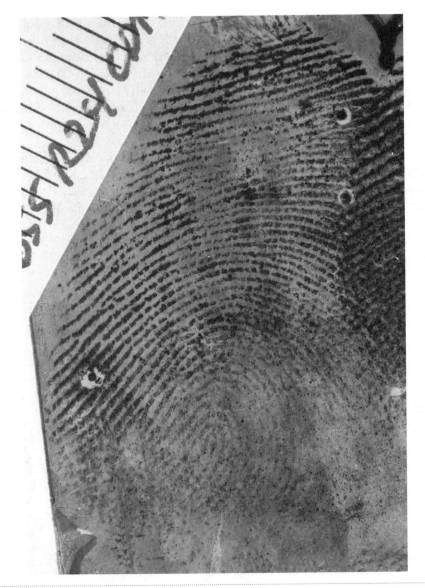

Figure 14–12 Lifted dust print.

Courtesy of Maine State Police Crime Laboratory

of individual characteristics from wear, breaks, or tears that, if numerous, will support an opinion that the cast or recovered impression came from one source and one source only—the suspect item (Saferstein, 1995).

The Burglary Investigation

Patrol officers typically are the first responders to burglaries and these officers consequently face the greatest risk. A burglary-in-progress call holds the potential for violence, although burglary is legally a property crime. Not until the initial call has been resolved does the investigator arrive on the scene. Once again, it is imperative that first responders be treated as members of the investigative team. Any investigation, if it is to be successful, depends largely on scene integrity, but none more so than a burglary investigation. In a homicide, the body and mess preclude rapid repopulation of the premises. In a burglary, the victims feel personally violated and hasten to remove evidence of that violation and determine how extensive it was and what was taken. It is the responding officers' responsibility to prevent anyone from degrading the integrity of the crime scene—that includes residents as well as patrol officers.

The patrol officers can be of assistance to the investigator in a number of ways, such as by doing the following:

- Locating or notifying owners of the burglary and keeping them at a distance until the investigator arrives
- Locating witnesses (anyone who has seen or heard anything that may assist in the investigation)
- Locating the party reporting the burglary if other than the owner
- Listing items taken if owners have already assessed their losses
- Securing the crime scene

Once the investigator arrives on the scene, the primary objective is to recognize and preserve possible sites of forensic evidence. This objective, however, is not the first addressed. The investigator will want to determine the point and **method of entry** onto the premises. The **point of entry** will provide information about the method of entry

OFFICER'S NOTEBOOK

Processing a Crime Scene in Which Tool Marks Are Apparent

It is an investigator's responsibility, whenever practical, to submit the entire object possessing the tool marks to the laboratory. If the object cannot be removed for submission, then photographs and cast impressions need to be provided. Neither photographs nor cast impressions will allow as definitive a comparison as would the actual object.

Under no circumstances should a suspect tool be fit into the impression. An attempt to do so will alter the impression and raise serious questions as to crime scene integrity and the quality of any comparison information provided by the crime laboratory.

If both a suspect tool and impression are available at the crime scene, they should be packaged separately so as to avoid any contact between the two. Failure to separately package and protect the suspect tool and impression could result in a cursory contact that might alter or add to the imperfections of either, rendering a comparison more difficult or impossible. In addition, a tool may bear paint or fiber trace evidence that could be contaminated or destroyed in the handling.

OFFICER'S NOTEBOOK

Processing a Crime Scene in Which Footprints Are Found

Footprints made on surfaces that lend themselves to fingerprint lifting can be lifted in the same fashion as a latent fingerprint. Lift tape large enough to accommodate a footprint is available commercially. The tape should be placed carefully over the impression, just as it would be placed over a fingerprint. A fingerprint roller can.be used to squeeze out any air bubbles created by the tape. The lifted footprint should be placed on a white or black backing, just as a fingerprint would be.

When shoe or tire impressions are left in dirt, preservation is achieved through photography first and a reproductive cast (**moulage**) second. If dirt or debris adheres to the cast, it should not be removed but packaged with the cast and transported to the crime laboratory.

and provide an indication as to the direction from which the burglar(s) approached the building. The area of approach may contain footprint, tire print, or eyewitness evidence that is easily destroyed, lost, or overlooked. Prior to examining the point of entry, the investigator should examine this area to discover whatever evidence there is and prevent its irretrievable loss. Examining a window from the outside without examining the grounds first may lead to the trampling of footprints or tire impressions. Likewise, finding out where the burglars parked will allow identification and preservation of any tire impressions, cigarette butts, litter, or vehicular fluid deposits left by the burglars and will prevent haphazard parking by the police and others from contaminating this part of the crime scene. Once the approach areas have been processed, an examination of the interior part of the crime scene can begin.

The most obvious points of entry are windows and doors. An absence of evidence of forced entry suggests that the burglar gained entry by using a key, lock pick, jimmy, bump keys, or by coming through an unsecured window or door. It should also raise the question of whether a member of the household assisted in or perpetrated the burglary. Burglaries are sometimes committed by a disenchanted or drug-using juvenile family member or by his or her friends and are also sometimes committed for the purpose of fraudulently acquiring an insurance payoff. Suspicions of household involvement must be handled tactfully and held in abeyance until they are corroborated by other evidence.

Once point of entry has been ascertained, the entry portal should be examined for tool marks, fiber evidence, and fingerprints. Any evidence of tool marks must be documented photographically and removed to the crime laboratory for examination. Reproductive casts are second best. Prior to making a cast or removing the tool-marked item, it should be examined for fibers and fingerprints. An alternative strategy is to handle the marked item as though it contains both and transport it to the crime laboratory to be processed for fibers and prints. A burglar crawling through a window will undoubtedly leave some fiber evidence; the trick is in finding it and processing it. Tool marks are so forensically valuable, however, that nothing should be done with them that is not absolutely necessary, thereby avoiding the possibility of altering them.

Once the point of entry and the **approach to entry** (the area that led to the entry of the crime scene) have been ascertained and processed, the investigator can turn to the interior of the crime scene. It is at this point that a walk-through with the owner can be instructive. The owner can point out the absence or presence of things that should not be there. A tool, used chewing gum, a cigarette butt, or other evidence might be otherwise overlooked. The owner can also assist in determining what things the burglar might have touched as he or she traveled through the dwelling. The crime scene, including avenues of approach, should be portrayed in a drawing, along with appropriate measurements.

Witnesses should be identified and interviewed, and in-depth interviews should be conducted with the owner and the entire family. A list of family associates, especially juveniles, should be compiled. Neighbors should be contacted, routinely, to help narrow down the time of the burglary based on what they may have heard or seen. Reducing the possible time frame can indicate whether the burglary was planned. Narrow time frames suggest two possibilities: the burglar was a very lucky amateur burglar, or the burglar was provided with information.

One very successful method of catching burglars and reducing the threat of burglary is to stamp serial numbers on valuables and record the numbers. Serial-numbered items are more readily identifiable than items for which only physical descriptions are provided. The serial number of a stereo can be included in statewide and nationwide computer databases used to identify stolen property. In addition, when receivers or purchasers of stolen items are confronted with the irrefutability of a serial number, they may become much more cooperative and willingly identify the persons from whom the property was received.

■ Motor Vehicle Theft

Historically cars have been stolen for five reasons: (1) joyriding, (2) parts, (3) resale, (4) insurance fraud, and (5) crime use. Temporarily depriving an owner of his or her vehicle, in many jurisdictions, does not rise to the level of auto theft. Most **joyriding** ends with the vehicle being abandoned and available for recovery. Not much in the way of investigation is required in joyriding cases if the culprits are not caught in possession of the vehicle. This section concentrates on the investigation of the remaining four types of auto theft.

Thefts generally occur at night, and autos are no exception. The most commonly reported crime is a stolen vehicle. Other crime data may reflect underreporting, but auto thefts are reported universally, probably because of the statutory requirement that autos be insured and because a police report is required to collect on insurance policies for damages or loss or to get a replacement rental vehicle. Unsurprisingly, young people have their vehicles stolen more often than do the elderly. Most vehicles are stolen by juveniles who are often in places that are popular hangouts for other juveniles. About half of all stolen vehicles are recovered in part or whole (Harlow, 1988).

Autos stolen for parts are generally **stripped** of the easily removed, easily transported parts, which are resold to individuals or salvage yard dealers (**Figure 14–13**). A vehicle may be stripped where parked or be stolen and transported to a location where it can be stripped at leisure. The objective is to remove as many valuable parts as possible, excepting the engine block and body, and then abandon the vehicle. Air bags have become a choice

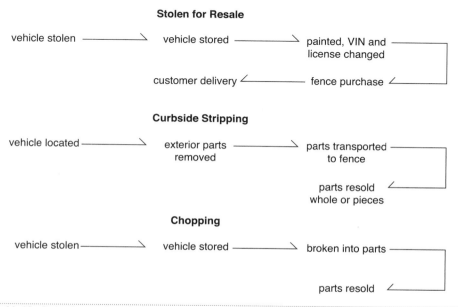

Figure 14–13 Stolen-for-resale, stripping, and chopping flowcharts.

item for thieves in the stripping business. The vehicle is usually recovered close to the place where the removal of parts took place. Most auto components are not stamped with numbers based on a universal numbering system and are therefore virtually impossible to trace. Investigative efforts should focus on storage rental facilities, gas stations, and public and private garages in the area surrounding the spot where the vehicle was abandoned.

Thieves who **chop** a vehicle have in mind the same objective as do those who strip a vehicle: the reduction of the vehicle to its parts. The focus is on the major body components, including doors, fenders, hood, bumpers, and windows—in fact, everything but the frame and the engine block. Auto body components historically have lacked identifying numbers. Manufacturers, aware of stripping and chopping, have begun putting a **vehicle identification number (VIN)** on auto components. The auto thief generally is not the individual who removes the parts. The thief sells the car to a chop shop, and a chopping team reduces it to rubble.

Occasionally a vehicle is stolen for the purpose of resale. The VIN is altered, a new title and license are obtained, and the vehicle is put on the block for sale. Vehicles can be stolen to order, or they can be stolen by a criminal enterprise specializing in appropriating late-model luxury vehicles and altering, transporting, and selling them, both inside and outside the United States.

A vehicle's VIN consists of 17 letters and numbers. Altered or false VINs can be recognized by someone who understands what the letters and numbers represent. The 1st symbol, which is a number, indicates the nation in which the vehicle was manufactured; the 2nd symbol, a letter, indicates the manufacturer (e.g., G stands for General Motors); and the 3rd, a number, indicates the make of the vehicle (e.g., Chevrolet). The next symbol indicates the type of restraints used in the vehicle (e.g., C for seatbelts). The next three symbols, all numbers, constitute the manufacturer's code for the position of the vehicle in the production line and the body type of the vehicle (e.g., van); the next symbol, a letter, indicates the type of engine. The 9th symbol, a number, is a check digit and is used to validate the VIN. The 10th symbol, a letter, tells the year the vehicle was made, and the 11th symbol, a letter, tells the city in which the auto plant is located. The remaining six symbols, all numbers, constitute the production number of the vehicle.

The vehicle most likely to be subjected to forensic examination is the vehicle stolen for use in a crime. The automobile becomes a focal point of the investigation of the crime and is processed for fingerprints, hair, fibers, and any other trace evidence that may linger. The automobile should be processed like any other crime scene.

Auto thefts are difficult to investigate. Those autos stolen for profit are usually stripped or disposed of with little evidence of their passing. Those taken for a joyride are abandoned quickly, leaving little usable evidence in their wake. The number of auto thefts occurring in any major metropolitan area is staggering and unmanageable. Thus, resources are best focused on autos used in other crimes. Most auto investigations proceed along the same lines. A checklist for such an investigation is given in the Officer's Notebook.

Carjacking

The robbery, theft, or attempted theft of a motor vehicle by force or threat of force is **carjacking**. Between 1987 and 1992, carjackings accounted for 2% of the 1.9 million vehicle thefts per year that occurred nationwide. An average of 35,000 completed and attempted carjackings took place each year in the United States between 1987 and 1992.

OFFICER'S NOTEBOOK

Checklist for Use in Vehicle Theft Cases
1. Make, model, license number, and VIN of the vehicle?
   - Names of all known operators of the vehicle
2. Where was the vehicle recovered?
3. How was entry made?
   - Break-in
   - Keyed
4. Who witnessed the theft?
5. When was the theft discovered?
   - By whom?
6. Where was the vehicle last legitimately used?
   - Who used it?
   - For what purpose?
7. Where was the operator at the time of the theft?
   - Witnesses to the operator's location and activities?
8. Where was the owner at the time of the theft?
   - Witnesses to the owner's location and activities?
9. Who has possession of keys to the vehicle?
   - Account for each set of keys.
10. Payment history?
11. Repair history?
12. Owner's financial circumstances?

In 52% of the carjackings, the offender succeeded in stealing the victim's motor vehicle (Klaus, 1998).

Most carjacking victims escape without injury. Offenders most often use a weapon; the weapons of choice are handguns. The potential for violence is high, and the high profile of the crime makes it deserving of serious police effort. It is not a car theft—it is an armed robbery. There are immediate victims and witnesses. The key to the investigation of carjackings is speed. The sooner a description of the vehicle and its occupant is broadcast, the greater the likelihood of capture and recovery.

Often carjacking investigations begin with the recovery of the vehicle or an interview of the victim. Although these are necessary components of the carjacking investigation, they are not the most important. Proximity is always an investigative index. There was a reason why a particular location was selected for the carjacking. Sometimes that reason will not be evident or discoverable, but often it is the answer to the question "Why was this car jacked here?" that will lead to the perpetrators. A number of propositions about the thief or thieves should occur to the carjacking investigator, such as the following:

- They reside in the area.
- They work in the area.
- They play in the area.
- They deal in the area.
- They prey on the area.
- They are known in the area.
- They were transported to the area.

- They walked to the area from nearby.
- They have been to the area before.
- The location was picked for a reason, such as:
  - Proximity to their destination
  - Availability of a vehicle
  - Availability of a particular type of vehicle

Should the vehicle be recovered, it should be processed as though it had been used in a homicide or kidnapping. The interior should be examined for hair and fiber as well as for fingerprints on all hard surfaces, concentrating on class characteristics. Ashtrays, under seats, and the floors may have been repositories for various debris deposited by the carjackers that has forensic value. If carjackers are not apprehended, they will most probably jack another car.

■ Applicable Case Law

Ownership

Generally, a **bona fide** (innocent) buyer of stolen goods receives only those ownership rights possessed by the seller. If the seller has stolen the items sold, then the buyer has no rights to possession or ownership, because the thief had none. The caveat, "Let the buyer beware," puts a bona fide buyer on notice that if the seller is not the owner and has no title to the property transfers, the lawful owner may reclaim the stolen item as having the greater right to possession. This principle can be seen in the case of *Greek Orthodox Church of Cyprus v. Goldberg et al.* (1990).

Intent to Commit Theft

Theft or larceny requires a **specific intent** to deprive an owner of possession of property. The intent to steal may be proved by direct evidence or by circumstantial evidence. Generally, the jury or judge infers intent to steal from the conduct and acts of the defendant. Intent may be obvious or ambiguous. It is the responsibility of the prosecution to prove intent by direct or circumstantial evidence.

CASE IN POINT

Greek Orthodox Church of Cyprus v. Goldberg et al., 1990

Peg Goldberg, an art dealer traveling in Europe in search of art purchases, was told of four early-Christian mosaics that were said to have been found in the rubble of a church in Cyprus and exported to Germany with the permission of the Cyprus government. In fact, they were stolen from the Greek Orthodox Church of Cyprus. While in Germany, she made an offer of purchase and bought them for $1,080,000. They were shipped to the United States. The Orthodox Church made claim for possession based on the fact that they had been stolen and transported to Germany and sold by the thief, not the church. Possession of the mosaics was returned to the church despite the substantial payment made by Ms. Goldberg.

The court held that when circumstances are as suspicious as those that faced Peg Goldberg, prospective purchasers would do best to do more than make a few last-minute phone calls. In such cases, dealers should take steps to ensure that the seller has legal possession of the items being sold. Ms. Goldberg could have had an authenticity check or a full background search of the seller done, could have asked to be provided with the seller's claim to title, or could have purchased buyer's insurance. Had she done any of these things, she might have discovered in time what she discovered too late: The church had a valid, superior, and enforceable claim to these mosaics and was entitled to receive them back.

CASE IN POINT

People v. Jaso, 1979
The defendant left a Sears department store with a bag of merchandise for which he did not pay. He was stopped in the parking lot by security. When confronted, he said that he was simply returning to his vehicle to get his wallet from his auto and that he had intended to return to pay for the merchandise. A struggle ensued, and Jaso was subdued and handcuffed. He was convicted, but on appeal it was determined that the instruction provided to the jury was defective, for it did not include an instruction that "in the crime of theft there must exist in the mind of the perpetrator the specific intent to take property of another and unless such intent so exists that crime is not committed."

CASE IN POINT

Commonwealth of Pennsylvania v. Muniem, 1973
Muniem was found leaving an empty warehouse. He was cooperative, had no loot, and did not resist police efforts to arrest him. He told police that he had to go to the toilet and had looked for a restroom in the empty building. The defendant had entered through an open door. Muniem was married, employed, and had no prior record. The Pennsylvania court ordered him released based on this reasoning:

> The only evidence produced against the appellant is his presence, perhaps as a trespasser, in a vacant building in daylight. . . . When found by the police, he was walking to the open door by which he testified he entered the building. The owner of the building testified that nothing was missing and there was no evidence of a forcible entry, or possession of any burglary tools, other tools or anything else.
>
> Each case must stand on its own facts in determining whether the Commonwealth has sustained its burden of proof. At best, the evidence of the Commonwealth may give rise to suspicion and conjecture of guilt but most certainly does not have such volume and quality capable of reasonably and naturally justifying an inference of a willful and malicious entry into a building with the intent to commit a felony so as to overcome the presumption of innocence and establish guilt beyond a reasonable doubt of the crime of burglary.

Intent in the Case of Burglary

If a defendant is caught in the act of stealing during a burglary, proving intent to commit theft is a fairly straightforward matter. If, however, there is no evidence of theft or of commission of a felony, proof of illegal entry into a premise that has items worthy of theft meets the requirement of proof of theft.

The Illinois Supreme Court held in *People v. Johnson* (1963) that intent must be proved, usually by inference. Proof of unlawful entry into a building that contains property that could be the subject of theft gives rise to an inference that will support the intent requirement for the offense of burglary. It may be assumed that the unlawful entry was not without purpose and that theft was the most likely purpose. However, in the case *Commonwealth of Pennsylvania v. Muniem* (1973), the court found that inconsistent evidence refuting theft after illegal entry was sufficient to dismiss the charge of burglary.

■ Summary

In this chapter we see that burglary can take many forms and that the investigation of burglaries requires attention to detail. Tool marks and impressions left at the scene are the grist of the investigation along with what neighbors see and hear.

Burglaries are the silent dread of everyone who has a lock on his or her door. Many years ago the author intended to enter through the locked gate to his rural home. The whole gate had been pulled down, including the 15-foot-tall, 10-inch cedar posts that held it in place. It was obvious that it had been done intentionally. The police were driving down the entry road and stopped to communicate that their investigation had been completed and that they would appreciate a list of anything that was missing. That moment is etched forever in memory. We often think of burglaries as crimes of property but forget that much of what we have we worked hard for and many things of value are worth more because of the sentiment attached to it. Those who say burglary is a property crime have never been burglarized.

Often burglaries are committed by people in search of or in need of drugs. Much of what is stolen in burglaries is fenced for as little as ten cents on the dollar. That money in many instances is used to fuel a drug habit. In the next chapter we will consider drugs; what they are, what they do, and how law enforcement carries on the war on drugs.

■ Key Terms

approach to entry: The area that led to the entry of the crime scene; often seen as a secondary crime scene, it may include parking areas, sidewalks, yards, and building exteriors

asportation: Movement of items taken from another; one of the three basic elements required for larceny in common law

bona fide: Innocent, genuine; the Latin means "in good faith"

breaking and entering: Term that was originally used for burglary because it required a *breaking* (forced entry) component and a physical entry into the premises

burglary: A crime involving (1) a person who (2) enters or remains on the premises (3) of another (4) without effective consent of the owner (5) for the purpose of committing a felony or theft

carjacking: The robbery, theft, or attempted theft of a motor vehicle by force or threat of force

chopping: Stealing an automobile to remove the major body components, including doors, fenders, hood, bumpers, and windows, in order to sell them

conversion: Using property entrusted to a person by another for the former's advantage and with the intent to deprive the owner of possession.

fence: Seller; the middleman necessary to let the majority of us who purchase stolen property pretend we have not been involved

jimmy: Tool used to pry open doors and windows

joyriding: Stealing an automobile for personal enjoyment

larceny: In common law, taking the property of another for the purpose of depriving that person of ownership; it required three basic elements: a taking; asportation (movement of the items taken); and an intent to deprive the owner

method of entry: The manner and direction from which the burglar(s) approached the building; it is determined by looking at the evidence at the point of entry

moulage: Reproductive cast

point of entry: Place where the criminal entered the premises; it is a location where forensic evidence is likely to be found

specific intent: Unambiguous purpose or reason; this must be proved in order to convict a person of theft or larceny

stripping: Removing and stealing the most easily removable and transportable parts from an automobile in order to resell them to individuals or salvage yard dealers

theft: An unlawful intentional appropriation of property

tire impression: Imprint left by a tire

tool mark: Any impression, cut, gouge, or abrasion caused by a tool coming into contact with another object

unauthorized use of a motor vehicle: Use of a vehicle by someone other than the owner without the owner's permission

vehicle identification number (VIN): Alphanumeric code consisting of 17 characters placed on automobile components to track them in the case of theft

■ Review Questions

1. What is the definition of larceny?
2. How does larceny differ from theft?
3. What has been the impact of consolidating theft offenses?
4. How does someone convert property that is not his or hers?
5. How does unauthorized use of a motor vehicle differ from auto theft?
6. What role does a fence play in the theft business?
7. Who supports the theft industry? How?
8. What is the value of tool marks to a burglary investigator?
9. What is the value of a moulage to a burglary investigator?
10. Of what value are the point of entry, method of entry, and approach to entry to the burglary investigator?
11. What is a VIN and of what value is it to a burglary investigator?
12. How does stripping a vehicle differ from chopping a vehicle?
13. What right to possession has a bona fide purchaser of stolen goods? Why?
14. What is meant by saying that "theft is a specific-intent offense?"
15. What propositions should come to the mind of the carjacking investigator?
16. Why might it be a good idea to photograph a tool impression prior to making a mold of it?
17. Why should tire impressions be taken with the tire still on the vehicle?
18. How might a footprint left in dust be lifted?

■ Bibliography

Harlow, C.W. (1988). *Motor vehicle theft*. Washington, DC: U.S. Department of Justice, Bureau of Justice Statistics.

Klaus, P. (1998). *Carjacking in the United States, 1992–1996*. Washington, DC: U.S. Department of Justice, Bureau of Justice Statistics.

Osterberg, J.W., & Ward, R.H. (1992). *Criminal investigation: A method for reconstructing the past*. Cincinnati, OH: Anderson.

Saferstein, R. (1995). *Criminalistics: An introduction to forensic science* (5th ed.). Englewood Cliffs, NJ: Prentice Hall.

■ Key Legal Cases

Commonwealth of Pennsylvania v. Muniem, 303 A.2d. 528 (Pa. Super. Ct. 1973).
Greek Orthodox Church of Cyprus v. Goldberg et al., 917 F.2d 278 (7th Cir. 1990).
People v. Jaso, 84 Cal. Rptr. 567 (Cal. Ct. App. 1979).
People v. Johnson, 28 Ill.2d 441, 192 N.E.2d 864 (1963).

Drug Offenses

CHAPTER

15

▶ ▶ STUDENT LEARNING OUTCOMES

Upon completion of this chapter students will demonstrate an understanding of:

- The various field tests available to presumptively determine that a substance is a drug
- The various type of laboratory tests available to determine a substance is a drug
- How cocaine/crack is made and used
- The various type of designer drugs presently in vogue
- How commonly abused drugs are made and abused

■ The Addict Myth

The United States has been engaged in a 25-year war it has been losing and seems doomed to lose. The media and Hollywood have convinced us that there is an epidemic of drug abuse in our cities that is threatening law-abiding citizens. We see ourselves as victims of a lawless under-society that resorts to violence in its efforts to corner the market on illicit drugs. One result is that prison populations are overflowing with drug-related offenders.

The reality is that poor people do not provide the impetus for this country's multi-billion-dollar-a-year drug industry. White polite society is irrevocably involved in the use of controlled substances. If addicts could be removed from our midst in the morning, there would still be a significant drug industry. When we examine the drug industry in all its facets, we see that a large portion of the drugs that are available are not the type generally used by the socioeconomically deprived. As Robin Williams, the actor and comedian, says, "Powdered cocaine is God's way of telling you that you have too much discretionary income." Hallucinogens, depressants, and stimulants are among the preferred recreational devices of the bored or jaded. Many pharmaceuticals find their way into the hands of men and women who have their doctor's permission to abuse drugs. College campuses are hotbeds of experimentation for curious students looking for newer and bigger kicks.

Legislatures have passed stiff penalties for violent drug offenders but they also provide funds for drug-abuse programs for those who qualify—generally people who are white, middle class, employed, educated, and financially secure. Two tiers of drug abuse have gripped our society; two tiers of enforcement strategies address the problem; and two tiers of legislation attempt to sanction the problem out of existence. It takes 500 times more powdered cocaine than crack cocaine to get an offender the same sentence. Our myopic view of drug abuse means that the law is draconian or hardly provides a sanction, depending on the socioeconomic status of the abuser.

Drug programs should not be a method for allowing individuals to avoid responsibility for their illegal behavior, nor should they be used in lieu of legal sanctions. If a war is to be waged (and there is no evidence that one has ever been conducted), then all persons should be subjected to the same legal process and the same sanctions for the same offenses. Attempting to focus on those who supply drugs is foolhardy, expensive, and not very effective in a society based on supply and demand. Removing a supplier only results in increased prices, more violence, and an opportunity for another to fill the created void.

Substance abuse habituation should carry special status only if addressed prior to arrest. Many professional organizations provide substance habituation rehabilitation without personal cost to the professional member. No stigma or loss of professional status is associated with voluntarily participating in a professional organization's substance abuse program. National funds should be made available to provide drug rehabilitation programs for persons voluntarily committing themselves for treatment prior to arrest. Any citizen should be able to seek and get the same type of treatment that professional organizations afford their members. No stigma should be attached to drug abusers seeking help, and they should be returned to their community and their employment upon successful completion of the program.

As a result of the widespread experimentation with drugs by young people, many lawyers do not see recreational drug use by middle-class society as a problem and attempt to differentiate the casual social user from the violent pusher. Any such perspective undermines the war effort. All drug involvement ultimately redounds to the benefit of the same people. When drug offenders are presented with a panoply of legal options, it is not surprising that respect for the law and for law enforcement deteriorates.

Regardless of what the legislators from state to state reflect in state statutes, citizens from those same states are voting with their cash ballot. Given the amount of money spent yearly on drugs and the cavalier way drug humor is bandied about on television and movies, it makes little sense for police to die over laws that the citizens of this country do not appear to support.

In Texas in 1975 possession of marijuana was a felony punishable by life imprisonment. Some years thereafter the legislature made the offense a citable misdemeanor. No one from the legislature bothered to explain the new policy to the spouses, parents, and children of those officers killed in the line of duty enforcing what came to be recognized as an unenforceable law. It is a shame that any law enforcement officer in this country should lose his or her life enforcing a law this country clearly vetoes every day with their cash ballots.

■ Drug Analysis

Forensic chemists are confronted with an array of substances in the specimens submitted to them for analysis. Their analyses must be specific and remove any doubt as to what drugs, if any, are involved. Furthermore, the identity of the drugs must be capable of proof at the time of trial. How does a chemist determine which drug is in a particular specimen? How does a chemist confirm that the probability of any other drug responding in an identical manner to the protocol selected is low enough to be not worth considering? He or she employs a two-stage protocol, consisting of screening tests and confirmatory tests.

Screening Tests

In a **screening test**, a specimen is subjected to a series of reagents that yield characteristic colors for commonly encountered drugs. Screening tests are used both in the lab and in the field. Ease of application makes color testing an efficient field-based method for achieving a tentative, presumptive identification of a drug. **Color reactions** are useful for screening purposes but do not result in a conclusive identification.

Five color test reagents are commonly used:

1. **Duquenois-Levine** is a test for marijuana (see **Figure 15–1**). When applied to marijuana, the reagent turns violet (**Figure 15–2**). The reagent is composed of three so-

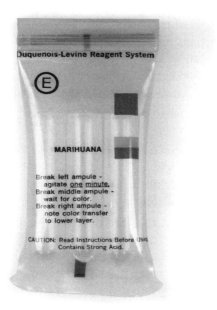

Figure 15–1 Duquenois-Levine marihuana.

Courtesy of Forensics Source

Figure 15–2 Marihuana field test.

@ Mikael Karlsson/Alamy Images

lutions: Solution A consists of 2% vanilla and 1% acetaldehyde in ethyl alcohol, solution B is concentrated hydrochloric acid, and solution C is chloroform.

2. The **Marquis test**, which screens for heroin, morphine, and opium derivatives, turns purple in their presence. The reagent can also be used for amphetamines and methamphetamines; in their presence, the mixture turns orange-brown. This reagent is composed of 2% formaldehyde in sulfuric acid.

3. Van Urk reagent, in the presence of LSD, turns blue-purple.

4. **Dillie-Koppanyi** is a test for barbiturates, in whose presence the reagent turns violet-blue.

5. The **Scott test** is a screen for cocaine. It renders a blue color upon application of solution A to a specimen containing cocaine. The blue transforms into pink upon application of solution B, and the blue color reappears in the chloroform layer upon addition of solution C.

Most labs and some field tests are completed using an open system with sealed bottles of solvents and reagents. The solvent dissolves and the reagent, an acid, causes a reaction. The color of that reaction has been recorded and can be expected of the appropriate solvent and reagent when placed on the questioned substance. The specimen to be tested is placed on a porcelain dish or in a petrie dish. The appropriate amount of solvent is placed on the specimen and allowed a few minutes to do its work. Once the suspect material has been dissolved, the appropriate reagent is then dropped onto the specimen. If the solution turns a particular color and that color is consistent for the drug being tested, the test is positive. The test is recorded and the record retained for further investigation and trial. The open containers of acid are broken or spilled easily, making the system hazardous; the Occupational Safety and Health Administration recognizes the procedure as highly hazardous.

A safer way to conduct field tests is to use commercial products that have solvent and reagent ampoules embedded into the package; the ampoules are broken in a particular sequence. This reaction takes place inside a sealed container, so the possibility of spills is eliminated from the testing equation. Each ampoule causes a reaction that is color coded to the drug for which the test is being conducted. The ampoules contain reagents that are acids and that when improperly broken may cause stains, burns, and damage to clothes, so care must be taken when conducting the tests. Disposable rubber gloves are fundamental to drug testing (natrile gloves are designed specifically for handling these types of substances).

Each drug testing kit provides the drug pouch or disposable chemical applicator, tubette and a small, sterile, toothpick-sized drug scoop. When preparing the pouches or tubettes, it is important to use only a sterile device for picking up the suspect drug and placing it into the package (**Figure 15–3**). Often investigators will use a knife or pen that is not sterile, thereby contaminating any test results. It is also important not to overload the pouch or tubette with the suspect drug; a very small quantity will produce the reaction. Whichever is being used, pouch or tubette, once the first ampoule is broken, after the test material has been added it must be agitated for a minimum of 30 seconds to one minute. This agitation allows the solvent to dissolve the drug and the reagent to react with the dissolved drug. After each ampoule is broken it must be agitated to facilitate the desired reaction.

Once the test is complete, it is important to document each step of the testing process (**TABLE 15–1**). The tests themselves are only determinative of probable cause and will

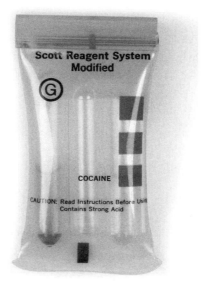

Figure 15–3 Pouch.

TABLE 15–1   Cocaine Salts and Base Reagent Checklist Protocol and Results

SUBJECT: _____ EVID #: _____

I.D. #: _____ DATE: _____ PKG #: _____ ITEM #: _____

EXAMINER: _____ DATE CERTIFIED: _____

EXAMINER SHALL READ, PERFORM AND CHECK EACH STEP.

☐   1. Weight _____ (grams)   ☐ Net   ☐ Gross *(Check One)*

☐   2. The Officer's opinion, based upon circumstances of seizure and appearance of the substance, indicates Cocaine HCl/Cocaine Base (Crack/Freebase).

☐   3. Hold the test with the printed side facing the operator.

☐   4. Check that all three (3) ampoules within the test are intact and are located in the left to right color sequence of Pink, Clear, Clear.

☐   5. Wearing disposable gloves, remove the plastic clip, open the test pouch and insert a small sample of the suspect material along with the plastic loading device into the bottom of the test pouch.

☐   6. Tap the pouch on a firm surface to move the suspect material and loading device into the bottom of the pouch and replace the closure clip.

☐   7. Break the left ampoule (Pink), at the middle of the ampoule and agitate for ten (10) seconds.

☐   8. Observe the development of a Blue Presence (Blue solution, Blue line along the bottom of the pouch, Blue in the corner of the pouch or a Pink field with small Blue flecks). IF NO BLUE COLOR IS PRESENT PROCEED TO STEP #14.

☐   9. Break the middle ampoule (Clear) and agitate for ten (10) seconds.

☐   10. Blue Presence will clear to a Pink solution. IF NO PINK COLOR IS PRESENT, GO TO STEP #14.

☐   11. Break the right ampoule (Clear) and agitate for ten (10) seconds.

☐   12. Tap the pouch firmly on one side to clear the field and gently roll the pouch back in the opposite direction to a 45° angle and allow the liquid to settle. Observe the color layering. Upper level Pink, lower level Blue.

☐   13. Result **POSITIVE** for: ☐ Cocaine HCl   ☐ Cocaine Base (Crack/Freebase)

☐   14. Result **INCONCLUSIVE** for Cocaine HCl/Crack/Freebase.

☐   15. Neutralize the test and dispose of using approved Department procedures.

_____   _____
Examiner Signature   Witness Signature

dissipate over time. They will not be available for trial, because once the test is complete and recorded, the specimen is disposed of or destroyed. The only thing left reflecting the test will be the record made in writing at the time of the field test.

In using a drug field-testing pouch for marijuana (Duquenois-Levine), first make sure that the test label is correct for the substance being tested. Examine the pouch and be sure there are three intact ampoules. The top of the pouch is clipped shut; to use the pouch, the clip must be removed. After removing the clip, insert into the pouch the following (also see **Figure 15–4**):

- Plant material—three or four quarter-inch-long particles
- Hashish—5–10 grams
- Hash oil—a pinhead's worth
- THC—a portion that fits on the tip of the loading device

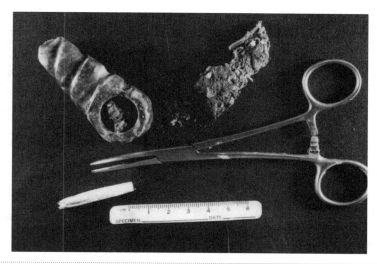

Figure 15–4 Hash and dried marijuana.

Courtesy of the Orange County Police Department

Once the suspect material has been inserted, the pouch must be clipped closed, then tapped to force the materials to the bottom. When the material has descended sufficiently, with the printed side of the pouch facing the user, the left ampoule can be broken and the pouch agitated for one minute. A very light tan color should form. When the middle ampoule is broken, the operator must pay close attention for the reaction, because, based on the quantity, quality, or freshness of the sample, the color may develop slowly or rapidly. As the purple color develops, there is a point at which the color will become darker. Too much development will spoil the reaction. Once the purple color has developed adequately, the third ampoule should be broken and the pouch agitated. By breaking the third ampoule the color remains fixed.

When analyzing the color, it should be noted that there was little reaction upon the breaking of the first ampoule (**Figure 15–5**). After breaking the second ampoule, the color turned purple, and upon breaking the third ampoule, the solution turned blue. When the pouch is tipped at an angle with the solution trapped in one corner, close examination will reveal a gray layer on top of a blue/purple layer. This is presumptively positive for *Cannabis sativa* (marijuana and its extracts).

Make sure to select the right tubette when testing for cocaine (Scott test). Crush the material to be tested into a powder; use only the amount that will fit onto the loading device. Open the tubette, add the suspect substance, and tap it to the bottom. Breaking the first (bottom) ampoule should reveal a blue color when agitated. Breaking the top (second) ampoule will also cause a blue sticky reaction. This reaction is presumptively cocaine hydrochloride. It can be used for all forms of cocaine, whether powder, crack, or base cocaine.

Color reactions differ based on the testing medium and method. The official definition of color reactions is a measurement and analysis of color by comparison with a standard, typically the colors are on the front of the pouch. In tubes, the standard is the color of the printing on the box or the color of the printing on the caps. We are seeking a match to the family of colors only, not the exact color shown.

Figure 15–5   First ampoule breaking in pouch.

@ US Coast Guard/AP Photos

There are three factors that affect the color reaction:

- Quality
- Quantity
- Agitation

The quality of the substance used for the test will affect the color intensity. A more pure substance may display darker colors and weaker substances lighter colors. The amount of the substance used will effect the intensity of the color reaction to varying degrees. It is necessary to agitate the sample vigorously to allow the chemistry to react properly with the substance itself. Depending on the agitation, color may increase or decrease.

Various cutting agents may create immediate heat and expansion within the test. If this reaction occurs, the clip on pouches can be canted 45 degrees, thereby allowing any generated heat or expansion to escape the pouch. Venting the pouch should dissipate most of the expansion and heat without destroying or contaminating the sample being tested. Once the pressure and heat have been reduced, the pouch can be reclosed and the clamp pushed back into position, allowing the reaction to develop fully and color analysis to continue.

Preparing Materials for Field Testing

All substances must be prepared properly prior to testing to facilitate the best reaction. The investigator must wear rubber gloves whenever testing or preparing to test, both for protection and to avoid allegations of cross-contamination. It is important to re-member that the purity of what is being tested is always in question. If what is found is pure and in powder or liquid form, the unclad hand may absorb the drug or the hands may transfer what has been picked up by the hands to the face and eyes. Once absorbed, there is no way to anticipate the drug reaction, which may be from mild to lethal. That is why the protocol always includes rubber gloves and field testing rather than barehanded handling of drugs and tasting them as a field test. Only an actor pretending to be an investigator would be so foolish as to taste something the purity and identity of which has yet to be determined.

If the substance to be tested is in capsules, the capsule can be separated by twisting the two parts of the capsule in opposite directions, allowing the contents to pour onto paper or a sterile surface. Sometimes the material in the capsule becomes caked and does not pour or comes out in chunks. Generally rolling the capsule half between forefinger and thumb will dislodge the contents; the powder can be crushed with a gloved finger and then lifted and placed inside the testing package.

Tablets must be reduced to powder or small fragments prior to testing. This can be done by crushing with the thumb or the heel of the hands. The powder will disperse beyond the hands, so it is important to have paper in place to capture as much of the powder as possible. Should it be necessary to use something harder than hand or fingers to crush the tablet, shroud the tool in an unused rubber glove before applying pressure to the tablet. Using something to crush the tablet that is not sterile will lead to allegations of cross contamination.

Powders often arrive or are distributed in large chunks (**Figure 15–6**). Reduce chunks to powder for testing. Break off a piece from the large chunk to obtain a sample that can be crushed in the same manner as tablets.

Liquids are the most dangerous controlled substances that may require field testing. The liquid may be highly volatile, or it may interact with water or other substances to cause an explosive reaction. The best rule to follow when dealing with liquids is to take them to the lab to be tested. Should it be necessary to field test liquids, do it carefully and use very small amounts. Moisten a sterile cotton swab with the liquid and then allow it to dry. Once dried, the swab portion can be cut off and deposited into the testing medium.

Figure 15–6 Dried and lumped cocaine.

Courtesy of DEA

Remember that any positive reaction is for probable-cause purposes only. Any evidence pertaining to the test at the time of trial will be based on the information recorded from the testing process.

Confirmatory Tests

Each screening test is insufficient by itself to prove a drug's identity, but the proper protocol will generate a combination of test results characteristic of only one chemical substance. Drug identification protocols generally rely upon a combination of test types to confirm a drug's identity, possibly including color tests, microcrystalline tests, chromatography, spectrophotometry, and mass spectrometry.

Microcrystalline Tests

Microcrystalline tests are more specific than tests based on color responses to chemical reagents. In a **microcrystalline test**, a small quantity of the substance is placed on a microscopic slide, and a drop of chemical reagent is added. The chemical reagent causes a precipitate reaction, creating crystals of a size and shape characteristic of a particular drug. The connection between types of crystals and types of drugs has become well established, and the results of microcrystalline tests are admissible at the time of trial. These tests can be conducted in the presence of diluents. Although the crystal structure and size may be altered by the diluents, experienced examiners can make the identification despite the alterations. When the appropriate color tests and microcrystalline tests are conducted in accordance with a standard protocol, the results point to only one drug (Siegel, 1988).

Chromatography

Both gas and thin-layer chromatography can be used to separate out diluents and identify the drug that remains. Chromatography involves a comparison of a known substance with an unknown substance. It is necessary to have some idea what the suspected substance is before drug analysis chromatography can be conducted. Generally, color and microcrystalline tests precede chromatography.

Gas Chromatography. Chromatography theory is based on the fact that chemical substances have a tendency to partially escape into their surroundings when dissolved in a liquid or when absorbed on a solid surface. In a beaker of water covered with a bell jar and kept at a constant temperature, the water in the beaker is in a liquid phase and the air above the beaker is in a gas phase. The molecules of oxygen and hydrogen escaping from the water through evaporation are in their gas phase, and those remaining in the water are in their liquid phase. As the gas molecules continue to escape, they will begin to accumulate above the water. The random movement of the molecules will carry some back into the water. A point will be reached at which the number of molecules escaping the water is equal to the number of molecules returning to the water. At this point the liquid phase and the gas phase are in equilibrium (Klein, Kruegel, and Sobol, 1979).

The distribution of a gas between its liquid and gas phases is dependent upon the solubility of the gas: the higher the solubility, the greater the tendency to remain in the liquid phase. During a chromatographic process, one phase is kept in continuous motion in a fixed direction. If two or more gases are dissolved in water, chromatography will occur when the air is forced to move continuously in one direction over the water. The gas with less solubility will have a greater number of molecules escaping into the gas phase than the other gas, and these molecules will travel faster than the molecules of the more soluble gas. After a period of time, the molecules of the two gases will become completely separated. The process can be viewed as a race. At first, the participating substances are mixed together at the starting line. As the race progresses, the substance that is more movable (moving phase) will charge ahead of the substance that prefers solubility (stationary phase) (Klein, Kruegel, and Sobol, 1979).

In **gas chromatography**, the moving phase, called the carrier gas, flows through a column constructed of glass (**Figure 15–7**). The stationary phase is a thin film of liquid contained within the column. As the carrier gas flows through the column, it carries along with it the components of a mixture that has been injected into the column. Those components having a greater affinity for the moving gas phase will travel through the column at a faster rate than those having a greater affinity for the stationary liquid phase. Eventually, after the mixture has traversed the length of the column, it will emerge separated into its component parts (Saferstein, 1995).

As the constituent components emerge from the column, they pass through a detector that creates a written record as a function of time. This written record of the separation is called a chromatogram. A typical chromatogram will show a series of peaks, each corresponding to a component of the mixture. The time required for a component to emerge from the column is known as the retention time. This serves as an identifying characteristic of a material. Two or more substances may have comparable retention times under similar chromatographic conditions; thus, the results of gas chromatography can only be considered presumptive and must be confirmed by other procedures.

An advantage of gas chromatography is that it can yield quantitative results. The amount of a substance passing through the detector is proportional to the peak recorded. By chromatographing a known concentration of a material and comparing the result with that of the sample, the concentration of the sample may be determined.

Thin-layer Chromatography. This type of chromatography incorporates a solid stationary phase and a moving liquid phase to separate the constituents of a mixture.

Figure 15–7 Gas chromatograph and spectrometer.

Courtesy of Austin Police Department, Austin, Texas

An absorbent plate is coated with a thin film of silica gel or aluminum oxide and is held in place with plaster of paris. If the specimen to be examined is a solid, it must first be dissolved in a solvent. A few microliters of the solution is spotted onto the lower edge of the plate, which is then placed upright in a closed chamber that contains a selected liquid to which fluorescent dye has been added. The placement is made so that only the bottom edge of the plate is resting in the liquid (test spots may not touch the liquid). The liquid will slowly rise up the plate (by capillary action). As the liquid moves past the test spots, the components of the sample will become distributed between the plate and the rising liquid. Those components that are the least soluble will travel up the plate faster than those components that are more soluble. When the liquid has traveled 10 cm past the test spots, the development is complete, and the plate is removed, dried, and examined (Klein, Kruegel, and Sobol, 1979).

The plates are placed under ultraviolet light, revealing those materials that fluoresce as bright spots on a dark background. Another method of visualization involves the use of a reagent spray that causes the separated spots to color. The unknown sample must be developed alongside a standardized sample on the same thin-layer chromatographic plate. If the standard and the test materials travel the same distances up the plate, they can tentatively be identified as being the same. The identification is not conclusive and requires confirmation (Klein, Kruegel, and Sobol, 1979).

The distance a spot has traveled up a thin-layer plate can be assigned a numerical value known as the Rf value. This value is defined as the distance traveled by the component divided by the distance traveled by the moving liquid phase. Because the liquid phase is allowed to travel 10 cm, the Rf value will be in tenths of a centimeter (e.g., if the spot moved 8 cm, the Rf value would be 0.8). Years of research and testing have produced much published data relating to the proper selection of thin-layer chromatography conditions for separating and identifying specific classes of substances, including drugs (Down and Gwyn, 1975).

Mass Spectrometry

The ability of gas chromatography to separate a complex mixture into its constituent parts, although reliable, predictable, and replicable, is still only presumptive. An expert cannot base his or her opinion solely on chromatographic retention time, but by coupling gas chromatography and **mass spectrometry**, a definitive identification can be made. After the mixture has been separated by the gas chromatograph, a direct connection of the chromatograph columns and the mass spectrometer (**Figure 15–8**) allows each component to flow into the spectrometer as it leaves the chromatograph. The material enters a high-vacuum chamber in which a beam of high-energy electrons is aimed at the sample molecules. The electrons collide with the molecules, causing them to lose electrons and to acquire a positive charge (i.e., to become ions). The ions are unstable and almost instantaneously decompose into numerous smaller fragments. The fragments are passed through an electric field, where they are separated according to their masses. Under carefully controlled conditions, no two substances produce the same fragmentation pattern. The fragmentation patterns are distinctive enough to be considered fingerprints (Yinon and Zitrin, 1977).

This technique can conclusively identify a chemical substance even in minute concentrations. The combination of gas chromatograph and mass spectrometer is further enhanced when linked to a computer system. Accuracy, speed, and sensitivity are added to the procedure, along with the capability to record and store data. The system is able to

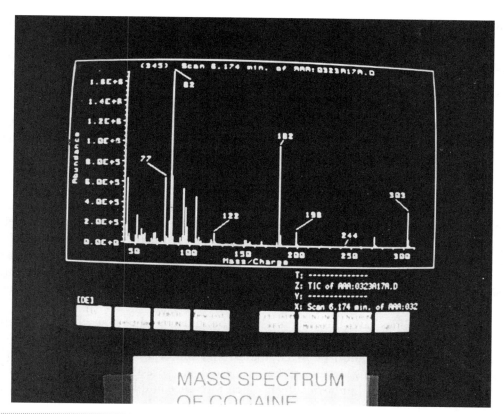

Figure 15–8 Analysis of crack cocaine sample by mass spectrometer.

Courtesy of Austin Police Department, Austin, Texas

detect and identify substances present in one millionth of a gram. Computer comparisons can be run of unknown substances, avoiding the necessity of a control specimen.

■ Narcotics

The source of most **narcotics** is opium. Narcotic drugs are analgesics that relieve pain by depressing the central nervous system. Their regular use will lead to physical dependence. Opium is extracted from the unripe pod of the opium poppy. The morphine content of the extracted opium is from 4% to 21%. Narcotics produce languor or even a stupor. To an addict, all else pales next to the effect of the opiates. All other tasks and responsibilities take a distant second to obtaining additional narcotics. Individuals are very lethargic while under the influence of a narcotic but may become extremely agitated when the drug begins to wear off and withdrawal sets in. It is at this point that rational behavior and communication become difficult.

The opium poppy will grow in a wide range of climates, but production of opium is labor intensive. The unripe seed pod is incised lightly multiple times. The milky fluid that collects on the surface is raw opium. After several hours, a collection of semi-dried material is taken from the surface. Each pod produces only a small amount of fluid, and thousands of pods have to be incised and harvested to produce a pound of raw opium. In 1945, over 200 tons of opium were imported into the United States for legitimate medical needs, and it was estimated that several times that amount was imported for illicit drug use. Today, in spite of the extensive use of synthetic analgesics, many tons of opium are imported into the United States legally, and the drug is still produced primarily in Asia, where labor is relatively cheap. Much of the illegal opium produced today is from an area referred to as the Golden Triangle. Some estimate that 5,000 to 20,000 pounds or more of illegal opium products, such as heroin, are brought into the United States each year.

The word *narcotic* is derived from the Greek word *narkotikon*, which means "to numb" or "benumbing." It refers to the principal effect of opium, which is to relieve pain. The term narcotic was originally used to refer to opium-derived drugs that produce analgesia or stupor, but common usage and legal definitions have expanded the use of the term to include other pain-relieving and stupor-inducing drugs.

In 1803, a German pharmacist isolated morphine from opium. Opium contains approximately 10% morphine. The compound was named after Morpheus, the Greek god of dreams, because of its effect of producing sleep. Eventually, **codeine**, occurring in opium at levels of 0.5%, was isolated. Morphine and codeine are the principal opium-derived alkaloids used today. Codeine is used as an analgesic and cough suppressant, morphine is used in several forms as an analgesic, and opium is used in preparations to treat diarrhea.

All true narcotics have shown themselves to be addictive when abused, even though several were originally introduced with the suggestion that they were nonaddictive. Addiction is a combination of psychological and physical dependence on a drug. As tolerance to the drug develops, the user requires more than the usual amount to experience the same euphoric effect. When tolerance and habitual use develop, a **physiologic dependence** also occurs, so withdrawal of the drug leads to clinical signs such as abdominal pains, nausea, and vomiting. Agitation and a feeling of distress generally resolve in several days. These physical signs can be prevented by renewing the drug levels or by substituting drugs such as methadone. Addiction is evident when the drug user has an overpowering desire or compulsion to obtain and take the drug and when there are physiologic effects upon withdrawal. It should be noted that some narcotic users are not addicts. These users, known as chippers (because they "chip" away at a habit), moderate their dosage in quantity and frequency. Opium is most typically taken orally (in a tincture such as laudanum) or smoked. Smoking vaporizes the opium, allowing morphine and other alkaloids to be absorbed from the smoke. Although the amount used initially is small, eventually large amounts are required to achieve an effect.

Heroin

Much like opium, morphine and heroin enjoyed wide over-the-counter acceptance. By 1900, some estimated that there were one million addicts in the United States. Heroin, introduced in 1898, was immediately proclaimed the most effective analgesic known. Thought to be nonaddictive, heroin was recommended specifically as treatment for addiction to other opium derivatives. It was sold as an elixir and in patent medicines until the early 1900s, when the danger was recognized. In 1914, the Harrison Narcotic Act made heroin and heroin-based medicines illegal (Baden, 1980).

The concentration and nature of heroin vary widely from region to region, as does the form. "Mexican brown" or "tar" heroin is popular on the West Coast (**Figure 15–9**), while a powdered form, "China white," is more popular on the East Coast. Concentrations are around 10% but can be higher. Cutting agents also vary from region to region, with

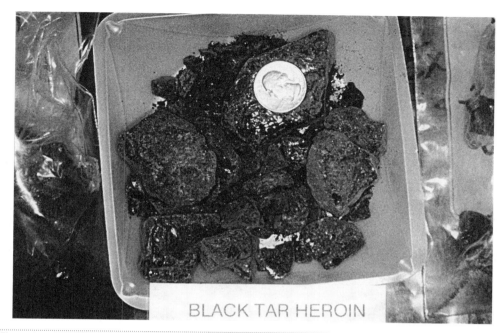

Figure 15–9   Black tar heroin.

Courtesy of Austin Police Department, Austin, Texas

quinine used on the East Coast and lidocaine on the West Coast. Aware of the variability of drugs and cutting agents, addicts prefer to buy from the same source.

Heroin usually is sold as a fine white powder in a glassine envelope or paper bundle, or as a tar wrapped in foil, within a balloon or condom, or in a small plastic bundle. To use, the contents of the container are emptied into a cooker. The cooker can be a spoon or wire-held bottle cap, but anything that will hold about 5 ml of fluid and allow heating over a flame will do. When water is added, most of the material is not dissolved immediately. A flame, usually from a match or cigarette lighter, is used to warm the solution to increase solubility. The liquid is aspirated into an insulin syringe (**Figure 15–10**), usually through a small piece of absorbent cotton, to remove insoluble material. The needle is inserted under the skin (skin popping) or into a vein, and a small amount of solution is injected as a test dose. The addict subjectively interprets how powerful the drug is and how much will be injected. This process of injecting a small amount and withdrawing some blood to keep the lumen open is called *registering, fooling,* and *booting.*

Individuals who may have difficulty finding a vein can employ another method of using heroin. Often the needle marks fester. Heroin can be rubbed onto the festering blisters, allowing the heroin to be introduced into the system. The skin erupts in lesions called *volcanoes* (**Figure 15–11**).

Heroin is made by reacting morphine with anhydride or acetyl chloride. The solution is cooled and neutralized with sodium carbonate. The heroin freebase is then purified by adding concentrated hydrochloric acid (Saferstein, 1995). The high associated with the use of heroin is short-lived, lasting three to four hours. The impact of the body's withdrawal from the effects of the drug—known as "keeping the sickness off"—accounts for the user's pursuit of another fix as much as does the high. A *jones* is the amount of money spent each day to keep the sickness off.

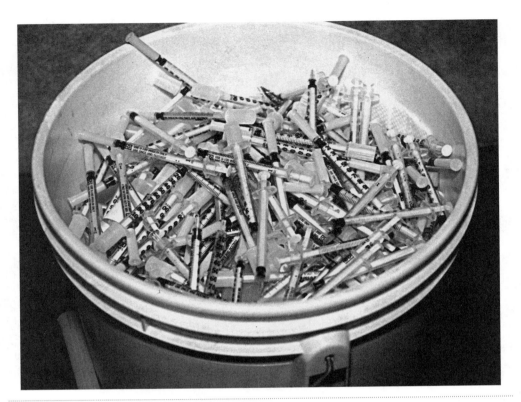

Figure 15–10 Hypodermic needles for disposal.

Courtesy of Austin Police Department, Austin, Texas

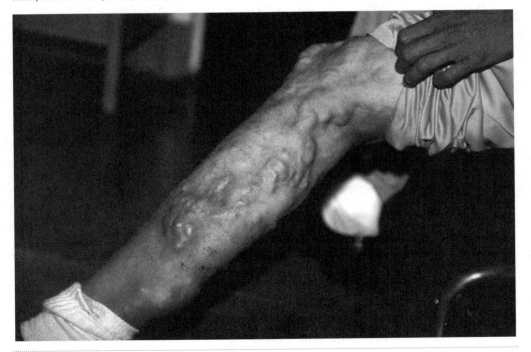

Figure 15–11 Heroin volcanoes.

© Michael Newman/PhotoEdit, Inc.

Common street-quality heroin is only 15% to 35% pure, because it is adulterated (stepped on) each time it changes hands. Traditionally, quinine was the choice of cut (diluent) for heroin. Contemporary pushers use other diluents such as starch, mannitol, procaine, and lactose. Mexican heroin is brown because of the refining process used. Mexican heroin is often cut with cocoa. Heroin comes in colors ranging from white to black (**Figure 15–12a and 15–12b**). The color may affect the field test. The darker the color

(A)

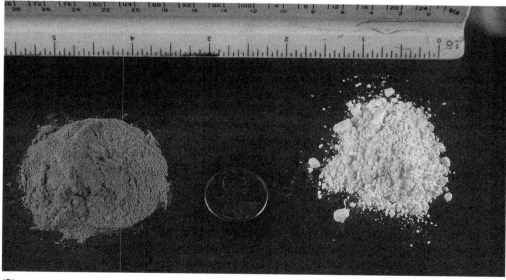

(B)

Figure 15–12 Heroin colors.

Courtesy of DEA

the more likely it is that it will interfere with the development of the green sought in the Mecke's field test (**Figure 15–13**). For that reason, it is a good practice to use less of the suspected material in the test as the color of the tested heroin darkens.

Syringes and cookers contain only small amounts of heroin, and street samples generally have low concentrations to begin with; both circumstances can make the task of proving heroin possession difficult. Swabbing the paraphernalia will allow sufficient residue to be picked up with which a field test can be conducted.

Balloons can be used to package heroin for sale. Heroin is placed in a balloon and the balloon is the twisted and rolled back over itself (**Figure 15–14**). Balloons sometimes are referred to on the street as *spitters,* from the practice of the seller placing the balloon in his mouth prior to sale. Once the sale is consummated the balloon is spit into the hand. Should a bust occur prior to the exchange, the dealer swallows the balloon.

Methadone

Some narcotics are not derived from opium. These drugs are nonetheless referred to as opiates because of the narcotic effect of the drugs. **Methadone** is a synthetic opiate used in maintenance programs for heroin addicts. When taking 80 to 120 mg a day of

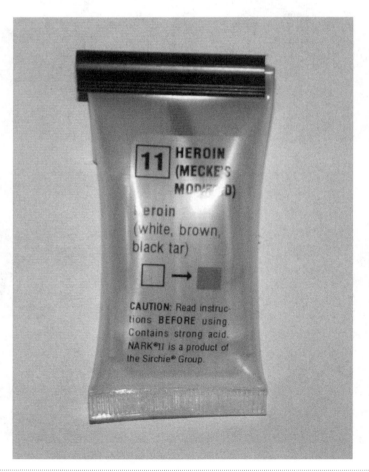

Figure 15–13 Mecke's pouch.

Figure 15–14 Heroin balloons.

Courtesy of DEA

methadone, heroin addicts will not experience the high associated with heroin or morphine use. The intent is to avoid the effects of withdrawal and the desire to get high for those people attempting to kick a heroin habit.

Codeine

Codeine is also present in opium but is usually prepared synthetically from morphine. It is used as a cough suppressant and is only one sixth as strong as morphine. Codeine is not a drug of choice for heroin users.

■ Hallucinogens

Hallucinogens are drugs that cause a distortion in thought processes and perceptions as well as changes in moods. Prolonged use can bring about permanent personality changes and loss of contact with reality. Persons under the influence of strong hallucinogens may not respond to verbal communication and may hallucinate to the extent that they are completely removed from reality. Users can be dangerous when confronted because of the distortion in their perceptions and vision. Contact with individuals under the influence must be cautious and humane. Hospitalization is preferable to incarceration because of the continuing danger these people may pose to themselves or others.

Marijuana

Marijuana is often classified as a hallucinogen for lack of anywhere else to put it. "The term *marijuana* encompasses all parts of the plant *Cannabis sativa* L., whether growing or not; the seeds thereof; the resin extracted from any part of such plant; and every compound, manufacture, salt, derivative, mixture, or preparation of such plant, its seeds or resins; but [does] not include the mature stalks of such plant, fiber produced from such stalks, oil or cake made from the seeds of such plant, any other compound, manufacture, salt derivative, mixture or preparation of such mature stalks (except the resin extracted therefrom), fiber, oil, or cake, or the sterilized seed of such plant which is incapable of germination" (Saferstein, 1995, p. 252).

The marijuana preparation consists of crushed leaves mixed in varying proportions with the flowers (buds), stems, and seeds (**Figure 15–15**). Often the quality of the marijuana is determined by the number of buds included in the bag (the more buds, the more potent the marijuana). Marijuana is usually smoked in a cigarette, or joint (**Figure 15–16**), or in a pipe or bong. Usual purchase amounts include the following:

- A joint or blunt (one hand-rolled cigarette)
- A matchbox (a small paper matchbox, about four joints' worth)
- A lid (approximately one ounce contained in a plastic bag)
- A pound (sold in paper and plastic bags)
- A key (a kilogram, or roughly 2.2 pounds)

Figure 15–15   Bales of marijuana leafs, stems, and seeds.

Courtesy of Austin Police Department, Austin, Texas

Figure 15–16 Partially smoked marijuana cigarette.
Courtesy of Austin Police Department, Austin, Texas

The plant secretes a sticky resin that is known as hashish (or hash). Hashish is sold by the gram or in compressed one-ounce bars about the size of a chocolate bar. The resinous material also can be extracted from the plant by soaking it in a solvent. Hashish oil is a resinous, viscous material, dark green to brown in color and having the consistency of tar. Hashish is smoked in a hash pipe (a metal or wooden device with a small bowl about the size of a dime) or a ceramic chillum (a straight-stemmed pipe without a filter but with a rock placed loosely over the hole in the bowl to prevent the hash from being sucked into the stem). Hash oil is dropped onto a marijuana cigarette to increase its potency or onto a regular cigarette. Increases in the distribution of hashish appear to coincide with lapses in the leaf marijuana market. Marijuana users prefer leaf use to the resinous hashish.

Marijuana was first introduced into the United States around 1920, most probably smuggled by Mexican laborers across the border into Texas. By 1937, 46 states and the federal government had laws prohibiting the use or possession of marijuana. Marijuana is a weed (and is sometimes referred to as "weed") that grows under most climatic conditions but flourishes in hot, tropical areas (**Figure 15–17**). The size of the plant and the potency of the marijuana depend on the amount of sunlight and rain it receives. The plant grows to a height of 15 feet and is characterized by an odd number of leaflets on each leaf (**Figure 15–18**). Each leaf contains five to nine leaflets, all having characteristic serrated edges.

In 1964, scientists isolated the psychoactive ingredient in marijuana: **tetrahydrocannabinol**, or **THC**. The discovery of THC allowed scientists to determine the potency of marijuana preparations and the effect those preparations have on individual users. The THC content in cannabis varies in different parts of the plant, with the resin and buds having the greatest potency. Marijuana, as generally used, and hashish have a THC content of 3% to 4%. The THC-rich resin extracted from the marijuana plant in the form of hash oil may have a THC content of 20% to 65% (Thornton and Nakamura, 1972).

There are two legal problems associated with the courts and cannabis. First, the defense may attempt to impeach the expert by demonstrating that the species of marijuana

Figure 15–17 Marijuana plant.

Courtesy of Austin Police Department, Austin, Texas

in question is suspect. Some botanists have asserted that there are numerous species of marijuana other than *Cannabis sativa*, and the defense, after establishing that the expert cannot testify as to the particular species, may argue that the allegations fail because the statute proscribes only *Cannabis sativa*. Most courts no longer recognize this defense, relying on congressional intent to control THC regardless of marijuana species.

The second problem occurs only in those jurisdictions that have separate penalties and definitions for hashish. When hashish is legally defined, it may be referred to as "a resinous extract of marijuana." The obvious question to be raised by the defense is, what is meant by resinous? Some chemists take the position that any oily preparation or cake made from marijuana is hashish. Others define hashish as the resin that contains THC

Figure 15–18 Marijuana leaf.

Courtesy of Austin Police Department, Austin, Texas

and argue that the presence of any plant material in an exhibit contaminates the pure resin, thereby disqualifying it as hashish. The issue is rendered moot in those jurisdictions that treat hashish the same as marijuana.

Lysergic Acid Diethylamide

Lysergic acid diethylamide (LSD) is synthesized from a type of fungus that attacks certain grasses and grains. Albert Hoffman, a Swiss scientist, first described the hallucinogenic effects of LSD after accidentally ingesting it in 1943. LSD was manufactured in a variety of forms, each having its advocates. The chemical itself is colorless and tasteless and can be distributed through a variety of shapes and forms, such as the following:

- Windowpane acid (1-mm by 2-mm rectangles of LSD-impregnated gelatin)
- Blotter acid (an aqueous solution of LSD poured evenly over absorbent perforated paper, usually about 1 cm square; **Figure 15–19**)

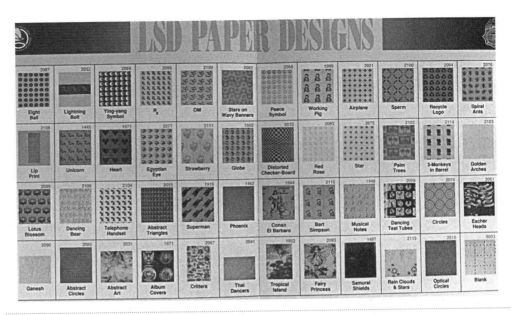

Figure 15–19 LSD paper designs.

Courtesy of Austin Police Department, Austin, Texas

- California sunshine (yellow tablets)
- Stamp acid (postage stamps with an aqueous solution of LSD dropped onto the adhesive surface)
- Sugar cubes (**Figure 15–20**)

The drug is very potent; as little as 25 µg is enough to start visual hallucinations that may last up to 12 hours. The acid trip is one of plateaus and peaks (periods of maximum hallucinations). The hallucinations begin 20 to 60 minutes after ingestion. More rapid absorption results when the material is dropped into the eye or injected. Subsequent

Figure 15–20 Sugar cube acid.

© Anette Linnea Rasmussen/ShutterStock, Inc.

dosages must be increased to obtain the same effects when LSD is used over an extended period. The drug may produce visual and auditory hallucinations as well as mood swings and feelings of anxiety, tension, and paranoia.

One common LSD-related legal problem is that the small amount of LSD in the submitted samples makes analysis difficult. The most common spot test for LSD is Erlich's test, in which the reagent turns purple in the presence of LSD. This spot test can be used to visualize LSD after thin-layer chromatography, thereby allowing two tests to be conducted on the same sample. In some states, LSD is proscribed, but isomers of LSD, such as lysergic acid methylpropylamide (LAMPA), are not. However, this issue is rendered moot in those jurisdictions that include LSD isomers in the proscriptive definition.

In instances of suspected LSD, first pass an ultraviolet lamp across the surface of the suspected material. Any areas that fluoresce purple under ultraviolet have LSD present. Each purple dot is a dose of LSD. Because of the possibility of abosorbing LSD through the skin only nitrile rubber gloves should be used. Nitrile gloves do not breathe and will not transmit LSD from the medium touched onto the investigator. Testing of suspected LSD is best left for the laboratory because of the ease of absorption.

Phencyclidine

Phencyclidine, once marketed by Parke-Davis as a large-animal tranquilizer, is a synthetic substance referred to on the street as PCP. PCP has appeared on the street in pill form (peace pills) and powder form (angel dust, tic, and dummy dust). Regardless of the delivery system, PCP is now generically referred to as angel dust. The preferred method of use is inhalation or ingestion. The drug can be placed in a solution into which marijuana cigarettes can be dipped and sold individually (sherm) (**Figure 15–21**). The dust can be

Figure 15–21 Marijuana cigarettes soaked in PCP.

Courtesy of Austin Police Department, Austin, Texas

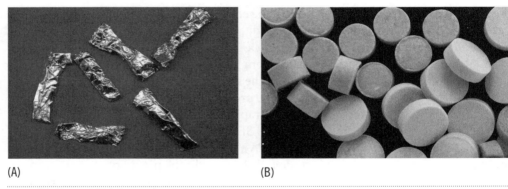

(A)   (B)

Figure 15–22   (A) PCP foil wrappers. (B) PCP pills.

Courtesy of DEA

sprinkled onto marijuana, which is then sold as an especially potent strain of marijuana. Because of availability, PCP is often sold as LSD, mescaline, or THC.

A chemist may be called upon to analyze material suspected of being PCP or to evaluate the manufacturing capabilities of a clandestine laboratory. A thorough knowledge of the chemistry used to manufacture PCP and any analogs of PCP will be necessary for the chemist to testify that PCP was being manufactured or was to be manufactured. The chemist will also need the ability to assess the production output of a clandestine laboratory based on the results of a police investigation and search.

PCP is a hallucinogen that should be treated as carefully as LSD (**Figure 15–22a and 22b**). Absorption through standard rubber gloves is possible, so the default gloving, again, is nitrile. PCP has a distinctive odor in powder or liquid form (**Figure 15–23**), whether

Figure 15–23   Liquid PCP.

© Michael Newman/PhotoEdit, Inc.

smoked in a marijuana cigarette or used as a powder. PCP smells like cat urine. This is another of those substances that should be transported to the crime lab as quickly as possible to avoid an accidental dosage. A field test created just for PCP should render a solid blue color.

■ Depressants

Because of the relaxing effects of **barbiturates**, they are generically referred to on the streets as downers. They act on the central nervous system and create a feeling of well-being and drowsiness. All barbiturates are derived from barbituric acid, first synthesized by a German chemist, Adolf Von Bauer. Of the 25 barbiturate derivatives used in medical practice, only 5 are common: amobarbital, secobarbital, phenobarbital, pentobarbital (**Figure 15–24**), and butabarbital (Saferstein, 1995). This drug is generally taken orally in 10- to 70-mg doses and is absorbed through the small intestines. Phenobarbital is absorbed slowly and is classified as a long-acting barbiturate. Abusers prefer the faster-acting barbiturates. The withdrawal from physical dependence on barbiturates is more severe than that for any other drug. Because of the large number of barbiturate derivatives manufactured, it is difficult to determine which specific derivative is in question.

Barbiturates are available through prescription and are made by numerous manufacturers. The marking on a barbiturate reflects the name of the manufacturer such as Lilly or Roche, or brand names such as Seconal, or a number/letter combination. Efforts to identify a particular tablet or capsule can include contacting the crime laboratory, a pharmacist, or using the *Physician's Desk Reference*. The *Physician's Desk Reference* is a

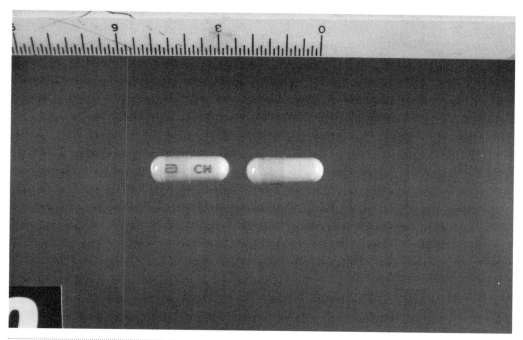

Figure 15–24 Nembutal sodium tablet (Pentobarbital).

Courtesy of DEA

> **OFFICER'S NOTEBOOK**
>
> **Treatment of a Clandestine Drug Lab**
> Good practice dictates that the lab remain undisturbed until a chemist or the person expected to testify about the lab and its production has had an opportunity to examine the premises and the equipment found on the site. It may be necessary for the prosecution to change the charges from "possession" or "manufacture" to "attempted manufacture" or "conspiracy to manufacture" based on the chemist's analysis of the lab's readiness.

compendium of all manufactured drugs; it provides all or some of the following information pertaining to a particular manufactured drug:

- Controlled Substance Act schedule
- A photograph of the imprints on either side of the substance
- The name under which the substance is sold
- A list of all active ingredients within a substance
- Photographs of the drug in the forms in which it is sold
- The manufacturer
- The marketer

■ Stimulants

Amphetamines

Amphetamines are synthetic central nervous system stimulants. Abusers collectively refer to them as uppers or speed and may inject the drug or take it orally. Injecting the drug provides for an immediate physiologic response (rush), followed by an intense feeling of pleasure. Individuals who prefer amphetamines to other drugs are called speed freaks and often binge, as do cocaine users. During a binge, a user may inject 500 to 1000 mg of amphetamines every 2 to 3 hours. The binge usually continues until all of the drug has been injected. Users report an increase in perception, information processing, and body function. Bingeing may produce hallucinations and paranoia. As the drug begins to wear off, users slip into a depression and prolonged periods of sleep.

The drug is primarily known for its stimulating properties, for it imparts a prolonged feeling of strength and well-being. Because it increases physiologic activity, tiredness is replaced by a feeling of energy. Amphetamines were used in the 1940s to increase productivity and allow prolonged activities that normally would be very tiring or tedious. Bomber pilots during World War II, for example, were given amphetamines to help them stay alert on long flights. Methamphetamine has garnered much attention in the media. It is known on the street as meth, crystal, crank, and speed; most of the chemical components are regulated, and many chemical syntheses leading to the same compounds are possible (Derlet and Heischober, 1990).

Methamphetamine may be a pure white crystal powder, but differences in recipes and cooking techniques can cause differences in color; color is not equated with purity. Meth can turn out in powder or chunks depending on the humidity during cooking and drying (**Figure 15–25a–d**). The high moisture content of meth can cause problems in weighing. The substance can lose up to 50% of its weight in evaporation, which must be taken into account at trial.

(A)   Courtesy of DEA   (B)   Courtesy of Orange County Police Department, Florida

(C)   Courtesy of Orange County Police Department, Florida   (D)   Courtesy of DEA

Figure 15–25 Methamphetamine color continuum.

Today there are primarily two methods of manufacture. One method (Red P) requires heat and is used to make large batches of meth; the other method utilizes anhydrous ammonia.

Each method starts with ephedrine or psuedoephedrine. Both of these chemicals are used in diet pills and over-the-counter cold remedies. In order to separate the ephedrine from the medication, it must first be extracted. The tablets are crushed (e.g., in blenders) and placed on a coffee filter, and denatured alcohol is poured over the powder. The alcohol is allowed to evaporate, and what remains is ephedrine. The next step in the Red P recipe calls for red phosphorus (from which the process receives its name), which is used in match striker plates. By cutting the striker plates from the matches and soaking them in denatured alcohol, the red phosphorus can be extracted: once the alcohol has evaporated, the remaining residue dries into red flakes of phosphorus. Solvents such as iodine and acetone are necessary to complete the process (**Figure 15–26a–d**).

Recently police have discovered covered jars of urine at clandestine laboratories. Methamphetamine is not metabolized completely, and urine contains as much as 80% of the original methamphetamine. Cooks who are also users may collect their urine and add a solvent. The solution is shaken and allowed to sit. The solvent will separate from the urine, carrying the unmetabolized methamphetamine (**Figure 15–27**). The solvent is drawn off and the methamphetamine is separated from the solvent.

One form of methamphetamine has received unusual press coverage. Known as ice, batu, or shabu, it has been called the most dangerous drug in existence. When volatile

(A)

(B)

(C)

(D)

© Shvaygert Ekaterina/ShutterStock, Inc.

(E)

Figure 15–26   (A-D) Meth production. (E) Phosphorus in solution.

methamphetamine oil is allowed to crystallize slowly in a refrigerator, large crystals form. White or slightly yellow in color, they are usually the size of rock salt, about one-quarter to one-half inch across (**Figure 15–28**).

The commonly used amphetamines can be smoked. The powder or crystals may be mixed with tobacco or marijuana, but more often they are heated to vaporize on the screen of a pipe so that the fumes can be inhaled. The pipe is usually a glass bulb with a hole in the top and a tube on one side, which acts as the mouthpiece. The drug is placed in the pipe, and the pipe is heated until white vapor appears as the drug melts. The finger sealing the hole on the top of the pipe is removed and the user inhales from the

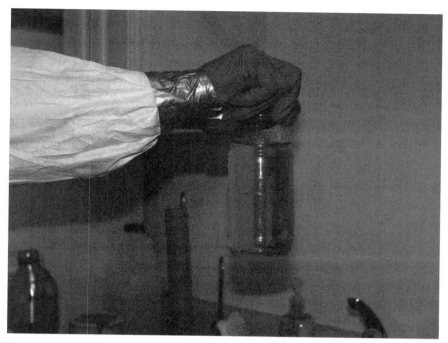

Figure 15–27 Urine meth.

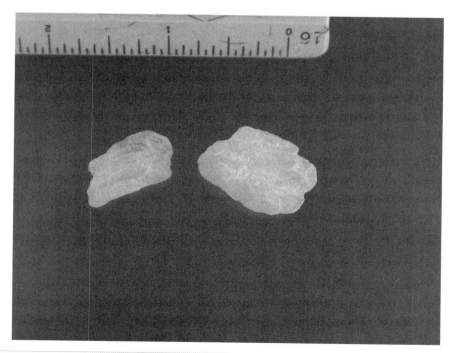

Figure 15–28 Meth ice.

tube as long as possible, holding the breath to allow absorption through the lungs. After inhalation, the pipe is immediately cooled with a wet cloth to condense the vaporized drug. A single crystal can be used several times before it is consumed completely, and, considering the length of the high, it would seem to be more economical than cocaine. A used pipe will have carbon on the outside bottom and a coating of white to gray crystals on the inside walls.

A significant problem associated with amphetamines is that they create in users a propensity toward paranoia and violent behavior, which may increase the likelihood that the user is carrying weapons.

The major problems in analyzing amphetamines are in distinguishing between the various isomers of an amphetamine and in differentiating amphetamine from methamphetamine. Furthermore, a forensic chemist not only must be able to analyze the substances submitted but also may be called upon to determine the exact status of a clandestine laboratory at the time it is seized. Investigators and police on the scene at the time of arrest must reduce the impact of their presence to a quantifiable minimum. Any changes in the scene resulting from the arrest will be noted by the defense. Photographs should be taken of the entire operation before, during, and after the processing of the crime scene. Gross changes in the features of these photos will require explanation by the investigators in charge and may provide means by which the defense may challenge statements regarding the production capabilities of the laboratory, possibly resulting in a reduced or dismissed charge.

Field testing for methamphetamine is a bit tricky. The Marquis field test will provide a positive reaction to meth and amphetamine (**Figure 15–29**). The only way to determine if the substance is methamphetamine rather than amphetamine is to conduct a second test that identifies both meth and Ecstasy. Knowing from the Marquis test that the sub-

Figure 15–29 Meth or MDMA field test.

Courtesy of Forensics Source

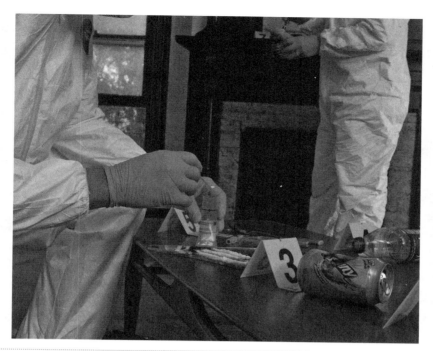

Figure 15–30 Meth or MDMA field test in action.

Courtesy of Forensics Source

stance is meth or amphetamine, a positive reaction of the meth/MDMA (Ecstasy) test by elimination will identify the substance as methamphetamine (**Figure 15–30**).

The meth/MDMA reagent will have three ampoules: upon breaking the third ampoule, a dark blue reaction will occur. The Marquis reagent contains a single ampoule. The color change from orange to brown indicates both amphetamines and meth (**Figure 15–31**).

Cocaine

History of Use

The word *coca* comes from the Aymara word *khoka*, meaning "the tree" (Karch, 1993). Measurable quantities of **cocaine** and nicotine have been detected in 3000-year-old Egyptian mummies (Balbanova, Parsche, and Pirsig, 1992). Boerhave favorably mentioned coca in his textbook on medicinal plants, published in 1708 (Mortimer, 1901).

Two events in 1884 significantly changed the pattern of cocaine use in the United States and Europe. The first was the publication of Freud's paper on cocaine (Stephens, 1993). The second was Koller's discovery that cocaine was a local anesthetic (Noyes, 1884). The availability of an effective local anesthetic had tremendous impact. Cocaine was propelled into the limelight, and physicians around the world were soon experimenting with the use of cocaine in a wide range of conditions (Karch, 1993). The first reports of cocaine toxicity appeared less than one year after Koller's and Freud's papers were published. An article in the *British Medical Journal* described the toxic reactions associated with cocaine use in ophthalmologic surgery ("Toxic Action of Cocaine," 1885). None of the negative reports appeared to have much impact. Patent medicine manufacturers continued to cash in on the popularity of coca by replacing low-concentration

Figure 15–31   Meth or MDMA field test photos.

© Mikael Karlsson/Alamy Images

cocaine extracts with high concentrations of refined cocaine hydrochloride. Thousands of cocaine-containing patent medicines flooded the market (Karch, 1993).

Until the early 1900s, cocaine had been taken mainly by mouth or by injection. The fact that the first cases of septal perforation and collapse were not reported until 1904 suggests that inhalation (snorting) had only become popular a year or so earlier (Maier, 1926). Between 1928 and 1973, there was only one reported fatality, and it involved a surgical misadventure. Suarez, Arango, and Lester (1977) first described the "body packer" syndrome, in which death results from the rupture of cocaine-filled condoms in a smuggler's intestines. The absence of case reports reflected a decline in use. Significant toxicity from the use of coca leaf and coca leaf extract was not a problem in the United States until purified cocaine became available. The small amounts of cocaine in patent medicines were apparently harmless, but the huge amounts of purified cocaine that could be ingested represented a quantum leap in dosage. With the appearance of crack cocaine in 1986, another order of magnitude increase in dosage occurred. Cocaine-related deaths and injuries are a product of more people using more of the drug in a more effective manner (Karch, 1993).

Production

Coca leaf has grown in the Andean subregion for thousands of years. Early explorers found it all along the eastern curve of the Andes, from the Straits of Magellan to the borders of the Caribbean. Coca grows best on the moist, warm slopes of mountains ranging from 1,500 to 5,000 feet. Coca shrubs grow to heights of 6 to 8 feet. Major growing areas in Bolivia share many characteristics. The Yungas Mountains, which are close to La Paz, have an average annual rainfall of 45 inches, and the Chapare River area, which is close to Cochabamba, has an annual rainfall of 102 inches. The plantations in the Yungas can

---

CASE IN POINT

Origins of a Legal Mass-Market Product

In 1857, Carl von Scherzer, chief scientist for a German training expedition sent around the world by Archduke Ferdinand, returned with 60 pounds of coca leaves. These were given to Albert Niemann, a graduate student in chemistry (Scherzer, 1861). Niemann was given the task of isolating coca's active principle. Purification of cocaine proved relatively simple, and Niemann published his PhD thesis, "On a New Organic Base in the Coca Leaves," in 1860 (Niemann, 1860). A *Lancet* editorial published in 1872 stated that "there is considerable difference of opinion as to its effects upon human subjects, and the published accounts are somewhat conflicting; but we think that there is strong evidence in favor of its being a stimulant and narcotic of a peculiar kind, and of some power" ("Coca," 1872, p. 746).

It was discovered that when alcohol and cocaine were combined, cocaethylene was formed, and the end product was as psychoactive as the cocaine itself. The French capitalized on this knowledge and began manufacturing wines containing coca. In early 1880, Parke Davis and Company began marketing a fluid extract containing 0.5 mg/ml of semipurified cocaine. In the United States, John Styth Pemberton began selling a "French Wine Cola." His initial marketing efforts were not very successful. In what proved to be a wise marketing move, Pemberton dropped the wine from the product and used a combination of cocaine and caffeine instead. The reformulated product was named Coca-Cola.

---

be harvested three times a year. Each harvest yields from 1 to 1.5 tons per hectare (890 to 1,336 pounds per acre) per year. The Chapare plantations are harvested four times a year, with a yield of 2 to 3 tons per hectare (1,789 to 2,672 pounds per acre) per year. The average coca plantation will produce for about 20 years, but after about the tenth year its yield steadily declines. More than 60% of all coca leaf is grown in Peru, with another 22% coming from Bolivia and 15% from Colombia. During processing, 400 pounds of leaf will yield 1 to 2 kg of coca paste (Abruzzese, 1989).

Cocaine extraction is a two- or three-step process, carried out in a series of laboratories. The first steps occur immediately after harvesting, when leaves are placed in a shallow pit lined with heavy plastic and then soaked in a solution of water and lime for three or four days. Gasoline or kerosene is then added to the mixture to extract the nitrogenous alkaloids. The coca leaf is discarded, and sulfuric acid is added to the extract. The gasoline or kerosene is removed, and the remaining solution is made alkaline by the addition of lime, causing the more basic alkaloids to precipitate out. This crude form of cocaine, called coca paste or pasta, is allowed to dry in the sun. (Brewer and Allen, 1991).

The site where the initial steps occur is referred to as a pasta lab. Laborers, called pisacocas, keep the alkali-coca leaf mulch mixed by stirring it with their hands and feet. The fluid is very corrosive and causes ulcers. The pisacocas tolerate the ulcers only because they are given a constant supply of coca paste to smoke (Weatherford, 1988).

Once the pasta is prepared, the clandestine manufacturer has two options. The pasta may be further purified at a base lab, or the producer may go directly to a crystal lab. At base labs, pasta is dissolved in dilute sulfuric acid. Potassium permanganate is added until the solution turns pink, thereby destroying the cinnamoyl-cocaine isomers present as impurities in the pasta. The reddish-pink solution is allowed to stand; then it is filtered, and the filtrate is made basic with ammonia. Cocaine base precipitates out. The precipitate is filtered, washed with water, and then dried. Finally, it is dissolved in diethyl ether or acetone. After filtering, concentrated hydrochloric acid and acetone are added, causing purified cocaine hydrochloride to precipitate out. This final step may be done on site, or the semipurified cocaine may be transported to a crystal lab, usually located in larger cities.

As much as 50 kg may be processed at one time in a crystal lab. The semipurified cocaine is dissolved in a solvent, often ether. Hydrochloric acid is added, along with acetone, and white crystals precipitate out. The crystals are collected by filtration. Traces of the solvent remain, and their presence can sometimes be used to identify the origin of cocaine samples. In producing countries, there is a significant market for the semipurified paste itself. Paste is smoked rolled up in pieces of newspaper or packed into cigarettes. The purity of confiscated cocaine is considered to be a good general indicator of availability. At wholesale levels, kilogram quantities that had been averaging 80% during 1990 increased to 87% purity during 1991. At the retail level, ounce specimens, which had been only 58% pure in 1990, had increased to 70% purity by 1991. The purity of the gram-sized samples sold on the street increased by only 2% during the same period. From 1990 through the first nine months of 1991, the price in the United States for kilogram quantities ranged from $11,000 to $40,000 (Karch, 1993). It is apparent that the market is volatile with no restraints other than what the market will bear.

Crack Cocaine

In the early 1970s, the organized production of cocaine lowered its street cost and increased its availability just as a wave of increased drug acceptance spread across the United States. Availability coupled with social acceptance led to a resurgence of cocaine use (Musto, 1991). As an acid or hydrochloride salt (**Figure 15–32**), the drug could be snorted or injected but not smoked. From the user's point of view it was still expensive—more expensive than heroin, and the pleasurable effects did not last as long.

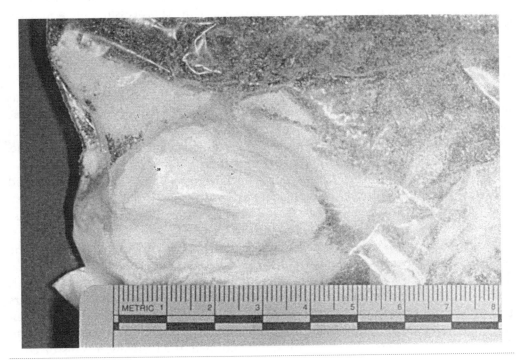

Figure 15–32   Powdered cocaine.

Courtesy of Austin Police Department, Austin, Texas

Crack cocaine, on the other hand, can be smoked (**Figure 15–33**). Rather than chemically decomposing, crack cocaine melts at 98°C and vaporizes. The vapor is absorbed by all mucous membranes and the lungs, rapidly producing a euphoric sensation that may last as long as 30 minutes. For many people, this effect is so overwhelming that they will sell or do anything to get more of the drug. The euphoric effect depends on the release of dopamine and other neurotransmitters, especially in the pleasure centers of the brain. Drug abusers state that the drug induces a feeling of power, self-esteem,

(A)

(B)

Figure 15–33   Crack cocaine and cocaine cookie crack (crack in the shape of the container in which it was formed).

Courtesy of Austin Police Department, Austin, Texas

and sensual well-being or sexual prowess, although prolonged use at high dosages has an adverse effect on sexuality.

Cocaine hydrochloride has been snorted or injected for years. However, by mixing it with ammonium hydroxide and then extracting the cocaine with ethyl ether, it could be changed into basic form and smoked. Smoking imparts a faster high, a more powerful onset of the drug's effect, and a longer-lasting high than the hydrochloride salt gives by injection. Inexperienced or intoxicated persons handling flammable solvents and open flames as they heated the extracted crystals of base on a pipe to vaporize and inhale the fumes suffered severe burns when the flammable solvent caught fire. As the amount of available cocaine became greater, prices dropped. A safer way to manufacture base cocaine using household chemicals was developed. Mixing the alkaline solution of cocaine with common sodium bicarbonate and heating the combination results in an opaque mass that is broken into chunks or rocks. Stoves were used to drive off the water and fix the base to the cocaine molecule, but microwave ovens are now commonly used for that purpose.

Many consider crack and freebase to be the same. They both begin as cocaine hydrochloride and both can be smoked. There is a distinct difference between them, in that freebase is virtually pure cocaine hydrochloride, whereas crack has the original impurities imparted from the cut in the powdered cocaine plus the residue of any baking soda that has not been strained out.

There are various methods of making crack. For example, soda can crack requires 6 grams of cocaine hydrochloride, 2 grams of flour, 2 grams of baking soda, a pinch of yeast, a carbonated drink, and the bottom of a beverage can. The dry ingredients are added first into the can bottom, with the beverage added next to form a thick liquid. The entire solution in the can bottom is then cooked on a low heat, stirring until the solution reduces into a thick paste. Once the paste dries it can be removed from the bottom of the can into one large crack cookie. The color of the crack will take on the color of the beverage used in the manufacturing of the crack.

Whichever method of making crack is employed, it is important to remember that each was made with, and contains, cutting agents and adulterants. When field testing crack, it is best not to scoop the bottom of the container for a sample: rather a chunk can be broken, thereby reducing the chances of just picking up loose cut in the bottom of the container.

Using Cocaine

Snorting involves making a line on a flat surface such as glass or a mirror. The thin 2- to 3-inch-long strip (the width of a match stick) of cocaine powder is inhaled (snorted). Single-edged razor blades are used to finely chop the cocaine powder and to construct the line for snorting. A rolled dollar bill (the denomination of the bill may be status related), a soda straw, a glass, silver, or gold tube, or a miniature spoon may be used for snorting (**Figure 15–34**). Regular users may grow the fingernail on the little finger of the dominant hand for use as an ersatz spoon.

The typical intravenous user injects the drug with an insulin syringe, leaving a pin-prick-size puncture site. Because cutting agents are usually soluble, the skin reaction, granulomas, and needle tracks seen with other drugs are not common in the case of cocaine.

Crack cocaine can be smoked in any manner that results in vaporizing the drug. It may be mixed with tobacco in a cigarette, in a regular pipe, in a pipe with a screen

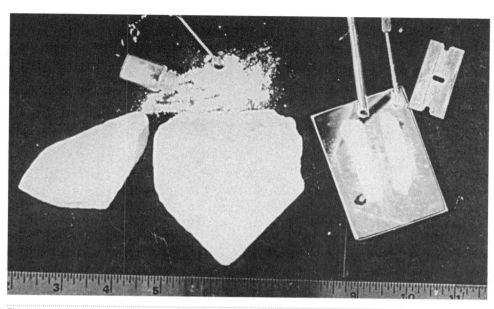

Figure 15–34 Cocaine powder, small bottle carrier and spoon lid, razor (to chop cocaine finely for inhalation), and metal straw (for inhalation "tooting").

Courtesy of Austin Police Department, Austin, Texas

to hold the tobacco and drug, or in a special crack pipe (**Figures 15–35 and 15–36**). Used by itself, the drug can be heated with a propane torch. Propane is preferred because other fuels are thought to impart an unpleasant taste to the vapors.

Field Testing for Cocaine

Cocaine is generally found in two forms in the field: rock or powder. The same tests are used for either, although it is important to remember that rock cocaine (whether crack or freebase) does not dissolve after the first testing ampoule is broken. The same reaction occurs, but the crack remains undissolved. No matter how hard you shake the pouch the rock remains rock.

In testing powdered or rock cocaine using the Scott reagent pouch, three ampoules must be broken and the proper color obtained after the breaking and agitation of each pouch. The standard color sequence is blue to pink to pink over blue. Anything other than this reaction indicates that what is being tested is not cocaine.

Often dealers will want to test cocaine to determine purity. Undercover investigators need to be aware of these various street testing techniques. The easiest is the burn method. A small quantity of the cocaine is placed on a four-inch square of foil. Enough water is added to dissolve the powder, after which heat is applied until the specimen is completely dissolved into a residue; the purer the cocaine, the browner the residue, and the whiter the specimen, the more cut has been added.

Legal Problems

No other controlled substance has been subjected to as many different types of scientific and legal attacks in court as cocaine. The reasons for this include the existence of numerous isomers of cocaine and the need to eliminate them analytically, the classification of cocaine as a narcotic for legal purposes, the public's perception of cocaine as being among the more dangerous drugs, and the relatively high income level of

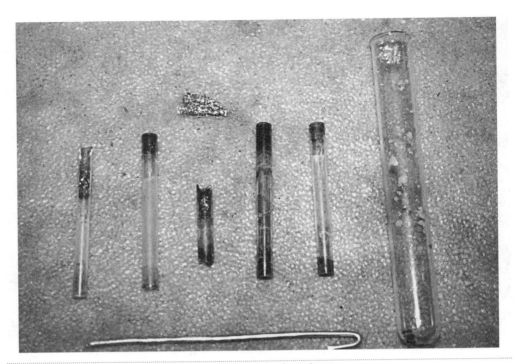

Figure 15–35   Crack cocaine pipes, filters (chore boy), and cleaning rod.

Courtesy of Austin Police Department, Austin, Texas

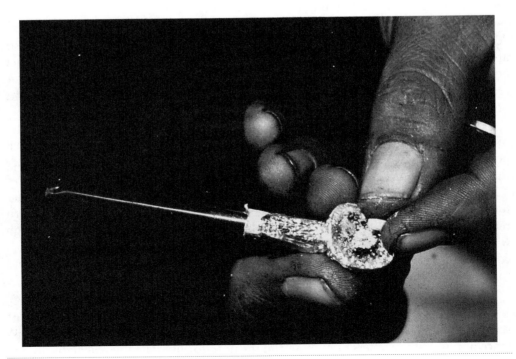

Figure 15–36   Crack pipe being smoked.

© Reuters/Howard Yanes/Landov

cocaine abusers, who have the resources to mount vigorous court defenses. The result has been an increased awareness on the part of drug chemists of the potential problems in cocaine analysis and consequently an increase in the number of tests performed in routine cocaine cases. The increase in tests has in turn caused an increase in the cost of cocaine analysis.

In some jurisdictions, most or all of the legal and scientific problems discussed here have been rendered moot through court decisions, changes in the wording of the cocaine laws, and increased levels of analysis. The major technical defenses in cocaine cases can be grouped into the following categories:

- Isomer defense 1: Diastereoisomers
- Isomer defense 2: Enantiomers
- Classification of cocaine as a narcotic
- The issue of aggregate weight

Isomer Defense 1: Diastereoisomers Diastereoisomers are chemical compounds that have the same chemical formula (isomers) and the same atomic bond arrangement but differ in the orientation of the molecules in three-dimensional space (stereoisomers). These isomers are not mirror images (mirror-image isomers are enantiomers). In general, diastereoisomers differ from one another in both physical and chemical properties. The diastereoisomers of cocaine are not available commercially, so a forensic chemist has nothing with which to compare a sample of alleged cocaine to positively eliminate the diastereoisomers. It is not enough that an analytical protocol yields results that are consistent with cocaine. The protocol results must also be inconsistent with all other substances, especially cocaine's isomers. Even with increased knowledge of the chemical and physical behavior of the diastereoisomers of cocaine, many chemists are still vulnerable to this challenge because they have not kept up with the literature or are not knowledgeable enough to grasp the concept of stereochemistry. Some state legislatures have responded to this chemical defense argument by changing the wording of the cocaine laws. In Michigan, for example, cocaine and all its stereoisomers are now controlled within Schedule II.

Isomer Defense 2: Enantiomers Because cocaine laws describe cocaine as a derivative of coca leaves, and only L-cocaine is a coca leaf derivative, this challenge was based on the failure of the chemist to eliminate enantiomeric D-cocaine (mirror-image cocaine) as a possibility. The most common response of the laboratories that were affected by the challenge was to add to the analytical protocol at least one test that would be able to eliminate D-cocaine from consideration.

Classification of Cocaine as a Narcotic The legal classification of cocaine, a central nervous system stimulant, as a narcotic by some jurisdictions is improper from a medical standpoint. In legal contexts, the term *narcotic* has been used for many years as a catchall term for dangerous drugs. There is no indication that any legislature meant to imply by this designation that cocaine is a narcotic medically. Nonetheless, the classification of cocaine as a narcotic in the criminal code means that it is treated as a narcotic for punishment purposes. Opponents of this classification claim that it is unfair to treat cocaine in this manner, because it is not, in their opinion, as dangerous a drug as heroin and the other narcotics. The argument has had only very limited success in the courts. Most courts have ruled that a legislature has every right to label cocaine as a narcotic for sanctioning purposes as long as there is no intent to medically classify cocaine as a narcotic.

Aggregate Weight Some states have passed laws linking the penalty for possession or distribution of drugs to the amount of the drugs. The laws are written in such a fashion that the crucial weight is that of the whole specimen, not the weight of the controlled substance. Under this aggregate-weight sentencing scheme, 100 g of a specimen of 1% cocaine would carry the same penalty as 100 g of pure cocaine. Some sentencing schemes increase the penalty based on weight. The forensic chemist will be asked to testify in cases where the aggregate weight is near the borderline between the two classes. Because the weighing of the drug is the responsibility of the laboratory, it is certain that there will be challenges to the accuracy of the balances used.

■ Club Drugs

Club drugs is a general term used for certain illicit substances, primarily synthetic, that are usually found at nightclubs, bars, and raves (all-night dance parties). Substances used as club drugs include, but are not limited to, MDMA (Ecstasy), GHB (gamma hydroxybutyrate—a date-rape drug), Rohypnol (a date-rape drug), ketamine (Special K), and methamphetamine (discussed earlier).

To some, club drugs seem harmless. Often, the raves where these drugs are used are promoted as alcohol-free events, which gives parents a false sense of security that their children will be safe attending such parties. These parents are not aware that raves may actually be havens for the illicit sale and abuse of club drugs.

Because club drugs are illegal and are often produced in unsanitary laboratories, it is impossible for the user to know exactly what he or she is taking. The quality and potency of these substances can vary significantly from batch to batch. Additionally, substitute drugs are sometimes sold in place of club drugs without the user's knowledge. For example, PMA (paramethoxyamphetamine) has been used as a substitute for MDMA. When users take PMA thinking they are really ingesting MDMA, they often think they have taken weak ecstasy because PMA's effects take longer to appear. They then ingest more of the substance to attain a better high, which can result in death by overdose.

■ Drug Regulation

The **Controlled Substances Act** is a federal law that establishes five schedules of classification for dangerous substances on the basis of potential for abuse, potential for physical and psychological dependence, and medical value. The criminal penalties for the manufacture, sale, or possession of controlled dangerous substances are related to the schedule as well (TABLE 15-2). The most severe penalties are for drugs listed in Schedules I and II.

Schedule I drugs are deemed to have a high potential for abuse, have no accepted medical use, and lack accepted safe protocols for use in treatment under medical supervision. Drugs controlled under this schedule include heroin, methaqualone, LSD, and marijuana.

Schedule II drugs have a high potential for abuse but have a current acceptable medical use. These drugs have a significant potential for severe psychological or physical dependence. Schedule II drugs include opium and derivatives of opium not listed in Schedule I; cocaine; methadone; phencyclidine; most amphetamine preparations; and most barbiturate preparations containing amobarbital, secobarbital, and pentobarbital. Dronabinol, the synthetic equivalent of the active ingredient in marijuana, has been

TABLE 15–2   Penalties for Controlled Substances Schedules Matrix

Controlled Substances Schedule	Penalty
I	0–20 years and/or $1 million
II	0–20 years and/or $1 million
III	0–5 years and/or $250,000
IV	0–3 years and/or $250,000
V	0–1 year and/or $100,000

Source: Reprinted from Drug Enforcement Agency

placed in Schedule II in recognition of its growing medical uses in treating glaucoma and chemotherapy patients (Saferstein, 1995).

Schedule III drugs have less potential for abuse than those in Schedules I and II and have a currently accepted medical use. These drugs have a potential for a low to moderate physical dependence or high psychological dependence. Schedule III controls all barbiturate preparations not covered under Schedule II and certain codeine preparations. Anabolic steroids were added to this schedule in 1991.

Schedule IV drugs have a low potential for abuse and have a current medical use. The abuse of these drugs may lead to limited dependence (less than that of Schedule III drugs). Drugs controlled in this schedule include propoxyphene (Darvon); phenobarbital; and tranquilizers such as meprobamate (Miltown), diazepam (Valium), and chlordiazepoxide (Librium).

Schedule V drugs have low abuse potential, have a medical use, and have less potential for producing dependence than Schedule IV drugs. Schedule V controls certain opiate drug mixtures that contain nonnarcotic medicinal ingredients.

The Controlled Substances Act includes a provision stipulating that an offense involving a controlled substance analog (i.e., a chemical substance substantially similar in chemical structure to a controlled substance) shall trigger penalties as if it were a controlled substance listed in Schedule I. This section is designed to combat the proliferation of so-called **designer drugs**. Designer drugs are substances that are chemically related to some controlled drugs and are pharmacologically very potent. These substances are manufactured in clandestine laboratories by skilled individuals who are aware that their products will not be covered by the schedules of the Controlled Substances Act.

Recent changes in the Controlled Substances Act constitute an effort to decrease the prevalence of clandestine drug laboratories designed to manufacture controlled substances. The act now regulates the manufacture and distribution of precursors, the chemical compounds used by clandestine drug laboratories to synthesize drugs of abuse.

■ Drug Investigations

The use of large amounts of unaccounted-for cash and the common arrest of persons who use or are addicted to controlled substances give the drug investigator a foothold in the fight against drugs. Most drug investigations are the result of police work, including the arrest of drug users who will cooperate with the police and the gathering of intelligence from the drug community. Information received from the drug community is always suspect. Informants do not provide information to police out of altruism. They generally have another agenda apart from the enforcement of laws and the enhancement of community safety.

The most effective tool to date in combating drug cartels has been the use of the Racketeer Influenced Corrupt Organization (RICO) Act, which provides for asset forfeiture. RICO laws were originally intended to combat organized criminal activity. Much of what is being done in contemporary drug distribution today fits the description of an organized criminal activity. RICO prohibits investing the proceeds of a pattern of racketeering activity in an enterprise that engages in interstate or foreign commerce; acquiring or maintaining an interest in such an enterprise by means of a pattern of racketeering activity; using a pattern of such activity in conducting the affairs of such an enterprise; and conspiracy to do any of the preceding (Osterburg and Ward, 2000). If a drug dealer is arrested based on proper probable cause, the government can seize property that has been used or obtained in violation of the law. The legal procedure employed in the forfeiture of such assets is civil rather than criminal in nature, requiring that a standard of a preponderance of evidence be applied by the state or federal government in proving the assets were the product of an organized criminal enterprise. Through asset forfeiture, state and federal police agencies have confiscated automobiles, money, houses, boats, airplanes, weapons, and other large consumer goods.

■ Drug Prevention

Many states are trying to change the message given to youths about drugs from "just do it" to "just say no." This latter message may fall on receptive ears if broadcast early enough. Teenagers, however, are listening to a different message conveyed by the media and the entertainment world. Late-night talk shows will invariably reveal comments about drugs, often flattering, frequently in jest. If we are facing an epidemic of drug abuse, if we are concerned about our children and their future, we need to change the perspective we bring to entertainment and education. Nothing is funny about drugs—about their use, their sale, and their consequences. Talk show guests do not jest about AIDS or breast cancer. The fact that drugs are ripe for comedic exploitation tells us two

---

OFFICER'S NOTEBOOK

Following Up on Informant's Tips

Police receiving information from informants are at risk in two ways: First, by receiving information that may or may not be true, and, second, by acting on information provided by people with ulterior motives. Yet the characterization of the enforcement of drug laws as a "drug war" prompts police to invest time and effort in responding to leads provided by informants.

Surveillance is the tool most often used by investigators to corroborate information provided by informants. Electronic, aural, and visual surveillance are part of the investigator's arsenal. Using electronic aural enhancement (wiretaps) to gather information can be arduous. The vocabulary of the drug world is unique and ever-changing. Investigators must have a working vocabulary that allows them to converse with drug-using informants as well as to interpret intercepted communications. Often, innocuous cellphone conversations carry the seeds of a drug transaction. The more sophisticated traffickers may use code words or numbers in describing locations, drug types, and monetary values. Beepers can use numbers to convey exactly that type of information. Having an opportunity to examine beeper logs may reveal a repeating number system that can be decrypted.

things: Drug use is more prevalent than we suspect, and drug use is more acceptable than we pretend.

One problem in educating young people about drugs is that the cast of characters we have fictionalized includes the evil drug user and the recreational drug user. It is a mistake to believe there is any difference between the two. The substances of abuse all come from the same place and support the same industry. Whether cocaine is abused in a crack house, dormitory, or penthouse is of little relevance to the cartel of drug producers and dealers who drive new autos and brandish 9-mm weapons. The purchase, regardless of location or use, contributes to the success of a growth industry as well as to the death of police fighting a winless war.

■ Summary

Drugs are the plague that is destroying America from the inside as those opposed to the United States watch and applaud as we self-destruct. Without sounding like an alarmist drugs are involved in the violation of virtually every criminal statute. They aggravate domestic disturbances, burglaries, and armed robberies. Even if drug use were decriminalized those without or unable to maintain gainful employment would still resort to crime to support their drug use. We have become so enamored with drugs that there is no ready solution. Prisons fill, gangs proliferate, and street crime continues to rise all fueled directly or indirectly by drugs. There are no casual users, the industry does not differentiate and cops die as comedians tell drug jokes and audiences laugh and wink.

Arson is an assault on an edifice, one of those crimes that can be fueled by something other than greed or malice. There are those who set fires because they like fire or the destruction the fire causes. Arson is also of interest to serial offender profilers. The next chapter presents material germane to the understanding of why people start fires and where the fire investigation begins.

■ Key Terms

amphetamines: Synthetic central nervous system stimulants

barbiturates: Depressants derived from barbituric acid that act on the central nervous system and create a feeling of well-being and drowsiness; they are generally taken orally in 10- to 70-mg doses and are absorbed through the small intestines

club drugs: A general term used for certain illicit substances, primarily synthetic, that are usually found at nightclubs, bars, and raves

cocaine: Stimulant drug derived from the coca plant

codeine: Narcotic that is used as an analgesic and cough suppressant

color reactions: Expected reactions to drug field tests

Controlled Substances Act: An act that established five schedules of classification for dangerous substances on the basis of potential for abuse, potential for physical and psychological dependence, and medical value and that set forth criminal penalties for the manufacture, sale, or possession of these controlled dangerous substances

crack cocaine: Form of cocaine that melts at 98°C and vaporizes; the vapor is absorbed by all mucous membranes and the lungs, rapidly producing a euphoric sensation that may last as long as 30 minutes

designer drugs: Substances that are chemically related to some controlled drugs and are pharmacologically very potent

Dillie-Koppanyi test: A test for barbiturates, in whose presence the reagent turns violet-blue

Duquenois-Levine test: A test for marijuana; when applied to marijuana, the reagent turns violet

forensic chemist: Person who performs chemical and physical analysis of physical evidence to determine the makeup of a substance or substances, including identifying drugs by their chemical properties

gas chromatography: A chromatographic technique in which a vaporized sample is carried by a gaseous mobile phase over a stationary phase (usually either a solid or a solid coated with a nonvolatile liquid), the amount of time required for each component to reach a detector is recorded, and the chromatogram that results will have a pattern of peaks that is used to identify the sample

hallucinogens: Drugs that cause a distortion in thought processes and perceptions as well as changes in moods

lysergic acid diethylamide (LSD): Hallucinogen that is synthesized from a type of fungus that attacks certain grasses and grains; the drug is very potent and as little as 25 mcg is enough to start visual hallucinations that may last up to 12 hours

Marquis test: Test used to screen for heroin, morphine, and opium derivatives; the reagent turns purple in their presence

mass spectrometry: Technique used to identify the masses of the component parts that were separated by gas chromatography; in the mass spectrometer, the sample is exposed to a beam of high-energy electrons that causes the sample to fragment, producing a characteristic fragmentation pattern that is distinctive enough to be considered a fingerprint

methadone: A synthetic opiate used to prevent the physical symptoms of narcotic withdrawal that would otherwise be felt by someone addicted to narcotics

microcrystalline test: Confirmatory test in which a small quantity of the substance is placed on a microscopic slide and a drop of chemical reagent is added; the chemical reagent causes a precipitate reaction, creating crystals of a size and shape characteristic of a particular drug

narcotics: Analgesics that relieve pain by depressing the central nervous system; the source of most narcotics is opium, and their regular use leads to physical dependence

phencyclidine (PCP): A synthetic substance that has appeared on the street in pill form (peace pills) and powder form (angel dust, tic, and dummy dust); now generically referred to as angel dust, and the preferred method of use is inhalation or ingestion

physiologic dependence: Dependance on the use of a drug such that withdrawal of the drug results in clinical signs such as abdominal pains, nausea, and vomiting

Scott test: Test used to screen for cocaine

screening test: Test in which a specimen is subjected to a series of reagents that yield characteristic colors for commonly encountered drugs

tetrahydrocannabinol (THC): The psychoactive ingredient in marijuana

thin-layer chromatography: Chromatography that incorporates a solid stationary phase and a moving liquid phase to separate the constituents of a mixture

■ Review Questions

1. What is the "two tiers of law" concept, and how does it apply to sanctions for the possession of cocaine?

2. What are the various presumptive tests that forensic chemists use to help them identify controlled substances?

3. Describe the following laboratory procedures: microcrystalline tests, gas chromatography, thin-layer chromatography, and mass spectroscopy.

4. How is heroin usually used, and from where does it come?

5. What makes a drug fall into the hallucinogenic classification?

6. What legal problems confront an investigator and a forensic scientist when dealing with a methamphetamine laboratory?

7. What was the result of the passage of the Controlled Substances Act?

8. What is crack cocaine?

9. What drugs pose the most serious withdrawal risks for those habituated?

10. What is a club drug?

11. What are some of the dangers associated with the use of club drugs?

12. Why should police not use a pocket knife to scoop drugs into a test kit?

13. In drug testing, does the sequence of progressive color change matter?

14. What are the three most likely factors responsible for reagent coloring?

15. Why is it important to document drug test procedures and results?

16. What kinds of information about a drug might be obtained from a PDR?

17. When handling drugs why are nitrile gloves preferable to common rubber gloves?

18. Describe the burn method for testing cocaine.

19. What is urine meth?

■ Bibliography

Abruzzese, R. (1989). Coca-leaf production in the countries of the Andean subregion. *Bulletin of Narcotics* 41, 95–104.

Baden, M.M. (1980). Investigation of deaths from drug abuse. In W.U. Spitz and R.S. Fisher (Eds.), *Medicolegal investigation of death* (2nd ed.). Springfield, IL: Charles C. Thomas.

Balbanova, S., Parsche, F., and Pirsig, W. (1992). First identification of drugs in Egyptian mummies. *Naturwissenschaften* 79, 358–371.

Brewer, L., and Allen, A. (1991). N-formyl cocaine: A study of cocaine comparison parameters. *Journal of Forensic Science* 36, 697–731.

Coca (1872). *Lancet,* May 25, 746.

Down, G.J., and Gwyn, S.A. (1975). Investigation of direct thin-layer chromatography-mass spectrometry as a drug analysis technique. *Journal of Chromatography* 103, 208–212.

Karch, S.B. (2002). *The pathology of drug abuse.* Boca Raton, FL: CRC Press.

Klein, M., Kruegel, A.V., and Sobol, S.P. (1979). *Instrumental applications in forensic drug chemistry.* U.S. Department of Justice, Drug Enforcement Administration, United States.

Maier, H.W. (1926). *Der Kokainismus.* (O.J. Kalant, Trans.). Toronto: Addiction Research Foundation.

Mortimer, W.G. (1901). Peru: The history and regulation of a dangerous drug. *Cornell Law Review* 58, 537.

Musto, D.F. (1991). Opium, cocaine and marijuana in American history. *Scientific American* 265(1), 40–47.

Niemann, A. (1860). Uber eine neue organische Base in den Cocablattern. Inaug-diss., University of Gottingen, Germany.

Noyes, H. (1884). Muriate of cocaine as a local anesthetic to the cornea: The ophthal-mological congress in Heidelberg. *Medical Record* 17, 418.

Osterburg, J.W., and Ward, R.H. (2000). *Criminal investigation: A method for reconstructing the past* (3rd ed.). Cincinnati, OH: Anderson Publishing.

Saferstein, R. (1995). *Criminalistics: An introduction to forensic science* (5th ed.). Englewood Cliffs, NJ: Prentice Hall.

Scherzer, K. (1861). *Narrative of the circumnavigation of the globe by the Austrian frigate "Novara."* London: Saunders, Otley and Co.

Siegel, J.S. (2005). Forensic identification of controlled substances. In R. Saferstein (Ed.), *Forensic science handbook* (Vol. 2). Englewood Cliffs, NJ: Prentice Hall.

Stephens, B.G. (1993). Investigations of death from drug abuse. In W.U. Spitz and R.S. Fisher (Eds.), *Medicolegal investigations of death* (3rd ed.). Springfield, IL: Charles C. Thomas.

Suarez, C., Arango, A., and Lester, J. (1977). Cocaine-condom ingestion. *JAMA* 238, 1391–1392.

Thornton, J.I., and Nakamura, G.R. (1972). The identification of marijuana. *Journal of Forensic Science Society* 14, 461.

"Toxic action of cocaine." (1885, November 21). *British Medical Journal,* 983.

Weatherford, J. (1988). Indian givers. In: *The drug connection.* New York: Crown.

Yinon, J., and Zitrin, S. (1977). Processing and interpreting mass spectral data in forensic identification of drugs and explosives. *Journal of Forensic Science* 22, 741–747.

■ Suggested Reading

Austin, J., and Krisberg, B.W. (1981). Wider, stronger, and different nets: The dialectics of criminal justice reform. *Journal of Research on Crime and Delinquency* 18(1), 165–169.

Collins, J. (1982). *Criminal justice clients in drug treatment.* Research Triangle Park, NC: Research Triangle Institute.

Finn, P. (1989). Decriminalization of public drunkenness: Response of the healthcare system. *Journal of Studies on Alcohol* 46(1), 7–16.

Galvin, J.J. (1977). Alternatives to prosecution: Instead of jail (Vol. 3.). Washington, DC: U.S. Government Printing Office.

Hayes and Associates. (1987). *TASC annual evaluation report.* Winston Salem, NC: Hayes and Associates.

Leonard, R. (1972). Deferred prosecution program. *The Prosecutor* 8(4), 36–41.

Mullen, J. (1974). *The dilemma of diversion.* Washington, DC: U.S. Government Printing Office.

Musto, D.F. (1973). *The American disease: Origins of narcotic control.* New Haven, CT: Yale University Press.

Nimmer, R. (1974). *Diversion: The search for alternative forms of prosecution.* Chicago: American Bar Foundation.

Plowman, T., and Rivier, L. (1983). Cocaine and cinnamoylcocaine of *Erythroxylum* species. *Annals of Botany* 51, 641.

President's Commission on Law Enforcement and Administration of Justice (1967). *The challenge of crime in a free society.* Washington, DC: U.S. Government Printing Office.

Saferstein, R. (1988). *Forensic science handbook* (Vol. 2). Englewood Cliffs, NJ: Prentice Hall.

Arson

▶ ▶ STUDENT LEARNING OUTCOMES

Upon completion of this chapter students will demonstrate an understanding of:

- What constitutes an arson
- Some of the motives for committing an arson
- The types of evidence to be sought at an arson crime scene
- The results of a vessel arson
- The importance of underwater crime scenes to counter terrorism

Arson is usually divided into two categories: arson and aggravated arson. The latter involves risk of human injury, whereas the former does not. Many states have recognized a number of different types of arson and have provided specific statutory prohibitions and sanctions for them. In Texas, a person can commit arson upon a fence, pasture, tree, auto, unoccupied dwelling, building, or structure. States having hot, dry summers have passed arson laws pertaining to fires that get out of hand and cause extensive property damage; although not technically arson (because of the absence of intent), they are nonetheless prohibited and may be cause for the application of legal sanctions.

■ Investigation of Arson

Traditionally, the responsibility for investigating fires fell to fire fighters. Just as they had equipment to conduct water rescues and were therefore given the responsibility for recovering drowning victims, they had expertise in fighting fires and were therefore given the responsibility for investigating them. Time has shown that specialized skill, experience, and equipment are required to conduct an effective arson investigation, prompting many fire departments to do one of two things: (1) report suspected arson to the police for investigation or (2) train fire fighters as arson investigators with police authority.

The role of fire fighters is generally to fight fires and in the process report anything suspicious that might indicate arson. They are not usually trained or equipped to investigate arson. Unfortunately, neither are most police investigators. The law enforcement community rarely paid much attention to deliberately set fires unless they were started to conceal a more serious offense such as homicide or burglary. The thinking generally has been that the insurance industry would handle the investigation and there was no sense in duplicating efforts. Although the insurance carrier's adjuster or investigator may investigate a fire, he or she will arrive on the scene long after the fire has been extinguished and long after prospective witnesses have disappeared and prospective evidence has been destroyed or removed.

Fires and explosions provide little information upon which an investigation can proceed. What information is available is generally circumstantial. Arson and bombings are committed with some degree of planning, and the arsonist or bomber is usually far from the scene when the crime is discovered and investigators respond. The extensive destruction at the scene renders most evidence unidentifiable or unusable. The laboratory can provide only limited assistance in identifying **accelerants** that may have been deployed or in reconstructing igniting or detonating devices. Although forensic scientists may be able to identify minute amounts of an accelerant in the materials provided for examination, there is no scientific test that will determine whether a particular arsonist used the accelerant, unless a suspect is taken into custody with evidence of the accelerant on clothing or in a container.

The cause of a fire may be readily apparent or may require extensive examination. Fires may be caused by accident or intent. One way of proving intent is by ruling out accidental causes of the fire. A final determination must take into consideration numerous factors and deserves a complete and meticulous investigation. Only properly trained and experienced investigators can conduct that type of investigation. Normally, an ordinary match will ignite fuels. However, other **ignitors** must be considered; electrical discharges, sparks, and chemicals may provide temperatures in excess of the **ignition temperature** of most fuels.

A fuel will interact with oxygen to produce a flame only when the fuel is in a gaseous state. This is true even if the fuel feeding the flame is wood, paper, cloth, plastic, or gasoline. In the case of a liquid fuel, the temperature must be high enough to vaporize the fuel. The vapor that forms burns when it mixes with oxygen. The **flash point** is the lowest temperature at which a liquid gives off sufficient vapor to form a mixture with air that will support combustion. Once the flash point is reached, the fuel can be ignited by some outside source of high temperature. The ignition temperature is always higher than the flash point. With a solid fuel, the process of generating vapor is more complex. Solid fuel will burn only when it is exposed to heat that is great enough to break down the solid into a gaseous product. The chemical decomposition is called **pyrolysis**. Gaseous fuel and air will only burn if their composition (the fuel-air mix) lies within certain limits. If the proportion of fuel to air is too low or too high (as in a flooded auto carburetor), combustion will not occur. The range in which air and fuel will support combustion is called the **flammable range**.

There are instances in which a fuel can burn without a flame. A burning cigarette or red-hot charcoal is an example of glowing combustion or smoldering. Combustion is taking place on the surface of a solid fuel in the absence of heat high enough to break down the fuel into a gaseous product (pyrolyze the fuel). This same phenomenon can be seen in wood fires once all the gases have been expended; the wood continues to smolder until all of the carbonaceous residue has been consumed (Saferstein, 1995).

Tabloids and tabloid television shows have convinced the public that fire may begin as the result of **spontaneous combustion**. Some have gone so far as to insist that humans can combust spontaneously. Regardless of what scriptwriters suggest, there is no documented case of a human spontaneously combusting. Spontaneous combustion of nonhuman materials is a product of a natural heat-producing process. This process is caused and maintained by poor ventilation. Hay stored in hot unventilated areas is a conducive medium for the growth of bacteria that generate heat. If left unventilated at elevated temperatures long enough, the hay may be ignited by the activity of the bacteria. Paint, oily rags, and various chemicals left in a hot unventilated area also may ignite. Spontaneous combustion is seldom the cause of a fire but often is invoked as the cause.

The focus of every arson investigation is the fire's **point of origin**. The investigation must begin as soon as possible after the fire has been reported, preferably while it is still burning. The fire itself may provide information about its nature and origin. The direction the fire travels will be helpful in determining where it began (**Figures 16–1 and 16–2**). If there are numerous fires spread out over a burning structure, arson should be presumed. Accelerants that may have been used to start the fire have detectable odors and smoke coloring. The inability of fire fighters to gain access to the building suggests that the fire began accidentally or that someone with a key started the fire. In addition

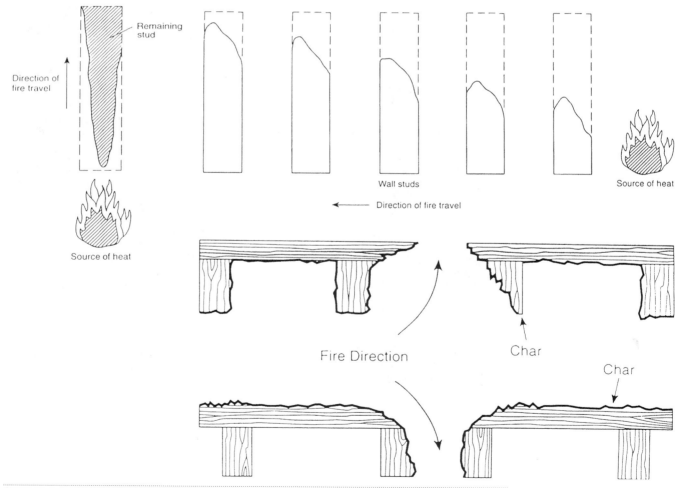

Figure 16–1   Direction of fire travel.

(A)

(B)

Figure 16–2   Direction of fire.

to what the fire can tell, witnesses on the scene may be helpful in gathering information about the fire. Investigators will want to note the following:

- When the fire was first discovered
- The size of the fire upon discovery
- Who discovered the fire
- Who reported the fire
- Unusual activity around the premises before the fire
- Unusual or unidentified persons in the area

Often a **pyromaniac** will return to the scene to enjoy the fruits of his or her labor. It is important to begin the investigation by taking pictures of those watching the fire to identify any known fire starters or persons who neither work nor live in the area. Professional arsonists may linger to determine if the fire set will be sufficient to destroy the building and the evidence of arson.

Once the fire has been extinguished, entry should be made as soon as it is safe. Recording the scene photographically is the first priority. A thorough search of the premises is required, for subsequent entries may have to be based on probable cause and a search warrant. Time is working against the investigator. Most fires are started or accelerated with petroleum-based hydrocarbons. Any remaining residue can evaporate in a matter of hours. Salvage operations may begin quickly, or a search of the premises for survivors or bodies may be conducted. It is imperative that the examination of the crime scene begin before it has been disturbed if possible; if it is not possible, the evidentiary value of the photographs will increase.

■ Arson Evidence

Two types of evidence are available to the arson investigator:

1. **Direct evidence** that links the arsonist to the fire, such as eyewitness identification or motive.
2. **Incendiary evidence**, which includes crime scene debris, observed burning characteristics, and an absence of accidental causation.

Motives for Arson

The motive for arson may be general (e.g., vandalism) or specific (e.g., commercial arson to collect insurance). Common motives include profit, vandalism, revenge, crime concealment, and thrill seeking (pyromania).

Fires for profit are common and are generally started as an alternative to financial failure or partner disenchantment. The target of the fire may not be the building alone. A thorough investigation of the paper trail associated with the business may not reveal anything confirming the fire. An absence of expanded or new insurance coverage might suggest that no profit motive exists. The relevant insurance, however, may be on the goods stored rather than the business itself. It is not unusual for fires to be set to rid the owner of a cumbersome or outdated inventory. There is usually some evidence to support the hypothesis that the fire was set to destroy the inventory. Valuable items that the owner does not wish to "liquidate" may be removed from the premises or replaced with outdated items insured at new-merchandise prices.

Automobile owners plagued with mechanical difficulties or monthly payments that they can no longer maintain may burn their autos for the insurance coverage and the relief of getting rid of a lemon. The vehicle will be reported stolen after the fire is set so that the owner avoids being stopped in a reportedly stolen vehicle. The time at which the vehicle was torched and the time it was reported stolen may be useful in investigating the auto arson. Additionally, items of commercial or sentimental value may have been removed from the vehicle prior to the burning. It is much more common for a stolen vehicle to be abandoned in a watery depository than for the thieves to burn it. If a vehicle is reported stolen and is subsequently discovered burnt, there is a very good possibility that it was an owner arson. The only practical reason fire would be used to destroy a stolen vehicle would be to cover up a more serious offense (a homicide, a robbery, or a hit and run).

Fires started by vandals cause untold property loss each year. The intent is generally to start a fire of a particular thing in a specific area for the "fun of it" or because "nobody was using it anyway." Schools and school-related buildings may be set on fire by disgruntled students (which would make the fire one of revenge rather than pure mischief). Field or forest fires started as a prank often grow into major fires that destroy thousands of acres. The investigation of a vandalistic fire begins at the point of origin, and the investigators attempt to locate witnesses who have seen young people playing in the area. Most of these types of fires are set by juveniles without much planning, using a match or lighter as an ignitor (sophisticated ignition systems are not going to be found at this crime scene). Most vandal arsonists remain uncaught.

Occasionally a fire fighter will set a fire that appears to be vandalism for the purpose of being part of the team called in to put out the fire. This type of arson, because of motive, falls in a category by itself. The ultimate objective may be for profit (fires keep fire fighters employed) or self-aggrandizement (the fire fighter has an opportunity to do something heroic). Obviously, a fire fighter arsonist is the most difficult type to catch, because he or she has extensive knowledge of fires and their investigation.

Fires for revenge are cowardly but nonetheless lethal. The cast of potential characters ranges from spurned suitors to disgruntled employees, and the motives range from racism to anger caused by a neighborly dispute. Once revenge has been selected as a possible motive, the list of suspects should be short and illuminating. These fires may be the product of long-range planning or may be fairly spontaneous. The modus operandi, which can range from igniting drapery in a hotel to setting ignition devices around the perimeter of a building, will vary, but the motive will steer the investigation.

Masking fires set to mask the commission of other crimes (e.g., homicides) are the major focus of arson investigations conducted by police agencies. The investigator must not only conduct a thorough arson investigation but also must observe the rudiments of, say, a homicide investigation at the same time. The main question confronting an investigator in arson with human victims is whether the fire was set to effect the death of the victims or whether the deaths were unintended consequences of the arson.

People love fire. It is hypnotic and simultaneously warming and comforting, not to mention romantic. People will turn the air conditioner on to be able to have a fire in the fireplace to create an intimate environment. Folks gathered around a campfire share not only its warmth but also each other's. Our love affair with fire has brought us to the pinnacle of technological refinement, but fire is also the source of a morbid fascination because of the havoc it can wreak when released. There are those among us who long to "release the beast"—those who set fires out of a sexual obsession and who

CASE IN POINT

The Happy Land Social Club Fire

In November 1988, the Happy Land Social Club was ordered to close down as a fire hazard because it had no fire exits, no fire alarm, and no sprinkler system. After a brief hiatus, the club was reopened, although the violations had not been addressed. On a weekend in April 1990, Julio Gonzalez, a Marielito (a member of the 1980 Cuban boatlift), engaged in a quarrel with his ex-girlfriend Lydia Feliciano. A bouncer ordered Julio off the premises. He left, saying he would be back and would shut the place down. Gonzalez told police that he purchased a dollar's worth of gasoline in a plastic milk jug and returned to the club. He splashed the gasoline through the front door of the club and then ignited it with a match. Most of the occupants were on the second floor and rushed toward two narrow stairways leading to the ground floor. Many were trampled in the panic; those who were not, found the front entrance blocked by flames. Ironically, the object of Julio's wrath managed to escape with four others. Eighty-seven people were killed, most from smoke inhalation. Gonzalez was indicted on 87 counts of felony murder (Magnuson, 1990).

will continue to set fires until stopped. Pyromaniacs (serial fire starters) are generally compulsive, and their fires are unplanned. Many believe this type of fire starting is one of a trilogy of behaviors that together are characteristic of serial killers (the other two are bedwetting and animal torture).

Incendiary Evidence

Fires tend to move upward, and therefore the point of origin is often the lowest point that shows intense burn characteristics. In addition, the arsonist may have used **trailers**, **streamers**, or **plants** to spread the fire (**Figure 16–3**). Gasoline-soaked rags, paper trails, or other devices used to ensure that fire starts and spreads may have not completely burned. Gasoline residue soaked into unburned furnishings or cracks in the flooring material may be retrievable, indicate the origin of the fire, and serve as evidence of arson.

Ignitor containers may be left at or near the scene. Most arson fires (except for those set by vandals) are started with the use of an ignitor other than a simple match. An ignition device allows the arsonist to exit the building safely or provides for ample time to secure an alibi for the time the fire was set. Ignitors can be very complex or deceptively simple. The more complex the igniting device, the more likely unburned remains will exist.

Collecting Evidence

The containers of choice for holding evidence in an arson investigation include unused paint cans (**Figure 16–5**) and mason jars. Both can be sealed airtight, and neither will react with suspect materials. Once evidence of arson has been discovered, the material should be placed in an airtight container, leaving one-third of the volume in the container empty. In order for the laboratory to run tests, three things are necessary:

1. An uncontaminated sample
2. A sufficient sample
3. A **background sample** (control)

Contamination is a byproduct of fire and the extinguishing of the fire. Additional contamination resulting from mishandling is what must be avoided. Containers made

(A)

(B)

(C)

(D)

Figure 16–3   Straw streamer, burning streamers, and burnt streamer.

OFFICER'S NOTEBOOK

Processing the Arson Scene

Once the point of origin has been located, it must be protected until a thorough examination has been completed. Again, photographs should be the first priority. The search for accelerants should not be forsaken because of the abundance of water left after the fire. Water does not interfere with laboratory methods used to detect flammable liquid residues. A **vapor detector,** also called a **sniffer,** helps in the detection of flammable fluids (**Figure 16–4**). The device detects the presence of volatile residues by sucking in air around the suspect sample. The air passes over a heated filament. A combustible vapor oxidizes and increases the temperature of the heated filament, measured by the detector's meter. A positive finding by the sniffer, however, is not determinative, only presumptive. Its value is that suspect samples can be tested at the scene. Any questionable samples must be properly handled, packaged, and transported to the laboratory.

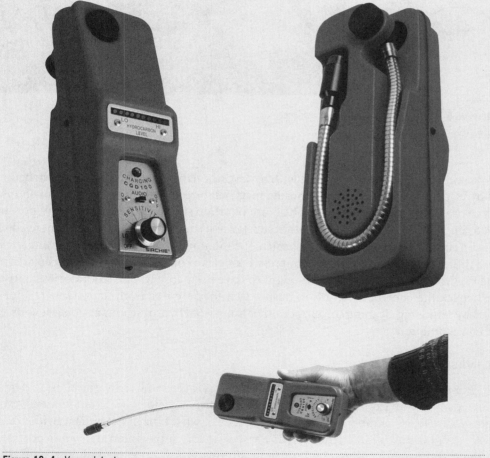

Figure 16–4   Vapor detector.

Figure 16–5 Unused paint can for storing evidence.

Courtesy of SIRCHIE Finger Print Laboratories, Inc.

of plastic or polyethylene will react with hydrocarbons and may result in the destruction of hydrocarbon vapors. When gathering material for collection, the investigator should try to preserve sizable specimens. The point of origin should produce a gallon of porous material, soot, and debris and any other substances thought to contain accelerant residue. It is important that all materials suspected of containing volatile liquids be accompanied by a thorough sampling of similar but relatively clean control specimens from an area of the fire in which accelerants are thought to have been absent. The laboratory scientists will check the control materials to ensure that they are free from flammable residues, thereby removing cleaning solvents or other household hydrocarbons as possible sources of contamination.

■ Vessel Arson

For the investigator, the main task in boat fires is the same as in land fires: to determine if a fire or an explosion was incendiary (arson) or accidental. To aid in the investigation, dive team members must have some idea of what type of incendiary evidence to look for. If the hull is intact, they can do a visual examination aimed at locating portions of the vessel that are charred and portions left unscathed. A detailed photographic log should be made, describing and documenting burn characteristics and any evidence discovered. Each piece of evidence to be recovered should be photographed in its original place and condition. The scene sketch should show the location of each piece of evidence within the search site.

Fires burn in boats in the same fashion as they do in buildings: from the ignition point upward. The probable point of origin will most likely be located closest to the lowest point that shows the most intense burn characteristics. The surface of charred wood

OFFICER'S NOTEBOOK

Arson Scene Evidence

Any empty or partially filled containers that may contain flammable substances should be collected and placed in sealed containers. Because a container is empty does not mean there are no traces of the contents left.

The search for ignitors should begin once the point of origin has been discovered. If a match was used, the fire will likely have consumed it, but this is not always the case. Something as insignificant as a match, ammunition, firearms, a Molotov cocktail (a bottle of gas with a gas-soaked rag as a wick), a cigarette, or a matchbook may be the key to the investigation. The match or cigarette may come from a matchbook or a pack of cigarettes on a suspect (a rare but not unknown event). The match can be identified as coming from a particular matchbook through comparison microscopy. The broken glass of a Molotov cocktail may bear fingerprints, or its wick may be matched to the cloth from which it was torn. If a suspect is in custody, his or her clothing should be examined for accelerants, and each article of clothing should be placed in a separate airtight container (Saferstein, 1995).

exhibits a pattern of crevices similar in appearance to the skin of an alligator (**Figure 16–6**). The probable point of origin is in the area where the smallest checks in the alligator pattern and the deepest charring are found. An ice pick pushed into the charred area may prove helpful in measuring the depth of charring. It is in this area that physical evidence of criminal design is most likely to be discovered, and wood samples should be taken from this area for laboratory examination for hydrocarbons (accelerants).

Nothing should be touched or moved before measurements and photographs have been taken and sketches made. The presence of hydrocarbon containers should be noted. In most arsons, an incendiary or detonation device of some type is employed to allow

Figure 16–6 Charred chair.

the arsonist to depart the scene or to establish an alibi. Such devices may be as complex as a remote control detonator or as simple as a candle embedded in gasoline. Remnants of **delay devices** may be discovered near the point of origin.

In the case of explosions, a larger area should be searched with the goal of discovering incendiary or detonation devices or their remains. Unburned fabric may retain measurable amounts of hydrocarbons. If the interior of the boat was splashed with diesel fuel, kerosene, or gasoline, any unburned porous material may retain traces of the accelerant. If streamers were used to aid in acceleration, unburned remains may be found. Cloth generally does not completely burn and, if used as a streamer, may still retain accelerant traces. Hydrocarbons dissipate more slowly in water. It is imperative that any pieces of evidence that may have hydrocarbon traces be packaged in water in watertight containers for delivery to the laboratory.

The gas chromatograph is the most reliable instrument for detecting flammable residues. Most arsons are initiated by petroleum distillates such as gasoline, diesel fuel, and kerosene, all of which are composed of a mixture of hydrocarbons. The gas chromatograph separates the hydrocarbon distillate into its components, giving a visual recording of the characteristic pattern of the specific petroleum product (Saferstein, 1995). In seeking evidence of suspected accelerants, it is necessary to test an uncontaminated control sample of the same material.

■ Vessel Explosions

The steps employed in the investigation of an explosion are generally the same as for arson, but there are several additional considerations. The chances of finding a large amount of trace evidence are remote. Like fire, an explosion is the product of combustion accompanied by the creation of gases and heat. It is the sudden buildup of expanding gas pressure at the point of detonation that produces the disruption of the explosion. Chemical explosions can be classified on the basis of the velocity of energy waves transmitted upon detonation.

Low-order explosives involve a relatively slow rate of conversion to a gaseous state. The energy wave generated travels at a speed of less than 1,000 meters per second. The most widely used explosives in the low-order group are black powder and smokeless powder. Low-order explosives can be ignited by heat and are usually ignited with a lighted fuse.

High-order explosives change rapidly to a gaseous state upon ignition. The energy wave created travels at a rate between 1,000 and 9,000 meters per second. Dynamite is the most common high-order explosive, although composition C-4 (made of RDX, the most popular and powerful of the military explosives) is also used. Unlike low-order explosives, high-order explosives must be detonated by an initiating device. The most common initiator is a blasting cap. However, the ignition switch on a boat can be used to provide the spark necessary to detonate high-order explosives.

The search should focus on locating the site of the device and identifying the type of explosive used. The point of detonation will often leave a gaping hole surrounded by scorching. The type of explosive used may be determined by inspecting the residue at the scene. Wood, metal, and fiberglass samples surrounding the **detonation point** should have sufficient residue to allow identification of the explosive. The entire area must be searched systematically to recover any trace of a detonating mechanism. Particles of explosives will be embedded in the pipe cap or threads of a pipe bomb. All materi-

OFFICER'S NOTEBOOK

Arson Checklist

The following data should be included in the report of a suspected arson or detonation.

1. General data
   a. Owner's name
   b. Insurer's name
   c. Date and time of fire
   d. Last user's name
   e. Time and date of last use
2. Owner data
   a. Financial condition of owner
   b. Prior loss history
   c. Prior criminal history
   d. Name of the insured
   e. Name of the insurer
   f. Claims history
   g. Other auto, building, or boat ownership, past and present
   h. Other insurers, past and present
   i. Owner satisfaction with auto, building, or vessel
   j. Property distribution (divorce or partner dissolution)
3. Vessel data (when applicable)
   a. Vessel condition prior to fire
   b. Value of the property
   c. Insured value of the property
   d. Payment history on boat mortgage
   e. Vessel furnishings (description of furnishings will be important in the chemical analysis of evidence)
   f. Condition and location of electrical wiring prior to fire
   g. Condition and location of diesel and gas lines prior to fire
   h. Condition and location of propane lines to galley stoves prior to fire
   i. Storage of flammable fluids (based on information provided by the owner)
   j. Types of fuels used
   k. Presence of ignition keys
4. Fire assessment
   a. Name of the party reporting the fire
   b. Name of party discovering fire
   c. Time interval between discovery and reporting
   d. Names of witnesses to the fire
   e. Witnesses to explosion (if any)
   f. Speed of travel of the fire
   g. Direction of spread of the fire
   h. Location of the vessel when fire was reported
5. Fire investigation
   a. Search site
   b. Recovery site
   c. Point of origin of the fire
   d. Evidence of accelerants
   e. Evidence of incendiary devices

(continued)

   f. Evidence of explosive devices
   g. Evidence of ignitors or detonators
   h. Burn characteristics (describe)
   i. Recovered evidence, its location, and manner of packaging
   j. Valuable items missing (e.g., telemetry system, television, stereo, speakers, backup engine, dingy)
   k. Insured's explanation of fire (the explanation should be consistent with the examination of the remains, specifically as to cause of fire, point of origin, type of smoke, and speed and direction of spread)

The major objective of every search and investigation is the recovery of evidence that will help resolve questions regarding the incident. Often special evidence technicians are available to assist in evidence collection in land investigations. Evidence technicians, arson investigators, explosive specialists, forensic scientists, criminalists, and forensic investigators have yet to get their feet wet, however. It is therefore incumbent upon the underwater recovery diver to be aware of possible evidence sites in order to preserve available evidence for laboratory examination.

OFFICER'S NOTEBOOK

FBI Joint Training

A super-tanker is moored offshore at an offloading facility delivering fuel to the thirsty automobiles of southern California. The facility is located in the Pacific Ocean, a short distance off the runways of Los Angeles International Airport (LAX). As the tanker is offloading fuel, a commuter pulled over along a nearby roadside observes several men unloading a small motor boat from a trailer parked illegally along the beach. He watches as the boat speeds out to sea in the direction of the tanker. A short time later the commuter sees an explosion offshore and notifies the authorities using his cell phone. Authorities determine that the tanker has not been hit but there is some debris on the surface of the water in the area pointed out by the first witness, whose story is later corroborated by the statements of other witnesses. It is quickly determined that a vessel has exploded but the circumstances are unknown. All activity at the fueling station is halted, as is incoming traffic at the nearby Port of Los Angeles/Long Beach. Air traffic at LAX is interrupted. Authorities at large commercial ports all around the United States are notified of the incident and placed on high alert. A thorough and proper underwater investigation must commence immediately in order to reopen the fueling station and return the ports and airports to normal operating conditions.

Terrifying Precedent

Despite the significant resources and attention that are focused on port security today, the above scenario (taken from a training scenario based on the USS *Cole* incident in Aden, Yemen) cannot be overlooked. This terrorist tactic has been tried repeatedly and proven effective, suggesting it will likely be tried again. Should a similar attack occur again, the ensuing underwater investigation will need to determine several very important things fairly quickly:

   1. Was the explosion of the small boat an innocent accident, or did it result from explosive materials intentionally placed onboard the vessel?
   2. Did the operators of the vessel intend to attack the super-tanker?
   3. What type and quantity of explosives, if any, were aboard the vessel?
   4. What type of device was intended to trigger the explosion at the tanker?

These and many other questions will be asked in the aftermath of such an incident, and their answers demanded quickly.

> **Preparing Dive Teams**
> **For Major Investigations**
> Law enforcement dive teams must be trained and equipped specifically for this type of complex underwater crime scene investigation. This was the idea behind a first-of-its kind course developed and taught jointly by bomb technicians from the Los Angeles Federal Bureau of Investigation (FBI), Los Angeles Police Department Bomb Squad, Los Angeles Sheriff's Department Arson Explosives Detail, and the U.S. Navy Explosive Ordnance Disposal (EOD) unit at Point Mugu, California. During their course planning, instructors recognized that while many public safety divers are well-trained in processing routine underwater crime scenes, most lack a robust training curriculum or certification for the specialized skills associated with major underwater crime scenes like those resulting from the use of an explosive device. The course would partner public safety divers with diver/bomb technicians so that evidence collected or located by divers could be quickly and adequately analyzed by the bomb techs—both in the water and along shore—in order to advance the work.
>
> Source: *FBI Law Enforcement Bulletin*

als gathered from the site of an explosion must be packaged in separate containers and labeled with all pertinent information.

Many manufacturers of dynamite include magnetic **microtaggants** in each stick. These fluorescent, color-coded, multilayered particles identify the residue as dynamite and indicate the source of manufacture. The color should make the taggants visible to ultraviolet light, and their magnetism should make them susceptible to a magnet. Electric shunts from blasting caps, clock mechanisms, batteries, and pieces of wrapper may survive the explosion and concomitant fire. In those instances where humans have been the victims of a vessel fire, their remains should be bagged. Their clothing should not be removed.

Insurance companies are anxious to cooperate with arson investigations, especially in those instances where the vessel, building, or goods were insured. The American Insurance Association in New York City has established a 24-hour computerized property insurance loss reporting system designed to detect patterns of arson and insurance fraud nationwide. Arsonists who change geographical location or insurance companies may be apprehended with the assistance of the property insurance loss reporting system.

In June of 2007 the author was contacted by the FBI and provided an unclassified Joint FBI/DHS (Department of Homeland Security) Intelligence Bulletin. The bulletin was not for public distribution but indicated an abiding concern for waterborne terrorism. Although criminal investigators do not see underwater crime scene processing as their responsibility, at each underwater crime scene there will be an investigator who has overall investigative responsibility in this new era of innovative terrorist targets. It is as foolish to presume that underwater crime scenes do not fall within the responsibility of investigators as it would be to presume that the results of the Twin Tower attack were not the responsibility of dry land investigators. In underwater crime scenes the investigator in charge may never get wet but s/he is nonetheless in charge of the investigation and as such should be aware of underwater protocols.

■ Relevant Case Law

Under what circumstances may investigators enter a building after a fire within the building has been extinguished? How long may they remain on the premises? How often may they return? What can be taken from the scene? These and other questions were answered by the U.S. Supreme Court's decision in *Michigan v. Tyler* (1978):

Prompt determination of a fire's origin may be necessary to prevent its recurrence. Immediate investigation may also be necessary to preserve evidence from intentional or accidental destruction. The sooner that officials finish their duties, the less subsequent interference there will be in the privacy and recovery efforts of the victims. Officials need no warrant to remain in a building for a reasonable time to investigate the cause of a blaze after it has been extinguished. If the warrantless entry to put out the fire and determine its cause is constitutional, the warrantless seizure of evidence while inspecting the premises for these purposes also is constitutional. . . . In determining what constitutes a reasonable time to investigate, appropriate recognition must be given to the exigencies that confront officials serving under these conditions, as well as to individuals' reasonable expectations of privacy (p. 502).

The Court used the terms *immediate* and *prompt* in describing the needs of investigators in examining the burnt premises. That language suggests that the examination should be conducted as soon as it is safe to enter the premises.

Investigators may remain on the premises as long as is necessary to determine whether there is a possibility of the fire rekindling and to discover the cause of the fire. The Court said that investigators can "remain in the building," which suggests that the investigation is an integral part of the firefighting effort. Their remaining in the building can only be for a "reasonable time"—the time necessary to complete the examination.

It appears from the language of this case that the examination of the premises must be conducted concomitantly with the extinguishing of the fire and its aftermath. Any subsequent visits must be accompanied by a warrant. During the initial examination, however, the investigators can take any evidence that they find.

■ Summary

Arson is a crime that is difficult to prevent and harder to investigate. Arson investigators need to know as much about fires as they do about investigation and law enforcement, which is why in most jurisdictions arson investigators are police officers who are also fire fighters. In addition to the usual type of fires that arson investigators have to investigate, there appears to be a new generation of fire setters waiting in the wings, the terrorist who uses explosives to cause ship, dam, or underwater cable damage. New times require new skills. Ten years ago an investigator could retire and never be involved with an underwater investigation. Today it appears to be the wave of the future.

The portion of this chapter that deals with prospective detonations in the water could have been presented just as easily in the next chapter on terrorism. Since September 11, 2001, we have been the target of many threats but few incidents. That may be a product of luck or of the covert operations employed by various intelligence organizations in this country. Whichever the case, 9/11 will not be the last attempt at causing serious damage on U.S. soil. The next chaper introduces some of the material available on terrorism; keep in mind that this small chapter only touches on that on which many others have written volumes.

■ Key Terms

accelerant: Any substance that has the effect of expanding the volume or intensity of a fire or propagating or communicating the fire

background sample: A control sample to compare against evidence found at the scene of a fire

delay device: An incendiary or detonation device of some type that is employed to allow the arsonist to depart the scene or to establish an alibi

detonation point: Location where an explosive was detonated

direct evidence: Evidence that links the arsonist to the fire, such as eyewitness identification or motive

flammable range: The range in which air and a fuel will support combustion

flash point: The lowest temperature at which a liquid gives off sufficient vapor to form a mixture with air that will support combustion

high-order explosives: Explosives that change rapidly to a gaseous state upon ignition; they must be detonated by an initiating device, such as a blasting cap

ignition temperature: Temperature provided by some outside source of heat that causes a fuel to ignite; the ignition temperature is always higher than the flash point

ignitor: An item or phenomenon that can start a fire by providing temperatures in excess of the ignition temperature of most fuels

incendiary evidence: Evidence from the fire itself, including crime scene debris, observed burning characteristics, and an absence of accidental causation

low-order explosive: Explosive that involves a relatively slow rate of conversion to a gaseous state; they can be ignited by heat and are usually ignited with a lighted fuse

masking fires: Fires set to mask the commission of other crimes

microtaggants: Fluorescent, color-coded, multilayered particles that identify a residue as dynamite and indicate the source of manufacture

point of origin: Location where a fire began; it generally evidences the deepest charring

pyrolysis: The chemical decomposition of a solid into a gaseous product

pyromaniac: A serial fire starter

spontaneous combustion: Combustion that is a product of a natural heat-producing process; it is caused and maintained by poor ventilation

trailers, streamers, and plants: Items used to spread a fire

vapor detector (sniffer): A device that detects the presence of volatile residues by sampling the air around a suspect area or sample

■ Review Questions

1. What distinguishes simple arson from aggravated arson?
2. How are ignitors and delay devices used in arsons?
3. What makes something burn?
4. What is the value of smoke color and odor to the arson investigator?
5. How does spontaneous combustion occur?
6. What kinds of evidence are available to the arson investigator?
7. How does an arsonist's motive assist in an arson investigation?
8. What are the most common motives for arson?

9. What is a masking fire?

10. What is a pyromaniac, and what is the serial killer trilogy?

11. What are streamers used for?

12. Where does the arson investigation begin?

13. What is the significance of the point of origin of the fire?

14. Why is it necessary to provide the laboratory with a background sample from the fire?

15. Why do fire departments investigate boat arsons?

16. What is an alligator pattern, and what is its significance to an arson investigator?

17. What is the difference between a high-order and low-order explosive?

18. What service does the American Insurance Association provide arson investigators?

19. What is the detonation point?

20. What are microtaggants?

21. Who will bear investigatory responsibility for waterborne terrorist acts?

22. Does the police agency in your town have a contingency plan for waterborne criminal/terrorist activity?

■ Bibliography

Magnuson, E. (1990, April 9). "The devil made him do it." *Time*, 38.

Saferstein, R. (1995). *Criminalistics: An introduction to forensic science* (5th ed.). Englewood Cliffs, NJ: Prentice Hall.

■ Key Legal Case

Michigan v. Tyler, 436 U.S. 499 (1978).

■ Key Arson-Related Terms

alligator charring: Char patterns on wood that resemble alligator skin

ambient: Surrounding, especially pertaining to the local environment, as in ambient air and ambient temperature

area of origin: The room or area where the fire began

arrow pattern: A fire pattern displayed on the cross section of a burned wooden structural member

backdraft: An explosion or the rapid burning of heated gases resulting from the introduction of air (oxygen in particular) into a building that is heavily charged with smoke and thus has a depleted oxygen content

ceiling layer: A buoyant layer of hot gases and smoke produced by a fire in a compartment

combustible: Capable of burning

combustible gas indicator: An instrument that samples air and indicates the presence of combustible vapors

drop down: The spread of fire by the dropping or falling of burning materials

failure analysis: A systematic examination of a system to determine the probability of a failure that may have contributed to or caused a fire

fire analysis: The process of determining the origin, cause, and development of a fire as well as the responsibility for the fire

fire scene reconstruction: The process of recreating the physical scene during a fire through the removal of debris and the replacement of contents or structural elements in their prefire positions

fire spread: The movement of fire from one place to another

flame: The luminous portion of burning gases

flammable: Capable of burning

flashover: In a contained fire, a situation in which surfaces exposed to heat reach ignition temperature simultaneously, causing the fire to spread rapidly

glowing combustion: Luminous burning of solid material without a visible flame

ignitable: Capable of fueling a fire

incendiary fire: A deliberately started fire

inflammable: Capable of burning; synonymous with flammable

overhaul: The search for and extinguishment of hidden fires

plume: The column of hot gases, flames, and smoke rising above a fire

point of origin: The exact physical location where a heat source and a fuel come in contact with each other to begin a fire

pointer: The difference in height of a series of fire-damaged vertical wood members; the tallest will have been farthest away from the source of heat, and the shortest will have been closest

pyromania: The inability to resist impulses to set fires

salvage: Procedures to reduce losses from smoke, water, and weather following a fire

smoke: An airborne particulate product of incomplete combustion suspended in gases

spalling: Chipping or pitting of concrete or masonry surfaces, which can be an indication of intense heat

trailer: A lone trail of combustibles or accelerants leading from the point of origin to some other area of the building; used to spread the fire

vector: An arrow used in a fire scene drawing to show the direction of heat, smoke, or flame flow

venting: The escape of smoke and heat through openings in a building

Terrorism

CHAPTER 17

▶ ▶ ▶ STUDENT LEARNING OUTCOMES

Upon completion of this chapter students will demonstrate an understanding of:

- Who terrorists are
- What terrorists want
- The weapons used by terrorists
- The tools available to the terrorism investigator
- The fundamentals of hostage negotiation

Every adult in the United States knows what he or she was doing on September 11, 2001, when they heard that a civilian passenger aircraft had crashed into the north tower of the World Trade Center. At approximately 8:45 A.M. on that date, the United States again became a casualty of **transnational terrorism**. The naiveté enjoyed by most Americans based on distance from the trouble spots of the world and on the illusion of being every other country's friend crumbled with the north tower. At approximately 9:03 A.M. of the same day, any hopes that the first incident was an accident disappeared as a second aircraft crashed into the south tower. We all waited, glued to our televisions and radios, for the other shoe to drop, and drop it did. Two other aircraft crashed: one into the Pentagon and the other in a field south of Pittsburgh. We continued to wait, stunned, wondering what was going to happen next. We watched people come together in New York City to help one another and mobilize government resources. We saw the mayor of New York step up and be counted, and we watched a President who promised that those responsible would pay.

It took time for the actions of government and law enforcement to come to light. We discovered that the Federal Aviation Administration (FAA) under the direction of the Federal Bureau of Investigation (FBI) closed all the airports in New York. The Port Authority of New York and New Jersey closed all New York–area bridges and tunnels. The FAA then grounded all U.S. flights. In retrospect, intelligence reveals that the rapid action of federal, city, and state agencies prevented further acts of planned terrorism.

As a result of the September 11th experience and in anticipation of future acts of terrorism, the President of the United States created a new cabinet-level department, the Office of Homeland Security. The role of the office is to bring together all of the government's antiterrorism resources under one head. As we move further away from 9/11, the Office of Homeland Security moves with us, and over time it will become further defined.

The homeland security advisory system is a product of the Office of Homeland Security. Based on intelligence gathered by various federal agencies, the nation is kept abreast of terroristic threats through a system of threat conditions. There are five stages to the system: low, guarded, elevated, high, and severe. Each stage is represented by a color:

- Green: low
- Blue: guarded
- Yellow: elevated
- Orange: high
- Red: severe

Bombings at the World Trade Center in 1993 and the Alfred P. Murrah Federal Building in Oklahoma City in 1995 awakened the United States to the realities of foreign and domestic terrorism. Prior to these two incidents, the United States had rested comfortably on the belief that terrorism was a phenomenon that occurred elsewhere. The arrival of terrorism on our shores was greeted with a variety of responses, and little in the law enforcement inventory existed to deal with it. We have had to learn. The FBI has become the investigative branch responsible for terrorism committed in the United States, although the first responders to a terroristic act will be the local police. The initial response will either advance the investigation and resolution of the crime or will retard it, depending on what the local agency knows about terrorism and hostage negotiations.

The FBI divides terrorism into two major groups with three subdivisons:

- *Domestic terrorism* involves two or more people with the intent to commit a terrorist act against the U.S. government or the American people
  - Animal rights groups
  - Ecological groups
  - Racial supremacy groups
- *International terrorism* involves terrorism aimed at the United States directed by a foreign government or foreign leader

The FBI has developed a strong response to the threats posed by domestic and international terrorism. Since 1993 the FBI has doubled its counterterrorism programs. With the latitude allowed through the patriot act, cooperation among law enforcement agencies at all levels represents an important component of a comprehensive response to terrorism. This cooperation assumes its most tangible operational form in the **joint terrorism task forces** (JTTF) that are now part of all FBI field divisions. These task forces are well-suited to respond to terrorism because they combine the national and international investigative resources of the FBI with the expertise of other federal law enforcement and local law enforcement agencies. The FBI currently has 84 JTTFs nationwide, one in each of the 56 field offices, and 28 additional annexes. By integrating the investigative abilities of the FBI with other federal law enforcement and local law enforcement agencies, these task forces represent an effective response to the threats posed to U.S. communities by domestic and international terrorists.

■ Terrorists

In the past, international terrorists did not operate in the United States. The distance from lines of supply, unfamiliarity with American geography and language, and a vigilant law enforcement community all militated against attempted terroristic acts. The bombing of the World Trade Center was not the first instance of international terrorism, but it was the one that brought to the world's attention the fact that the United States is vulnerable.

It also allowed an inside look at the structure of a terrorist group. The organizational unit of international terrorist groups is the **cell**, a small cadre of zealots who will sacrifice their lives in furtherance of a religious, political, or social cause. The membership of each cell is small, and its members know only each other, not other members of the larger group, in order to protect the larger group if a member is captured and interrogated.

Terrorist groups are developing two types of operations: one based on sleeper cells and one on transient cells. A **sleeper cell** comprises individuals who immigrate (e.g., to the United States), establish a residence and an identity, find employment, and await orders from their overseas comrades in arms to begin terroristic acts or to lay the groundwork for future terroristic acts. They receive money and material from others in the group and may begin stockpiling weapons and explosives in a safe house for use when others in the group arrive. A **transient cell** is a group that arrives in a country solely for the purpose of conducting a terroristic act or campaign. The transient cell will rely on a sleeper cell to provide the logistics for its activities.

A working definition of terrorism can be helpful in determining whether a group's behavior rises to the level of terrorism. We might say that terrorism is the threat of violence, individual acts of violence, or a campaign of violence designed primarily to instill fear (Jenkins, 1975). In addition to violence for the purpose of instilling fear, there is generally a political component. Most terrorist organizations attempt to further a political agenda. Absent the political component, gangland extortion and threats would meet the definition of terrorism.

Violence for effect is the ultimate objective of the terrorist—not the effect it has on the victims, but the effect it has on the society at large. A terrorist act absent the media would affect only the victims and the immediately surrounding area. It is only through the media that such acts are publicized, causing widespread appreciation of their horror. The intended effect is to make the public feel fear and concern.

It is important to remember that the violence wrought upon hapless victims is not the objective of the violence. The bombing of Pan American Airlines Flight 103 over Lockerbie, Scotland, was intended to influence the public, who would be informed by the media of the deaths of the passengers. It has been suggested that the rest of the world follow in the footsteps of Britain, which has passed laws limiting news coverage of terrorist events (Shipler, 1988). There is no absolute right of the press to have access to information not available to the public at large. If the public can be restricted in what they hear and see at a crime scene, so then can the press. Attributing a terroristic act to a terrorist group is free publicity. A newspaper would consider it unethical to accept an advertisement from a terrorist group claiming credit for a terroristic act. What the press will not allow terrorists to buy, it gives them for nothing.

In discussing terrorism, it is helpful to categorize terroristic acts into four groups:

1. **Domestic terrorism** evolves within a state (or country). Disgruntled citizens engage in terrorist acts that, although brought down upon the heads of individuals, are aimed at bringing about social or political change. White supremacist groups such as the Ku Klux Klan and the Aryan Nation, along with militant antiabortion, militia, and environmental groups, may pose the greatest threat of terrorism in the United States.

2. **State-sponsored terrorism** is used by a government to manipulate its own citizens. Saddam Hussein's use of gas on the Kurdish population of Iraq to bring about conformity was an example of state-sponsored terrorism, as was the Third Reich's divestment of German Jews' status as citizens and its attempt to exterminate them. A vocal minority bent on change may be seen as a serious threat by a sitting government, which might then apply force to bring about a resolution to the political controversy.

3. **Transnational terrorism** is conducted by terrorists against citizens of another country. Transnational terrorist groups are not directly supported by a state but may receive indirect support from various regimes for services rendered. Hezbollah and Fatah are examples of terrorist groups that travel throughout a region irrespective of geographic boundaries, furthering a cause through terrorism that transcends nations, states, and their citizens.

4. **International terrorism** is conducted by state-supported terrorists but involves the citizens of more than one state. The Palestine Liberation Organization (PLO), has historically operated in a number of geographic regions (Mullins, 1997).

Terrorists are not as easily identifiable as most think. They do not generally wear indices of country or group affiliation before the terroristic act. There are generally no outwardly discernible characteristics that distinguish them from the population at large. Most are dedicated and highly motivated supporters of social or political causes. Often their frustration with peaceful efforts to effect what they believe to be fundamental and necessary change has led to desperation, and they believe that their only avenue to success is to erode the will of the government that remains deaf to their cause. Those who come together out of political frustration, desperation, and disenfranchisement unify and compound their assets, resolve, dedication, and strength.

Terrorist groups are linear (rather than hierarchical), highly mobile, flexible, efficient, self-contained, and, most important, closed. They are difficult if not impossible to infiltrate, and law enforcement is still looking for the tools with which to deal with them. The United States has identified 81 terrorist organizations worldwide and has identified North Korea, Iran, Sudan, Syria, and Cuba as sponsors of terrorism.

■ Weapons of Terrorism

The weapons of terrorism will become more deadly. The use of nuclear, biological, and chemical agents has become more of a threat. **Nuclear terrorism** would involve terrorists detonating a nuclear device. Although the technical expertise necessary to construct a nuclear device is not beyond the capabilities of terrorists, the technological means probably are, and a more realistic avenue to nuclear terrorism would involve the theft or purchase of a nuclear device. The Georgian states of the former Soviet Union have a stockpile of over 13,000 nuclear weapons left after the collapse of the Soviet Union. These weapons have been offered at auction to any organization or state that can afford to purchase them, with no regard for political agenda or affiliation (Mullins, 1997).

The possession of a nuclear device is not necessary for terrorists to pose a **nuclear threat**. A nuclear facility could be taken hostage, and, with sufficient expertise, a core meltdown could be threatened or actualized. Dozens of countries have joined the nuclear community, most recently Pakistan and Egypt. What security precautions have been effected in the far-flung reaches of the nuclear community to prevent the sabotage or ransoming of nuclear facilities (from which fissionable material could be had)? What procedures have been employed for nuclear materials accountability? What types of criminal history and background checks are required of persons working in the industry? In addition to the panoply of security deficits in our country and among our nuclear neighbors, there are terrorists who may receive support from governments that want to break into the nuclear monopoly.

Biological weapons are among the oldest weapons of warfare. Various terrorist groups have at their disposal a variety of biological weapons, including botulinum toxin, one of the deadliest toxins on earth; anthrax can be ordered from biological supply houses (Mengel, 1979). The disadvantage of using biological agents is the difficulty of controlling the spread. Once an agent is released, many people other than those targeted might be affected, including the terrorists. Cloning and genetic engineering are making biological agents more target-specific. Once perfected, these weapons will become an attractive addition to the terrorists' arsenal.

Of the three types of weapons—nuclear, biological, and chemical—the latter has the greatest potential for terrorist use. **Chemical weapons** are easy to obtain or make and also to disperse. Only small quantities of chemicals such as sarin are needed to immobilize an entire city. Furthermore, chemical dispersal may be delayed, allowing the terrorists to escape without fear of contamination. Chemical weapons may become the new weapons of choice for terrorists. Joyner (1993) suggested two reasons for this. First, terrorist killing and property damage have become a matter of routine for both terrorists and the viewing public. It will take larger acts of violence to precipitate fear and garner media coverage. Second, terrorists are becoming better funded and more technologically proficient.

Another potential weapon is technology. The United States is the most technologically advanced nation in the world, but technology is a double-edged sword and leaves us open to **technological terrorism**. Many of us cannot remember a time when grocery cashiers used a mechanical cash register. When computers go down, businesses go down. We have become simultaneously technologically advanced and dependent. Our infatuation with technology has thus created a window of opportunity for terrorism. Using a computer as a weapon, terrorists may target metropolitan water supplies, public utility companies, dams, electrical power grids, transmission lines and transformers, petroleum refineries and pipelines, and power plants.

An immediate responsibility in the case of a suspected terrorist bombing is the evacuation of personnel to insure their safety. Unexploded improvised explosive devices (IEDs) require an evacuation area be created and maintained. That responsibility will fall to the patrol force under the supervision of the investigator in charge.

Biological Threats

Botulinum Toxins
- Initial symptoms appear several hours to one to two days after exposure and include
  - Blurred vision
  - Drooping eyelids
  - Difficulty understanding language
  - Difficulty speaking
  - Muscle weakness
- Day one
  - Mucous in throat
  - Neuromuscular symptoms
  - Respiratory distress
  - Difficulty swallowing
- Day four
  - Indistinct speech
  - Dilated pupils
  - Retarded eye motion
  - Mental numbness

Smallpox
- Incubation average 12 days
  - Phase one symptoms
    - Malaise
    - Fever
    - Chills
    - Vomiting
    - Headache
    - Backache
    - Rash
  - Phase two symptoms
    - Facial rash
    - Eruptions on mucous membranes
    - Eruptions on extremities
    - Eruptions extend to the trunk of the body

Cutaneous anthrax
- Incubation 1 to 5 days; initial symptoms include
  - Small bumps
  - Blisters
  - Painless lesions
  - Ulcerated necrotic tissue (ulcer of dead skin)

Inhalation anthrax
- Nonproductive cough (dry cough)
  - Chest pain
  - Respiratory distress
  - Difficulty breathing
  - Purple coloration of mucous membranes
  - Shock and death within 24 hours

Source: National Counterterrorism Center's 2007 Counterterrorism Calendar

The mechanism whereby terrorists injure and kill is not necessarily anything overly exotic. Substantial damage can be done with limited resources. No one considered a passenger aircraft a terrorist explosive device. The standard in the airline industry has long been to cooperate with hijackers; nonresistance was the objective, with ultimate release the outcome when the hijackers reached their destination. It is important to remember that the damage inflicted is to further a political aim. The sites are chosen based on vulnerability, value as a terrorist target, and maximum impact. Communities will have to examine their infrastructures, determine which

© Ramzi Hachicho/ShutterStock, Inc.

Chemical Agents

Nerve agents
- Tabun (GA)
  - Colorless
  - Fruity smell
- Sarin (B)
  - Colorless
  - Odorless
- Soman (GD)
  - Colorless
  - Fruity odor
  - Oil of camphor odor
- VX
  - Colorless to straw colored
  - No odor

Vessicants (blister agents)
- Sulfur mustard (HD)
  - Pale yellow to brown
  - Garlic or mustard odor
- Lewsite (L)
  - Amber to brown
  - Smells like geranium

Pulmonary (lung) agents
- Chlorine (CL)
  - Clear to yellow gas
  - Smells like bleach
- Phosgene (CG)
  - Colorless gas
  - Smells like freshly-mown hay

Blood agents
- Hydrogen cyanide (AC)
  - Gas
  - Bitter almond odor
- Cyanogen chloride
  - Gas or liquid
  - Pungent odor

Source: National Counterterrorism Center's 2007 Counterterrorism Calendar

are the most-vulnerable but also which are the most-needed potential targets. A city has limited resources and cannot harden all targets; the objective in vulnerability analysis is to determine not only what is most vulnerable but also what is a priority with regard to operational necessity. What targets are those that are most essential to the welfare of the citizens of a particular community and how can they be hardened. Target hardening does not prevent a terrorist attack, it simply discourages one. A good home security system does not prevent burglaries, it just sends burglars to a place that is easier to burglarize.

The new world of counterterrorism begins with education. Much of what we have done and believed about antiterrorism instruction in the past is now invalid. Universities, including the university at which the author is employed, are developing curricula in homeland security. Terrorism and counterterrorism is multifaceted and no one course can adequately prepare a student to manage homeland security issues relevant to terrorism. The following curriculum was provided in partnership with the Naval Postgraduate School and is being offered as a master's program at Chaminade University of Honolulu:

- Introduction to homeland security
- **Technology for homeland security:** The 21st-century terrorist is computer literate and understands how computers can be used to further a terrorist's objective. New technology in biotechnology assists federal, state, and local law enforcement. Technology is an integral part of international conspiracies and makes the smallest opposition a large threat.
- **Asymmetric conflict and homeland security:** The word "terrorism" no longer describes the conflict between the United States and terrorists. This course includes traditional

terrorism subject matter but from a much broader perspective, recognizing that the concept of warfare does not include an invisible enemy, with no recognizable army or territory, and that traditional notions of terrorism do not include strategic planning, prevention, preparation, containment, and rehabilitation as subject matter.

- **Critical infrastructure vulnerability analysis and protection:** What do we protect? What can we afford to protect? What do we absolutely need to protect?
- **Strategic planning and budgeting for homeland security:** How do we intend to use our resources and manpower? What is a strategic plan and why is it important we have one?
- **The law and homeland security:** A multidisciplinary approach—U.S. laws, international laws, conventions, and treaties, and their impact on gathering intelligence and hunting terrorists.
- **Intelligence for homeland security:** The most effective investigative tool in the war on terrorism is information. How do you get it and what do you do with it?
- **The psychology of fear:** Why do terrorists commit terroristic acts and why are we so afraid (or should be)?

Through curricula such as these, investigators, fire fighters, emergency medical personnel, city managers, civil defense, nongovernmental agencies, etc., are discovering that terrorism is a complicated issue and that traditional methods of instruction are now of little help in dealing with the management of homeland security agencies and responsibilities. Of course the keystone for homeland security preparation is interagency communication and cooperation. In the future, single agencies and local investigators will be working within an incident management system involving a much larger group of homeland security experts in the prevention and investigation of terrorist acts.

■ Investigating Terrorism

Terrorism is an act or series of acts that includes a crime. It is the responsibility of the investigating agency to apply traditional methods, perhaps on a much larger scale, to investigate the underlying criminal offenses that accompany the terrorism. Terrorists most commonly commit the following crimes:

- Conspiracy
- Kidnapping
- Skyjacking
- Murder
- Assault (including aggravated assault)
- Burglary (to commit a felony other than theft)
- Bombing and arson
- Extortion

These crimes are the same as those committed by any other offender, except they are committed by a dedicated group of well-trained and prepared professionals motivated by political goals. The primary investigative tool for terrorist acts is patience; the primary investigative tool for suspected terrorist groups is intelligence (information).

The initial crime scene in a terroristic kidnapping is the location from which the victim was kidnapped. A second crime scene is the location to which the victim was taken. In fact, each place used by the terrorists in advancing their kidnapping scheme should be considered a separate crime scene. If a vehicle was used and abandoned, it too should be processed as a crime scene.

Keep in mind that in this type of investigation, what seems unimportant now may prove to be important later. It takes training, skill, and experience to determine what is evidence and what is not, and it is best to err on the side of prudence and bag it all. Dirt, stones, hairs, and fibers are as important in a kidnapping as they are in a homicide. The dirt and stones may reveal a location that the victim or the terrorists may have previously visited. Hair and fiber may provide comparison evidence when a suspect is apprehended. The trunk of the vehicle should be examined carefully, for it is often used by kidnappers to transport the victim, and fragments of rope, tape, or fabric used to bind the victim may be found there. Mud, dirt, and other debris on the undercarriage of the vehicle may indicate other stops made by the suspects prior to abandoning the vehicle. Stolen license plates may have been used. It may prove fruitful to process the vehicle from which the plates were stolen for fingerprints (Osterburg and Ward, 1992).

Gathering Intelligence

Successful investigation of a suspected terrorist group requires, in addition to massive amounts of patience, the ability to appreciate the group's motivation; efforts to establish lines of communication with any and all agencies that may have information about the group and its individual members; and the compilation of a database containing personal information about individual group members, suspected prior terrorist acts, and cross references for all items recovered at any terroristic crime scene or discovered safe house.

The intelligence efforts should focus on the group's

- Membership
- Possible local affiliations
- Stated and unstated goals
- Resource base
- Propensity toward violence
- Level of proficiency
- Preferred tactical approach (types of weapons, explosives, etc.)
- Method of communication (e.g., Web site, in the case of some domestic terrorist groups)
- Method of funding
- Organizational structure

Some domestic groups may espouse positions opposed to the majority and the government; espousal of such positions in itself is not actionable. Civil disobedience is protected under the First Amendment. It is when a group moves past unpopular opinions and civil disobedience and incites actions in violation of the law that First Amendment protection ends and investigative inquiry begins.

Often the most accessible information about a suspected organization or individual has to do with their financial activity. Large financial transactions leave paper or digital trails. The following list can be useful in seeking indicators of suspicious financial activity:

- Account transactions that are inconsistent with past deposits or withdrawals
- Transactions involving a high volume of incoming or outgoing wire transfers with no logical or apparent purpose that come from, go to, or transit sanctioned countries, non-cooperative nations, or sympathizers.
- Unexplainable clearing or negotiation of third-party checks and their deposits in foreign bank accounts
- Breaking transactions larger than $10,000 into smaller amounts by making multiple deposits or withdrawals or by buying cashier's checks, money orders, or other monetary instruments to evade IRS bank reporting requirements
- Corporate layering; transfers between bank accounts of related entities or charities for no reason
- Wire transfers by charitable organizations to companies located in countries know to be bank or tax havens
- Charitable bank deposits that lack signs of fund-raising activity (absence of small checks or donations)
- Use of multiple accounts to collect funds that are transferred to the same foreign beneficiaries
- Transactions without logical economic purpose
- Overlapping corporate officers, bank signatories, or other identifiable similarities associated with the same addresses, references and financial activities
- Cash-debiting schemes in which deposits in the United States correlate directly with ATM withdrawals in countries of concern
- Issuance of checks, money orders, or other financial instruments, often numbered sequentially, to the same or similarly named person or business (National Counterterrorism Center, 2007)

Collection and Preservation of Evidence

One of the most important tasks of a terrorism investigation is the collection and preservation of evidence. Most terrorist acts involve bombing or kidnapping (taking hostages). In bombings, the focus of the investigation will be on searching the site of the detonation in an effort to recover parts of the bomb, its packaging, or the detonating device. Bomb parts can be helpful in determining the manufacturer of the bomb's material components and may also have fingerprints that can be processed. If the terrorists have launched a campaign of terroristic bombings, the bombings may be linked by the components used in each of the explosive devices. If, as in the 1993 World Trade Center bombing, suspects are identified, bomb components may be matched with materials recovered from the suspects, or residues may be matched with those found on the suspects' clothes.

The most common type of explosive weapon used in the United States is a pipe bomb filled with fragmentation material (e.g., nails) and black powder. The detonator is a fuse. All of the materials needed to make such a device are available at sporting goods and hardware stores. The Internet has made access to recipes for bombs and explosives a keystroke away, from sophisticated devices to agricultural fertilizer containing ammonium nitrate mixed with diesel fuel, as was used in the Oklahoma City bombing (see TABLE 17-1 and Figure 17-1).

TABLE 17–1   Commonly Available Plastic Explosives and Their Physical Properties

Name	Explosive Material	Velocity	Color	Origin
C-4	RDX	26,400 fps	White	US/Canada
PE-4	RDX	27,000 fps	White	UK
Rowenex	RDX	26,200 fps	Orange	UK
Demex	RDX	26,900 fps	White	UK
Plastex	PETN	23,000 fps	Clear	Switzerland
Plastrite4	RDX	25,000 fps	Yellow	Russia
Semtex H	RDX/PETN	24,300 fps	Orange	Czech
Seismoplast	PETN	23,800 fps	Red	Germany
Semtex 1A	PETN	24,000 fps	Red	Czech

Source: National Counterterrorism Center's 2007 Counterterrorism Calendar

Expray is an example of an aerosol-based field test kit for the detection and identification of Group A explosives such as TNT (trinitrotoluene) and Group B explosives such as Semtex H and C4, as well as compounds containing inorganic nitrates that are used in improvised explosives. Expray is commonly used as:

- A preblast, analytical tool
- A postblast investigative tool
- A screen against potential terrorist elements

Figure 17–1   C4 compound.

Courtesy of Mass Communication Specialist 2nd Class Michael Zeltakalns/U.S. Navy

The testing process is fast and efficient. No glass ampoules, spatulas, or waiting periods are required. Results appear in seconds. No additional tools or equipment are required. The identification/detection process requires no special training and testing can be performed on the spot. For both law enforcement and investigative personnel, Expray is a proven tool for increasing the accuracy, efficiency, and number of interdictions. For forensic and environmental laboratories, it has proven to reduce the number of samples submitted for testing. Expray is sold in a kit configuration that provides three aerosol sprays, collection papers, and an RDX-impregnated verification pad (verification pad is used to ensure that the spray still contains active reagents).

Expray-1 is used to search for Group A-type explosives, which include TNT, Tetryl, TNB (trinitrobenzene), DNT (Compound 9), and picric acid and its salts. The investigator wipes the suspected surface with a collector pad and sprays the collector pad with the aerosol can marked Expray-1. If a dark brown-violet color appears, this indicates the presence of TNT; an orange color indicates the presence of Tetryl and other Group A explosives.

Expray-2 is used to search for Group B type explosives, which include dynamite, nitroglycerine, RDX, Petn, Semtex, nitrocellulose, and smokeless powder. If there is no color change after spraying Expray-1, spray Expray-2. The almost immediate appearance of a pink color change indicates the presence of Group B explosives. Most plastic types of explosives belong to this group, including C-4 and Semtex.

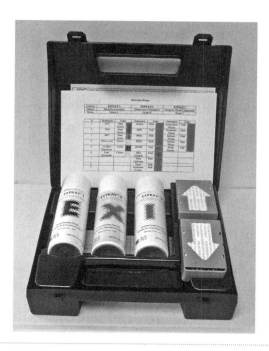

Figure 17–2 Expray kit.

Courtesy of Medimpex United Inc.

Expray-3 is used to search for nitrate-based explosives, which include ANFO (ammonium nitrate-fuel oil), commercial and improvised explosives based on inorganic nitrates, black powder, flash powder, gun powder, potassium chlorate and nitrate, sulfur powder, and ammonium nitrate (both fertilizer and aluminum). If there is still no reaction after using the Expray cans 1 and 2, but presence of explosives is still suspected, spray the same paper with Expray-3. A pink reaction indicates the presence of nitrates, which could be part of an improvised explosive (see **Figure 17–2**).

■ Hostage Negotiation

Often a kidnapping will result in a hostage situation, sometimes because the purpose of the kidnapping was to take the victim hostage. The common choice is a victim who will garner sympathy and notice. Part of every hostage situation is the decision by authorities to negotiate or to respond tactically. The contemporary perspective is to negotiate until one of three things occurs:

1. The siege ends.

2. The negotiation resolves the situation.

3. A hostage is injured.

There are a limited number of options available to authorities confronted with a situation similar to that at the Munich Olympics in 1972:

- Acquiesce to terrorist demands
- Respond tactically (attack)
- Use surgical strikes (sniper fire)

CASE IN POINT

The Birth of Contemporary Terrorism

In 1972, the world, with breath held, watched as 13 Arabs invaded the Israeli Olympic compound in Munich, Germany, killed two Israelis, and took nine athletes hostage. The captors demanded the release of 200 Palestinian prisoners being held in Israel. These prisoners were not released, and after hours of unsuccessful negotiation the terrorists left the compound with their hostages. The police confronted the terrorists at the municipal airport as the terrorists approached the helicopter they had ordered. Following a 15-minute firefight in which 10 Arabs, all of the Israeli hostages, and one police officer died, police captured three surviving terrorists.

- Use chemical intervention (tear gas)
- Contain and negotiate

In response to the Munich disaster, the New York City Police Department (NYPD) asked Harvey Schlossberg to help develop guidelines for hostage negotiations. Schlossberg (1979) emphasized the importance of containing the situation and negotiating until all negotiable avenues are exhausted or the situation is resolved. He stressed three fundamental rules of hostage negotiation (see Officer's Notebook).

In understanding the motivation of the hostage takers, the first step is to accept the proposition that all behavior is understandable, goal-oriented, pleasure-seeking, and problem-solving in nature. To understand seemingly meaningless and irrational behavior, the negotiator needs to understand the hostage takers' history, goals, and problem-solving abilities. The NYPD built the first hostage recovery program in the United States, emphasizing hostage negotiation over **tactical response**.

The Stockholm Syndrome

In 1973, a lone gunman attempting to rob the Sveriges Kredit Bank in Stockholm, Sweden, began a 131-hour standoff with the police. He demanded the release of the man who had been his cellmate while he was incarcerated, and this man joined the gunman and four hostages in the bank's vault. During the siege, the hostages came to fear the police more than the hostage takers. The hostages came to believe they knew better than the police what needed to be done to gain their release and save their lives. They sided with the hostage takers and attempted to advance the goals of the hostage takers. This phenomenon became known as the **Stockholm syndrome**.

OFFICER'S NOTEBOOK

Fundamental Rules of Hostage Negotiation

1. **Contain and negotiate,** which requires a patrol force that understands the security needs of a negotiating situation and can provide the proper secured perimeter within which the negotiations can be conducted.
2. Attempt to understand the hostage takers' motivation and personality, which requires intelligence gathering and psychological input during the negotiations.
3. Slow the incident down, because time works in the negotiator's favor.

The syndrome is important to hostage negotiators for two reasons. First, the hostages may come to feel sympathy for the hostage takers, to the disadvantage of the authorities during debriefing or during a tactical response. Understanding the dynamics of the syndrome will assist police in dealing with what appears to be aberrant hostage behavior. Hostages may deny abuse or aggressiveness on the part of the hostage takers and may make statements to the media in support of the hostage takers and their cause. It is for this reason that hostages must be isolated from the media and that intelligence provided by them during debriefing should be treated skeptically.

Second, investigators should be aware that the syndrome can be used by the police or the hostages to build rapport between the hostage takers and the hostages that may help resolve the standoff or save a hostage's life (McMains and Mullins, 1996).

Hostage Taker Demands

All hostage takers make demands. Without demands there would be no hostage situation. The demands of the criminal hostage taker will be part of a **freedom package**. Escape, no prison time, an investigation of prison conditions, removal of all police, and money may all be part of the package. Terrorists may want publicity or concessions from the government.

Often negotiators will make promises they have no intention of keeping. The courts have been consistent in determining that such contracts are a product of duress and that a contract under duress is unenforceable at law (*United States v. Crosby,* 1983). Neither is there an obligation to provide hostage takers with Miranda warnings prior to or during negotiations. Anything said during the course of negotiations may be used at the time of trial without fear of exclusion for Miranda violations (*United States v. Mesa,* 1980). In order for Miranda to apply, two fundamental elements are necessary—custody and interrogation—and neither is present in a hostage negotiation situation.

Negotiable Demands

All **negotiable demands** should be accompanied by a counteroffer. Demands are a trade in progress. Always get something for something given. The obvious choice is a hostage. The situation will dictate how much of a demand should be provided and how much simply should be negotiated without being paid off. The more professional the hostage takers, the more careful must be promises and demand negotiations. Following is a list of common items often requested by hostage takers that are susceptible to negotiation. Any item delivered may possess characteristics that will allow a listening device to be planted.

- Food
- Cigarettes
- Beverages (Neither alcohol nor drugs is generally bartered, although a consulting psychologist may authorize bartering such items in certain situations.)
- Media coverage. It has been standard practice in the past to refuse to provide press coverage. Given today's technology, it is impossible to completely bar the press. If allowed to operate within specific parameters, the press may provide an opportunity for additional intelligence to be gathered regarding the hostages and the hostage takers' location.
- Transportation may be negotiated without being provided, although once it is promised, some evidence of its delivery should be made apparent to the hostage takers.

- Money should be treated the same way as transportation—negotiated but hesitantly delivered.
- Freedom may be negotiable even if it is undeliverable.
- Heat
- Air conditioning
- Clothing
- Medicine has historically been on the short list of nonnegotiables. It is best to negotiate for release and medical treatment rather than to provide medicine but, in the face of adamant hostage takers, there may be no alternative to providing medical care for sick or wounded hostages.

Nonnegotiable Demands

Some argue that all demands are negotiable, even though some may not be deliverable. However, common sense dictates that some demands cannot be negotiated, and when a refusal to negotiate a demand is properly delivered to the hostage takers, it is generally expected and accepted. Weapons and illicit drugs top the list of **nonnegotiable demands**, followed by hostage exchanges and prisoner releases (McMains and Mullins, 1996).

It may be the responsibility of the local police agency to provide an immediate response to a terrorist hostage situation. This chapter presents the minimum that investigators and patrol officers must know to deal with the situation adequately until hostage negotiation and tactical teams arrive. By following the principles given, first responders can avoid jeopardizing the chance for negotiations. The material is not presented in the hopes of making readers into hostage negotiators. It would take a book on hostage negotiations equal in size to this one to accomplish that task.

■ Summary

It is impossible to include in one chapter everything investigators need to know to investigate terrorism and terrorist organizations. This chapter introduced students to the subject matter. Those interested will find a library full of information available to them.

What is known today is not nearly enough to combat terrorism. As much time and effort that the United States employs in thwarting terrorism, the same amount of time and effort is expended by terrorist organizations around the world in circumventing U.S. counterterrorism efforts. It is a world where the targets stay a step behind the terrorists and exhaust resources and manpower trying to second guess where the next major terrorist incident might occur. We have learned a lot as a nation since September 11, 2001, but there is no guarantee that we are learning enough or learning fast enough. We have a short collective memory and forget the turmoil this country was in after 9/11 and the demands we made of our government. Everything that was done as a result of that day has now become an inconvenience or a violation of someone's rights. In any discussion about terrorism there must be included the question: How free can we be and still be safe?

In the next chapter we will see that the same kinds of tools used to battle terrorism are used to combat organized crime. It is strange that the horrific legacy of organized crime can be glamorized for our entertainment on television and in the movies. From an investigator's perspective the only entertaining part of organized crime is watching sealed indictments being issued.

■ Key Terms

biological weapons: Biological agents chosen because of their harmful properties and used to spread disease or cause death

cell: A small cadre of zealots whose members know only each other, not other members of the larger group

chemical weapons: Chemical compounds used to harm or kill people; they are easy to obtain or make and also to disperse, and the chemical dispersal may be delayed, allowing the terrorists to escape without fear of contamination

contain and negotiate: First of the fundamental rules of hostage negotiation, it requires a patrol force that understands the security needs of a negotiating situation and can provide the proper secured perimeter within which the negotiations can be conducted

domestic terrorism: Terrorism that evolves within a state (or country); disgruntled citizens engage in terrorist acts that, although brought down upon the heads of individuals, are aimed at bringing about social or political change

Expray: Explosives field test kit

freedom package: Conditions hostage takers want met in exchange for the hostages; conditions may include escape, no prison time, an investigation of prison conditions, removal of all police, or money

international terrorism: Terrorism conducted by state-supported terrorists but that involves the citizens of more than one state

joint terrorism task forces: Interagency cooperation fighting terrorism

negotiable demands: Demands made by hostage takers that can be bargained; all negotiable demands should be accompanied by a counteroffer, usually the return of a hostage in exchange for the item requested

nonnegotiable demands: Demands made by hostage takers that will under no circumstances be fulfilled by authorities

nuclear terrorism: Involves terrorists detonating a nuclear device

nuclear threat: The potential for terrorists to acquire nuclear weapons or take actions against nuclear facilities

sleeper cell: A terrorist cell that comprises individuals who immigrate, establish a residence and an identity, find employment, and await orders

state-sponsored terrorism: Terrorism used by a government to manipulate its own citizens

Stockholm syndrome: When hostages come to trust or sympathize with the hostage takers more than with the authorities, and begin to help the hostage takers advance their cause

tactical response: An assault by a special operations or response team

technological terrorism: Use of computers as weapons to target such locations as metropolitan water supplies, public utility companies, dams, electrical power grids, transmission lines and transformers, petroleum refineries and pipelines, and power plants

transient cell: A group that arrives in a country solely for the purpose of conducting a terroristic act or campaign

transnational terrorism: Terrorism that is conducted by terrorists against citizens of another country; these groups are not supported by a state but may receive support from various regimes in various countries and locations

■ Review Questions

1. What is the basic organizational unit of terroristic groups?
2. What is the difference between sleeper and transient cells, and what role does each play in a terrorist organization?
3. What role does the media play in fostering terrorism?
4. What are the definitions of domestic terrorism, international terrorism, transnational terrorism, and state-supported terrorism?
5. What is the definition of terrorism?
6. What is nuclear terrorism and what is the most serious threat of nuclear detonation by terrorists? Why?
7. What are the differences between investigating a terroristic act and investigating a suspected terrorist group?
8. How does the First Amendment apply to terrorism?
9. What occurred in Munich, Germany, that led to the development of hostage negotiation teams?
10. What role did the New York City Police Department play in the development of hostage negotiation teams?
11. What is meant, in the context of hostage negotiations, by the phrase "contain and negotiate"?
12. What is the Stockholm syndrome, and how might it influence hostage negotiations?
13. What is a freedom package and what is generally included in it?
14. What impact did the cases *United States v. Mesa* and *United States v. Crosby* have on hostage negotiation operations?
15. What role did federal agencies play after the September 11, 2001, terrorist attack?
16. Which hostage taker demands are negotiable and which are nonnegotiable? Why?
17. What is the Office of Homeland Security?
18. What are the alert stages associated with homeland security?
19. What is technological terrorism?
20. What are the tools of technological terrorism?
21. What role does the Joint Terrorism Task Force play in fighting terrorism?
22. Which countries are the major sponsors of terrorism?
23. Which plastic explosive has the greatest velocity? Where is it made?
24. List five indicators of illicit financial transactions.

■ Bibliography

Jenkins, B.M. (1975). International terrorism: A new mode of conflict (Research Paper 48, California Seminar on Arms Control and Foreign Policy). Los Angeles: Crescent.
Joyner, C.C. (1993). Chemoterrorism: Rethinking the reality of the threat. In J.J. Han (Ed.), *Terrorism and political violence: Limits and possibilities of legal control*. Dobbs Ferry, NY: Oceana.

McMains, M.J., and Mullins, W.C. (1996). *Crisis negotiations: Managing critical incidents and hostage situations in law enforcement and corrections.* Cincinnati, OH: Anderson.

Mengel, R.W. (1979). Terrorism and new technologies of destruction: An overview of the potential risk. In A.R. Norton and M.H. Greenberg (Eds.). *Studies in nuclear terrorism.* Boston: Hill.

Mullins, W.C. (1997). "Future trends in terrorism." *Justice Professional* 10, 31–46.

Osterburg, J.W., and Ward, R.J. (1992). *Criminal investigation: A method of reconstructing the past.* Cincinnati, OH: Anderson.

National Counterterrorism Center (2007). 2007 Counterrorism Calendar.

Schlossberg, H. (1979). *Hostage negotiations.* Presentation at the Texas Department of Public Safety's Terrorism School, Austin, Texas.

Shipler, D.K. (1988). "Future domestic and international terrorism: The media perspective." *Terrorism* 11, 543–545.

■ Key Legal Cases

United States v. Crosby. 713 F.2d 1066 (5th Cir. 1983), cert. denied, 104 S.Ct. 516.

United States v. Mesa. 638 F.2d 582 (3rd Cir. 1980).

Organized Crime

▶ ▶ STUDENT LEARNING OUTCOMES

Upon completion of this chapter students will demonstrate an understanding of:

- What constitutes organized crime
- Various major organized crime groups
- Methods of investigating organized crime
- The role of intelligence in combating organized crime
- The role of the task force in combating organized crime

Organized crime is not a recent phenomenon. It has been with us at least as long as has our ability to organize. Crime is socially defined, so it would appear that the human ability to form social groups and define acceptable behavior accompanied the efforts by some to work together to frustrate behavioral guidelines to their advantage. It is difficult to pinpoint when in history humans first organized themselves into groups for personal gain in contravention of social demands.

Howard Abadinsky (1997) defines organized crime as:

a nonideological enterprise that involves a number of persons in close social interaction, organized on a hierarchical basis for the purpose of securing profit and power by engaging in illegal and legal activities. Positions in the hierarchy and positions involving functional specialization may be assigned on the basis of kinship or friendship, or rationally assigned according to skill. The positions are not dependent on the individuals occupying them at any particular time. Permanency is assumed by the members who strive to keep the enterprise integral and active in pursuit of its goals. It eschews competition and strives for monopoly over particular activities on an industry or territorial basis. There is a willingness to use violence to achieve ends or to maintain discipline. Membership is restricted, although nonmembers may be involved on a contingency basis. (p. 5)

■ Organized Crime Groups

The basic attributes of an organized crime group as defined include the following:

- *Absence of political ideology.* What is best for the organization regardless of political affiliation is what is embraced and supported. When the group is involved in politics, the group's objective is to gain protection or leverage for its members and activities.

- *A hierarchical structure* designed to insulate those at the top from the conduct of those at the bottom. Those at the top are accorded respect and deference based on position rather than personality. As in the military, the lesson is to salute the uniform, not the man.
- *A limited membership* based on race (as in black gangs and white supremacist organizations), ethnicity (as in the Jewish and Italian organizations), kinship, or criminal history (as in the Aryan Brotherhood and some motorcycle gangs). Once minimal qualifications have been met, the new member must be sponsored and must perform an act of initiation, usually involving a criminal act.
- *Longevity into perpetuity.* The ultimate objective, after procuring profit, is to ensure that the organization and its activities withstand the death or incarceration of leaders. The assurance that the organization will take care of its own (taken as a promise or a threat) provides the impetus for loyalty and a disincentive for cooperating with the authorities. Ask yourself this simple question: Who would you rather have hunting you, an angry organized crime group or the FBI?
- *Division of labor.* Certain positions and functions are performed by members who have a demonstrated proclivity and skill for the task. An **enforcer** in an organized crime group carries out the commands for violence or murder. A **fixer** may have the responsibility for ensuring that politicians and law enforcement agents are on the organization's payroll. A **cleaner** may be called upon to sterilize a crime scene, usually the scene of a murder. A **launderer** is responsible for finding pathways for the organization's money to appear legitimately earned.
- *Anticompetitiveness.* As nature abhors a vacuum, so do organized crime groups abhor competition. When violence occurs today among criminal organizations, it is generally precipitated by disputes over territory.
- *A set of rules* (written or oral). The violation of any rule is sanctioned severely. Not many sanctions are imposed, but when one is, the result is usually serious injury or death.

Organized crime groups share additional commonalities regarding goals and methods. First, their illegal activities are conspiratorial. Second, in at least some of their activities, they commit or threaten to commit acts of violence or other acts intended

CASE IN POINT

Suspected Casino Laundering

In Las Vegas, Nevada, the author was learning how to play a card game called baccarat. A young woman who worked for the casino was expertly explaining the nuances of the game when a man wearing considerable gold jewelry around his neck and on his hands approached the table. He offered the dealer $15,000 for chips, played one game, and left the table. Inquiry was made about the unusual behavior, and the casino employee indicated that the gentleman would now cash in his chips at the casino window. He would show a $14,900 gain, would later fill out the appropriate IRS forms, and would have just successfully laundered a decent chunk of money. This procedure repeated at numerous casinos throughout the city could result in a large amount of laundered currency.

to intimidate. Also, they conduct their activities in a methodical, systematic, or highly disciplined and secret fashion.

Organized crime groups insulate their leadership from direct involvement in illegal activities by their intricate organizational structure. They attempt to gain influence in politics and commerce through corruption, graft, and legitimate means. And finally, they have economic gain as their primary goal—gain not only from patently illegal activities such as drug dealing, gambling, and loan sharking, but also from laundering illegal money and investing in legitimate businesses (Abadinsky, 1997).

Organized crime can itself be viewed as a business, for it provides training, uses merit promotion, and depends for success on a peer group who operates with substantial amounts of capital. The greed of the early "robber barons" provides an example of how wealth can be squeezed from the timid through adroit application of daring, intelligence, and violence. Many of the great family fortunes of the 20th century were made by bending or breaking laws and by applying force when necessary.

The inclination of Americans to attempt to legislate morality creates an environment ripe for the picking. Outlawing some things based on morality has proven an exercise in futility. If enough people demand something that is immoral, the demand will sustain enterprises whose purpose is to supply that thing, be it gambling, alcohol, prostitution, or drugs. The law will not necessarily reduce the supply or the demand. Bear in mind that many who vote for or support morality legislation are also involved in subverting that legislation. Such legislation raises the risks associated with providing the illegal goods or services, thus providing a lucrative cartel for those willing to assume the risks. Scarcity allows prices to be raised, increasing the attractiveness of the illegal activity. The American dream places significant emphasis on material accumulation, but avenues for obtaining material possessions are not readily available to a large segment of the population. Organized crime is a response to this social and legal reality.

Several distinct groups have the characteristics of a criminal organization:

- Italian-American crime families
- Latin-American crime families
- Independent white criminal organizations
- Black criminal organizations
- Outlaw motorcycle gangs

Italian-American Crime Families

Because of their notoriety and propensity for violence, the Italian-American crime families have been the most closely scrutinized by law enforcement agencies. Whether art imitates life or life imitates art, we have seen a plethora of "wise guy" movies, often showing crime family members in a sympathetic way. These portrayals have given rise to an American icon—part myth, part reality, but all violent. Following are some of the activities associated with these organized crime families.

- **Extortion (procuring money for protection):** Generally the protection sold was to other unallied Italian immigrants, who had to pay a price for doing business in a particular neighborhood or suffer damage to their inventory or premises or injury to family members or themselves.
- **Drug dealing:** After the repeal of Prohibition, the routes for smuggling alcohol established by the crime families lay dormant until it was decided that some of the families would use the smuggling routes to distribute heroin.

- **Loan sharking:** In loan sharking, money is lent at usurious rates, and collection is based on the premise that violence will be used if debts are not repaid. The objective is not violence but collection (with the probability of repeat business). Violence is a last resort in dealing with deadbeats. Generally, loan sharks make two kinds of loans. The "knockdown loan" has a specified schedule of repayment, including principal and interest. The "vig" loan arrangement requires total payment at a particular date, interest (vigorish) included. Bankruptcy laws cannot be invoked to protect the insolvent.
- **Fencing:** Fencing operations allow thieves a ready source of income for their stolen goods, albeit at less than pawnshop prices. Without their fences, most heroin addicts could not support their habits. Fencing became a twofold blessing for the mob in that it provides cheap goods for resale and allows heroin users a steady income source to continue buying mob-supplied heroin. A fence connected to a crime family can be relied upon to have large amounts of cash available on short notice, and by dealing with a "connected" fence, thieves are assured they will not be victimized by other thieves posing as fences.
- **Organized theft:** Organized theft rings are made up of individuals who have chosen a career as thieves and con artists. The experience of hijacking the opposition's booze trucks during Prohibition pushed some mob-connected criminals toward truck hijacking and auto theft. One example of a mob scam is the "in and out," in which a sham business is established, and furniture and equipment are either leased with little money advanced or purchased on a 30-day payment contract. As the furniture and equipment are delivered through the front door, they are removed for resale out the back.
- **Kidnapping:** Kidnapping has historically been seen as a lucrative type of crime, especially if the person kidnapped possessed political or economic stature.
- **Assassination:** The assassination of political, law enforcement, and media figures was often an objective (although in some cases an unachieved objective). Although most historical slayings involved crime family against crime family, many innocent bystanders were injured and significant property damage occurred.
- **Labor union corruption: Labor racketeering** involves the infiltration, domination, and use of a union for personal benefit by illegal, violent, or fraudulent means. It uses many means, including strike breakers (violent thugs used to disperse picketers), picket protectors (violent thugs used to protect picketers), the obtaining of lucrative union contracts without the necessity of competitive bids (providing substandard material and workers to enhance profit), and initiating and resolving strikes (generally to increase union coffers with the intent of using the money or stealing it). The first casinos in Las Vegas were mob run and purchased with union money (in the form of no-interest loans).

The following is adopted from the FBI Organized Crime Web site:

Since their appearance in the 1800s, the Italian criminal societies known as the Mafia have infiltrated the social and economic fabric of Italy and the world. They are one of the most notorious and widespread of all criminal societies. There are several groups currently active in the United States:

- the Sicilian mafia
- the Camorra or **Neapolitan mafia**

- the 'Ndrangheta or **Calabrian mafia**
- the Sacra Corona Unita or United Sacred Crown

The FBI estimates that the four groups have approximately 25,000 members total, with 250,000 affiliates worldwide. There are more than 3,000 members and affiliates in the United States, scattered mostly throughout the major cities in the Northeast, the Midwest, California, and the South. Their largest presence centers around New York, southern New Jersey, and Philadelphia. Their criminal activities are international, with members and affiliates in Canada, South America, Australia, and parts of Europe. They are also known to collaborate with other international organized crime groups from all over the world, especially in drug trafficking.

Charles "Lucky" Luciano, a Mafioso from Sicily, came to the United States in the 1920s and is credited for making the American **La Cosa Nostra** what it is today. Luciano structured the La Cosa Nostra after the Sicilian Mafia. When Luciano was deported back to Italy in 1946 for operating a prostitution ring, he became a liaison between the Sicilian Mafia and the U.S. La Cosa Nostra.

The Neapolitan mafia, also known as the Camorra, derives its name from the word *camorra* which means "gang." The Camorra first appeared in the mid-1800s in Naples, Italy, as a prison gang. Once released, members formed clans in the cities and continued to grow in power. The Camorra has more than 100 clans and approximately 7,000 members, making it the largest of the Italian organized crime groups.

In the 1970s, the Sicilian mafia convinced the Camorra to convert their cigarette smuggling routes into drug smuggling routes with the Sicilian mafia's assistance. Not all Camorra leaders agreed, leading to the Camorra Wars. Opponents of drug trafficking lost the war. The Camorra now specializes in cigarette smuggling and receives payoffs from other criminal groups for any cigarette traffic through Italy. The Camorra is also involved in money laundering, extortion, alien smuggling, robbery, blackmail, kidnapping, political corruption, and counterfeiting. It is believed that nearly 200 Camorra affiliates reside in the United States.

The Calabrian mafia is also known as the 'Ndrangheta mafia, from the word *'Ndrangheta,* which comes from the Greek meaning "courage" or "loyalty". The 'Ndrangheta formed in the 1860s when a group of Sicilians was banished from the island by the Italian government. They settled in Calabria (the toe of the Italian boot) and formed small criminal groups. There are about 160 'Ndrangheta cells with roughly 6,000 members. They specialize in kidnapping and political corruption, but also engage in drug trafficking, murder, bombings, counterfeiting, gambling, frauds, thefts, labor racketeering, loan-sharking, and alien smuggling. Cells are loosely connected family groups based on blood relationships and marriages. In the United States, there are an estimated 100 to 200 members and associates, primarily in New York and Florida.

Law enforcement became aware of the Sacra Corona Unita in the late 1980s. Like other groups, it started as a prison gang. As its members were released, they settled in the Puglia region in Italy and continued to grow and form links with other mafia groups. The Sacra Corona Unita is headquartered in Brindisi, Italy, located in the southeastern region of Puglia.

The Sacra Corona Unita consists of about 50 clans with approximately 2,000 members and specializes in smuggling cigarettes, drugs, arms, and people. It is also involved in money laundering, extortion, and political corruption. The organization collects payoffs from other criminal groups for landing rights on the southeast coast of Italy, a natural gateway for smuggling to and from postcommunist countries like Croatia, Yugoslavia, and Albania. Very few Sacra Corona Unita members have been identified in the United States, although some individuals in Illinois, Florida, and New York have links to the organization.

La Cosa Nostra is the foremost organized criminal threat to American society. Literally translated into English it means "this thing of ours." It is a nationwide alliance of criminals—linked by blood ties or through conspiracy—dedicated to pursuing crime and protecting its members. La Cosa Nostra, or the LCN as it is known by the FBI, consists of different families or groups that are generally arranged geographically and engaged in significant and organized racketeering activity. It is also known as the Mafia, a term used to describe other organized crime groups. LCN is most active in the New York metropolitan area, parts of New Jersey, Philadelphia, Detroit, Chicago, and New England. It has members in other major cities and is involved in international crimes.

Historical highlights include:

- **1951:** A U.S. Senate committee led by Democrat Estes Kefauver of Tennessee determined that a "sinister criminal organization" known as the Mafia operated in this nation.
- **1957:** The New York State Police uncovered a meeting of major LCN figures from around the country in the small upstate New York town of Appalachian. Many of the attendees were arrested. The event was the catalyst that changed the way law enforcement battles organized crime.
- **1963:** Joseph Valachi became the first La Cosa Nostra member to provide a detailed look inside the organization. Recruited by FBI agents, Valachi revealed to a U.S. Senate committee numerous secrets of the organization, including its name, structure, power bases, codes, swearing-in ceremony, and members of the organization.

Over the years, FBI investigations have revealed how organized criminal groups have proliferated and affected much of the world. Partnerships with foreign law enforcement agencies are essential to combat global organized crime groups. Through the project, two FBI investigators are detailed to the headquarters of the Italian National Police, while the FBI hosts two Italian officers. The investigators work side by side with host agents and other law enforcement officials to help investigate the Sicilian mafia and La Cosa Nostra. They also work on Albanian organized crime.

Labor racketeering is the domination, manipulation, and control of a labor movement in order to affect related businesses and industries. It can lead to the denial of workers' rights and inflicts an economic loss on the workers, business, industry, insurer, or consumer.

The historical involvement of La Cosa Nostra in labor racketeering has been thoroughly documented:

- More than one third of the 58 members arrested in 1957 at the Appalachian conference in New York listed their employment as "labor" or "labor-management relations."
- Three major U.S. Senate investigations have documented La Cosa Nostra's involvement in labor racketeering. One of these, the McClellan Committee, in the late-1950s, found systemic racketeering in both the International Brotherhood of Teamsters and the Hotel Employees and Restaurant Employees International Union.

- In 1986, the President's Council on Organized Crime reported that five major unions—including the Teamsters and the Laborers International Union of North America—were dominated by organized crime.
- In the early 1980s, former Gambino family boss Paul Castellano was overheard saying, "Our job is to run the unions."

Labor racketeering has become one of La Cosa Nostra's fundamental sources of profit, national power, and influence. FBI investigations over the years have clearly demonstrated that labor racketeering costs the American public millions of dollars each year through increased labor costs that are eventually passed on to consumers. Labor unions provide a rich source for organized criminal groups to exploit in the form of their pension, welfare, and health funds. There are approximately 75,000 union locals in the United States, and many of them maintain their own benefit funds. In the mid-1980s, the Teamsters controlled more than 1,000 funds with total assets of more than $9 billion. Labor racketeers attempt to control health, welfare, and pension plans by offering sweetheart contracts, peaceful labor relations, and relaxed work rules to companies, or by rigging union elections.

Labor law violations occur primarily in large cities with both a strong industrial base and strong labor unions, like New York, Buffalo, Chicago, Cleveland, Detroit, and Philadelphia. These cities also have a large presence of organized crime figures. The FBI uses several investigative techniques to root out labor law violations, including electronic surveillance, undercover operations, confidential sources, and victim interviews.

There are also numerous criminal and civil statutes to use, primarily through the **Racketeer Influenced and Corrupt Organization (RICO) Act**. The civil provisions of the RICO statute have proven to be very powerful weapons. They are often more productive because they attack the entire corrupt entity instead of imprisoning individuals, who can easily be replaced with other organized crime members or associates.

Industrialists who capitalized on economic opportunities using fair means and foul to enrich themselves and their descendants set the standard for the criminal organizations that followed. Most Italians who immigrated to the United States came from the poorest parts of southern Italy in the late 1800s. They encountered an economy with no place for the powerless or for ethnic minorities. Many sought through illegal and immoral means the success that the Morgans and Vanderbilts had achieved. Instead of forming corporations, bureaucracies, and industrial hierarchies, some Italian-Americans created **patrimonial organizations** centered around families, heads of families, and patrons. The emphasis was on traditional values and the use of rituals to foster emotional bonding among men. The world was divided into those whom one could trust because of strong personal relationships and the rest of the world (Collins, 1975).

To be eligible for membership in an Italian-American crime family, a young man must be of Italian descent. He needs a sponsor and must have a long history of successful criminal activity or possess certain skills required by the family. Every potential member is expected to participate in a murder as executioner or assistant and to be a proven moneymaker. Each member is an independent contractor, not an employee, and may bring together non-Italian nonmembers (who might be attracted by the connections available to the family member) as associates who can provide information about prospective criminal endeavors. As a member generates substantial income for himself and the family (which takes a percentage of all income), his position and status within the family increase.

> ### CASE IN POINT
>
> **Origin of the Hell's Angels**
>
> After World War II, a group of California veterans with military skills that did not transfer well into polite society formed a motorcycle club dedicated to mocking social values, staying intoxicated, and "raising hell." Eventually, this and other fun-loving and hell-raising motorcycle clubs evolved into self-perpetuating, structured, and disciplined organizations whose major source of income was from criminal activity and who controlled the methamphetamine drug market. Using violence, they have been able to restrict market entry and monopolize most of California, with distribution points (local Hell's Angels chapters) throughout the United States.

Outlaw Motorcycle Gangs

Not all motorcycle clubs are gangs or engage in criminal activity, although up until the late 1970s any male who drove a Harley-Davidson motorcycle but was not a policeman was suspected of gang affiliation. Furthermore, not all motorcycle gangs are sophisticated criminal organizations. Some bikers engage in random acts of violence and perpetrate property crimes to uphold their image as tough guys, but few claim affiliation with the known outlaw gangs, such as the **Hell's Angels** or the Bandidos.

In contrast to the Italian-American crime families, the biker groups developed organizational configurations similar to those of the military and industry. Today, groups such as the Hell's Angels and the Bandidos are essentially highly structured bureaucracies. The leader of the national group, the national president, has offices at the national headquarters. He surrounds himself with specifically chosen members who serve as enforcers and bodyguards and from whose ranks come the individuals delegated to leadership positions. Each chapter has a president, vice president, and secretary-treasurer as well as an enforcer and a sergeant at arms. Prospective members enter on a probationary status through a sponsor and must be unanimously nominated for club membership. They carry out all menial jobs at the clubhouse and for club members.

When a man is finally admitted to membership, he is allowed to "fly the **colors**" of the organization by displaying an insignia that includes the name of the club and the chapter location. Also sewn onto the member's sleeveless denim jacket or leather jacket is a variety of patches that differ in color and content. A patch with the number 13 is often worn, for the 13th letter in the alphabet, M, indicates a propensity for the use of marijuana. Other common patches display a Nazi insignia, the numbers 666 (from the Book of Revelations pertaining to Satan), 1% (representing the percentage of interest the wearer has in society at large), and wings of different colors representing dubious club accomplishments (yellow distinguishes the wearer as having drunk female urine, and red indicates the wearer has performed oral sex on a menstruating female). The significance of the wings are twofold: They demonstrate the low regard in which women associates ("old ladies," "mamas," or "sheep," depending on their relationship to the members) are held, and they serve as a proclamation that the wearer is not a policeman (on the assumption that police would not stoop to this level of behavior).

Illegal income is derived from stolen motorcycles and motorcycle parts, the sale of customized motorcycles, prostitution, exotic dancers, massage parlors (to which female associates are lent), and the sale of automatic weapons and explosives. Bikers have accepted contracts from Italian-American crime families for murder and have been used by them to provide the muscle in their collection activities. The clubs' most lucrative enterprise is the manufacture and distribution of methamphetamines.

New Wave Organized Crime Groups

New organized crime groups have arisen that are fueled by the desire for and attainment of drug income. Some have adopted the business techniques of corporate America, including use of upper managers, accountants, bookkeeping, and computers for tracking distribution and income. Their characteristics include **vertical integration** (structuring the group so that it controls both the lines of manufacture and of distribution and thus eliminates the middleman) and insulation of leaders from the activities of those involved in manufacture and distribution.

The drug trade has proven lucrative and elusive. Violence provides the continuity and the method of control. The diversity of new wave organizations increases as new entrants strive to become the most violent kid on the block. Recent participants in these types of endeavors include black, Asian, Jamaican, and Colombian groups.

As with some Italian immigrants, some of these new arrivals or socially disenfranchised groups look to illegal means to obtain material success. The black gangs have come to an accommodation among themselves, agreeing to geographic parceling to avoid continued conflict. They finally recognized that they were killing more black gang members than the police were. They also recognized that warring over turf made little sense when so much drug money was available for those who could compromise.

The drug business is a fluid one, ever-changing in players and in product requirements. Regional distribution rights are subject to the law of survival of the fittest. In order to break into the monopolistic industry, a group must demonstrate no reluctance for violence. The new kids on the block are the Jamaican posses, violent and homogeneous, based on ethnicity, race, and culture. They pose a formidable social and law enforcement problem. They are politically and profit motivated. They funnel money and guns back to Jamaica, where local gangs attempt to control the political process (Lyman, 1993).

About 30,000 violent street gangs, motorcycle gangs, and prison gangs with approximately 800,000 members operate in the United States today. Many are sophisticated and well organized; all use violence to control neighborhoods and boost their illegal money-making activities, which include drug trafficking, robbery, theft, fraud, extortion, prostitution rings, and gun trafficking. To help curb the growth of gangs, in 2005 the FBI created the **National Gang Intelligence Center (NGIC)**. The NGIC is a multiagency center that integrates gang intelligence from across the country on the growth, migration, criminal activity, and association of gangs that pose a threat to the United States. The mission of the NGIC is to support law enforcement by sharing information and introducing strategic and tactical analysis of intelligence gathered about gangs.

■ Organized Crime and Applicable Laws

RICO

The business of organized crime requires the violation of many federal and state laws. It is the large variety of laws violated that provides law enforcement agencies, grand juries, and prosecutors the means for effective enforcement and prosecution.

The most important of these laws is the 1970 RICO Act, which authorizes asset forfeiture and other civil sanctions to be used against an organized crime group. Under

RICO, many offenses that do not ordinarily constitute a violation of federal law may be federal offenses if they occur as a product of racketeering. The law itself has a laundry list of offenses that may be litigable under federal auspices but would not ordinarily be federal violations:

- Bribery
- Embezzlement
- Trafficking in contraband cigarettes
- Drug trafficking
- Wire fraud
- Sports bribery
- Obstruction of justice

RICO also increases the sanctions for certain offenses that have historically been under federal jurisdiction, including counterfeiting, bankruptcy fraud, Hobbs Act violations (the act prohibits foreign or interstate travel or the use of interstate facilities to advance illegal activities), and Mann Act violations (the act prohibits transporting a woman across state lines for illegal purposes). The criminal and civil sanctions for violating RICO are significant: a fine not to exceed $25,000 and/or 20 years in prison, along with the possibility of both civil and criminal **forfeiture** of any property used in or proceeding from the proscribed criminal activity.

Conspiracy Laws

A **conspiracy** is an agreement by two or more persons to commit an act that would be in violation of some criminal statute, accompanied by an overt act in furtherance of the conspiracy. The agreement itself becomes the essential element of the crime, and a crime is committed even if the object of the agreement is not achieved. What makes conspiracy so attractive to those investigating organized criminals is that there is no need to establish that an organization's leader committed a physical act furthering a criminal act, only that he or she can be shown to have been a party to the agreement.

Howard Abadinsky (1997) provides a summary of some of the legal aspects of conspiracy:

- Statements by one of the conspirators are binding on the other members of the conspiracy.
- A co-conspirator need not have joined the conspiracy at its inception. Upon joining the conspiracy, each co-conspirator validates the prior acts and statements of his or her co-conspirators.
- To be found guilty of a conspiracy, all that must be proven is that the suspect had knowledge of the conspiracy and its essential objective.
- The statute-of-limitations period does not begin until completion of the last conspiratorial act, which may be an act of hampering an investigation into a matter that occurred long ago.
- A defendant who claims to have withdrawn from a conspiracy has the burden of presenting proof that he or she did withdraw—which means proving that he or she performed some affirmative action of withdrawal.
- Venue in a conspiracy prosecution generally lies in the judicial district in which the agreement was made or in any judicial district in which one of the overt acts was committed.

- A party to a conspiracy is responsible for any offense committed by a co-conspirator in furtherance of the conspiracy even though he or she did not participate in the offense or lacked knowledge of the offense.

■ Investigating Organized Crime

Organized crime crosses all boundaries—geographic, social, and political. Consequently, the fundamental problem associated with investigating organized crime is cooperative communication among federal, state, and local agencies. To overcome communication failures among federal agencies (who have often preferred not to divulge information to anyone), in 1961 Attorney General Robert Kennedy set up a system of area coordinators, consisting of federal attorneys delegated to visit assigned areas to ensure that information about organized crime was being shared and used. From this endeavor grew the concept of the **strike force** (National Association of Attorneys General, 1977). Strike force members came from the FBI; Drug Enforcement Administration; Internal Revenue Service; Bureau of Alcohol, Tobacco, and Firearms; Immigration and Naturalization Service; Customs Service; Department of Labor; and Postal Inspection Service.

According to Robert Stewart (1980), four strike force characteristics are essential:

1. The strike force is interdisciplinary, because it combines investigative and prosecutorial personnel and such specialists as accountants, and it includes investigators from federal, state, and local agencies.

2. The strike force is insulated, being free from local pressures and politics, which can inhibit effective enforcement.

3. The strike force is offender-focused rather than offense-focused. The main target is the offender who is involved in a lengthy list of offenses over a long period of time.

4. The strike force is proactive, free to roam at large seeking out targets, assessing relevant organized crime intelligence data, and targeting specific organized crime groups for investigation.

Gathering Intelligence

Information about organized crime groups is referred to as intelligence (Dintino and Martens, 1983). Intelligence data are collected for both tactical and strategic purposes. **Tactical intelligence** is information that contributes directly to the achievement of an immediate law enforcement objective. **Strategic intelligence** is information that contributes to producing sound judgments with respect to long-range law enforcement objectives. The information is collected over time and put together by an **intelligence analyst** to reveal new patterns of organized criminal activity.

Analysis is the heart of the intelligence system. A copious quantity of unrelated information is useless until organized and analyzed. It must be processed and stored in a manner that makes it legally useful, readily understandable, and easy to retrieve. The collecting and storing of intelligence data may not seem like exciting law enforcement. And indeed, the results of intelligence gathering are never immediate or dramatic. Furthermore, information analysis often does not impress decision makers in charge of allocating funds.

Robert Stewart (1980) provides a list of common sources of intelligence data:

- Court records
- Real estate transactions
- Clerk of the deeds of record

- Attorney general incorporation records and minutes
- Business records
- Intelligence and open files from other agencies
- Newspapers and periodicals
- Utility company records
- Electronic surveillance records
- Statements from accomplices, informants, and victims

Since 1980, the U.S. Department of Justice has funded six regional information-sharing systems that provide services to state and local law enforcement officers. Each system has a computerized law enforcement database that contains entries pertaining to major crime figures. Each system also offers investigative analysis support; loans investigative equipment; and provides confidential funds, timely bulletins with crime-related information, and training.

Investigative Grand Juries

A grand jury is composed of between 9 and 24 citizens who have been selected according to law and sworn to hear evidence against an accused party to determine if there is probable cause to bring the accused before the court for trial. The grand jury is also empowered to investigate criminal activity. To meet this responsibility, the jury can compel testimony (with grants of immunity and threats of contempt), issue subpoenas (to require appearance), and issue subpoenas duces tecum (to require that named documents be produced). The Organized Crime Control Act of 1970 requires that an investigative grand jury (**special grand jury**) be impaneled every 18 months in federal judicial districts with populations greater than 1 million. The objective of such a grand jury is to collect evidence as part of a larger inquiry into organized crime and corrupt public officials.

The investigative grand jury is the single most useful tool by which to attack the traditional forms of organized crime. Members of an organized criminal group can be required to appear and be questioned about their superiors and the illegal activity of the organization and its leaders. Grants of **immunity** can be given to compel testimony, at which time Fifth Amendment protection against self-incrimination no longer applies. If the grant is ignored, the witness may be incarcerated for contempt until he or she decides to testify. If a witness testifies truthfully, that witness will be ostracized from the criminal community and thereby neutralized as an organized crime operative. The defection of one member of a criminal organization may serve to topple the dominoes, forcing others to cooperate with the government (Stewart, 1980).

As long as there are consumers clamoring for illegal goods, there will be criminal organizations willing to accept the risks associated with providing those goods. One argument in support of removing "victimless" crimes such as drug use, gambling, and prostitution (although it has victims, there is generally no complainant) from criminal statutes is that by doing so we fire a fatal bullet into the heart of organized crime. Perhaps the legalization of these crimes will occur, but it is not very likely. A moral society will attempt to ensure its morality by outlawing activities that appear to threaten it. As long as there is a national appetite for illicit sex, drugs, and vice, there will be organizations to provide them. The battle against these organizations sometimes seems like an exercise in futility, although many believe it must be fought. For every crime organization that is broken asunder, there is another waiting to step into its place. Legislating morality has never been effective, and law enforcement has always had to, and perhaps always will have to, bear the onus of being unable to eradicate vice. Organized crime, vice, and narcotics are not only legal problems, but also social problems, and they will not disappear as a result of laws and their enforcement.

■ Summary

Organized crime reaches into every household throughout the country. The corruption of labor unions passes on the cost of organized crime to the consumer. Drug trafficking carries with it a social cost with which this country has yet to contend. Organized criminals claim to provide a service for which people are willing to pay. Without a willing buyer there would be no illicit trafficking in drugs or anything else. As prevalent as organized crime is in this country some serious soul searching needs to be done to appreciate the role the consumer of illicit products plays in sustaining organized crime and gang activity.

As new minority group members arrive in this country without an education or entrepreneurial capital, the world of gangs and organized criminal activity awaits them. The most effective tool against organized crime is information and the combined federal task force. Although the mafia may not be the syndicate it once was, black, Hispanic, and Jamaican gangs, supremacist groups, and terrorists have taken their place. There is little fear that organized crime will disappear.

The next chapter deals with the new wave criminal and the tools used to commit white collar crime. Although street crime still exists it is the world of computers and scams where the real money is being made. A quick look at your email in-box will reveal the solicitations for partnerships in foreign endeavors involving emerging nations and unaccounted for large sums of money ostensibly available to be removed from that country. The shear number of these solicitations received daily begs the belief that anyone would be foolish enough to participate.

■ Key Terms

Calabrian mafia: Known as the 'Ndrangheta mafia, from the word *'Ndrangheta,* which comes from the Greek, meaning "courage" or "loyalty"

cleaner: Person in an organized crime group who may be called upon to sterilize a crime scene, usually the scene of a murder

colors: Insignia of an organization, which includes the name of the club and the chapter location, worn by members of that organization

conspiracy: An agreement by two or more persons to commit an act that would be in violation of some criminal statute, accompanied by an overt act in furtherance of the conspiracy

enforcer: Person in an organized crime group who carries out the commands for violence or murder

fixer: Person in an organized crime group who may have the responsibility for ensuring that politicians and law enforcement agents are on the organization's payroll

forfeiture: Giving up any property used in or proceeding from a proscribed criminal activity

Hell's Angels: A California motorcycle club that evolved into a self-perpetuating, structured, and disciplined organization whose major source of income was criminal activity and who controlled the methamphetamine drug market

immunity: Offer that can be given to compel witness testimony, at which time Fifth Amendment protection against self-incrimination no longer applies

intelligence analyst: Person who collects intelligence information and puts the information together to reveal new patterns of organized criminal activity

labor racketeering: The manipulation of labor unions

La Cosa Nostra: Refers to the American mafia

launderer: Person in an organized crime group who is responsible for finding pathways for the organization's money to appear legitimately earned

National Gang Intelligence Center: A multi-agency center that integrates gang intelligence from across the country

Neapolitan mafia: Known as the Camorra and derives its name from the word *camorra,* which means "gang"

patrimonial organizations: Organizations centered around families, heads of families, and patrons that emphasize traditional values and the use of rituals to foster emotional bonding among men

Racketeer Influenced Corrupt Organization (RICO) Act: Law that authorizes asset forfeiture and other civil sanctions to be used against an organized crime group

special grand jury: An investigative grand jury, impaneled every 18 months in federal judicial districts with populations greater than 1 million, having the objective of collecting evidence as part of a larger inquiry into organized crime and corrupt public officials

strategic intelligence: Information that contributes to producing sound judgments with respect to long-range law enforcement objectives

strike force: An interdisciplinary team composed of investigative and prosecutorial personnel from federal, state, and local agencies who seek out offenders who are involved in a lengthy list of offenses over a long period of time, assess relevant organized crime intelligence data, and target specific organized crime groups for investigation

tactical intelligence: Information that contributes directly to the achievement of an immediate law enforcement objective

vertical integration: Structuring a group so that it controls both lines of manufacture and lines of distribution and thus eliminates the middleman

■ **Review Questions**

1. What are the attributes of an organized crime group?
2. What are the roles of the enforcer, fixer, cleaner, and launderer in the organized crime family?
3. What are the contributions to American life of the Italian-American crime families?
4. Who and what are the Hell's Angels?
5. What are biker colors? Describe some of the patches that bikers wear.
6. What are vertical integration and insulation, and what role do they play in the new wave organized crime groups?
7. What are the provisions of RICO?
8. What are criminal and civil forfeiture, and what is the burden of proof for each?
9. Where did the idea of an organized strike force come from?

10. What is a strike force?

11. What is a conspiracy?

12. What advantage does the crime of conspiracy possess for investigators attempting to fight against organized crime?

13. What is intelligence? Include a discussion of the difference between strategic and tactical intelligence.

14. What services does an intelligence analyst provide?

15. What is the function of the special grand jury, and what powers does it have to assist it in performing that function?

16. What is labor racketeering?

17. What type of efforts does the FBI employ to weed out labor racketeers?

18. What is the purpose of the National Gang Intelligence Center?

19. Who makes up the Neapolitan mafia?

20. Who are the Sacra Corona?

21. Who are the Calabrian mafia?

■ Bibliography

Abadinsky, H. (1997). *Organized crime.* Chicago: Nelson-Hall.

Collins, R. (1975). *Conflict sociology.* New York: Academic Press.

Dintino, J.J., and Martens, F.T. (1983). *Police intelligence systems and crime control.* Springfield, IL: Charles C. Thomas.

Lyman, M.D. (1993). *Criminal investigation: The art and science.* Englewood Cliffs, NJ: Prentice Hall.

National Association of Attorneys General. (1977). *Organized crime control units.* Raleigh, NC: Committee on the Office of Attorney General.

Stewart, R.C. (1980). *Identification and investigation of organized criminal activity.* Houston, TX: National College of District Attorneys.

White-Collar Crime

CHAPTER 19

▶ ▶ STUDENT LEARNING OUTCOMES

Upon completion of this chapter students will demonstrate an understanding of:

- The prevalence of white-collar crime
- The role of the questioned document examiner in investigating white-collar crime
- The use of computers in perpetrating theft
- The problems in searching computers and peripherals
- The problems in seizing computers and peripherals
- How someone's identity can be stolen

In most jurisdictions, white-collar crime is not a statutory offense in and of itself but rather is an area of criminality encompassing certain kinds of theft and trespass. Traditionally, local jurisdictions have had little to do with white-collar crime and white-collar criminals, and it was thought that white-collar criminals were responsible for only a small portion of the total amount of ill-gotten gain. High finance, computers, and a federal interest in some types of white-collar crime have changed that. Local and state agencies are often ill equipped to deal with sophisticated white-collar crimes, especially those that involve computers. The key to apprehending white-collar criminals is specialized training and agency hiring based on specific skill selection.

Nonviolent crimes committed for personal or financial gain accomplished through deception or the use of computers may be classified as white-collar crime. The name denotes crimes committed by workers using their brains rather than their brawn. Blue-collar workers generally are involved in some type of manual labor, whereas white-collar workers are professional or management personnel who do not get their hands dirty. The distinction in labor gave rise to the distinction in crime. Most white-collar criminal activity involves money laundering, confidence games, and computer crimes.

■ Money Laundering

The advent and growth of the drug industry in the United States have given groups of drug dealers more cash than they have the ability to spend. An ever-vigilant federal government, with the help of various types of national legislation aimed at preventing **money laundering**, has made it difficult for drug cartels to dispose of large quantities of money. The cartels' very success in garnering large profits has placed them in constant fear of detection by federal officials—which could lead to asset forfeiture and prison sentences. They have managed to ward off federal attention by finding methods of making their illegal profits appear to be legitimate income. The process of legitimizing illegal income can take many forms. Launderers may commingle illegal income with proceeds from legitimate businesses that deal primarily in cash (Italian-American crime families used bowling alleys, restaurants, casinos, saloons, and night clubs), or they may use international financial practices to muddy their trail.

Illegal drug transactions are cash based. Each participant is compensated in cash, and equipment is purchased with cash. It is necessary for traffickers to channel their income in a way that allows ready access without attracting unnecessary attention. Storing money is risky (the money is vulnerable to theft, fire, or extortion) and, if large quantities are involved, can be cumbersome. Most street transactions are conducted using small denominations. The small denominations must be changed for larger denominations for ease of transport and use. Banks would seem to be the solution.

The 1970 Bank Secrecy Act, however, requires U.S. banks to maintain records of all transactions in excess of $10,000. Any transfers to foreign banks in excess of $5,000 also must be recorded. A report must be filed whenever currency or monetary instruments of more than $5,000 are taken into or out of the country. Yet there are so many techniques used to launder money that investigations of laundering are extremely complex. The authority given federal agencies to investigate money laundering has prompted many traffickers to use **offshore financial institutions**. Drug traffickers seek out countries that have little or no tax on income and have strict bank secrecy laws, such as the Cayman Islands.

One of the first obstacles confronting drug traffickers is finding a financial institution that has access to international transfer facilities and can accommodate large deposits of money on a regular basis. Traffickers know that once the money is introduced into a banking system, it becomes indistinguishable from any other money with which it is mingled. Having an international bank as an ally allows money to be moved in and out of the institution quickly and quietly. The banking laws and procedures intended to protect legitimate depositors and investors help conceal drug profits and make the investigation of laundering difficult if not impossible.

Offshore financial institutions often exist for the purpose of laundering drug money. A visit to the Cayman Islands reveals numerous storefront financial institutions that exist in name only. Their primary role is to deposit money in legitimate financial institutions on the islands through local channels. As the United States brings diplomatic and economic pressure to bear on these offshore sites, new countries will likely enter the laundering arena.

■ Confidence Swindles

For centuries, criminals have attempted to relieve the foolish, greedy, and gullible of their cash. The perpetration by **con artists** (confidence swindlers) of **con games** (confidence swindles) on the unsuspecting public is a tried and true criminal activity. For centuries swindling was not prohibited by law. Under common law, there was no theft, because the person voluntarily parted with his or her property. Most states have incorporated theft by swindle into their theft statutes, recognizing that voluntary relinquishment of possession does not transfer ownership without specific intent to do so.

All cons contain an element of dishonesty or gain without an expenditure. It is an old axiom, but generally true, that you cannot con an honest man. Most cons tap into the little bit of larceny in the soul of each of us, without which most cons cannot work. Many people are looking for something for nothing. The best defense is to keep in mind this rule of thumb: If it looks too good to be true, it probably is. Many swindles go unreported because of the embarrassment associated with admitting one's duplicity or naiveté.

The most damaging cons are those that take advantage of elderly people, who are often less vigilant, have less contemporary sophistication, and are susceptible to offers of a bargain because they live on a fixed budget. The oldest scam perpetrated on the elderly is the **home repair scam**, which may take many forms but requires initial entry to the premises. The con artist makes a telephone inquiry about termites, siding, window heat loss, or some other home problem. The con artist offers a free examination and the examiner inevitably discovers some malady, which is then repaired at an exorbitant price. It is a scam because either the malady did not exist (and the substantiating evidence was fabricated) or it could have been repaired better for less money.

Conning has also gone online and into telemarketing. One con game involves offering a free product (a vacation, an appliance, software, or pornographic pictures) in exchange for answering a few consumer profile questions. The mark is told that the profile will not be sold or given to anyone but will be used internally for marketing purposes. The catch is that there is generally a shipping cost associated with providing the product. The mark is told the amount can be charged to any credit card. The ultimate objective, of course, is to obtain the credit card number. With the information provided in the consumer profile, that number can now be used for online cash transfers, for charging an inflated postage and handling fee, or for the purchase of products.

Investigation of confidence swindles is difficult because of the efforts of con artists to cover their tracks. Often the con and the con artist have moved on by the time the victims have discovered they have been swindled. Telephone and credit card records can be useful but generally lead to disconnected phone banks, pseudonyms, and vacant rental space. Databases of various swindles and their modi operandi are helpful in tracking con games and may assist in associating a con game with a suspect. The modus operandi can only be provided by the victim, making the victim interview the most important part of the investigation.

From a preventive standpoint, the best approach is to issue a public advisory describing the type of swindle and its variations. The hope is that someone will contact the police before actively participating in the scam, thereby allowing the police an opportunity to build a sting operation.

■ Forgery and Check Fraud

The ever-expanding consumer marketplace has driven check writing to a new high. Everyone has a checking account or needs one. All business that is not conducted by computer financial exchange is conducted by check writing. Payrolls are met by check, and citizens meet their monthly financial obligations by check. It should be no surprise that theft through **forgery** or alteration of checks is also at a new high. Forging a check involves signing another's name to a check without authority (with intent to defraud). Forgery of government checks (e.g., Social Security, welfare, and unemployment checks) is the most common, and the investigation of such forgery may require a joint effort by state and federal law enforcement agencies. As in all criminal investigations, the necessary elements of the offense must be established. In check forgery and check alteration cases, this means that the prosecution must prove an intent to defraud and the suspect's knowledge of the false nature of the check. The suspect is generally prepared to authenticate the forged check with some type of false identification. The checks may have been stolen, found, or manufactured by computer. The name on the check may be fictitious. Blank checks may be forged to someone's account, or a check made payable to a particular person may have been found or stolen and fraudulently endorsed, allowing another to receive the proceeds of the check.

Check alteration involves the rearrangement of preexisting information, erasures, obliterations, or additions. An altered check may have been written to the suspect, who then alters the amount, making forgery and false identification unnecessary. Corporate checks are prime candidates for alteration, because they require less identification to cash and are subjected to less scrutiny during the cashing process.

■ Questioned-Document Examination

Any object that contains handwritten or typewritten markings whose source or authenticity is in doubt may be referred to as a **questioned document**. Questioned documents can even include walls, windows, doors, or any other object containing writing or other symbols. **Document examination**, besides providing a variety of information, may allow the following:

- The connection of a specific document to a specific suspect
- The connection of a specific document to a specific typewriter or computer printer
- The detection of alterations, forgeries, or erasures and restoration of the document to its original form

Paper documents submitted for examination should be placed in a transparent protective folder and handled as little as possible.

Handwriting Comparison

No two individuals write exactly alike. The style of writing acquired by a learner is that which is fashionable at the particular time and place. Unsurprisingly, many pupils in a handwriting class tend at first to have writing styles that are similar to each other. A child normally reaches the stage where the nerve and motor responses associated with the act of writing become subconscious. The individual's writing now begins to take on innumerable habitual shapes and patterns that are unique. Variations are expected in angularity, slope, speed, pressure, letter and word spacing, relative dimensions of letters, connections, pen movement, writing skill, and finger dexterity. The arrangement of writing on paper may be as distinctive as the writing itself. Margins, spacing, crowding, insertions, and alignment are all results of personal habits.

It may be relatively easy to change one's writing style for a few words or sentences, but the task of maintaining the style grows more difficult with each additional word. When there is a large amount of writing available to a questioned-document examiner, a person's attempt at disguise will generally fail. It is imperative that an adequate number of **known writings** from the suspect be provided so the examiner can perform a comparison between a suspect sample and known samples. The known writings should contain some of the word and letter combinations present in the questioned document (Saferstein, 1995).

Documents may be altered after preparation so that their original content may be hidden. One of the most common alteration methods is to try to erase parts of the document by abrading or scratching the paper's surface. All erasures disturb the upper fibers of the paper. These disturbances can be seen when examined under a microscope or by allowing light to strike the paper obliquely from one side. Sometimes so much of the paper has been removed that it is impossible to identify the original contents.

According to the decision in *Gilbert v. California* (1967), there is no right to counsel when obtaining handwriting samples before a suspect has been formally charged with having committed a crime. The court also was of the opinion that the prohibition against self-incrimination contained in the Fifth Amendment is a testimonial protection and that a handwriting sample is not testimony. In *United States v. Mara* (1973), the U.S. Supreme Court held that obtaining a handwriting sample was not a Fourth Amendment violation, because the common use of handwriting in public and for public purposes removes the expectation of privacy required for Fourth Amendment protection.

Typewriter Comparison

The two questions investigators ask questioned-document examiners most often are these: Can you determine the make and model of the typewriter used to type the questioned document? Can you confirm that a particular suspect typewriter typed the document?

To answer the first question, an examiner must have access to a complete reference collection of past and present typefaces used by typewriter manufacturers. Although there may be a dozen manufacturers using a particular typeface, many of these are readily distinguishable upon comparison of the type style, shape, and size. The use of a typewriter will result in wear and damage to the machine's moving parts. The changes will occur in a manner that is both random and irregular, imparting individual characteristics to the typewriter and the type. Variations in vertical and horizontal alignment and perpendicular misalignment of characters, as well as defects in each character, are valuable for establishing the identity of the typewriter.

Associating a particular typewriter with a typewritten document requires a comparison of the questioned document and exemplars typed on the suspect typewriter.

Computer Printer Comparison

Recently forensic scientists have used microscopical reflection-absorption spectroscopy for analyzing the resins contained in dry, black printer copies. The technique uses heat transfer of toner from a document to the reflective surface of aluminum foil. Once the toner has been scraped from the surface of the document and placed on the foil, microscopical reflection-absorption spectroscopy analyzes the polymer resins contained in the toner. The result of the analysis is a graphic display of the component polymers. That graphic display is compared to the graphic display from the toner taken from the suspect printer. Once the two graphs are compared, the analyst can determine with a high degree of reliability if the toner on the document was printed from the computer's printer.

■ Computer-Assisted Crime

How dependent upon computers have we become? It is difficult to imagine what life was like before the advent of computers. Inventories, transactions, shipments, money, and receipt of goods are now computer dependent. A movie rental shop operator with computer problems closes the establishment rather than conduct business without the assistance of computers. Grocery stores using barcodes to price and inventory merchandise shut down when their computers go down. The computer has become much more than a tool; it has become an artificial limb without which we cannot conduct the majority of business. As we grow more dependent upon computers, there are those who recognize the criminal opportunities presented by the ubiquity of computers. A criminal with computer sophistication can unlock doors that most of us do not know exist. This is the information age, and information is power. The vast amount of information stored in computer systems makes information highly available to those who know how to get it. It has fallen to law enforcement to keep abreast of technological developments and obtain the expertise necessary to combat technological crime, especially crime committed with the assistance of computers.

The major tool for investigators is the same as for any type of criminal investigator: the search warrant. Problems arising from search and seizure issues as they pertain to computers extend beyond the Fourth Amendment to embrace the free speech and free press guarantees contained in the First Amendment. The foundation upon which all searches and seizures are based is the "reasonableness" of police behavior. A search and seizure conducted within the parameters of a valid warrant is presumed reasonable. Conversely, any search and seizure conducted without the benefit of a warrant is presumed unreasonable (until proven otherwise). Warrant validity is based on the existence of probable cause as sufficiently stated in the affidavit supporting the warrant (particularity).

Computer Particularity and Probable Cause

When computers are the subject of a warrant, the areas of particularity and probable cause create new headaches for police investigators. Most computer investigations will be the result of considerable intelligence gathering and analysis.

Computer criminals must use devices that allow them access to other computers and databases. It is necessary to determine the computer's role in the alleged crime in order to meet probable cause requirements for a search and/or a seizure. The computer's role will determine if the machine itself is to be seized or simply searched onsite. It will also determine whether the peripherals (printer, modem, keyboard, etc.) are to be seized or searched onsite. The determination of these issues can only be made based on extensive information about the crime that has been committed and the way it was committed. That information will establish the probable cause upon which the investigator may act.

A probable cause affidavit must contain statements to the effect that:

1. A crime has been committed.
2. Evidence of a crime exists.
3. The evidence of the crime can be found at the search site.

It is the second probable cause element that requires investigators to know the exact role that the computer played in the commission of the offense. If the computer was used as a tool to commit a crime, then probable cause would justify the seizure of the entire computer system and allow a subsequent search of the system at the crime laboratory. If the computer was used simply to store information of a criminal offense, then probable cause would be established to seize data records (printouts) from the computer. In order to establish probable cause to seize both the computer system and its data records, the police have to show that the computer was used to commit the criminal offense and that data pertaining to that offense (or others) were contained in the computer. In other words, there must be an affirmative link between the items listed to be seized and the criminal activity alleged. Absent a showing of this link, the system seizure or the data seizure may be suppressed.

Warrant Particularity

Under the Fourth Amendment, a valid warrant must "particularly describe the place to be searched and the persons or things to be seized." When dealing with an online computer system, it is not always possible to determine exactly what type of computer system was used to commit the crime or store evidence of it. The police must describe the computer system as precisely as the facts allow. In many cases, they may only be able to state that the criminal used some type of computer, keyboard, monitor, and means of connection to other computers, servers, Internet service providers, etc. A "particular" search and seizure cannot be conducted by an investigator who does not understand the basics of computer technology and how that technology is normally applied.

What separates computer data records from other records is the form in which computer records may be found. They could be stored electronically on a hard drive (which can be inside the computer or externally added to increase the size of the internal hard drive), on optical or magnetic discs, on tapes, or on a CD or DVD. However, it is the information sought that must be particularly described, not necessarily the form in which it exists. If the records sought are particularly described, the simple addition to the search warrant affidavit of the statement that the records sought may be written or electronic should allow seizure of the records regardless of their form. If the investigator has only general information about the records sought, the warrant must include a **limiting phrase** to help separate the information to be seized from information that may be legally permissible to possess. The limiting phrase may contain language that describes the information sought in general terms, with the added constraints of a particular time frame, author, or subject matter. It is vital that the limiting phrase restrict the scope of the search so that it remains within the boundaries of probable cause set forth in the affidavit.

Computers and the First Amendment

Under the First Amendment, citizens of the United States enjoy freedom of speech and freedom of the press. When searching and seizing an online computer system, investigators can view the system as not merely a data repository but a "publishing and distribution operation" (Rose, 1995). While a search and seizure of a computer used for data storage may only involve Fourth Amendment issues, a search and seizure of an online computer system might also involve the protections of the First Amendment. If a suspect is using a computer to download (transfer information from one computer to another) illegal pornography, the First Amendment will not provide a defense against a charge of possession of the illegal material. If the host (sending computer) is targeted by the investigators, however, their attempts to search and seize that system will be met with First Amendment challenges. Obviously, illegal pornography is not protected speech or press under the First Amendment, but other items contained in the host computer may be. Seizing the host computer system and all its contents may involve the seizure of constitutionally protected items.

Conducting the Search and Seizure

The investigative team that carries out the physical search and seizure of the online computer system needs to be thoroughly familiar with the special requirements present in an online computer case (TABLE 19-1). The investigators may have all the probable cause they need and may be familiar with all of the rights and issues involved, but if the execution of the search and seizure is done improperly, the records sought may be destroyed. Traditionally, search warrants have authorized searches for objects that occupy a place in space and time and obey physical laws. But in the world of online computer systems, things are less physical and more virtual (existing in time, not necessarily in space).

Generally, the search team will know where the computer in question resides and, if it is networked, where the other computers are that make up the network. Should a search reveal an online relationship that was not anticipated and indicate that incriminating information is being stored off-site, the team may have to obtain another warrant. If, however, the team is in an office or university building and the second computer is in an adjacent or nearby office of the same building, the initial warrant may have been drafted broadly enough to justify a search of the other computers. Language in the warrant allowing a search and seizure of any evidence that is stored in **off-site computers** that are readily and routinely accessed by the primary computer and serve regularly as components of the primary computer's network will justify extending the search. The warrant language must be supported by statements in the affidavit that establish the probability that unknown off-site computers exist, suggest the location of these computers, and describe the alleged link between the primary computer and the off-site computers (Computer Search and Seizure Working Group, 1994).

It is difficult to assess the costs of computer crime nationwide because there is very little information available regarding the number of computer crimes committed and the losses associated with those crimes. In many instances the crime is never discovered or discovered so belatedly that all traces of the crime have been erased.

The fast-growing industry of computer crime has required a concomitantly fast-growing computer forensics industry. But it must be kept in mind those committing computer crimes spend all their time figuring out ways to circumvent existing laws and computer systems. In truth the thieves stay a step or two ahead of the police. Computer forensics deals with the identification, gathering, packaging, and preserving of evidence to assure that all evidence is admissible at the time of trial. In addition to an understanding of the forensic aspects of computer investigation, the competent investigator must also be able to testify knowledgeably and understandably about every aspect of the investiga-

---

TABLE 19–1   Computer Search Checklist

- Probable cause
- Description of the computer and peripherals to be seized
- Description of the system (networked, bbs, Web site)
- Description of constitutional issues
- Computer expertise needed
- Storage and examination area
- Nature of the data being sought
- How data are to be distinguished from other protected data
- How data are to be retrieved with minimum damage to original
- When search will be executed
- How the premises with be secured

tion. Juries often prefer a simpler, rather than a more complex theory or explanation. The types of evidence that a computer forensic investigator must deal with live in both the physical and virtual world. The physical components involve the computer and peripherals, which are subject to all constitutional restraints pertaining to the search or seizure of the computer and related hardware. The hardware itself is seldom a legal problem although unplugging it or pressing any key on an unattended computer may result in a command to reformat the drives and destroy any information contained on the hard drive.

Gathering and preserving data requires the examination of log files, Internet access, and stored and transmitted data, which may give rise to major problems. An investigator must not alter the original data in efforts to extract it. In most instances a mirror image of all data on a computer is made and it is the image that is manipulated so that the original computer and data remains unaffected and amenable to admissibility during trial. The basic protocol in handling any evidence is that it be maintained in the same condition as when it was found. Anything done to the evidence while in the custody of the police must be logged into chain-of-custody log sheets and the evidence must be maintained and available to the defendant for independent defense testing requests.

The basic rules in dealing with computer investigations are:

- Procure all necessary warrants
  a. To enter the premises
  b. To seize computer and peripherals
  c. To examine data
- Do not let anyone access the computer, most particularly anyone who lives on the premises
  a. Especially police who think they know something about computers
  b. Only access to be made is by a computer forensic specialist
- Do not execute any programs on the computer at the crime scene except those necessary to save data in temporary files or memory
- Do not alter anything contained on or in the computer and peripherals
- Maintain chain of custody information for everything seized
- Leave copies of warrants and receipts for everything taken
- Write narrative summaries of all that occurred in the seizure process
- Store all items in a temperature controlled environment

No-Knock Warrants

A **no-knock warrant** justifies entry into the evidence site without knocking and announcing that the persons entering are police. In order to enter without knocking and announcing in a computer search and seizure case, the investigators need to be able to articulate, in the probable cause affidavit, reasonable grounds for believing that the evidence might be destroyed otherwise or that an occupant might escape. The primary concern would be the preservation of evidence. In some instances, **computer hackers** (computer users with sophisticated understanding of computer and software functions who are engaged in invading computer systems other than their own) have been known to use time-delay devices or **hot keys** to permit quick disposal of incriminating evidence. A time-delay function is programmed into the computer, and, while activated, monitors the keyboard for activity. If a certain period of time goes by without any keys being depressed, the program activates a kill function that erases all of the data stored in the system. A hot-key program activates the erasure of data when a certain key or combination of keys is depressed.

Computer Experts

Criminal investigators may think that a fellow officer is a computer expert because the officer has a computer and spends a lot of time working with computers. A well-meaning officer who thinks he or she has enough computer knowledge to assist during a search of a computer system can be much more dangerous than an officer who knows he or she is computer illiterate and refrains from assisting in the actual seizure. Seizing a computer is a highly technical endeavor and should be attempted only by those with specific training.

It is not necessary for every member of the search team to understand in detail the process for carrying out the search of a computer system. The individual doing the data searching on the computer will most likely be the computer forensic expert. It is this individual's responsibility to determine the nature of the operating system, and he or she may find it necessary to boot the system (start the computer) with an uncontaminated disk. Using **utility software**, the expert will begin searching through the accumulated data. By using or modifying utility software, a search can be tailored to meet the requirements of the search warrant.

Determining What to Seize

Just because investigators have probable cause to seize a computer does not necessarily mean they can seize the entire system. The peripheral items may not be relevant and therefore, according to the **independent component doctrine**, not subject to lawful seizure. Each component of the computer system must be examined individually for probable cause elements prior to seizing. The requirements of the independent component doctrine are easier to deal with prior to a seizure than afterward.

It is a mistake to presume that any item connected to a suspect computer is seizable. A network may have thousands of computers connected to each other. A warrant to search and seize the suspect computer would never be construed as allowing a search and seizure of all the other computers in the network. Just because it is convenient to seize a computer does not mean it is constitutional. Currently, it is acceptable to seize the computer, the monitor, and the keyboard. These are the essentials needed for input and output of data. Any other items seized must be independently addressed in the probable cause affidavit and the warrant. The physical examination of a computer's contents may need to occur off-site. It may take days or weeks to completely examine the computer and the data it contains.

CASE IN POINT

United States v. Henson

In this case, investigators searched several used car dealerships, looking for evidence of an odometer roll-back scheme. Among the evidentiary items seized were several computer systems. Because of the volume of evidence listed in the warrant to be seized, the court upheld the seizure of entire systems, including peripherals. The court reasoned that it would have been impractical for investigators to remain onsite at the dealerships for days, searching and sorting through the evidence.

The Search

Controlling the premises in an online computer search is essential for success. Because of the ease with which evidence can be destroyed, the search team must take complete and absolute control of the search site. Once control has been asserted, the computer system's communication links must be broken to prevent remote access and remote destruction of evidence. Even something as simple as disconnecting the computer may have disastrous results when attempted by anyone other than an expert. The key to finding the evidence described in the search warrant is to look in the right places and thoroughly exhaust all possible computer storage areas. In their zeal to access the data inside a computer, investigators should not overlook the possibility of fingerprints and handwritten notations (which may be passwords).

In addition to hard drives, disks, and CDs, other sites that may harbor data are available only to the knowledgeable and prepared. Trained computer specialists are often able to pull various amounts of data from input and output devices. Print spoolers hold data to be printed, and a print spooler may be holding unprinted data if it was unable to send the data to the printer (because the printer was out of paper, for example, or was turned off before printing). Printer drivers may contain a hard drive that stores information before it is printed and will keep the stored information until its memory limit is reached and it begins to write over the oldest data with new data (Computer Search and Seizure Working Group, 1994).

Whereas most forensic scientists' search and seizure procedures have been honed over the years, computer forensic experts are only beginning to craft widely accepted guidelines to ensure that evidence seized can be admitted at the time of trial. Computer evidence is tough to authenticate in court because it can be altered so easily. The International Association of Computer Investigative Specialists has developed a procedure in which investigators can extract a mirror image of the information in the computer without altering the original, thereby preserving the original to demonstrate that the data retrieved have not been changed.

Besides authentication issues, courts are also grappling with the admissibility of evidence that computer investigators find concerning one crime while searching for evidence of another offense. In traditional searches of a suspect's home, auto, business, or files, the police must limit their search to evidence relevant to the crime outlined in the warrant but may also seize evidence of an unrelated crime if it is in plain view. A major question yet to be answered by the courts is whether an investigator can use information against the suspect about an unknown offense that was discovered while searching a computer for information about another offense. Using federal wiretap procedures as an analogy, it would appear prudent to obtain a second warrant for the stumbled-upon offense.

Applicable Case Law

The U.S. Supreme Court, in *Andresen v. Maryland* (1976), determined that under certain circumstances it is reasonable to expect that computer records seen three months previously would still be present at the location in which they were observed.

The U.S. Court of Appeals in *Application of Lafayette Academy, Inc.* (1979), ruled that the limiting phrase used to circumscribe the computer records that could be seized was insufficiently narrow (see Case in Point).

Messages sent back and forth via computer (e-mail) are stored until read and deleted. If a stored electronic message is less than 180 days old, police must obtain a warrant to

> ## CASE IN POINT
>
> ### Application of Lafayette Academy, Inc.
> Lafayette Academy was being investigated for fraudulent activities involving the Federally Insured Student Loan Program. The warrant authorized the seizure of "books, papers, rosters of students, letters, correspondence, documents, memoranda, contracts, agreements, ledgers, worksheets, books of account, student files, file jackets and contents, computer tapes, disks, computer operation manuals, computer tape logs, computer tapes, computer tape printouts, Office of Education documents and forms which constitute evidence of the commission of violations of the laws of the United States, that are violations of 18 U.S.C. Sections 286, 287, 371, 1001, and 1014." The court invalidated the search warrant because the limiting phrase allowed the seizure of items for crimes beyond the scope of the probable cause. The probable cause in this case had only been established for frauds pertaining to the Federal Insured Student Loan Program. The statutes cited in the warrant covered a wide range of crimes. The court felt the warrant authorized the search and seizure of documents related to crimes other than the crime for which probable cause had been established.

search for and seize the message. Once the message has been stored for longer than 180 days, all that is needed to search for and seize the communication is an administrative subpoena and advance notice given to the parties involved. The U.S. Court of Appeals, in *Steve Jackson Games, Inc. v. United States Secret Service* (1979), determined that if a message has been sent but has not been read, the message is a stored message rather than a communication in transmission, and thus a subpoena will allow examination of the message.

In *Michigan v. Summers* (1981), the U.S. Supreme Court determined that a warrant to search for certain items carries with it the power to detain individuals found upon the premises until the search has been completed.

Identity Theft

Identity theft and identity fraud are terms used to refer to all types of crime in which someone wrongfully obtains and uses another person's personal data in some way that involves fraud or deception, typically for economic gain. Unlike fingerprints, which are unique and cannot be given to someone else for his or her use, personal data—especially Social Security numbers, bank account or credit card numbers, telephone calling card numbers, and other valuable identifying data—can, if they fall into the wrong hands, be used to personally profit at the owner's expense.

In the United States and Canada, many people have reported that unauthorized persons have taken funds out of their bank or financial accounts, or, in the worst cases, taken over their identities altogether, running up vast debts and committing crimes while using the victims' names. In many cases, a victim's losses may include not only out-of-pocket financial losses but also substantial additional financial costs associated with trying to restore his or her reputation in the community and correcting erroneous information for which the criminal is responsible.

Many people do not realize how easily criminals can obtain personal data without having to break into someone's home. In public places, criminals may engage in shoulder surfing—watching from a nearby location as the mark punches in his or her telephone calling card number or credit card number—or may listen in while the mark gives his or her credit card number over the telephone to a hotel or rental car company.

Even the area near a person's home or office may not be secure. Some criminals go through garbage cans or a communal trash bin to obtain copies of canceled checks, credit card or bank statements, or other records that typically bear the name, address, and even telephone number of the person whose identity they intend to steal. These types of records make it easier for criminals to get control over accounts and assume a mark's identity.

Discarded applications for preapproved credit cards that have not been shredded may result in criminals trying to activate the cards for their use. (Some credit card companies have adopted security measures that allow a card recipient to activate the card only from his or her home telephone number, but this is not yet a universal practice.) Also, if mail is delivered to a place where others have ready access to it, criminals may simply intercept and redirect the mail to another location.

In recent years, the Internet has become an appealing place for criminals to obtain identifying data, such as passwords or even banking information. In their haste to explore the exciting features of the Internet, many people respond to spam—unsolicited e-mail that promises them some benefit but requests identifying data—without realizing that in many cases the requester has no intention of keeping the promise. Criminals use computer technology to obtain large amounts of personal data. With enough identifying information about an individual, a criminal can take over that individual's identity to conduct a wide range of crimes: for example, false applications for loans and credit cards, fraudulent withdrawals from bank accounts, fraudulent use of telephone calling cards, or obtaining other goods or privileges that the criminal might be denied if he or she were to use his or her real name. If the criminal takes steps to ensure that bills for the falsely obtained credit cards, or bank statements showing the unauthorized withdrawals, are sent to an address other than the victim's, the victim may not become aware of what is happening until the criminal has already inflicted substantial damage on the victim's assets, credit, and reputation.

In 1998, Congress passed the Identity Theft and Assumption Deterrence Act. This legislation created a new offense of identity theft and prohibits:

knowingly transfer[ring] or us[ing], without lawful authority, a means of identification of another person with the intent to commit, or to aid or abet, any unlawful activity that constitutes a violation of Federal law, or that constitutes a felony under any applicable State or local law (18 U.S.C. A4 1028(a)(7)).

Federal prosecutors work with federal investigative agencies such as the FBI, the United States Secret Service, and the U.S. Postal Service to prosecute identity theft and fraud cases.

Phishing is a scam where criminals send messages via the Internet to obtain personal and financial information from unsuspecting victims. Often the messages will appear to be from government agencies, banks, or other financial institutions. They may even contain a link to the real institution they are imitating or professing to be a part of. All phone numbers will be answered by the online criminals as though it were a working institutional telephone number, in an effort to extract personal information sufficient to steal an identity. Once that identity is stolen, access to credit cards and bank funds are available to the thief. Some thieves send an e-mail that appears to be from a legitimate business and ask to be called at a phone number to update your account or obtain a refund.

Antivirus software and firewalls can protect from inadvertently accepting unwanted files, but nothing can protect against voluntary disclosures of personal information. Antivirus software scans incoming communications for troublesome files. A firewall blocks all communications from unauthorized sources. It is especially important to utilize a firewall if the Internet is accessed through a broadband connection. Operating systems (like Windows or Linux) or browsers (like Internet Explorer or Firefox) also may offer free software patches to close holes in the system that hackers or phishers could exploit. The key to thwarting phishing is to remember reputable lending agencies and all government agencies do not solicit personal information through e-mails.

■ Summary

White-collar crime has come of age; instead of confidence swindles and stings, computers are the tool for the new-age swindler. There are a lot of very imaginative and talented computer thieves thinking of new ways to separate the unwary from their money. Is it possible to be sufficiently vigilant so as to not be a victim? It is not only money; in some instances it has been more than money. Those tempted to help these overseas thieves not only provide money to assist in the transfer of foreign sums to their account, in some instances they have been foolish enough to meet these people to effect the transfer of funds and become victimized again.

As this is written a bridge in Minneapolis stretching over the Mississippi river has collapsed. Reports say the bridge was rated "structurally deficient." It may be an accident or it may be criminal negligence. If the latter, everything that is underwater will become important in a criminal prosecution. If it is determined that the collapse was criminal neglect, what we are watching is an underwater investigation. The following chapter discusses the role of the underwater investigator in the investigative process.

■ Key Terms

computer hacker: Computer user with sophisticated understanding of computer and software functions who is engaged in invading computer systems other than his or her own

con artists: Confidence swindlers

con games: Confidence swindles

document examination: Inspection of a questioned document for clues about its origin

forgery (check): Signing another's name to a check without authority (with intent to defraud)

home repair scam: Scam requiring initial entry to the premises, which may be initiated by a telephone inquiry about termites, siding, window heat loss, or some other home problem; a free examination is typically provided, and the examiner inevitably discovers some malady, which is then repaired at an exorbitant price

hot keys: A certain key or combination of keys that, when depressed, activate the erasure of data

identity theft: Type of crime in which someone wrongfully obtains and uses another person's personal data in some way that involves fraud or deception, typically for economic gain

independent component doctrine: Doctrine stating that peripheral items may not be relevant and therefore not subject to lawful seizure

known writings: Writing samples from a suspect that can be used by the examiner to perform a comparison between a suspect sample and known samples and that should contain some of the word and letter combinations present in the questioned document

limiting phrase: Phrase in a warrant that helps separate the information to be seized from information that may be legally permissible to possess

money laundering: The process of legitimizing illegal income

no-knock warrant: Warrant that justifies entry into the evidence site without knocking and announcing that the persons entering are police

offshore financial institutions: Financial institutions located in countries that have little or no tax on income and have strict bank secrecy laws, such as the Cayman Islands; they are often sought out and used by drug traffickers

off-site computer: Computer that is readily and routinely accessed by the primary computer being searched and serves regularly as a component of the primary computer's network

phishing: A scam where criminals send messages via the Internet to obtain personal and financial information from unsuspecting victims

questioned document: Any object that contains handwritten or typewritten markings whose source or authenticity is in doubt

utility software: Software used by a computer expert to begin searching through the accumulated data in a computer

■ Review Questions

1. What difficulties do drug traffickers face in disposing of their illegal profits?
2. What is the role of offshore financial institutions in drug traffickers' disposal of their illegal profits?
3. What is a confidence swindler?
4. How are the elderly victimized by confidence swindlers?
5. How does forgery differ from alteration of a document (check)?
6. What is the role of the questioned-document examiner?
7. What questions may a questioned-document examiner answer?
8. What are "known writings" and of what use are they to the questioned-document examiner?
9. In drafting a computer search warrant affidavit, of what value is a limiting phrase? Provide an example of one.
10. What First Amendment issues may arise during the execution of a computer search warrant?
11. What is a computer hacker?
12. What are hot keys?
13. How do computer search experts use utility software?
14. In the case of searching data on a computer, what issue pertaining to the "plain view" exception to the warrant requirement has yet to be resolved?
15. What is the independent component doctrine, and how does it apply to computer peripherals?
16. What has the International Association of Computer Investigative Specialists contributed to the investigation of computer crimes?

17. What is identity theft?

18. How can identity theft be perpetrated?

19. What steps has the federal government taken in an effort to combat identity theft?

20. Is it possible to tell if a document printed by a computer printer was printed by a particular printer? If so, how? If not, why not?

21. Why is it important to make a mirror image of all computer data seized?

22. What are the basic rules for computer investigations?

■ Bibliography

Computer Search and Seizure Working Group. (1994). Federal guidelines for searching and seizing computers. http://epic.org/security/computer_search_guidelines.txt. Accessed July 15, 2008.

Saferstein, R. (1995). *Criminalistics: An introduction to forensic science* (5th ed.). Englewood Cliffs, NJ: Prentice Hall.

■ Key Legal Cases

Andresen v. Maryland, 427 U.S. 463 (1976).

Application of Lafayette Academy, Inc., 610 F.2d 1 (1st Cir., 1979).

Gilbert v. California, 388 U.S. 263 (1967).

Michigan v. Summers, 452 U.S. 692 (1981).

Steve Jackson Games, Inc. v. United States Secret Service, 36 F.3d 457 (1979).

United States v. Henson, 848 F.2d 1374 (6th Cir., 1988).

United States v. Mara, 410 U.S. 19 (1973).

18 U.S.C. A4 1028(a)(7)

Underwater Investigations

▶ ▶ STUDENT LEARNING OUTCOMES

Upon completion of this chapter students will demonstrate an understanding of:

- The myths associated with underwater recovery operations
- The process employed in processing an underwater crime scene
- The methods used to preserve submerged evidence
- Medicolegal aspects of underwater death
- Vessel collision investigation

Earth is the water planet. The United States has water boundaries on three sides and inland waterways too numerous to measure. More and more human activity is taking place on America's waterways. As our water-related activities increase, so do the problems associated with enforcing laws on the nation's most popular playgrounds, and so do the number of accidents, drownings, violent crimes, and homicides. Criminals often seek a watery repository for weapons and other evidence of wrongdoing. It has become an integral part of the police function to provide resources that can be deployed to retrieve this evidence.

■ Myths of Underwater Recovery Operations

An investigative perspective on underwater evidence recovery operations dispels a number of myths. For many years it was common practice for divers to recover submerged items and bring them to the surface. Little regard was given to the possibility of submerged evidence retaining forensic information. A series of experiments showed that submerged evidence does not necessarily lose its forensic value.

A working forensic protocol began to emerge, as did a set of propositions based on the way operations had been conducted (see Chapter 3 for list of myths.)

■ Elements of Underwater Investigation

Many agencies have begun to recognize the value of an underwater recovery team and have begun to understand that submerged items may have forensic value. The dive team and the underwater investigators on that team cannot operate in a vacuum. It serves little purpose to train **underwater investigators** if other members of the criminal justice family do not appreciate what it is underwater investigators do or can do. Because the objective of all investigations is to obtain a conviction, it becomes apparent that underwater investigators are part of a larger team, a team made up of those who will assist in preparing, testing, and preserving evidence recovered by underwater investigators.

The original challenge in underwater recovery work was to teach dive teams a scientific protocol to apply to recovery operations and to the evidence obtained as a result of those operations. The world of the underwater investigator began with reinventing the role of public safety diving based on solid forensic perspectives. The public safety diving industry has done a good job in educating those who are interested in being educated. Most dive teams have underwater investigators who understand the steps involved in processing an **underwater crime scene**. The weak link in the chain has been the lack of success in bringing other members of the criminal justice team to the table. Administrators, dry-land investigators, forensic personnel, and prosecutors have not been as quick as dive teams to learn about a new perspective in underwater recovery operations. The work of underwater investigators will not reach its maximum potential until the other members of the criminal justice team become as knowledgeable as those processing underwater crime scenes.

The Team

The basic structure of a dive recovery team includes, minimally, the following:

- Scene commander
- Line tender
- Primary diver
- Backup diver (90% diver)
- Safety diver (Hendrick, 2000)

Scene Commander

The scene commander is responsible for all aspects of the operation, but the most vital task lies in the commander's responsibility to conduct a risk/benefit analysis based on the requirements of a dive operation, the training and experience of the team, and the equipment available (and that which the team is trained to use). The risk/benefit analysis is an ongoing responsibility, beginning at the time of the first dispatch and continuing until the last diver is out of the water.

In the usual diver operation, the commander is responsible for the following:

1. Risk analysis
2. Call out (contacting team members)
3. Predive briefing
4. Role assignment
5. Deployment
6. Establishing crime scene parameters
7. Determining the search method(s) to be employed
8. Operational oversight
9. Postdive briefing

Line Tenders

Line tenders are the eyes and ears of the underwater investigator. Although underwater communication systems are available, the price is often more than the dive team budget will allow. The underwater recovery process began with divers being tethered to a tended line (**Figure 20–1**). The line tender and the diver communicated through a process of predetermined line tugs that signaled change of direction, ascent, entanglement, and so on. Line pulls are still the most common method of communication during police dive recovery operations. During operations of limited and no visibility (which are the bulk of police dive operations), the underwater investigator is dependent on line pulls for guidance and communication.

Additionally, the tender assists in the staging of all operational equipment and is responsible for dressing each diver. The donning of diver gear is cumbersome, especially when dealing with dry suits, weight harnesses, and tanks. The tender does the lifting and exertion, thus reserving the divers' strength and composure for the operation.

Divers

The three divers work together in providing support and confidence for each other. The primary diver has the operational rudder. The integrity of the search is based on this diver. The quality of a search depends on the pattern selected and the methodology employed. It is axiomatic to say that a successful search is one that:

- Discovers what is being sought, or
- Is conducted in such a fashion that search integrity is maintained, that is, confidence in the pattern selected and employed is so high as to be able to conclude unequivocally that the item sought is not within the completed pattern.

It is to the primary diver that the success or failure of the mission is attributed.

The backup diver is the next person in rotation to take the place of the primary diver. Most operations limit each diver's underwater time to 25 minutes. Attention spans and maximum efficiency peak during that 25-minute period. Having sufficient divers to continue a rotation until the item sought is found is the responsibility of the scene commander. The backup diver is 90% prepared to enter the water. In addition to being the next diver in the search rotation, this diver also serves as safety diver should the safety diver be deployed.

Figure 20–1   Tethered diver and tended diver.

Courtesy of Lt. Chester Leonard Dixon, TDPS ret.

The sole responsibility of the safety diver is to be 100% suited and prepared to enter the water. This diver is often deployed in the water so the diver remains cool, because body temperature increases the temperature inside the diver's wet or dry suit. It is this diver's responsibility to track the course of the search and make suppositions as to what the searching diver is encountering. Should there be a need for assistance, this diver can be deployed immediately. Once the safety diver is deployed, the 90% diver completes dressing and becomes the default safety diver (Hendrick, 2000).

Training

In the beginning, anyone with basic recreational dive certification was considered for participation on public safety recovery dive teams. Over time, it became apparent that recreational diving and recreational training had little to do with the responsibilities of the public safety diver. Formalized training began at various venues around the country. Dive Rescue International began providing public safety diver instruction, as did Southwest Texas State University in the formation of its Underwater Institute. Slowly, training programs began to develop around the country to address the unique characteristics of public safety diving.

An integral part of the advancement of training was the recognition that what public safety divers were doing was evidence recovery; thus, the next evolution in training included forensic considerations in the processing of what came to be known as underwater crime scenes. The Underwater Institute at Southwest Texas State University was one of the first universities in the country to begin offering training in underwater investigation. The first underwater investigation course was included in a criminal justice curriculum in the summer

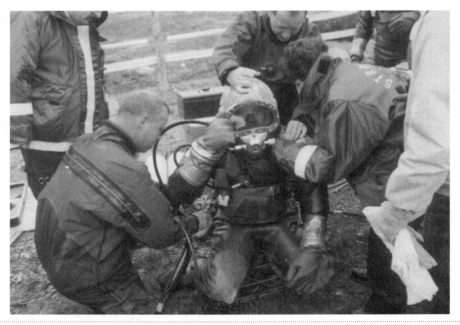

Figure 20–2 Helmet and dry suit.

Courtesy of Lt. Chester Leonard Dixon, TDPS ret.

of 2003 at a small university in Honolulu, Hawaii. In the summer of 2003, Chaminade University of Honolulu offered CJ 480 (Underwater Forensic Investigation) for college credit.

Equipment

As underwater investigation evolves, so does the need for particular types of equipment. The needs range from inflatable body bags to face masks with heads-up displays showing depth and air pressure. Much of the equipment that public safety divers use is borrowed from commercial divers. Helmets, dry suits, hard-wired communication systems, and surface-supplied air are all employed in processing underwater crime scenes. It was not so long ago that all recovery diving was done with scuba gear. Part of the advancement in underwater investigation has been an appreciation for the contaminated circumstances in which most recovery diving is done. Scuba gear poses serious dangers of infections and disease for divers when used in highly contaminated water. Many criminals pick waters that are visually impenetrable, with that invisibility being caused by contaminants in the water. Operations in contaminated water cannot be conducted safely without dry suits, full-face masks, or helmets (**Figure 20–2**). As we learn and grow, we discover that equipment that was once acceptable has become unworkable.

■ Recovering Submerged Firearms

The recovery of submerged firearms is a straightforward proposition. No expensive lift equipment is necessary, and the time involved in the recovery is minimal once the firearm has been located. The location and mapping of submerged firearms should be handled in the same fashion as for important evidence uncovered in a land investigation. However, the recovery method usually employed is to hand the weapon to someone on shore or in a boat. The handling of weapons in such a cavalier fashion demonstrates a lack of appreciation for the effect of water on ferrous metals and the potential for transient evidence to remain on any firearm used in the commission of a crime.

Purposes of Recovery

The recovery and preservation of firearms have four main purposes:

1. Medicolegal examination
2. Ballistic comparisons
3. Weapon identification
4. Fingerprint examination

The likelihood of discovering fingerprints on a weapon that has been submerged even for a short period of time is remote. However, in 1993 scientific divers began the recovery of the S.S. *Brother Jonathan,* which was sunk in July of 1865. On board was a reputed treasure trove of gold and silver. Gold coins were recovered, corroded and virtually unrecognizable. The coins were placed in the hands of a numismatic team who carefully dissolved the adhered calcium and residue without using polish, abrasives, or any other substance that would be harmful to the coins. After the dirt was removed, the majority of the coins were no different in appearance than if they had been stored in a bank vault over the last century. Under the corrosion on one coin was an intact and discernible human fingerprint, awaiting the light of day.

There are parts of a submerged firearm that may render a classifiable latent print. New technology is constantly being developed to assist investigators, and a product called Wet Print has been created that allows fingerprints to be developed on a wet surface without the necessity of drying the surface first. Any ammunition in the weapon may retain fingerprint impressions. The ammunition in these weapons should be considered live and the weapon loaded until rendered otherwise.

A firearm retrieved from salt water after lengthy submersion may appear relatively unaffected. Once retrieved and subjected to the air, however, **oxidation** will begin immediately, and thorough rusting may progress in less than an hour, rendering a ballistics examination impossible. It is therefore crucial to keep the weapon immersed in water until the preservation procedure can begin. When a firearm is properly retrieved and maintained, preservation techniques may allow ballistics tests to be conducted on the weapon and its ammunition. All firearms need to be preserved for testing, and the preservation process begins with the divers who recover the weapon.

Serial Numbers

Every firearm is stamped with a variety of numbers. The serial number is useful in determining the original owner of the weapon. It may be more readily apparent immediately upon discovery than after mishandling and oxidation have occurred. One of the initial acts of the on-scene dive team should be to record and photograph the serial number in the water if visibility allows. Once rusting begins (and it happens very quickly), retrieval of the serial number may be difficult or impossible.

The serial number is usually stamped with hard metal dies. These dies strike the metal surface with a force that allows each digit to sink into the metal at a prescribed depth. Restoration of serial numbers can be accomplished, because the metal crystals in the stamped zone are placed under a permanent strain that extends a short distance beneath the original numbers. When an **etching agent** is applied, the strained area will dissolve at a slower rate thus permitting the underlying number pattern to appear. The recovery of a serial number using etching acids is governed by the extent of corrosion of the firearm. Obviously, corrosion of the firearm must be confined to what has already occurred at the time of recovery and should not be added to by exposing the firearm to oxidizing agents.

Barrel Blowback

In addition to fingerprint and ballistic evidence, a firearm, especially a handgun, may contain hair, tissue, blood, and fibers. The muzzle blast of a gun fired in contact with a body and the negative pressure in the barrel following discharge may cause blood, hair, tissue fragments, and fabric to be found several inches back inside the barrel (Spitz, 1993). Additionally, fibers and identifiable debris from pockets, beneath car seats, inside glove compartments, and so on, may cling to the outside of the barrel or may have been forced into the barrel. As the weapon sinks to its resting place, water fills the barrel from the outside in, trapping any such evidence against the breach wall. It is only when the firearm is brought to the surface and raised aloft by the barrel that the water pressure is released and the barrel successfully flushed of all evidence. By placing the weapon in water in a water-tight container while still submerged (so that water pressure is equalized on both sides of the barrel), investigators can ensure that the evidence continues to be trapped inside the barrel.

■ Body Recovery

Once a body has been located and measurements recorded, it must be raised to the surface. It is during the recovery portion of the operation that investigators can preserve evidence or irredeemably destroy or contaminate it.

Medicolegal Aspects of Underwater Death

All bodies should be **bagged** in the water. There are cases in which rigor and putrefaction make underwater bagging difficult, but a failure to bag in the water may result in the loss of transient evidence, such as hair or fibers, and the destruction or contamination of trace evidence, such as accelerant residue. Hands should also be bagged to preserve any tissue, broken fingernails, fiber, or gunpowder that may be retrieved from the hands and fingers. Hands may also suffer postmortem damage as the result of the recovery operation. If hands are bagged, the nature of such damage becomes readily apparent.

Feet and shoes should be bagged to preserve any trace evidence in the shoe soles and to enable comparison of **wear patterns** of footwear. Footwear is easily dislodged during traditional body recovery operations. Trace evidence lodged in the soles of shoes may also be lost in the recovery process. Evidence gained from footwear will be especially important if the victim is not identified immediately, is a homicide victim, or has been in an aircraft disaster in which body parts are strewn about. All bags should be placed firmly around the body parts, with due consideration for any possible premortem ligature marks. All evidence recovered from water should be accompanied by a sample of the bottom structure as a control for laboratory analysis. The **bottom structure sample** will allow the lab technicians to definitively state that any residue on a body or any evidence lodged in shoes was not a product of the submersion and picked up from the bottom.

Fingerprints

In experiments conducted at the Southwest Texas State University's Underwater Institute, a variety of materials were submerged to determine what surfaces might maintain fingerprint impressions and what procedures would best develop them. The results revealed that metal, glass, and mirrored surfaces can retain fingerprint impressions for as long as 36 hours.

Identification of Submerged Bodies

An investigation of an unattended death may focus on the question of the victim's identity. Whether it is an accidental death or homicide, the identity of an unknown decedent is important. Identification begins where and when the body is found and proceeds backward, gravitating toward individuals in contact with, activities engaged in by, and places visited by the unidentified person prior to death. Evidence at the scene of where the deceased was going or had been are the pathways leading to identification.

Identification methods may be described as primary or secondary. Primary identification methods include direct questioning of friends and relatives, comparing teeth and dental records, comparing evidence of prior injuries, surgeries, and x-rays, and comparing actual fingerprints and recorded fingerprints. Secondary methods include all other methods of confirming or excluding identity. These include the use of jewelry, eyeglasses, birthmarks, congenital abnormalities, tattoos, scars, race, hair color, blood type, sex, and age to narrow the field of possibilities. The key to identification is to discover characteristics of an unidentified body that correspond exactly to the documented characteristics of a missing person.

Personal Effects

Personal effects, clothing, and gross anatomical features are the first items available for examination in attempting to determine identification. In mass disasters, descriptions of clothing and personal effects are provided by the next of kin. Billfolds contain driver's licenses, credit cards, and personal papers. Jewelry is often unique and engraved. Keys are often distinctive in design and can be recognized as door keys, auto keys, briefcase keys, and suitcase keys. A successful unlocking provides a tentative identification.

Dental Comparisons

Teeth resist decomposition and therefore are a common means of positive identification. The major problem associated with teeth is the care necessary during the recovery procedure to ensure that all teeth in and around **skeletonized remains** have been found. A person's occupation or oral habits may have an impact on his or her teeth. Carpenters and electricians who grip nails between their teeth may have notched upper incisors. Tailors may have similar smaller notches. Musicians who play wind instruments often clench the mouthpiece between their teeth, leaving broad worn areas on the upper teeth. Longtime pipe smokers may have developed a diamond-shaped gap between upper and lower clenched teeth. Nicotine stains will be found on the surfaces of the teeth of heavy pipe and cigarette smokers. The presence of poor oral hygiene, many decayed teeth, and swollen gums is indicative of low economic status.

Shoe Wear

The shod foot survives burning, decomposition, marine animal depredation, and water damage more consistently than do hands and especially fingers. The investigator's focus is generally on hands—on fingerprints and palm prints. Yet soft, unprotected tissues are the first sites to suffer marine animal depredation and are least likely to exhibit discernible, classifiable characteristics. Feet and shoes may provide readily available identification information. The wear patterns of the outer and inner soles of shoes and boots are sufficiently unique to permit comparisons for exclusionary purposes.

Postmortem Changes

After death, physicochemical changes occur that lead to the dissolution of all soft tissues. The importance of these changes is that they occur in a regular sequence and can be used to arrive at an approximate time of death. Knowledge of these changes will also prevent investigators from mistaking them for premortem injuries. Among the most useful postmortem changes for determining the time of death are putrefaction, ocular changes, and postmortem lividity.

Putrefaction

Putrefaction is one of death's realities with which underwater investigators must contend. Attempting to raise a decomposing body by attaching lines or towing by an arm or leg will prove less than satisfactory. Decomposing bodies must be bagged in the water; the alternative is to retrieve them in bits and pieces.

Rigor mortis of the involuntary muscles and putrefaction are often viewed as indices of time of death. The rate of putrefaction depends on the physical environment in which the body reposes. It is generally accepted that putrefaction in air is more rapid than in water, which is more rapid than in soil. One week in air equals two weeks in water and eight weeks in soil (Perper, 1993). Once a body has been removed from the water, however, putrefaction will accelerate. In temperate climates, decomposition on the surface begins within 24 to 30 hours. In water, decomposition generally begins within 48 to 60 hours. Putrefaction in sea water is slower than in fresh water because the salt retards the growth of bacteria. In stagnant water, bacteria usually abound and decomposition is swift.

Water temperature will also affect the rate of decomposition. As water depth increases, water temperature generally decreases and the rate of decomposition slows. In evaluating postmortem changes, it is important to consider the outside temperature, the temperature at the water surface, and the temperature at the depth from which the body was recovered. Often investigators are anxious to discover the body, and when searching proves unproductive, they begin to discuss how long it might be before the body will float to the surface. The flotation of a drowned body is dependent upon the production of gases as decomposition progresses. Carbon dioxide, methane, sulfur dioxide, ammonium sulfide, and hydrogen sulfide make up the bulk of these gases, and they all have two characteristics that militate against postmortem flotation: they are **water soluble** (dissolve in water) and easily compressed (underwater pressure increases 14.7 pounds every 33 feet of depth). At greater depths, the decomposition rate will decrease (because of colder temperature), the production of gases will be suppressed, and the gases will be more compressed. In a drowning where the water exceeds 100 feet and the water temperature is less than 38°F, the body may never float. Trying to assess the time to flotation is a waste of energy, and depending on flotation to deliver the body is usually foolhardy.

Once the body has completely decomposed and has been fully skeletonized, the bones may last for centuries (**Figure 20–3**). Bones that have been immersed for long periods may demineralize and turn to dust upon touching.

Ocular Changes

Eyes may exhibit the earliest postmortem changes. A thin corneal film may begin to develop within minutes of death. Corneal cloudiness develops within 3 hours of death. If the eyes are closed, the appearance of corneal filming and clouding may be delayed for 24 hours or longer. Often the deceased has what is known as a **lazy eyelid**, where the lack of muscle rigidity allows the lid to fall over half the eye. An examination of the eye will reveal that the lower, exposed half has developed corneal filming while the upper half, still damp and protected from the air, has not. As the result of water immersion, the

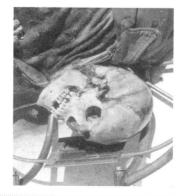

Figure 20–3 Skeletal remains.

Reproduced from Teather, Robert. *Encyclopedia of Underwater Investigation*. Best Publishing Company, 1994

corneal filming that ordinarily occurs on dry land should not be evident in a drowning victim (**Figure 20–4**), and the existence of corneal filming in a drowning victim calls for an explanation. The body may have floated to the surface and resubmerged as a result of the accumulation, then dissipation, of body gases (purged more quickly and easily on the surface). Yet, since the normal flotation posture is face down, corneal filming in drownings is indeed difficult to explain.

Postmortem Lividity

Once the heart no longer circulates blood through the body, gravity causes blood to pool in the lower parts of the body. The pooled blood imparts a purple color to the lower body parts and a paleness to the upper body. **Lividity** is most apparent in bodies that have lain on land. Blood pooling can indicate that a body discovered on land has been moved after death. If the body is placed in a position other than the position of death, an absence of lividity in the lower portions suggests the body has been moved. Bodies in water should show little evidence of lividity because of the water's buoyancy. Should lividity be prominent, death prior to submersion should be suspected. Lividity can be manufactured in fast-moving water, where the current creates a gravitational pull independent of the earth's gravity. Lividity in those circumstances should appear in the downstream parts of the body.

Common Errors in Interpreting Postmortem Changes

Postmortem changes may be misinterpreted, which will slow an investigation. The following is a partial list of misinterpretations that may occur as a result of postmortem changes.

- Postmortem bloating of the body may create an appearance of obesity.
- Purged fluid may be mistaken for blood caused by an antemortem trauma. Although mouth-purged fluids are associated with drownings, they may also be present in a heart attack or drug overdose.

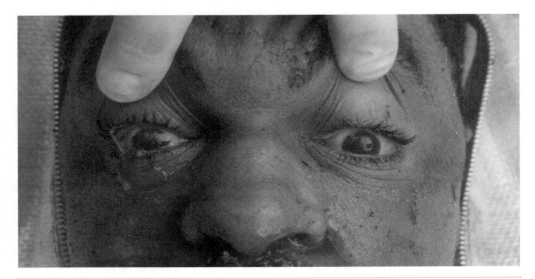

Figure 20–4 Absence of corneal filming.

Reproduced from Teather, Robert. *Encyclopedia of Underwater Investigation*. Best Publishing Company, 1994

> **CASE IN POINT**
>
> **The Chappaquiddick Drowning**
> The significance of bloodstained foam in the respiratory passages of a body recovered from water was an important issue at a 1969 court hearing in Wilkes-Barre, Pennsylvania, regarding the death of Mary Jo Kopechne. At this hearing, arguments were heard regarding whether Kopechne's body should be exhumed for autopsy to determine the cause of death. The judge refused to order an exhumation based on the testimony that a large amount of pinkish foam exuded from her nose and mouth after she was recovered from the water. This finding led to the conclusion that Kopechne died by drowning and was thus still alive when the car in which she was a passenger drove off a bridge at Chappaquiddick, Massachusetts (Spitz,1993).

- Postmortem dilatation and flaccidity of the vagina and anus may produce the appearance of a sexual attack.
- The diffusion of blood into tissues may be difficult to distinguish from antemortem bruising.
- Skin shedding may be misperceived as an antemortem thermal injury.
- Skin discoloration may cause erroneous racial classification.

The problem in relying upon the results of rigor mortis and putrefaction in determining time of death is that many environmental variables and individual characteristics affect postmortem processes. The time of death, therefore, can only be broadly estimated within a variable time frame. The longer the time between death and discovery, the less accurate are time-of-death estimates and the wider the time frame. Keeping in mind the shortcomings inherent in estimating the time of death, the following approach is generally applied.

1. An initial wide window of death is established and subsequently narrowed as additional information becomes available. The window of death is defined as the time interval from positive ascertainment of life to time of discovery of the remains. The window of death should be set based on the most reliable testimony or evidence as to when the individual was last alive.

2. Using individual postmortem changes and taking into consideration temperature and physical characteristics of the deceased, a conservative range for time of death can be established.

■ Drowning

Most drownings are accidental, some are suicidal, and occasionally police investigators are confronted with a body that has been placed in the water for purposes of disposal. Underwater investigators thus have to know the differences between cases of drowning and **postmortem immersion**. Several phases are recognized in drowning:

- Breath holding lasts until accumulating carbon dioxide in the blood and tissues causes stimulation of the respiratory center in the brain and inhalation of water.
- Swallowing of water is followed by coughing, vomiting, and rapid loss of consciousness.
- Convulsions associated with gasping precede respiratory arrest, which is followed by failure of the heart, brain damage, and death.

CASE IN POINT

Clues to Accidental Drowning

A young man was found in shallow water. A short distance from the body was an empty wine bottle. The wine bottle cap was screwed in place. Upon examination of the deceased, it was noted that his pants zipper was open. The initial impression was that the young man was intoxicated and fell into the water while urinating. Subsequent autopsy findings confirmed that he had a blood alcohol level of 0.21. Lack of turbulence of the water in which the man was found suggested that the water in his stomach was from drowning as opposed to turbulent water action. An examination of the crime scene and the young man's clothing strongly suggested drowning as opposed to foul play. The investigator's theory was borne out by the autopsy results.

The central question in body recovery from waterways is whether the individual was alive at the time of submersion. The scene surrounding the drowning and the deceased person's clothing may provide information as to how the body came to be in the water (see Case in Point).

Exudate

Abundant foam can be found exuding from the mouth and nostrils of many drowning victims (**Figure 20–5**). An attempt at resuscitation may apply sufficient pressure on the chest to cause the **exudate** to become visible. The foam is a mixture of mucus, air, and water. The presence of this mixture in the airway suggests that the victim was alive at the time of submersion. As decomposition progresses, the fluid turns foul-smelling and brown.

Changes in Skin

Skin of the hands and feet wrinkled by immersion in water is frequently referred to as **washerwoman's skin** (**Figure 20–6**). Contrary to a common misconception, washerwoman's

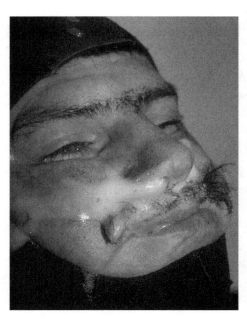 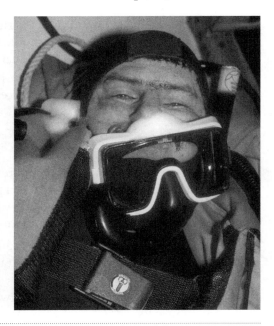

Figure 20–5 Drowning exudate.

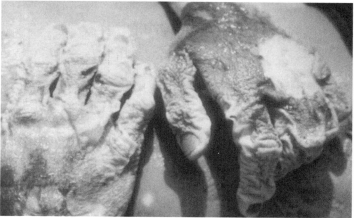

Figure 20–6   Gloving (top) and washerwoman's skin (bottom).

Reproduced from Teather, Robert. *Encyclopedia of Underwater Investigation.* Best Publishing Company, 1994

skin has nothing to do with drowning but is a product of immersion. Skin wrinkling can begin after only 30 minutes of immersion in water of 50°F. Gloving begins in warm water within several hours but may not begin in cold water for several days. When the skin sheds from the hands and feet, the fingernails and toenails are shed also. The shed skin may be inked to obtain fingerprints and sole prints for the purpose of identification. Both the inner and outer surfaces of shed skin will render a print.

Flotation

A body in fresh water sinks to the bottom unless air is trapped in the clothing (although infants may float). In salt water, a body may float several feet below the surface and be visible to low-flying search aircraft. In either case, the body may surface completely when tissue gas has formed as a result of putrefaction. Gas formation generally begins in the gastrointestinal tract. The time of the reappearance of the body depends on water temperature and the person's antemortem diet. Gases formed are easily compressed; in cold, deep water, gas formation may be suppressed or not occur at all. There are a number of commercial products available that allow the charting of water temperature to arrive at a reflotation time. The variables affecting postmortem gas formation are such that any estimate of reflotation time based on any theory is strictly guesswork.

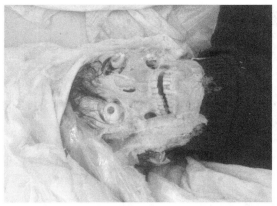

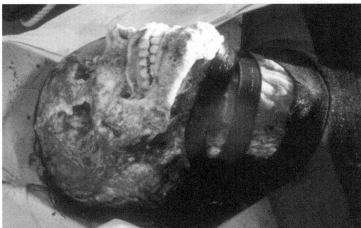

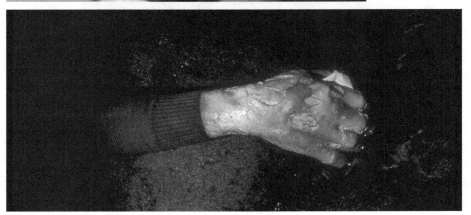

Figure 20–7 Anthropophagy.

Reproduced from Teather, Robert. *Encyclopedia of Underwater Investigation.* Best Publishing Company, 1994

Marine Depredation

Marine life feeds on the soft part of the victim's face, an act known as anthropophagy (**Figure 20–7**). Often postmortem injuries to the eyelids, lips, nose, and ears are mistaken for traumatic antemortem injuries. A variety of algae may cover the exposed parts of the body, giving a green or black hue to those areas. A body may be so covered with algae

CASE IN POINT

Algae Clues

In April 1976, the body of a woman without head or hands was found floating in an upstate New York lake. She had a peculiar gash under the left breast. The corpse was covered with green algae. The medical examiner, who was a hospital pathologist, determined that the slim, athletic body belonged to a woman in her late twenties and that she had been dead for three weeks. Broadcasts on television and radio brought no response that was of help in identifying the decapitated woman.

Dr. Michael Baden, chief medical examiner for the city of New York, examined the body and determined that the woman's age was closer to 55 and that there had been an identifiable scar or tattoo removed from under the breast to prevent identification. Dr. Baden sent samples of the algae to a biologist, who examined it and discovered two generations of algae. Fresh green algae had formed during the recent year, and dead algae was present from a prior year, pointing to the conclusion that the woman had been dead for at least a year and a half. Following the public announcement of the new age, time of death, and possible identifying scar, the body was promptly identified by the woman's sister, who suspected that her brother-in-law had killed his wife.

as to give the impression it is covered in mud and make identification of the victim and determination of time of death more difficult, as shown by the Case in Point.

■ Auto, Aircraft, and Vessel Recovery

Vehicular Drownings and Vehicle Recoveries

Stolen autos are commonly retrieved from various waterways. Stolen auto recovery is such an integral part of underwater recovery operations that it has become standard procedure to assume that a submerged vehicle is simply a stolen vehicle. This perspective can lead to the destruction of evidence if the vehicle was used in a crime or if a crime was committed within the vehicle. Human remains and other objects that repose within the vehicle will be unnecessarily thrown about the interior. Most agencies place a hooked cable around the axle of the submerged vehicle and then have it winched to shore by a tow truck or barge. If the vehicle has filled with water, the pressure of the water within the vehicle may burst the windows. Anything within the vehicle that floats will be jettisoned with the water, including clothing, paper, bodies, and plastic or items contained in plastic, all of which may have provided information about a crime that was committed in the vehicle or with the vehicle.

Most divers will give the interior of a submerged vehicle a cursory examination before winching it to the surface. More experienced divers will roll the windows down, if possible. Although most vehicle recovery is done by tow truck, floating (lifting) vehicles with air bags reduces internal disturbance and exterior damage, including undercarriage damage, to a minimum. Companies that distribute salvage equipment have pontoon bags that can be attached to the side of the vehicle with a yoke and inflated simultaneously using a topside air compressor.

Case Study

In June 1997, Travis County prosecutor Ronnie Earl was seeking the death penalty for two teenagers charged in a carjacking that resulted in the deaths of two men. Ahmad McAdoo and Derrick Williams, both 17, were indicted for capital murder for placing University of Texas students Juan Cotera (25 years old) and Brandon Shaw (20 years old) in the trunk of Shaw's Volvo and pushing the car into Town Lake in Austin, Texas. An autopsy showed that both men were still alive when the car entered the water and that they died from drowning.

Shortly after the indictment the district attorney's office contacted the author and Lt. Lynn Dixon, commander of the Texas Department of Public Safety Dive Team. We were asked if it was possible to reconstruct the incident and film the interior of the trunk to demonstrate to the jury the "heinous" nature of being entombed in a trunk as it slowly filled with water.

In Texas it is incumbent upon the prosecutor to prove aggravating circumstances in order to charge the jury with a capital offense. It was the prosecutor's intention to meet that responsibility by making the death of Shaw and Cotera as graphic and real as possible. Lt. Dixon organized and supervised the in-water operations, and the author consulted on the evidentiary and forensic aspects of the simulation. We discussed the location of the camera in the trunk to effectively film its filling. We discussed the likely difficulties in reproducing the drowning. We could use the same car or a similar auto, and we would have to put something in the trunk that approximated the volume of the two men. We also discussed the placement of the camera, and to determine the camera's location we needed to know:

1. How deep the water was
2. Whether the vehicle had landed on the roof or its wheels
3. If there was any damage to the trunk lid that would affect the rate the trunk would fill

In order for a court simulation to be admitted, it must be a simulation that accounts for the relevant variables of the original occurrence. For example, water would have to enter at approximately the same rate and volume as in the original instance.

The prosecutor wanted to use the same vehicle in which the drowning had occurred. We asked if there was any visible damage to the trunk lid that would significantly affect the fill rate. He later reported that there was damage to the lid. We then asked if the recovering team had noted the damage prior to recovery or whether it was a product of the recovery. The question was crucial to the simulation, in that if the lid damage had been present prior to the recovery, the simulation would be accurate, but if the damage was a product of the recovery we would have to use another auto of the same make and model as the original.

The following day the prosecutor's office reported that there were no written notes, reports, or statements reflecting the recovery or the state of the vehicle before or after its recovery. Based upon that lack of information the state changed tactics and offered McAdoo and Williams a plea with a sentence of two counts of life imprisonment, which both accepted.

It was this experience that prompted the author to consider a method that divers could employ to tactilely examine the exterior of an upright submerged auto. We know that many of these vehicles end up on their roofs and the top of the vehicle as well as the trunk lid are seriously damaged. Not much in the way of an underwater examination can take place. Vehicles that submerge upright are amenable to a cursory examination, and it is for those that the underwater swim around was conceived.

Part of the daily flight protocol for a private pilot involves a walk-around. The idea was to discover any gross anomalies, leaks, or nonworking apparatuses before taking off. The same procedure could be employed in a swim-around.

Automobile Swim-Around and Exterior Examination

Investigators should perform an exterior examination of the vehicle that is similar to the preflight walk-around conducted by pilots of small aircraft (**Figure 20–8**). During the swim-around, the divers, if they have an underwater slate, can record gross anomalies of the exterior of the vehicle.

All exterior damage should be sketched, noted, and, if possible, photographed. If the vehicle was used in a hit and run, there will be external evidence of the incident. All windows should be assessed and described. An impact burst pattern in a window may have resulted from an occupant striking the window or a pedestrian striking the window. Without a written or photographic record of the pattern, there will probably be no evidence of it after salvage, because the damaged window is likely to burst when the vehicle is raised by its rear axle.

Often exterior vehicle damage is of little evidentiary value because it is impossible to determine if the damage occurred before the vehicle was submerged, during submersion, or as a result of the salvage operation. Any damage to the undercarriage and

License Plate Number

VIN

WINDOWS LOWERED PRIOR TO LIFTING   yes   no

Auto Swim Around

Occupants
lf   mf   rf
lr   mr   rr

Windows Intact

windshield	yes	no
rear	yes	no
left front	yes	no
left rear	yes	no
right front	yes	no
right rear	yes	no

Driver's Window Open   yes   no

Keys in Ignition   yes   no

Headlights Intact   yes   no

Taillights Intact   yes   no

Glove Compartment
Content   bagged

Reported Stolen   yes   no

Crime Vehicle   yes   no

Owner Contacted   yes   no

Figure 20–8 Automobile swim-around.

hoses must be presumed to have resulted from the salvage operation. Even in water of minimal visibility, there are some procedures that can be performed to minimize loss of trace evidence.

The most obvious indication that a vehicle has been stolen is the absence of ignition keys. Other indications of theft might include hot wires; a blocked steering wheel or gas pedal; intrusion marks on doors, windows, and the trunk; and the absence of valuable accessories, such as a radio, CD player, speakers, a cellular phone, or hubcaps. Generally, the driver-side window will be down or driver-side door unlocked to allow someone standing outside the vehicle to accelerate the vehicle. Should the keys be found in the ignition, the probability of the vehicle having been stolen drops significantly. A hand search of the interior of the vehicle for ignition keys can be performed in water of limited visibility.

CASE IN POINT

Importance of a Swim-Around
In 1997, in Austin, Texas, two men carjacked a Volvo with two male occupants. The occupants were bound and placed in the trunk, and the vehicle was driven into Lake Travis. As the result of a thorough investigation, the perpetrators were caught and charged with capital murder. The prosecution wanted to seek the death penalty and decided that it would enter evidence during the sentencing stage of the trial demonstrating what the filling of the trunk with water was like from the perspective of two entombed and drowning men. The prosecutor contacted the author to assist in the reconstruction. An inquiry was made as to the condition of the trunk, and it was determined that there was damage to the trunk lid. The damage to the lid was such as would affect the rate at which the trunk compartment would fill. It could not be determined, however, whether the damage to the trunk existed prior to the vehicle's recovery or was incident to that recovery. The inability to answer that crucial question denied the prosecution the opportunity to reconstruct the filling of the trunk. Had a swim-around been conducted and had the divers determined that there was trunk lid damage prior to recovery, the simulation could have been accomplished.

If the vehicle has been stolen and used in the commission of a crime, fruits or instrumentalities of the crime may be lost during recovery. The license plate number and the vehicle identification number (VIN), if retrievable, may allow a computer check to determine the status of the vehicle. In water of limited visibility, license plate numbers and VINs can be read through a water bath, which is a plastic bag filled with clear water. When pressed against a license plate, the water bath allows a diver to place his or her face mask against the bag and view the plate through clear water. However, some stolen vehicles are not reported immediately, nor are some crimes that were committed using a stolen auto. The best policy is to treat each vehicle to be recovered as a possible tool in the commission of an offense and as a possible source of trace evidence (unless, of course, it is known otherwise).

If the vehicle has been involved in an accident or a hit and run, it will probably be subjected to a vigorous examination by the investigating officers. If there are dents, scratches, fabric, or paint on the exterior that may have been transferred from another vehicle or body, all scuba and salvage equipment will have to be eliminated as possibilities before any trace evidence can be considered useful. Therefore, the salvage operation should be done with the least adverse impact upon the vehicle, and all scuba and salvage equipment should be logged and specifically described to allow for exclusion of possible contamination by the dive and recovery team.

Evidence Collection

A considerable amount of information can be obtained from a submerged vehicle before efforts are made to raise it. If access into the vehicle is practicable and can be accomplished safely, an examination of the glove compartment can be made. All items in the glove compartment should be removed and placed in plastic bags (leave water in the bags with the contents). The floors of the vehicle can be examined, photographed, and if anything is discovered, tagged and bagged. The most innocuous of items may prove to be useful. The underside of seats and behind the rear cushions should be examined and any items discovered retrieved. Occupant recovery should be conducted in the water when possible. Much evidentiary information will be lost if the occupants are left in the vehicle during the recovery operation. Postmortem injuries to the body resulting from contact with the interior of the vehicle during recovery will complicate the autopsy.

It should be remembered that all items packaged wet (i.e., in a water solution) must ultimately be removed from their plastic container and dried before they can be properly examined. Items that are recovered in the water should be completely immersed in the medium from which they were retrieved, not just kept damp, because mildew will begin rapidly. Turning the items over to the lab wet transfers the responsibility for drying and preserving the items to the laboratory technicians.

Lights

It would be helpful to the investigation to know whether the lights were intact prior to recovery, because they too are often a casualty of the salvaging operation. Determining whether the light lenses are intact prior to raising the vehicle provides a bit of evidentiary information. If there are pieces of the lens still in place, they will probably not be in place following recovery. The pieces, therefore, should be photographed, bagged, and tagged prior to lifting the vehicle. The fact that the light switch is on or off is not always indicative of whether the lights were on or off at the time the vehicle entered the water. In salvage operations, the light switch will likely be struck by debris or bodies thrown

> **OFFICER'S NOTEBOOK**
>
> **Checklist for Recovery of a Submerged Auto**
> - Photos should be taken whenever possible from all cardinal directions and from above.
> - A swim-around inventory should be done of all gross features of the vehicle, including windows, doors, tires, body, and trim. All information gathered from the swim-around should be recorded.
> - A specific examination of lights and lenses should be conducted.
> - A check for intrusion marks on the body of the vehicle should be done.
> - The divers should check for license plates (front and back).
> - The VIN (vehicle identification number) should be recorded.
> - The vehicle should be examined for occupants.
> - The divers should check for evidence of contraband.
> - The contents of the glove compartment should be bagged.
> - The sun visors should be examined.
> - The divers should keep in mind that certain surfaces, such as glass and mirrors, will retain fingerprints even in water.

forward as the vehicle is raised by its rear axle. The light bulbs can reveal whether the lights were on when the vehicle entered the water. Retrieval of the light bulbs may thus prove to be useful as the investigation progresses.

Burning light filaments break in a characteristic fashion upon impact (their breakage differs from that of filaments that break when not lighted or after they have burnt out). It is important not to remove the bulbs from their housings when bulb comparisons may be necessary, but to instead remove the entire light assembly so that damage to the bulbs and filaments will be kept to a minimum. The direction of an external impact (to the front or rear of the vehicle) can be ascertained by the direction in which the filament is distorted.

Small Aircraft Recovery Operations

The crash of a small aircraft poses a different challenge to the underwater recovery team. Such aircraft are often intact, for deceleration speeds are not as great as those of large passenger aircraft. Large passenger aircraft may have begun their descent from as high as 30,000 feet, whereas small aircraft descend from altitudes of less than 5,000 feet. This difference in altitude will also provide for rescue opportunities. The deceleration is not so great as to necessarily cause death and dismemberment. If occupants are conscious, they may be able to escape alive. Most of these small craft have electronic locating devices that may assist in locating the crash site. Many small craft crashes are a product of bad weather. The same bad weather that was a significant component in the chain of events that led to the crash may inhibit search efforts. By the time the weather clears, the locating devices may no longer be emitting a signal. It is more difficult to locate the crash site itself than to locate the aircraft once the site has been determined.

Once the crash site has been located, investigators must determine what type of operation is needed—rescue versus recovery. Many dive teams handle both rescue and recovery operations. Most do not; however, recovery teams may find themselves in a position to provide rescue service.

In the investigation of this type of crash, divers should conduct a preliminary swim-around to ascertain gross features of the aircraft, passengers, and cargo (**Figure 20–9**).

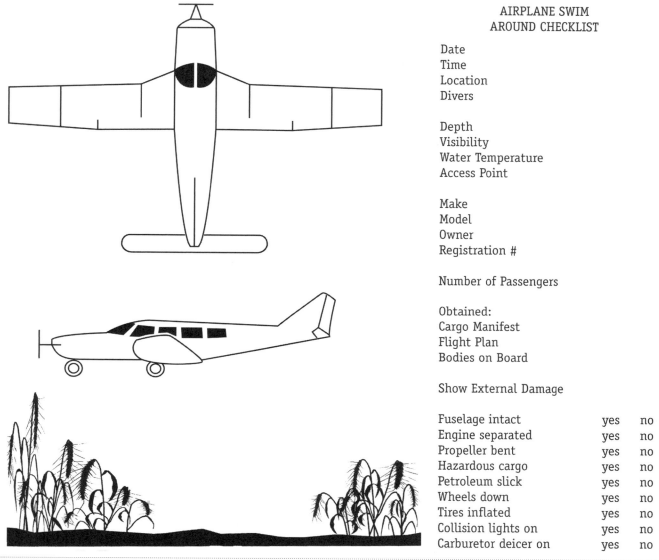

AIRPLANE SWIM
AROUND CHECKLIST

Date
Time
Location
Divers

Depth
Visibility
Water Temperature
Access Point

Make
Model
Owner
Registration #

Number of Passengers

Obtained:
Cargo Manifest
Flight Plan
Bodies on Board

Show External Damage

Fuselage intact	yes	no
Engine separated	yes	no
Propeller bent	yes	no
Hazardous cargo	yes	no
Petroleum slick	yes	no
Wheels down	yes	no
Tires inflated	yes	no
Collision lights on	yes	no
Carburetor deicer on	yes	no

Figure 20–9 Aircraft swim-around checklist.

Occupants may still be strapped into their seats. In many instances, the entire aircraft and occupants can be lifted intact to the surface without disturbing the interior of the craft or destroying evidence. Most small aircraft have lift points that can be used in the recovery operation if the aircraft is intact and structurally sound.

Proper processing includes the geographical location of the craft (measurement) and the recovery of the debris and bodies in such a fashion as to lend to the preservation of both. The objective in aircraft recoveries is to reconstruct the events leading to the crash in order to determine the presence of criminal enterprise. This is best accomplished by treating the crash site as a crime scene and handling all debris and human remains as though they were evidence. The presumption in small aircraft crashes is that they are accidents. It would better serve the interests of all parties to presume the crash site is a crime scene and to process it accordingly.

Vessel Recoveries

Boating accident investigation is a specialty that requires considerable training and experience. Boating accidents increase each year. More people and vessels are competing for space in recreational waterways than ever before. It is not surprising that when growing recreational populations, watercraft, and alcohol come together, a formula for destruction is in the offing. To that mix come local, state, and federal enforcement agencies charged with making the nation's waterways safe for a variety of recreational activities. When motorized watercrafts come together, the results are dramatic and traumatic. Speeds attainable on water are sufficient to cause catastrophic property damage, injury, and death. Underwater investigators will be called to these scenes to aid in the processing of the evidence and the bodies.

Automobile accident reconstruction can serve as a model for the procedures that should be applied in vessel accident reconstruction. Securing the perimeter on land is relatively easy, but in the water, part or all of the vessels that need to be examined may be underwater. It will be necessary to determine the parameters of the operation based on the debris field resulting from the collision. Locating the site of impact is usually fairly straightforward; it is the processing and reconstruction that tax the skills of the underwater investigator. Recovery proceeds as in any other crime scene:

1. Secure the boundaries of the operation.
2. Photograph the debris field, visibility permitting.
3. If vessels are intact, a tactile examination of the exterior of the vessels may be conducted, similar to the swim-around used for autos and aircraft.
4. Geographically locate the vessel and its component parts. Measurement of the vessels at rest will provide valuable information for the accident reconstructionist to determine fault, direction of travel, speed, right of way, and penetration.
5. Begin recovery of the submerged craft, components, and contents.
6. Do not overlook evidence of alcohol or drug use.
7. If the collision took place at night, evidence regarding use of lights will be important.

Although vessel investigations are a specialized activity, police agencies will call upon underwater investigators to assist in the recovery and investigation of the accident.

Vessel and aircraft catastrophes often leave the underwater investigator with bodies and debris that have been burned and that require specific recovery and investigative procedures. Vessel and aircraft explosions may result in fires. Aircraft crashes are often accompanied by fires. Whether the explosion and fires are the product of accident, negligence, or criminal enterprise, the investigation will focus on the underwater recovery site and the evidence obtained therefrom. Underwater investigators may mistake seriously burned bodies recovered from underwater as displaying signs of advanced putrefaction.

Boat Accident Investigation

Boat collisions differ markedly from auto collisions. The automobile accident reconstructionist generally deals with automobiles that remain on the ground and leave visible traces of their passage. Occasionally a vehicle will vault and become airborne, but ultimately the path of the vehicle can be traced by the marks left prior to vaulting and those left when the vehicle returns. The automobile accident investigator deals with two dimensions. Not so for the underwater investigator who is trying to reconstruct a boat collision. If two boats collide, one generally rides up onto the other. There are no skid marks in the traditional sense to reveal the path of the boats or their impact points, but boats do have evidence of having come into contact with one another, and marks borne by the boats can reveal much about the directions of travel, impact point, and right of way. Keeping in mind that boat investigations involve three dimensions, some of the information that will be available to the investigator may be submerged. Point of impact can be confirmed by debris left as a result of the impact. Just as in auto collisions, there is a beginning and end to the debris left at the accident site. Finding the beginning of the debris puts the investigator very close to the point of impact. So too, underwater debris that can be associated with one or more of the vessels involved in a collision can assist in determining point of impact.

Of what value is point of impact? In auto collisions the point of impact and the resting point of the vehicles can assist in approximating speed at time of impact; to a lesser degree, point of impact can assist in determining right of way and speed in boat collisions. In those witnessed collisions where the **impacting boat** is launched over the **impacted boat**, the distance traveled can assist in determining speed of the impacting vessel. Most boating accidents do not occur in a vacuum. Someone survives; someone witnessed the collision or the boats prior to collision. With the extensive use of recreational waterways today there is almost always someone watching if not videotaping or photographing in the area. Those who may be witnesses need to be identified as soon as possible and interviewed. Photographs and video footage should be examined for other observers or witnesses, and boats or automobiles in the background (Hickman, 2002).

When boats collide, one of two patterns generally results. If the impacting boat is hydroplaning its bow will be elevated. If the collision occurs with the impacting boat bow elevated, it is likely to pass over or onto the impacted boat. In those situations, there will be evidence of that passing on the bottom of the impacting boat. Any scratches on the bottom of the impacting boat that are attributable to the collision will impart a direction to the impact. In addition to the damage caused by the boat, there may also be evidence of damage or injury resulting from the propeller or bow cleat (tie down). If the impacting boat does not pass over or onto the impacted boat, damage should be to the hull of the impacted boat and to the bow of the impacting boat. The speed of the impacting boat and its weight will contribute to the depth of penetration in these collisions. There are no standard depth penetration tables based on make and model of boats as there are for automobiles, but the depth of penetration can partially explain what happened before, during, and after the collision (see **Figures 20–10a, 20–10b, 20–11, and 20–12**).

Occasionally the dynamics of a crash can be best understood by reenacting the crash and documenting the collision and its aftermath.

The collision may result in the destruction of a boat's tachometer and/or speedometer. When this happens it is reasonable to conclude that the speed or horsepower reflected in the damaged instrument reflects the speed of the boat at the time of impact. Upon impact the indicator needle of the instrument may slap the back of the gauge and lodge there.

Occupants will collide with the interior of their boats or be thrown from them. The occupant of a boat involved in a collision will be thrown in the direction opposite the collision impact. Often, secondary impacts leave evidence of the change in speed during the collision. Misshapen or broken steering wheels and cracked windshields are evidence

(A)

(B)

Figure 20–10   Vaulting boat collision.

Photos courtesy of William Chilcott, P.E.

Figure 20–11   Launching boat.

Photos courtesy of William Chilcott, P.E.

Figure 20–12 Vaulted boat damage.

Photos courtesy of William Chilcott, P.E.

of passenger impact and can be used to ascertain speed. The type of steering wheel or windshield can be subjected to laboratory testing applying force sufficient to duplicate the damage on the original item, thus giving some indication of the velocity necessary to create the deforming force.

Propeller Injuries

Boating accidents may cause an occupant to be thrown from the boat. If the occupant is the only person on board, the vessel may begin a slow circle at high speed heading back to the point at which the occupant was lost. Most boats today are equipped with safety mechanisms that turn the engine off should the driver be thrown from the boat, but many boaters fail to use this mechanism, making them subject to the high-speed turning boat.

It is not uncommon for boats to run over swimmers, snorkelers, divers, water skiers, or other boats. In instances when injury or death arises from the incident, some conclusions may be drawn from the **propeller injuries** on the body. Different types of boat engines impart unique characteristics to propeller cuts. Deformities in the propeller may also be evident in the injuries produced by the propeller. In investigations involving propeller injuries or death it is important to obtain the motors and propellers from the boat. An examination of the propeller may immediately rule out a particular boat or tests may be needed to determine whether the propeller in question caused the injuries or death.

The character of the wound may suggest a number of things (see **Figure 20–13**):

- Straight cuts occur when a propeller is performing at maximum efficiency (moving rapidly in or through the water). The cuts are fairly equidistant in spacing, with substantial distance between cuts.

- Curved cuts occur when a propeller is performing at less than its maximum efficiency (moving slowly in or through the water). The slow movement of the propeller cuts and pushes tissue backward.
- Cuts close together generally indicate a propeller in reverse gear, in that the backward motion of the vessel is substantially reduced by gear ratios, thereby depositing numerous cuts very close to each other.

Much of what needs to be known about propeller cuts can be discovered as a product of experimentation with limb prosthetic devices or anatomically correct dummies.

Propellers can provide information about a crash, property damage, human injury and death. A thorough examination of the propeller will reveal that it has come into contact with something. The bends and dents may be a product of general use, but serious distortion prevents the propeller from operating without shaking the boat apart. Serious distortion is a product of contact with something hard enough to damage the propeller. In injury and death it may be necessary to remove the propeller from the motor and package it so as to preserve it for laboratory examination. A gross examination of a propeller will reveal it has hit something, but a microscopic examination may reveal the source of the impact. Blood, tissue, hair, and fiber may cling to the propeller. Suspect boats should have propellers packaged in such a fashion as to avoid the loss or damage of trace evidence.

Fire

Fire is a natural consequence of using gasoline to power a boat. When taking on fuel or storing it, the vapor will settle to the lowest part of the boat. Many boats have bilge blowers that will cleanse the air from fueling prior to starting the boat. We often forget how volatile gasoline is, and that can lead to fires and explosions. The problem in investigating fires is that most of the boat and virtually all of the evidence has been consumed, and the boat may sink. One of the most important parts of examining a boat

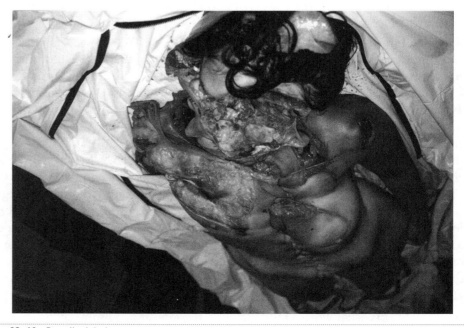

Figure 20–13 Propellor injuries.

Photos courtesy of William Chilcott, P.E.

Boat Accident Report

Boat data:

Operators' names _____

Addresses _____

Owners' names _____

Addresses _____

Rented or owned _____

Age of operators _____

Number of persons in each boat _____

Type of boat

    Motorboat _____

    Personal watercraft _____

    Sail boat _____

    Raft _____

    Canoe _____

    Other (specify) _____

Hull material

    Wood _____

    Aluminum _____

    Steel _____

    Fiberglass _____

    Other (specify) _____

Boat number _____

Boat name _____

Boat manufacturer _____

Boat model _____

Mfgr. hull identification number _____

Propulsion

    Outboard _____

    Inboard _____

    Sail _____

    Paddle _____

Boat measurements

    Length _____

    Width abeam _____

    Depth (transom to keel)

    Year built _____

    Number of engines _____

    Make _____

    Horsepower _____

Accident data:

Date _____

Time _____

Name of waterway _____

Location (fed and measured) _____

    City, county, state _____

Weather conditions

    Wind _____

    Speed _____

    Direction _____

Water conditions _____

Visibility _____

Type of accident

    Sinking _____

    Capsizing _____

    Collision with fixed object _____

    Collision with floating object _____

    Collision with vessel _____

    Fire or explosion _____

    Other (specify) _____

Activity

    Towing _____

    Cruising _____

    Racing _____

    Rowing _____

    Fishing _____

    Scuba diving, swimming etc. _____

    Water skiing _____

    Other (specify) _____

Narrative

    Accident causation

        Alcohol/drug use _____

        Right of way _____

        Speed _____

        Inattention _____

        Other (specify) _____

Operator culpability

    What happened _____

    How it happened _____

    Why it happened _____

fire is to determine what role arson may have played in setting it. Boats are susceptible to fires set for the purpose of defrauding an insurance company. Boat arson is one way of getting rid of a boat that has lost its appeal, lost its resale value, or taxes the financial ability of the owner.

Case Study

Dr. William Chilcott, a boat accident reconstructionist living in Sweetgrass, California, was involved in an investigation in Alaska that involved the death of a child and his mother in a boat fire. The father reported an accidental fire that began at the engines with smoke so thick from the engine area as to be impenetrable. He reported high seas that prevented him from assisting his family. During the course of the investigation by local police, the father stated that he had time to retrieve an exposure suit and two dogs, and escape into a 24-foot twin-engine boat he was towing as a safety boat. He motored to shore as the boat burned to the water line. He went to his accountant's home, which was close by, to report the accident.

A check on the insurance of the boat revealed that the boat had been heavily insured and was described as a 50-foot Hatteras. The U.S. Coast Guard arrived on the scene to film the last few minutes of the burning prior to the boat sinking. Dr. Chilcott was called in as an expert witness to examine the film footage. He first determined that the location of the swim hatch was on the wrong side of the boat to be a Hatteras and that the two burned spots on the swim step flew in the face of the father's testimony that the seas were heavy. If seas had been heavy, in Dr. Chilcott's opinion, the steps should not have burned. Based on the misrepresentation to the insurance company of the make of the boat, its being heavily insured, and the burns on the swim step, it was Dr. Chilcott's opinion that the boat was set on fire and that the deaths may have been a homicide. He recognized his responsibility to contact the FBI to report a homicide on international waterways.

The FBI, U.S. Navy, and the state of Alaska assisted in the recovery of the boat. The Coast Guard was able to locate the point at which the sinking took place and the Navy found the sunken boat using submersibles; the boat was a 48-foot Meridian, not a 50-foot Hatteras as described and insured. Using barges and cranes, the boat was rigged around the engines to be lifted to the surface. However, bottom suction prevented the lifting of the boat and the cranes pulled the two motors free. The motors were recovered and examined. A 9-mm bullet casing was found in the motor. The bottoms of the engines were unscathed, flying in the face of the man's statement that the fire had started at the engines. Based on the investigation's findings, the man was charged with murder and arson.

Prior to trial, the man was involved in a high-speed collision and rendered a quadriplegic. The state of Alaska, having no correctional facilities for handling the medical needs of a quadriplegic, relegated him to house arrest with an ankle-monitoring device. Prior to trial his body was discovered, still in his wheelchair, in five feet of water at the end of the pier at his home.

Dr. Chilcott's expertise and help allowed the FBI and the state of Alaska to complete an investigation into the deaths of the woman and child. It was Dr. Chilcott's understanding of fire, burning dynamics, and arson that allowed the investigation to progress to a successful conclusion.

Light Filaments

Lighting can be an important ingredient in determining the cause of a boating accident. The same understanding of light bulb filaments that is employed in automobile reconstruction can be helpful in determining if the colliding boats were rigged with the appropriate array of lights and, during nighttime boating, if those lights were on. Considering the immense areas of operation available to boats, it is absolutely imperative that nighttime boating be visible to other boaters. When the underwater investigator is gathering evidence, lights, bulbs, and filaments should be considered. The fact that the light switch is on or off is not always indicative of whether the lights were on at the time of the collision. During impact or recovery debris or persons thrown about the boat will likely strike the light switch. The light bulbs from the lights themselves can often reveal whether or not the lights were on when the accident occurred. A retrieval of the light bulbs may prove to be useful as the investigation progresses (Becker, 1995).

We know that filaments break in a highly characteristic fashion depending on temperature. That understanding should apply to boat accidents and recoveries as well as to automobile recoveries. Additionally, if light filaments do not break, they may bend in the opposite direction of the impact, providing information on direction of travel and direction of impact.

It should be remembered that all items recovered from a boat that are wet, other than lights and bodies, must be completely immersed in the medium from which they were retrieved. The laboratory will dry any wet materials before subjecting the material to laboratory testing.

■ Summary

In this chapter we learned that there is a whole new world of investigative challenges. Many police agencies have adopted a forensic approach to processing underwater crime scenes, but many have not. Fire departments in many parts of the country are still providing services to police agencies that such agencies would do better to provide themselves. We do not send police to fight fires, and we should not send fire fighters to process crime scenes, on land or in water. Investigators should remember that:

- Submerged evidence can retain forensic information.
- The FBI has dive recovery teams.
- The Bureau of Alcohol, Tobacco, Firearms (BATF) has dive recovery teams.
- The Naval Criminal Investigative Service (NCIS) has dive recovery teams.
- The U.S. Army CID has dive recovery teams.
- Many progressive metropolitan police agencies have dive recovery teams.
- Many states have dive recovery teams.

Throughout this text we have talked about the bigger team, the next chapter talks about three players on that bigger team, the prosecutor, the defense lawyer, and the investigator.

■ Key Terms

bagged: Placed in a sealable bag for preservation of evidence

boat accident report: A report that documents a vessel collision and its investigation

bottom structure sample: Control sample used for comparison with evidence recovered from water during laboratory analysis

etching agent: Substance used to retrieve serial numbers from firearms; when the etching agent is applied to the firearm, the strained area will dissolve at a faster rate than the underlying uncorroded metal, thus permitting the underlying number pattern to appear

exudates: A foam mixture of mucus, air, and water oozing from the mouth and nostrils of many drowning victims

lazy eyelid: In a deceased person, the lack of muscle rigidity that allows the lid to fall over half the eye

impacted boat: A boat that is the target of a vessel collision

impacting boat: A boat that provides the direction and force of a vessel collision

light filaments: A source of evidence and information in boat collisions

lividity: Purple color found on the lower parts of a deceased person's body, due to gravity causing blood to pool those areas; because of this, the upper parts of the body are pale

oxidation: Corrosion of a metal caused by its exposure to and combination with oxygen

postmortem immersion: Immersion of a body underwater after the person has already died

propeller injuries: Damage caused to human occupants in colliding vessels by a craft's propeller

skeletonized remains: The skeletal portion of a deceased person that is left after all of the soft tissue has decomposed

swim-around: An underwater tactile examination of a submerged vehicle

underwater crime scene: Area located under a body of water that contains evidence from a crime

underwater investigator: Member of a dive team who understands the steps involved in processing an underwater crime scene

washerwoman's skin: The wrinkling of the skin of the hands and feet as a result of immersion in water

water soluble: Dissolvable in water

wear patterns: Patterns that result from the slow removal of portions of an item caused by motion of or against that item

■ **Review Questions** ▬▬▬▬▬▬▬▬▬▬▬▬▬▬▬▬▬▬▬▬▬

1. What is the difference between traditional methods of handling drownings and an investigative approach to handling drownings?

2. What effect does oxidation have on submerged firearms, and how should that be taken into consideration during recovery operations?

3. How might firearm serial numbers be developed if oxidized?

4. What can the shoes of a drowning victim reveal to an investigator?

5. What is exudate, and what role did it play in the investigation of the Mary Jo Kopechne drowning?

6. How is washerwoman's skin caused, and what does it indicate about cause of death?

7. What is a common drowning position?

8. What is an automobile swim-around?

9. What kinds of things can be ascertained from a swim-around?

10. How do small aircraft crashes differ from large commercial passenger aircraft crashes?

11. Of what value is measurement in vessel accident reconstruction?

12. What is a successful underwater recovery operation?

13. Who is on the underwater investigation dive team?

14. What is the objective of an underwater recovery operation?

15. Of what value is a submerged auto swim-around?

16. What steps would you take in a submerged vessel investigation?

17. What damage on a boat may demonstrate it was the impacting vessel?

18. What information can propeller cuts impart to the investigator regarding speed and direction?

19. What kind of evidence might be found on a propeller of a craft that impacted a human?

20. What information might light filaments provide an investigator investigating a boat collision?

21. How is evidenced retrived from a submerged vessel packaged?

■ Bibliography

Becker, R.F. (1995). *The underwater crime scene:* Underwater crime investigative techniques. Springfield, IL: Charles C. Thomas.

Hendrick, W., Zafers, A., and Nelson, C. (2000). *Public safety diving.* Saddle Brook: Penn Well.

Perper, J.S. (1993). Time of death and changes after death. In W.U. Spitz (Ed.), *Medicolegal investigation of death* (3d ed.). Springfield, IL: Charles C. Thomas.

Spitz, W.U. (1993). Injury by gunfire. In W.U. Spitz (Ed.), *Medicolegal investigation of death* (3d ed.). Springfield, IL: Charles C. Thomas.

■ Suggested Reading

Bass, W.M. (1987). *Human osteology: A laboratory and field manual* (3rd ed.). Columbia, MO: Missouri Archaeological Society.

Bray, M. (1984). The eye as a chemical indicator of environmental temperature at the time of death. *Journal of Forensic Science* 29, 389–395.

Bray, M. (1985). Chemical estimation of fresh water immersion intervals. *American Journal of Forensic and Medical Pathology* 6, 133–139.

Bray, M., Luke, J.L., and Blackbourne, B.D. (1983). Vitreous humor chemistry in deaths associated with rapid chilling and prolonged freshwater immersion. *Journal of Forensic Science* 28, 589–593.

Davis, J.H. (1986). Bodies found in the water. *American Journal of Forensic and Medical Pathology* 7, 291–297.

DiMaio, D.J., and DiMaio, V.J.M. (1989). Airplane crashes. In D.J. DiMaio and V.J.M. DiMaio (Eds.), *Forensic pathology.* New York: Elsevier.

Fierro, M.F. (1993). Identification of human remains. In W.U. Spitz (Ed.) *Medicolegal investigation of death* (3rd ed.). Springfield, IL: Charles C. Thomas.

Fisher, R.S., Spitz, W.U., Breitenecker, R., and Adams, J.E. (1965). Techniques of identification applied to 81 extremely fragmented aircraft fatalities. *Journal of Forensic Science* 10, 121–127.

Giertsen, J.C., and Morild, I. (1989). Seafaring bodies. *American Journal of Forensic and Medical Pathology* 10, 25–27.

Henahan, J.F. (1980). Fire. *Science* 80(1), 29–38.

Jungbluth, W.O. (1986). Inner sole footwear comparison. *Identification News* 5, 13.

Lonsdale, M.V. (1989). *SRT diver: A guide for special response teams.* Los Angeles: Specialized Tactical Training Unit.

Luntz, L.L. (1967). Dental radiography and photography in identification. *Dental Radiography and Photography* 40, 83.

McCormick, M.M. (1980). The National Transportation Safety Board and the investigation of civil aviation and transportation accidents. *American Journal of Forensic and Medical Pathology* 1, 239–243.

Rivers, R.W. (1980). *Traffic accident investigators' handbook.* Springfield, IL: Charles C. Thomas.

Simson, L.R. (1980). Aircraft death investigation: A comprehensive review. In W.J. Curran, A.L. McGarry, and C.S. Petty (Eds.), *Modern legal medicine, psychiatry and forensic science.* Philadelphia: Davis.

Smerecki, C.J., and Lovejoy, C.O. (1986). Identification via pedal morphology. *Identification News,* May, 3–5, 15.

Stahl, C.J., III. (1993). Identification of human remains. In W.U. Spitz and R.S. Fisher (Eds.), *Medicolegal investigation of death* (2nd ed.), Springfield, IL: Charles C. Thomas.

Teather, R.G. (1983). *The underwater investigator.* Fort Collins, CO: Concept Systems.

U.S. Navy. U.S. naval flight surgeon aircraft mishap investigation pocket reference (2nd ed.) (1989). Norfolk, VA: Naval Safety Center, Aeromedical Division.

Wagner, G.L., and Froede, R.C. (1993). Medicolegal investigation of mass disasters. In W.U. Spitz (Ed.), *Medicolegal investigation of death* (3rd ed.). Springfield, IL: Charles C. Thomas.

Warfel, G.H. (1979). *Identification technologies.* Springfield, IL: Charles C. Thomas.

Defense Lawyers, Prosecutors, and Investigators

CHAPTER

21

▶ ▶ STUDENT LEARNING OUTCOMES

Upon completion of this chapter students will demonstrate an understanding of:

- The responsibility of the defense in a criminal trial
- The responsibility of the prosecution in a criminal trial
- The responsibility of the investigator in preparing to testify in a criminal trial
- The responsibility of the investigator in testifying in a criminal trial
- The value of a prosecution summary

■ The Defense

All states require lawyers to adhere to a code of professional responsibility. Each code requires attorneys to maintain client confidentiality and provide the best possible defense allowed by law and propriety. The conventional wisdom is that if the defense does its job, the prosecution does its job, and the police do their job, a just verdict will result. The only consolation a defense lawyer has in defending a client he or she believes to be guilty is that justice will be done on the condition that all participants in the legal process act competently.

A defense lawyer does not inquire into a client's guilt or innocence. It is not in the client's best interest to confess guilt, and most clients do not. On the other hand, it could injure the quality of a defense lawyer's preparation of the defendant's case if he or she were to rely heavily on the defendant's protestations of innocence. Believing in the defendant's innocence may prevent the lawyer from examining certain evidence or interviewing witnesses and thus revealing conflicts best discovered before trial. It is virtually an axiom of criminal law that a defense attorney should not assume a client has told the whole truth. Valuable information may be lost to an attorney who places too much confidence in the statements of a criminal client.

Defensive Burden and Affirmative Defenses

The legal burden generally borne by the defendant can be summed up succinctly: none. It is the responsibility of the defense lawyer to ensure that the defendant receives a fair trial and that neither the prosecution nor the court trespasses upon the due process rights of the defendant. Certain defenses require a preliminary showing of the applicability of the defensive position to the offense. These defenses are referred to as **affirmative defenses**.

The state generally has the responsibility to carry the burden of proof. It always has the responsibility to carry the burden of persuasion. In specific situations enumerated by statutes (codes of criminal procedure), the defense has the responsibility to put forth certain defenses, the most common being self-defense. The list of affirmative defenses is not a long one. It varies from state to state but typically includes the following:

- Insanity
- Incompetence
- Self-defense
- Coercion
- Entrapment

In most states, the defense must notify the prosecution in writing before trial that it intends to put forth an affirmative defense and must specify which defense it will use. One common result of an affirmative defense is that a new and separate procedure is required, such as a competency hearing. A competency hearing determines the state of mind of the defendant at the time of trial, whereas an insanity hearing determines the state of mind of the defendant at the time of the crime. If found by the court to be incompetent, the defendant will be sent to a mental institution until his or her competency has been restored, at which point the defendant will be required to stand trial for the offense charged.

In a competency hearing, the burden is upon the defendant to produce clear and convincing proof that he or she (1) does not understand the nature of the proceeding against him or her and (2) is unable to assist in his or her own defense. It is the defense lawyer's job to put forth all applicable defenses and to attempt to impeach the credibility of all witnesses and attack the admissibility of all evidence.

Defense Strategies

There are basically three ways the defense can win a criminal trial:

1. By impeaching the evidence
2. By impeaching the police
3. By creating confusion and delay

Impeaching Evidence

The **chain of custody** is one of the more commonly litigated pretrial issues. An investigator may view his or her role as completed once the evidence has been discovered or bagged. But a case may fail because of the inability of the prosecution to prove the whereabouts of certain evidence—not that it has been lost, but that it was unaccounted for at some point between the time it was discovered and the present moment. The prosecution has the responsibility to establish the location of the evidence every second after it came into the custody of the police. It would be very embarrassing to discover for the first time while undergoing cross-examination by the defense that there was a break in the chain of custody. Like any chain, the chain of custody is only as strong as its weakest link.

It is the investigating officer's responsibility to examine the trail of documentation that accounts for the whereabouts of the evidence to be admitted. Every person who has removed the evidence from its repository should be identified in the evidence logs and evidence tags. Any breach in the chain should be discovered well before trial and remedied, if possible. The problem with a break in the chain of custody is that it is often impossible to repair without altering documentation and committing perjury.

If there is a break in the chain, it is the prosecutor's job to determine whether the break is so complete as to render the evidence inadmissible. If the evidence is inadmissible, the prosecutor must then decide whether sufficient untainted evidence exists to win a conviction. Under the common law, a chain of custody must be shown from the moment evidence was discovered until it appears in the courtroom, so that the court can be satisfied that what the prosecutor is attempting to have entered into evidence is the same item discovered by the police and that the item has not been altered. Evidence should be handled only by people with a need to handle it. That need should be predicated on something other than curiosity.

The investigator who recovers a particular item of evidence will be responsible for testifying about what happened to the item once it was taken from the search site. Other than packaging, storing, and testing, the best thing that can happen to evidence is nothing. Every removal of evidence from storage should be recorded. If persons other than the testifying officer have handled the evidence, they may be called by the defense to testify. They will be asked to explain the purpose of the removal, the procedures of removal, where the evidence was taken, what was done to it, and, most important, whether there is any way to be certain that the item labeled as a specific piece of evidence is really the item recovered and not another similar item.

Evidence should be checked against the evidence log compiled during the investigation to ensure that all evidence has been retrieved. Chain-of-custody testimony is basically the same for all evidence. The chain of custody is not proven until the evidence has been identified appropriately. **Authentication** is a process separate from establishing the chain of custody, and its exact nature depends on the specific evidence to be entered. Authentication before the court is often referred to as establishing an evidentiary foundation or a predicate for admissibility.

Officers or investigators should be familiar with the questions and answers that establish the chain of custody during a trial. It is the responsibility of the testifying investigator to understand the rules of evidence well enough to be able to testify competently, and the investigator should anticipate chain-of-custody inquiries about any evidence. Once the witness has been identified and the chain of custody established, the court will require authentication of the evidentiary item. Chain-of-custody testimony evolved to ensure that items admitted into evidence have not been altered, and authentication evolved to help establish that evidentiary items are what the lawyers claim them to be.

A self-authenticating item is one that requires no assistance in establishing its authenticity; a certified copy of a birth certificate requires no elaborate protocol to establish that it is in fact a certified birth certificate. State and federal rules of evidence usually set out which items are self-authenticating. The testimony of the investigator typically is the predicate (foundation) for authenticity of evidentiary items that are not self-authenticating.

Overlooked evidence and contaminated evidence are errors that do not readily lend themselves to repair. It is best to discover any such errors prior to trial. Bringing them to the attention of the prosecuting attorney will allow a legal analysis of the tainted evidence and its impact on the remaining evidence. If it is determined that the remaining evidence is also tainted or insufficient for winning a conviction, the charges can be dropped and the investigation resumed. If the case is dismissed after the jury has been sworn in or acquittal has been won, the investigation will remain closed forever.

The time to admit or discover errors is before trial. A conscientious investigator and a conscientious prosecutor should never lose a case based on investigative error or contaminated evidence. Such problems should be uncovered long before trial and a tactical decision made as to the viability and vulnerability of the prosecution.

Impeaching the Police

Closely tied to the issue of inadmissible evidence is the question of the competence and credibility of the police. Obviously, an attack on the training, education, and experience of the officers involved would be one way to try to discredit the evidence, a main defense objective. This strategy is sometimes referred to as "striking the evidence over the shoulder of the police". If training, education, and experience issues can be raised, they could affect a jury's view of the credibility of the testifying witness and everything he or she has touched in the course of the investigation. If even one small bit of evidentiary procedure is wanting in the conduct of the investigating team, the whole team will be viewed more skeptically. A discredited police officer reflects discredit on the entire investigative team and on the investigative process.

Police are subject to greater personal scrutiny than any other type of witness. An officer's entire personnel record, job performance, and personal life, as well as any complaints made against the officer, will be examined prior to trial, and anything that can be used to undermine the officer's testimony will be admissible on the grounds of challenging the officer's competence and credibility.

Suppose a prosecutor discovers for the first time at trial that the chief investigator in a racially charged case is a racist. The options confronting the prosecution are fairly straightforward: Call the witness or do not call the witness (keeping in mind that a questionable witness can still be called by the defense as a hostile witness). If the prosecution decides to call the witness, it must be prepared to deal with the racial issue. No purpose will be served by attempting to distance itself from its own witness. In the law, it is understood that the party calling a witness in effect vouches for that witness. A questionable witness can only reflect badly upon himself or herself and the prosecution.

The questions the prosecution has to ask in deciding to call a questionable witness are these:

- Is the witness vital to the prosecution's case?
- Is there sufficient evidence absent this witness to win a conviction?

If the witness is vital to the prosecution's case, two further questions need to be asked:

- Can the witness's questionable behavior, attribute, or opinion be presented in such a way that it will not alienate the jury?
- If the behavior, attribute, or opinion cannot be so presented, what impact will it have on the jury?

If sufficient evidence exists to win a conviction without this witness, other questions arise:

- Will the defense call the witness?
- If so, what impact will this witness have when called by the defense as a **hostile witness** (a witness who is favorable to the other side)?

When the analysis of the situation has been completed, the prosecution must decide whether to go forward with its case or dismiss it. No matter how odious the crime, insufficient evidence and impeachable witnesses (persons whose veracity is open to question) undermine not only the case in question but also the criminal justice system as a whole. It is too late to ask the necessary questions at the time of trial.

The prosecutor's remedy for tainted evidence or unreliable witnesses is dismissing a case. Unfortunately, police, investigators, and prosecutors sometimes compound the problem by attempting to engage in **damage control**. That is a fatal mistake. Sometimes prosecutors become so emotionally involved in a case that they cannot distance themselves enough to objectively assess the impact of prospective damaging evidence or testimony. They want a conviction so badly that they lose sight of their professional duty, which is to see that justice is done. When objectivity is lost, disaster looms if a case that should be dismissed is not. The trial then becomes a series of damage control skirmishes that ultimately will sink the prosecution's case and undermine the judicial system.

Confusion and Delay

There is an old legal defense axiom: If you can't win on the facts, argue the law; if you can't win on the law, argue the facts; if you can't win on either, delay. The U.S. Constitution guarantees a defendant a speedy trial. The truth is, most defendants do not want a speedy trial. As long as the trial is not held, a verdict of guilty is not rendered. As long as a trial is not held, the defendant (if bonded) remains free. The longer the trial is delayed, the greater the chance the state will lose a witness and the dimmer memories will become. Most defendants do not benefit by rushing to the courthouse and have everything to gain by waiting.

There are competing components of the U.S. Constitution that come into play in getting a defendant to trial. The U.S. Supreme Court has handed down many decisions dealing with proper legal representation and efforts put forth in preparing a defense. The defendant's right to have sufficient time to prepare a defense conspires against a speedy trial. The very nature of the U.S. criminal justice system also influences how soon a defendant comes to trial. Most judges and prosecutors face a crowded criminal trial docket and therefore do not oppose postponing criminal trial proceedings except in a high-profile case. But while the wheels of justice slowly turn, police witnesses change agencies and eyewitnesses move, their memories wane, or they die. A speedy trial is virtually a mythical beast in today's judicial forums.

Another old defense axiom is that a good defense lawyer can make the simplest cases complex. Many cases involve forensic evidence and complicated expert testimony. The more difficult the testimony is to understand, the more room the defense has to sow confusion. Trials in which DNA testimony occurs are so convoluted that even people who understand DNA typing often lose track of the testimony and its significance. Instead of discussing forensic aspects of blood and its genetic composition, the defense attorney, in cross-examination, might bring up population statistics, laboratory procedures, and other matters of little relevance to the question of who left blood at the crime scene. This approach uses two defense principles: impeach the evidence and confuse the jury. Without actually impeaching the evidence, the defense attorney so obscures the forensic procedures that a jury member might mistake confusion for a reasonable doubt. All testifying witnesses must have the ability to make the difficult easy to comprehend and must understand what they are testifying about so well that they can provide clear answers to questions intended to obfuscate. A cross-examination conducted by a competent defense attorney can be a fearsome thing and should not be underestimated by the witness or the prosecution.

Suppression Hearings

More cases are lost in **suppression hearings** than by a verdict of acquittal. Indeed, investigators spend more time in these hearings than they do testifying at trial, for it is in these hearings that most of the important judicial decisions regarding evidence, confessions, and police conduct (or misconduct) are raised and resolved. A suppression hearing gives defendants an opportunity to see what kind of case the prosecution has and what caliber of witnesses it is facing. In most instances, if a defendant's motion to suppress illegally obtained evidence and statements is granted, the prosecution dismisses the case for lack of evidence. It is important to remember that the prosecution's burden is to prove the offense beyond a reasonable doubt, which represents a substantial increase over the burden of proof that police need to arrest.

Motions to suppress are heard long before a jury is picked or a trial date set. The defense need not worry about the impression the jury will get from harsh treatment of the testifying witnesses. Investigating officers can be made to feel like criminals through vigorous and vehement cross-examination. The defense can use the suppression hearing to assess the opposition.

The best way to avoid a suppression hearing is to ensure that all police conduct is above question. An investigator should presume that any investigation will end up at trial and at a motion to suppress. It might not be true, but no one is able to distinguish beforehand between investigations that will lead to a trial and those that will not. The investigation that has taken evidentiary shortcuts is almost certainly doomed, but it may be years before the trial reveals that to the investigating team. In the realm of criminal investigation, there are no sure things and no unimportant pieces of evidence.

The two most commonly litigated issues in criminal cases are illegal searches and seizures and illegally obtained statements. Given the quantity of time and effort that goes into training criminal investigative teams, one would think that team members would know the difference between a legal and an illegal search, a legal and an illegal arrest, and legally and illegally obtained confessions. But the rate of suppressed evidence strongly suggests that the performance of many police is deficient. Either the training they received was inadequate or they have chosen to ignore the training and conduct the investigation in a way inconsistent with their training.

■ The Prosecution

In a trial, the prosecution has the burden to prove four things: subject matter jurisdiction, venue, identification of the party charged, and elements of the offense. Each criminal trial is a competition involving these four issues. Although a trial may take a day, week, month, or even longer to complete, the basic requirement of the prosecution is to prove beyond a reasonable doubt each and every element of the offense with which the defendant has been charged. The prosecution must also establish that the court trying the matter has jurisdiction of the case, that the venue is proper, and that the person standing trial today is the one charged with the offense.

Jurisdiction

Each state has a tiered system of trial courts, ranging from small-claims courts to courts like those featured on television to courts of last review (often referred to as appellate or supreme courts). Trial courts are granted the authority to hear cases based on their subject matter and/or the amount of money at stake. Criminal courts are generally divided into two categories: courts handling serious crimes (felonies) and courts handling less serious offenses (misdemeanors). Court **jurisdiction** has nothing to do with geography; it has to do with statutory authority. It should not be confused with police jurisdiction. Police jurisdiction is geographic in nature, for it sets the territorial boundaries within which police may act. Court jurisdiction in a criminal case is determined by the type of offense. If it is a felony case, it is heard in district court; if a misdemeanor case, it is heard in a lesser court. Lesser courts are referred to as courts of limited jurisdiction.

It is necessary to show the court in which a case is being tried that the offense charged is covered by the court's statutory or constitutional authority. Proof of the court's appropriateness is generally accomplished through the testimony of the criminal investigator. Such proof is most crucial in states that determine the seriousness of theft offenses based on the sum stolen. If stealing something that has a value of more than $750 is a felony, there must be testimony offered by the state proving the value of the item stolen in order to establish for the record that the offense was in fact a felony over which the court has felony jurisdiction. Absent that showing, the state has failed to prove an essential ingredient of its case and may be subject to a motion for a **directed verdict of acquittal** when the defense raises the issue to the judge. Upon a motion for a directed verdict, the court will direct the court reporter to examine the record for any testimony pertaining to the value of the item stolen. Should that testimony not be there, the defendant's motion may be granted, which results in a dismissal of the case. The **transcript** typed by the court stenographer is the official record of what has taken place during the course of the trial. Upon appeal, the only issues that will be reviewed by the court are those raised at the time of trial and memorialized in the trial record (transcript).

Venue

The geographical area over which a court presides is called its **venue**. (The concept of a court's venue can be understood by comparing venue to police jurisdiction.) The prosecutor has the responsibility to establish through competent testimony that the crime with which the defendant is charged has occurred in an area over which the court has authority. The state generally proves this element through police testimony. The Sixth Amendment to the U.S. Constitution requires that the defendant be tried in the geographical area in which the offense was committed. An investigator must testify that the crime occurred in the state, county, and city over which the court has authority. Failure to do so will result in a motion by the defendant for a directed verdict of acquittal. It should be noted that double jeopardy attaches once the jury has been sworn in, so that a dismissal prevents the prosecution from re-filing the case, and the defendant goes free.

In-Court Identification

In every criminal case, the prosecution must assure the court that the individual in court is the same person charged with the offense of which he or she stands accused. The **in-court identification** of the defendant is not necessarily a cursory affair. The prosecutor may ask a witness to confirm the defendant's identity and receive that confirmation, but it is not only the judge who must be satisfied that the defendant has been identified as the perpetrator. On appeal, the reviewing court will look to the trial transcript (record) in determining whether the identification was made acceptably.

The problem with "letting the record reflect" identification (e.g., that the witness pointed to the defendant) is that the record reflects only words and conduct. It is the testimony of the prosecutor that has established the identity of the defendant, but the

OFFICER'S NOTEBOOK

Proper In-Court Identification of a Defendant
An in-court identification of a defendant should be made in the following way to withstand appellate review.

Q: Officer, is the man whom you saw leaving the scene of the crime and whom you arrested for the crime in the courtroom today?

A: Yes.

Q: Where is he sitting?

A: In front of the bar at the defense counsel table with his attorney.

Q: Would you describe what he is wearing?

A: He is wearing a blue sport coat, gray pants, a white shirt, and a red tie.

It is unnecessary to use the dramatic Hollywood gesture of a pointed finger. The record now does reflect an appropriate in-court identification.

prosecutor is not a competent witness, and what he or she says is not evidence. It should be apparent that this method of identifying the defendant does not meet legal requirements (unless the trial is videotaped). It helps if the witness and the prosecutor know what is required for making a proper in-court identification of the defendant. The protocol outlined in the Officer's Notebook is one that has withstood appellate review.

Elements of the Offense

That the burden of the prosecution is to prove the **elements of an offense** may seem self-evident, but proving this is not always as simple as it seems. The prosecution and the testifying investigator have the responsibility of knowing what the elements of an offense are and what facts to be admitted into evidence support each and every element of the offense.

Many investigators have a superb familiarity with the penal code of their state and can quote line and verse in discussing various arrests and prosecutions in which they have been involved. Yet it is an entirely different skill to be able to recognize from a labyrinth of information and facts exactly what crime has been committed and what can be charged. Relying on the state penal code will always leave a gap in an investigator's understanding of the legal elements of various offenses. Applicable case law helps to interpret code provisions when ambiguity arises. There are a number of relevant cases that accompany every section and offense enumerated in the penal code. The well-prepared investigator has an annotated version of the penal code that assists in fully understanding the elements of an offense.

For example, according to most penal codes, burglary of a habitation occurs when a person enters or remains on the premises of another, without effective consent of the owner, for the purpose of committing theft or another felony. By this definition, can a person burglarize his or her own home? It would seem not. If a person, seeing an open window, pushes a pole through the window and lifts up and removes a purse resting on the table without any part of his or her person entering the dwelling, has a burglary been committed? Not if we literally apply the penal definition. Or if a person, seeing an open window and a purse on a table, sends in a trained monkey to retrieve the purse, has a burglary been committed? The answer to this question as well will not be determinable without annotated cases interpreting the code. A well-trained investigator knows not only the codified elements of an offense but also where to find the cases to assist in interpreting the codes when an element of human ambiguity enters the fray. (For the curious, yes, a person can burglarize his or her own home. And using a pole device or trained animal has been seen by the courts as extending the human arm and thus as constituting burglary.)

A failure to prove jurisdiction, venue, in-court identification, or the elements of the offense charged will result in a verdict for the defendant and a loss for the prosecution. Remember, the prosecution is part of the criminal investigation team, and when the prosecution loses, the investigator and the investigation lose.

■ Investigators and Trials

Testimonial Devices to Avoid the Truth

There are numerous opportunities during the course of a criminal investigation for things to go wrong. Conducting an error-free investigation is impossible, and what is done to address the errors that occur will often determine the outcome of the investigation and the trial. Once an error has been made, there are three ways of dealing with it:

1. Deny it ever occurred (denial)
2. Blame someone or something else for the error (scapegoating)
3. Admit the error and examine various ways to address it (growth)

Denial

Denying that an error has been made may result in perjured testimony. If the error is not acknowledged in the documentation, the trial can become very uncomfortable for the testifying investigator. An investigator who intends to participate in successful prosecutions must excel at two things: documentation and testifying. It serves no purpose for the best of investigators to take the witness stand without adequate documentation in support of the investigation. Trials often occur months and sometimes even years after the investigation has been completed. The only reliable record of the investigation is the documentation prepared by the investigator. If that documentation is sparse, inaccurate, or compositionally inept, the testifying investigator risks having to try to remedy those shortcomings on the witness stand. A catastrophe will usually occur if the officer testifies to facts not included in the documentation. Such testimony is a gift to the defense. If the facts are important enough to tell the jury, then why were they not included in the original report? The inference obviously is that they would have been important enough had they actually happened.

A failing memory that recovers in time for the trial is also risky. If a report was made soon after the crime, would it not be a more accurate rendition of the facts than an uncorroborated distant recollection? Obviously, a contemporaneous recording of significant events is more reliable than remembrances occurring months or years later, and any suggestion to the contrary is viewed as suspect.

Good trial lawyers are not born, they are made. Competent police witnesses are also shaped by their training and experience. Further, a superbly skilled but unprepared trial lawyer will lose to a well-prepared trial lawyer of modest talents every time. This suggests that any witness who enters the gladiatorial arena of the law must be well prepared in order to handle a good trial lawyer's questions (Becker, 1995). The quality of a witness's testimony is a reflection of the witness's preparation. The quality of the preparation is, in turn, a reflection of the quality of the documentation completed by the investigating officers, the time spent in studying that documentation, and the sources of that documentation.

A testifying police investigator can be a defense lawyer's ally or worst nightmare. In selecting the jury, defense lawyers inquire into every **venireperson's** (prospective juror's) occupational background. Anyone with police relatives or police friends will most likely be struck from a jury. Prospective jurors will be asked if they believe that a police officer is more believable than any other witness. They will be asked if they are of the opinion that police officers do not make mistakes. They will be asked if they are of the opinion that police officers do not lie. Anyone answering these questions with a yes will likely be **peremptorily struck** (struck without reason) from the jury. Why do defense lawyers place so much emphasis on police officers? They know that the entire case may rest on the testimony of the police and the investigation they performed. They also know that each officer is bestowed with an invisible "shroud of veracity" by virtue of the esteem with which police are generally held in the community.

Many people believe and want to believe that police officers are honest and lack deceit. The whole jury has anticipated, since the **voir dire** (jury selection), the moment that the testifying investigator is called by the bailiff as a witness. That officer is scrutinized the moment he or she steps through the door and enters the courtroom. If the officer walks confidently, is dressed professionally, and shows personal pride in his or her appearance, many on the jury will extend the courtesy of belief. The officer's believability cannot usually be damaged by anything that the defense may have done or attempt to do, but it can be stripped away by incompetent, insincere, or dishonest testimony. The penalty for false testimony for any other witness is to be labeled a perjurer and to be forgotten. The penalty for a criminal investigator who is incompetent or dishonest is a verdict of acquittal for the defendant and a prosecutor who will be extremely reluctant to prosecute that officer's cases.

Habit is a tool or a vice. If over a period of time all investigations are conducted with the same meticulousness, a habit aimed at success will eventually be established. That habit is difficult to cultivate, because police know that the majority of investigations leading to arrest will never go to trial. If a case is not likely to be tried, why invest time and effort in providing documentation, processing evidence, and interviewing witnesses? Presuming a case will not go to trial or that another officer will do the writing ensures embarrassment or dishonesty if the presumption is proved false. The only foolproof way to avoid falling victim to the plea-bargain presumption is to prepare every case as though it were going to trial. This level of preparation may be tedious, but it certainly provides practice. And when a case does go to trial, the high quality of the preparation will make the defense lawyer's life much more difficult.

An investigator with experience testifying will not wait until the day of trial to review the case. The prudent course is to examine the paperwork, evidence, logs, photographs, diagrams, sketches, and charts that will be admitted through the officer's testimony. Reviewing the condition of all evidence, including markings, labels, and the chain of custody, is also important. All diagrams, reports, statements, notes, and sketches should have been constructed with the trial in mind and lend themselves to quality enlargements that will assist the jury in understanding the investigator's testimony. It is a mistake to use technical language and jargon if not absolutely necessary. Keeping it simple is the surest way to avoid complications during cross-examination.

Scapegoating

We have grown accustomed to referring to automobile collisions as accidents, or something that occurred by chance. In truth, chance has little to do with most traffic collisions. Speed, tailgating, intoxication, and lack of attention are the precipitating causes of collisions—not fortune, chance, or fate.

Similarly, police will euphemistically say that a defendant got off on a technicality. In such instances, the police probably failed to do their job or failed to do it correctly. There are no technicalities upon which a defendant may be released. Only police (or prosecutorial or judicial) misconduct of constitutional dimensions can result in the defendant being released on a technicality. Is coercing a confession a technicality? Some police believe it is. Is searching a person or his or her home or effects without probable cause a technicality? Some police believe it is. By reducing an infringement of the U.S. Constitution to the level of a technicality, police show their disdain for the Bill of Rights and the blueprint of American due process. Defense lawyers for the most part point out and exaggerate the errors of the police and the prosecution; they seldom manufacture them.

Aiming for Error-Free Investigations

There will be mistakes during the investigation and during the trial. There are no perfect trials or investigations. A perfect investigation is suspect. Yet if police officers cannot conduct a perfect, error-free investigation, why should they try?

Although error-free investigations are unattainable, attempting to achieve them is highly desirable. The never-ending efforts of the police to perform the perfect investigation will be recognized and will bear fruit both in and out of the courtroom. The investigator who leaves no stone unturned will be more successful in investigating crime than the investigator who rushes to judgment based on hastily gathered information and evidence—that is, if we define success as conducting investigations that lead to convictions or rigorous plea bargains.

Loose ends are errors of omission and can be just as costly as errors of commission. It is not very helpful to discover at the time of trial that the defense has found a witness who places the defendant at a different location than that alleged in the indictment or who has him or her departing the scene hours before the crime was committed. Errors of omission are the easiest to avoid. If investigators do the job they are paid to do in the way they are paid to do it, errors of omission will be kept to a minimum.

How do you explain to a prosecutor that you failed to discover the existence of an alibi witness? How do you dispute testimony that you never knew existed? How do you prepare for trial when there is relevant information missing? How do you explain to the jury your efforts to convict a possibly innocent person? How do you explain the failure to discover **exculpatory evidence** (evidence indicating innocence)? All these are questions that investigators, prosecutors, and judges would rather avoid. They can be avoided by striving for perfection and following all leads even after the puzzle has seemingly been solved.

Ethical Testimony

Prior to a suppression hearing or a trial, prosecutors may discover problems with the case being prepared. Hasty conferences with investigators may be called and a joint exercise in damage control undertaken. If damage control is accomplished by modification of the investigating officer's recollection of an event, handling of evidence, or personal philosophy, the result is perjury no matter the motivation. It is easy to believe that the end justifies the means—that the defendant has done a bad thing and deserves to be punished and therefore that lying to ensure punishment is okay. Months, sometimes years of hard investigative work, might be at stake.

It should not be difficult to tell the truth, even when you know that the truth may set free a defendant you believe to be guilty. It is at this point that one's personal philosophy becomes an issue. The decision to lie, fabricate evidence, or deny **culpability** (criminal responsibility) is determined well before the opportunity to lie, fabricate evidence, or deny culpability arises. An individual's character and personal philosophy are part of what he or she carries around in dealing with the world. The formation of a personal philosophy begins in early childhood and continues in the home, church, school, and on the street. An individual's personal philosophy never achieves finished form but is constantly evolving. If nurtured, it grows in the right direction; if not, it grows in the other.

It is not the big issues, such as police corruption, but rather the day-to-day decisions that reflect what a police officer's personal philosophy is. A personal philosophy does not come hardwired from the factory. A person does not awaken one morning and make the decision to be honest or dishonest. That decision is the result of a long series of incremental steps. Many in criminal justice believe we need to teach ethics by preaching about what is right and pointing fingers at those who do wrong. Yet the basis of ethical conduct resides in the personal philosophy we bring to our encounters. It is not unique to police work. The same philosophy accompanies us no matter what it is we choose to do with our lives. The early lessons we learned have stuck and grown or they have died. If the latter, their death was not a quick and painless one. Those values and lessons die a slow, lingering death—but they nonetheless die unless they are nourished. Nourishment is easy: you just use them. Every time an opportunity arises to do the right thing and you do it, the probability of doing the right thing in the future has increased. As

OFFICER'S NOTEBOOK

Checklist for Testimony Preparation

1. Complete all documentation in a timely fashion (as information, evidence, and data are obtained).
2. Examine all evidence prior to trial.
3. Compare all evidence to references in documentation and relocate any identifying markings or characteristics.
4. Gather all field notes and sketches and place them in a separate folder (examine for extrinsic information).
5. Confer with the prosecutor prior to trial in anticipation of trial.
6. Contact all lab technicians and forensic scientists and discuss laboratory findings.
7. Contact the medical examiner and discuss the examination and documentation provided by his or her office.
8. Contact all witnesses to reconfirm information provided and the validity of statements made.
9. Select appropriate apparel and ensure appropriate grooming.
10. Arrive at the courthouse early.
11. Remain at the courthouse until dismissed by the prosecutor.
12. Testify objectively and truthfully.
13. Treat the defense attorney with the same courtesy that was extended to the prosecution (especially if the defense attorney's conduct does not warrant it). The old adage, "Don't get mad, get even" is self-defeating and should be replaced with the saying, "Don't get mad, don't get even—win."
14. After testifying, do not leave the courthouse until excused by the judge.

you sit reading this book, you know whether you are an honest or a dishonest person. Nothing in an ethics curriculum, nor anything that could be included in this book, can change your degree of honesty.

Preparing for Trial

When preparing for trial, the investigator must meet with the prosecutor a few days before the scheduled date of the trial. It is during this pretrial conference that the choreography for the trial will be mapped out. Between the two the following will be determined:

- What role the investigator and the investigative team will play
- The order of testimony, based on the chronology of events and the need for a human conduit in the admission of various types of evidence
- The order of presentation of evidence; each item of evidence is preceded by its proof in the chain of custody
- Strong points; every case has them
- Weak point; every case has these too, and the trick is to discover them before the defense does
- Trial strategy, including anticipated witness impact, anticipated victim impact, types of favorable jurors, damage control.

Additionally, the lead investigator can review the following:

- The rules of evidence, including evidentiary predicates, chain of custody, authentication rules
- The location and health of all evidence, evidence logs, photos, and photo logs
- Documentation such as witness statements, offense reports, confessions, Miranda warnings, waivers, medical records
- Availability of testifying witnesses
- Expert witness testimony, along with the evidence and documentation it will be based upon

Expected Courtroom Demeanor

The public has expectations of how a testifying officer should look and sound, which are sometimes unrealistic and influenced by Hollywood and television images. They do expect officers to testify professionally and objectively. The greatest gift a testifying officer can give the defense is the loss of his or her self-control. The witness stand is not a place from which to do battle. The system is adversarial, but it is the truth that the prosecution uses to build its case and it is the truth that the prosecution expects to get from all state witnesses. Any discourtesy by the defense lawyer is a matter to be attended to by the prosecutor and the judge—not the witness.

The expectations of the court and the public require that the officer who intends to testify consider the following before entering the courtroom:

- Ensure appropriate dress and appearance—from head to toe (shoes are the most often neglected aspect; haircuts fall in second place).
- People encountered in, around, and outside of the courthouse should be treated with respect, even adverse witnesses. This is a rule that should be followed all the time but is most important in regard to trials. Jurors, the defense, the press, or the public may be watching.

- Do not discuss the case outside of the courtroom, the prosecutor's office, or the police station.
- Arrive early and get a feel for the courtroom to which the case has been assigned. Walk around. Make it yours.
- Engage in no discussions with the defense or anyone on the defense team without the presence of the prosecutor.

When testifying, it is important to remember that you represent the state and that you carry a burden, responsibility, and benefit in your testimony. You are entitled to be believed and enjoy that presumption until proven unworthy. The following are guidelines for testifying.

- Make eye contact with the attorney while he or she is asking you questions. Look to the jury when you answer. The lawyer who inquired knows that the answer he or she is seeking is for the benefit of the jury, so respond directly to them.
- The truth is your only weapon. You know more about the subject in question than anyone in the room. Do not be intimidated.
- Listen to the question, because an objection may be lodged and the question may have to be rephrased. By listening to and remembering the first question, you will know what the prosecutor is asking in the rephrased question.
- If more than one question is asked, answer the first one and then ask for the second one to be repeated. Watch for a series of quick questions that require either all yes or all no answers: You may be hit with one to which the prior answers do not apply.
- Remember that you are in control. You cannot be asked another question until you have answered the one initially posed. Take your time. Do not relinquish the tempo of the questioning. It relinquishes control.
- Answer yes or no whenever possible to defense questions. Let the defense ask for elaboration.
- If your answer sounds bad, wait for the prosecution to ask a rehabilitating question. That is the prosecutor's job, not the witness's.
- If you do not know the answer, do not be reluctant to say so without explanation unless asked. Again, the prosecution will ask the rehabilitating question for you to answer.
- Use exact Miranda waiver language—read it.
- Use approximations in times, distance, and measurements
- "Yes, sir" and "No, sir" or "Yes, ma'am" and "No ma'am" are good ways to address both the prosecution and the defense.
- Using notes to refresh your memory entitles the defense to see them. Be sure there is nothing offensive in your field notes.
- Be sure there are no notes from other investigations in your notebook: The defense gets to look at all of whatever you bring to the witness stand.
- Testify about what you know, not what you think or suspect, unless specifically asked to do so. The more vigorous the examination, the more thought and time you should put into your answers.

- Do not hesitate to admit that you have talked to others about this case. These others might include the prosecution, witnesses, suspects, victims, and fellow officers.
- Be courteous. There is no excuse for a combative police witness, ever.

Prosecution Summary

In each case, the investigating officer should prepare a prosecution summary. The reasons and content have been discussed earlier. In preparing to testify, a check of the prosecution summary and a review of its contents will help an officer anticipate the flow of the trial and the nature of the testimony. Some of the things in the summary that will assist the investigator in gearing up for trial include the following:

1. The indictment
   - Penal code offense: The elements of the crime that the state must prove and that the investigator must be prepared to address
2. Probable cause as it applies to any searches or arrests
   - Any exceptions that may have allowed a search or an arrest on less than probable cause should be noted
   - All search and arrest warrants should be examined
3. Statements made by the defendant or on behalf of the defendant
   - Revisit the documentation supporting any waiver of rights to legal assistance and to remain silent.
   - Anticipate the defense that will be presented
   - Anticipate any affirmative defenses that may be pled
4. Witness statements
   - Inconsistencies within a statement
   - Inconsistencies between statements
   - Remember that in the real world, no two people perceive an event in exactly the same way; expect inconsistencies.
   - Assessment of the reliability of the witnesses
5. Review all evidence.
   - Tags
   - Logs
   - Pictures
6. Prepare all diagrams and sketches for enlargement and trial use.

■ Summary

What most people know about criminal trials they have learned from television. Unfortunately what they have seen has not been a realistic portrayal. Considering that criminal trials take days or weeks, trying to summarize a trial in 15 minutes or less is going to be surreal at best. The movies portray only the emotional highpoints. Few ever portray an appropriately conducted jury selection process. Many lawyers believe that a trial can be won or lost during the jury selection process. Whether that is true or not it is the only time that lawyers get to speak personally with each juror and it may well be a pivotal point in a trial.

Pretrial hearings are often where cases are decided. Most criminal cases will never reach a jury trial. All of our preconceived ideas about a trial are irrelevant until a trial that catches our attention is aired. We become experts on trial procedure based on Judge Judy or some other theatrical portrayal, not recognizing that trying a criminal case is as much about procedure as it is about style. In truth, little happens in a well-tried criminal trial that would hold the attention of an audience for more that twenty minutes.

Whenever a criminal investigator testifies s/he enjoys a special place among the witnesses that will testify. Fact witnesses may only testify about what they saw or heard. Expert witnesses can express opinions based on what they saw and heard and think. Criminal investigators are expert witnesses. The next chapter tells us what is so special about that witness they call expert.

■ Key Terms

affirmative defense: Defense that requires a preliminary showing of the applicability of the defensive position

authentication: Often referred to as establishing an evidentiary foundation or a predicate for admissibility, it is a process separate from establishing the chain of custody that depends on the specific evidence to be entered

chain of custody: The record of the transfer of physical evidence from one person to the next

culpability: Criminal responsibility

damage control: Distorting evidence and records to try to salvage a case that should otherwise be dismissed

directed verdict of acquittal: Dismissal of a case that results from the prosecution's failure to prove that the court hearing the case has the jurisdiction to do so

elements of the offense: The crime that has been committed and what can be charged

exculpatory evidence: Evidence indicating innocence

hostile witness: Witness who is favorable to the other side

in-court identification: Assuring the court that the individual in court is the same person charged with the offense of which he or she stands accused; the prosecution this must do this in every criminal case

jurisdiction: The statutory authority of a court to hear a case; in general, it is the authority to apply the law or govern

peremptorily struck: Struck (from the jury) without a reason

suppression hearing: A pretrial hearing in front of a judge to determine constitutional issues related to the admissibility of evidence

transcript: The official record of what has taken place during the course of the trial, typed by the court stenographer

venireperson: A prospective juror

venue: The geographical area over which a court presides

voir dire: Jury selection process

■ Review Questions

1. How can a lawyer ethically defend a defendant he or she believes is guilty? Include in your discussion comments on the ethical obligation a lawyer has to a client.
2. What must the state prove in each and every criminal case that it tries?

3. How does police jurisdiction differ from judicial jurisdiction?

4. What is a motion for a directed verdict of acquittal?

5. Why is an in-court identification of the defendant required, and how is it made?

6. What role does case law play in understanding penal code offenses?

7. What is an affirmative defense, and what effect does it have on the burden of proof in a criminal trial?

8. What are the three basic tactics employed by the defense in an effort to win a criminal trial?

9. What is the chain of custody, and what problems arise in attempting to maintain it?

10. How is a personal philosophy formed and how does it evolve?

11. What are the advantages to a defendant in delaying a trial?

12. What is a motion to suppress evidence, and what role does it play in a criminal investigation? What issues should arise when the prosecutor and investigator meet to prepare for trial?

13. What things might a testifying investigator consider before entering the courtroom?

14. How might a prosecution summary assist an investigator in preparing for trial?

■ Bibliography

Becker, R.F. (1995). *The underwater crime scene: Underwater crime investigative techniques.* Springfield, IL: Charles C. Thomas.

CHAPTER

22

Expert Testimony

▶ ▶ STUDENT LEARNING OUTCOMES

Upon completion of this chapter students will demonstrate an understanding of:

- What an expert witness is
- The history of expert witnesses
- The test for the admissibility of scientific evidence
- The test for admissibility of expert witnesses
- The role of contemporary expert witnesses in criminal trials
- The role of the police expert witness in the criminal trial

■ Expert Witnesses: A Brief History

The Feudal Era

In tracing the roots of the use of expert witnesses to resolve disputes, it is necessary to begin in the feudal era. Medieval history reveals that the roots of feudalism were in the third through the sixth centuries and many practices were established between the sixth and ninth centuries. Merovingian and Carolingian kings paid their generals and administrators with grants of land; in the ninth century these fiefs became hereditary and semi-independent (Durant, 1950). In those times, Western European society consisted of freemen, serfs, and slaves. Freemen included nobles, clerics, professional soldiers, practitioners of the professions, most merchants and artisans, and peasants who owned their land or leased it from a feudal lord.

The feudal law of property recognized three forms of land possession:

1. The **allod**, land held by unconditional ownership
2. The **fief**, land whose use but not ownership was granted to a vassal on condition of service
3. **Tenure**, land use granted on condition of payment

Typically, the serf tilled a plot of land owned by a lord or baron, who gave him a life tenure and military protection as long as the serf paid an annual rent in products, labor, or money. In feudal theory, only the king had absolute ownership of the land. The loftiest of nobles was only a tenant (Durant, 1950).

As disputes involving land use and succession arose, manorial courts were established to settle disputes between tenants, or between tenant and lord; disputes between lord and

> **CASE IN POINT**
>
> **Truth by Ordeal**
> Truth by ordeal has a history that extends beyond the Old Testament and has been applied by aborigines of the Australian Outback, Africans, and Scandinavians (Holland, 1995). The Old Testament speaks of poison as a truth determiner, and it was used in that vein in Africa and India (Holland, 1995). The ordeal was superstition applied to resolve legal disputes: the belief that a supreme being would not let an innocent person suffer provided the foundation. God or the gods were called upon to serve as an expert in assisting the trier of fact in determining guilt or innocence. The ordeal took many forms, from walking on red-hot plowshares to being bound and thrown in a pond. The conventional wisdom was that witches would not allow themselves to drown, and the innocent would sink. Dead but guiltless was the desired outcome. Obviously, an "expert" postulated the "facts" that witches float and that innocent people walking across red-hot plowshares will not be burned.

vassal or lord and lord were submitted to juries of men of equal standing and of the same fief. Procedure in feudal law attempted to substitute public penalties for private revenge. In a regime where judges and executors of law were usually illiterate, custom and law were largely one. When questions arose as to law or penalties, the oldest members of the community were asked what had been the custom thereon in their youth. Age and recall were the required characteristics for admitting their learned opinion. The community itself was the chief source of law, and the elders of the community were called as experts by the court to assist in a consistent application of an unwritten law and its penalties.

The Inquisition

Any nation preparing for war is well advised to—and often does—seek out minor skirmishes to prepare troops and equipment for major engagements. The Church of Rome was no exception. The continuing war on heresy that culminated in the **papal inquisition** began with a series of inquisitional skirmishes that had their justification steeped in the Old Testament. The Old Testament laid down a simple code for dealing with heretics: they were to be carefully examined; and if three reputable witnesses testified to their having "gone and served other gods," the heretics were to be led out from the city and "stoned with stones until they die" (Deuteronomy 17:25).

In classical Rome, where the gods were allied with the state in close harmony, **heresy** and blasphemy were classed with treason and were punishable with death. Where no accuser could be found to denounce an offender, the Roman judge summoned the suspect and made an **inquisitio**, or inquiry, into the case; from this procedure the medieval inquisition took its form and name.

It was the general assumption of Christians that the Son of God had established the Church. On this assumption, any attack upon the Catholic faith was an offense against God Himself. The stubbornly disobedient heretic could only be viewed as an agent of Satan sent to undo the work of Christ, and any man or government that tolerated heresy was serving the devil. The Church looked upon heresy precisely as the state looked upon treason: it was an attack upon the very foundation of social order. "The civil law," said Pope Innocent III, "punishes traitors with confiscation of their property, and death. . . . All the more, then, should we excommunicate, and confiscate the property of those who are traitors to the faith of Jesus Christ; for it is an infinitely greater sin to offend the divine majesty than to attack the majesty of the sovereign" (Durant, 1950, p. 777).

Before the 13th century, inquisition into heresy had been left to local bishops, who waged local wars against a rising tide of heresy. Berthold of Regensburg estimated there were 150 heretical sects in the 13th century. Most of these were harmless groups who gathered to study the Bible without the assistance of a priest and to interpret various passages as they saw fit. Many felt that priests should live in poverty, as did Christ. The Franciscan movement arose as such a sect, and narrowly escaped being treated as heretical.

In 1185, Pope Lucius III, dissatisfied with the negligence of the bishops in pursuing heresy, ordered them to visit their parishes at least once a year to arrest all suspects, to reckon as guilty any who would not swear full loyalty to the Church, and to hand over such recalcitrants to the government. Papal legates were empowered to depose bishops negligent in stamping out heresy. In 1215, Innocent III required all civil authorities, on pain of death, to swear publicly to exterminate all heretics from the lands subject to their obedience.

When Gregory IX mounted the papal throne (1227), he found that despite prosecutions, heresy was growing in most of Italy and France. Pope Gregory appointed a board of inquisitors, headed by a Dominican monk, to sit in Florence and bring the heretics to judgment. This in effect was the beginning of the papal Inquisition. The Inquisition was now officially established under the control of the popes.

After 1227, Gregory and his successors sent out an increasing number of special inquisitors to pursue heresy. Inquisitorial procedure might begin with the summary arrest of all charged heretics, sometimes also of all suspects; the visiting inquisitors might summon the entire adult population of a locality for a preliminary examination. Heretics who did not confess were cited before the inquisitorial court. Accused persons could be tried in their absence and condemned to death. Two condemnatory witnesses were required. After 1254, the inquisitors were required to submit all evidence to a group of men of high repute from the community. Often a board of experts (*periti*) was called upon to pass judgment on the evidence.

During this process, three legal precedents were established that have endured to our benefit:

1. Confessions must be voluntary.
2. A suspect cannot be convicted on the uncorroborated testimony of an accomplice.
3. The concept of burden of proof rests upon the accusing party.

Interestingly, the rationale for using torture to solicit incriminating statements was based on a benevolent motive. The Church believed that it was necessary to prove guilt beyond not just a reasonable doubt but beyond all doubt. The only way that all doubt could be removed was through self-incrimination. The end sought was admirable; it was the means to that end that we now question.

Experts and the Common Law

In early English common law history, there seems to have been two modes of using expert knowledge:

1. To select as jurymen such persons as were by experience especially fitted to know the class of facts that were before them
2. To call to the aid of the court skilled persons whose opinion it might adopt or not as it pleased

The first mode has been lost, but the second is alive and well, along with a third, more contemporary, application of having the parties in dispute bring forth skilled persons to testify.

The first method was to impanel a **special jury**, which in this context means a jury of persons especially fitted to judge the peculiar facts of the case in issue. The first recorded incidence of such a special jury was in 1838 (*Rey v. Wyoherly,* 8 C&P, 1838). A jury of persons especially skilled in landlord-tenant relations was impaneled, and the court followed its opinions in disposing of the matter. This specially impaneled jury was no anomaly; its use in resolving trade disputes was common in the city of London throughout the 14th century (Riley, 1868).

The special jury continued as an institution of England. We find in 1645 that the court summoned a jury of merchants to try merchants' affairs because it was conceived they might have a better understanding of the issues in dispute than others who were not of the profession (Hand, 1901).

The second method discussed was to summon the advice of certain skilled persons to help the court out of its difficulties. In 1345, in an appeal of mayhem, the court summoned surgeons from London to aid them in determining whether or not a wound was fresh (Riley, 1868). In 1409 and 1555, documents submitted to the court that were partly in Latin prompted the justices to seek grammatical masters to assist in the interpretation and construction of the documents (*Buckley v. Thomas, I Plow.* 118, 1555). Lord Holt of the Kings Bench, in deciding the celebrated case of *Buller v. Crips* (1703), asked the opinion of London merchants as to the effect of refusing negotiability of promissory notes.

Originally, and for many years under common law trial practice, the jury had no witnesses present before them at all. They were advised of the issues in dispute and were allowed to cast about at their own discretion in gathering what facts might be available. Those facts were brought with them to the court and considered among the jurors during their deliberations. It was not until the middle of the 15th century that the courts developed the practice of summoning witnesses for the purpose of providing testimony, and it was still later that compulsory process became available (Hand, 1901).

The rules of evidence in England evolved slowly and were focused upon the regulation of what evidence the jury could see and hear. Through successive court decisions, judges gradually restricted the material that witnesses might present to the jury. The rule that a witness may not testify to mere opinion was promulgated. The rule was designed to eliminate irrelevant and redundant testimony. An exception to this rule was made for experts.

Obviously, the exception for experts was an anomaly in procedural law that was the resort of the court when an issue was reached that was beyond its ken. This anomaly for the benefit of the court was extended to trial adversaries in 1678 in the case of *Rex v. Green.* This was a trial for murder, and the question was raised as to the cause and mechanism of death. Out of an abundance of caution, the court allowed both sides to present physicians as witnesses, thereby balancing the latitude granted the parties. The court thus delegated the exception that it had reserved unto itself to trial adversaries in the hopes that expert opinion to assist the court could be anticipated and provided for by the litigant. This case gave birth to the fledgling industry of expert witnesses, as the common law of England was applied to the trial practice of the United States.

■ Contemporary Expert Witnesses

Who Is a Scientific Expert?

Scientific evidence can come before the jury only from the mouth of an expert witness. Occasionally, controversy surrounds a particular practice, bringing into question whether such a practice or procedure is in fact scientific (see the Case in Point). In 2004, we have seen courts deny fingerprint experts the latitude to testify that fingerprint comparisons are a "match."

The U.S. Supreme Court in 1993 decided in ***Daubert v. Merrill Dow Pharmaceuticals*** that federal trial court judges were obligated to evaluate the basis of expert testimony in order to determine its reliability and value to the jury. Since 1993, the Supreme Court has decided another expert testimony case, ***Kumho Tire Co. v. Carmichael*** (1999). These two cases have established the criteria for the admissibility of expert testimony in federal and state courts.

Lower courts have been busy defining and applying the new expert witness standards to the various circumstances in which experts may be called to testify. Historically, anyone with information that could assist the judge or jury in understanding facts relevant to issues in question could be admitted as an expert witness. The *Daubert* decision and its line of cases suggest that the Supreme Court favors expert testimony and the opinions expressed therein that are based on replicable data gathered through acceptable scientific methodology. This has meant that experts with no research support for their opinions have found courts unwilling to qualify them as experts.

Courts struggled with the task of determining the reliability of expert testimony for the better part of the 20th century. In 1923, the circuit court of appeals for the District of Columbia developed the first test for assessing expert testimony. In ***Frye v. United States*** (1923), the court held that for novel scientific evidence to be admissible, the party offering it must establish that the expert testimony and the techniques used to generate the results have been generally accepted as reliable in the scientific community. The "general acceptance" test was plagued with problems from the outset. The terms were vague and susceptible to subjective interpretation by the courts, allowing trial judges to control the admissibility of expert testimony based on what they personally believed was credible and reliable.

CASE IN POINT

Questionable Experts of the Past

Experts can be a source of chicanery and ignorance as well as insight. In 1781, Sir William Herschel, the British astronomer who discovered the planet Uranus, was convinced and publicly pronounced that the "sun was richly stored with inhabitants" (Gardner, 1957). Physicians of the 19th century were encouraged by Dr. Linard Williams, the medical officer to the Insurance Institute of London, to treat people with wide-set eyes as one would horses or cows because the set of their eyes suggested they were not evolved from meat-eating predators but rather from vegetarian bovines and equines (Gardner, 1957). Even the noted physicist Lord Kelvin believed that x-rays were a hoax (Gardner, 1957). Had these scientists been called as expert witnesses in their questionable areas of expertise, what havoc would have been wreaked upon an unsuspecting jury and court? Although Sir William Herschel was an eminent astronomer, could he and should he have been allowed to testify as to the inhabitants of the sun?

EXHIBIT 22-1   Federal Rule of Evidence 702

> If scientific, technical, or other specialized knowledge will assist the trier of fact to understand the evidence or to determine a fact in issue, a witness qualified as an expert by knowledge, skill, experience, training or education may testify thereto in the form of an opinion or otherwise.

The attack on the general acceptance test escalated in the years following the 1975 adoption of the Federal Rules of Evidence. Proponents for the elimination of the test argued that the federal rules superseded *Frye* and were void of any reference to the general acceptance standard. In 1993, the debate over *Frye* reached a climax when the Supreme Court granted certiorari in *Daubert* and decided that ***Federal Rule of Evidence 702*** superseded the Frye test (**EXHIBIT 22-1**).

Proponents of the general acceptance *Frye* test argued that this ruling would open the floodgates to unfounded and unreliable evidence. They feared that juries would be misled and confused by evidence that was not credible and generally accepted in the scientific community. The Court addressed these concerns by laying the task of managing the admission of evidence on the trial judge. The Court listed four nonexclusive factors to be considered when evaluating expert testimony:

1. Whether the theory can be tested
2. Whether the theory or technique has been subjected to peer review as well as publication
3. The potential rate of error
4. The existence and maintenance of standards controlling the technique's operation

The Court in *Daubert* attempted to address what it saw as an inflexible and problematic test for determining admissibility under *Frye*. Despite the Court's attempt to liberalize the admission of expert testimony, the *Daubert* ruling resulted in more confusion. Rather than liberalize the standards for expert testimony, many courts used *Daubert* to create a more stringent test for expert evidence admissibility.

In 1999 the Supreme Court decided the case of *Kumho Tire Co. v. Carmichael*. The intent of the holding in *Kumho* was to grant trial courts broader discretion in determining the reliability of expert testimony. The Court stated that the expert checklist provided in *Daubert* was merely advisory and that courts were free to employ a broad spectrum of discretion in admitting expert testimony. The list was never intended to be exhaustive or all-inclusive.

Because of the Court's recent decision on expert testimony and the lack of uniformity in the district courts in applying *Kumho*, the advisory committee for the Federal Rules of Evidence proposed an amendment to Rule 702 that reads:

If scientific, technical, or other specialized knowledge will assist the trier of fact to understand the evidence or to determine a fact in issue, a witness qualified as an expert by knowledge, skill, experience, training, or education may testify thereto in the form of an opinion or otherwise if (1) the testimony is based upon sufficient facts or data, (2) the testimony is the product of reliable principles and methods, and (3) the witness has applied the principles and methods reliably to the facts of the case. (Committee on Rules of Practice and Procedure, 26)

The proposed amendment, consistent with Kumho, would provide that all types of expert testimony be subject to an admissibility determination by the trial court based on evidence of reliability.

The standards set forth by Mark McCormick are as relevant today as they were in 1982 in providing guidance regarding the probative value of proffered scientific evidence. McCormick offered the following factors to be considered in a probative analysis of the admissibility of scientific evidence (McCormick, 1982):

- The potential error rate in using the technique
- The existence and maintenance of standards governing its use
- Analogy to other scientific techniques whose results are admissible
- The extent to which the technique has been accepted by scientists in the field involved
- The nature and breadth of the inference adduced
- The clarity and simplicity with which the technique can be described and its results explained
- The extent to which the basic data are verifiable by the court and jury
- The availability of other experts to test and evaluate the technique
- The probative significance of the evidence in the circumstances of the cases
- The care with which the technique was employed in the case

Expert witness testimony has become a growth industry. Courts are becoming more reliant on scientific evidence. This reliance appears to be the product of three correlative factors. First, society is becoming ever more dependent on technology to provide answers. Second, forensic applications were greatly enhanced when the federal government approved an infusion of funds into the Law Enforcement Assistance Administration (LEAA) for the upgrade of law enforcement. And finally, the U.S. Supreme Court under Chief Justice Earl Warren restricted the admissibility of evidence under the Fourth, Fifth, and Sixth Amendments that had been secure under traditional police methods and admonished that new investigative skills needed to be developed and applied to criminal investigations (Farley, 1993).

The number of criminal trials relying in whole or part on scientific evidence and expert testimony has increased dramatically. The police misconduct that the Supreme Court has been concerned with to a large extent has been replaced by forensic investigation and evidence. More professionals are spending more time testifying in criminal cases than ever before. Expert witness fees may exceed $600 per hour. Professional bar journals abound with advertisements for expert trial assistance. The classified section of many bar journals, heretofore the purview of those seeking to fill legal positions, is rapidly giving way to experts hawking their wares.

In the midst of a technical revolution in the courtroom, police, investigators, prosecutors, defense lawyers, jurors and judges prepare to do battle by focusing on scientific circumstantial evidence admitted or refuted by expert witnesses. For every prosecution expert, there will be an equally credentialed opposing expert ready and willing to take exception to the work of prosecution experts.

The Police Expert in Criminal Trials

Although police are not scientists, they are experts and are often granted the latitude of an expert witness in their testimony. The example that most readily comes to mind is that of a police officer testifying as to the intoxicated state of a motorist. After it has been demonstrated that the officer has had experience dealing with people who have been proven to be intoxicated, the examining attorney will often ask if in the officer's opinion the motorist was intoxicated. Prior to breath analysis and video cameras, a police officer's testimony was the only vehicle through which intoxication could be proven. When a defendant refuses to provide a breath sample, police may resort to the traditional speech, gait, and bloodshot eye trilogy during their testimony. This type of testimony usually went something like this:

Q: Was there anything notable about the defendant's speech?
A: Yes, his speech was slurred.
Q: Was there anything notable about the defendant's gait?
A: Yes, his gait was unsteady.
Q: Was there anything notable about the defendant's eyes?
A: Yes, his eyes were bloodshot.
Q: Was there anything notable about the defendant's breath?
A: Yes, the defendant's breath smelled as though he had consumed alcoholic beverages.
Q: Have you seen people who in your estimation were under the influence of alcohol?
A: Yes.
Q: On one occasion or many occasions?
A: On many occasions.
Q: Based on your observations of the defendant, have you an opinion as to whether or not the defendant was intoxicated?
A: Yes.
Q: And what is that opinion?
A: I believe the defendant was intoxicated at the time of the arrest.

Police and investigators testify as **police experts** in identifying the odor of burning marijuana, caliber of firearms, approximate speeds, entrance wounds, exit wounds, and so on every day somewhere. It should be apparent that college educations and doctoral degrees are not the only expert services that the court may rely upon.

Criminal investigators today are more scientifically oriented than ever before. Much of what they do involves threshold scientific principles. In discussing the discovery of fibers, fingerprints, blood, drugs, and bodies and their decomposition, however, it is important to remember that the expertise that investigators have in these areas is limited and does not make them scientists. Any testimony by an investigator regarding forensic evidence must be limited to its discovery and initial identification. Laboratory testing and lab results are the domain of forensic experts with scientific training that generally exceeds that of the average investigator. Opinions regarding forensic evidence are generally a product of a technician or scientist's work, and the role these opinions play in an investigation should be identified as the product of the efforts of the scientists and technicians who originated the opinion. In simplest terms, leave **scientific testimony** to the scientist.

■ Summary

It is good that the last chapter focuses on the role investigators provide that is the least appreciated. The role of the investigator is summed up in most films as:

- Arrive on the crime scene
- Make astounding assumptions based on observations
- Track a suspect endlessly
- Get involved in a high-speed pursuit
- Get involved in a shootout
- Arrest or recover the body of the perpetrator
- Go to closing credits

The real work of the investigator is reflected in the documents prepared in support of the investigation and ultimately in the testimony of that investigator in a court of law. Absent competent, sincere, credible testimony based on documents reflecting a Constitutionally permissible investigation it all comes to naught. Sitting and testifying from the witness box may not be exciting, but it is where we do our best work.

■ Key Terms

allod: Land held by unconditional ownership.

Daubert v. Merrill Dow Pharmaceuticals: Case in which the Supreme Court decided in 1993 that federal trial court judges were obligated to evaluate the basis of expert testimony in order to determine its reliability and value to the jury

Federal Rule of Evidence 702: A federal rule stating that if scientific, technical, or other specialized knowledge will assist the trier of fact to understand the evidence or to determine a fact in issue, a witness qualified as an expert by knowledge, skill, experience, training or education may testify thereto in the form of an opinion or otherwise

fief: Land whose use but not ownership was granted to a vassal on condition of service

Frye v. United States: Case in which the first test for assessing expert testimony was developed; in this 1923 case, the circuit court of appeals for the District of Columbia held that for novel scientific evidence to be admissible, the party offering it must establish that the expert testimony and the techniques used to generate the results have been generally accepted as reliable in the scientific community

heresy: A belief inconsistent with a religion's dogma

inquisitio: Inquiry

Kumho Tire Co. v. Carmichael: An expert testimony case, decided by the Supreme Court in 1999, that has helped establish the criteria for the admissibility of expert testimony in federal and state courts

papal inquisition: The trying of heretics by the authority of the pope

police experts: Police officers who are often granted the latitude of expert witnesses in their testimony

scientific testimony: Testimony about information gathered from the evidence by scientific analysis, this type of testimony can only be performed by a science expert

special jury: In common law, a jury of persons especially fitted to judge the peculiar facts of the case in issue

tenure: land use granted on condition of payment

■ Review Questions

1. What were the allod, fief, and tenure as they related to feudal land?
2. What role did experts play in land ownership during the feudal period?
3. What precipitated the papal inquisition?
4. What role did a panel of experts play during the inquisition?
5. What did the inquisition contribute to contemporary American law?
6. Discuss the evolution of the use of expert testimony in early English law.
7. Who can be an expert for trial purposes?
8. How is it determined whether a person deserves expert status?
9. Discuss *Daubert, Kumho,* and *Frye* as they apply to expert testimony.
10. What constitutes an expert under Federal Rule of Evidence 702?

■ Bibliography

Committee on Rules of Practice and Procedure, Judicial Conference of the United States. (2001). *Preliminary draft of proposed amendments to the Federal Rules of Civil Procedure and Evidence.*

Durant, W. (1950). *The age of faith.* New York: Simon and Schuster.

Farley, M. (1993). Legal standards for the admissibility of novel scientific evidence. In F. Saferstein (Ed.), *Forensic science handbook, Vol. III.* Englewood Cliffs, NJ: Prentice Hall.

Gardner, M. (1957). *Fads and fallacies in the name of science.* New York: Ballantine.

Hand, L. (1901). Considerations regarding expert testimony. *Harvard Law Review* 1, 40–58.

Holland, B. (1995 March). Do you swear that you will well and truly try. . .? *Smithsonian,* 108–117.

McCormick, M. (1982). Scientific evidence: Defining a new approach to admissibility. *67 Iowa Law Review* 879, 911–912.

Riley, H.T. (1868). *Memorials of London and London life in the 13th, 14th, and 15th centuries.* London: Longmans, Green & Co.

■ Key Legal Cases

Buckley v. Thomas, I Plow. 118 (1555).
Buller v. Crips, 6 Mod. 29 (1703).
Daubert v. Merrill Dow Pharmaceuticals, Inc., 509 U.S. 592 (1993).
Frye v. United States, 293 F. 1013 (DC Cir., 1923).
Kumho Tire Co. v. Carmichael, 526 U.S. 137 (1999).
Rex v. Green, 6 Howell, State Trials (1678).
Rey v. Wyoherly, 8 C&P (1838).

Direct Examination of Fingerprint Experts

APPENDIX

A

■ Investigator Who Discovered and Lifted Prints

What follows is a sample of a direct examination of an investigator who discovered and lifted a latent fingerprint at a crime scene.

Q: Would you state your name please?

A: [Responds with full legal name.]

Q: Where do you live?

A: [This is a completely irrelevant question that the witness may choose not to answer. This question is so commonly asked that few lawyers bother to ask what relevance it may have to the testimony about to be elicited. If an investigator prefers that his or her home not be a matter of public record, the prosecutor should not ask this question.]

Q: What is your occupation [profession]?

A: [Gives specific function and organization.]

Q: How long have you served in that capacity?

A: [States approximate length of tenure and indicates answer is an approximation.]

Q: For whom did you work prior to holding this position?

A: [This question should initiate a review of all professional employment, with no gaps unaddressed. Approximate times and dates should suffice. The witness should describe one position at a time and wait for a prompt from the prosecutor before continuing. Keep in mind that the opposition has checked the witness's work history and may have a better command of that work record than does the witness.]

Q: Returning to your current employment, what is your responsibility pertaining to fingerprints and crime scenes?

A: Locating, visualizing [developing], photographing, and lifting fingerprints.

Q: To perform the type of work that you do, are there any educational or training requirements?

A: [Describes fully all relevant education, training, workshops, and seminars.]

Q: Is there a certification process required for the type of services you provide?

A: [Describes all certification requirements.]

Q: Have you testified in court before pertaining to fingerprint identification? ["Identification" may need to be replaced if objected to by the defense. Possible substitutes include "visualization," "development," and "lifting."]

A: Yes.

Q: How many times?

A: [An approximation may be acceptable if the number is large and the exact number is not known. An estimate must be identified as such.]

Q: In the course of your employment as a criminal investigator, approximately how many fingerprints have you discovered?

A: [An approximation will do.]

Q: In the course of your employment as a criminal investigator, approximately how many fingerprints have you developed using fingerprint powder?

A: [An approximation will do.]

Q: In the course of your employment as a criminal investigator, approximately how many fingerprints have you photographed?

A: [An approximation will do.]

Q: In the course of your employment as a criminal investigator, approximately how many fingerprints have you "lifted"?

A: [An approximation will do. Although not required in most jurisdictions, this is the point where a formal offer to the court would be made of the officer as having been qualified as an expert in the field of fingerprint discovery, fingerprint development, fingerprint photography, and fingerprint lifting. Once the officer is qualified and withstands impeachment efforts during the defendant's voir dire, the examination can continue and begin to focus on the evidence as opposed to the investigator's qualifications.]

Q: Can you tell us what a fingerprint is?

A: The pattern of the finger friction skin ridges left on a touched surface.

Q: Can you explain what you mean by finger friction skin ridges?

A: The raised ridges on the surface of the fingers and thumbs.

Q: Does everyone have such ridges?

A: Yes.

Q: Are these ridges unique to each individual?

A: To date, millions of fingerprints have been taken, and no two people have been found to have the identical fingerprint. [Simple answers are understandable and believable. The responsibility of the lawyer and the investigator is to conspire to make the complex understandable and the difficult simple. Language should facilitate communication. Technical jargon enhances communication between individuals who share the same vocabulary but it can be used for purposes other than communication, such as intimidation and sowing confusion. Unexplained technical jargon has no place in the courtroom. Simply put, any hard-to-grasp statement, whether made in a foreign language or a technical language, can be translated into words a well-educated 15-year-old can understand. If it cannot, the statement is not expressing a genuine thought or the speaker does not understand what he or she is saying. As a final reminder, keep it simple, keep it understandable, keep it believable.]

Q: Are there different types of fingerprints that can be left at a crime scene?

A: Yes.

Q: Can you describe them for us?

A: Visual, plastic, and latent.

Q: What is a visual print?

A: One that can be seen with the naked eye.

Q: Can you give the jury an example?

A: If a finger contacts oil, paint, blood, or some similar material, it may leave an impression of the finger ridges.

Q: What is a plastic print?

A: The best example of a plastic print would be the impression left after a child pressed his or her hand onto a wet cement sidewalk. [If another example was especially relevant to the case, it should be cited instead.]

Q: What is a latent print?

A: Finger friction skin ridges have pores through which sweat is released. These friction ridges may also pick up oils as a result of hand and finger contact with the face and hair. These oils and sweat may be deposited on a surface in the pattern of the friction skin ridges of the finger or fingers that made contact with that surface.

Q: Will you describe to the jury how such an invisible fingerprint is found at a crime scene?

A: There are two general ways in which a latent print can be found: by randomly applying powder to various surfaces the suspect may have touched or by shining upon such surfaces certain types of lights at an angle.

Q: Once you have found a latent print, what then do you do with it?

A: If it appears upon examination under a magnifying glass that the print has sufficient ridge characteristics, we will develop it, photograph it, and lift it. If the number of identifiable ridge characteristics is small, it is likely that cross-examination will focus on whether there is a sufficient number of identifiable ridge characteristics. A comparison of a crime scene latent print having few ridges and the defendant's inked fingerprint impression can still be meaningful if a chart-sized enlargement is used to show the similarities. Such demonstrative evidence can be introduced at this juncture.

Q: I hand you what has been marked as State's Exhibit No. 1 and ask you if you can identify it.

A: It is an enlargement of a fingerprint. [Any objection at this point should be overruled if the enlargement is simply being used for demonstrative purposes and not as evidence. If the enlargement is of the defendant's inked fingerprint and this enlargement is going to be used for comparison purposes, it can be admitted later. Reference to this enlargement will again be made during the direct examination of the expert who is going to provide comparison testimony, and it will be proven up and entered into evidence at that time. Assume that this witness will not provide comparison testimony.]

Q: Will you point out for the jurors where the finger friction skin ridges are represented?

A: [Approaches the enlargement and does so.]

Q: Once you have discovered a latent print with sufficient ridge characteristics, what would you do with it?

A: Photograph it.

Q: Would you take the photograph?

A: Yes.

Q: What type of camera do you use to photograph the latent impression once you have found it on an object at a crime scene?

A: It is a camera specially designed for fingerprint photography.

Q: How does it work?

A: The lens tube is placed around the latent impression so that the impression is centered and the lens and camera produce a negative that is the same size as the impression. It is a 35-mm single-reflex, autofocus camera operating with a set of four strobe lights.

Q: After you photograph a latent fingerprint that you have made visible, what do you do with it?

A: It is marked, lifted, and mounted.

Q: How do you mark a fingerprint?

A: There is a paper backing upon which the fingerprint will be mounted after being lifted. That paper backing has information lines for time, date, case identification number, and technician name. This information is recorded prior to lifting the print.

Q: What do you do with the latent print after you have marked it?

A: I lift the print.

Q: Will you explain to the jury what you mean when you say you lift the print?

A: A lift is a transparent tape backed by a silicon-treated piece of paper. The tape is hinged at one end of the paper to allow the transparent tape to be separated from the paper, allowing the tape to be placed over the visualized impression, adhesive side down. The tape is smoothed over the impression, then lifted straight up. When the procedure is done correctly, the powder, in the shape of the impression, will then stick to the adhesive side of the tape, which is then placed back on top of the silicon-treated paper and smoothed out again.

Q: Once the latent impression has been photographed, marked, and lifted, what is done with it?

A: It is submitted to the laboratory for identification, classification, and comparison.

Q: Did you do the identification, classification, and comparison?

A: [The answer to this question will depend on department's resources and standard procedure. Often the lifting investigator does not provide any further services, in which case an additional witness would be required to answer the questions pertaining to classification and comparison.]

Q: Have you ever been to [location of crime scene]?

A: Yes.

Q: When specifically?

A: [Provides the dates of any and all visits.]

Q: Did you discover any latent prints on any of those visits?

A: [A simple yes may be the proper answer, or it may be necessary to state that other investigators or technicians discovered the prints.]

Q: How many?

A: [States total discovered, total developed, total photographed, and the total lifted.]

Q: What did you do with the various impressions that you discovered?

A: Developed [visualized], photographed, marked, lifted, and submitted them to the laboratory.

Q: When you first arrived on the scene, were there any other persons present?

A: Yes.

Q: Who?

A: [Names all persons on the premises.]

Q: Were there finger impressions found at the scene that belonged to any of these people?

A: Yes, there were impressions left by the victim and occupants of the residence as well as those of certain police personnel.

Q: How did you determine that these individuals left fingerprint impressions at the crime scene?

A: We took inked impressions of all persons whom we knew to have been on the premises.

Q: What is an inked impression?

A: Finger friction skin ridge patterns resulting from placing individual fingers and thumbs from both hands onto an inked pad, then pressing those fingers and thumbs onto a piece of white cardboard. The ink transfers the finger friction skin ridge patterns onto the cardboard. These inked impressions can then be compared to the latent prints lifted at the crime scene to eliminate the prints of those who had legitimate access to the premises.

Q: What types of objects did you dust for latent prints?

A: [Lists all surfaces dusted.]

Q: Referring to State's Exhibit No. 2, would you point out the location of the broken glass [item] you dusted?

A: [Points out the location of the glass on the crime scene diagram of the glass dusted. If the exhibit is placed at a distance from the witness stand, it will be necessary to approach the diagram.]

Q: Now will you please mark the glass represented on the diagram you are referring to with your initials, and today's date in black ink?

A: [Does so.]

Q: I now hand you what has been marked as State's Exhibit No. 3 and ask you if you recognize it.

A: Yes, I recognize it.

Q: What is it?

A: It is a piece of the glass from the crime scene from which I lifted a number of latent prints.

Q: How do you know this is the same piece of glass?

A: I marked the glass with my initials, the case number, and the date I lifted the print [or: I tagged the evidence, including my name, the date, and the case number].

Q: Has this item been changed in any way since last you saw it?

A: No.

Q: Would you demonstrate for the judge and jury the manner in which you dusted State's Exhibit No. 3 for development of latent impressions?

A: [A very effective demonstrative method is to use an overhead projector. Placing the thumb on the glass will leave a latent print that cannot be seen until the fingerprint powder is dropped and the excess powder removed. The entire process can be projected onto a large screen, and the judge and jury can actually see the print visualized as the excess powder is removed. The witness should provide an oral description of what he or she is doing. Once the impression has been dusted, the investigator should write in the dust his or her name, the crime scene location, and the case identification number. These etchings can be lifted along with the print, tagging and mounting the print simultaneously.]

Q: I again hand you what has been labeled as State's Exhibit No. 3 and ask you where you discovered the latent impressions on it.

A: [Points out from where the latents were lifted.]

Q: What did you do with the latent impressions after you visualized them?

A: I photographed them.

Q: Using the type of camera you have previously described?

A: Yes.

Q: Did you examine the camera before you used it?

A: Yes.

Q: What did you find?

A: It was in good working order.

Q: What did you do after you photographed the latent impressions?

A: I lifted them and the marked information written in the excess fingerprint powder.

Q: Will you demonstrate how you lifted those impressions and the writing in the excess fingerprint powder?

A: [Returning to the overhead projector, the witness demonstrates how the hinged lift was placed onto the print and writing, smoothed, and lifted. The witness also demonstrates how the lifted materials were mounted on the silicon-backed paper. The witness should provide a running narrative describing the procedure.]

Q: Once you lifted the impression, what did you do with it?

A: I turned it over and printed on the back of the silicon-backed paper my initials, the time, the date, the location of the premises, and the location within the premises where the lift was taken.

Q: I now hand you State's Exhibit No. 4 and ask you if you recognize it.

A: Yes.

Q: Does State's Exhibit No. 4 truly and accurately portray the latent impressions that you observed on the surface of the glass found at the scene of the crime on the date in question?

A: It does.

Q: At what time did you leave the crime scene with the latents represented in State's Exhibit No. 4?

A: [Gives approximate time, but answer must be substantiated by evidence logs.]

Q: At what time did you arrive at the crime laboratory?

A: [Gives approximate time, but answer must be substantiated by evidence log.]

Q: Was State's Exhibit No. 4 in your possession during that time? [This question and its answer are necessary for chain-of-custody purposes.]

A: Yes. [If it was not, witness must account for all times not in possession.]

Q: I now hand you what has been marked as State's Exhibit No. 5 and ask you if you recognize it.

A: Yes.

Q: What is it?

A: A photographic negative.

Q: A photographic negative of what?

A: A photographic negative of the latent impressions on the glass found at the crime scene.

Q: A photographic negative of the latent impressions that you have previously identified as State's Exhibit No. 4?

A: That's correct.

Q: When was the first time you saw this photographic negative?

A: [Provides the specific date and time the film was developed.]

Q: Whose writing appears within the photographic negative on the card located next to the impression?

A: Mine.

Q: What does that writing say?

A: [Reads name, date, time, location, and case identification number.]

Q: Is that from the identifying card you placed next to the prints?

A: Yes.

Q: Is it a fair and accurate representation of the latent impressions as you observed them on the surface of the glass found on the floor in the living room of the house at [address of the crime scene] that you lifted on [date lifted]?

A: Yes.

Q: Did you submit the negative described as State's Exhibit No. 5 to the identification and comparison section of the police laboratory?

A: Yes.

Q: Has it been changed in any way?

A: [If any identifying information has been appended to the photographic negative, it should be described as a change.]

Q: Other than what you have told us, has this photographic negative been altered in any way?

A: No.

The above authentication and chain-of-custody predicate must be provided for each group of latent impressions lifted that is going to be used in evidence, minus the developing, marking, and lifting demonstrations. If latents are discovered on fixed objects that cannot be carried into the courtroom, the locations of these objects should be indicated by stating, in feet and inches, how far they lie from recognizable points and in what direction (e.g., 6 inches below the doorknob on the bedroom door in the southeast bedroom of the premises).

■ Latent Fingerprint Identification Expert

Q: Would you state your name please?

A: [Responds with full legal name.]

Q: Where do you live?

A: [Although having nothing to do with the facts at issue, background questions are designed to put the witness at ease by asking nonthreatening questions that require little thought. However, it may not be prudent to provide such intimate information to the defendant, friends of the defendant, or other potential assailants.]

Q: What is your occupation [profession]?

A: [Gives specific function and organization.]

Q: How long have you served in that capacity?

A: [States approximate length of tenure and indicates answer is an approximation.]

Q: For whom did you work prior to this position?

A: [This question should initiate a review of all professional employment.]

Q: Returning to your current employment, what is your present assignment?

A: I work with the fingerprint identification section of [name of agency].

Q: To perform the type of work that you do, are there any educational or training requirements?

A: [Describes fully all relevant education, training, workshops, and seminars.]

Q: Is there a certification process required for the types of services you provide?

A: [Describes all certification requirements.]

Q: Have you ever published an article pertaining to your work? [This question should be asked only if such publications exist.]

A: Yes [or no].

Q: Describe each relevant article.

A: [Gives title, publisher, and summary.]

Q: Do you belong to any professional organizations? [This question should be asked only if such membership exists and is relevant.]

A: Yes [or no].

Q: Have you taught any seminars, workshops, or classes pertaining to your area of specialization? [This question should be asked only if such teaching has occurred.]

A: Yes [or no].

Q: Have you ever testified in court pertaining to fingerprint identification?

A: Yes.

Q: How many times?

A: [An approximation may be acceptable if the number is large and the exact number is not known. An estimate must be identified as such.]

Q: How many times have you testified on behalf of the state?

A: [An approximation will do if the specific number is not known.]

Q: In the course of your employment in fingerprint identification, approximately how many fingerprints have you identified?

A: [An approximation will do.]

Q: In the course of your employment in fingerprint identification, approximately how many fingerprint comparisons have you completed?

A: [An approximation will do.]

Q: What is the purpose of the crime laboratory identification section?

A: To maintain fingerprint files and databases, arrest records, photographic files, and mug shots of people who have been arrested as well as files of active fingerprint impressions that are part of ongoing investigations.

Q: What is the function of the latent fingerprint section?

A: To receive photographs, negatives, and lifts of latent fingerprints that have been processed by the crime laboratory technicians and to evaluate these impressions to determine if they are suitable for comparison purposes and, upon request, to perform fingerprint comparisons.

Q: Can you tell me what fundamental principles the science of fingerprints is based on?

A: It is based on the immutability and uniqueness of skin patterns. As regards immutability, the skin that covers the inside of the fingers, the palms, and the soles of the feet is formed in about the fourth month of fetal life, and the skin patterns remain unchanged throughout a person's life until destroyed by death and decomposition. As regards uniqueness, no given area of friction skin is ever duplicated on the body of the same person or the body of another person.

Q: In your study of the science of fingerprints and in your years of experience, have you ever encountered, read about, or heard about two people who had identical fingerprints?

A: No.

Q: What is a latent fingerprint or impression?

A: The word latent means "hidden from view" or "invisible." In the science of fingerprints, only those fingerprints that cannot be seen with the unaided eye are latent prints. But as a result of police and media usage, latent print has come to mean any fingerprint impression that has inadvertently been left on a relatively smooth surface at the scene of a crime.

Q: What is an inked impression or inked fingerprint?

A: An impression of the friction ridges on a finger or thumb that results from applying ink to the finger or thumb and then pressing that digit onto a piece of nonabsorbent paper attached to a fingerprint card.

Q: What is the difference between an inked impression and a latent print?

A: An inked impression is recorded intentionally and a latent print is left inadvertently.

Q: Does finger friction ridge skin form identifiable patterns?

A: Yes.

Q: Would you explain what these patterns are?

A: There are three basic types: loops, whorls, and arches. [It would be helpful at this juncture for the witness to refer to various exhibits depicting these patterns while describing each.]

Q: Of what value is the ability to identify fingerprint pattern types?

A: It assists us in making comparisons between inked impressions and latent fingerprints.

Q: Does everyone have loop, whorl, and arch patterns?

A: No. The most common ridge characteristics are loops. About 65% of all fingerprint patterns on file are loops. Whorls make up about 35% of all patterns on file, and arches, the least common, make up about 5% of fingerprint patterns.

Q: Do ridge characteristics differ from person to person?

A: No, the lines that make the ridges and patterns are common stuff; however, their location and their relationship to one another differ. We may have any combination of patterns: only loops; loops and arches; loops and whorls; arches and whorls; and loops, arches, and whorls. Sometimes there is more than one pattern in a print.

Q: Can you describe for the jury the procedure that you employ in comparing a latent impression with an inked impression?

A: I examine the prints by placing both under a dual-lens magnifying glass. By adjusting the focus, I can examine both prints simultaneously. [If a fingerprint comparator is used, it needs to be described.] It is readily apparent if the patterns are of the same type. If they are, a closer examination of the ridges that make up the pattern will display a similarity in length, spacing, forking, and divergence. By grouping these characteristics in one print, I should be able to readily determine if that group of characteristics is present in the other. It is not necessary that an entire pattern be recognized in order to compare two prints. Parts of a latent pattern have characteristics that can be grouped and used to compare them to an inked impression. Two characteristics within a pattern will allow me to count the ridges between those characteristics, providing further assistance in identifying the latent print. [At this point, it would be helpful to demonstrate to the jury how this process is conducted. Again using an overhead projector, the expert can place a partial thumbprint on the projector screen in full or partial display. Once developed, the print should be covered with a lift but not lifted. Next to the developed partial print, the expert can roll a full impression of his thumb and develop it, covering the rolled impression with a lift. Now the grouping of characteristics and ridge counting can be conducted while the entire jury watches. It can be helpful to point out the core of the print, bifurcations, deltas, and other distinguishing features on both impressions. If the witness works in a computer-literate agency, he or she could use one of a number of software programs to capture the same procedure on computer disk. The entire demonstration can be prepared prior to trial and displayed using a computer projection panel and a screen. However, there is much to be gained by using the overhead projector method, because it demonstrates the development techniques, thereby reinforcing their familiarity and reliability.]

Q: In examining a latent fingerprint left at a crime scene, is it common to have the entire finger friction ridge skin pattern of that finger?

A: No. More often than not, the pattern is fragmentary. You seldom get an entire fingerprint.

Q: How much of the finger friction skin ridge pattern of a latent print is required in order to compare that latent print with an inked impression?

A: An identification can be made from a latent print that is an eighth of the size of the inked impression of the same finger if sufficient ridge characteristics are present. [The danger here is in trying to quantify how many ridge characteristics are enough; this can only be addressed by the expert's prior experience and training. The thing to remember is that the witness is the expert, and although opinions may differ, the witness's opinion, based on his or her experience and training, is as valid as that of another expert who may disagree. As questioning progresses, the use of enlargements of the latent and inked impressions and the pointing out of the comparable characteristics may make it apparent to the untrained eye that these prints are identical, obviating the issue of whether sufficient ridge characteristics exist.]

Q: Now, I would direct your attention to the morning of [appropriate date]. Were you working that morning?

A: Yes.

Q: How late did you stay?

A: [Gives departing time.]

Q: I hand you what has been marked as State's Exhibit No. 3 and ask you if you recognize it.

A: Yes.

Q: What is it?

A: A fingerprint that has been lifted after development or a photograph of a developed latent print.

Q: Do you know where this lift [photograph] came from?

A: Yes, it was provided to me by [name of lifting technician].

Q: When was that?

A: [Gives time and date.]

Q: What were you asked to do with this fingerprint?

A: To compare it to inked impressions.

Q: Were you provided inked impressions?

A: Yes.

Q: By whom?

A: [Gives name of the officer who took the inked impressions. Generally these inked impressions will be proven up (the predicate laid) by the investigating officer or the jail booking officer. If the witness has taken the inked impressions, then it will be necessary to ask the following questions.]

Q: I hand you what has been marked as State's Exhibit No. 6 and ask you to identify it.

A: It is a fingerprint card.

Q: What is on the card?

A: Inked fingerprint impressions.

Q: Who took these impressions?

A: I did.

Q: From whom were these inked impressions taken?

A: The defendant [name of the defendant].

Q: Is the man from whom these inked impressions were taken in the courtroom today?

A: Yes.

Q: Would you identify him please? [Having the witness point out the defendant is not a sufficient court identification. The proper identification method is to give a physical description of the defendant, including clothing and hair, and to state the defendant's location in the courtroom.]

Q: Was anyone else present when these impressions were taken?

A: Yes [or no].

Q: Who?

A: [Names all who witnessed the fingerprinting.]

Q: Is this fingerprint card dated?

A: Yes.

Q: What is the date?

A: [Provides the date.]

Q: Is this card signed?

A: Yes.

Q: By whom?

A: It bears my signature.

Q: After you took these impressions, what did you do with them?

A: I made them a part of case file [appropriate case file number].

Q: And where did you obtain them from in anticipation of your testimony here today?

A: From case file [appropriate case file number].

Q: Has this card been altered or changed in any way since the impressions were taken?

A: No.

Q: Did you provide the comparison that was requested of you?

A: Yes.

Q: What did you determine from your comparison of the impression lifted from the crime scene and the inked impressions of the defendant?

A: Based on ridge characteristics, I determined that these prints are identical.

Q: How many points of comparison did you establish between the latent print and the inked impression?

A: Eight. [Hopefully the number of points of comparison is no less than eight.]

Q: I hand you what has been marked as State's Exhibit No. 7 and ask you if you recognize it.

A: Yes.

Q: What is it?

A: An enlargement of the latent impression lifted at the crime scene.

Q: An enlargement of the same latent impression that has been entered as State's Exhibit No. 3?

A: Yes.

Q: Is the enlargement a fair and accurate representation of the latent as you recall it?

A: Yes.

Q: I hand you what has been marked as State's Exhibit No. 8 and ask you if you recognize it.

A: Yes.

Q: What is it?

A: An enlargement of one of the inked impressions of the defendant's finger from which inked impressions were taken.

Q: An enlargement of an inked impression contained in State's Exhibit No. 6?

A: Yes.

Q: Is the enlargement a fair and accurate representation of the inked impression as you recall it?

A: Yes.

Q: Will you take the two enlargements and point out and explain to the jury the first point of comparison you discerned that convinced you that these prints were identical?

A: Point 1 on the latent impression is an ending ridge.

Q: Point 1 on the inked impression?

A: An ending ridge.

Q: Point 2 on the latent impression?

A: Point 2 on the latent impression is an ending ridge.

Q: Point 2 on the inked impression?

A: Point 2 on the inked impression is an ending ridge.

Q: Point 3 on the latent impression?

A: Point 3 on the latent impression is an ending ridge.

Q: Point 3 on the inked impression?

A: Point 3 on the inked impression is an ending ridge.

Q: Point 4 on the latent impression?

A: Point 4 on the latent impression is a bifurcation.

Q: Point 4 on the inked impression?

A: Point 4 on the inked impression is a bifurcation.

Q: Point 5 on the latent impression?

A: Point 5 on the latent impression is a short ridge.

Q: Point 5 on the inked impression?

A: Point 5 on the inked impression is a short ridge.

Q: Point 6 on the latent impression?

A: Point 6 on the latent impression is an ending ridge.

Q: Point 6 on the inked impression?

A: Point 6 on the inked impression is an ending ridge.

Q: Point 7 on the latent impression?

A: Point 7 on the latent impression is an ending ridge.

Q: Point 7 on the inked impression?

A: Point 7 on the inked impression is an ending ridge.

Q: Point 8 on the latent impression?

A: Point 8 on the latent impression is an ending ridge.

Q: Point 8 on the inked impression?

A: Point 8 on the inked impression is an ending ridge.

Q: How many points of comparison are required in order to positively identify a latent impression?

A: The precise number is dependent upon how clear, complete, and unusual the characteristics are. In my opinion, no fewer than 8. Most authors agree that in no case are more than 12 necessary to positively establish identity.

Q: Based upon your experience, education, and training and the comparisons of the latent prints and the defendant's inked impressions, do you have an opinion, based on a reasonable scientific certainty, as to whether or not the same person made the latent impression and the inked impression?

A: Yes, I do.

Q: What is that opinion?

A: It is my opinion that the impression lifted at the crime scene is identical with fingerprint number 7 from the inked fingerprint card taken from the defendant and that they therefore were made by the same person.

Q: Based on your examination of the latent print lifted at the crime scene, do you have an opinion, based on a reasonable scientific certainty, as to the force with which it was applied?

A: It is my opinion, from an examination of the latent impression, that there was considerable force applied to the glass from which the print was lifted.

Q: How were you able to determine that?

A: The skin on the hand is pliable and the ridge structure will broaden when pressure is applied. In the latent impression, portions of the ridge structure have been broadened, narrowing the distance between ridges, which suggests the application of force.

Using this predicate as a guideline, there should be no procedural obstacles to the admissibility of the prints by the prosecution. However, the expert must be prepared to defend his or her testimony during cross examination by the defendant's attorney. The chain of custody may be questioned or the points of comparison may be challenged. The use of enlargements, however, should allow the jury to come to the same conclusion as the witness if the witness's testimony was credible and not reaching. An attempt to manufacture points of comparison will usually backfire. Use only those points of comparison upon which reasonable persons would agree.

Direct Examination of the Forensic Chemist

Following is a list of questions that a prosecuting attorney is likely to ask a forensic chemist during examination:

- What college degrees do you have?
- What on-the-job training have you undergone?
- Have you done postgraduate work?
- How many hours of university chemistry have you taken?
- Have you taken any courses in the following subjects: drug assay, spectroscopy, botany, and organic qualitative analysis?
- Has your analytical chemistry education included training in the analysis of abused drugs?
- How many prior court appearances have you made?
- For whom have you made these appearances?
- Do you or does your laboratory have a general protocol for the analysis of drugs? (See the end of the appendix for a description of an appropriate protocol.)
- Does your laboratory have a uniform set of tests that must be performed by all chemists before a suspected sample is reported as an illegal drug?
- Did you do a gross morphological analysis of the suspected controlled substance? If so, what information was yielded?
- Did you record your observations in a notebook?
- Did you do a microscopic analysis of the suspected controlled substance? If so, what information was yielded? [The witness should describe exactly what he or she saw. If marijuana was examined, were cystolith hairs seen? Many plants have cystolith hairs, and horse urine, like marijuana, will give a positive result when subjected to the Duquenois-Levine test. Forensic chemists often arrive at an identification of a drug based on nonspecific spot tests and refrain from doing confirmatory tests, to the misfortune of prosecuting attorneys.]
- Did you conduct a thin-layer chromatography on the suspected controlled substance? If so, what information did this test reveal? [Thin-layer chromatography is a method of separation and, absent a standard test run simultaneously, renders only a presumptive identification. Many chemicals have the same Rf (retention time).]
- Did you make a photocopy of the chromatographic plate? [Obviously, such a photocopy will go a long way toward defusing defense arguments.]
- Did you do a spectrophotometric analysis of the suspected controlled substance? If so, what information was yielded by this analysis? [If a mass spectroscopy

analysis was performed, the defense attorney will likely ask these two questions: Was the observed spectrum from the defendant's sample or could it have been from a trace residue in the injector? Was a background spectrum obtained?]

- How many different samples have you tested during your career?
- Who prepared each of the reagents used?
- Where were the reagents from the time of preparation to the time of use?
- Were each of the reagents tested on a control sample to ensure viability?
- Did you attempt to identify any other or all substances in the sample other than the suspected controlled substance? [The witness, in response, would state the identity of each such substance.]
- How was identification of these contaminants made?
- Could contaminants affect the analysis results?
- State the date and time you received the suspected controlled substance.
- Describe the condition of the sample upon receipt. [The description should remove any question as to possible tampering with or cross-contamination of the sample as well as the sufficiency of the sample.]
- From whom did you receive the sample?
- Were you told the suspected identity of the sample before or during your analysis? [Defendants believe that analysts "find what they are looking for," which is why a "general unknown" protocol is applied and explained to investigators, prosecutors, and defendants.]
- Did you preserve the sample upon which you conducted your procedures? If so, where is it? [The defense will most likely have already filed motions to be present at the time of testing, to restrict destructive testing, and to have defense experts conduct their own tests. However, such requests may be reserved until the time of trial as a delaying tactic.]
- To whom did you transfer the sample?
- When did you transfer the sample?
- What was the condition of the sample when it was transferred?
- Where was the sample stored while in your custody?
- Who had access to the sample while in your custody?
- What records reflect the storage and access to the sample? [All the previous 11 questions concern the chain of custody.]
- When did you tell the prosecutor of your results? [The prosecutor has a responsibility to use due diligence in advising the defendant of testing and test results. This question can be used by the defense to try to establish less than due diligence on the part of the prosecutor.]

Which questions the prosecutor asks of the forensic chemist will depend partly on the conduct of the investigator and the handling of any samples that are presented to the laboratory for analysis. Any additional contamination resulting from processing the crime scene or later handling of the evidence will serve the defendant's interests.

The following is a general protocol for the analysis of drugs (Saferstein, 1988):

- Visual examination of the exhibit is the first step, followed by examination under a low-power microscope. Gross and net weight are determined.

- Examination proceeds from the general to the specific. Each test narrows down the number of possible substances. The progression from the general to the specific, known as the "general unknown" method, includes these steps:
  1. Preliminary visual examination of all exhibits
  2. Weighing of all exhibits
  3. Selection of representative samples
  4. Screening tests (usually spot tests)
  5. Separation tests
  6. Confirmatory tests
  7. Quantitative analysis
- Analytical schemes and tests conform to those already in general practice in the field. Courts and juries will put more weight on the results obtained from an analytical scheme if other chemists in other laboratories are doing substantially the same tests. The defense will attempt to present evidence of other tests and examinations that could have been performed, and thus it is the responsibility of the testifying chemists to know which tests are being generally used.
- Whenever possible, at least one test performed should be specific for the drug in question. Such a confirmatory test should be analytically different from those tests used in the presumptive and separation phases of the examination. In most drug analyses, the confirmatory tests of choice are infrared spectrophotometry and gas chromatography-mass spectroscopy. A confirmatory test in an analytical scheme is more reliable and easier to defend in court than a collection of presumptive tests.
- Some attention must be paid to conserving the drugs present in an exhibit.
- If there is insufficient material to subject the drug to a complete analysis, nondestructive tests should be performed in preference to destructive ones.
- Tests should do double duty. Tests that are used for quantitative analysis, such as gas chromatography, are also good qualitative tests if run properly.

■ Bibliography

Saferstein, R. (1988). *Forensic science handbook* (Vol. 2). Englewood Cliffs, NJ: Prentice Hall.

September 24, 1964

The President
The White House
Washington, D.C.

Dear Mr. President:
Your Commission to investigate the assassination of President Kennedy on November 22, 1963, having completed its assignment in accordance with Executive Order No. 11130 of November 29, 1963, herewith submits its final report.

Respectfully,

Earl Warren, Chairman
Richard B. Russel
John Sherman Cooper
Hale Boggs
Gerald R. Ford
Allen W. Dulles
John J. McCloy

Clinical Record—Autopsy Protocol
Date 11/22/63 1300 (CST)
Prosecuter: CDR J. J. Humes, MC, USA
Assistant: CDR "J" Thornton Boswell, MC, USN, LCOL, Pierre A. Finck, MC, USA
    (04 043 322)
Full Autopsy
Ht. - 72 1/2 inches
Wt. - 170 pounds
Eyes - blue
Hair - Reddish brown
Pathological diagnosis: Cause of Death: Gunshot wound, head.
Signature: J. J. Eumes, CDS, MC, USN
Military organization: President, United States
Age: 46
Sex: Male
Race: Caucasion
Autopsy No. A63-272
Patient's Identification: Kennedy, John F., Naval Medical School

■ Clinical Summary

According to available information the deceased, President John F. Kennedy, was riding in an open car in a motorcade during an official visit to Dallas, Texas, on 22 November 1963. The President was sitting in the right rear seat with Mrs. Kennedy seated on the same seat to his left. Sitting directly in front of the President was Governor John B. Connally of Texas and directly in front of Mrs. Kennedy sat Mrs. Connally. The vehicle was moving at a slow rate of speed down an incline into an underpass that leads to a freeway route to the Dallas Trade Mart where the President was to deliver an address.

Three shots were heard and the President fell forward bleeding from the head. (Governor Connally was seriously wounded by the same gunfire.) According to newspaper reports (*Washington Post* November 23, 1963), Bob Jackson, a Dallas *Times Herald* photographer, said he looked around as he heard the shots and saw a rifle barrel disappearing into a window on an upper floor of the nearby Texas School Book Depository Building.

Shortly following the wounding of the two men the car was driven to Parkland Hospital in Dallas. In the emergency room of that hospital the President was attended by Dr. Malcolm Perry. Telephone communication with Dr. Perry on November 23, 1963, develops the following information relative to the observations made by Dr. Perry and procedures performed there prior to death.

Dr. Perry noted the massive wound of the head and a second much smaller wound of the low anterior neck in approximately the midline. A tracheostomy was performed by extending the latter wound. At this point bloody air was noted bubbling from the wound and an injury to the right lateral wall of the trachea was observed. Incisions were made in the upper anterior chest wall bilaterally to combat possible subcutaneous emphysema. Intravenous infusions of blood and saline were begun and oxygen was administered. Despite these measures cardiac arrest occurred and closed chest cardiac massage failed to re-establish cardiac action. The President was pronounced dead approximately thirty to forty minutes after receiving his wounds.

The remains were transported via the Presidential plane to Washington, D.C., and subsequently to the Naval Medical School, National Naval Medical Center, Bethesda, Maryland, for postmortem examination.

General Description of the Body

The body is that of a muscular, well-developed, and well-nourished adult Caucasian male measuring 72 $^1/_2$ inches and weighing approximately 170 pounds. There is beginning rigor mortis, minimal dependent livor mortis of the dorsum, and early algor mortis. The hair is reddish brown and abundant, the eyes are blue, the right pupil measuring 8 mm in diameter, the left 4 mm. There is edema and ecchymosis of the inner canthus region of the left eyelid measuring approximately 1. 5 cm in greatest diameter. There is edema and ecchymosis diffusely over the right supra-orbital ridge with abnormal mobility of the underlying bone. (The remainder of the scalp will be described with the skull.) There is clotted blood on the external ears but otherwise the ears, nares, and mouth are essentially unremarkable. The teeth are in excellent repair and there is some pallor of the oral mucous membrane.

Situated on the upper right posterior thorax just above the upper border of the scapula there is a 7 × 4 mm oval wound. This wound is measured to be 14 cm from the tip of the right acromion process and 14 cm below the tip of the right mastoid process.

Situated in the low anterior neck at approximately the level of the third and fourth tracheal rings is a 6.5 cm long transverse wound with widely gaping irregular edges. (The depth and character of these wounds will be further described below.)

Situated on the anterior chest wall in the nipple line are bilateral 2 cm long recent transverse surgical incisions into the subcutaneous tissue. The one on the left is situated 11 cm cephalad to the nipple and the one on the right 8 cm cephalad to the nipple. There is no hemorrhage or ecchymosis associated with these wounds. A similar clean wound measuring 2 cm in length is situated on the antero-lateral aspect of the left mid arm. Situated on the antero-lateral aspect of each ankle is a recent 2 cm transverse incision into the subcutaneous tissue.

There is an old well-healed 8 cm McBurney abdominal incision. Over the lumbar spine in the midline is an old, well-healed 15 cm scar. Situated on the upper antero-lateral aspect of the right thigh is an old, well-healed 8 cm scar.

Missile Wounds

1. There is a large irregular defect of the scalp and skull on the right involving chiefly the parietal bone but extending somewhat into the temporal and occipital regions. In this region there is an actual absence of scalp and bone producing a defect which measures approximately 13 cm in greatest diameter.

From the irregular margins of the above scalp defect tears extend in stellate fashion into the more or less intact scalp as follows:

1. From the right inferior temporo-parietal margin anterior to the right ear to a point slightly above the tragus.
2. From the anterior parietal margin anteriorly on the forehead to approximately 4 cm above the right orbital ridge.
3. From the left margin of the main defect across the midline antero-laterally for a distance of approximately 8 cm.
4. From the same starting point as c. 10 cm postero-laterally.

Situated in the posterior scalp approximately 2. 5 cm laterally to the right and slightly above the external occipital protuberance is a lacerated wound measuring 15 x 6 mm. In the underlying bone is a corresponding wound through the skull which exhibits beveling of the margins of the bone when viewed from the inner aspect of the skull.

Clearly visible in the above described large skull defect and exuding from it is lacerated brain tissue which on close inspection proves to represent the major portion of the right cerebral hemisphere. At this point it is noted that the falx cerebri is extensively lacerated with disruption of the superior saggital sinus.

Upon reflecting the scalp multiple complete fracture lines are seen to radiate from both the large defect at the vertex and the smaller wound at the occiput. These vary greatly in length and direction, the longest measuring approximately 19 cm. These result in the production of numerous fragments which vary in size from a few millimeters to 10 cm in greatest diameter.

The complexity of these fractures and the fragments thus produced tax satisfactory verbal description and are better appreciated in photographs and roentgenograms which are prepared.

The brain is removed and preserved for further study following formalin fixation.

Received as separate specimens from Dallas, Texas, are three fragments of skull bone which in aggregate roughly approximate the dimensions of the large defect described above. At one angle of the largest of these fragments is a portion of the perimeter of a roughly circular wound presumably of exit which exhibits beveling of the outer aspect of the bone and is estimated to measure approximately 2.5 to 3.0 cm in diameter. Roentgenograms of this fragment reveal minute particles of metal in the bone at this margin. Roentgenograms of the skull reveal multiple minute metallic fragments along a line corresponding with a line joining the above described small occipital wound and the right supra-orbital ridge. From the surface of the disrupted right cerebral cortex two small irregularly shaped fragments of metal are recovered. These measure 7 × 2 mm and 3 × 1 mm. These are placed in the custody of Agents Francis X. O'Neill, Jr., and James W. Sibert, of the Federal Bureau of Investigation, who executed a receipt therefore (attached).

2. The second wound presumably of entry is that described above in the upper right posterior thorax. Beneath the skin there is ecchymosis of subcutaneous tissue and musculature. The missile path through the fascia and musculature cannot be easily proved. The wound presumably of exit was that described by Dr. Malcolm Perry of Dallas in the low anterior cervical region. When observed by Dr. Perry the wound measured "a few millimeters in diameter," however it was extended as a tracheostomy incision and thus its character is distorted at the time of autopsy. However there is considerable eccymosis of the strap muscles of the right side of the neck and of the fascia about the trachea adjacent to the line of the tracheostomy wound. The third point of reference in connecting these two wounds is in the apex (supra-clavicular portion) of the right pleural cavity. In this region there is contusion of the parietal pleura and of the extreme apical portion of the right upper lobe of the lung. In both instances the diameter of contusion and ecchymosis at the point of maximal involvement measures 5 cm. Both the visceral and parietal pleura are intact overlying these areas of trauma.

Incisions

The scalp wounds are extended in the coronal plane to examine the cranial content and the customary (Y) shaped incision is used to examine the body cavities.

Thoracic Cavity

The bony cage is unremarkable. The thoracic organs are in their normal positions and relationships and there is no increase in free pleural fluid. The above described area of contusion in the apical portion of the right pleural cavity is noted.

Lungs

The lungs are of essentially similar appearance the right weighing 320 gm, the left 290 gm. The lungs are well aerated with smooth glistening pleural surfaces and gray-pink color. A 5 cm diameter area of purplish red discoloration and increased firmness to palpation is situated in the apical portion of the right upper lobe. This corresponds to the similar area described in the overlying parietal pleura. Incision in this region reveals recent hemorrhage into pulmonary parenchyma.

Heart

The pericardial cavity is smooth walled and contains approximately 10 cc of straw-colored fluid. The heart is of essentially normal external contour and weighs 350 gm. The pulmonary artery is opened in situ and no abnormalities are noted. The cardiac chambers contain moderate amounts of postmortem clotted blood. There are no gross abnormalities of the leaflets of any of the cardiac valves. The following are the circumferences of the cardiac valves: aortic 7.5 cm, pulmonic 7 cm, tricuspid 12 cm, mitral 11 cm. The myocardium is firm and reddish brown. The left ventricular myocardium averages 1.2 cm in thickness, the right ventricular myocardium 0.4 cm. The coronary arteries are dissected and are of normal distribution and smooth walled and elastic throughout.

Abdominal Cavity

The abdominal organs are in their normal positions and relationships and there is no increase in free peritoneal fluid. The vermiform appendix is surgically absent and there are a few adhesions joining the region of the cecum to the ventral abdominal wall at the above described old abdominal incisional scar.

Skeletal System

Aside from the above described skull wounds there are no significant gross skeletal abnormalities.

Photography

Black and white and color photographs depicting significant findings are exposed but not developed. These photographs were placed in the custody of Agent Roy E. Kellerman of the U. S. Secret Service, who executed a receipt therefore (attached).

Roentgenograms

Roentgenograms are made of the entire body and of the separately submitted three fragments of skull bone. These are developed are were placed in the custody of Agent Roy H. Kellerman of the U. S. Secret Service, who executed a receipt therefore.

■ Summary

Based on the above observations it is our opinion that the deceased died as a result of two perforating gunshot wounds inflicted by high velocity projectiles fired by a person or persons unknown. The projectiles were fired from a point behind and somewhat above the level of the deceased. The observations and available information do not permit a satisfactory estimate as to the sequence of the two wounds.

The fatal missile entered the skull above and to the right of the external occipital protuberance. A portion of the projectile traversed the cranial cavity in a posterior-anterior direction (see lateral skull roentgenograms) depositing minute particles along its path. A portion of the projectile made its exit through the parietal bone on the right carrying with it portions of cerebrum, skull and scalp. The two wounds of the skull combined with the force of the missile produced extensive fragmentation of the skull, laceration of the superior sagittal sinus, and of the right cerebral hemisphere.

The other missile entered the right superior posterior thorax above the scapula and traversed the soft tissues of the supra-scapular and the supra-clavicular portions of the base of the right side of the neck. This missile produced contusions of the right apical parietal pleura and of the apical portion of the right upper lobe of the lung. The missile contused the strap muscles of the right side of the neck, damaged the trachea and made its exit through the anterior surface of the neck. As far as can be ascertained this missile struck no bony structures in its path through the body.

In addition, it is our opinion that the wound of the skull produced such extensive damage to the brain as to preclude the possibility of the deceased surviving this injury. A supplementary report will be submitted following more detailed examination of the brain and of microscopic sections. However, it is not anticipated that these examinations will materially alter the findings.

/s/
J. J. HUMES
CDR, MC, USN (497831)

/s/
"J" THORNTON BOSWELL
CDR, MC, USN (489878)

/s/
PIERRE A. FINCK
LT COL, MC, USA
(04-043-322)

■ **Supplementary Report of Autopsy Number A63-272**
   President John F. Kennedy Pathological Examination Report No. A63-272

Gross Description of the Brain

Following formalin fixation the brain seighs 1500 gms. The right cerebral hemisphere is found to be markedly disrupted. There is a longitudinal laceration of the right hemisphere which is para-sagittal in position approximately 2.5 cm to the right of the of the midline which extends from the tip of the occipital lobe posteriorly to the tip of the frontal lobe anteriorly. The base of the laceration is situated approximately 4.5 cm below the vertex in the white matter. There is considerable loss of cortical substance above the base of the laceration, particularly in the parietal lobe. The margins of this laceration are at all points jagged and irregular, with additional lacerations extending in varying directions and for varying distances from the main laceration. In addition, there is a laceration of the corpus callosum extending from the genu to the tail. Exposed in this latter laceration are the interiors of the right lateral and third ventricles.

When viewed from the vertex the left cerebral hemisphere is intact. There is marked engorgement of meningeal blood vessels of the left temporal and frontal regions with considerable associated sub-arachnoid hemorrhage. The gyri and sulci over the left hemisphere are of essentially normal size and distribution. Those on the right are too fragmented and distorted for satisfactory description.

When viewed from the basilar aspect the disruption of the right cortex is again obvious. There is a longitudinal laceration of the mid-brain through the floor of the third ventricle just behind the optic chiasm and the mammillary bodies. This laceration partially communicates with an oblique 1.5 cm tear through the left cerebral peduncle. There are irregular superficial lacerations over the basilar aspects of the left temporal and frontal lobes.

In the interest of preserving the specimen coronal sections are not made. The following sections are taken for microscopic examination:

1. From the margin of the laceration in the right parietal lobe.
2. From the margin of the laceration in the corpus callosum.
3. From the anterior portion of the laceration in the right frontal lobe.

4. From the contused left fronto-parietal cortex.

5. From the line of transection of the spinal cord.

6. From the right cerebellar cortex.

7. From the superficial laceration of the basilar aspect of the left temporal lobe.

During the course of this examination seven (7) black and white and six (6) color 4 × 5 inch negatives are exposed but not developed (the cassettes containing these negatives have been delivered by hand to Rear Admiral George W. Burkley, MC, USN, White House Physician).

■ Microscopic Examination

Brain

Multiple sections from representative areas as noted above are examined. All sections are essentially similar and show extensive disruption of brain tissue with associated hemorrhage. In none of the sections examined are there significant abnormalities other than those directly related to the recent trauma.

Heart

Sections show a moderate amount of sub-epicardial fat. The coronary arteries, myocardial fibers, and endocardium are unremarkable.

Lungs

Sections through the grossly described area of contusion in the right upper lobe exhibit disruption of alveolar walls and recent hemorrhage into alveoli. Sections are otherwise essentially unremarkable.

Liver

Sections show the normal hepatic architecture to be well-preserved. The parenchymal cells exhibit markedly granular cytoplasm indicating high glycogen content which is characteristic of the "liver biopsy pattern" of sudden death.

Spleen

Sections show no significant abnormalities.

Kidneys

Sections show no significant abnormalities aside from dilatation and engorgement of blood vessels of all calibers.

Skin Wounds

Sections through the wounds in the occipital and upper right posterior thoracic regions are essentially similar. In each there is loss of continuity of the epidermis with coagulation necrosis of the tissues at the wound margins. The scalp wound exhibits several small fragments of bone at its margins in the subcutaneous tissue.

Final Summary

This supplementary report covers in more detail the extensive degree of cerebral trauma in this case. However neither this portion of the examination nor the microscopic examinations alter the previously submitted report or add significant details to the cause of death.

/s/
J. J. HUMES
CDR, MC, USN, 497831

Date: 6 December 1963

From: Commanding Officer, U. S. Naval Medical School
To: The White House Physician
Via: Commanding Officer, National Naval Medical Center
Subj: Supplementary report of Naval Medical School autopsy No. A63-272, John F. Kennedy; forwarding of

1. All copies of the above subject final supplementary report are forwarded herewith.

/s/
J. H. STOVER, JR.

6 December 1963

First Endorsement

From: Commanding Officer, National Naval Medical Center
To: The White House Physician
1. Forwarded.

/s/
C. B. GALLOWAY

Index

Note: Italicized page locators indicate a figure/photo; tables are noted with a *t*.